Lecture Notes in Computer Science 4991

Commenced Publication in 1973
Founding and Former Series Editors:
Gerhard Goos, Juris Hartmanis, and Jan van Leeuwen

Editorial Board

David Hutchison
　Lancaster University, UK
Takeo Kanade
　Carnegie Mellon University, Pittsburgh, PA, USA
Josef Kittler
　University of Surrey, Guildford, UK
Jon M. Kleinberg
　Cornell University, Ithaca, NY, USA
Alfred Kobsa
　University of California, Irvine, CA, USA
Friedemann Mattern
　ETH Zurich, Switzerland
John C. Mitchell
　Stanford University, CA, USA
Moni Naor
　Weizmann Institute of Science, Rehovot, Israel
Oscar Nierstrasz
　University of Bern, Switzerland
C. Pandu Rangan
　Indian Institute of Technology, Madras, India
Bernhard Steffen
　University of Dortmund, Germany
Madhu Sudan
　Massachusetts Institute of Technology, MA, USA
Demetri Terzopoulos
　University of California, Los Angeles, CA, USA
Doug Tygar
　University of California, Berkeley, CA, USA
Gerhard Weikum
　Max-Planck Institute of Computer Science, Saarbruecken, Germany

Liqun Chen   Yi Mu   Willy Susilo (Eds.)

Information Security Practice and Experience

4th International Conference, ISPEC 2008
Sydney, Australia, April 21-23, 2008
Proceedings

 Springer

Volume Editors

Liqun Chen
Hewlett-Packard Laboratories
Filton Road, Stoke Gifford, Bristol BS34 8QZ, UK
E-mail: liqun.chen@hp.com

Yi Mu
Willy Susilo
University of Wollongong
School of Computer Science & Software Engineering
Centre for Computer and Information Security Research
Northfields Avenue, Wollongong, NSW 2522, Australia
E-mail: {ymu, wsusilo}@uow.edu.au

Library of Congress Control Number: 2008924370

CR Subject Classification (1998): E.3, C.2.0, D.4.6, H.2.0, K.4.4, K.6.5

LNCS Sublibrary: SL 4 – Security and Cryptology

ISSN   0302-9743
ISBN-10   3-540-79103-5 Springer Berlin Heidelberg New York
ISBN-13   978-3-540-79103-4 Springer Berlin Heidelberg New York

This work is subject to copyright. All rights are reserved, whether the whole or part of the material is concerned, specifically the rights of translation, reprinting, re-use of illustrations, recitation, broadcasting, reproduction on microfilms or in any other way, and storage in data banks. Duplication of this publication or parts thereof is permitted only under the provisions of the German Copyright Law of September 9, 1965, in its current version, and permission for use must always be obtained from Springer. Violations are liable to prosecution under the German Copyright Law.

Springer is a part of Springer Science+Business Media

springer.com

© Springer-Verlag Berlin Heidelberg 2008
Printed in Germany

Typesetting: Camera-ready by author, data conversion by Scientific Publishing Services, Chennai, India
Printed on acid-free paper   SPIN: 12254644   06/3180   5 4 3 2 1 0

Preface

The 4th Information Security Practice and Experience Conference (ISPEC 2008) was held at Crowne Plaza, Darling Harbour, Sydney, Australia, during April 21–23, 2008. The previous three conferences were held in Singapore in 2005, Hangzhou, China in 2006 and Hong Kong, China in 2007. As with the previous three conference proceedings, the proceedings of ISPEC 2008 were published in the LNCS series by Springer.

The conference received 95 submissions, out of which the Program Committee selected 29 papers for presentation at the conference. These papers are included in the proceedings. The accepted papers cover a range of topics in mathematics, computer science and security applications, including authentication and digital signatures, privacy, encryption and hash-function algorithms, security analysis, network security, access control, security devices, pairing and elliptic curve-based security practice, security computation and so forth. The conference proceedings contain revised versions of the selected papers. Since some of them were not checked again for correctness before publication, the authors (and not the Program Committee) bear full responsibility for the contents of their papers.

In addition to the contributed papers, the program comprised two invited talks. The invited speakers were Vijay Varadharajan (Macquarie University, Australia) and Robert Huijie Deng (Singapore Management University, Singapore). Special thanks are due to these speakers.

We would like to thank all the people who helped with the conference program and organization. First, we thank the Steering Committee for their guidance on the general format of the conference. We also heartily thank the Program Committee and the sub-reviewers listed on the following pages for their hard efforts and time contributed to the review process, which took seven weeks. Each paper was carefully evaluated by at least two or three people. There was significant online discussion about a large number of papers.

The submission and review process was run using the iChair software, written by Thomas Baigneres and Matthieu Finiasz (EPFL, Switzerland).

We wish to thank all the authors who submitted papers, and the authors of accepted papers for revising their papers according to referee suggestions and sending their final versions on time. We thank the staff at Springer for their help with producing the proceedings.

Finally, we would like to thank the Organizing Committee for their excellent contribution to the conference.

April 2008   Liqun Chen
                                                                                                                        Yi Mu
                                                                                                                  Willy Susilo

The 4th Information Security Practice and Experience Conference (ISPEC 2008)

Steering Committee

Feng Bao Institute for Infocomm Research, Singapore
Robert H. Deng Singapore Management University, Singapore

General Chair

Willy Susilo University of Wollongong, Australia

Program Chairs

Liqun Chen HP Laboratories, UK
Yi Mu University of Wollongong, Australia

Program Committee

Joonsang Baek Institute for Infocomm Research, Singapore
Colin Boyd QUT, Australia
Ernie Brickell Intel Corporation, USA
Liqun Chen HP Laboratories, UK
Michael Cheng Middlesex University, UK
Sabrina De Capitani
  di Vimercati University of Milan, Italy
Cunsheng Ding Hong Kong University of Science Technology, China
Ed Dowson QUT, Australia
Dengguo Feng Chinese Academy of Sciences, China
Dieter Gollmann TU Hamburg, Germany
Guang Gong University of Waterloo, Canada
Amir Herzberg Bar-Ilan University, Israel
Hongxia Jin IBM, USA
Kwangjo Kim ICU, Korea
Steve Kremer ENC Cachan, France
Taekyoung Kwon Sejong, Korea
Xuejia Lai Shanghai Jao Tong University, China
Pil Joong Lee Pohang University of Science and Technology, Korea
Benoit Libert UCL, Belgium

Javier Lopez   University of Malaga, Spain
Masahiro Mambo   Tsukuba University, Japan
Atsuko Miyaji   JAIST, Japan
Chris Mitchell   RHUL, UK
Yi Mu   University of Wollongong, Australia
Josef Pieprzyk   Macquarie University, Australia
Jean-Jacques Quisquater   UCL, Belgium
C. Pandu Rangan   Indian Institute of Technology, India
Mark Ryan   University of Birmingham, UK
Ahmad-Reza Sadeghi   Ruhr University Bochum, Germany
Willy Susilo   University of Wollongong, Australia
Tsuyoshi Takagi   Future University, Japan
Vijay Varadharajan   Macquarie University, Australia
Huaxiong Wang   Nanyang Technological University, Singapore
Duncan S. Wong   City University of Hong Kong, China
Fangguo Zhang   Sun Yat-Sen University, China
Ning Zhang   University of Manchester, UK
Jianying Zhou   Institute for Infocomm Research, Singapore
Huafei Zhu   Institute for Infocomm Research, Singapore

Organizing Committee

Man Ho Au   University of Wollongong, Australia
Xinyi Huang   University of Wollongong, Australia
Shams Ud Din Qazi   University of Wollongong, Australia
Pairat Thorncharoensri   University of Wollongong, Australia
Wei Wu   University of Wollongong, Australia
Tsz Hon Yuen   University of Wollongong, Australia

External Referees

Koichiro Akiyama   Zheng Gong   Joseph K. Liu
Shane Balfe   Goichiro Hanaoka   Hans Loehr
Andrew Brown   Xuan Hong   Yu Long
Chris Charnes   Xinyi Huang   Yi Lu
Sherman Chow   Shaoquan Jiang   Mark Manulis
Baudoin Collard   Naoki Kanayama   Krystian Matusiewicz
Stéphanie Delaune   Jin Ho Kim   Aybek Mukhamedov
Dang Nguyen Duc   Young Mok Kim   Pablo Najera
Xinxin Fan   Izuru Kitamura   Mototsugu Nishioka
Gerardo Fernandez   Divyan M. Konidala   Takeshi Okamoto
Kazuyoshi Furukawa   Eun Jeong Kwon   Kyosuke Osaka
Sebastian Gajek   Vinh The Lam   Hasan Qunoo
Shen Tat Goh   Vo Duc Liem   Anongporn Salaiwarakul

Jae Woo Seo
Jong Hoon Shin
Masaaki Shirase
Jason Smith
Ben Smyth
Yinxia Sun
Damien Vergnaud

Guilin Wang
Qihua Wang
Marcel Winandy
Mu-En Wu
Guomin Yang
Yeon-Hyeong Yang
Qiu Ying

Jin Yuan
Zhenfeng Zhang
Zhifang Zhang
Chang-An Zhao
Xingwen Zhao

Table of Contents

Verification of Integrity and Secrecy Properties of a Biometric
Authentication Protocol 1
    A. Salaiwarakul and M.D. Ryan

An On-Line Secure E-Passport Protocol 14
    Vijayakrishnan Pasupathinathan, Josef Pieprzyk, and
    Huaxiong Wang

Secure Multi-Coupons for Federated Environments: Privacy-Preserving
and Customer-Friendly 29
    Frederik Armknecht, Alberto N. Escalante B., Hans Löhr,
    Mark Manulis, and Ahmad-Reza Sadeghi

1-out-of-n Oblivious Signatures 45
    Raylin Tso, Takeshi Okamoto, and Eiji Okamoto

A Formal Study of the Privacy Concerns in Biometric-Based Remote
Authentication Schemes 56
    Qiang Tang, Julien Bringer, Hervé Chabanne, and David Pointcheval

Private Query on Encrypted Data in Multi-user Settings 71
    Feng Bao, Robert H. Deng, Xuhua Ding, and Yanjiang Yang

Towards Tamper Resistant Code Encryption: Practice and
Experience 86
    Jan Cappaert, Bart Preneel, Bertrand Anckaert,
    Matias Madou, and Koen De Bosschere

A New Public Key Broadcast Encryption Using Boneh-Boyen-Goh's
HIBE Scheme 101
    Jong Hwan Park and Dong Hoon Lee

RSA Moduli with a Predetermined Portion: Techniques and
Applications 116
    Marc Joye

Variants of the Distinguished Point Method for Cryptanalytic Time
Memory Trade-Offs 131
    Jin Hong, Kyung Chul Jeong, Eun Young Kwon, In-Sok Lee, and
    Daegun Ma

Secure Cryptographic Precomputation with Insecure Memory 146
    Patrick P. Tsang and Sean W. Smith

Securing Peer-to-Peer Distributions for Mobile Devices 161
  *André Osterhues, Ahmad-Reza Sadeghi, Marko Wolf,
  Christian Stüble, and N. Asokan*

Unified Rate Limiting in Broadband Access Networks for Defeating
Internet Worms and DDoS Attacks................................ 176
  Keun Park, Dongwon Seo, Jaewon Yoo, Heejo Lee, and Hyogon Kim

Combating Spam and Denial-of-Service Attacks with Trusted Puzzle
Solvers 188
  Patrick P. Tsang and Sean W. Smith

PROBE: A Process Behavior-Based Host Intrusion Prevention
System 203
  Minjin Kwon, Kyoochang Jeong, and Heejo Lee

Towards the World-Wide Quantum Network......................... 218
  Quoc-Cuong Le, Patrick Bellot, and Akim Demaille

Synthesising Monitors from High-Level Policies for the Safe Execution
of Untrusted Software 233
  Andrew Brown and Mark Ryan

Mediator-Free Secure Policy Interoperation of Exclusively-Trusted
Multiple Domains 248
  Xingang Wang, Dengguo Feng, Zhen Xu, and Honggang Hu

Privacy of Recent RFID Authentication Protocols................. 263
  Khaled Ouafi and Raphael C.-W. Phan

A New Hash-Based RFID Mutual Authentication Protocol Providing
Enhanced User Privacy Protection 278
  Jihwan Lim, Heekuck Oh, and Sangjin Kim

An Efficient Countermeasure against Side Channel Attacks for Pairing
Computation 290
  Masaaki Shirase, Tsuyoshi Takagi, and Eiji Okamoto

Efficient Arithmetic on Subfield Elliptic Curves over Small Finite Fields
of Odd Characteristic 304
  Keisuke Hakuta, Hisayoshi Sato, and Tsuyoshi Takagi

Secure Computation of the Vector Dominance Problem 319
  Jin Yuan, Qingsong Ye, Huaxiong Wang, and Josef Pieprzyk

Rational Secret Sharing with Repeated Games 334
  Shaik Maleka, Amjed Shareef, and C. Pandu Rangan

Distributed Private Matching and Set Operations 347
  Qingsong Ye, Huaxiong Wang, and Josef Pieprzyk

Computational Soundness of Non-Malleable Commitments 361
    David Galindo, Flavio D. Garcia, and Peter van Rossum

Square Attack on Reduced-Round Zodiac Cipher..................... 377
    Wen Ji and Lei Hu

Analysis of Zipper as a Hash Function 392
    Pin Lin, Wenling Wu, Chuankun Wu, and Tian Qiu

On the Importance of the Key Separation Principle for Different Modes
of Operation 404
    Danilo Gligoroski, Suzana Andova, and Svein Johan Knapskog

Author Index 419

Verification of Integrity and Secrecy Properties of a Biometric Authentication Protocol

A. Salaiwarakul and M.D. Ryan

School of Computer Science,
University of Birmingham, UK
{A.Salaiwarakul, M.D.Ryan}@cs.bham.ac.uk

Abstract. In this paper, we clarify and verify an established biometric authentication protocol. The selected protocol is intended to have three properties: effectiveness (integrity checks are carried out on all hardware before enabling transmission of biometric data), correctness (the user is satisfied that integrity checks have been executed correctly before transmission of biometric data occurs), and secrecy (unauthorized users cannot obtain biometric data by intercepting messages between the system's hardware components). We analyse the clarified protocol using applied pi calculus and the ProVerif tool, and demonstrate that it satisfies the intended properties of the protocol. Moreover, this paper shows that the verification result between the naive interpretation and the clarified interpretation is different.

1 Introduction

1.1 Biometric Authentication Protocols

Biometric authentication complements other methods of authentication such as passwords or smartcards. It may be used as an alternative to these, or in combination. Passwords used on their own are known to have certain weaknesses: users are liable to choose easily guessable passwords, transfer passwords between each other in ways not desired by the system owners, use the same password on multiple systems, or forget their passwords. Authentication using smart cards also has some of these weaknesses, such as undesired transfer between, or theft from, users. Biometric user authentication can be utilised in a variety of applications, from logging into a local PC, to passenger identification at a border control, to authentication on a remote server in e-commerce transactions or online banking.

Potential biometric techniques include fingerprint and hand geometry, as well as voice, retina, face and behavioural characteristics. The rapid move towards the use of biometrics in user authentication comes from the method's promise to offer secure and reliable authentication. In well-designed and engineered systems for biometric authentication, user A cannot authenticate as another user B, even with B's cooperation. In contrast to other types of credential, such as password or smartcard, which can be transferred or stolen, biometric authentication promises a "non-transferability" property, which means that users cannot lose their credentials or acquire those belonging to others.

However, there are many obstacles to overcome before this potential can be realised. Biometric authentication depends on biometric protocols, i.e. the way biometric data is transmitted and stored. But protocol design is known to be very difficult. The well-known paper that identified attacks on the Needham-Schroeder protocol that was believed to be invulnerable and had been used successfully for more than a decade [1]is one example of how accurate protocol verification is crucial. The focus of this paper concerns the handling and storage of biometric data. Biometric data cannot be considered a secret in the way that private keys or passwords can. In contrast with private keys, biometric data is given to potentially hostile hosts when a user wishes to authenticate herself, and unlike passwords, biometric data cannot be replaced - a user cannot conveniently choose different biometric data to present to different hosts in the way that one might use a different (and lower security) password for a webmail account as for a bank account. Moreover, in contrast with keys and passwords, biometric data such as the user's facial characteristics and fingerprints should be considered to be in the public domain, and can be captured without the user's consent or knowledge.

In spite of this, we take the view that biometric data should be kept private as a matter of good practice. In this respect, it is rather like credit card numbers; they are not really private, as we voluntarily cite them on the phone and by unencrypted email and allow restaurant and other retail staff to handle the cards, often in our absence. Nevertheless, it seems sensible not to allow such data to be spread around without restriction. The same idea applies to biometric data; even if a user's biometric data could be captured by agents having access to smooth surfaces the user touches, or agents to whom the user authenticates, it should not be made unnecessarily easy for malicious agents to acquire it. However, biometric authentication methods cannot assume that biometric data is secret. Such an assumption is false.

+**Long version.** The full paper that presents the ProVerif model is available at http://www.cs.bham.ac.uk/~mdr/research/papers/

1.2 Our Contribution

To demonstrate verification of biometric authentication protocols, we use an established protocol, CPV02 [2], as a case study, and prove whether its intended properties are satisfied.

In order to verify the properties of the biometric authentication protocol, we need to clarify the operation of the protocol. We show that it is easy to interpret the protocol incorrectly, and that this would affect the security properties. An example of a naive interpretation and its verification result is given in a later section.

We set out and formalise the intended properties of the protocol. We present the verification result of the naive interpretation, and clarification of the protocol's detail that is necessary in order to achieve successful verification. Moreover, we show that the verification outcome of the naive interpretation of the protocol identifies an attack while the result of the clarified one is different.

To obtain our findings, we use the verification tool ProVerif [5]. We explain the protocol, clarify it, and provide a formal model of the protocol and its properties. We then give the outcome of the verification, and some analysis.

2 The CPV02 Protocol

In [2], Chen, Pearson and Vamvakas present a protocol for biometric authentication that we call CPV02. This protocol prevents disclosure of biometric data both during data transmission and within all system hardware. This is achieved through integrity metric checking. The protocol is a generic protocol for biometric authentication. It can be used as a protocol in applications that require authentication before the user is allowed to proceed.

The system under consideration is composed of three connected components: a smartcard (SC), a trusted computing platform (TCP) and a trusted biometric reader (TBR).

The SC is used for storing credential information such as the user's biometric code or the user's signature. The TBR is a device for reading the user's biometric data for use later in the matching process. In this protocol, the TBR and the SC generate session keys to transfer the user's submitted biometric data (BD) and the user's stored biometric code (BC).

A TCP is a device that behaves in an expected manner for the intended purpose and is resistant to attacks by application software or viruses [3]. This is achieved because the TCP contains a Trusted Platform Module (TPM), which stores keys and can perform cryptographic operations. The TPM can check the integrity of the TCP. Specifically, it can create an unforgeable summary of the software on the TCP, allowing a third party to verify that the software has not been compromised. This can be accomplished by presenting a certificate to the third party to confirm that it is communicating with a valid TPM. Table 1 summarises notations and meanings that will be used through out the paper. Figure 1 shows the basic system for this model. Informally, it can be described as a user holding a smart card that contains her previously stored biometric code, e.g. fingerprint code. To authenticate herself to the system, she first inserts the smart card into a smart card reader. This triggers part of the protocol during which the integrity of the computing platform and the biometric reader are checked and the result is returned to the smart card. If the smart card is satisfied that the computing platform and biometric reader have not been tampered with, it indicates this to the user, e.g. by releasing a special image to be displayed by the computing platform. The user recognises that image as an indication that the integrity checks have been successful and proceeds to the second step, which is biometric authentication. To achieve that, she submits her biometric data, e.g. by placing her fingerprint on a biometric reader. The biometric code stored on the smart card and the submitted biometric data from the biometric reader are then sent to the computing platform, which will validate whether

Table 1. Notations and Meanings

Notation	Meaning
BC	User's stored biometric code
BD	User's submitted biometric data
TPM	Trusted Platform Module
TCP	Trusted Computing Platform
TBR	Trusted Biometric Reader

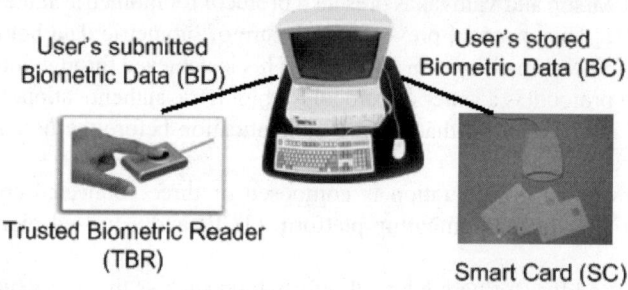

Fig. 1. The basic setup for CPV02 consists of a trusted biometric reader (TBR), a trusted computing platform (TCP) that supports a trusted platform module(TPM), and a smart card device (SC)

they match. If they match, the smart card will release the user's credential data, e.g. her signature on a message, to the computing platform.

The BC is stored in the SC and will be transferred to the TPM for comparison with the BC. However, before this transmission is performed, the TPM and the SC must authenticate each other by sending an authentication message, which includes a nonce and integrity metric. The integrity metric is a measurement of the trustworthiness of the component. Depending on its policy, the challenger will decide, based on this value, whether to trust or allow any action to be performed.

The SC sends a nonce n1 and its identity to the TPM. The TPM generates a nonce n2 and a message including n1, n2, the identity of the SC and integrity metric D3. The integrity metric D3 is used to trigger the components involved in the communication to do the integrity checking. The message sent back to the SC will be signed by the TPM so that the SC can check its origin and the correctness of n1. After the authentication's success, the SC generates the session key SK1, shared by the SC and the TPM, for encrypting the BC, before sending it together with the authentication messages. After the TPM has verified the message, it then stores the BC.

When the TBR is presented to the system, it also performs mutual authentication with the TPM and generates a session key to share between the TBR and the TPM. In the same way as that in which the TPM and the SC authenticated each other, the TBR sends an integrity metric D7 to the TPM. If the TPM has successfully verified the message it receives, it will send back a message MF5. The TBR verifies the message. After the authentication has succeeded, the TBR generates a session key SK2, shared by the TBR and the TPM, for use in encrypting the BD from the TBR to the TPM.

The BD is encrypted by using the session key created in the previous stage to the TPM. This data will be compared with the BC. After the message is verified, the TPM decrypts the encrypted message and verifies the validity of the BD. If they match, the user is allowed to use the system or perform the request. For example, the SC releases the user's signature. The message sequence of this protocol is shown in Figure 2.

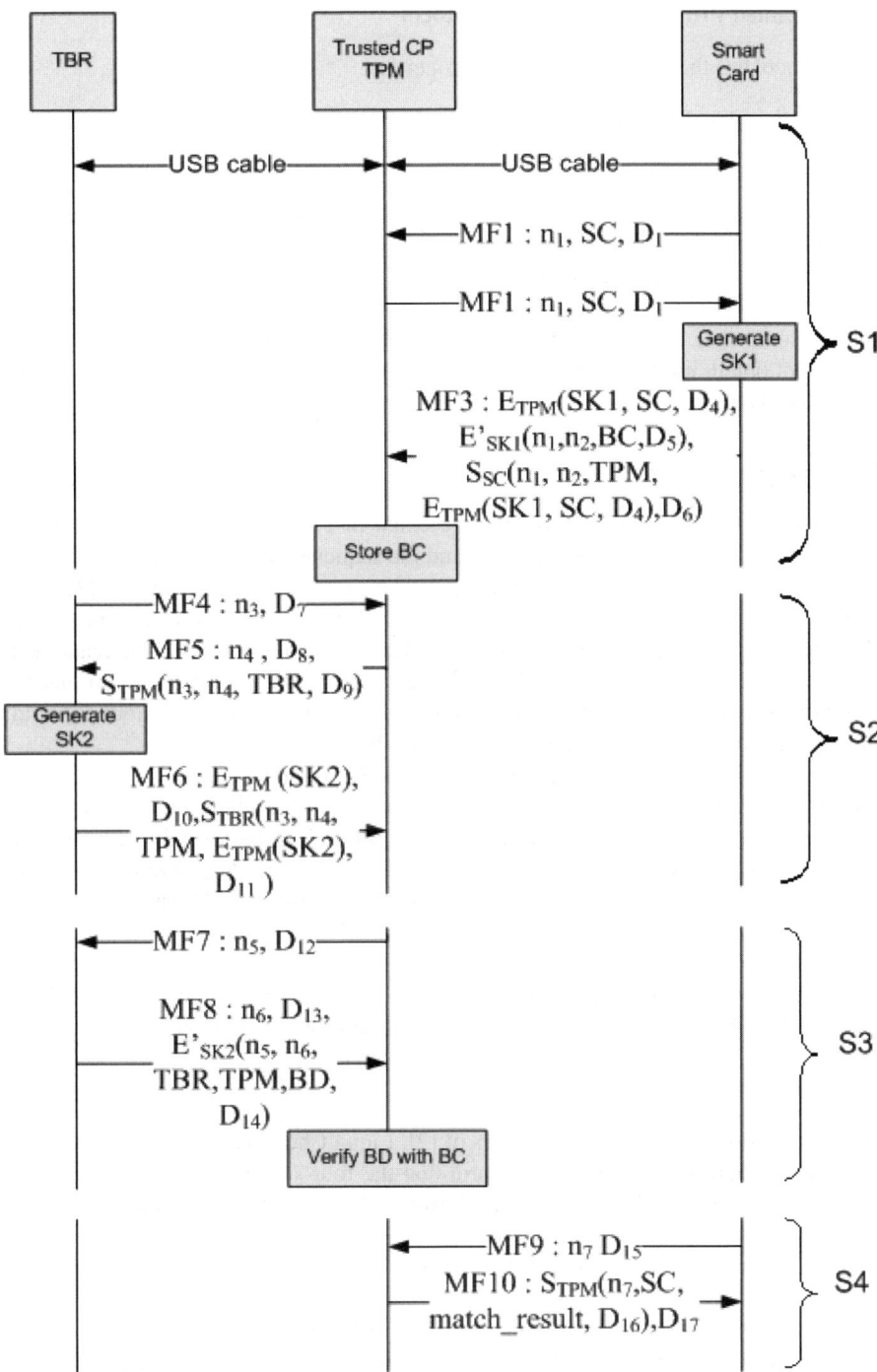

Fig. 2. Message Sequence Chart for CPV02 Protocol

2.1 Intended Properties of CPV02 Protocol

The protocol has the following intended properties:

1. *Effectiveness.* The accessed computing platform is given neither the user's stored biometric code nor the user's submitted biometric data until the integrity of both the computing platform and biometric reader are checked by the smart card.
2. *Correctness.* The biometric reader is not given the user's submitted biometric data until the user is convinced of the correctness of both the computing platform and biometric reader integrity checking.
3. *Secrecy.* An unauthorised entity that can listen to a message between the smart card and computing platform, or between the biometric reader and computing platform, cannot obtain either the user's stored biometric code or the user's submitted biometric data.

2.2 Problem Encountered

To verify the three protocol properties presented in 2.1, we need to gain a detailed understanding of how the protocol works and the sequence of messages.

If a naive verifier were to interpret the CPV02 protocol as it is presented in [2] (page 7-9), it would identify an attack. The sub-protocols are presented in a sequence order, and since nothing is said about the order in which they should be run, the reader can assume they are run in the order presented. We performed the verification on that assumption. The result of the verification shows that one of the properties does not hold: the biometric data is released before the TPM is checked.

The ProVerif model of this interpretation is shown in the full paper[+]. Let us briefly describe this model. The code consists of 4 processes (excluding the main process): TPM, TBR, SC and ProcessK. Processes TPM, TBR and SC perform the operations of the TPM, TBR and SC respectively (as mentioned in section 2). ProcessK distributes the verification key certificates to the three processes TPM, TBR and SC. The main process generates private keys for each component and distributes them via private channels, running these processes concurrently.

The result of the verification shows that the TCP is sent the BC before the TBR is checked. This breaks one of the intended properties of the protocol: *effectiveness.*

2.3 The Clarified CPV02 Protocol

Email discussion with one of the authors of [2], Liqun Chen, has given us further vital information about CPV02. We have learnt that the four sub-protocols can run at any time and in any order. Moreover, the result from one sub-protocol may affect the other sub-protocols. For example, sub-protocol (S1) cannot be run successfully without also running sub-protocol (S2). These facts cannot be easily extracted from the paper without the discussion and they are important in order to successfully verify the protocol.

Let us consider the message sequence chart of CPV02 in Figure 2. The protocol consists of four sub-protocols (S1), (S2), (S3), and (S4) which can run in any order and at any time. In (S1), the encrypted BC is sent from the SC to the TPM. In (S2), a session key is created for use between the TPM and the TBR when the BD is encrypted. In (S3), the encrypted BD is sent from the TBR to the TPM. In (S4), a matching result on the BC and BD is sent from the TPM to the SC.

The detailed ProVerif model for verifying the properties according to the clarified protocol is presented in section 4.

3 Applied Pi Calculus and ProVerif

3.1 Applied Pi Calculus

Applied pi calculus is a language for describing concurrent processes and their interactions [4]. It is based on pi calculus, but is intended to be less pure and therefore more convenient to use. Properties of processes described in applied pi calculus can be proved by employing either manual techniques or automated tools such as ProVerif [5]. As well as reachability properties that are typical of model-checking tools, ProVerif can in some cases prove that processes are observationally equivalent [6].

To describe processes in applied pi calculus, one starts with a set of names (which are used to name communication channels or other constants), a set of variables, and a set of function symbol which will be used to define terms. In the case of security protocols, typical function symbols will include **enc** for encryption (which takes plaintext x and a key k, and returns the corresponding cipher text) and **dec** for decryption (which takes cipher text and a key k and returns the plaintext x). One can also describe equations which hold on terms constructed from the function. For example:

$$\textbf{dec}(\textbf{enc}(x,k),k) = x$$

Terms are defined as names, variables, and function symbols applied to other terms. Terms and function symbols are sorted, and of course function symbol application must respect sorts and arities. In the applied pi calculus, one has (plain) processes and extended processes. Plain processes are built up in a similar way to processes in the pi calculus, except that messages can contain terms (rather than just names) [4,7].

3.2 ProVerif

ProVerif is a protocol verifier developed by Bruno Blanchet [8]. This tool has been used to prove the security properties of various protocols [7,9]. It can be used to prove secrecy, authenticity and strong secrecy properties of cryptographic protocols. It can handle an unbounded number of sessions of the protocol and an unbounded message space. The grammar of processes accepted by ProVerif is described in the long version of the paper.

In order to verify properties of a protocol, query commands may be made. The query 'attacker: m' is satisfied if an attacker may obtain the message m by observing the messages on public channels and by applying functions to them. The query $ev : f(x_1, \ldots, x_n) \Rightarrow ev : f'(y_1, \ldots, y_m)$ is satisfied if the event $f'(y_1, \ldots, y_m)$ must have been executed before any occurrence of the event $f(x_1, \ldots, x_n)$.

An advantage of using ProVerif as a verfier is it models an attacker which is compliant with the Dolev-Yao model [10] automatically. We do not need to explicitly model the attacker.

4 Modelling the Clarified CPV02 in ProVerif

Now we model the CPV02 protocol based on the derived message sequence chart (shown in Figure 2) from clarification and the following assumptions:

1. All the components, TPM, SC and TBR, hold the public key of certificate authority.
2. The integrity metric measurements have been made and are stored in the tamper-resistant storage. Therefore we model it, as it is a stored secret value, and verify its correctness with the challenger's stored value.

The ProVerif code consists of signature and equational theory, a main process, a process for certificate distribution, S1 process, S2 process, S3 process, and S4 process. A detailed description of each process will be given in a later section.

4.1 Signature and Equational Theory

Our ProVerif model involves public key and host functions. We model cryptographic function as *enc* and *dec*. Similarly, the symmetric cryptography is modelled as *senc* and *sdec*. In order to introduce digital signature, function *sign* is added and function *checksign* is used to verify the origin of messages.

The public key cryptography is represented in the first equation. To decrypt messages from symmetric cryptography, the second equation permits us to do so. In the interest of verifying the origin of messages; the checksign equation is introduced in our model.

```
equation dec(enc(x,pk(y)),y) = x.
equation sdec(senc(x,k),k) = x.
equation checksign(sign(x,y),pk(y)) = x.
```

4.2 Main Process

In the main process, the public keys, private keys, and the identities of each component are created and distributed in the public channel. Moreover, the components can run at any time and in any order.

4.3 Certificate Distribution

This process is intended to distribute the certificates of verification keys for the integrity checking process and distribute them through the private channel to guarantee that each identity will obtain them correctly.

4.4 (S1) Sending the Encrypted Biometric Code

This sub-protocol includes two processes: TPM1 and SC1. The mutual authentication between the TPM and the SC is performed before the encrypted BC is transmitted. Firstly, the TPM and the SC obtain their certificates. The TPM generates a fresh random nonce. Then it sends its integrity metric with this nonce to the SC. The SC checks the certificate it receives from the TPM and retrieves the public key of the TPM. The

SC verifies the validity of messages and generates a session key and then sends the BC encrypted by the key to the TPM. The TPM verifies the accuracy of the received message, decrypts it, and stores the BC in its secure storage. Moreover, from email discussion, we have learnt that (S1) cannot run successfully before (S2) has run. So we add state checking to check that (S2) has run.

4.5 (S2) Creating a Session Key for Encrypting the User's Submitted Biometric Data

This sub-protocol represents mutual authentication between the TPM and the TBR. It also creates a session key for sharing between the TPM and the TBR. This sub-protocol runs when a TBR has been introduced to the system.

This sub-protocol includes the two processes TPM2 and TBR2. The certificates are obtained via the private channels. Note that the TPM has already obtained this certificate in the previous sub-protocol. TPM1 and TPM2 are indeed the same trusted platform modules but they are run in different sub-protocols and therefore require distinct names. So we model TPM2 to receive the certificate again but the certificate it receives is the same certificate as that received by TPM1.

The TBR has to authenticate itself to the TPM using an integrity checking mechanism. It creates a fresh random number and sends it with its integrity metric. If the TPM is satisfied with the checking result, it will send its certificate along with the authentication message to the TBR. The TBR retrieves the public key of the TPM. It then checks the correctness of the message. If it is valid, the TBR will create a session key SK2 for the encryption and decryption of the BD.

While the processes TPM1, TPM2, TPM3, and TPM4 are on the same trusted platform module, as seen in section 2, in order to fit the CPV02 protocol they need to run as separate sub-protocols. This fact also applies to TBR2 and TBR3. All variables created or received in one TPM process should be known to others. Hence, in the process TPM2, two private channels are set up. One is used for acknowledging that S2 has run and the other is used for transferring the session key SK2 from the process TPM2 to the process TPM3. Similarly, a private channel is set up in process TBR2 to transmit the session key from the process TBR2 to the process TBR3.

4.6 (S3) Sending Encrypted User's Submitted Biometric Data from the Biometric Reader to the Trusted Platform Module

The processes TPM3 and TBR3 run in sub-protocol (S3). Firstly, the TPM obtains the session key SK2 via the private channel. The TBR also obtains the identity of the TPM and the session key via the private channels from TBR2.

The TPM generates a fresh random nonce and sends it to the TBR. Again, from email discussion about the sequence of the processes, (S3) cannot run successfully before (S1) has run. The TBR verifies the message and sends back the BD encrypted by the session key created in the previous stage. The TPM verifies the received message and decrypts it to retrieve the BD. In order to check protocol properties later, after the BD is received, an *event tcpgetBD()* is launched.

4.7 (S4) Sending a Matching Result

The last sub-protocol (S4) represents the transfer of a matching result on the BC and BD from the TPM to the SC. This sub-protocol includes process TPM4 and process SC4. We model it to check the correctness of the messages received.

The TPM acquires its certificate via the private channel. The SC creates a fresh random number and sends it with a request. The TPM verifies the message. It then signs the match result message and sends it to the SC. We model a match result as a fresh value since we are not concerned with the mechanism by which the TPM carries out the matching process. The SC will check the signature and the correctness of the message. If it is correct, the SC may release the user's credential to the TPM. We do not model how the SC releases this credential since it goes beyond the definition of the protocol.

5 Analysis

As described in section 2.2, if a naive interpretation of the protocol is applied, an attack is found. After the clarification of the protocol is introduced, we intend to analyse the properites of the protocol to see if the result of the verification is different.

We have analysed the three properties of CPV02, *effectiveness*, *correctness* and *secrecy*, using ProVerif. All three properties of the protocol are satisfied.

Using ProVerif as a verification tool means we can model a Dolev-Yao style attacker that can compose and decompose messages (provided it has relevant cryptographic keys), and has full control over messages that pass over public interfaces and networks.

In the case of the CPV02 protocol, the USB cables are considered part of the public network, since an attacker can interfere with them. The smart card interfaces are also considered public. A prototype device is presented in [11] that can listen to the signal between smart card and smart card reader. This sort of device could be used by an attacker to try to capture a user's biometric code.

5.1 Effectiveness

The TCP will not be given either the BC or the BD unless the integrity of the TPM and TBR has been checked by the SC.

According to the protocol, the BC is transferred from the SC to the platform, and the BD is read from the TBR and sent to the platform; then the two are compared. To protect the BD from a malicious attacker, the device holding this data has to be convinced that the destination to which it will transfer the data can be trusted before the transmission is carried out. This is done by means of integrity checks.

To analyse this property, we use the *event* and *query* command. These two commands are used to check the correctness of sequences of events. While the *event* command is used for launching an event when a certain action is executed, the *query* command is used to prompt ProVerif to verify the correctness of the sequence of events that we specify. If the sequence is not correct, an attack is identified.

In order to verify this property in ProVerif, we encode the integrity check which ensures that the SC is satisfied with the integrity metric of the TCP and the TBR before

Verification of Integrity and Secrecy Properties of a Biometric Authentication Protocol

the trusted platform module receives the user's stored biometric code and user's submitted biometric data. The event *tcpChecked()* is inserted after the SC has checked the integrity of the TCP via the TPM, and the event *tcpgetBC()* is inserted after the TCP has received the BC^+.

Similarly, to verify that the integrity metric of the TBR is checked by the SC before the BD is transferred, an event *tbrChecked()* is launched after the SC has checked the integrity metric of the TBR.

It should be noted that there is no direct communication between the TBR and the SC, so the TPM is responsible for checking the integrity metric of the TBR on behalf of the SC. To model this situation, we code it in such a way that if the TPM is satisfied with the integrity metric of the TBR, an event *tbrChecked()* is triggered. The TBR then sends the encrypted BD to the TPM. The TPM verifies the message, stores the BD, and then an event *tcpgetBD()* is inserted$^+$.

We need to check that these events are executed in the correct order, i.e. that the TPM's integrity metric and the TBR's integrity metric have been examined before the TPM receives the BD. This should be the case even in the presence of an attacker that can control the order of the subprotocols and the messages on the network. This check is implemented using ProVerif's *query* command:

query ev: tcpgetBD() $\Rightarrow$ ev: tcpChecked() & ev : tbrChecked().
query ev: tcpgetBC() $\Rightarrow$ ev: tcpChecked() & ev : tbrChecked().

5.2 Correctness

The TBR is not given the BD until the user is satisfied with the integrity checks on both the TCP and TBR.

This property aims to protect the BD from being read by a malicious biometric reader, the user places her biometric data only on the biometric reader that she trusts. This property is important because if the BD is stolen or accidentally disclosed, it cannot be altered, replaced or regenerated.

To verify this property, we check that the biometric reader (TBR) receives the BD after the integrity metric of the TCP and the integrity metric of the TBR have been checked.

To achieve this, we launch an event *tbrgetBD()* after the BD is created in the process TBR3$^+$. The event would not be triggered without satisfactory integrity checking. To check the correct order of events, we use the query command:

query ev: tbrgetBD() $\Rightarrow$ ev: tcpChecked() & ev : tbrChecked().

5.3 Secrecy

An unauthorised entity that can listen to a message between the SC and TCP, or between the TBR and TCP, cannot obtain either the BC or the BD.

As we remarked in section 1, the secrecy of biometric data cannot be relied upon. The security of a protocol should not depend on the secrecy of biometric data. Indeed, this protocol does not depend on it, since it uses a trusted biometric reader to guard against disclosure. Nevertheless, it is good practice to prevent widespread dissemination, and this property verifies that the protocol does not give an attacker easy access to that data.

To model this property we use the *query* command to ask ProVerif whether an attacker can access the BC or the BD. The commands for this verification are

$$query\ attacker : BC.$$
$$query\ attacker : BD.$$

Using these commands to check whether the specified arguments are secret, ProVerif will exhaustively check whether there is any way that an attacker could obtain the information, BD and BC, that we want to protect. If an attacker can obtain the data, then a potential attack has been identified.

6 Conclusion and Future Work

We have presented a specification of the CPV02 biometric authentication protocol, obtained after clarifying details of the protocol through email discussion with one of the authors. We modelled the clarified protocol using the applied pi calculus and the ProVerif verification tool. We have encoded three intended properties of the protocol, namely *effectiveness*, *secrecy* and *correctness*. The positive results from the verification show that the properties of the protocol hold.

The protocol is successfully verified against the properties. Without this clarification, verification of one of the properties fails.

The CPV02 protocol uses trusted computing platform and involves integrity checking. The trusted computing platform module is an essential part of the protocol in order to guarantee that the components that involved in biometric authentication data cannot be tampered by an intruder. Similar to other classical protocols, nonces are used for checking the freshness of message received and encryption and decryption are also used for the secrecy of message content.

In future work, we will select other protocols with different properties and verify that they hold in a similar way. We would also like to investigate biometric authentication protocol which can be used for unsupervised remote authentication, such as in online banking.

Acknowledgement. Many thanks to Liqun Chen, one of the authors of [2], for detailed email discussion, which was crucial in clarifying the protocol and our understanding of it.

References

1. Lowe, G.: An attack on the Needham-Schroeder public-key authentication protocol. Information Processing Letters 56, 131–133 (1995)
2. Chen, L., Pearson, S., Vamvakas, A.: Trusted Biometric System (2002), http://www.hpl.hp.com/techreports/2002/HPL-2002-185.pdf
3. Pearson, S.: How Can You Trust the Computer in Front of You? (2002), http://www.hpl.hp.com/techreports/2002/HPL-2002-222.pdf

4. Abadi, M., Fournet, C.: Mobile values, new names, and secure communications. In: Proceedings of the 28th Annual ACM Symposium on Principles of Programming Languages, pp. 104–115 (2001)
5. Blanchet, B.: An efficient cryptographic protocol verifier based on prolog rules. In: Schneider, S. (ed.) 14th IEEE Computer Security Foundations Workshop, pp. 82–96. IEEE Computer Society Press, Los Alamitos (2001)
6. Blanchet, B.: Automatic Proof of Strong Secrecy for Security Protocols. In: IEEE Symposium on Security and Privacy, pp. 86–100 (2004)
7. Kremer, S., Ryan, M.: Analysis of an Electronic Voting Protocol in the Applied Pi Calculus. In: Sagiv, M. (ed.) ESOP 2005. LNCS, vol. 3444, pp. 186–200. Springer, Heidelberg (2005)
8. Blanchet, B.: ProVerif Automatic Cryptographic Protocol Verifier User Manual (2005)
9. Delaune, S., Kremer, S., Ryan, M.: Coercion-resistance and Receipt-freeness in Electronic Voting. In: 19th Computer Security oundations Workshop, IEEE Computer Society Press, Los Alamitos (2006)
10. Dolev, D., Yao, A.C.: On the Security of Public Key Protocols. In: Proceedings of 22nd IEEE Symposium on Foundations of Computer Science, pp. 350–357 (1981)
11. Bond, M.: Chip and Pin (EMV) Point-of-Sale Terminal Interceptor (2007), http://www.cl.cam.ac.uk/~mkb23/interceptor/

An On-Line Secure E-Passport Protocol

Vijayakrishnan Pasupathinathan[1], Josef Pieprzyk[1], and Huaxiong Wang[2]

[1] Centre for Advanced Computing - Algorithms and Cryptography (ACAC)
Department of Computing
Macquarie University, Australia
{krishnan,josef}@ics.mq.edu.au
[2] Nanyang Technological University, Singapore
hxwang@ntu.edu.sg

Abstract. The first generation e-passport standard is proven to be insecure and prone to various attacks. To strengthen, the European Union (EU) has proposed an Extended Access Control (EAC) mechanism for e-passports that intends to provide better security in protecting biometric information of the e-passport bearer. But, our analysis shows, the EU proposal fails to address many security and privacy issues that are paramount in implementing a strong security mechanism.

In this paper we propose an on-line authentication mechanism for electronic passports that addresses the weakness in existing implementations, of both The International Civil Aviation Organisation (ICAO) and EU. Our proposal utilises ICAO PKI implementation, thus requiring very little modifications to the existing infrastructure which is already well established.

1 Introduction

Due to increased risk of terrorism, countries are adopting biometric enabled passport as a preventive measure to monitor and strengthen their border security. The ICAO, an United Nation body responsible for setting international passport standards, established five task forces under the New Technology Working Group (NTWG) to develop a standard for Machine Readable Travel Documents (MRTD) [1]. The ICAO standard DOC 9303 [1] for MRTD describes a contactless smart card microchip that conforms with ISO-14443 [2], embedded within an e-passport booklet. The microchip duplicates the information that appears on an passport's bio-data page and which is recorded in the Machine Readable Zone (MRZ). The e-passport standard provides details about establishing a secure communication between an e-passport and an Inspection System (IS), authentication of an e-passport, details on storage mechanism and biometric identifiers that should be used.

Ari Juels, *et al.* [3] presented some security and privacy issues that apply to the first generation e-passports. The authors express concerns regarding the fact that the contactless chip embedded in an e-passport allows the e-passport contents to be read without direct contact with an Inspection System (IS) and, importantly, with the e-passport booklet closed. The authors also raise concerns as to whether data on the chip could therefore be covertly collected by means of "skimming" or "eavesdropping". Because of low entropy, the key would be also vulnerable to brute force attacks as demonstrated by [4]. The risk of eavesdropping is increased by the surveillance environment in which border checks occur, particularly, as the border control becomes more and more automated (as discussed in [5]), this will ultimately assist in a covert collection of e-passport data. Kc and Karger [6] presented the "splicing attack", "fake finger attack" and other attacks that can be carried out when an e-passport bearer presents the passport to hotel clerks.

In [7], V. Pasupathinathan et al. made a formal analysis and found that the e-passport protocol does not satisfy security goals for data origin authentication as it can be subject to replay and grandmaster chess attacks, and the weakness can be exploited in cases where problems with facial biometric exists. They also pointed out that data confidentiality is also compromised when an attacker is able to obtain encryption and MAC keys stored in the e-passport chip using information stored in MRZ. They were able to formally verify and prove that security goals like, mutual authentication, key freshness and key integrity are also not satisfied.

To address these concerns the NTWG has planned further discussions in 2007 about standardising the next generation of e-passports that will support Extended Access Control (EAC), which is based on EU's proposal [8] for EAC. A primary goal of EAC is to provide mutual authentication (in particular, authentication of IS) and additional security for biometrics. The first generation e-passports have a single biometric identifier, based on the facial biometric, whereas the second generation will include both finger prints and iris scan biometric identifiers.

This paper analyses the security features of the current proposal for EAC, identifies its weaknesses and proposes an alternative mechanism. We believe that, EAC proposal fails to provide adequate security and has introduced security weaknesses and implementation issues on its own. Our proposed solution addresses the drawbacks in the current EU EAC proposal and provides the following enhanced security features: (1) prevention of biometric information being released to a malicious IS in possession of MRZ details, (2) enhancement of communication security between an e-passport and a IS, (3) protection against passport skimming and (4) reduction of PKI implementation.

1.1 Organisation

In Section 2 we provide a brief overview of EAC protocol and highlight some security issues and weaknesses in proposed authentication mechanisms. In Section 3, we propose our protocol for EAC that covers the entire e-passport protocol suite. In Section 4, we provide a security analysis of our proposed system and finally, Section 5 concludes our work.

2 EU Extended Access Control

EU has issued an e-passport specification [8] for EAC and is intended to restrict access to secondary biometric identifiers like finger prints and iris scans.

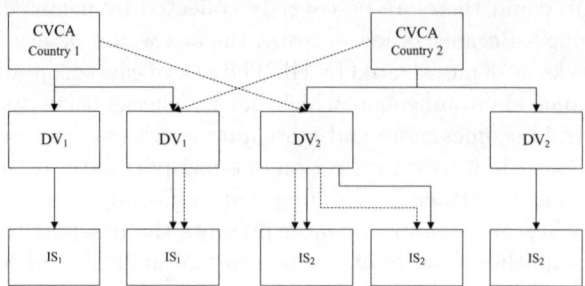

Fig. 1. EAC PKI

The guideline is based on authentication techniques proposed by D. Klüger from Federal Office for Information Security (BSI) [9,10]. Klüger proposed two protocols, Chip Authentication (CA) and Terminal Authentication (TA). His proposal also included modifications to the existing PKI. Country Signing Certification Authority (CSCA) is required to certify Document Verifiers (DV) in other countries which in turn certifies Inspection Systems (IS) present at a country's border security checkpoint. Figure 1 provides an overview of the modified PKI hierarchy.

2.1 E-Passport Operation with EAC

The EU EAC proposal for e-passports involves the following four protocols:

1. An e-passport bearer presents his/her document to a border security officer who scans the MRZ on the e-passport through a MRZ reader and then places the e-passport near an IS to fetch data from the chip. The e-passport and the IS establish an encrypted communication channel by executing the Basic Access Control (BAC) protocol (described in Appendix A).
2. The IS and the e-passport then perform a mandatory chip authentication.
3. The chip authentication is followed by passive authentication as in the first generation passport (described in Appendix A).
4. Terminal authentication.

Only if all protocols are completed successfully, the e-passport releases sensitive information like secondary biometric identifiers. If an IS does not support EU EAC, the e-passport performs the collection of protocols as specified in the first generation e-passports.

2.2 Chip Authentication (CA)

Chip Authentication protocol is a mandatory EU EAC mechanism that replaces active authentication proposed in the first generation e-passports. It involves a Diffie-Hellman key agreement and is followed by *passive authentication*. It is performed after a successful BAC and provides both an authentication of the chip and generation of a session key. The chip sends its public key (PK_{chip}) and its

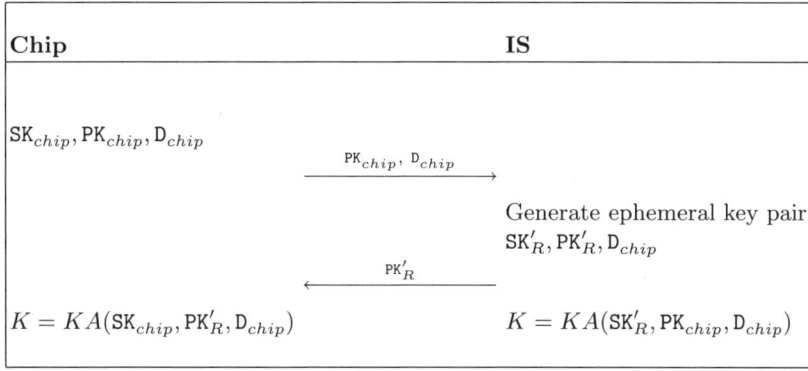

Fig. 2. Chip Authentication

domain parameters (D_{chip}) to IS. IS then generates an ephemeral D-H key pair (SK'_R,PK'_R) using the same domain parameters and sends the newly generated public key to the chip. Both the chip and IS derive a new session key K. The chip authentication is immediately followed by a passive authentication. This allows IS to verify whether PK_{chip} is genuine.

2.3 Terminal Authentication (TA)

Terminal Authentication is also a mandatory EU EAC mechanism that involves a two-pass challenge-response protocol and allows the chip to authenticate an IS. TA is only carried out after a successful run of chip authentication and passive authentication as it provides only an unilateral authentication of IS. During TA, the IS is required to send a certificate chain ($CERT_{IS}\langle\rangle$, $CERT_{DV}\langle\rangle$, $CERT_{CVCA^H}\langle\rangle$). The certificate $CERT_{CVCA^H}\langle\rangle$ represents a certificate issued by the e-passport's home country's CA, which is also stored in the e-passport. The

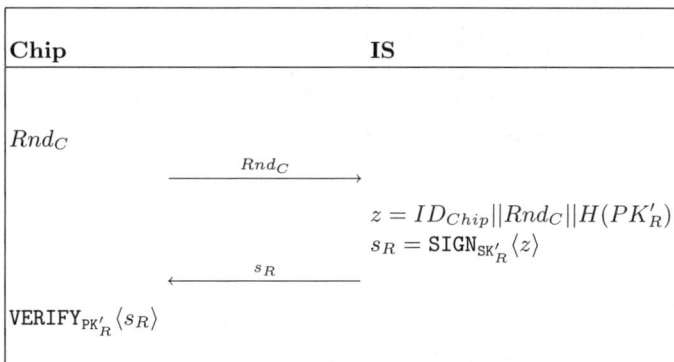

Fig. 3. Terminal Authentication

chain indicates that the visiting country's IS is certified by a visiting country's Document Verifier (DV), which in turn is certified by a e-passport's home country CVCA. After a certificate chain is validated by the e-passport, it sends a challenge to IS. IS responds with a digitally signed message that contains the received challenge, the IS's ephemeral public key used in the chip authentication and e-passport ID (ID_{chip}), where, ID_{chip} is the document ID obtained from the e-passport's MRZ. The e-passport verifies the signature received and if the verification holds then it has successfully authenticated IS.

2.4 Security Issues in Second Generation E-Passports

EU proposal for EAC in e-passports provides much better security compared to the first generation e-passports. Nevertheless, EAC proposal still relies on BAC to derive the initial session key needed to access e-passport bearer's details including their facial biometric. Because of the inherent weaknesses of BAC as previously described (e.g. keys that have insufficient entropy), the EAC proposal also suffers from the same weaknesses.

EAC proposal makes extensive use of PKI. Both chip and terminal authentication protocols requires verification of certificates that invovles the entire certification hierarchy. The e-passport initially contains the root level certificate ($\text{CERT}_{CVCA^H}\langle\rangle$) that was written by its document verifier at the time of issue. As the e-passport chips are time-less devices, i.e they do not have any internal clock, this makes them vulnerable to attacks using expired certificates. Klüger [9,10] acknowledges this vulnerability and proposed that the e-passport should write $\text{CERT}_{CVCA^H}\langle\rangle$ with the latest certificate it obtains when it performs a terminal authentication with a visiting country's IS. During the first run of terminal authentication the time of expiry of $\text{CERT}_{CVCA^H}\langle\rangle$ that was initially written is used as a reference time to validate visiting country's IS certificate and after a successful run of the protocol the e-passport will store the $\text{CERT}_{CVCA^H}\langle\rangle$ that is present in the certificate chain received from an IS. But, the protocol is still vulnerable to attacks using expired IS certificates. Validity of IS certificates are considerably shorter when compared to CVCA certificates. A compromised IS even if its certificate was expired would still be able to authenticate itself to an e-passport and obtain access to sensitive e-passport information including finger prints and iris scans, that were intended to be protected by EAC. The attack is more effective for infrequently used e-passports, because they have only the initially written $\text{CERT}_{CVCA^H}\langle\rangle$ which themselves may be expired. As the e-passport uses the time on $\text{CERT}_{CVCA^H}\langle\rangle$ as a reference point, it would accept any certificate, as long as its validity is before the current reference time recorded on the e-passport.

The approach of sending certificate chains can also lead to a Denial-of-Service (DOS) attack on an e-passport. Since an IS terminal is not authenticated during or before chip authentication, a malicious terminal could flood the chip by sending lots of public keys and certificates. Because of the limited memory that is available in an e-passport chip, the chip could run out of memory and essentially stopping the chip from functioning in a desired manner.

The EAC proposal also has some new weaknesses. The e-passport should now have write access to the chip, to update its $\text{CERT}_{CVCA^H}\langle\rangle$. This could be used by an illegitimate e-passport bearer to update the chip with false information. The EAC proposal does not specify how write access would be controlled by the chip. Another drawback of EAC proposal is the cross certification among countries. Every country implementing EAC would be required to certificate other country's document verifiers. That essentially means that each document verifier that certifies IS will need to be certified by CSVA of every participating country. EAC recommends the validity of document verifier certificates be one third of CVCA certificate's validity period. This becomes an extremely complex undertaking for each country, with respect to certifying other participating country's document verifiers and maintenance of revocation lists. EAC also does not address Grandmaster Chess Attack [11] to which the first generation passports were vulnerable to. The BAC protocol is used only to form a session key for an encrypted communication channel between a chip and IS and does not provide authentication. Therefore the chip establishes a session key even though it is not sure if IS is genuine. EU EAC also does not provide any guarantees regarding freshness or origin of messages.

There are also concerns regarding privacy of the e-passport bearer. The chip sends its identification details (public key) during CA, even before it has authenticated the IS. Therefore, this would make very easy for an attacker to track an e-passport bearer, as an attacker is not required to authenticate to an e-passport before obtaining details from an e-passport. H. Scherzer *et al.* from IBM developed a secure operating system called Caernarvon [12] for smart cards. In the Caernarvon protocol a smart card reader authenticates itself to a smart card chip using its public key first and then engages in the Diffie-Hellman key agreement to form a session key. This makes the Caernarvon protocol more secure compared to the current implementation in EAC, but the Caernarvon protocol shares the same weaknesses EAC has with certificate verification as discussed above.

3 On-Line Secure E-Passport Protocol (OSEP Protocol)

In this section we present an on-line secure e-passport protocol. An on-line authentication system for e-passport is similar to the current e-passport system (or as in the standard non-electronic passport). Currently, most security organisations are involved in passive monitoring of border security checkpoints. When a passport bearer is validated at a border security checkpoint, the bearers details are collected and entered into a database. The security organisation compares this databases against the databases of known offenders (e.g. terrorists and wanted criminals). The OSEP protocol changes this to an active monitoring system. The border security check-point or the DV can now cross check against the database of known offenders, simplifying the process of identification of criminals.

Our proposal provides the following security features:

- An e-passport discloses its information stored on the chip only after a successful authentication of IS. This prevents revealing e-passports identity to a

third party that is not authorised or cannot be authenticated. This prevents covert collection of e-passport data from "skimming" or "eavesdropping" attacks that were very effective against both the ICAO e-passport and the EU EAC standards.
- The OSEP protocol provides proof of freshness and authenticity for messages between participating entities.
- The OSEP protocol uses existing ICAO PKI implementation (first generation passports) and eliminates the need for cross certification among participating countries as required by EU EAC (second generation passports).
- The OSEP protocol eliminates the need for certificate chain verification by an e-passport. Only the top level certificate (CVCA) is required to be stored in an e-passport chip, reducing memory requirements and thus prevents a malicious reader from performing a DOS attack on an e-passport.
- The OSEP protocol also requires an IS to provide proof of correctness for public key parameters to an e-passport. This allows an e-passport to verify that an IS is using correct domain parameters and to prevent related attacks [13,14].

3.1 Initial Setup

All entities involved in the protocol share the public quantities p, q, g where:

- p is the modulus, a prime number of the order 1024 bits or more.
- q is a prime number in the range of 159-160 bits, such that $q|(p-1)$.
- g is a generator of order q, where $\forall i < q, g^i \neq 1 \mod p$.
- Each entity has its own public key and private key pair (PK_i, SK_i), where $\text{PK}_i = g^{(\text{SK}_i)} \mod p$
- Entity i's public key (PK_i) is certified by its root certification authority (j) and is represented as $\text{CERT}_j \langle \text{PK}_i, i \rangle$.
- Public parameters p, q, g used by an e-passport are also certified by its root certification authority.

3.2 Phase One - IS Authentication (ISA)

Step 1 ($\mathcal{IS}$): When an e-passport is presented to an IS, the IS reads MRZ information using an MRZ reader and issues the smart card command GET CHALLENGE to the e-passport chip.

Step 2 ($\mathcal{C}$): The e-passport chip then generates a random $c \in_R 1 \leq c \leq q-1$ and computes $K_c = g^c \mod p$, playing its part in the key agreement process to establish a session key. Chip replies to the GET CHALLENGE command by sending K_c and its domain parameters p, q, g.

$$\mathcal{C} \longrightarrow \mathcal{IS} : K_c, p, q, g$$

Step 3 ($\mathcal{IS}$): On receiving the response from the chip, the IS generates a random $is \in_R 1 \leq is \leq q-1$ and computes its part of the session key as $K_{is} = g^{is} \mod p$. IS digitally signs the message containing MRZ value of the e-passport and K_c.

$$S_{\mathcal{IS}} = \text{SIGN}_{\text{SK}_{\mathcal{IS}}}\langle MRZ \| K_c \rangle$$

It then contacts the nearest DV of the e-passports issuing country and obtains its public key. IS encrypts and sends its signature $S_{\mathcal{IS}}$ along with e-passports MRZ information and K_c using DV's public key $\text{PK}_{\mathcal{DV}}$.

$$\mathcal{IS} \longrightarrow \mathcal{DV} : \text{ENC}_{\text{PK}_{\mathcal{DV}}}\langle S_{\mathcal{IS}}, MRZ, K_c \rangle, \text{CERT}_{\mathcal{CVCA}}\langle \text{PK}_{\mathcal{IS}}, \mathcal{IS} \rangle$$

Step 4 ($\mathcal{DV}$): DV decrypts the message received from IS and verifies $\text{CERT}_{\mathcal{CVCA}}\langle \text{PK}_{\mathcal{IS}}, \mathcal{IS} \rangle$ and the signature $S_{\mathcal{IS}}$. If the verification holds, DV knows that IS is genuine and creates a digitally signed message $S_{\mathcal{DV}}$ to prove IS's authenticity to the e-passport.

$$S_{\mathcal{DV}} = \text{SIGN}_{\text{SK}_{\mathcal{DV}}}\langle MRZ \| K_c \| \text{PK}_{\mathcal{IS}} \rangle, \text{CERT}_{CVCA}\langle \text{PK}_{\mathcal{DV}}, \mathcal{DV} \rangle$$

DV encrypts and sends the signature $S_{\mathcal{DV}}$ using the public key $\text{PK}_{\mathcal{IS}}$ of IS.

$$\mathcal{DV} \longrightarrow \mathcal{IS} : \text{ENC}_{\text{PK}_{\mathcal{IS}}}\langle S_{\mathcal{DV}}, [\text{PK}_{Chip}] \rangle$$

DV may choose to send the public key of the chip if required. This has an obvious advantage, because the IS system now trusts DV to be genuine, it can obtain a copy of e-passport chip's PK to verify during E-passport authentication.

Step 5 ($\mathcal{IS}$): IS on decrypting the message received, computes the session key $K_{cis} = (K_c)^{is}$ and encrypts the signature received from DV, the e-passport MRZ information and K_c using K_{cis}. It also digitally signs its part of the session key K_{is}.

$$\mathcal{IS} \longrightarrow \mathcal{C} : K_{is}, \text{SIGN}_{\text{SK}_{\mathcal{IS}}}\langle K_{is}, p, q, g \rangle, \text{ENC}_{K_{cis}}\langle S_{\mathcal{DV}}, MRZ, K_c \rangle$$

Step 6 $\mathcal{C}$: The chip on receiving the message from IS computes the session key $K_{cis} = (K_{is})^c$. It decrypts the message received using the session key and verifies signature $S_{\mathcal{DV}}$ and $\text{VERIFY}_{PK_{\mathcal{IS}}}\langle \text{SIGN}_{\text{SK}_{\mathcal{IS}}}\langle K_{is}, p, q, g \rangle \rangle$. On successful verification, the chip is convinced that the IS system is genuine and can proceed further in releasing its details. All further communication between an e-passport and IS is encrypted using the session key K_{cis}

3.3 Phase Two - E-Passport Authentication (EPA)

Step 1 $\mathcal{C}$: The IS issues an INTERNAL AUTHENTICATE command to the e-passport. The e-passport on receiving the command creates a signature $S_{\mathcal{C}}$ = $\text{SIGN}_{\text{SK}_{chip}}\langle MRZ \| K_{cis} \rangle$ and sends its domain parameter certificate to IS. The entire message is encrypted using the session key K_{cis}.

$$\mathcal{C} \longrightarrow \mathcal{IS} : \text{ENC}_{K_{cis}}\langle S_{\mathcal{C}}, \text{CERT}_{DV}\langle \text{PK}_{\mathcal{C}} \rangle, \text{CERT}_{DV}\langle p, q, g \rangle \rangle$$

Step 2 ($\mathcal{IS}$): IS decrypts the message and verifies $\text{CERT}_{DV}\langle p, q, g \rangle$, $\text{CERT}_{DV}\langle \text{PK}_{\mathcal{C}} \rangle$ and $S_{\mathcal{C}}$. If all three verification holds then IS is convinced that the e-passport is genuine and authentic.

During ISA, IS sends the e-passports MRZ information to the nearest e-passport's DV, which could be an e-passport country's embassy. Embassies are DV's as they are allowed to issue e-passport to their citizens and as most embassies are located within an IS's home country, network connection issues will be minimal.

Sending MRZ information is also advantageous, as the embassy now has a list of all its citizens who have passed through a visiting country's border security checkpoint. We do not see any privacy implications, because, most countries require their citizen to register at embassies when they are visiting a foreign country.

4 Analysis of E-Passport Scheme

In this section we identify important security goals required in an e-passport protocol and perform a security analysis of our proposed OSEP protocol.

4.1 Requirement Analysis

The two most important requirements for border security are,:identification of the passport bearer and authentication of the passport data. Due to the digital nature of data stored in an e-passport, it is easy for the data to be copied or modified. An e-passport protocol will need to address security requirements that will affect electronic data storage and transmission. The references [9,1] provided a brief overview of security goals for e-passports. The description in the references was limited and did not consider goals that are essential in the analysis of cryptographic protocols. Our security goals for an e-passport system are:

Goal 1 *Identification*: After a successful completion of an e-passport protocol, both an e-passport and IS must obtain guarantees (unforgeable proof) of the other party's identity.

Goal 2 *Authenticity*: After a successful completion of an e-passport protocol, both an e-passport and IS must be sure about authenticity of messages received during the conversation with each other, and should also have an undeniable proof of the origin of messages.

Goal 3 *Data confidentiality*: Data confidentiality during an e-passport protocol run is guaranteed by the security of session key agreed between an e-passport and IS, therefore, if the e-passport completes a single protocol run with the view that it has negotiated a session key K with IS, then the e-passport is guaranteed that no other third-party has learnt key K and if IS completes the protocol run then it associates the key K with the e-passport. Data confidentiality of information stored in the e-passport chip is not considered as it is protocol independent, but is necessary for an e-passport protocol to detect if information was tampered, which is provided by our integrity goal.

Goal 4 *Integrity*: Integrity of data in an e-passport chip is guaranteed by signatures, therefore, in a run of an e-passport protocol, if an IS successfully verifies and validates signatures on messages from the e-passport, then the

IS obtains guarantee about information held in the e-passport chip has not been modified by any third party or the e-passport bearer after chip's initialisation by DS.

Goal 5 *Privacy*: In every run of an e-passport protocol, the e-passport bearer is assured that, his/her e-passport's digital identity is revealed only to an authenticated IS involved in the current protocol run.

Goal 6 *Session key security*: Both entities, an e-passport and IS have proof that, each run of the e-passport protocol is unique and compromise of long term keys does not compromise session keys derived in the previous protocol runs.

4.2 Security Analysis of the OSEP Protocol

In this section we present a brief security analysis of the OSEP protocol. We first list our assumptions and then our claims about the OSEP protocol's security that corresponds to our security goals described in Section §4.1.

Assumptions

- In the OSEP protocol both an e-passport and IS instantiate a non-concurrent protocol run (session) between them, whereas session connections between IS and DV may run concurrently.
- IS is always the initiator of a protocol run and an e-passport is always the responder.
- The underlying security for Diffie-Hellman (DH) key exchange, the Decisional Diffie-Hellman (DDH) assumption holds.
- Cryptographic primitives like, symmetric and public key encryption, digital signatures, message authentication codes and hash functions are secure under the standard security notions.

Lemma 1. *If the encryption scheme used in the protocol is secure against the CCA2 attack then at the end of the OSEP protocol, both $\mathcal{C}$ and $\mathcal{IS}$ will complete matching sessions and get the same session key.*

Proof (Sketch): Since the signature algorithm is secure against existential forgery under the adaptive chosen-message attack (by assumption), the MRZ information along with randomness of K_c and K_{is} guarantees the freshness of the message and binds the message with the two communicating parties. Therefore an attacker cannot forge or modify a message. For an attacker to forge or modify a message that is acceptable by $\mathcal{IS}$ or $\mathcal{C}$, he would need to forge the signature on $\texttt{SIGN}_{\texttt{SK}_{IS}}\langle K_i, p, q, g\rangle$ in phase 1, step 5 or forge the signature on $S_\mathcal{C}$ in phase 2, step 1. This contradicts our assumptions.

Furthermore, the digital signature by $\mathcal{C}$ contains the freshly generated session key K_{cis}. This prevents replay of messages from a previous run by an adversary who is not able to to generate signatures on both K_c and K_{cis}. □

Theorem 1. *The protocol provided in Section 3 is SK-secure if the encryption scheme used is secure against the CCA2 attack.*

Proof. In order to prove our protocol is SK-secure [15], we have to prove that $\mathcal{C}$ and $\mathcal{IS}$ get the same session key after they complete matching sessions and that an adversary cannot distinguish the session key K_{cis} from a random value with a non-negligible advantage. The former directly follows Lemma 1 and the following lemma provides proof for later.

Lemma 2. *Assuming DDH and the signature scheme is secure, then an attacker cannot distinguish the session key K_{cis} from a random value with a non-negligible advantage.*

Proof (Sketch): The proof is by contradiction. Lets assume that an attacker can distinguish the session key K_{cis} from a random value with a non-negligible advantage η. In the C-K model [15], the key exchange attacker is not permitted to corrupt the *test session* or its *matching session*, so an attacker cannot directly get the session key K_{cis} from an attack on the OSEP protocol. Therefore, the attacker has two possible method to distinguish K_{cis} from a random value.

- The attacker learns the session key K_{cis}.
- The attacker successfully establishes a session (other than a test or its matching session) that has the same session key as the test session.

The first methods means that given g, g^c, g^{is}, g^α, the attacker is able to distinguish $\alpha = K_{cis}$ from random. This contradicts our DDH assumption. For the second method, there are two strategies an attacker can take. (A) After $\mathcal{C}$ and $\mathcal{IS}$ complete the *matching sessions*, the attacker establishes a new session with either $\mathcal{C}$ or $\mathcal{IS}$. But this session key will be not the same as K_{cis} as the values c and is are chosen randomly by $\mathcal{C}$ or $\mathcal{IS}$. (B) The attacker intervenes during the run of the protocol and makes $\mathcal{C}$ and $\mathcal{IS}$ get the same session key but not complete *matching sessions*. But this is not feasible according to Lemma 1 and we know that an attacker cannot succeed. □

Thus from Lemma 1 and Lemma 2, we know that $\mathcal{C}$ and $\mathcal{IS}$ will get the same session key after the completion of matching sessions and the attacker cannot distinguish the session key from a random value with a non-negligible advantage. In accordance with definition of SK-security [15](Definition 1) the OSEP is SK-secure.

Theorem 2. *The OSEP protocol provides undeniable proof of identification of both $\mathcal{C}$ and $\mathcal{IS}$.*

Proof (Sketch): The message sent to $\mathcal{C}$ by $\mathcal{IS}$ in Step 5 of ISA includes the values, $S_{\mathcal{DV}}$, MRZ and K_c. The signed message $S_{\mathcal{DV}}$ contains public key of $\mathcal{IS}$ verified by $\mathcal{DV}$, so it is sufficient for $\mathcal{C}$ to verify $S_{\mathcal{DV}}$ to successfully identify $\mathcal{IS}$ as genuine.

An adversary wishing to falsely identify of IS will need to forge $S_{\mathcal{DV}}$. $S_{\mathcal{DV}}$ can be only generated with a valid DV's secret key ($\text{SK}_{\mathcal{DV}}$). The adversary cannot forge $S_{\mathcal{DV}}$ as he does not know $\text{SK}_{\mathcal{DV}}$.

An adversary who does not have K_{cis} and $\text{SK}_{\mathcal{C}}$, will not be able to identify as a genuine $\mathcal{C}$, because, in EPA $\mathcal{C}$ is required to digitally sign its MRZ and the freshly generated session key K_{cis}. Therefore, the OSEP protocol provides non-repudiable proof of identity for both $\mathcal{IS}$ and $\mathcal{C}$. □

Remark 1. The strict privacy requirement is, the e-passport protocol guarantees no information about an e-passport bearer is available to any unauthorised entities and the relaxed privacy requirement is, when the e-passport protocol guarantees that digital identity or biometric information of an e-passport bearer is not be available to any unauthorised entities. The OSEP protocol provides partial forward secrecy under the strict privacy requirement as loss of the long-term secret key of both $\mathcal{IS}$ and $\mathcal{DV}$ will reveal the MRZ information of an e-passport. But, compromise of long term key does not compromise the previous session keys established. Also, any loss of session key in the previous protocol does not compromise future runs of an e-passport protocol. Thus under the relaxed privacy requirement, the OSEP protocol provides perfect forward secrecy.

In addition, in the OSEP protocol, an e-passport bearer is sure about protection of his/her digital identity against an unauthenticated $\mathcal{IS}$ and *unknown adversaries* as the digital identity of an e-passport bearer $\text{PK}_{\mathcal{C}}$ is revealed only in the step one of EPA. EPA follows a successful ISA, therefore $\mathcal{C}$ is also sure about the $\mathcal{IS}$ identity. The digital identity is also protected from any adversary eavesdropping on the communication as it is encrypted using the fresh secure session key established during ISA.

The OSEP protocol also provides tamper detectable integrity check for data in an e-passport's chip. Integrity of e-passport data provided in OSEP is similar to what was provided by both first generation and second generation passports. The data stored in an e-passport's chip is hashed and digitally signed by the e-passport's DS at the time of initialisation. Therefore as a consequence of the assumption four, that hash functions and digital signatures are secure, the OSEP protocol provides integrity verification. An adversary wishing to authenticate modified data will need to forge the digital signature of DS on the hash values. This is infeasible as the adversary does not know the DS's private key $\text{SK}_{\mathcal{DS}}$.

To summarise, OSEP is a simple and efficient protocol. Its main advantages are that it not only protects the chip's data during communication from an eavesdropper, but also restricts access to an unauthenticated IS. The protocol requires very little modification to existing PKI implemented by the first generation e-passport standard. A disadvantage of the OSEP protocol is, its on-line nature of authentication mechanism. IS is required to contact the e-passport countries DV and authenticate itself before it can continue communication with an e-passport. This process might incur some delay, but we expect this delay to be minimal as the communication between IS and DV will be through a high-speed network.

5 Conclusion

Security techniques implemented in both the first and second generation of e-passports do not adequately protect an e-passport bearer. The first generation e-passport standard is vulnerable to brute force attacks because session keys generated have a very low entropy. The second generation e-passport proposal requires extensive modifications to exiting infrastructure and it still relies on the first generation standards to provide a secure connection to protect primary biometric identifiers. Both the standard have ignored the need to protect e-passports details during setting up a communication, which makes the e-passport bearer vulnerable to identity theft and covert surveillance.

We have presented an on-line e-passport protocol that addresses many weaknesses in both the first and second generation e-passport protocols. Our proposal also offers significant security advantages. The security measures will make an e-passport extremely hard for a malicious user to authenticate as a genuine e-passport bearer or as an IS. The proposed protocol also protects the details of an e-passport bearer from an unauthorised IS thus reducing the threat of identity theft. The OSEP protocol also uses existing PKI infrastructure in place for the first generation e-passport standard and eliminates the need for sending certificate chain as proposed in the second generation e-passport standard, making an e-passport in OSEP protocol less vulnerable to DOS based attacks. Electronic passports are an important step in the right direction. They enable countries to digitise their security at the border control and provide faster and safer processing of an e-passport bearer. The OSEP protocol strengthens this process by providing an enhanced e-passport security measure.

Acknowledgments

The work is supported by Australian Research Council grants DP0663452, DP0558773 and DP0665035.

References

1. ICAO: Machine readable travel documents. Technical report, ICAO (2006)
2. ISO/IEC: Iso/iec14443, identification cards – contactless integrated circuit(s) cards – proximity cards (2000)
3. Juels, A., Molnar, D., Wagner, D.: Security and privacy issues in e-passports. In: IEEE SecureComm. 2005 (2005)
4. Laurie, A.: Rfidiot (2007)
5. Australian Customs Service: Smartgate (2006)
6. Kc, G.S., Karger, P.A.: Preventing attacks on machine readable travel documents (mrtds) (2005), http://eprint.iacr.org/
7. Pasupathinathan, V., Pieprzyk, J., Wang, H.: Formal analysis of icao's e-passport specification. In: Brankovic, L., Miller, M. (eds.) Australasian Information Security Conference (AISC2008). Conferences in Research and Practice in Information Technology (CRPIT), vol. 81, Australian Computer Society (2008)

8. Justice and Home Affairs: Eu standard specifications for security features and biometrics in passports and travel documents. Technical report, European Union (2006)
9. Kügler, D.: Security concept of the eu-passport. Security in Pervasive Computing 85 (2005)
10. Kügler, D.: Adavance security mechanisms for machine readable travel documents. Technical report, Federal Office for Information Security (BSI), Germany (2005)
11. Desmedt, Y., Goutier, C., Bengio, S.: Special uses and abuses of the fiat-shamir passport protocol. In: Pomerance, C. (ed.) CRYPTO 1987. LNCS, vol. 293, pp. 21–39. Springer, Heidelberg (1988)
12. Scherzer, H., Canetti, R., Karger, P.A., Krawczyk, H., Rabin, T., Toll, D.C.: Authenticating mandatory access controls and preserving privacy for a high-assurance smart card. In: Snekkenes, E., Gollmann, D. (eds.) ESORICS 2003. LNCS, vol. 2808, pp. 181–200. Springer, Heidelberg (2003)
13. Wiemers, A.: Kommentare zu application interface for smart cards used as secure signature creation device, part 1 - basic requirements. Technical Report Version 0.14, Bonn, Germany (2003)
14. ANSI: Public key cryptography for the financial services industry, key aggreement and key transport using elliptic curve cryptography. Technical report, American National Standards Institute (ANSI 2001) (2001)
15. Canetti, R., Krawczyk, H.: Analysis of key exchange protocols and their use for building secure channels. In: Pfitzmann, B. (ed.) EUROCRYPT 2001. LNCS, vol. 2045, pp. 453–474. Springer, Heidelberg (2001)

A Basic Access Control and Passive Authentication

Basic access control is an optional security mechanism that uses ISO 11770-2 *Key Establishment Mechanism 6* to form a secure channel between IS and a chip. The protocol uses two secret keys (K_{ENC}, K_{MAC}) that are stored in a chip. IS derives both these keys using scanable data present in MRZ, namely passport number, date of birth of the passport bearer, date of passport validity and check digits for those values. The three pass challenge-response protocol is initiated by IS which requests a challenge from the chip. On receiving the challenge (Rnd_{C2}) IS creates a checksum according to ISO/IEC 9797-1 *MAC algorithm 3* over the cipher text that contains IS's response to chip's challenge Rnd_{R2} and keying material K_R. The chip on obtaining IS's response creates a checksum that includes its keying material K_C. Both IS and the chip verify the MAC obtained and decrypt the message to reveal both keying materials, to form the "key seed" K_{seed}. K_{seed} is used to derive a shared session key using the key derivation algorithm described in [1] (*Appendix 5*). Passive authentication (PA) provides only a basic level of security, as it is still vulnerable to skimming and eavesdropping attacks. PA is used to verify the integrity and to authenticate data stored in an e-passport. The e-passport bearer information is digitally signed by DS (Documemnt Signer) and verified by IS during PA.

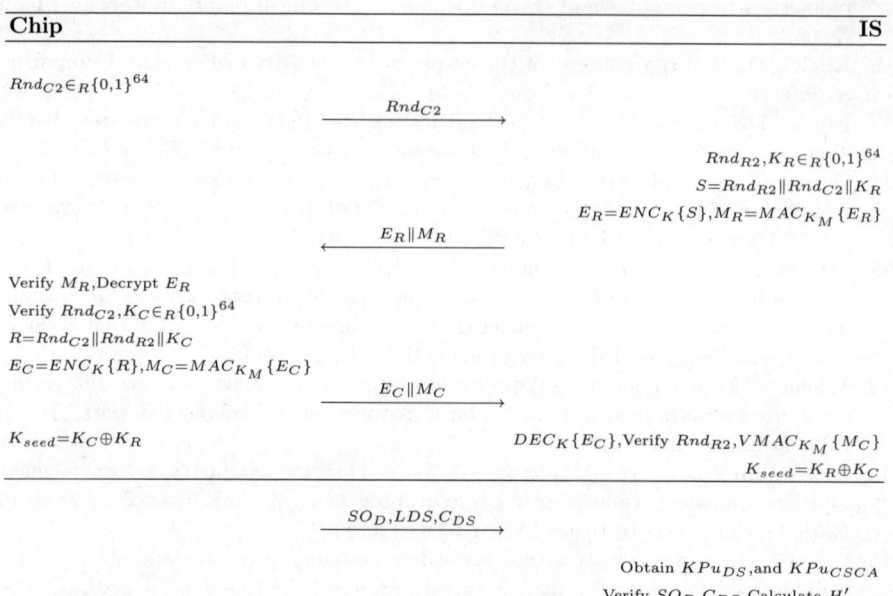

Fig. 4. Basic Access Control and Passive Authentication

Secure Multi-Coupons for Federated Environments: Privacy-Preserving and Customer-Friendly

Frederik Armknecht[1], Alberto N. Escalante B.[1], Hans Löhr[1], Mark Manulis[2], and Ahmad-Reza Sadeghi[1]

[1] Horst Görtz Institute for IT Security
Ruhr-University of Bochum, Germany
{frederik.armknecht,alberto.escalante,
hans.loehr,ahmad.sadeghi}@trust.rub.de
[2] UCL Crypto Group, Université Catholique de Louvain, Belgium
mark.manulis@uclouvain.be

Abstract. A digital multi-coupon is similar to a paper-based booklet containing k coupons that can be purchased from one vendor and later redeemed at a vendor in exchange for services. Current schemes, offering privacy-protection and strong security properties such as unsplittability of multi-coupons, address business scenarios with a single vendor and multiple customers, and require customers to redeem coupons in some fixed order.

In this paper, we propose a multi-coupon scheme for federated environments that preserves the security and privacy properties of existing schemes, as well as their asymptotic communication and computation complexity. We define a generic formal security model and show that our scheme meets the formal requirements of this framework. Moreover, in contrast to previous solutions, we allow customers to redeem their coupons in an arbitrary order.

Keywords: coupons, privacy, unlinkability, unsplittability, payment system, loyalty, federation.

1 Introduction

Coupons are the basis for successful business models and are widely used in practice. Companies distribute (paper-based) coupons to customers for various marketing purposes, like encouraging loyalty, providing discounts, setting up prepayment models, and attracting new customers. A special variant are coupon booklets, where all coupons are contained in a booklet and are only valid as long as they are attached to the booklet. This ensures a property we call *unsplittability*: the single coupons cannot be redeemed autonomously; instead, they can only be shared among customers by giving away the entire booklet each time a coupon is spent.

We call coupon booklets (and their electronic equivalents) *multi-coupons (MCs)*. A vendor provides a customer with a new multi-coupon in the *issue* procedure. The customer can then use the coupons from this multi-coupon in the *redeem* procedure to pay the vendor. During redemption, the vendor verifies that the coupon is valid and authentic, and provides the customer with the specified good or service. Each coupon in a multi-coupon can be used only once. In the following, we denote by *object* the good or service implied by a coupon. Any item that can be bought may become an object in practice, e.g., clothes, songs, books, videos, tickets, and even services, such as discounts, access to computer resources, etc.

Multi-Coupons in a Vendor Federation. Until now, multi-coupons were proposed in use cases with a single vendor. Hence, one approach to make MCs more user-friendly is to make them usable in a more general scenario, where a federation of vendors is involved. For instance, consider a cooperation between transportation companies, different cultural institutions, restaurants, and shops offering joint coupons to tourists who can then visit any of the indicated places of interest, eat at the participating restaurants, and buy goods from the listed shops at discount prices. Note that paper-based variants of such cooperations exist in many cities (e.g., [1,2,3]) and enjoy popularity. The general case is that tourists buy a special card which is accompanied with coupons offering discounts. This card should be presented prior to using any of the coupons (i.e., coupons are unsplittable).

Obviously, it would be more convenient if a tourist could buy the MC at *any* involved vendor and would not be forced to go to a central place like the tourist information. A trivial solution could be to connect each vendor to one central server which issues the electronic MCs, but more intelligent solutions which allow the vendors to act autonomously as much as possible are certainly preferrable. Moreover, there might be several competing vendors in the federation that provide the same service, e.g., different restaurants, where a customer could get a meal at a reduced price. In such cases, it might be desirable that the vendor who actually provided the service – e.g., the restaurant which served the meal – obtains money for it. In our scheme, a vendor can prove that a customer redeemed a coupon to him, and hence he could charge the coupon issuer.

We remark that the above scenario is just a use case where a digital multi-coupon scheme maintained by a federation of vendors would be of potential interest, and that the scheme designed in this paper is general and could be employed in different business models through the specification of its object types.

Electronic *multi-coupon schemes (MCSs)* are in several ways superior to paper-based schemes. Despite the lower production costs and the possibility to buy and generate them over the Internet, they enable finer business models tailored to the different types of customers. However, new and specific security considerations need to be taken into account.

Security and Privacy Considerations. In contrast to paper-based coupon booklets, it is very easy to create a perfect copy of an electronic MC. Further, when dealing with an MCS, we must also consider attacks in which different users collude and attempt to cheat on vendors. Moreover, privacy and anonymity of customers become more important since the vendor may try to infer and store additional information about them including purchase habits, gender, age, etc. This would harm privacy and allow client profiling and price discrimination [17]. For optimal user privacy, vendors should not be able to link different transactions to one user (i.e., *unlinkability* should be provided).

Unforgeability and *unsplittability* are essential properties of an MCS (see [8,10,15]). The users should not be able to forge coupons or share ("split") an MC in such a way that several users can spend coupons from one MC independently. In the literature, *weak unsplittability* (also called *all-or-nothing sharing*) has been proposed (see, e.g., [10]): a user who wants to share a single coupon with someone else has to share the entire MC and all the secret data associated with that MC. Our scheme fulfills a stronger definition, called *unsplittability* (cf. [11]): If two users share coupons from an MC, then if one of them redeems, the second one cannot redeem any coupon from the same MC without interaction with the first user, even if both users know the entire secret data. To support business models where the vendor which provides the user with a service can charge money from the issuer of the coupon, additional requirements must be met. During the redemption protocol, the issuer of the coupon must be identifiable, and other vendors must be protected from being incorrectly held responsible for issuing this coupon. In Section 3, we actually define two requirements, *framing resistance* (the requirement of the issuer) and *claimability* (the requirement of the redeeming vendor).

Although payment issues are important for the deployment of an MCS in practice, they cannot be completely solved by cryptographic techniques. Hence, these issues are out of scope of this paper. Here, we assume that it suffices that a judge can execute an algorithm Claim to verify that a coupon, issued by a given issuer, has been redeemed to a given vendor.

Contribution. We introduce a new multi-coupon scheme deployable for a federation of vendors. Our scheme provides unlinkability, unsplittability, unforgeability, framing resistance and claimability. We introduce a formal security framework with definitions of these properties in which we prove the security of our scheme.

Previous MCSs suffer from the problem that they either do not provide unsplittability, or all the coupons in a multi-coupon have to be redeemed in sequential order (fixed during issue). If an MCS is to be used with a federation of vendors, such a restriction can be a strong limitation: imagine that the vendors want to offer an MC with coupons for different types of goods. In that case, customers certainly would want to decide themselves in which order they want to redeem their coupons. Hence, we need a *non-sequential* MCS, where the coupons can be redeemed in arbitrary order. However, the scheme of [11] offers nice features that we want to retain, in particular, *coupon objects*. These allow to have different types of coupons in one MC. We improve and extend this scheme in two important aspects: our scheme can be used by a group of vendors, which also introduces new security requirements. Moreover, we do not require the order of redemption of the single coupons to be fixed when the MC is issued. Furthermore, MCs can be created and issued offline without any connection to the vendors at which the coupons can be redeemed. For instance, this allows in practice to install a variety of selling booths in the tourist card example mentioned above.

Redeem complexity (both computation and communication) is constant w.r.t. the size k of the MC (i.e., the number of coupons it contains), and complexity of the protocol for issuing MCs is linear in k, which is the best we can get when each coupon has individual attributes (like coupon objects). If all coupons in an MC are the same (i.e., no coupon objects are used), ideas from [6] can be used to further reduce the complexity.

Organization. First, we give an overview of our scheme, define general multi-coupon schemes and describe our realization in Section 2. In Section 3, we give a formal framework with game-based formal definitions of the requirements, and provide sketches for security proofs. We discuss related work in Section 4. Finally, we conclude our article in Section 5. Further details can be found in the extended version.[1]

2 Our Federated Multi-Coupon Scheme

2.1 Informal Description of a Multi-Coupon's Lifecycle

In our scheme, a group of vendors $\mathcal{V}$ with common databases DB, DB' (trusted by the vendors) executes protocols with users $\mathcal{U}$ to issue and redeem coupons. The databases

---
[1] See http://www.trust.rub.de/home/publications

are used only during the redeem protocol. A multi-coupon M contains k individual coupons, which include, among other information, a coupon identifier id. The coupons are all cryptographically tied to M, which has an MC identifier mid and a freshness identifier fid. To simplify the description below, we temporarily omit coupon objects ob and the MC identifier mid.

In the Issue protocol, a user U obtains an MC from a vendor V with one signature on each individual coupon, and one signature validating the freshness fid, signed by the issuing vendor V. The signatures on the individual coupons (on id) prevent U from forging coupons, whereas the signature on the MC (on fid) ensures its freshness, which is used to prevent splitting.

In the Redeem protocol, the user U redeems a single coupon from an MC to a vendor V'. For this, he has to prove knowledge of a signature on the single coupon and that the MC is fresh. Double redemption of coupons is prevented by the vendor V' through a lookup in a central database DB of coupon identifiers. Similarly, V' queries the central database DB' of freshness IDs to verify the freshness of the MC. If the current coupon id and freshness ID fid have not already been used, then they are inserted into the corresponding database. Afterwards, the database DB sends a signature $cert_{DB}$ to the vendor V' certifying that V' is responsible for the redemption of this coupon. V' will need this signature as an evidence to charge the coupon issuer. At the end of Redeem, a new fid is generated and signed by V', so that this protocol can be executed repeatedly, as long as there are coupons left in the MC.

After redemption, the Claim algorithm can be executed by any party to verify that a user redeemed a coupon originally issued by a vendor V to a vendor V', and thus, that V' is entitled to charge V for the corresponding coupon. The input to this algorithm is the coupon ID id, a (non-interactive) proof of knowledge of a signature on id, and the certificate $cert_{DB}$ given by DB to V' during Redeem. The certificate is used to prevent double charging. Note that the databases do not participate in this algorithm.

2.2 Components of a General Federated MCS

Basic Notation. For a finite set S, $s \in_R S$ denotes the assignment of an element sampled uniformly from S to the variable s. Let Alg_A be a probabilistic algorithm. By $\text{out}_A \leftarrow \text{Alg}_A(\text{in}_A)$ we denote that the variable out_A is assigned the output of Alg_A's execution on input in_A. We denote by $(\text{Alg}_A(\text{in}_A), \text{Alg}_B(\text{in}_B))$ a pair of interactive algorithms with private inputs in_A and in_B, respectively, and write $(\text{out}_A, \text{out}_B) \leftarrow (\text{Alg}_A(\text{in}_A), \text{Alg}_B(\text{in}_B))$ to denote the assignment of Alg_A's and Alg_B's private outputs after their interaction to the variables out_A and out_B, respectively.

Here, we adapt the basic framework from [11] to our scenario with a federation of vendors. The involved parties are a set of vendors $\mathcal{V}$ and a set of users $\mathcal{U}$, where $n_{\mathcal{V}} = |\mathcal{V}|$ denotes the number of vendors in the federation. We will refer to any particular user simply by U, and V, V' will denote particular vendors. We assume that each vendor V has a unique identity ID_V which is publicly known. Common system parameters for the cryptographic building blocks (like commitment and signature schemes) will be omitted in the notation for better readability.

Definition 1 (Multi-Coupon Scheme). *A multi-coupon scheme (MCS) for a federation of vendors $\mathcal{V}$ consists of a set of protocols and algorithms {Setup, Issue, Redeem, Claim}:*

Setup *algorithm.* $(PK, \{SK_{V_i}\}_{1 \leq i \leq n_{\mathcal{V}}}) \leftarrow \text{Setup}(1^\kappa, n_{\mathcal{V}})$ *is the (in general, distributed) initialization algorithm executed by the vendors once to generate one instance* of the MCS, where κ is the security parameter, $n_\mathcal{V}$ is the number of vendors. It outputs a public key PK (which includes 1^κ and $k_{\max}$, the maximum allowed number of coupons per MC), and a set of secret keys $\{SK_{V_i}\}_{1 \leq i \leq n_\mathcal{V}}$. The vendors' states are initialized to the empty string.

Issue protocol. In order to obtain an MC with k coupons, U performs the following protocol with a vendor V: $((res_u, M), res_v) \leftarrow (\texttt{Issue}_u(k, V, PK, ob_0, \ldots, ob_{k-1}),$ $\texttt{Issue}_v(k, SK_V, ob_0, \ldots, ob_{k-1}))$ where, from now on, the subindices u and v denote user and vendor algorithms, respectively. The common input $ob_0, \ldots, ob_{k-1}$ specifies coupon objects (individual attributes) for the k individual coupons in the MC that is to be issued. The output flags $res_u, res_v \in \{acc, rej\}$ indicate success or failure. $\texttt{Issue}_u$ outputs res_u and a multi-coupon M, whereas $\texttt{Issue}_v$ only outputs res_v.

Redeem protocol. A multi-coupon M (issued by V) is redeemed to V' via the protocol $((res_u, M'), (res_v, crn, ob, \pi, s')) \leftarrow (\texttt{Redeem}_u(M, m, PK), \texttt{Redeem}_v(s, SK_{V'}))$. The parameters to $\texttt{Redeem}_u$ are the multi-coupon M from which the user wants to redeem a coupon, a specification m of the coupon to be redeemed[2], and the public key PK of the MCS. The vendor algorithm takes the vendors' state s and the private key of the redeeming vendor $SK_{V'}$ as input. $\texttt{Redeem}_u$ outputs an updated multi-coupon M' and a flag res_u just like in $\texttt{Issue}$, and $\texttt{Redeem}_v$ outputs a new state s' of the vendors, a unique coupon reference number crn, an object ob, a proof π that a user redeemed a coupon to V' (with reference number crn and object ob, issued by V), and a flag res_v.

Claim algorithm. To verify that a coupon with reference number crn issued by V has indeed be redeemed to vendor V', the (public) algorithm $\texttt{Claim}$ can be run to verify a proof π, i.e., $res \leftarrow \texttt{Claim}(crn, ob, \pi, V', V)$. The result res is true if π proves that V issued a coupon with object ob that was redeemed to V' with reference number crn; otherwise, res is false. crn is used to identify a redeemed coupon, i.e., it can be noticed, when the same redeemed coupon is claimed twice.

Correctness (informal). Any MCS must fulfill the correctness requirement: if all participants in the protocol are honest, each individual coupon from each MC that was issued by any vendor can be redeemed successfully at any vendor (equal to or different from the issuer), regardless of the order of redemption, i.e., a user can redeem any coupon that she hasn't spent yet at any time.

2.3 Building Blocks

Commitment Scheme (CS). We use the integer CS from [7], based on the scheme in [12], with two bases $g, h \in \text{QR}_n$ (quadratic residues modulo n), and a special RSA modulus n as a public key. A commitment to x has the form $C_x = g^x \cdot h^r$, where r is a random value.

Proofs of Knowledge (PoK). We use a number of honest-verifier statistical zero-knowledge PoKs. By $\text{PoK}\{(\tilde{x}_1, \ldots, \tilde{x}_n) : R(\tilde{x}_1, \ldots, \tilde{x}_n)\}$ we denote an interactive PoK, where a prover proves to a verifier that she knows a witness $(\tilde{x}_1, \ldots, \tilde{x}_n)$ (denoted by tilded variables) such that relation R holds, and the verifier does not gain any useful information beyond this assertion.

Proof of Equality of Representations. $\mathcal{P}$ proves that she is able to open two commitments C_1 and C_2 (for two possibly different instances of the commitment scheme), such

---

[2] Details depend on the scheme; e.g., m could be the index in a list of all coupons in a multi-coupon or an ID.

that certain components of the openings are equal. For example, PoKEqRep$\{(\tilde{x}, \tilde{r}_x, \tilde{y}, \tilde{r}_y) : C_1 = g_1^{\tilde{x}} g_2^{\tilde{r}_x} \wedge C_2 = \hat{g}_1^{\tilde{y}} \hat{g}_2^{\tilde{r}_y} \wedge \tilde{x} = \tilde{y}\}$ denotes the proof that the exponents $\tilde{x}$ and $\tilde{y}$ are equal.

Camenisch Lysyanskaya signature scheme (*CLS*). The *CLS* [7] is a signature scheme with efficient protocols based on the *strong RSA assumption*. The protocols for this scheme allow signing committed values, and proving knowledge of a signature (see below). The following description is done in the context of our scheme.

$CLS.\text{Setup}(1^\kappa)$. The signer $\mathcal{S}$ generates a special RSA modulus $n = pq$, such that n has size $\ell_n := 2\kappa$, where κ is a security parameter. Then he chooses numbers $a, b, c \in_R \text{QR}_n$, where a, b are called bases. The public key CLS_{PK} is (a, b, c, n), and the secret key CLS_{SK} is the prime p.

$CLS.\text{Sign}(x, CLS_{SK})$. To sign a message $x \in [0; 2^{\ell_m})$, the signer chooses a random prime e of size $\ell_e := \ell_m + 2$, a random number s of size at most $\ell_s := \ell_n + \ell_m + \ell$, where ℓ is another security parameter, $\mathcal{S}$ computes $v \leftarrow (a^x b^s c)^{e^{-1}} \pmod{n}$, and outputs (e, s, v).

$CLS.\text{Verify}(x, \sigma, CLS_{PK})$. For $(e, s, v) := \sigma$, the algorithm tests if $v^e \equiv a^x b^s c \pmod{n}$, $x \in [0; 2^{\ell_m})$, $s \in [0; 2^{\ell_s})$, e is ℓ_e bits long, and outputs *true* or *false*.

The signature allows the following useful protocols:

Signature on a committed value and PoK of this signature [7]. Signature generation is a protocol from [7] between a user U and a signer $\mathcal{S}$, who knows the secret key CLS_{SK}. Let $CLS_{PK} := (a, b, c, n)$ be the corresponding public key. The common input to U and $\mathcal{S}$ is a commitment C_x, for which U (supposedly) knows an opening $(x, r_x) : C_x = a^x b^{r_x}$. At the end of the protocol U obtains a signature $\sigma := (e, s, v)$ on x, while x is statistically hidden from $\mathcal{S}$. We denote this protocol as: $\sigma \leftarrow \text{SigOnCommit}\{U(x, r_x), \mathcal{S}(CLS_{SK})\}(C_x)$.

For a commitment C'_x, U can prove knowledge of (x, r'_x, e, s, v) [7], such that (x, r'_x) is an opening of C'_x, and (e, s, v) is a valid signature on x, where x and σ are hidden by the zero-knowledge property of the protocol. We denote this protocol as: PoKSigOnCommit$\{(\tilde{x}, \tilde{r}'_x, \tilde{\sigma}) : C'_x = a^{\tilde{x}} b^{\tilde{r}'_x} \wedge CLS.\text{Verify}(\tilde{x}, \tilde{\sigma}, CLS_{PK})\}$.

This signature scheme can be extended to sign message tuples $(x_1, \ldots, x_k)$ by introducing k bases a_i [7]. The extended scheme for k-tuples will be denoted by $CLSk$. The protocols above can be extended to support multiple messages, and selective message disclosure. E.g., abusing notation, we denote by SigOnCommit$\{U(\tilde{x}_1, \tilde{r}_{x_1}), \mathcal{S}(CLS3_{SK})\}(C_{x_1}, x_2, x_3)$ a protocol to generate a signature on a 3-tuple (x_1, x_2, x_3), where the message x_1 is blinded by a commitment C_{x_1}, and two messages x_2 and x_3 are disclosed in clear. Similarly, by PoKSigOnCommit$\{(\tilde{x}_3, \tilde{r}_{x_3}, \tilde{\sigma}) : C_{x_3} = a_3^{\tilde{x}_3} b^{\tilde{r}_{x_3}} \wedge CLS3.\text{Verify}((x_1, x_2, \tilde{x}_3), \tilde{\sigma}, CLS3_{PK})\}$ we denote the corresponding PoK that U knows a signature σ on a tuple (x_1, x_2, x_3), where x_1 and x_2 are disclosed to the verifier, but x_3 is kept blinded. Again, the variables with ˜ are kept secret.

Non-interactive proofs and signatures of knowledge. Using a cryptographic hash function, the PoKs described above can be turned into non-interactive PoKs by the Fiat-Shamir heuristic [13]. We add the prefix NI- ("non-interactive") to the PoKs to indicate that a non-interactive proof is used instead of an interactive protocol, e.g., NI-PoKSigOnCommit to denote a non-interactive proof of knowledge of a signature on a commitment. If additional data (a "message") is hashed, the NI-PoK becomes a signature on this message (as in [19]) and is called a *signature of knowledge (SoK)*. Since the actual protocol remains the same, we use the same notation with simply appending the message (as in NI-PoKSigOnCommit$\{\ldots\}(m)$). The security of SoKs can be shown in the *random oracle model*. In practice, it is assumed that this heuristic is secure, as long as the hash function which is used is cryptographically strong. For a more general and formal treatment of SoKs, see [9].

2.4 Concrete Construction

Overview. A multi-coupon M of size $k \leq k_{\max}$ consists of its identifier mid, a freshness identifier fid, a signature σ' on the pair (fid, mid), and a list of k individual coupons, where $k_{\max}$ is the maximal number of coupons an MC can contain. Each individual coupon (id, ob, σ) is specified by a coupon identifier id, a coupon's object ob (i.e., the good or service represented by the coupon[3]), and a signature σ on the tuple (id, ob, mid). Depending on the business model, the object IDs in an MC could either be chosen by the user, or they could be determined by the issuer. We model object IDs as common input to the issue protocol, leaving this decision to the concrete application.

We require that all signatures and non-interactive proofs in the protocols are always verified by the recipient. If the verification fails, the protocol is aborted, and the respective party outputs *rej* (subsequently, verification steps will be omitted). All public keys and parameters for the underlying protocols are known to all participants in the scheme (e.g., the federation of vendors could maintain a server with a directory of all public keys). The coupon reference number crn from our formal definitions is implemented by a unique ID id_i for each individual coupon.

Setup. For the setup of the MCS, the vendors have to create keys[4]: one common $CLS2$ key pair (PK_{Fed}, SK_{Fed}) for the federation, where all vendors know the private key, and one $CLS3$ key pair (PK_V, SK_V) for each individual vendor V. Moreover, the vendors have to create two empty common databases DB (for coupon IDs) and DB' (for freshness IDs), where all vendors can create new entries (of course, this can be implemented by two tables in one database). Every vendor is allowed to insert entries into the databases, but no vendor is allowed to delete them. DB possesses a key pair (PK_{DB}, SK_{DB}) of an arbitrary signature scheme, e.g., RSA, to issue certificates to vendors which inserted coupon IDs.

Remark. In this instantiation, the public key mentioned in Def. 1 consists of PK_{Fed} and PK_{V_i}; the secret key from Def. 1 includes SK_{Fed} and SK_{V_i}.

Issue. The Issue protocol is shown in Fig. 1. In step 1, the multi-coupon identifier mid is selected by the vendor, whereas the freshness ID fid_0 and IDs for the individual coupons id_i are chosen by the user. The vendor only obtains commitments $C_{fid_0}, C_{id_0}, \ldots C_{id_{k-1}}$ to the values chosen by the user. In step 2, the user receives a signature σ'_0 on (mid, fid_0) with the secret key of the federation SK_{Fed}, and in step 3, he obtains signatures σ_i on (C_{id_i}, mid, ob_i) with the signing key SK_V of the issuer.

Redeem. The Redeem protocol for the $(j+1)$-th redemption from a multi-coupon, where $0 \leq j \leq k-1$, is shown in Fig. 2. During the first Redeem from a multi-coupon (i.e., $j = 0$), the freshness ID fid_0 and corresponding signature σ'_0 from Issue is used and updated; in subsequent redemptions, the freshness ID and signature from the previous execution of Redeem are used and updated. In step 1, the user blinds mid by commitments (otherwise, the vendor could use mid to link transactions), and sends the data of the coupon he wants to redeem (id_i, ob_i, fid_j), together with the ID of the issuer ID_V, to the vendor V'. In step 2, U proves that the two commitments to mid are

---

[3] The vendors must publish an encoding of coupon's objects as integers.

[4] We do not use group signatures, because coupon issuers should be identifiable.

```
Common input: public keys $PK_V = (a_1, a_2, a_3, b, c, n)$, $PK_{Fed} = (\hat{a}_1, \hat{a}_2, \hat{b}, \hat{c}, \hat{n})$,
    number of single coupons $k$, object identifiers $ob_i$, $i = 0, \ldots, k-1$
User's input: –
Vendor's input: private keys $SK_V = p$, $SK_{Fed} = \hat{p}$
            User $U$                                                             Vendor $V$
Step 1:
    $fid_0 \in_R (0; 2^{\ell_m})$; $r_{fid_0} \in_R (0; 2^{\ell_n})$;                    $mid \in_R (0; 2^{\ell_m})$;
    $C_{fid_0} \leftarrow \hat{a}_1^{fid_0} \hat{b}^{r_{fid_0}}$;         ←——— $mid$ ———
    for each $i = 0, \ldots, k-1$ do
        $id_i \in_R (0; 2^{\ell_m})$;
        $r_{id_i} \in_R (0; 2^{\ell_n})$;
        $C_{id_i} \leftarrow a_1^{id_i} b^{r_{id_i}}$;
    end for;                      ——— $C_{fid_0}, C_{id_0}, \ldots, C_{id_{k-1}}$ ———→
Step 2:
    $\sigma'_0$       ←       SigOnCommit$\{U(fid_0, r_{fid_0}), V(SK_{Fed})\}(C_{fid_0}, mid)$
Step 3:
    for each $i = 0, \ldots, k-1$ do
        $\sigma_i$    ←       SigOnCommit$\{U(id_i, r_{id_i}), V(SK_V)\}(C_{id_i}, mid, ob_i)$
    end for;
    return $(mid, fid_0, \sigma'_0, \{(id_i, \sigma_i)\}_{0 \le i < k})$;                              return $accept$;
```

Fig. 1. Issue Protocol

actually commitments to the same number. In step 3, the user proves knowledge of the signature σ_i, and the vendor obtains a signature of knowledge π' that allows him later to prove that this coupon was redeemed to him. In step 4, the user proves knowledge of a signature σ'_j on (fid_j, mid). The vendor has to verify that both id_i and fid_j are fresh by quering the databases (i.e., he checks that these values are not yet in DB and DB'), and inserts these entries. After insertion, the database DB signs id_i and sends the signature to V'. To prevent races between vendors, which open the door to some attacks, only one vendor at any time is allowed to "query and insert", as an atomic operation.

In step 5, U chooses a new random freshness ID fid_{j+1} for this MC and sends a commitment to fid_{j+1} to V'. At the end of the protocol (in step 6), the user obtains a new freshness signature σ'_{j+1} for this MC. The vendor sets $\pi \leftarrow (\pi', \text{cert}_{DB}, C_{mid})$, and returns (id_i, ob_i, π).

A malicious user cannot abuse $C_{fid_{j+1}}$ to obtain signatures with SK_{Fed} on arbitrary messages, because the second part of the signed message is proven to be a valid commitment to mid. All signatures with SK_{Fed} on such messages will always be interpreted as freshness signatures, thus this protocol cannot be used as signature oracle. For efficiency reasons, the NI-PoKs and NI-SoKs could all be combined into one NI-SoK.

Claim. The deterministic Claim algorithm verifies the SoK that a vendor V' obtained during the Redeem protocol and the certificate given by DB to V'. It uses only public information and hence can be run by anyone, for example, by a judge in case of dispute. Double charging is prevented because a vendor will only pay back once for each coupon identifier. The vendor V' can always charge the issuing vendor unless DB generates

```
Common input: public keys $PK_V = (a_1, a_2, a_3, b, c, n)$, $PK_{Fed} = (\hat{a}_1, \hat{a}_2, \hat{b}, \hat{c}, \hat{n})$
   bases $g, h, \hat{g}, \hat{h}$ for internal use of PoKSigOnCommit protocols
User's input: single coupon $(id_i, mid, ob_i, fid_j, \sigma_i, \sigma'_j)$ issued by vendor $V$, issuer's ID $ID_V$
Vendor's input: private key $SK_{Fed} = \hat{p}$, databases $DB, DB'$
```

User U		Vendor V'

Step 1:
  $\tilde{r}_{mid}, \tilde{r}'_{mid} \in_R (0; 2^{\ell_n})$;
  $\tilde{C}_{mid} \leftarrow a_2^{\tilde{mid}} b^{\tilde{r}_{mid}}$;
  $\tilde{C}'_{mid} \leftarrow \hat{a}_2^{\tilde{mid}} \hat{b}^{\tilde{r}'_{mid}}$; $\xrightarrow{ID_V, id_i, \tilde{C}_{mid}, ob_i, fid_j, \tilde{C}'_{mid}}$

Step 2:
  NI-PoKEqRep$\{(\tilde{mid}, \tilde{mid}', \tilde{r}_{mid}, \tilde{r}'_{mid}) : \tilde{C}_{mid} = a_2^{\tilde{mid}} b^{\tilde{r}_{mid}} \wedge \tilde{C}'_{mid} = \hat{a}_2^{\tilde{mid}'} \hat{b}^{\tilde{r}'_{mid}} \wedge \tilde{mid} = \tilde{mid}'\}$ $\rightarrow$

Step 3:
  NI-PoKSigOnCommit$\{(\tilde{mid}, \tilde{r}_{mid}, \tilde{\sigma}_i) : \tilde{C}_{mid} = a_2^{\tilde{mid}} b^{\tilde{r}_{mid}} \wedge CLS3.\text{Verify}((id_i, \tilde{mid}, ob_i), \tilde{\sigma}_i, PK_V)\}(ID_{V'})$ $\rightarrow$
  $\pi' \leftarrow$ output of step 3;

Step 4:
  NI-PoKSigOnCommit$\{(\tilde{mid}, \tilde{r}'_{mid}, \tilde{\sigma}'_j) : \tilde{C}'_{mid} = \hat{a}_2^{\tilde{mid}} \hat{b}^{\tilde{r}'_{mid}} \wedge CLS2.\text{Verify}((fid_j, \tilde{mid}), \tilde{\sigma}'_j, PK_{Fed})\}$ $\rightarrow$

Step 5:   cert$_{DB} \leftarrow$ insert id_i into DB;
  $fid_{j+1} \in_R (0; 2^{\ell_m})$; $r_{fid_{j+1}} \in_R (0; 2^{\ell_n})$;   insert fid_j into DB';
  $C_{fid_{j+1}} \leftarrow \hat{a}_1^{fid_{j+1}} \hat{b}^{r_{fid_{j+1}}}$; $\xrightarrow{C_{fid_{j+1}}}$

Step 6:
  $\sigma'_{j+1} \leftarrow$ $\xleftarrow{\text{SigOnCommit}\{U(fid_{j+1}, r_{fid_{j+1}}, mid, r'_{mid}), V'(SK_{Fed})\}(C_{fid_{j+1}}, C'_{mid})}$

  return $(fid_{j+1}, \sigma'_{j+1})$; $\pi \leftarrow (\pi', \text{cert}_{DB}, C_{mid})$;   return (id_i, ob_i, π);

Fig. 2. Redeem Protocol

```
Claim(id, ob, π, V', V):
   parse π as (π', cert_DB, C_mid);
   verify cert_DB w.r.t. id, PK_DB;
   verify π' w.r.t. id, ob, C_mid, PK_V, ID_V';
```

Fig. 3. Claim Algorithm

two certificates for the same coupon identifier. However, this misbehavior can always be identified.

Efficiency. The communication (and computation) complexity of the Issue protocol is linear in the number k of individual coupons in the multi-coupon to be issued. Correspondingly, the size of the MC data is also linear in k. The Redeem protocol is constant w.r.t. to k. The operations performed by DB and DB' (search, insert and sign) do not depend on the size k of the MCs (but, of course, on the security parameter κ), and they should not impact the efficiency unless the communication between the vendors and the databases is slow. If coupon objects are not necessary, ideas from [6] could be used to obtain logarithmic complexity (in k) for Issue, and also logarithmic size of the MC data. Compared to the MCS from [11], one additional SigOnCommit protocol has to be run instead of a local signature generation during Issue. In the Redeem protocol, two additional IDs (V and fid_j) are sent to the vendor in the first step, and we need an extra round to send a commitment to the vendor. Another difference is that we use non-interactive versions of the protocols during Redeem, which slightly increases efficiency – but this could also be done in the MCS from [11].

3 Security Framework and Analysis

Here, we generalize the adversarial model from [11] to a federation of vendors. The security requirements are defined by *games*, and it can be shown that our scheme meets these requirements. We only present some proof sketches and refer the reader to the full version of this paper for more details. An adversary is a p.p.t. algorithm $\mathcal{A}$, which can play the role of either a collusion of vendors and users, or only of a group of users. W.l.o.g., we let the adversary be specified by a sequence of algorithms (e.g., $\mathcal{A} := (\mathcal{A}_1, \mathcal{A}_2, \mathcal{A}_3)$). Honest parties are assumed to communicate over secure channels.

We consider two types of users (resp. vendors): *honest* and *corrupted* users (resp. vendors). Users (resp. vendors) belonging to the set of honest users (resp. vendors) execute algorithms of the MCS if requested by $\mathcal{A}$, but remain honest otherwise. $\mathcal{A}$ has full control over the corrupted users and vendors, and he is provided with their previous protocol views. Similar to [14], we allow $\mathcal{A}$ to interact with the system through a set of queries[5] handled by an *interface*, which partially simulates the MCS, executes protocols with $\mathcal{A}$, and records certain user's or vendor's activities. Note that the interfaces do not restrict $\mathcal{A}$ in any way – they control the actions of the honest parties on behalf of $\mathcal{A}$. Correctness of the scheme can be easily verified (proof omitted).

Framing resistance and claimability. During the redemption protocol, the original issuer of the coupon must be identifiable (to allow the redeeming vendor to claim money from the issuer), and other vendors must be protected from false claims. It must be ensured that a vendor who issued an MC can always be held responsible for all coupons from this MC. We break down this property into two requirements: (1) **framing resistance**: a collusion of vendors and users must never be able to claim that another vendor issued a coupon with a specific object, when he didn't; and (2) **claimability**: an honest vendor who redeemed a coupon must always be able to claim money for it.

Interface I_1. In the games defining "claimability" and "framing resistance", the adversary $\mathcal{A}$ plays the role of a coalition of all users and has the capability to corrupt vendors.

Counters $ctrC_{V,ob}$ (initially 0) for each coupon object ob are defined for each vendor V, counting the coupons with object ob, that were issued by V. The following queries are provided to $\mathcal{A}$.

$I_1.\text{Issue}_v(V, k, ob_0, \ldots, ob_{k-1})$. If $k \in [1; k_{\max}]$ and V is an honest vendor, the Issue_v algorithm is executed. The counter for each coupon object ob is increased by the number of times ob occurs in the MC issued by V, i.e., $\forall \lambda \in [0; k-1]$: $ctrC_{V,ob_\lambda}$++.

$I_1.\text{Redeem}_v(V', V)$. If V' is an honest vendor, the Redeem_v protocol is executed for V', i.e., $\mathcal{A}$ wants to redeem a coupon (issued by V) to V'.

$I_1.\text{Corrupt}(V)$. $\mathcal{A}$ receives all secrets of V (and V is removed from the set of honest vendors).

In the $FrameGame$ (see Fig. 4), $\mathcal{A}$ can interact with the system via the interface I_1. $\mathcal{A}$ outputs the identity V of the vendor he wants to "frame" (in order to win this game,

---

[5] Like in existing schemes, queries must not be executed concurrently, which simplifies model and construction.

$FrameGame(\mathcal{A}, \kappa, n_V)$:
  $(PK, \{SK_{V_i}\}_{1 \leq i \leq n_V}) \leftarrow$
    $\text{Setup}(1^\kappa, n_V)$;
  $(V, ob, CRN, \Pi) \leftarrow \mathcal{A}^{I_1}(1^\kappa, PK)$;
  if (V uncorrupted $\land |CRN| > ctrC_{V,ob} \land$
    $(\forall crn \in CRN \colon \exists (\pi, V') \in \Pi$:
    $\text{Claim}(crn, ob, \pi, V', V) = true))$
    return $broken$;
  else return $unbroken$;

$ClaimGame(\mathcal{A}, \kappa, n_V)$:
  $(PK, \{SK_{V_i}\}_{1 \leq i \leq n_V}) \leftarrow$
    $\text{Setup}(1^\kappa, n_V)$;
  $(V', V, s_\mathcal{A}) \leftarrow \mathcal{A}_1^{I_1}(1^\kappa, PK)$;
  if V' corrupted
    return $unbroken$;
  $(Res_\mathcal{A}, (res_v, crn, ob, \pi, s')) \leftarrow$
    $(\mathcal{A}_2(s_\mathcal{A}), I_1.\text{Redeem}_v(V', V))$;
  if ($res_v = acc \land$
    $\text{Claim}(crn, ob, \pi, V', V) = false)$
    return $broken$;
  else return $unbroken$;

Fig. 4. The games $FrameGame$ and $ClaimGame$

$\mathcal{A}$ has to choose an uncorrupted vendor), an object ob, and a set of coupon reference numbers CRN with a corresponding set Π of pairs (π, V') of proofs that V' was involved in the redemption of a coupon with object ob issued by V. If Claim succeeds for all of these proofs and there are more elements in CRN than coupons (with object ob) issued by V (i.e., $|CRN| > ctrC_{V,ob}$), $\mathcal{A}$ wins the game, because then $\mathcal{A}$ must be able to claim coupons V did not issue. (Of course, all elements of the set must be distinct – i.e., $\mathcal{A}$ cannot "replay" the same crn multiple times).

Definition 2 (Framing resistance of an MCS). *An MCS is resistant against framing if there is no p.p.t adversary $\mathcal{A}$ that can win the FrameGame in Fig. 4 (i.e., Frame-Game$(\mathcal{A}, \kappa, n_V)$ = broken for some number of vendors $n_V \geq 1$) with non-negligible probability (in κ).*

Theorem 1 (Framing resistance). *Assuming the security of CL signatures against existential forgery, the proposed MCS is resistant against framing, i.e., for all p.p.t adversaries $\mathcal{A}$ and for all $n_V \geq 1$, $Pr[FrameGame(\mathcal{A}, \kappa, n_V) = broken]$ is negligible (in κ) in the random oracle model.*

Proof (sketch). Assume a successful adversary $\mathcal{A}$ which breaks $FrameGame$ with non-negligible probability. From that, we construct an algorithm $\mathcal{B}$ that, given a signature oracle for an instance of the $CLS3$ signature scheme, produces an existential forgery for this instance.

$\mathcal{B}$ has to simulate the $FrameGame$ towards $\mathcal{A}$ in the random oracle model. To do so, $\mathcal{B}$ has to guess which issuer V will be "attacked" by $\mathcal{A}$. The $CLS3$ signature oracle is used by $\mathcal{B}$ for V's signatures – the keys for the other vendors and for the federation are generated honestly by the respective algorithms. If $\mathcal{A}$ corrupts a vendor different from V, $\mathcal{B}$ delivers the corresponding secret key to $\mathcal{A}$. If $\mathcal{A}$ corrupts V, the simulation fails. Assuming that $\mathcal{A}$ corrupts all vendors but one, the probability to guess the right vendor is $1/n_V$. In [7], it is shown how to simulate the building blocks for our protocols.

In the Issue and Redeem protocols, it can be assumed that $\mathcal{B}$ can extract all secrets (by rewinding) for each PoK and SoK from $\mathcal{A}$ (it is shown in [7] that efficient knowledge extractors exist for the sub-protocols we use). Since rewinding can be done for all sub-protocols independently, $\mathcal{B}$ is still efficient.

When $\mathcal{B}$ executes Issue for V, $\mathcal{B}$ stores σ_i together with the signed tuple (id_i, mid, ob_i) (where id_i is obtained by knowledge extraction). This information is used to identify a forged CL signature: $\mathcal{B}$ extracts the secrets from all SoKs that are returned by $\mathcal{A}$

(in the set Π in the *FrameGame*). The condition $|CRN| > ctrC_{V,ob}$ in the *FrameGame* ensures that there are more distinct coupon IDs id_i than signatures for coupons with object ob have been queried by V. Therefore, one of the NI-SoKs π does not correspond to a coupon issued by V and $\mathcal{A}$ must have produced a forgery of a CL signature. $\mathcal{B}$ can identify the forgery using the data stored during Issue, and outputs it as the required existential forgery of a $CLS3$ signature. Of course, this only works, if the vendor challenged by the adversary is actually the vendor V guessed by $\mathcal{B}$ at the beginning of the simulation.

Since the probability of an adversary to forge a CL signature is negligible, so is the probability of $\mathcal{A}$ to win the *FrameGame*. □

To break the *ClaimGame* (see Fig. 4), $\mathcal{A}$ successfully redeems a coupon to an uncorrupted vendor V', but V' cannot claim money for it (i.e., the Claim algorithm fails). In the first phase, A_1 can interact arbitrarily with the honest vendors via I_1. He must output an issuer V of a coupon (possibly corrupted) and an uncorrupted vendor V', and an arbitrary state $s_\mathcal{A}$ for the second phase. To win the game, A_2 must be able to redeem a coupon, allegedly issued by V, to V', but Claim must fail for this coupon. A_2's output $Res_\mathcal{A}$ is discarded.

Definition 3 (Claimability of an MCS). *An MCS is* claimable *if there is no p.p.t adversary $\mathcal{A} := (A_1, A_2)$ that can win the ClaimGame in Fig. 4 (i.e., ClaimGame($\mathcal{A}, \kappa, n_\mathcal{V}$) = broken for some number of vendors $n_\mathcal{V} \geq 1$) with probability > 0.*

Theorem 2 (Claimability). *The proposed MCS provides claimability, i.e., for all p.p.t adversaries $\mathcal{A}$ and for all $n_\mathcal{V} \geq 1$, $Pr[ClaimGame(\mathcal{A}, \kappa, n_\mathcal{V}) = broken] = 0$.*

Proof (sketch). The checks in the Claim algorithm are a subset of the checks performed in Redeem by the vendor. Therefore, the condition in the *ClaimGame* that V' accepts, but Redeem fails, is a contradiction (i.e., $\mathcal{A}$ can never win). □

Unforgeability and unsplittability. No coalition of users should be able to redeem more coupons than have been issued by the vendors. Moreover, multi-coupons should be *unsplittable* (cf. [11]): We require that if a user U_0 shares an MC with a user U_1, as soon as one user redeems a single coupon, the other one cannot redeem any more without interacting with the user who redeemed first (note that sharing can always be achieved by copying all the data).

In the games, we have to restrict the queries that are available to $\mathcal{A}$: he is not allowed to corrupt vendors, because a vendor could issue as many coupons as he likes – and hence "unforgeability with corrupted vendors" would make no sense. Moreover, we consider unsplittability to be a requirement of the entire federation. Therefore, we do not need to model corruptions: We assume that in the games defining unforgeability and unsplittability, *all users* but *no vendors* are corrupted.

```
SplitGame(A, κ, n_V):
  (PK, {SK_{V_i}}_{1≤i≤n_V}) ← Setup(1^κ, n_V);
  (s, V, V'_{j_0}, ..., V'_{j_K}) ← A_1^{I'_1}(1^κ, PK)
  if K < ctrM_V
    return unbroken;
  for λ ← 0 to K do:
    (res_A, res_v) ←
       (A_2(s), I'_1.Redeem_v(V, V'_{j_λ}));
    if (res_v ≠ acc)
      return unbroken;
  return broken;
```

Fig. 5. The game defining unsplittability (*SplitGame*), where I'_1 is the interface I_1 without Corrupt queries

Furthermore, we have to count the difference between the coupons (separately for each object ob) a vendor V issued, and the number of coupons (issued by V, with ob) that were already redeemed, i.e., the number of coupons issued by V with object ob that are available to the adversary. Thus, a counter $ctrD_{V,ob}$ (initially 0) is introduced for each issuer V, which is increased during issue, and decreased after a successful Redeem (possibly at a different vendor V'). For the definition of unsplittability, it is important to know how many MCs issued by V that still contain redeemable coupons the users may have. In an unlinkable MCS, this cannot be done precisely; therefore, the MC counter $ctrM_V$ (initially 0) is just an upper bound on the users' MCs (with valid redeemable coupons). To count the MCs the users might have, $ctrM_V$ is increased by one whenever V issued a coupon. After successful redemption, the MC counter is adjusted if the number of coupons issued by V that are still available to $\mathcal{A}$ is smaller than the number of MCs (issued by the same vendor): $ctrM_V \leftarrow \min(ctrM_V, ctrD_V)$.

Interface I_1'. The modified interface I_1 without Corrupt queries, but with counters $ctrM_V$ and $ctrD_{V,ob}$ is denoted by I_1'.

Intuitively, to win the splittability game (see Fig. 5), $\mathcal{A}$ has to create more (in the game: $K+1$) "shares" than he has MCs (at most $ctrM_V \leq K$), which can be redeemed *independently* from each other. The state of A_2 is reset after each Redeem to the state s that was output by A_1; i.e., information gained in one execution of Redeem is not available in the other executions.

Definition 4 (Unsplittability of an MCS). *An MCS is* unsplittable *if there is no p.p.t adversary $\mathcal{A}$ that can win the SplitGame in Fig. 5 (i.e., SplitGame($\mathcal{A}, \kappa, n_\mathcal{V}$) = broken for some number of vendors $n_\mathcal{V} \geq 1$) with non-negligible probability (in κ).*

Theorem 3 (Unsplittability). *Assuming the security of CL signatures against existential forgery, our MCS is unsplittable, i.e., for all p.p.t adversaries $\mathcal{A}$ and for all $n_\mathcal{V} \geq 1$, the probability $Pr[SplitGame(\mathcal{A}, \kappa, n_\mathcal{V}) = broken]$ is negligible (in κ) in the random oracle model.*

Proof (idea). We can show unsplittability by a reduction, similar to the one in the proof of Theorem 1: Assuming an adversary $\mathcal{A}$ against *SplitGame*, we construct an adversary $\mathcal{B}$ against the security of the CL signature scheme (i.e., $\mathcal{B}$ will produce an existential forgery of a CL signature). $\mathcal{B}$ has to simulate the interface I_1', and play the *SplitGame* with $\mathcal{A}$. To do so, $\mathcal{B}$ has black-box access to signature oracles for the $CLS2$ and the $CLS3$ signature schemes (these oracles can be used in the simulation because vendors cannot be corrupted). If $\mathcal{A}$ wins the game, $\mathcal{B}$ has to come up with an existential forgery of one of the signature schemes. The simulation proceeds like in the proof of Theorem 1, and it can be proven that the counter $ctrM_V$ ensures that a forgery occurs, which can be extracted from the adversary by rewinding. In this way, $\mathcal{B}$ produces an existential forgery of one of the CL signature schemes. □

In the unforgeability game, the adversary $\mathcal{A}$ can interact with the system via I_1', and he has to output the identity of an arbitrary vendor, an object ob of his choice. If more coupons (with object ob) issued by this vendor have been redeemed than the vendor originally issued (i.e., $ctrD_{V,ob} < 0$), $\mathcal{A}$ wins. Due to space restrictions, we omit the formal definition, theorem, and proof (which are analogous to unsplittability).

Unlinkability. To ensure privacy and anonymity of the customers, we require that the vendors should not be able to link a Redeem procedure of a customer to the corresponding Issue procedure, nor to another Redeem procedure where the customer used the same MC. Unlinkability for one user has to be provided against a collusion of vendors and other users.

Informally, unlinkability is achieved because the vendor's knowledge about elements of a single coupon depends on the actual procedure. During Issue, id and fid_0 are hidden, whereas mid, σ, σ'_0 are known to the vendor. During Redeem, id and fid_0 are disclosed to the vendor, but mid, σ, σ'_0 are hidden. fid_j ($0 \leq j < k$) is hidden from the vendor during the j-th run of Redeem, but disclosed during the $(j+1)$-th run; σ'_j ($0 \leq j < k$) is known to the vendor during the j-th run of Redeem, but hidden during the $(j+1)$-th run. The objects ob are known to the vendor during both Issue and Redeem. If a certain coupon object is unique to a user, this could be used for linking. Hence, the formal definition has to exclude "trivial linking" by objects. But if there are more users with coupons of a given object, it cannot be used for linking. We assume that in a system with many users, for each object there should be several users with a corresponding coupon. Hence, privacy should be preserved, for practical purposes.

For a formal definition, theorem, and proof (which are quite similar to [11]), we refer the reader to the extended version of this paper.

4 Related Work

Syverson et al. [20] introduced the concept of unsplittability in the context of unlinkable serial transactions to discourage sharing, and suggested an extension of their scheme to implement coupon books. Later, Chen et al. [10] described the properties that a privacy-protecting MCS must provide, and proposed an unforgeable, unlinkable, and weakly unsplittable scheme. However, their construction is less practical because redemption complexity is linear in k (i.e., the number of coupons in the MC).

More recently, Nguyen [15] addressed some disadvantages of [10], and defined a security model for MCSs, followed by an efficient construction based on a verifiable pseudorandom function and bilinear groups. Its issue and redeem complexity is constant w.r.t. k, it offers the same security properties as in [10], and adds a new feature to *revoke* MCs. One drawback the schemes from [15,10] is that every issued MC must contain the same number of coupons, i.e., k is a system parameter fixed for all MCs. This limitation, as pointed out in [15], can be overcome in both schemes at the cost of efficiency, by extending the issue protocol in a way that MCs with fewer than k coupons can be issued. Another drawback of these schemes is that they do not provide coupon objects (or coupon types [8]), and they support only one vendor.

Finally, a privacy-protecting MCS scheme with strong protection against splitting has been proposed in [11]. In this scheme, the number k of coupons in an MC can vary with different MCs. Moreover, coupon objects are supported, and the proofs for the security (unforgeability, unlinkability, and unsplittability) are sketched. However, all coupons in an MC must be redeemed in a sequential order that has to be fixed during the issue protocol, and only a single vendor is considered.

As explained in [10,15], most related schemes (e.g., e-cash, digital credentials) cannot be employed as privacy-protecting unsplittable MCSs because they have different usage patterns [18,4], are inefficient in this setup [16], or lack at least one of the required properties [5], in particular unsplittability. Some e-cash systems (e.g., [6]) can be used as unlinkable or at least anonymous MCSs (cf. [8]). However, they are at most weakly unsplittable. Although [6] provides logarithmic issue complexity (and size) in k, it cannot support individual attributes per coupon. If coupon objects would be introduced, the issue complexity (and multi-coupon size) would also be linear in k, as in our scheme, but would not provide unsplittability.

5 Conclusion and Future Work

In this paper, we proposed a generic security model for multi-coupon schemes, suitable for a federation of vendors. We designed an efficient scheme where coupons can be redeemed in arbitrary order, and which is provably secure in this model. Future work may focus on dynamic aspects of the scheme, considering the case where vendors join and leave the federation, or on the design of more efficient schemes.

References

1. Paris Visite (October 2007), http://www.ratp.info/touristes/
2. Roma Pass (October 2007), http://www.romapass.it/english/index.html
3. Vienna Card (October 2007), http://www.wienkarte.at/EN/?l=e
4. Blundo, C., Cimato, S., De Bonis, A.: Secure e-coupons. Electronic Commerce Research 5(1), 117–139 (2005)
5. Brands, S.: A technical overview of digital credentials. research report (February 2002), http://www.xs4all.nl/#brands/
6. Camenisch, J., Hohenberger, S., Lysyanskaya, A.: Compact e-cash. In: Cramer, R.J.F. (ed.) EUROCRYPT 2005. LNCS, vol. 3494, pp. 302–321. Springer, Heidelberg (2005)
7. Camenisch, J., Lysyanskaya, A.: A signature scheme with efficient protocols. In: Cimato, S., Galdi, C., Persiano, G. (eds.) SCN 2002. LNCS, vol. 2576, pp. 268–289. Springer, Heidelberg (2003)
8. Canard, S., Gouget, A., Hufschmitt, E.: A handy multi-coupon system. In: Zhou, J., Yung, M., Bao, F. (eds.) ACNS 2006. LNCS, vol. 3989, pp. 66–81. Springer, Heidelberg (2006)
9. Chase, M., Lysyanskaya, A.: On signatures of knowledge. In: Dwork, C. (ed.) CRYPTO 2006. LNCS, vol. 4117, pp. 78–96. Springer, Heidelberg (2006)
10. Chen, L., Enzmann, M., Sadeghi, A.-R., Schneider, M., Steiner, M.: A privacy-protecting coupon system. In: S. Patrick, A., Yung, M. (eds.) FC 2005. LNCS, vol. 3570, pp. 93–108. Springer, Heidelberg (2005)
11. Chen, L., Escalante, A.N.B., Löhr, H., Manulis, M., Sadeghi, A.-R.: A Privacy-Protecting Multi-Coupon Scheme with Stronger Protection against Splitting. In: Dietrich, S., Dhamija, R. (eds.) FC 2007 and USEC 2007. LNCS, vol. 4886, pp. 29–44. Springer, Heidelberg (2007)
12. Damgård, I., Fujisaki, E.: A statistically hiding integer commitment scheme based on groups with hidden order. In: Zheng, Y. (ed.) ASIACRYPT 2002. LNCS, vol. 2501, pp. 125–142. Springer, Heidelberg (2002)
13. Fiat, A., Shamir, A.: How to prove yourself: practical solutions to identification and signature problems. In: Odlyzko, A.M. (ed.) CRYPTO 1986. LNCS, vol. 263, pp. 186–194. Springer, Heidelberg (1987)
14. Kiayias, A., Tsiounis, Y., Yung, M.: Traceable signatures. In: Cachin, C., Camenisch, J.L. (eds.) EUROCRYPT 2004. LNCS, vol. 3027, pp. 571–589. Springer, Heidelberg (2004)
15. Nguyen, L.: Privacy-protecting coupon system revisited. In: Di Crescenzo, G., Rubin, A. (eds.) FC 2006. LNCS, vol. 4107, pp. 266–280. Springer, Heidelberg (2006)
16. Nguyen, L., Safavi-Naini, R.: Dynamic k-times anonymous authentication. In: Ioannidis, J., Keromytis, A.D., Yung, M. (eds.) ACNS 2005. LNCS, vol. 3531, pp. 318–333. Springer, Heidelberg (2005)

17. Odlyzko, A.: Privacy, economics, and price discrimination on the internet. In: ICEC 2003: Proceedings of the 5th international conference on Electronic commerce, pp. 355–366. ACM Press, New York (2003)
18. Persiano, P., Visconti, I.: An efficient and usable multi-show non-transferable anonymous credential system. In: Juels, A. (ed.) FC 2004. LNCS, vol. 3110, pp. 196–211. Springer, Heidelberg (2004)
19. Schnorr, C.-P.: Efficient signature generation by smart cards. Journal of Cryptology, IACR 4(3), 161–174 (1991)
20. Syverson, P.F., Stubblebine, S.G., Goldschlag, D.M.: Unlinkable serial transactions. In: Hirschfeld, R. (ed.) FC 1997. LNCS, vol. 1318, pp. 39–56. Springer, Heidelberg (1997)

1-out-of-n Oblivious Signatures

Raylin Tso[1], Takeshi Okamoto[2], and Eiji Okamoto[2]

[1] Department of Computer Science,
National Chengchi University,
No.64, Sec.2, ZhiNan Rd., Taipei City, 11605, Taiwan
raylin@cs.nccu.edu.tw
[2] Department of Risk Engineering
Graduate School of Systems and Information Engineering
University of Tsukuba,
1-1-1 Tennodai, Tsukuba, Ibaraki, 305-8573, Japan
ken@risk.tsukuba.ac.jp,
okamoto@risk.tsukuba.ac.jp

Abstract. An oblivious signature with n keys (or messages) is a signature that the recipient can choose one of n keys (or messages) to get signed while the signer cannot find out on which key (or message) the recipient has got the signature. This kind of signature is firstly introduced by L. Chen in 1994. However, the previous reference does not crisply formalize the notion. Furthermore, the proposed constructions are less efficient in both communication and computation. In this paper, we first give formal definitions on the model of oblivious signatures. Then, based on the Schnorr signature, we propose our efficient oblivious signature scheme. A comparison result is also provided in this paper which shows that our scheme is more efficient than Chen's schemes and those using a combination of a signature scheme and an oblivious transfer protocol.

Keywords: 1-out-of-n signature, oblivious signature, oblivious transfer, Schnorr signature.

1 Introduction

Nowadays, as consumers increasingly rely on the internet for shopping, banking and other activities, privacy has become more and more important for consumers who worry about how personal information is used. Motivated by the increasing interest in issues relating to the protection of personal privacy, L. Chen in 1994 proposed the concept of oblivious signatures [4].

In [4], L. Chen considered two types of oblivious signature schemes. The first one is an oblivious signature scheme with n keys and the second one is an oblivious signature scheme with n messages.

Oblivious signature with n keys could be considered a complement of group signature [5]. This scheme is a multiparty protocol. The participants are a group of n signers $S_1, \cdots, S_n$ (or a signer with n different keys) and a recipient R. The scheme has the following characteristics.

1. By executing the protocol, the recipient R can get a message signed with one of n keys which is chosen by himself.
2. The possible signers, even the holder of the accepted key, cannot find out with which key the message is got signed.
3. When necessary, R can show that he has got a signature (on the message) with one of the n keys without revealing with which special one.

The application of this scheme is made in the case of accessing sensitive databases. In this case, a database can only be accessed with a permit (which is possibly a signature signed by the administrator of the database) from the administrator of the database. But the information about which database interests the user may be sensitive. So the user chooses n databases and get the permit (ie., a signature) for only one of n databases without revealing which one.

The second scheme involves a signer S and a recipient R. The common input for both R and S contains n messages. The scheme has the following characteristics.

1. By executing the protocol, the recipient R can choose only one the the n messages to get signed.
2. The signer cannot find out on which message the recipient has got the signature.
3. When necessary, R can show that he has got a signature on one of the n messages without revealing which special one.

This scheme is useful in the case of internet shopping. In this case, the user will buy a software from the seller. In order to prevent illegitimate use, the software can be used if and only if it is signed by the seller. However, the information about which product interests the user may be sensitive in some stage. So the user can choose n softwares and get one and only one signed by the seller without revealing which one.

Motivation. Although the concept of oblivious signatures is not completely new, previous references do not crisply formalize the notion, the model of the schemes as well as the security model. Moreover, previously proposed constructions are less efficient in both communication and computation. For example, in L. Chen's schemes [4], to generate an oblivious signature, a round of interaction consisting of three movies between a signer and a recipient is required. Overall overhead during the interaction of the schemes is at least $3072n$ bits, where n is the number of keys or messages. The size of the generated signature is also a problem. In L. Chen's schemes, a signature consists of 9 parameters with more than 7000 bits in total.

Our Contributions. Motivated by the above mentioned problems, in this paper, we first give formal definitions on the model of oblivious signature schemes and give the security requirements of the scheme. Then, based on the Schnorr signature [14], we propose our efficient oblivious signature scheme. A comparison result is also provided in this paper which shows that our scheme is more efficient than Chen's schemes and those using a combination of a signature scheme and an oblivious transfer protocol.

1.1 Related Works

Oblivious Transfer. Oblivious transfer was firstly introduced in 1981 by M. Q. Rabin [13]. It is a protocol by which a sender sends some information to the receiver while remains oblivious to what is received. Theoretically, an oblivious signature can be implemented by an oblivious transfer. However, to construct an oblivious signature in this way is inefficient.

Blind Signature. In cryptography, a blind signature, as introduced by D. Chaum [3], is a form of digital signature which allows a user to get a message signed by a signer without revealing *any information* about the message to the signer. The resulting blind signature can be publicly verified in the manner of a regular digital signature. Examples of applications include digital election systems and digital cash schemes.

Note that we cannot use a blind signature to construct an oblivious signature on n messages since, in this case, there is no guarantee that the message getting signed is actually the one of n predetermined messages. In other words, a recipient may construct some other messages on which the signer is not going to offer the signature. Furthermore, an oblivious signature with n keys cannot be generated from a blind signature since there is only one signer with one private/public key-pair in a blind signature schemes.

2 Preliminaries

This section gives some cryptographic primitives and definitions required for our construction.

Definition 1. Discrete Logarithm (DL) Problem: Let G be a cyclic group of prime order p and g be a generator of G. The DL problem to the base g means the following problem:

Given $g, h \in G$, where $h = g^x \mod p$ for some unknown x, find x.

The DL problem is believed to be difficult and also to be the hard direction of a one-way function.

Definition 2. Forking Lemma[12]: Let $(\mathcal{K}, \mathcal{S}, \mathcal{V})$ be a digital signature scheme with security parameter 1^k, with a signature of the form $(m, \sigma_1, h, \sigma_2)$, where $h = \mathcal{H}(m, \sigma_1)$ and σ_2 depends on σ_1 and h only. Let $\mathcal{A}$ be a probabilistic polynomial time Turing machine whose input only consists of public data and which can ask $q_h > 0$ queries to the random oracle. Assume that, within time bound T, $\mathcal{A}$ produces, with probability $\epsilon \geq 7q_h/2^k$, a valid signature $(m, \sigma_1, h, \sigma_2)$. Then, a replay of the attacker $\mathcal{A}$, where interactions with the signer are simulated, outputs two valid signature $(m, \sigma_1, h, \sigma_2)$, and $(m, \sigma_1, h', \sigma_2')$ such that $h \neq h'$, within time $T' \leq 84480Tq_h/\epsilon$.

3 Definition of Oblivious Signature

In this section, we formally define the notion of an oblivious signature and the security requirements behind the oblivious signature. One important modification to the original definitions in [4] is that the characteristic of *ambiguous verification*[1] is neglected in our definition. This is because that, by implementing the technique of *universal 1-out-of-n signatures* recently proposed by R. Tso et. al. in [15], this characteristic can be easily achieved for *any* three-move type signature schemes [7]. Consequently, we should not consider ambiguous verification as a unique feature of obvious signatures. It should be considered as an additional feature for all three-move type signatures.

There are two types of oblivious signatures: a 1-out-of-n oblivious signature with n keys and a 1-out-of-n oblivious signature with n messages. Due to the space limitations, we only give the formal model for 1-out-of-n oblivious signatures with n messages. However, we emphasize that the formal model for 1-out-of-n oblivious signatures with n keys can be easily defined accordingly.

3.1 Formal Model of Oblivious Signatures with n Messages

A 1-out-of-n oblivious signature scheme (abbreviated to $\mathcal{OS}_1^n$) with n messages involves three types of entities: a recipient $\mathcal{R}$, an oblivious signer $\mathcal{S}$ and a verifier $\mathcal{V}$.

- **A recipient $\mathcal{R}$:** for any input of n messages, $m_1, \cdots, m_n$, $\mathcal{R}$ can choose any one of these n messages to get signed by $\mathcal{S}$.
- **An oblivious signer $\mathcal{S}$:** $\mathcal{S}$ is able to sign the message chosen by $\mathcal{R}$ but is not able to learn which one of the n messages is actually signed.
- **A verifier $\mathcal{V}$:** $\mathcal{R}$ converts the oblivious signature into a generic signature σ and transmits σ to $\mathcal{V}$. $\mathcal{V}$ is able to verify the validity of the signature without any secrete information.

The following definition gives the formal model of a $\mathcal{OS}_1^n$.

Definition 3. An oblivious signature protocol $\mathcal{OS}_1^n$ consists of four tuples, $(\mathcal{G}, \mathcal{S}, \mathcal{R}, \mathcal{V})$, where $\mathcal{S}, \mathcal{R}$ are two interactive Turing Machines, $\mathcal{G}$ is a probabilistic polynomial-time algorithm and $\mathcal{V}$ is a deterministic polynomial-time algorithm.

- $(para, pk, sk) \leftarrow \mathcal{G}(1^k)$: A probabilistic polynomial-time algorithm $\mathcal{G}$ which takes a security parameter 1^k as input and the output is the public parameters, $para$. Based on $para$, a public/private key pair (pk, sk) of a signer $\mathcal{S}$ can be defined accordingly.
- $(completed/notcompleted, \sigma/fail) \leftarrow interact(\mathcal{S}(para, pk, sk, m_1, \cdots, m_n), \mathcal{R}(para, pk, m_l))$: $\mathcal{S}$ and $\mathcal{R}$ are a pair of polynomially-bounded probabilistic interactive Turing machines. Both machines have the following tapes: a read-only input tape, a write-only output tape, a read/write work tape, a

---

[1] The characteristic that, when necessary, the recipient can show that he has got a signature with one of n keys (or messages) without revealing with which special one.

read-only random tape, a read-only communication tape and a write-only communication tape. The input tape of $\mathcal{S}$ is given the public parameter, $para$, the public/private key pair (pk, sk) and n messages $(m_1, \cdots, m_n)$. The input tape of $\mathcal{R}$ is given $para, pk$ and a message $m_l \in \{m_1, \cdots, m_n\}$. The length of all inputs must be polynomial in the security parameter 1^k of the algorithm $\mathcal{G}$. Then $\mathcal{S}$ and $\mathcal{R}$ engage in the interactive protocol of some polynomial number of rounds. At the end of this protocol, the output tape of $\mathcal{S}$ contains either *completed* or *notcompleted* and the output tape of $\mathcal{R}$ contains either fail (if $\mathcal{S}$ outputs "*notcompleted*") or a signature σ (if $\mathcal{S}$ outputs "completed") where σ is a generic signature on the message m_l.
- $1/0 \leftarrow \mathcal{V}(\sigma, para, pk, m_l)$: A deterministic polynomial-time algorithm $\mathcal{V}$ which takes the signature σ, the public parameters $para$, a public key pk of a signer $\mathcal{S}$ and a messages m_l as input, returns 1 or 0 for accept or reject, respectively.

3.2 Security Requirements

We now define the securities required for oblivious signatures. The securities defined in this section are modified from the security definitions of blind signatures defined in [1] and [9].

In the coming definitions, $negl(n)$ denotes any function which grows slower than $\frac{1}{n^c}$ for sufficiently large n and some constant c.

Definition 4. (Completeness) If $\mathcal{S}$ and $\mathcal{R}$ follow the signature issuing protocol properly and, at the end of the protocol, $\mathcal{S}$ outputs completed and $\mathcal{R}$ outputs σ, then, with probability at least $1 - negl(n)$, σ satisfies $\mathcal{V}(\sigma, para, pk, m_l) = 1$. The probability is taken over the coin flips of $\mathcal{G}, \mathcal{S}$ and $\mathcal{R}$.

The signature σ on messages m_l is said valid with regard to $(para, pk)$ if it leads $\mathcal{V}$ to accept.

Except the completeness of the protocol, in order to define security, we discuss separately protecting the recipient and the signer. The security for signers is the unforgeability of signatures and the security for recipients is the ambiguity in selected messages (against signers). The security for signers is protected in the sense of computational security and the security for recipients is protected in the sense of unconditional security.

To define the security for signers, we first introduce the following game.

Definition 5. (Game A) Let $\mathcal{R}^*$ be a probabilistic polynomial time forging algorithm. $\mathcal{R}^*$ executes the recipient's part and tries to forge a new signature σ^* on a message, m^*.

1. $(para, pk, sk) \leftarrow \mathcal{G}(1^k)$,
2. $\mathcal{R}^*(para, pk)$ engages in the signature issuing protocol with $\mathcal{S}(para, pk, sk)$ for any message-set $\mathcal{M}_i$ and any message $m_{(i,j)} \in \mathcal{M}_i$ which are adaptively chosen by $\mathcal{R}$. This step can be executed in polynomially many number of times where $\mathcal{R}^*$ can decide in an adaptive fashion when to stop. In each

execution, when $\mathcal{S}$ outputs completed, then $\mathcal{R}^*$ obtains a valid signature σ_i on the message $m_{(i,j)} \in \mathcal{M}_i$. Let t denote the number of executions where $\mathcal{S}$ outputs completed, and $m_{(i,j_i)}$ denote the message corresponding to the signature σ_i, $1 \leq i \leq t$.

3. $\mathcal{R}^*$ outputs a new signature σ^* on a message, m^*, where $m^* \notin \{m_{(1,j_1)}, \cdots, m_{(t,j_t)}\}$.

Definition 6. (Security for signers:Unforgeability) An oblivious signature scheme provides the security for signers if, for any probabilistic polynomial-time forging algorithm $\mathcal{R}^*$ that plays the above game, we have

$$Pr\left(\mathcal{V}(\sigma^*, para, pk, m^*) = 1\right) < negl(n).$$

The probability is taken over the coin flips of $\mathcal{G}, \mathcal{S}$ and $\mathcal{R}^*$.

Intuitively, the security for signers means that, except the signatures σ_i on $m_{(i,j_i)}$, $1 \leq i \leq t$, it is *computationally* infeasible, without the knowledge of the private key sk of $\mathcal{S}$, to produce any valid signature which will be accepted by $\mathcal{V}$. This part is similar to the notion of Existential Unforgeability against Adaptive Chosen Message Attack (EUF-ACMA) [8] for any standard publicly verifiable signature scheme.

The security for recipients is defined through Game B.

Definition 7. (Game B) Let $\mathcal{S}^*$ be an attacking algorithm with unlimited computation power which executes the signer's part and $\mathcal{R}$ be an honest recipient that follows the signature issuing protocol. Let m_0, m_1 be two messages randomly picked by $\mathcal{S}^*$ and $\mathcal{M} \supseteq \{m_0, m_1\}$ be a set of messages which is also determined by $\mathcal{S}^*$. Let $b \in_R \{0,1\}$ which is kept secret from $\mathcal{S}^*$. The message m_b is put on the input tape of $\mathcal{R}$ which is also kept secret from $\mathcal{S}^*$. The purpose of $\mathcal{S}^*$ is to predict b via the execution of the following game.

1. $(para, pk, sk) \leftarrow \mathcal{G}(1^k)$,
2. $\{m_0, m_1\} \leftarrow \mathcal{S}^*(para, pk, sk, \mathcal{M})$,
3. $\mathcal{S}^*$ engages in the signature issuing protocol with $\mathcal{R}(para, pk, m_b), b \in_R \{0,1\}$,
4. $\mathcal{S}^*$ outputs a bit $b' \in \{0,1\}$ according to the view from steps 1, 2, and 3 (ie., $\mathcal{S}^*$ is not allowed to view the output of $\mathcal{R}$ at the end of the signature issuing protocol).

We say that the attacking algorithm $\mathcal{S}^*$ wins the game if $b' = b$.

Definition 8. (Security for recipients against signers: Ambiguity in selected messages) An oblivious signature scheme provides unconditional security for recipients against signers if, for any attacking algorithm $\mathcal{S}^*$ executing the signer's part, $\mathcal{S}^*$ wins in Game B with probability at most $1/2 + negl(n)$. The probability is taken over the coin flips of $\mathcal{G}, \mathcal{R}$ and $\mathcal{S}^*$.

Intuitively, the security for recipients against signers means that it is *unconditionally* infeasible for any attacker $\mathcal{S}^*$ to find out which one of the messages in $\mathcal{M}$ is chosen by a recipient $\mathcal{R}$.

4 Proposed Schemes

In this section, we propose our 1-out-of-n oblivious signatures with n messages. In some applications, the message-set $\{m_1, \cdots, m_n\}$ (in which one of them will get signed) may be decided by the signer, while in other applications, they may be decided by the recipient. In either case, they should not affect the security of the scheme. In the following scheme, we assume that they are decided by the recipient.

4.1 Proposed 1-out-of-n Oblivious Signatures with n Messages

System Setting: On input a security parameter 1^k, a signer $\mathcal{S}$ runs the System-Setup algorithm $\mathcal{G}$. The following output forms the public parameters of the scheme.

- p, q: two large primes such that $q|(p-1)$,
- g, h: two elements of $\mathbb{Z}_p^*$ of the same order q where the discrete logarithm $\log_g^h$ is unknown to all.
- $\mathcal{H} : \{0,1\}^* \to \mathbb{Z}_q^*$: an one way hash function.

Key Generation: $\mathcal{S}$ picks a random number $x \in \mathbb{Z}_q^*$ and computes $y \leftarrow g^x \bmod p$. x is kept secret as her private key and y is public as her public key.

Signature Generation: Assume that a recipient $\mathcal{R}$ would like to get a signature σ on a message $m_l \in \{m_1, \cdots, m_n\}$ which is obliviously signed by $\mathcal{S}$, then $\mathcal{R}$ executes the following protocol with $\mathcal{S}$:

Step 1. $\mathcal{R}$ starts the protocol by picking a random number $r \in \mathbb{Z}_q^*$, then computs $c = g^r h^l \bmod p$ and sends c together with the n messages $m_1, \cdots, m_n$ to the signer $\mathcal{S}$. Here l is the value of the subscript of m_l.

Step 2. For $i = 1, \cdots, n$, $\mathcal{S}$ picks a random number $k_i \in_R \mathbb{Z}_q^*$ and computes:
- $K_i \leftarrow g^{k_i} \bmod p$,
- $\hat{e}_i \leftarrow \mathcal{H}(m_i, K_i c/(gh)^i \bmod p)$, and
- $\hat{s}_i \leftarrow k_i - x\hat{e}_i \bmod q$.

$\mathcal{S}$ then sends $(\hat{e}_i, \hat{s}_i)$, $1 \leq i \leq n$, to $\mathcal{R}$.

Step 3. For $1 \leq i \leq n$, $\mathcal{R}$ computes $\delta_i \leftarrow g^{(r-i)} h^{(l-i)} \bmod p$ and accepts the oblivious signature if and only if

$$\hat{e}_i = \mathcal{H}(m_i, g^{\hat{s}_i} y^{\hat{e}_i} \delta_i \bmod p) \quad 1 \leq i \leq n.$$

Step 4. To convert the oblivious signature into a generic (Schnorr) signature, $\mathcal{R}$ computes:
- $e \leftarrow \hat{e}_l$, and
- $s \leftarrow r - l + \hat{s}_l \bmod q$,

The signature on m_l is $\sigma \leftarrow (e, s)$.

Signature Verification: Any verifier $\mathcal{V}$ accepts the signature σ as a valid signature on m_l if and only if

$$e = \mathcal{H}(m_l, g^s y^e \bmod p)$$

4.2 Security

Lemma 1. The proposed scheme is complete.

Proof. The completeness of the signature $\sigma = (e, s)$ is depended on the Schnorr signature. So, we only show the completeness of the oblivious signature $\sigma' = \left(\sum_{1 \leq i \leq n'}(\hat{e}_i, \hat{s}_i, \delta_i)\right)$ in Step 3 of the Signature Generation Algorithm. For any $(\hat{e}_i, \hat{s}_i, \delta_i)$ of $m_i \in \{m_1, \cdots, m_n\}$, we have

$$\mathcal{H}(m_i, g^{\hat{s}_i} y^{\hat{e}_i} \delta_i \bmod p)$$
$$= \mathcal{H}(m_i, g^{k_i - x\hat{e}_i} y^{\hat{e}_i} g^{(r-i)} h^{(l-i)} \bmod p)$$
$$= \mathcal{H}(m_i, g^{k_i - x\hat{e}_i} g^{x\hat{e}_i} g^{(r-i)} h^{(l-i)} \bmod p)$$
$$= \mathcal{H}(m_i, g^{k_i} g^{(r-i)} h^{(l-i)} \bmod p)$$
$$= \mathcal{H}(m_i, K_i g^r h^l / (gh)^i \bmod p)$$
$$= \mathcal{H}(m_i, K_i c / (gh)^i \bmod p)$$
$$= \hat{e}_i.$$

□

We than proof that the proposed scheme provides the security for signers.

Theorem 1. If there exists an adaptively chosen message attacker $\mathcal{B}$ which wins Game A with an advantage ϵ within a time T, then there exists an algorithm $\mathcal{A}$ which can solve the DL problem with the same advantage within a time $T' \leq 84480 q_h T/\epsilon$, where q_h is the number of hash queries.

Proof: $\mathcal{A}$ is given a DL problem (p, q, g, y) where p, q are two large primes such that $q|(p-1)$, and g, y are two elements of $\mathbb{Z}_p^*$ of the same order q. The purpose of $\mathcal{A}$ is to find $\log_g^y$, which is the solution to the DL problem.

In order to solve the problem, $\mathcal{A}$ utilizes $\mathcal{B}$ as a black-box. To get the black-box $\mathcal{B}$ run properly, $\mathcal{A}$ simulates the environments of the proposed $\mathcal{OS}_1^n$ scheme. In the following proof, we regard the hash function $\mathcal{H}$ as a random oracle. On the other hand, in the following proof, we assume that $\mathcal{B}$ is well-behaved in the sense that it always queries the random orale $\mathcal{H}$ on the message m^* that it outputs as its forgery. According to [2], we know that it is trivial to modify any adversary-algorithm $\mathcal{B}$ to have this property.

$\mathcal{A}$ picks a random number $h \in <g>$ and sets (p, q, g, h) as the system-wide parameters. Here $<g>$ denotes the subgroup of $\mathbb{Z}_p^*$ generated by g. In addition, $\mathcal{A}$ sets y as the signer's public key. $\mathcal{A}$ gives (p, q, g, h) and y to $\mathcal{B}$ and allows $\mathcal{B}$ to run via Game A.

In Game A, via an interactive way with $\mathcal{A}$, $\mathcal{B}$ takes part as a recipient in order to get a signature obliviously signed by the signing key $\log_g^y$. In order to respond for this query, for each $\mathcal{M}_i = \{m_{i_1}, \cdots, m_{i_n}\}$ and $c_i = g^{r_i} h^{l_i}$ chosen by $\mathcal{B}$, $\mathcal{A}$ does the following steps:

- For each $j = 1, \cdots, n$, $\mathcal{A}$ picks a random number $k_{i_j} \in_R \mathbb{Z}_q^*$ and
  - computes $K_{i_j} = g^{k_{i_j}} \bmod p$,

- picks $\hat{s}_{i_j} \in_R \mathbb{Z}_q^*$,
- sets $\hat{e}_{i_j} \leftarrow \mathcal{H}(m_{i_j}, K_{i_j} c_i/(gh)^j \mod p)$.
- $\mathcal{A}$ returns $(\hat{e}_{i_j}, \hat{s}_{i_j}), 1 \leq i \leq n$, to $\mathcal{B}$ and records $(\mathcal{M}_i, c_i, K_{i_1}, \cdots, K_{i_n}, \hat{e}_{i_1}, \cdots, \hat{e}_{i_n}, \hat{s}_{i_1}, \cdots, \hat{s}_{i_n})$ to a Sign-List which is assumed to be initially empty.

The above execution can be executed at most t times. After the execution, $\mathcal{B}$ outputs its forgery $\sigma^* = (e^*, s^*)$ on a message m^*. Assume σ^* is a valid forgery and $\mathcal{B}$ wins Game A. According to the protocol, we have

$$e^* = \mathcal{H}(m^*, y^{e^*} g^{s^*} \mod p).$$

Since $\mathcal{B}$ is assumed to be well-behaved, we have $e^* = \mathcal{H}(m_{i_j}, K_{i_j} c_i/(gh)^j \mod p) = \hat{e}_{i_j}$ for some $\hat{e}_{i_j}$ and $m^* = m_{i_j}$ which are on the Sign-List.

We are now ready to apply the Forking Lemma [12]. By replaying the game with the same random tape but different choices of oracle $\mathcal{H}$, at the end of the second run, we obtain another valid forgery $(m^*, e^{*'}, s^{*'})$. Since $s^* = k_{i_j} + r_i - l_i + x_a e^*$ and $s^{*'} = k_{i_j} + r_i - l_i + x_a e^{*'}$ for the same $k_{i_j} + r_i - l_i$ (according to the Forking Lemma), we obtain $x_a = \frac{s^* - s^{*'}}{e^* - e^{*'}} \mod q$. This is the solution to the DL problem. The advantage of $\mathcal{A}$ is the same as the advantage of $\mathcal{B}$ and the total running time T' of $\mathcal{A}$ is equal to the running time of the Forking Lemma [12] which is bound by $84480 q_h T/\epsilon$. Here q_h is the number of hash queries in the game. □

Theorem 2. *The proposed scheme provides perfect security for recipients. In other words, the proposed scheme provides unconditional security on the ambiguity of the selected message.*

Proof: It is sufficient to show that an attacker $\mathcal{F}$, taking parts as a signer, wins Game B with probability exactly the same as random guessing of $b \in \{0, 1\}$.

Assume $\mathcal{M} = \{m_1, \cdots, m_n\}$ and $c = g^r h^l, l \in \{1, \cdots, n\}$, where c is chosen by the recipient $\mathcal{R}$. It is easy to see that for any such c, there exists an $r_i \in \mathbb{Z}_q$ such that

$$c = g^r h^l = g^{r_1} h^1 = \cdots = g^{r_i} h^i = \cdots = g^{r_n} h^n \mod p.$$

Consequently, we conclude that $\mathcal{F}$ wins Game B with probability exactly the same as random guessing of b. This ends the proof. □

5 Discussions and Performance Comparisons

In Chen's schemes [4], the signature consists of two random signatures: $\sigma_{(g,y)}(m')$ and $\sigma_{(\mathcal{H}(m_l),m')}(m_l)$. $\sigma_{(g,y)}(m')$ is the signature on a random message m' with secret key $x = \log_g^y$ and $\sigma_{(\mathcal{H}(m_l),m')}(m_l)$ is the signature on message m_l with the random secret key $e = \log_{\mathcal{H}(m_l)}^{m'}$. On the other hand, $\sigma_{(g,y)}(m')$ is generated by $\mathcal{S}$ in an interactive way with $\mathcal{R}$ but $\sigma_{(\mathcal{H}(m_l),m')}(m_l)$ is computed by $\mathcal{R}$ individually,

Table 1. Performance Comparison 1

Scheme	Numbers of Communication	Communication Cost		
		Communication Over Head		
		$\mathcal{S} \to \mathcal{R}$ ($\approx bits$)	$\mathcal{R} \to \mathcal{S}$ ($\approx bits$)	$\mathcal{R} \to \mathcal{V}$ ($\approx bits$)
New	2	$2n|q|$ ($\approx 320n$)	$|q|$ (≈ 160)	$2|q|$ (≈ 320)
Chen [4]	3	$3n|p| + n|q|$ ($\approx 3232n$)	$|q|$ (≈ 160)	$7|p| + 2|q|$ (≈ 7488)
DSA-OT	2	$2n|p| + 2n|q|$ ($\approx 2368n$)	$|p|$ (≈ 1024)	$2|q|$ (≈ 320)

Table 2. Performance Comparison 2

Scheme	Computation Cost		
	Signer: $\mathcal{S}$	Receiver: $\mathcal{R}$	Verifier: $\mathcal{V}$
New	$2nEx.$	$(2n+2)Ex.$	$2Ex.$
Chen [4]	$3nEx.$	$(2n+10)Ex.$	$8Ex.$
DSA-OT	$5nEx.$	$3Ex.$	$2Ex.$

so the oblivious property (from signer's viewpoint) is preserved. The verification of these two signatures assures anyone that the signer $\mathcal{S}$ with public key y indeed signed the message m_l.

Although, in Section 4, we only showed the construction of a 1-out-of-n oblivious signature with n messages, we emphasize that the proposed scheme can be easily modified into a 1-out-of-n oblivious signature with n keys. The technique is to use the signing key y_l in the proposed scheme instead of h. In this way, the signing key can be designated by a recipient. We omit the details and focus only on oblivious signature with n messages due to the space limitations.

In the following tables, we compare the efficiency of our scheme with that of Chen's scheme and the combination of the oblivious transfer (OT) scheme defined in [16] and DSA signature standard [10]. We denote Ex the exponentiation in $\mathbb{Z}_p$ and ignore other operations such as reversion and hash in all schemes.

In Table 1, we see that Chen's scheme requires three movies of communication between the signer $\mathcal{S}$ and the recipient $\mathcal{R}$ whereas our scheme and DSA-OT require only two movies of communication. In addition, our scheme enjoys small size of communication over head comparing with these two schemes. Table 2 shows the computation cost of each scheme and we can see that our scheme is more efficient than Chen's scheme in every step and more efficient than DSA-OT in the signing phase.

6 Conclusion

Oblivious signature is first proposed by Chen in 1994. However, previous references do not crisply formalize the notion, the model of the schemes as well as the security model. Moreover, previously proposed constructions are less efficient in both communication and computation. In this paper, we give formal definitions on the model of oblivious signature schemes and give the security requirements of the scheme. We also propose a new oblivious signature scheme which is more efficient than Chen's scheme and the scheme based on DSA and oblivious transfer. Based on the discrete logarithm problem, the security of our scheme is proved in the random oracle model.

References

1. Abe, M., Okamoto, T.: Provably secure partially blind signatures. In: Bellare, M. (ed.) CRYPTO 2000. LNCS, vol. 1880, pp. 271–286. Springer, Heidelberg (2000)
2. Boneh, D., Lynn, B., Shacham, H.: Short signatures from the Weil pairing. In: Boyd, C. (ed.) ASIACRYPT 2001. LNCS, vol. 2248, pp. 514–532. Springer, Heidelberg (2001)
3. Chaum, D.: Blind signatures for untraceable payments. In: Advances in Cryptology –CRYPTO 1982, pp. 199–203. Plenum Press (1983)
4. Chen, L.: Oblivious signatures. In: Gollmann, D. (ed.) ESORICS 1994. LNCS, vol. 875, pp. 161–172. Springer, Heidelberg (1994)
5. Chaum, D., van Heijst, E.: Group signatures. In: Davies, D.W. (ed.) EUROCRYPT 1991. LNCS, vol. 547, pp. 257–265. Springer, Heidelberg (1991)
6. Chen, L., Pedersen, T.: New group signature schemes. In: De Santis, A. (ed.) EUROCRYPT 1994. LNCS, vol. 950, pp. 163–173. Springer, Heidelberg (1995)
7. Fiat, A., Shamir, A.: How to prove yourself: A randomized protocol for signing contracts. In: Odlyzko, A.M. (ed.) CRYPTO 1986. LNCS, vol. 263, pp. 186–194. Springer, Heidelberg (1987)
8. Goldwasser, S., Micali, S., Rivest, R.: A digital signature scheme secure against adaptively chosen message atttacks. SIAM Journal on Computing 17(2), 281–308 (1988)
9. Juels, A., Luby, M., Ostrovsky, R.: Security of blind digital signatures. In: Kaliski Jr., B.S. (ed.) CRYPTO 1997. LNCS, vol. 1294, pp. 150–164. Springer, Heidelberg (1997)
10. NIST (National Institute for Standard and Technology), Digital Signature Standard (DSS), FIPS PUB, vol. 186 (1994)
11. Pointcheval, D., Stern, J.: Security proofs for signature schemes. In: Maurer, U.M. (ed.) EUROCRYPT 1996. LNCS, vol. 1070, pp. 387–398. Springer, Heidelberg (1996)
12. Pointcheval, D., Stern, J.: Security arguments for sigital signatures and blind signatures. Journal of Cryptology 13(3), 361–396 (2000)
13. Rabin, M.O.: How to exchange secrets by oblivious transfer, Technical Report TR-81, Aiken Computation Laboratory, Harvard University (1981), http://eprint.iacr.org/2005/187.pdf
14. Schnorr, C.P.: Efficient signature generation by smart cards. Journal of Cryptology 4(3), 161–174 (1991)
15. Tso, R., Okamoto, T., Okamoto, E.: Universal 1-out-of-n signatures. In: Proceedings of the Symposium on Cryptography and Information Security 2007 (SCIS 2007), vol. 2B4-3 (2007)
16. Tzeng, W.G.: Efficient 1-out-of-n oblivious transfer schemes with universal usable parameters. IEEE Transactoins on Computer 53(2), 232–240 (2004)

A Formal Study of the Privacy Concerns in Biometric-Based Remote Authentication Schemes*

Qiang Tang[1,**], Julien Bringer[2], Hervé Chabanne[2], and David Pointcheval[3]

[1] DIES, EWI, University of Twente, the Netherlands
[2] Sagem Sécurité
[3] Departement d'Informatique, École Normale Supérieure
45 Rue d'Ulm, 75230 Paris Cedex 05, France

Abstract. With their increasing popularity in cryptosystems, biometrics have attracted more and more attention from the information security community. However, how to handle the relevant privacy concerns remains to be troublesome. In this paper, we propose a novel security model to formalize the privacy concerns in biometric-based remote authentication schemes. Our security model covers a number of practical privacy concerns such as identity privacy and transaction anonymity, which have not been formally considered in the literature. In addition, we propose a general biometric-based remote authentication scheme and prove its security in our security model.

1 Introduction

Privacy has become an important issue in many aspects of our daily life, especially in an era of networking where information access may go far beyond our control. When sensitive information such as biometrics is used, the privacy issues become even more important because corruption of such information may be catastrophic for the relevant applications. In this paper we focus on the issue of handling the privacy concerns in remote biometric-based authentication schemes.

1.1 Related Work

Biometrics, such as fingerprint and iris, have been used to a higher level of security in order to cope with the increasing demand for reliable and highly-usable information security systems, because they have many advantages over typical cryptographic credentials. For example, biometrics are believed to be unique, unforgettable, non-transferable, and they do not need to be stored. One of the most important application areas is biometric-based authentication schemes, where an authentication is simply a comparison between a reference biometric template

---

* This work is partially supported by French ANR RNRT project BACH.
** The work was done when the author worked as a postdoc researcher at École Normale Supérieure.

and a new template extracted during the authentication process. Note that, depending on the type of biometrics, comparison may mean image matching, binary string matching, etc.

Despite of its advantages, in practice, there are some obstacles in a wide adoption of biometrics.

First, biometrics are only approximately stable over the time, therefore, they cannot be directly integrated into most of the existing systems. To address this issue, error-correction concept is widely used in the literature (e.g. [3,4,8,10,11,18,19,25,29]). Employing this concept, some intermediate information (referred to as helper data in some work) is firstly generated based on a reference biometric template, and later, a newly-extracted template could help to recover the reference template or some relevant information if the distance between the templates is small enough (depending on the type of biometrics). Instead of employing this concept, a number of authors also suggest to compare biometric templates directly (e.g. [1,12,34]). Atallah et al. [1] propose a method, in which biometric templates are treated as bit strings and subsequently masked and permuted during the authentication process. Du and Atallah [12,34] investigate a number of biometric comparison scenarios by employing secure multiparty computation techniques. Schoenmakers and Tuyls [27] propose to use homomorphic encryption schemes for biometric authentication schemes by employing multi-party computation techniques.

Second, biometrics are usually regarded to be sensitive because they uniquely identify an individual. The sensitivity of biometrics lies in the fact that disclosure of biometrics in a certain application leads to the disclosure of the true identity of the involved users in this application. In addition, if the same type of biometrics of a user is used in two applications, then there is an undeniable link for the user's activities in both applications. Nonetheless, it is worth stressing that biometrics are normally considered to be public information. In [20,28,29,31,33], the authors attempt to enhance privacy protection in biometric authentication schemes, where the privacy means that the compromise of the database will not enable the adversary to recover the biometric template. Ratha, Connell, and Bolle [2,24] introduce the concept of *cancelable biometrics* in an attempt to solve the revocation and privacy issues related to biometric information. Ratha *et al.* [23] intensively elaborate this concept in the case of fingerprint-based authentication systems. Recently, Bringer *et al.* [5,6] propose a number of biometric-based authentication protocols which protect the sensitive relationship between a biometric feature and relevant pseudorandom username.

Practical concerns, security issues, and challenges about biometrics have been intensively discussed in the literature (e.g. [2,17,21,24,26,32]). Tuyls, Skoric, and Kevenaar [30] present a summary of cryptographic techniques for dealing with biometrics.

1.2 Motivation and Contributions

The stability problem concerned with biometric measurements has been paid pretty much attention and investigated very well at this moment. However, privacy issues concerned with biometrics have not been understood well. With respect to biometric-based authentication schemes, we do not have a general formalization of privacy concerns based on a clear system structure. In practice, privacy may mean much more than the adversary cannot recover the user's biometric template. For instance, a user may also want the relationship between its biometric template and username to remain secret in a service, where the user uses a personalized (pseudorandom) username instead of his true name. This requirement might become much stronger if the user wants to multiple registrations under different usernames at the service provider.

In the rest of this paper, we consider the following scenario for biometric-based authentication schemes: Suppose a human user registers at a service provider to consume some service and would like to authenticate himself to the service provider using his biometric (say, his iris). Typically, the user will choose a personalized username and register his reference biometric information under this username. In order to authenticate himself to the service provider, the user presents his username and some fresh biometric information, and then the service provider will perform a matching between the reference biometric information and the fresh biometric information. The contributions of this paper can be summarized as follows.

First, we propose a new system structure for biometric-based remote authentication schemes. In the new structure, there are four types of components, including human user, sensor client, service provider, and database. There are two motivations for us to assume sensor client and service provider to be independent, which means the service provider does not control the sensor client.

1. One is to protect human users' privacy against a malicious service provider. If a malicious service provider controls the sensor client, then it can easily obtain human users' biometric information and potentially manipulate the information.
2. The other is based on the fact that human users may wish to access the service provider wherever they are. In this case, it is natural to make the assumption that sensor client could be provided by another party which has business agreement with the service provider.

Different from any previous system, the database is assumed to be independent from the service provider and serve as a secure storage for biometric information. The motivations for the detachment are as follows.

1. The first is that a user may not trust a service provider to store his biometric template regardless of the transformation which might be applied to the template.
2. The second is that the service provider's access to the biometric information can be minimized, so is the database's access. This structure makes it possible to protect human users' privacy against a malicious service provider or a malicious database. Under the traditional structure, where the service

provider controls the database, we do not see how to achieve our privacy goal[1].
3. The third is that, in practice, the service provider has avoided the responsibility for storing biometric templates. As data breaches for service providers are reported more and more frequently nowadays, the need for the separation becomes stronger and stronger.

With respect to the new structure, we formalize the following attributes related to privacy concerns which have not been formally considered in the literature.

- The security for private relationship between personalized username and biometric template is defined to be an attribute *identity privacy*.
- The security for user's transaction statistics is defined to be an attribute *transaction anonymity*.

Note that, for non biometric-based (authentication) schemes, the requirement of identity privacy might not be as significant as in our case because cryptographic credentials are not bound to an individual permanently.

Second, we propose a general biometric-based remote authentication scheme by employing a Private Information Retrieval (PIR) protocol [7,9,15] and the ElGamal public-key encryption scheme [13]. The security of the scheme is based on the semantic security of ElGamal, namely the DDH assumption. Instead of ElGamal, other homomorphic encryption schemes can also be used for the same purpose but the computational load will stay in a similar level. Our proposal is not focused on a specific biometric, but rather on such type of biometrics that can be represented as binary strings in the Hamming space and authentication can be done through a binary string matching. For example, iris is one type of such biometrics [16]. For other biometrics, how to construct a secure authentication scheme in our security model remains as an open problem.

1.3 Organization

The rest of the paper is organized as follows. In Section 2 we provide some preliminary definitions. In Section 3 we provide the security and privacy definitions for biometric-based remote authentication schemes. In Section 4 we present a new biometric-based remote authentication scheme. In Section 5 we provide security analysis for the new scheme in our security model. In Section 6 we conclude the paper.

2 Preliminary Definitions

2.1 The System Structure

In the new system structure for biometric-based authentication schemes, we consider four types of components.

---
[1] Especially, applying a one-way function to the biometric template will not be enough to achieve our privacy goal.

- Human user, which uses his biometric to authenticate himself to a service provider.
- Sensor client, which captures the raw biometric data and extracts a biometric template, and communicates with the service provider.
- Service provider, which deals with human user's authentication request by querying the database.
- Database, which stores biometric information for users, and works as a biometric template matcher by providing the matching service to the service provider.

Remark 1. Different from the local authentication environment, sensor client and service provider are assumed to be independent components in our structure. We consider this to be an appropriate assumption in the remote authentication environment, where human users access the service provider through sensor clients, which are not owned by the service provider but have a business agreement with the service provider.

Remark 2. In practice, there might be only very few organizations that can be trusted by human users to store their biometric information though they may want to use their biometrics for the authentication purpose at many service providers. Therefore, in practice we suggest an scenario like that of Single Sign-On systems [22], where biometric information for all service providers are centralizedly stored and managed. In addition, in our security model the centralized database won't be a bottleneck in the sense of security.

For the simplicity of description, in the following discussions, we assume N users U_i $(1 \leq i \leq N)$ register at a service provider $\mathcal{S}$, these users authenticate themselves through a sensor client $\mathcal{C}^2$, and the database is denoted as $\mathcal{DB}$. Moreover, we would expect users to conduct their authentication services at different service providers while registering their biometric templates in the same (trusted) database.

2.2 The Authentication Workflow

Like most existing biometric-based cryptosystems, we also assume that a biometric-based authentication scheme consists of two phases: an enrollment phase and a verification phase.

1. In the enrollment phase, user U_i registers his reference biometric information, which is computed based on his reference biometric template b_i, at the database $\mathcal{DB}$ and his personalized username ID_i at the service provider $\mathcal{S}$. Note that a human user may have multiple registrations at the same service provider.
2. In the verification phase, user U_i issues an authentication request to the service provider $\mathcal{S}$ through the sensor client $\mathcal{C}$. $\mathcal{S}$ matches U_i's biometric templates with help from the database $\mathcal{DB}$.

---

[2] In practice, there may be a number of sensor clients for human users to access the service provider, but this simplification will not affect our security result.

2.3 Assumptions and Trust Relationships

We make the following assumptions.

1. Biometric Distribution assumption: Let H be the distance function in a metric space (in this paper, we assume it to be Hamming space). Suppose b_i and b_j are the reference biometric templates for Alice and Bob, respectively. There is a threshold value λ, the probability that $\mathsf{H}(b_i, b'_j) > \lambda$ is close to 1 and the probability that $\mathsf{H}(b_i, b'_i) \leq \lambda$ is close to 1, where b'_i and b'_j are the templates captured for Alice and Bob at any time.
2. Liveness assumption: We assume that, with a high probability, the biometric template captured by the sensor is from a live human user. In other words, it is difficult to produce a fake biometric template that can be accepted by the sensor.
3. Security link assumption: The communication links between components are protected with confidentiality and integrity. In practice, the security links can be implemented using a standard protocol such as SSL or TLS.

The biometric distribution and the liveness assumptions are indispensable for most of biometric-based cryptosystems and they are considered as a prerequisite for the adoption of biometrics. Note that biometrics are public information, additional credentials are always required to establish security links in order to prevent some well-known attacks (e.g. replay attacks). Therefore, the security link assumption is indeed also assumed in most cryptosystems, though it is not as standard as others.

In a biometric-based authentication system, we assume the following trust relationships.

1. Sensor client is always honest and trusted by all other components. By assuming this trust relationship, the liveness assumption is extended from sensor client to service provider in the following sense: when the service provider receives a username and some fresh biometric information, it can confirm with a high probability that the the fresh biometric information is extracted from a human user which has presented the username to the sensor client.
2. With respect to authentication service, service provider is trusted by human users to make the right decision, and database is trusted by human users and the service provider to store and provide the right biometric information. Only an outside adversary may try to impersonate an honest human user.
3. With respect to privacy concerns, both service provider and database are assumed to be malicious which means they may deviate from the protocol specification, but they will not collude. In reality, an outside adversary may also pose threats to the privacy concerns, however, it has no more advantage than a malicious system component.

3 Security Model for Biometric-Based Authentication

We first describe some conventions for writing probabilistic algorithms and experiments. The notation $x \xleftarrow{R} S$ means x is randomly chosen from the set S.

If $\mathcal{A}$ is a probabilistic algorithm, then $\mathcal{A}(\mathsf{Alg};\mathsf{Func})$ is the result of running $\mathcal{A}$, which can have any polynomial number of oracle queries to the functionality Func, interactively with Alg which answers the oracle queries issued by $\mathcal{A}$. For the clarity of description, if an algorithm $\mathcal{A}$ runs in a number of stages then we write $\mathcal{A} = (\mathcal{A}_1, \mathcal{A}_2, \cdots)$. As a standard practice, the security of a protocol is evaluated by an experiment between an adversary and a challenger, where the challenger simulates the protocol executions and answers the adversary's oracle queries. Without specification, algorithms are always assumed to be polynomial-time and the security parameter is assumed to be ℓ.

Specifically, in our case, there are two functionalities Enrollment and Verification, where Enrollment can be initiated only once to simulate the enrollment phase and Verification can be initiated for any user to start an authentication session for any polynomial times. Without loss of generality, if Verification is initiated for U_i, we write Verification(i).

In addition, we have the following definitions for negligible and overwhelming probabilities.

Definition 1. *The function $P(\ell) : \mathbb{Z} \to \mathbb{R}$ is said to be negligible if, for every polynomial $f(\ell)$, there exists an integer N_f such that $P(\ell) \leq \frac{1}{f(\ell)}$ for all $\ell \geq N_f$. If $P(\ell)$ is negligible, then the probability $1 - P(\ell)$ is said to be overwhelming.*

3.1 Soundness and Impersonation Resilience

Definition 2. *A biometric-based authentication scheme is defined to be sound if it satisfies the following two requirements:*

1. *With an overwhelming probability, the service provider will accept an authentication request in the following case: sensor client sends (ID_i, b) in an authentication request, where $\mathsf{H}(b, b_i) \leq \lambda$ and b_i is the reference template registered for ID_i.*
2. *With an overwhelming probability, the service provider will reject an authentication request in the following case: sensor client sends (ID_i, b) in an authentication request, where $\mathsf{H}(b, b_i) > \lambda$ and b_i is the reference template registered for ID_i.*

If b, where $\mathsf{H}(b, b_i) \leq \lambda$, is extracted from a user different from the user registered under b_i, then we say false accept occurs. Otherwise, if b, where $\mathsf{H}(b, b_i) > \lambda$, is extracted from the user registered under b_i, then we say false reject occurs. From a cryptographic point of view, the false reject rate and the false accept rate may be very high. However, this issue is irrelevant to our privacy concerns, hence, how to handle them is beyond the scope of our paper.

For authentication schemes, impersonation resilience should be the primary goal, nonetheless, under the security link assumption and the liveness assumption, soundness implies impersonation resilience in our case so that we omit the formalization.

3.2 Identity Privacy

In practice, a malicious service provider or a malicious database may try to probe the relationships between personalized usernames and biometric templates, though they do not need such information in order to make the system work. Informally, the attribute identity privacy means that, for any personalized username, the adversary knows nothing about the corresponding biometric template. It also implies that the adversary cannot find any linkability between registrations in the case that the same human user has multiple registrations at the service provider.

Definition 3. *A biometric-based authentication scheme achieves identity privacy if* $\mathcal{A} = (\mathcal{A}_1, \mathcal{A}_2)$ *has only a negligible advantage in the following game, where the advantage is defined to be* $|\Pr[e' = e] - \frac{1}{2}|$.

$$\mathbf{Exp}_{\mathcal{A}}^{Identity\text{-}Privacy}$$
$$\begin{vmatrix} (i, ID_i, b_i^{(0)}, b_i^{(1)}, (ID_j, b_j)(j \neq i)) \leftarrow \mathcal{A}_1(1^\ell) \\ b_i = b_i^{(e)} \qquad\qquad\qquad \overset{R}{\leftarrow} \{b_i^{(0)}, b_i^{(1)}\} \\ \emptyset \qquad\qquad\qquad\qquad \leftarrow \textsf{Enrollment}(1^\ell) \\ e' \qquad\qquad\qquad\qquad \leftarrow \mathcal{A}_2(Challenger; \textsf{Verification}) \end{vmatrix}$$

Note that the symbol ∅ means that there is no explicit output (besides the state information) for the adversary. In the experiment, presumably, the adversary $\mathcal{A}_2$ will obtain the corresponding information[3] from the challenger. The attack game can be informally rephrased as follows:

1. The adversary $\mathcal{A}_1$ generates N pairs of username and relevant biometric template, but provides two possible templates $(b_i^{(0)}, b_i^{(1)})$ for ID_i.
2. The challenger randomly chooses a template $b_i^{(e)}$ for the username ID_i, and simulates the enrollment phase to generate the parameter for the sensor client, the service provider, and the database.
3. The adversary $\mathcal{A}_2$ can initiate any (polynomial) number of protocol instances for the verification protocol, and terminates by outputting guess e'.

In this definition (and Definition 4), the adversary can freely choose the username and biometric template pairs for the enrollment phase, therefore, it models the security for any type of biometric regardless of its distribution in practice. It is worth stressing that, if a scheme achieves identity privacy, then neither a malicious service provider or a malicious database (or an outside adversary which has compromised any of them) can recover any registered biometric template.

As to our knowledge, none of the existing biometric-based authentication schemes (including those in Section 1) achieve identity privacy under our definition. Informally, these scheme suffers from the following vulnerability: Suppose that human users use their iris to authenticate themselves to a service provider $\mathcal{S}$.

---

[3] The information refers to that of the malicious component at the end of the enrollment phase.

If $\mathcal{S}$ is malicious (or a hacker which has compromised the biometric database of $\mathcal{S}$), then it can easily determine whether a human being, say Alice, has registered.

3.3 Transaction Anonymity

Since the database is supposed to store biometric information, therefore, it might obtain some transaction statistics about the service provider and registered human users. Informally, the attribute transaction anonymity means that, for every query issued by the service provider, a malicious database knows nothing about which user is authenticating himself to the service provider.

Definition 4. *A biometric-based authentication scheme achieves transaction anonymity if an adversary $\mathcal{A} = (\mathcal{A}_1, \mathcal{A}_2, \mathcal{A}_3)$ has only a negligible advantage in the following game, where the advantage is defined to be $|\Pr[e' = e] - \frac{1}{2}|$.*

$$\mathrm{Exp}_{\mathcal{A}}^{Transaction\text{-}Anonymity} \begin{vmatrix} (ID_j, b_j)(1 \leq j \leq N) \leftarrow \mathcal{A}_1(1^\ell) \\ \emptyset \leftarrow \mathsf{Enrollment}(1^\ell) \\ \{i_0, i_1\} \leftarrow \mathcal{A}_2(Challenger, \mathsf{Verification}) \\ i_e \stackrel{R}{\leftarrow} \{i_0, i_1\} \\ \emptyset \leftarrow \mathsf{Verification}(i_e) \\ e' \leftarrow \mathcal{A}_3(Challenger; \mathsf{Verification}) \end{vmatrix}$$

As the adversary is a malicious database, presumably the adversary $\mathcal{A}_2$ will obtain the corresponding information from the challenger. The attack game can be informally rephrased as follows:

1. The adversary $\mathcal{A}_1$ generates N pairs of username and relevant biometric template.
2. The challenger simulates the enrollment phase to generate the parameters.
3. The adversary $\mathcal{A}_2$ can then initiate any (polynomial) number of protocol instances for the verification protocol. At some point, $\mathcal{A}_2$ chooses two users U_{i_0}, U_{i_1} and asks the challenger to initiate an instance for the verification protocol.
4. The challenger chooses U_{i_e} and initiates an instance for the verification protocol.
5. The adversary $\mathcal{A}_3$ can continue to initiate any number of protocol instances, and terminates by outputting guess e'.

4 A General Biometric-Based Authentication Scheme

In this section we describe a general biometric-based authentication scheme, where the biometric template matching can be done through binary string comparison. We first describe the enrollment phase and the verification phase, and then provide some remarks.

4.1 The Enrollment Phase

In the enrollment phase, every component initializes its parameters as follows.

- $\mathcal{C}$ generates a key pair (pk_c, sk_c) for a signature scheme (KeyGen, Sign, Verify) and publishes the public key pk_c. In addition, $\mathcal{C}$ implements a $(\mathcal{M}, m, \tilde{m}, \lambda)$-secure sketch scheme (SS, Rec) [11], where $\mathcal{M}$ is the space of biometric template, m and $\tilde{m}$ can be any values, and λ is the threshold value in the biometric distribution assumption described in Section 2.3.
- $\mathcal{DB}$ generates an ElGamal key pair (pk_{db}, sk_{db}), where $pk_{db} = (\mathbb{G}_{db}, q_{db}, g_{db}, y_{db})$, $y_{db} = g_{db}^{x_{db}}$, and $sk_{db} = x_{db}$, and publishes pk_{db}.
- $\mathcal{S}$ generates an ElGamal key pair (pk_s, sk_s), where $pk_s = (\mathbb{G}_s, q_s, g_s, y_s)$, $\mathbb{G}_s = \mathbb{G}_{db}$, $g_s = g_{db}$, $y_s = g_s^{x_s}$, and $sk_s = x_s$, and publishes pk_s.
- U_i generates his personalized username ID_i and registers it at the service provider $\mathcal{S}$, and registers B_i at the database $\mathcal{DB}$, where b_i is U_i's reference biometric template and

$$B_i = \mathsf{Enc}((g_s)^{ID_s||ID_i||b_i}, pk_s)$$
$$= (B_{i1}, B_{i2})$$

Note that B_i has two components since the encryption scheme is ElGamal. In addition, U_i (publicly) stores a sketch $sketch_i = \mathsf{SS}(b_i)$.

4.2 The Verification Phase

If U_i wants to authenticate himself to the service provider $\mathcal{S}$ through the sensor client $\mathcal{C}$, they perform as follows.

1. The sensor client $\mathcal{C}$ extracts U_i's biometric template b_i^* and computes the adjusted template $b_i' = \mathsf{Rec}(b_i^*, sketch_i)$. If $H(b_i^*, b_i') \leq \lambda$, $\mathcal{C}$ sends $(ID_i, M_{i1}, M_{i2}, \sigma_i)$ to the service provider S, where

$$X_i = \mathsf{Enc}((g_s)^{ID_s||ID_i||b_i'}, pk_s)$$
$$= (X_{i1}, X_{i2}),$$
$$M_{i1} = \mathsf{Enc}(X_{i1}, pk_{db}), \ M_{i2} = \mathsf{Enc}(X_{i2}, pk_{db}),$$
$$\sigma_i = \mathsf{Sign}(ID_s||M_{i1}||M_{i2}, sk_c).$$

   Otherwise, $\mathcal{C}$ aborts the operation.
2. $\mathcal{S}$ first retrieves the index i for ID_i and then forwards $(M_{i1}, M_{i2}, \sigma_i)$ to the database $\mathcal{DB}$.
3. $\mathcal{DB}$ first verifies the signature σ_i. If the verification succeeds, $\mathcal{DB}$ decrypts M_{i1} and M_{i2} to recover X_i. For every $1 \leq \ell \leq N$, the database randomly selects $s_t \in \mathbb{Z}_{q_s}$ and computes $R_t = (X_i \oslash B_\ell)^{s_t}$, where, for any integer x and two ElGamal ciphertexts (c_1, c_2) and (c_3, c_4), the operator $\oslash$ is defined as follows: $((c_1, c_2) \oslash (c_3, c_4))^x = ((\frac{c_1}{c_3})^x, (\frac{c_2}{c_4})^x)$.
4. The server runs a PIR protocol to retrieve R_i. If $\mathsf{Dec}(R_i, sk_s) = 1$, $\mathcal{S}$ accepts the request; otherwise rejects it.

4.3 Remarks on the Proposed Scheme

It is well known that, with ElGamal scheme, we need to encode the plaintext in a certain way in order to obtain semantic security, however, there is no encoding method which will fully preserve the homomorphic property. In our case, we set $\mathbb{G}_s = \mathbb{G}_{db}$ and $g_s = g_{db}$, so that all plaintexts are exponentiations of g_s and we avoid the encoding problem.

Under the original definition given in [11], a secure sketch scheme is typically used to preserve the entropy of the input and allow the reconstruction of the input in the presence of a certain amount of noise. In our case, we only need the second functionality, namely the secure sketch scheme is used to remove the noise in the fresh biometric template. Therefore, we allow the parameters m and $\tilde{m}$ to be any values. The choice of λ depends on both the type of biometric and the underlying application's requirements on false accept and false reject rates.

User U_i does not need to register any information, either public or private, at the sensor client, though it need to store some public information, namely the secure sketch. The authentication is conducted through an exact equivalence comparison between the reference template and the adjusted fresh template (say, the output from the secure sketch scheme). As a result, we avoid the need to perform approximate biometric matchings on the service provider side and are able to use the underlying cryptographic techniques. This makes the scheme more scalable and flexible than other similar schemes. Compared with the existing remote authentication schemes (e.g. those in [3,4,8]), the proposed scheme demonstrates our concept of detaching biometric information storage from the service provider and shows a way to enhance human users' privacy in practice. In addition, our scheme also demonstrates a method to transform the existing schemes to satisfy our security definition, i.e. using a combination of plaintext equivalence test and PIR.

The computational complexity is dominated by that of the database $\mathcal{DB}$ which has to perform $O(N)$ exponentiations, the sensor client needs to perform 6 exponentiations and sign one message for each authentication attempt, while the service provider only needs to decrypt one message (one exponentiation) to make a decision. In addition, there is some computational load in running the PIR protocol. The communication complexity is dominated by the PIR protocol. If it is instantiated to be the single-database PIR protocol of Gentry and Ramzan [14], then the communication complexity between the service provider and the database is $O(\ell + d)$, where d is the bit-length of an ElGamal ciphertext and $\ell \geq \log N$ is the security parameter.

5 Security Analysis of the Proposed Scheme

5.1 Soundness and Impersonation Resilience

From the biometric distribution assumption and the soundness of the secure sketch, it is straightforward to verify that the proposed authentication scheme is sound under Definition 2. In addition, U_i's biometric templates b_i and b'_i are encoded in the form $(g_s)^{ID_s||ID_i||b_i}$ and $(g_s)^{ID_s||ID_i||b'_i}$. Hence, if the entropy of the adopted biometric is high, then the service provider and the database, even if they collude, cannot recover the biometric templates based on the Discrete Logarithm assumption.

5.2 Security Proof for Identity Privacy

In the verification protocol, even if security sketch is adopted, it is not guaranteed that $b'_i = b_i$. Therefore, in the security proof, we assume that the difference pattern, i.e. the distribution of $b'_i - b_i \mod q$, is denoted as $pattern_i$. In fact, the security results are independent from the difference patterns. Due to the page limit, the proofs for both lemmas will appear in the full version of this paper.

Lemma 1. *The proposed scheme achieves identity privacy against malicious $\mathcal{S}$, based on the semantic security of the ElGamal scheme and the existential unforgeability of the signature scheme.*

Lemma 2. *The proposed scheme achieves identity privacy against malicious $\mathcal{DB}$, based on the semantic security of the ElGamal scheme.*

5.3 Security Proof for Transaction Anonymity

We next show that the proposed scheme achieves transaction anonymity. The proof of this lemma will appear in the full version of this paper.

Lemma 3. *The proposed scheme achieves transaction anonymity against malicious $\mathcal{DB}$, based on the semantic security of the ElGamal scheme and the security (user privacy) of the PIR protocol.*

5.4 Further Remarks

In our security analysis, as to an outside adversary, we only considered the case where it has not compromised any system component. If the adversary has compromised the sensor client $\mathcal{C}$, then it may impersonate an honest user to the service provider if it obtains this user's biometric template (note that biometrics are public information). This is a common problem for many authentication systems, unless we adopt a tamper-resistant sensor client. If the adversary has compromised the service provider $\mathcal{S}$ or the database $\mathcal{DB}$, then the identity privacy property is still preserved. A possible vulnerability when $\mathcal{DB}$ is compromised is that it may be able to impersonate any user in the system by impersonating $\mathcal{DB}$ to the service provider. Again, this is a common problem for most authentication systems, and one possible solution is to adopt a layered security design. For example, tamper-resistant hardware can be used for establishing communication links. Then, even if the adversary has compromised the database, the ciphertexts of biometric templates will not help him to impersonate any honest user.

6 Conclusion

In this paper we have proposed a specifically-tailored system structure and security model for biometric-based authentication schemes. In our security model, we describe two privacy properties, namely identity privacy and transaction anonymity, which are believed to be serious concerns because of the uniqueness of biometrics. We have also proposed a general authentication scheme which fulfills the security properties described in our security model. An interesting characteristic of our scheme is that, assuming biometric template and secure sketch to be public, a user does not need to store any private information and register any information at the sensor client. In addition, the security requirements on the secure sketch scheme can be greatly relaxed (entropy preservation is not required). As a further research direction, it is interesting to investigate more efficient solutions in our security model.

References

1. Atallah, M.J., Frikken, K.B., Goodrich, M.T., Tamassia, R.: Secure biometric authentication for weak computational devices. In: Patrick, A.S., Yung, M. (eds.) FC 2005. LNCS, vol. 3570, pp. 357–371. Springer, Heidelberg (2005)
2. Bolle, R.M., Connell, J.H., Ratha, N.K.: Biometric perils and patches. Pattern Recognition 35(12), 2727–2738 (2002)
3. Boyen, X.: Reusable cryptographic fuzzy extractors. In: Atluri, V., Pfitzmann, B., McDaniel, P.D. (eds.) CCS 2004: Proceedings of the 11th ACM conference on Computer and communications security, pp. 82–91. ACM Press, New York (2004)
4. Boyen, X., Dodis, Y., Katz, J., Ostrovsky, R., Smith, A.: Secure remote authentication using biometric data. In: Cramer, R.J.F. (ed.) EUROCRYPT 2005. LNCS, vol. 3494, pp. 147–163. Springer, Heidelberg (2005)
5. Bringer, J., Chabanne, H., Izabachène, M., Pointcheval, D., Tang, Q., Zimmer, S.: An application of the Goldwasser-Micali cryptosystem to biometric authentication. In: Pieprzyk, J., Ghodosi, H., Dawson, E. (eds.) ACISP 2007. LNCS, vol. 4586, pp. 96–106. Springer, Heidelberg (2007)
6. Bringer, J., Chabanne, H., Pointcheval, D., Tang, Q.: Extended private information retrieval and its application in biometrics authentications. In: Bao, F., Ling, S., Okamoto, T., Wang, H., Xing, C. (eds.) CANS 2007. LNCS, vol. 4856, Springer, Heidelberg (2007)
7. Chor, B., Kushilevitz, E., Goldreich, O., Sudan, M.: Private information retrieval. J. ACM 45(6), 965–981 (1998)
8. Crescenzo, G.D., Graveman, R., Ge, R., Arce, G.: Approximate message authentication and biometric entity authentication. In: Patrick, A.S., Yung, M. (eds.) FC 2005. LNCS, vol. 3570, pp. 240–254. Springer, Heidelberg (2005)
9. Crescenzo, G.D., Malkin, T., Ostrovsky, R.: Single database private information retrieval implies oblivious transfer. In: Preneel, B. (ed.) EUROCRYPT 2000. LNCS, vol. 1807, pp. 122–138. Springer, Heidelberg (2000)
10. Dodis, Y., Katz, J., Reyzin, L., Smith, A.: Robust fuzzy extractors and authenticated key agreement from close secrets. In: Dwork, C. (ed.) CRYPTO 2006. LNCS, vol. 4117, pp. 232–250. Springer, Heidelberg (2006)

11. Dodis, Y., Reyzin, L., Smith, A.: Fuzzy extractors: How to generate strong keys from biometrics and other noisy data. In: Cachin, C., Camenisch, J.L. (eds.) EUROCRYPT 2004. LNCS, vol. 3027, pp. 523–540. Springer, Heidelberg (2004)
12. Du, W., Atallah, M.J.: Secure multi-party computation problems and their applications: a review and open problems. In: NSPW 2001: Proceedings of the 2001 workshop on New security paradigms, pp. 13–22. ACM Press, New York (2001)
13. ElGamal, T.: A public key cryptosystem and a signature scheme based on discrete logarithms. In: Blakely, G.R., Chaum, D. (eds.) CRYPTO 1984. LNCS, vol. 196, pp. 10–18. Springer, Heidelberg (1985)
14. Gentry, C., Ramzan, Z.: Single-database private information retrieval with constant communication rate. In: Caires, L., Italiano, G.F., Monteiro, L., Palamidessi, C., Yung, M. (eds.) ICALP 2005. LNCS, vol. 3580, pp. 803–815. Springer, Heidelberg (2005)
15. Gertner, Y., Ishai, Y., Kushilevitz, E., Malkin, T.: Protecting data privacy in private information retrieval schemes. In: Proceedings of the Thirtieth Annual ACM Symposium on the Theory of Computing, pp. 151–160 (1998)
16. Hao, F., Anderson, R., Daugman, J.: Combining crypto with biometrics effectively. IEEE Transactions on Computers 55(9), 1081–1088 (2006)
17. Woodward Jr., J.D., Orlans, N.M., Higgins, P.T.: Biometrics (Paperback). McGraw-Hill/OsborneMedia (2002)
18. Juels, A., Sudan, M.: A fuzzy vault scheme. Des. Codes Cryptography 38(2), 237–257 (2006)
19. Juels, A., Wattenberg, M.: A fuzzy commitment scheme. In: ACM Conference on Computer and Communications Security, pp. 28–36 (1999)
20. Linnartz, J.M.G., Tuyls, P.: New shielding functions to enhance privacy and prevent misuse of biometric templates. In: Kittler, J., Nixon, M.S. (eds.) AVBPA 2003. LNCS, vol. 2688, pp. 393–402. Springer, Heidelberg (2003)
21. Maltoni, D., Maio, D., Jain, A.K., Prabhakar, S.: Handbook of Fingerprint Recognition. Springer, Heidelberg (2003)
22. Pashalidis, A., Mitchell, C.J.: A taxonomy of single sign-on systems. In: Safavi-Naini, R., Seberry, J. (eds.) ACISP 2003. LNCS, vol. 2727, pp. 249–264. Springer, Heidelberg (2003)
23. Ratha, N., Connell, J., Bolle, R.M., Chikkerur, S.: Cancelable biometrics: A case study in fingerprints. In: ICPR 2006: Proceedings of the 18th International Conference on Pattern Recognition, pp. 370–373. IEEE Computer Society Press, Los Alamitos (2006)
24. Ratha, N.K., Connell, J.H., Bolle, R.M.: Enhancing security and privacy in biometrics-based authentication systems. IBM Systems Journal 40(3), 614–634 (2001)
25. Safavi-Naini, R., Tonien, D.: Fuzzy universal hashing and approximate authentication. Cryptology ePrint Archive: Report 2005/256 (2005)
26. Schneier, B.: Inside risks: the uses and abuses of biometrics. Commun. ACM 42(8), 136 (1999)
27. Schoenmakers, B., Tuyls, P.: Efficient binary conversion for paillier encrypted values. In: Vaudenay, S. (ed.) EUROCRYPT 2006. LNCS, vol. 4004, pp. 522–537. Springer, Heidelberg (2006)
28. Tuyls, P., Akkermans, A.H.M., Kevenaar, T.A.M., Schrijen, G.J., Bazen, A.M., Veldhuis, R.N.J.: Practical biometric authentication with template protection. In: Kanade, T., Jain, A., Ratha, N.K. (eds.) AVBPA 2005. LNCS, vol. 3546, pp. 436–446. Springer, Heidelberg (2005)

29. Tuyls, P., Goseling, J.: Capacity and examples of template-protecting biometric authentication systems. In: Maltoni, D., Jain, A.K. (eds.) BioAW 2004. LNCS, vol. 3087, pp. 158–170. Springer, Heidelberg (2004)
30. Tuyls, P., Skoric, B., Kevenaar, T.: Security with Noisy Data. Springer, London (2008)
31. Tuyls, P., Verbitskiy, E., Goseling, J., Denteneer, D.: Privacy protecting biometric authentication systems: an overview. In: EUSIPCO 2004 (2004)
32. Uludag, U., Pankanti, S., Prabhakar, S., Jain, A.K.: Biometric cryptosystems: Issues and challenges. In: Proceedings of the IEEE, vol. 92(6), pp. 948–960 (2004)
33. Verbitskiy, E., Tuyls, P., Denteneer, D., Linnartz, J.P.: Reliable biometric authentication with privacy protection. In: SPIE Biometric Technology for Human Identification Conf. (2004)
34. Atallah, M.J., Du., W.: Protocols for secure remote database access with approximate matching. Technical report, CERIAS, Purdue University. CERIAS TR 2000-15 (2000)

Private Query on Encrypted Data in Multi-user Settings

Feng Bao[2], Robert H. Deng[1], Xuhua Ding[1], and Yanjiang Yang[2]

[1] School of Information Systems, SMU
{robertdeng,xhding}@smu.edu.sg
[2] Institute for Infocomm Research, Singapore
baofeng@i2r.a-star.edu.sg, yjyang@smu.edu.sg

Abstract. Searchable encryption schemes allow users to perform keyword based searches on an encrypted database. Almost all existing such schemes only consider the scenario where a single user acts as both the data owner and the querier. However, most databases in practice do not just serve one user; instead, they support search and write operations by multiple users. In this paper, we systematically study searchable encryption in a practical multi-user setting. Our results include a set of security notions for multi-user searchable encryption as well as a construction which is provably secure under the newly introduced security notions.

1 Introduction

With the prevalence of network connectivity, a typical paradigm of many enterprise database applications is for multiple users to access a shared database via a local area network or the Internet. For business-critical or security-sensitive data, encryption is often used as the last line of defense to combat unsolicited data accesses. Consider the following application example. A federation of healthcare institutes plans to establish a medical database so that their medical practitioners and researchers can share clinic records and research results. To reduce the operational cost, management of the database is outsourced to a database service provider. The database is encrypted in order to comply with patient privacy related laws, such as HIPPA in the United States, and yet the encrypted database must be searchable by authorized users.

Searchable encryption is a cryptographic primitive that enables users to perform keyword-based searches on an encrypted database just as in normal database transactions [8,10,12,19]. However, all the existing schemes are limited to the single-user setting where the database owner who generates the database is also the single user to perform searches on it. To support multi-user searches, Curtmola et. al. [8], by directly extending their single-user schemes, suggest to share the secret key for database searching among all users. Their scheme allows only one user to write to the database, though multiple users are able to search. Unfortunately, many practical applications (e.g., the aforementioned healthcare federation example) require a database to support both write and search operations by multiple users. Moreover, user revocation in their scheme is based on broadcast encryption, where a revocation affects all non-revoked users.

Extending a single-user scheme to a *full-fledged* multi-user scheme by sharing secret keys (or the private keys of public key based systems (see Section 2)) among all users is a naïve approach with several serious shortcomings. First, there is no feasible means to determine the originator of a query in a provable manner, since all queries are generated from the same key. This becomes unacceptable when accountability of queries is desired by the database application. Secondly, user revocation can be prohibitively expensive. In a multi-user application, user revocation is a routine procedure. For a key-sharing based scheme, revocation often implies a new round of key distribution involving all non-revoked users. Obviously, this is not scalable for large and dynamic systems where user revocation may occur frequently. One may suggest using access control to complement key sharing in order to address the problem of user revocation (i.e., user revocation does not entail key renewal). However, deployment of access control in practice is prohibitively expensive as pointed out in [8], and worse yet, users have to maintain an additional set of secrets. Thirdly, many searchable encryption schemes follow the symmetric access paradigm, i.e., the same key is used for index generation and search. Therefore, once a revoked user breaks the security perimeter of a database system and gains illegal access to the encrypted database, she is still able to search it at her will. One remedy could be to update the indexes after every user revocation. However, it is obviously infeasible for large databases due to the immense cost it entails.

In this paper, we systematically study searchable encryption in the multi-user setting. We formulate a system model and define its security requirements. We also propose an efficient construction, which offers not only the conventional query privacy, but also the following new features.

- Our system allows a group of users, each possessing a distinct secret key, to insert their encrypted data records to the database while every user in the group is able to search *all* the records using her chosen keywords with the assistance from a semi-trusted database server.
- Our system allows the user management of the database owner organization to dynamically and efficiently revoke users. Our revocation does not require distribution of new keys, nor needs to update the encrypted database including the indexes. After a revocation, the revoked users are no longer able to search the database, while the revocation process is transparent to those non-revoked users. Our system also allows for dynamic user enrollment, since a user joining does not affect other user's settings.
- Our system offers *query unforgeability* in the sense that neither a dishonest user nor the database server is able to generate valid queries on behalf of another user unless her secret key is compromised.

The rest of the paper is organized as follows. In the next section, we discuss the related work and highlight the difference between our work and other searchable encryption schemes. Then, we define the system and formulate security requirements in Section 3. Our proposed construction, together with a rigorous security analysis and a performance evaluation, are presented in Section 4. Concluding remarks are in Section 5.

2 Related Work

Our work is under the umbrella of *searchable encryption*, which in general allows a user to search among encrypted data and find the data containing a chosen keyword. The first practical scheme of this kind is due to Song et al [19], who consider searches across encrypted keywords within a file with an overhead linear to the file size. Goh [12] and Chang and Mitzenmacher [10] propose to search encrypted indexes of a set of documents. Their approaches improve the search efficiency at the cost of a large storage for the constructed indexes (the bit-length of the index for each document is proportional to the total number of keywords). A formal security notion of searchable encryption is defined in [8] which also constructs schemes provably secure against non-adaptive and adaptive adversaries. Yang et al [20] apply the concept of searchable encryption to dynamic databases. The work of [4] considers the variation of simultaneous search of conjunctive keywords.

The first public-key based searchable encryption scheme is due to Boneh et al [2], where the private key holder can perform a search among messages encrypted under the corresponding public key. Park et al [18] and Hwang et al [15] propose variations of conjunctive keywords search in the public key setting. Abdalla et al [1] further analyze the consistency property of public key based searchable encryption, and demonstrate a generic construction by transforming an anonymous identity-based encryption scheme.

Note that while public key based schemes allow for multi-user writing, only the key holder who knows the private key can perform searches. As a result, applying public key based searchable encryption schemes to the multi-user setting would face the same problem as that of symmetric key based ones. Although Curtmola et al. suggest in [8] to employ broadcast encryption to allow multiple user search, it only allows a single user to write to the database. Moreover, their scheme is more suitable for a static collection of documents than a dynamic database. By contrast, our work in this paper studies searchable encryption in database applications where a group of users share data in a way that all users are able to write to and search an encrypted database without sharing their secrets.

3 Model and Definitions

3.1 System Model

We consider a database system $\{D, UM, Serv, \mathcal{U}\}$, where D is a database; UM is the user manager of the data owner organization that is responsible for the management of users, e.g., user enrolment and user revocation; $Serv$ is the database server providing the search service; $\mathcal{U}$ is a group of users.

The database D consists of m records $\{d_1, \cdots, d_m\}$ of multiple attributes. One of the attributes is the *keyword* used for search (note that it is straightforward to consider multiple keyword attributes). The domain of the keyword attribute is denoted by $\mathcal{W}$. The keyword of d_i is denoted by $d_i.w$. $Serv$ does not host the database D directly; instead, it hosts an encrypted version of D, denoted by $D' = \{d'_1, \cdots, d'_m\}$, where $d'_i = \langle E(d_i), I(d_i.w) \rangle$: the first component is an encryption of d_i and the second is the output of an index generation function $I(\cdot)$ on $d_i.w$. Let $E_D = \{E(d_1), \cdots, E(d_m)\}$ and $I_D = \{I(d_1.w), \cdots, I(d_m.w)\}$.

Table 1. Notations

Notation	Semantic
k_{UM}	the secret key of UM
e	the encryption key for record encryption
$qk_u, ComK_u$	user u's query key and her complementary key, respectively
U-ComK	a list of 2-tuples $(u, ComK_u)$ maintained by $Serv$

With the assistance of $Serv$, an authorized user $u \in \mathcal{U}$, is allowed to insert data records to D' and to search data records including those inserted by others based on her chosen keywords. We use $q_u(w)$ to denote a query from user u on keyword $w \in \mathcal{W}$. On receiving query $q = q_u(w)$, $Serv$ is expected to return $a_q = \{E(d_i) \mid d_i \in D, d_i.w = w\}$. Whenever necessary, UM may revoke a user's privilege of searching the database. Therefore, the user set $\mathcal{U}$ is divided into an authorized user set $\mathcal{U}_A$ and a revoked user set $\mathcal{U}_R$. Only users in $\mathcal{U}_A$ are allowed to successfully search and write to the database.

UM is an offline user manager of the data owner organization and is responsible for user enrollment and revocation; therefore we assume that UM is trusted and all interactions with UM are secure (Please do not confuse UM with the system administrator of the database server). We consider a semi-trusted $Serv$ as in [13], in the sense that it does not deviate from the prescribed protocol execution while it may try to derive as much information as possible from user queries and database access patterns. In particular, we assume that it will not launch active attacks such as collusion with users. Our trust model for $Serv$ is based on the following observation. In practice, most database hosting services are run by large and reputable IT service providers which clearly understand the paramount importance of corporate reputation for business success. Therefore, it is logical to assume that the database hosting server follows trusted-but-curious (semi-trusted) behavior. Active attacks are easy to detect/notice and therefore risk the server from being caught. Even a rumor of violation of rules will result in very bad publicity and damage a company's reputation.

Throughout the rest of the paper, we use the following notations. For a set S, we write $x \in_R S$ to denote that x is selected uniformly at random from S, and write $|S|$ to denote the size of S. For an algorithm A, $x \leftarrow A$ denotes that A outputs x. A function $\nu : \mathbb{N} \to [0, 1]$ is negligible if for any polynomial p, there exists $k_p \in \mathbb{N}$ such that for all $k \geq k_p$, $\nu(k) \leq 1/p(k)$. For convenience of reference, other notations used in the sequel are listed in Table 1.

3.2 Definitions

We now define the multi-user encrypted database system and its security notions. A multi-user encrypted database system, denoted by Γ, consists of the following algorithms:

- Setup(1^κ). A probabilistic algorithm executed by UM to set up the system and to initialize system-wide parameters, where κ is the security parameter. The algorithm outputs a secret key k_{UM} for UM and the record encryption key e for a semantically secure symmetric key encryption scheme.

- Enroll(k_{UM}, u). Executed by UM to enroll user u to the system. Taking as input k_{UM} and user identity u, it outputs a pair of query key and complementary key ($qk_u, ComK_u$) for u. qk_u and e are then securely transported to user u, and $ComK_u$ is securely passed to $Serv$ who then updates the U-ComK list by inserting a new entry ($u, ComK_u$).
- GenIndex($qk_u, w; ComK_u$). An interactive algorithm run between user u and $Serv$ to generate an index for keyword w. User u sends an index request on w to $Serv$, who then computes a response using the corresponding $ComK_u$. Finally, u outputs $I(w)$ based on $Serv$'s response.
- Write($qk_u, e, d_i; ComK_u$). Run between user u and $Serv$ to write an encrypted record d_i' to D'. The user u first invokes GenIndex($qk_u, d_i.w; ComK_u$) to generate $I(d_i.w)$, then computes $E(d_i)$ using e, and finally passes $d_i' = \langle E(d_i), I(d_i.w) \rangle$ to $Serv$ which appends it to D'.
- ConstructQ(qk_u, w). Run by a user u to construct a query. It takes as input the secret query key qk_u and a chosen keyword w, and outputs a query $q_u(w)$.
- Search($q_u(w), ComK_u, D'$). Run by $Serv$ to search D' for records containing w. Namely, on a query $q_u(w)$, it outputs $a_q = \{E(d_i) \mid d_i \in D, d_i.w = w\}$.
- Revoke(u). Run by UM to evict a user from the system. On an input user identity u, it revokes u's search capability. As a result, $\mathcal{U}_A = \mathcal{U}_A \setminus \{u\}, \mathcal{U}_R = \mathcal{U}_R \cup \{u\}$, and u is no longer able to search the database.

A multi-user encrypted database system Γ is *correct* if an authorized user can always get the correct query reply. More formally, $\forall u \in \mathcal{U}_A, \forall w \in \mathcal{W}$,
Search(ConstructQ(qk_u, w), $ComK_u, D'$) = $\{E(d_i) \mid d_i \in D, d_i.w = w\}$.

We also formalize several security requirements of the multi-user encrypted database system, including *query privacy, query unforgeability* and *revocability*.

Query Privacy. A common security requirement for all searchable encryption schemes is *query privacy*, which is a security notion on the amount of information leakage to the *server* regarding user queries. As discussed in [8], any searchable encryption scheme inevitably reveals certain query traces (defined shortly) to the server, unless using the *private information retrieval* techniques, or PIR for short [9]. We refer interested readers to [3,9,16,17] for various discussions on PIR. For searchable encryption, the server always observes the database access patterns (e.g. two queries have the same reply), albeit the server is unable to determine the keyword in a query. However, apart from the information that can be acquired via observation and the information derived from it, no other information should be exposed to the server.

For a record d_i, we use $id(d_i)$ to denote the identifying information that is uniquely associated with d_i, such as its database position or its memory location. For a query q and its reply (i.e., the outputs of Search) a_q, we define $\Omega(q) = \{u_q, id(a_q)\}$, where u_q is the issuer of q and $id(a_q)$ represents the identifying information of each record in a_q. Let $Q_t = (q_1, \cdots, q_t)$ be a sequence of t queries from the user group, and let $W_t = (w_1, w_2..., w_t)$ be the corresponding queried keywords, and $A_t = (a_1, a_2, ..., a_t)$ be the corresponding t replies, where $t \in \mathbb{N}$ and is polynomially bounded. We define V_t as the *view* of an adversary (i.e., $Serv$) over the t queries as the transcript of the interactions between $Serv$ and the involved query issuers, together with some common knowledge. Specifically, $V_t = (D' = (E_D, I_D), id(d_1'), ..., id(d_{|D'|}'), \text{U-ComK list}, Q_t, A_t)$.

Following the notation from [8], the *trace* of the t queries is defined to be: $T_t = (|D'|, id(d'_1), ..., id(d'_{|D'|}), \Omega(q_1), ..., \Omega(q_t), |\mathcal{U}_A|)$, which contains all the information that we allow the adversary to obtain. Note that $|\mathcal{U}_A|$ equals the number of entries in the U-ComK list. A simulation-based definition of query privacy is formally presented as follows.

Definition 1 (Query Privacy). *A multi-user encrypted database system Γ achieves query privacy if for all database D, for all $t \in \mathbb{N}$, for all PPT algorithm $\mathcal{A}$, there exists a PPT algorithm (the simulator) $\mathcal{A}^*$, such that for all V_t, T_t, for any function f:*

$$|\Pr[\mathcal{A}(V_t) = f(D, W_t)] - \Pr[\mathcal{A}^*(T_t) = f(D, W_t)]| < \nu(\kappa)$$

where the probability is taken over the internal coins of $\mathcal{A}$ and $\mathcal{A}^*$.

Intuitively, the notion of query privacy requires that all information on the original database and the queried keywords that can be computed by $Serv$ from the transcript of interactions she obtains (i.e., V_t) can also be computed from what it is allowed to know (i.e. T_t). In other words, a system satisfying query privacy does not leak any information beyond the information we allow the adversary to have. Note that query privacy implies record secrecy, i.e. the encrypted database $D' = (E_D, I_D)$ does not reveal information on the original database.

REMARK We stress that in the definition of query privacy, user-server collusion is not included in our adversarial model. As we argued earlier, this is a practically rational assumption. On the other hand, from a technical perspective, user-server collusion is able to comprise any searchable encryption scheme, since the sever can always compare the access patterns between a target user and the colluding user.

Query Unforgeability. In our system, queries issued by user u is generated by her individual secret query key, which is distinct to any other user's query key. It is thus a basic requirement that neither another user nor the server can generate a *legitimate* query on behalf of u. We refer to this property, which is only applicable to the multiple-user setting, as *query unforgeability*. Query unforgeability allows a query to be uniquely bound to its issuer in a provable way. Therefore, it is the security basis of other system features, e.g. accountability and non-repudiation.

To define query unforgeability, we first define the legitimacy of user queries. For a user $u \in \mathcal{U}$, we define u's legitimate query set as $Q_u = \{q_u(w) | q_u(w) \leftarrow \textsf{ConstructQ}(qk_u, w), w \in \mathcal{W}\}$. Namely, a query is user u's legitimate query if it is indeed constructed by running ConstructQ with qk_u. Therefore, an informal meaning of query unforgeability is that for any user u, no adversary is able to compute q satisfying $q \in Q_u$ without compromising qk_u.

Query unforgeability is defined based on a game between an adversary and a challenger. We consider two types of adversaries: malicious users (possibly in a collusion) and $Serv$. They have different knowledge and attack capabilities. Let $\mathcal{A}_U$ be the adversary representing malicious users and $\mathcal{A}_S$ representing $Serv$. Let $\hat{u}$ be the target user. In $\mathcal{A}_U$'s game, the challenger simulates the execution of Γ and offers an oracle $\mathcal{O}$ which answers $\mathcal{A}_U$'s queries on the executions of Enroll, GenIndex, Write, Search, and $\textsf{ConstructQ}(qk_{\hat{u}}, \cdot)$ which allows $\mathcal{A}_U$ to obtain queries on keywords of her choices with respect to user $\hat{u}^1$. In $\mathcal{A}_S$'s game, she has the knowledge of all users' complementary keys and a collection of $\hat{u}$'s queries (gathered when $\hat{u}$ searches the database). Thus the challenger gives $\mathcal{A}_S$ the oracle access to $\mathsf{ConstructQ}(qk_{\hat{u}}, \cdot)$.

The game is the following: the adversary (either $\mathcal{A}_U$ or $\mathcal{A}_S$) first picks her target user $\hat{u}$. Then for $\mathcal{A}_U$, she is given the query keys of the remaining users, and she queries $\mathcal{O}$ at her will with the restriction that the number of queries is polynomial-bounded. For $\mathcal{A}_S$, she is given the complementary keys of all users including the target user, and the oracle access to $\mathsf{ConstructQ}(qk_{\hat{u}}, \cdot)$. In the end, the adversary halts and returns a query q. Let $Q'_{\hat{u}}$ denote the set of $\hat{u}$'s queries obtained by the adversary from querying $\mathsf{ConstructQ}(qk_{\hat{u}}, \cdot)$. The adversary wins the game if and only if $q \in Q_{\hat{u}} \setminus Q'_{\hat{u}}$. The advantage of the adversary against query unforgeability is defined as the probability of she winning the game. We summarize the notion of query unforgeability as follows.

Definition 2 (Query Unforgeability). *A multi-user encrypted database system Γ achieves* query unforgeability *if for any $\hat{u} \in \mathcal{U}$, for all PPT algorithms $\mathcal{A}_U$ and $\mathcal{A}_S$:*

$$\Pr[q \in Q_{\hat{u}} \setminus Q'_{\hat{u}} : (k_{UM}, e) \leftarrow \mathsf{Setup}(1^\kappa);$$
$$\forall u \in \mathcal{U} \ (qk_u, ComK_u) \leftarrow \mathsf{Enroll}(k_{UM}, u);$$
$$q \leftarrow \mathcal{A}_U^{\mathcal{O}}(\{qk_u | u \in \mathcal{U} \setminus \{\hat{u}\}\})$$
$$\text{or} \ \ q \leftarrow \mathcal{A}_S^{\mathsf{ConstructQ}(qk_{\hat{u}}, \cdot)}(\{ComK_u | u \in \mathcal{U}\})$$
$$] < \nu(\kappa)$$

where the probability is taken over the internal coins of $\mathcal{A}_U$, $\mathcal{A}_S$, Setup, and Enroll.

REMARK Since each user possesses a distinct query key, it would be a natural requirement to maintain *secrecy of query keys*, i.e., a query key is only known to its owner. It is straightforward to observe that if a system is query unforgeable, it also preserves *secrecy of query keys*. Otherwise, the knowledge of the target's query key easily leads to generating a legitimate query.

Revocability. User eviction is an indispensable part of a multi-user application. It is desirable to allow UM to revoke the search capabilities of users who are deemed no longer appropriate to search the database. Since the incapability of searching the database indexes is implied by the incapability of distinguishing them, we define revocability based on index indistinguishability.

An adversary's advantage in attacking revocability is defined as her winning probability in the following game. The adversary $\mathcal{A}$ runs in two stages, $\mathcal{A}_1$ and $\mathcal{A}_2$: In the first stage, $\mathcal{A}_1$ acts as an authorized user and is allowed to access the oracle $\mathcal{O}$ as in Definition 2. At the end of the first stage, $\mathcal{A}_1$ chooses two new keywords w_1 and w_2, which have not been queried thus far. Let $state$ represent the knowledge $\mathcal{A}_1$ gains during the first stage. In the second stage, $\mathcal{A}_2$ is revoked, and is given the index of one of the two keywords. $\mathcal{A}_2$ finally outputs a bit b'. $\mathcal{A}$ wins the game if and only if $b' = b$. We summarize the notion of revocability as follows.

Definition 3 (Revocability). *A multi-user encrypted database query system Γ achieves* revocability *if for all PPT algorithms $\mathcal{A} = (\mathcal{A}_1, \mathcal{A}_2)$:*

---

[1] An malicious user may observe $\hat{u}$'s queries by attacking her system or the communication channel.

$$\Pr[b' = b : \quad (k_{UM}, e) \leftarrow \textsf{Setup}(1^\kappa);$$
$$\forall u \in \mathcal{U}_A \ (qk_u, ComK_u) \leftarrow \textsf{Enroll}(k_{UM}, u);$$
$$(qk_\mathcal{A}, ComK_\mathcal{A}) \leftarrow \textsf{Enroll}(k_{UM}, \mathcal{A});$$
$$(state, w_0, w_1) \leftarrow \mathcal{A}_1^\mathcal{O}(qk_\mathcal{A});$$
$$\textsf{Revoke}(\mathcal{A});$$
$$b \in_R \{0, 1\}, I(w_b) \leftarrow \textsf{GenIndex}(qk_u, w_b; ComK_u)_{u \in_R \mathcal{U}_A};$$
$$b' \leftarrow \mathcal{A}_2(state, I(w_b), w_0, w_1),$$
$$] < 1/2 + \nu(\kappa)$$

where the probability is taken over the internal coins of $\mathcal{A}$, Setup, Enroll, and the instance of u.

Intuitively, the definition demands that all successful searches rely on the assistance from $Serv$ using the corresponding complementary keys. With this feature, UM is able to efficiently revoke a user by instructing $Serv$ to delete the relevant key.

REMARK. The definition of revocability based on the index indistinguishability addresses the cryptographic strength of the searching protocol. A revoked user might mount attacks on the system or the communication channel in order to perform a search. For instance a replayed query may help a revoked user to search the database. We argue that this type of attacks can be neutralized by deploying secure communication channels or a user authentication mechanism, which are out of the scope of this paper.

4 Our Construction

4.1 Technical Preliminaries

Pseudorandom Function and Pseudorandom Permutation. A pseudorandom function is a function whose outputs cannot be efficiently distinguished from the outputs of truly random functions. A keyed cryptographic hash function is often modeled as a pseudorandom function. The main difference between a pseudorandom function and the random oracle is that the former can be accessed only by the key holder, while the latter is publicly accessible. If a pseudorandom function is a permutation, then it is *pseudorandom permutation*. Symmetric key encryption schemes are often modeled as pseudorandom permutations.

Bilinear Map. Let G_1 and G_2 be two groups of prime order p. A bilinear map is a function $\hat{e}: G_1 \times G_1 \to G_2$, satisfying the following properties:

1. Bilinear: For all $g_1, g_2 \in G_1$ and all $x_1, x_2 \in Z_p^*$, $\hat{e}(g_1^{x_1}, g_2^{x_2}) = \hat{e}(g_1, g_2)^{x_1 x_2}$.
2. Non-degenerate: If g is a generator of G_1, then $\hat{e}(g, g)$ is a generator of G_2.
3. Computable: $\hat{e}(g_1, g_2)$ can be efficiently computed for any $g_1, g_2 \in G_1$.

Note that the G_1 is a Gap-Diffie-Hellman group (GDH group), where the Decisional DH problem (DDH) is easy while the Computational DH problem (CDH) is still hard. The CDH problem is to compute g^{ab}, given g, g^a, g^b; and the DDH problem is to determine $c \stackrel{?}{=} g^{ab}$, given g, g^a, g^b, c, where G is a cyclic group generated by g of prime order p, $c \in_R G$, and $a, b \in_R Z_p^*$.

BLS Short Signature. Boneh et al. proposed a short signature scheme in [6] based on bilinear maps. A brief recall of the scheme is as follows: Let $G_1, G_2, \hat{e}$ be defined as the above, and g be a generator of G_1; $h : \{0,1\}^* \to G_1$ be a collision resistant hash function. A user's key pair is $(x \in Z_p^*, y = g^x \in G_1)$, where x is the private signing key. Then, the signature on a message m is defined to be $\sigma = h(m)^x$. Signature verification is to check $\hat{e}(g, \sigma) \stackrel{?}{=} \hat{e}(y, h(m))$. The BLS short signature achieves existential un-forgeability if h is modeled as a random oracle.

4.2 Protocol

We now present our construction. Let G_1, G_2 be two cyclic groups of a prime order p, and a bilinear map $\hat{e} : G_1 \times G_1 \to G_2$ between them as defined above. Let g be the generator of G_1. Let $[m]_k$ denote an encryption of a message $m \in \mathcal{M}$ under a secure symmetric encryption scheme with the secret key $k \in \mathcal{K}$, where $\mathcal{M}$ is the message domain and $\mathcal{K}$ is the domain of the secret key. We use $\langle c \rangle_k$ to denote its decryption. Let $h : G_2 \to \mathcal{K}$ be a collision-resistant hash function mapping an element in G_2 to an element in $\mathcal{K}$, and $h_s : \mathcal{S} \times \mathcal{W} \to G_1$ be a keyed hash function under a seed $s \in \mathcal{S}$ that maps a keyword to an element in G_1, where $\mathcal{S}$ is the domain of the secret seeds. The details of our protocol for the multi-user encrypted database system (MuED) are shown in Figure 1. In this construction, the encryption of records is performed using a semantically secure symmetric key encryption $E()$ with the key e. Note that $[.]_k$ and $E()$ can be different symmetric encryption schemes (in fact, $[.]_k$ is not necessarily semantically secure), so we distinguish them for clarity reason.

Note also that while the database server $Serv$ maintains a Com_K list, the list is not intended to enforce access control, or to make any verification on the legitimacy of the user or the relationship between the user and the complementary key $ComK_u$. $Serv$ simply uses the complementary key indicated by the querying user in the algorithm of **Search**.

4.3 Correctness

The correctness of the protocol is straightforward. Suppose that a record $\langle E(d_i), I(w) \rangle$ is generated by user u, where $d_i.w = w$ and $I(w) = \langle r, [r]_k \rangle$. Note that k essentially is equal to $h(\hat{e}(h_s(w), g)^x)$. Consider a user $\bar{u}$ with a secret key $x_{\bar{u}}$ and a complementary key at $Serv$ being $ComK_{\bar{u}}$. Her query on the keyword w is $q_{\bar{u}}(w) = h_s(w)^{x_{\bar{u}}}$; and the key used in **Search** is thus $k' = h(\hat{e}(q_{\bar{u}}(w), ComK_{\bar{u}})) = h(\hat{e}(h_s(w)^{x_{\bar{u}}}, g^{\frac{x}{x_{\bar{u}}}})) = h(\hat{e}(h_s(w), g)^x)$. Since $k = k'$, $E(d_i)$ is inserted into the reply set and returned to $\bar{u}$ according to the protocol. We remark that since $h(\cdot)$ and $h_s(\cdot)$ are collision resistant hash functions, the probability of computing the same key from two different keywords are negligible.

4.4 Security Analysis

In this section, we analyze the security of our protocol, and in particular show that the construction of MuED in Figure 1 satisfies the security requirements in Section 3.

Query Privacy. We first prove that our protocol achieves query privacy in the following theorem.

Setup(1^κ) :	UM sets up public system parameters G_1, G_2, and $\hat{e}$; selects $x \in_R Z_p^*$ and assigns $k_{UM} = x$; selects the random data encryption key e for $E()$ and a random seed $s \in \mathcal{S}$ for the keyed hash function h_s.
Enroll(k_{UM}, u):	UM sets $\mathcal{U}_A = \mathcal{U}_A \cup \{u\}$; selects $x_u \in_R Z_p^*$ and computes $ComK_u = g^{\frac{x}{x_u}} \in G_1$; securely sends $qk_u = (x_u, s)$ and e to user u, and sends $ComK_u$ to $Serv$, who then inserts a new entry $(u, ComK_u)$ to U-ComK.
GenIndex($qk_u, w; ComK_u$):	To generate an index for keyword w, user u first selects a random blinding element $r_w \in_R Z_p^*$, and computes and sends $(u, h_s(w)^{r_w})$ to $Serv$. Upon receiving the *generate index* request, $Serv$ returns $e_w = \hat{e}(h_s(w)^{r_w}, ComK_u)$ to u who then computes $k = h(e_w^{x_u/r_w}) \in \mathcal{K}$, and sets the index for w as $I(w) = \langle r, [r]_k \rangle$, where $r \in_R \mathcal{M}$. Outputs $I(w)$.
Write($qk_u, e, d_i; ComK_u$):	To write a record d_i to $Serv$, user u first generating the index of $d_i.w$ (i.e., $I(d_i.w)$) by invoking GenIndex($qk_u, d_i.w; ComK_u$). Then u computes $E(d_i)$ using e, and passes $d'_i = \langle E(d_i), I(d_i.w) \rangle$ to $Serv$.
ConstructQ(qk_u, w):	User u computes $q_u(w) = h_s(w)^{x_u}$ and outputs $(u, q_u(w))$ as her query on the keyword w.
Search($q_u(w), ComK_u, D'$):	$Serv$ scans U-ComK to find $ComK_u$. If no result, she outputs $\bot$. Otherwise, using $ComK_u$, she computes $k' = h(\hat{e}(q_u(w), ComK_u))$ and sets $a_{q_u(w)} = \emptyset$. For each $I_i \in I_D$ in the form (A, B), she sets $a_{q_u(w)} = a_{q_u(w)} \cup \{E(d_i)\}$ if $A = \langle B \rangle_{k'}$. Finally, she returns $a_{q_u(w)}$ to user u.
Revoke(u):	UM sets $\mathcal{U}_A = \mathcal{U}_A \setminus \{u\}$ and $\mathcal{U}_R = \mathcal{U}_R \cup \{u\}$. Then she instructs $Serv$ to delete the entry of $(u, ComK_u)$ from the U-ComK list.

Fig. 1. The Construction of MuED

Theorem 1. *MuED achieves query privacy in Definition 1 if $E(\cdot)$ and $[\cdot]_k$ are pseudorandom permutations and $h_s(\cdot)$ is a pseudorandom function.*

Proof. It suffices for us to construct a PPT simulator $\mathcal{A}^*$ such that for all $t \in \mathbb{N}$, for all PPT adversaries $\mathcal{A}$, all functions f, given the trace of t queries T_t, $\mathcal{A}^*$ can simulate $\mathcal{A}(V_t)$ with non-negligible probability. More specifically, we show that $\mathcal{A}^*(T_t)$ can generate a view V_t^* which is computationally indistinguishable from V_t, the actual view of $\mathcal{A}$. Recall that $T_t = (|D'| = m, 1, ..., m, \Omega(q_1), ..., \Omega(q_t), |\mathcal{U}_A|)$ and $V_t = (E_D = \{E(d_1), ..., E(d_m)\}, I_D = \{I_1, ..., I_m\}, 1, ..., m, \text{U-ComK}, Q_t, A_t)$.

For $t = 0$ ($Q_t = \emptyset$, $A_t = \emptyset$), $\mathcal{A}^*$ builds $V_t^* = (E_D^* = \{E(d_1)^*, ..., E(d_m)^*\}, I_D^* = \{I_1^*, ..., I_m^*\}, 1, ..., m, \text{U-ComK}^*)$ as follows. For $1 \leq i \leq m$, it selects $E(d_i)^* \in_R \{0,1\}^{|E(d_i)|}$, and sets $I_i^* = \langle I_i^*[1], I_i^*[2] \rangle$, where $I_i^*[1] \in_R \mathcal{M}$ and $I_i^*[2] \in_R \mathcal{M}$. To construct U-ComK*, for each entry $\mathcal{A}^*$ selects a random user identity and sets the corresponding complementary key as a random element from G_1 (the total number of entries is $|\mathcal{U}_A|$, which is contained in T_t). It is easy to check that V_t^* and V_t are computationally indistinguishable if the symmetric encryption (i.e., used to instantiate E and $[\cdot]_k$) is pseudorandom permutation. Note that in this proof, we did not consider the process of generating D', and assume that D' is already in place. In fact, the generation of D' in MuED does not provide $\mathcal{A}$ any additional knowledge on the keywords, since the only extra information $\mathcal{A}$ obtains by observing the generation of D' is $h_s(w)^{r_w}$ for each w

($r_w \in_R Z_p^*$), which clearly is computationally indistinguishable from a random element from G_1.

For $t > 0$, $\mathcal{A}^*$ builds $V_t^* = (E_D^*, I_D^*, 1, ..., m, \text{U-ComK}^*, Q_t^*, A_t^*)$ as follows. To be general, we suppose that all queries in Q_t are from distinct users (recall that the querier of a query can be seen from $\Omega(q_i)$), but some of them may query the same keywords. For $1 \leq j \leq |\mathcal{U}_A|$, it selects $x_j^* \in_R Z_p^*$ and sets $x^* = x_1^* \times ... \times x_{|\mathcal{U}_A|}^*$.

- Generating E_D^*: Generation of E_D^* is the same as in the case of $t = 0$, where each $E(d_i)^*$ is a random value.
- Generating Q_t^*: Recall that from $\Omega(q_1), ..., \Omega(q_t)$ contained in V_t, $\mathcal{A}^*$ can determine which queries ask the same keyword. For each $\Omega(q_i)$, it selects a random user identity u_i^* as the querier, and picks up an element from $\{x_1^*, ..., x_{|\mathcal{U}_A|}^*\}$, say x_i^*, for u_i^*. If there does not exist $j < i$ such that $\Omega(q_j) = \Omega(q_i)$ (note that $\Omega(q_j) = \Omega(q_i)$ means that q_i and q_j ask the same keyword), selects a random element $r_g \in_R G_1$ and computes $q_i^* = r_g^{x_i^*}$. Otherwise, re-uses the same r_g for q_j^* to compute q_i^*.
- Generating U-ComK*: We actually associate each x_i^* with a user in $\mathcal{U}_A$. Accordingly, the complementary key corresponding to x_i^* is computed as g^{x^*/x_i^*}. To organize the U-ComK*, the users together with the corresponding complementary keys involved in generating Q_t^* should be placed to the appropriate positions according to $\Omega(q_1), ..., \Omega(q_t)$, while the remaining users and complementary keys can be placed randomly to fill the remaining entries of the list.
- Generating I_D^*: From $\Omega(q_i), 1 \leq i \leq t$, $\mathcal{A}^*$ knows which records are retrieved by query q_i. Recall that for $\Omega(q_i)$, q_i^* is computed as $r_g^{x_i^*}$. Computes $k^* = h(\hat{e}(r_g, g)^{x^*})$, and for each of the records retrieved by q_i, the index is set as $\langle r \in_R \mathcal{M}, [r]_{k^*} \rangle$. At last, the index of each of the remaining records (i.e., those are not retrieved by Q_t) is set as $\langle r_1 \in_R \mathcal{M}, r_2 \in_R \mathcal{M} \rangle$.
- Generating A_t^*: Generation of A_t^* is straightforward. A_t^* is simply the set of records from E_D^* whose id's are contained in $\Omega(q_1), ..., \Omega(q_t)$.

We show that V_t^* is computationally indistinguishable from V_t by comparing them component by component. It is easy to see that if E is a pseudorandom permutation, E_D^* and E_D are computationally indistinguishable. For Q_t^* and Q_t, let us consider an actual query $q_u(w) = h_s(w)^{x_u}$ and a simulated query $q_u^* = r_g^{x_u^*}$, where $r_g \in_R G_1$: $q_u(w)$ and q_u^* are computationally indistinguishable if h_s is a pseudorandom function. For U-ComK* and U-ComK, an actual complementary key g^{x/x_u} and a simulated complementary key g^{x^*/x_u^*} is indistinguishable, since x_u and x_u^* are random values. It is also not hard to see that I_D^* and I_D are computationally indistinguishable if $[\cdot]_k$ is pseudorandom permutation. Finally, given the above indistinguishability results, the indistinguishability between A_t^* and A_t is straightforward. □

Query unforgeability. In the following, we prove that our protocol satisfies query unforgeability.

Theorem 2. *If there exists a PPT adversary (either $\mathcal{A}_U$ or $\mathcal{A}_S$) that breaks the query unforgeability of MuED in Definition 2 with an advantage ϵ, then there exists a PPT adversary $\mathcal{B}$ who can succeed in forging BLS short signatures with the same amount of advantage.*

Proof. We prove the theorem relative to $\mathcal{A}_U$ and $\mathcal{A}_S$, respectively. Given a BLS short signature scheme as specified in Section 4.1, where x is the secret signing key and y is the public key. Let $\mathcal{B}$ be a PPT adversary attempting to forge a short signature with respect to y.

CASE 1 (For $\mathcal{A}_U$): Intuitively, $\mathcal{A}_U$ obtains a set of queries $Q = \{h_s(w_1)^{x_{\hat{u}}}, h_s(w_2)^{x_{\hat{u}}}, ...\}$ of the target user $\hat{u}$ through the ConstructQ$(qk_{\hat{u}}, \cdot)$ oracle. Note that since $\mathcal{A}_U$ knows s, h_s cannot be modeled as a pseudorandom function; rather, it is modeled as a random oracle. As a result, these queries are essentially the BLS short signatures under the signing key $x_{\hat{u}}$. If $\mathcal{A}$ computes $h_s(w)^{x_{\hat{u}}}$ from Q, it clearly forges a signature on w. The detail of the proof follows.

The proof involves constructing $\mathcal{B}^{\mathcal{O}(x)}(\mathsf{Desc}(\mathcal{O}(x)))$, on input of $\mathsf{Desc}(\mathcal{O}(x))$ which is a description of an instance of the BLS short signature scheme, and is provided the signing oracle $\mathcal{O}(x)$. Note that $\mathsf{Desc}(\mathcal{O}(x))$ includes $g \in G_1$, the public key $y = g^x$, hash function h used in the signature scheme, $\hat{e} : G_1 \times G_1 \rightarrow G_2$, and possibly other parameters describing the scheme. The main idea is to set the signing key x to be the secret query key of the target user. As such, the most challenging part of the simulation is that if k_{UM} is selected randomly as in the original protocol construction, we have difficulty in computing the complementary key of the target user, which should be $g^{k_{UM}/x}$, since we only know g^x. The trick we have is to let $\mathcal{B}$ choose k_{UM} in a "controlled" way, but $\mathcal{A}_U$ does not detect the difference. Specifically, the details of the simulation are as follows.

1. **Setup:** In setting up the system, $\mathcal{B}$ uses $G_1, G_2, \hat{e}$ of the BLS short signature scheme as system parameters. $\mathcal{B}$ then selects a random seed s and a random data encryption key e. To generate k_{UM}, $\mathcal{B}$ chooses a set $X = \{x_1, ..., x_j, ...x_{max}\}$, where $x_j \in_R Z_p^*$ and max is the maximum number of user in the system which is polynomially bounded by the security parameter κ. Then $\mathcal{B}$ sets $\tilde{k}_{UM} = y^{\prod_{j=1}^{|X|} x_j} = g^{x \cdot \prod_{j=1}^{|X|} x_j} \in G_1$. Note that $\mathcal{B}$ actually does not need to know the discrete logarithm of k_{UM}.

2. **Enroll:** To enroll users in $\mathcal{U}$ to the system, $\mathcal{B}$ assigns a random element from X to a user as the query key. In particular, for each $u_i \in \mathcal{U} \setminus \{\hat{u}\}$, chooses a distinct $x_i \in X$, and sets $(qk_{u_i}, ComK_{u_i}) = ((x_i, s), y^{x_1 \cdots x_{i-1} x_{i+1} \cdots x_{|X|}})$. for the target user $\hat{u}$, it sets $ComK_{\hat{u}} = g^{\prod_{i=1}^{|X|} x_i}$ (as a result, $x = x_{\hat{u}}$ is a component of $qk_{\hat{u}}$, which $\mathcal{B}$ tries to compute); $\mathcal{B}$ then gives $qk_{u_i}, u_i \in \mathcal{U} \setminus \{\hat{u}\}$, together with e to $\mathcal{A}_U$.

3. **Answer $\mathcal{O}$ queries:** $\mathcal{B}$ needs to answer the following types of queries from $\mathcal{A}_U$: Enroll, GenIndex, Write, Search, and ConstructQ$(qk_{\hat{u}}, \cdot)$. It should be clear that $\mathcal{B}$ can trivially answer the queries of Enroll, GenIndex, Write Search, because she has the correct complementary keys of all users. We thus focus on how $\mathcal{B}$ answers ConstructQ$(qk_{\hat{u}}, \cdot)$ queries. $\mathcal{A}_U$ can ask for queries on keywords of her choice constructed using the target user's query key. To answer a ConstructQ$(qk_{\hat{u}}, \cdot)$ query, $\mathcal{B}$ resorts to its oracle $\mathcal{O}(x)$: on receiving a keyword w, $\mathcal{B}$ submits the word to $\mathcal{O}(x)$; on getting the reply from $\mathcal{O}(x)$, $\mathcal{B}$ tests the validity of the reply using the verification algorithm of the signature scheme. If it is not valid, $\mathcal{B}$ continues

to query $\mathcal{O}(x)$ until gets a valid reply. $\mathcal{B}$ then returns to $\mathcal{A}_U$ the reply it gets from $\mathcal{O}(x)$. Note that implicitly, $\mathcal{O}(x)$ simulates the random oracle $h(\cdot)$, and provides the oracle access to $\mathcal{B}$. Moreover, since $\mathcal{A}_U$ knows s, $\mathcal{B}$ needs to simulates $h_s(\cdot)$ to $\mathcal{A}_U$. To simulate $h_s(\cdot)$, $\mathcal{B}$ uses the oracle $h(\cdot)$ from $\mathcal{O}(x)$: in particular, whenever getting a message from $\mathcal{A}_U$ querying $h_s(\cdot)$, $\mathcal{B}$ asks the same message to $h(\cdot)$, and returns to $\mathcal{A}_U$ what is returned from $\mathcal{O}(x)$. As a result, the set of $\{h_s(w_1)^{x_{\hat{u}}}, h_s(w_2)^{x_{\hat{u}}}, ...\}$ obtained by $\mathcal{A}_U$ is actually $\{h(w_1)^{x_{\hat{u}}}, h(w_2)^{x_{\hat{u}}}, ...\}$, which is a set of the BLS signatures.
4. $\mathcal{B}$ finally outputs what $\mathcal{A}_U$ outputs.

CASE 2 (For $\mathcal{A}_S$): The proof is similar to Case 1. To avoid redundancy, we only highlight the differences between two proofs. $\mathcal{A}_S$ also obtains a set of queries $Q = \{h_s(w_1)^{x_{\hat{u}}}, h_s(w_2)^{x_{\hat{u}}}, ...\}$ of the target user $\hat{u}$ through the ConstructQ$(qk_{\hat{u}}, \cdot)$ oracle, but $\mathcal{A}_S$ does not know the seed s. This intuitively suggests that forging a query is much harder for $\mathcal{A}_S$ than for $\mathcal{A}_U$. In the actual proof, $\mathcal{B}$ does not choose s at all in Setup (the trick is actually that $\mathcal{B}$ does not use any key for the hash function). Moreover, $\mathcal{B}$ does not provides $\mathcal{A}_S$ the oracle access to $h_s(\cdot)$, since $\mathcal{A}_S$ does not know s and thus does not have access to $h_s(\cdot)$.

The simulation by $\mathcal{B}$ is perfect in both cases. It is obvious that if q on w output by $\mathcal{A}_U$ or $\mathcal{A}_S$ is a legitimate query of the target user $\hat{u}$, then q must be equal to $h(w)^{x_{\hat{u}}}$, which is a valid BLS short signature on w. This completes the proof. □

Revocability. The following theorem establishes that the construction of MuED satisfies revocability.

Theorem 3. *MuED achieves revocability in Definition 3 if $[\cdot]_k$ is a secure encryption scheme.*

Proof. The proof is pretty straightforward, and we only state the intuition behind the proof. The indexes of the two keywords w_1 and w_2 are $I(w_1) = \langle r_1, [r_1]_{k(w_1)} \rangle$ and $I(w_2) = \langle r_2, [r_2]_{k(w_2)} \rangle$, where $r_1, r_2 \in_R \mathcal{M}$, and $k(w_1)$ and $k(w_2)$ denote the secret keys generated from w_1 and w_2, respectively. Since the complementary key of a revoked user is deleted from the U-ComK list, the revoked user can never get $k(w_1)$ and $k(w_2)$ from the keywords and the query key it has; moreover, it cannot get the keys either if $[\cdot]_k$ is a secure encryption scheme that does not expose the encryption key. As a result, $I(w_1)$ and $I(w_2)$ are independent of w_1 and w_2, respectively, from the perspective of the revoked user. So the advantage of the adversary guessing the correct bit cannot be significantly more than 1/2. □

4.5 Performance

We focus on the online query process, as other procedures (algorithms) have constant computational overhead. For query issuance, the main computation at the user side is simply an exponentiation operation. Thus its computational complexity is $\mathcal{O}(1)$. For a query process, the main computation at the server side includes a pairing operation, and n symmetric key decryption, where n is the number of records. Thus the computational complexity is asymptotically $\mathcal{O}(n)$. Note that all existing single-user searchable encryption schemes except those in [8] require $\mathcal{O}(n)$ server computation. This suggests that the searching efficiency of our protocol does not downgrade due to supporting multiple users.

The computation cost of [8] is linear to the size of the keyword set, instead of the document set. This performance gain is due to a preprocessing of all documents so that the index of a keyword links together all relevant documents. However, it introduces more cost in document deletion or insertion. An optimization approach for our scheme is for the server to group the records retrieved by a reply together by sharing a common index (since they contain the same keyword). It saves the server from repetitively searching the same keyword. As the system proceeds, this can greatly reduce the server computation overhead.

5 Conclusion

Existing efforts on searchable encryption have focused on single-user settings. Directly extending a searchable encryption scheme for the single-user setting to the multi-user setting has several downsides, e.g., the considerable costs associated with re-distributing query keys and re-generating the encrypted database. To solve theses problems, in this paper we presented a systematic study on searchable encryption under a practical multi-user database setting. We first formulated a system model as well as a set of security requirements, then presented a concrete construction which provably satisfies those requirements. In our construction, each user employs a distinct key, and consequently, user revocation does not entail updating of query keys and re-encryption of the database, and is transparent to the non-revoked users. Moreover, each authorized user can also insert and search the database, an important feature to data sharing in the multi-user setting. Our construction is efficient, achieving similar performance as most of the existing single-user schemes.

Acknowledgement

This research is partly supported by the Office of Research, Singapore Management University.

References

1. Abdalla, M., Bellare, M., Catalano, D., Kiltz, E., Kohno, T., Lange, T., Lee, J., Neven, G., Paillier, P., Shi, H.: Searchable Encryption Revisite: Consistency Properties, Ration to Anonymous IBE, and Extensions. In: Shoup, V. (ed.) CRYPTO 2005. LNCS, vol. 3621, pp. 205–222. Springer, Heidelberg (2005)
2. Boneh, D., di Crescenzo, G., Ostrovsky, R., Persiano, G.: Public key encryption with keyword search. In: Cachin, C., Camenisch, J.L. (eds.) EUROCRYPT 2004. LNCS, vol. 3027, pp. 506–522. Springer, Heidelberg (2004)
3. Beimel, A., Ishai, Y., Kushilevitz, E., Raymond, J.-F.: Breaking the $o(n^{1/(2k-1)})$ barrier for information-theoretic private information retrieval. In: Proc. FOCS 2002, pp. 261–270 (2002)

4. Ballard, L., Kamara, S., Monrose, F.: Achieving Efficient Conjunctive Keyword Searches over Encrypted Data. In: Qing, S., Mao, W., López, J., Wang, G. (eds.) ICICS 2005. LNCS, vol. 3783, pp. 414–426. Springer, Heidelberg (2005)
5. Bellare, M., Rogaway, P.: Random oracles are practical: A paradigm for designing efficient protocols. In: Proc. ACM Conference on Computer and Communications Security, CCS 1993, pp. 62–73 (1993)
6. Boneh, D., Lynn, B., Shacham, H.: Short Signatures from the Weil Pairing. In: Boyd, C. (ed.) ASIACRYPT 2001. LNCS, vol. 2248, pp. 514–532. Springer, Heidelberg (2001)
7. Canetti, R., Goldreich, O., Halevi, S.: The random oracle methodology, revisited. In: Proc. STOC 1998, pp. 209–218 (1998)
8. Curtmola, R., Garay, J., Kamara, S., Ostrovskey, R.: Searchable Symmetric Encryption: Improved Definitions and Efficient Constructions. In: Proc. ACM Conference on Computer and Communications Security, CCS 2006, pp. 79–88 (2006)
9. Chor, B., Kushilevitz, E., Goldreich, O., Sudan, M.: Private information retrieval. Journal of the ACM (1995)
10. Chang, Y., Mitzenmacher, M.: Privacy Preserving Keyword Searches on Remote Encrypted Data. In: Ioannidis, J., Keromytis, A.D., Yung, M. (eds.) ACNS 2005. LNCS, vol. 3531, pp. 442–455. Springer, Heidelberg (2005)
11. Fiat, A., Shamir, A.: How to prove yourself: Practical solutions to identification and signature problems. In: Odlyzko, A.M. (ed.) CRYPTO 1986. LNCS, vol. 263, pp. 186–194. Springer, Heidelberg (1987)
12. Goh, E.: Secure Indexes (2003), http://crypto.stanford.edu/~eujin/papers/secureindex/secureindex.pdf
13. Goldreich, O.: Foundations of Cryptography, vol. 2. Cambridge University Press, Cambridge (2004)
14. Goldreich, O., Ostrovsky, R.: Software Protection and Simulation on oblivious RAMs. Journal of ACM 43(3), 431–473 (1996)
15. Hwang, Y.H., Lee, P.J.: Public Key Encryption with Conjunctive Keyword Search and Its Extension to a Multi-User System. In: Proc. International Conference on Pairing-Based Cryptography, Pairing 2007 (2007)
16. Kushilevitz, E., Ostrovsky, R.: Replication is not needed: single database, computationally private information retrieval. In: Proc. FOCS 1997, pp. 364–373 (1997)
17. Lipmaa, H.: An oblivious transfer protocol with log-squared communication. In: Zhou, J., López, J., Deng, R.H., Bao, F. (eds.) ISC 2005. LNCS, vol. 3650, pp. 314–328. Springer, Heidelberg (2005)
18. Park, D.J., Kim, K., Lee, P.J.: Public Key Encryption with Conjunctive Field Keyword Search. In: Lim, C.H., Yung, M. (eds.) WISA 2004. LNCS, vol. 3325, pp. 73–86. Springer, Heidelberg (2005)
19. Song, D., Wagner, D., Perrig, A.: Practical Techniques for Searches on Encrypted Data. In: Proc. IEEE Symposium on Security and Privacy, S&P 2000, pp. 44–55 (2000)
20. Yang, Z., Zhong, S., Wright, R.N.: Privacy-Preserving Queries on Encrypted Data, Proc.

Towards Tamper Resistant Code Encryption: Practice and Experience

Jan Cappaert[1], Bart Preneel[1],
Bertrand Anckaert[2], Matias Madou[2], and Koen De Bosschere[2]

[1] Katholieke Universiteit Leuven
Department of Electrical Engineering, ESAT/SCD-COSIC
Kasteelpark Arenberg 10
B-3001 Heverlee, Belgium
{jan.cappaert,bart.preneel}@esat.kuleuven.be
[2] Universiteit Gent
Department of Electronics and Information Systems, ELIS/PARIS
Sint-Pietersnieuwstraat 41
B-9000 Gent, Belgium
{banckaer,mmadou,kdb}@elis.ugent.be

Abstract. In recent years, many have suggested to apply encryption in the domain of software protection against malicious hosts. However, little information seems to be available on the implementation aspects or cost of the different schemes. This paper tries to fill the gap by presenting our experience with several encryption techniques: bulk encryption, an on-demand decryption scheme, and a combination of both techniques. Our scheme offers maximal protection against both static and dynamic code analysis and tampering. We validate our techniques by applying them on several benchmark programs of the CPU2006 Test Suite. And finally, we propose a heuristic which trades off security versus performance, resulting in a decrease of the runtime overhead.

1 Introduction

In the 1980s application security was achieved through secure hardware, such as ATM terminals, or set-top boxes. Since the 1990s, however, secure software has gained much interest due to its low cost and flexibility. Nowadays, we are surrounded by software applications for online banking, communication, e-voting, ... As a result, threats such as piracy, reverse engineering and tampering have emerged. These threats are exacerbated by poorly protected software. Therefore, it is important to have a thorough threat analysis (e.g., STRIDE [10]) as well as software protection schemes. The techniques discussed in this paper protect against reverse engineering and tampering.

The goal of encryption is to hide the content of information. Originally, it was applied within the context of communication, but has become a technique to secure all critical data, either for short-term transmission or long-term storage. More recently, commercial tools for software protection have become available.

These tools need to defend against attackers who are able to execute the software on an open architecture and thus, albeit indirectly, have access to all the information required for execution.

Even though encryption is one of the best understood information hiding techniques and has been used previously for software protection, little details on its practical application and performance impact are available. In this paper we discuss a number of practical schemes for self-encrypting code and report on our experience. Furthermore, we introduce an on-demand decryption scheme which operates at function granularity and which uses the hash of other code sections as the decryption key.

The remainder of this paper is structured as follows. Section 2 describes software security and its threats. Section 3 provides an overview of related work. In Sect. 4 we discuss our on-demand code decryption scheme. A numerical evaluation is given in Sect. 5. Section 6 discusses several attack scenarios and possible countermeasures. Finally, conclusions are drawn in Sect. 7.

2 Software Security and Threats

Protecting code from reverse engineering is one of the main concerns for software providers. If a competitor succeeds in extracting and reusing a proprietary algorithm, the consequences may be major. Furthermore, secret keys, confidential data or security related code are not intended to be analyzed, extracted, stolen or corrupted. Even if legal actions such as patenting and cyber crime laws are in place, reverse engineering remains a considerable threat to software developers and security experts.

In many cases, the software is not only analyzed, but also tampered with. Nowadays examples are cracks for gaming software or DRM systems. In a branch jamming attack, for example, an attacker replaces a conditional jump by an unconditional one, forcing a specific branch to be taken even when it is not supposed to under those conditions. Such attacks could have a major impact on applications such as licensing, DRM, billing and voting.

Before changing the code in a meaningful way, one always needs to understand the internals of a program. If one would change a program at random places one could no longer guarantee the correct working of the application after modification. Several papers present the idea of *self-verifying code* [4,9] that is able to detect any changes to critical code. These schemes, however, do not protect against analysis of code. In this paper tries to solve analysis and tampering attacks simultaneously through encryption.

We focus on software-only solutions because of their low cost and flexibility. Clearly, code encryption is more powerful if encrypted code can be sent to a secure co-processor [21]. But when this component is not available, as is the case on most existing systems, the problem becomes harder to tackle. Essentially, such a co-processor can be assumed to be a black-box system, where the attacker is only able to monitor I/O behavior. Software-only solutions against malicious hosts need to work within a white-box environment, where everything can be inspected and modified at will.

3 Related Work

There are three major threats to software: piracy, reverse engineering and tampering. In recent years, a number of countermeasures have been treated in the literature. Software watermarking, for example, aims at protecting software reactively against piracy. It embeds a unique identifier into an application such that it can be proved that a specific copy belongs to a specific individual or company. As a result, one can trace copied software to the source unless the watermark is destroyed.

A second countermeasure, code obfuscation, protects against reverse engineering. Code obfuscation aims to generate a semantically equivalent, but less intelligible version of a program.

The goal of a third countermeasure is to make software more tamper-resistant. As this paper studies protection mechanisms against malicious analysis and tampering, we will not elaborate on software watermarking.

3.1 Code Obfuscation

Once software is distributed, it is largely beyond the control of the software provider. This means that attackers can analyze, copy, and change it at will. Not surprisingly, a substantial amount of research has gone into making this analysis harder. The developed techniques range from tricks to counter debugging, such as code stripping, to complex control flow and data flow transformations that try to hide a program's internal operation. The goal is to achieve the security objective of *confidentiality*. For example, when Java bytecode was shown to be susceptible to decompilation – yielding the original source code – researchers began investigating techniques to protect the code [6,13]. Protection of low-level code against reverse engineering has been addressed as well [24].

3.2 Tamper Resistance

Tamper resistance protects *data authenticity* where, in this context, 'data' refers to the program code. In '96 Aucsmith [1] introduced a scheme to implement tamper-resistant software. Through small, armored code segments, referred to as integrity verification kernels (IVKs), the integrity of the code is verified. These IVKs are protected through encryption and digital signatures such that it is hard to modify them. Furthermore, these IVKs can communicate with each other and across applications through an integrity verification protocol. Many papers in the field of tamper resistance base their techniques on one or more of Aucsmith's ideas.

Several years later, Chang et al. [4] proposed a scheme based on *software guards*. Their protection scheme relies on a complex network of software guards which can mutually verify each other's integrity and that of the program's critical sections. A software guard is defined as a small piece of code performing a specific task (e.g., checksumming or repairing). When checksumming code detects a modification, repair code is able to undo this malicious tamper attempt. The security of the scheme relies partially on hiding the obfuscated guard code and the complexity of the guard network. Horne et al. [9] discuss a related concept called 'testers', small hash functions that verify the program at run time. These testers can be combined with embedded software watermarks to result in a unique, watermarked, self-checking program.

Other related research is *oblivious hashing* [5], which interweaves hashing instructions with program instructions and which is able to prove to some extent whether a program operated correctly or not.

However, in some cases, programmers might opt for self-checking code instead of self-encrypting code, based on some of the following disadvantages:

- limited hardware support: self-modifying code requires memory pages to be executable and writable at the same time. However some operating systems enforce a W^X policy as a mechanism to make the exploitation of security vulnerabilities more difficult. This means a memory page is either writable (data) or executable (code), but not both. Depending on the operating system, different approaches exist to bypass – legally – the W^X protection: using mprotect(), the system call for modifying the flags of a memory page, to explicitly mark memory readable and executable (e.g., used by OpenBSD) or setting a special flag in the binary (e.g., in case of PaX). A bypass mechanism will most likely always exist to allow for some special software such as a JVM that optimizes the translation of Java bytecode to native code on the fly.
- implicit reaction to tampering: if an encrypted code section is tampered with the program will crash after incorrect decryption, assuming that it is hard to target bits flips in the plaintext by manipulating the ciphertext. Furthermore, even if one succeeds in successful tampering with a specific function, our dependency scheme will propagate faulty decryption along the functions on the call stack whenever the modified function is verified (i.e. a decryption key is derived from its code), which will sooner or later make the program crash as well. However, crashing is not very user-friendly. In the case of software guards [4,9], detection of tampering could be handled more technically by triggering another routine that for example exits the program after a random time, calls repair code that fixes the modified code (or a hybrid scheme, which involves both techniques), warns the owner about the malicious attempt through a hidden channel, ...

3.3 Code Encryption

This section provides an overview of dynamic code decryption and encryption; one often refers to this as a specific form of self-modifying or self-generating code. Encryption ensures the confidentiality of the data. In the context of binary code, this technique mainly protects against static analysis. For example, several encryption techniques are used by polymorphic viruses and polymorphic shell code [18]. In this way, they are able to bypass intrusion detection systems, virus scanners, and other pattern-matching interception tools.

Bulk Decryption. We refer to the technique of decrypting the entire program at once as *bulk decryption*. The decryption routine is usually added to the encrypted body and set as the entry point of the program. At run time this routine decrypts the body and then transfers control to it. The decrypting routine can either consult an embedded key or fetch one dynamically (e.g., from user input or from the operating system). The main advantage of such a mechanism is that as long as the program is encrypted, its internals are hidden and therefore protected against static analysis.

Another advantage is that the encrypted body makes it hard for an attacker to statically change bits in a meaningful way. Changing a single bit will result in one or more bit flips in the decrypted code (depending on the encryption scheme) and thus one or more modified instructions, which may lead to program crashes or other unintended behavior due to the brittleness of binary code.

However, as all code is decrypted simultaneously, an attacker can simply wait for the decryption to occur before dumping the process image to disk.

On-demand Decryption. In contrast to bulk decryption, where the entire program is decrypted at once, one could increase granularity and decrypt small parts when they are needed at run time. Once they are no longer needed, they can be re-encrypted. This technique is applied, a.o., by Shiva [14], a binary encryptor that uses obfuscation, anti-debugging techniques, and multi-layer encryption to protect ELF binaries. Viega et al. [23] provide a related method to write self-modifying programs in C that decrypt a function at run time.

On-demand decryption overcomes the weaknesses of revealing all code in the clear at once as it offers the possibility to decrypt only the necessary parts, instead of the whole body. The disadvantage is an increase in overhead due to multiple calls to the decryption and encryption routines.

4 On-demand Decryption Framework

In this section, we introduce our on-demand decryption scheme. The granularity of this scheme is the function level, meaning that we will decrypt and encrypt an entire function at a time.

4.1 Basic Principle

The scheme relies on two separate techniques, namely integrity checking and encryption. The techniques from integrity-checking are used to compute the keys for decryption and encryption. The integrity checking function can be a checksum function or a hash function. Essentially, it has to map a vector of bytes, code in this case, to a fixed-length value, in such a way that it is hard to produce a second image resulting in the same hash.

The basic idea is to apply the integrity checking function h to a function a to obtain the key for the decryption of another function b. Using the notation of D for decryption and E for encryption, this results in $b = D_{h(a)}(E_{h(a)}(b))$. To this end, b needs to have been encrypted with the correct key on beforehand (i.e. $E_{h(a)}(b)$, denoted by $\bar{b}$). We will refer to this scheme as a *crypto guard*.

We would like the guard to have at least the following properties:

- if one bit is modified in a, then 1 or more bits in b should change (after decryption); and
- if one bit is modified in $\bar{b}$, then 1 or more bits should change in b after decryption.

For the first requirement, a cryptographic function with a as key could be used. For example, Viega et al. [23] use the stream cipher RC4 where the key is code of another function. The advantage of an additive stream cipher is that encryption and decryption are the same computation, thus the same code. It is also possible to construct stream ciphers out of block ciphers (e.g., AES) using a suitable mode of operation. For more on the cryptographic properties of these functions, we refer to [15]. The major disadvantage of these ciphers is that they are relatively slow for our case, and relatively large as well. However, note that we still require the integrity-checking function that also serves as a one-way compression function, because each cipher requires a fixed, limited key size.

From a cryptographic point of view we require a second image resistant hash function and secure encryption mode with suitable error propagation properties (e.g., PCBC). However, size and speed of these algorithms is essential for the overall performance of the protection scheme as its security assumes inlining the guard code. This results in more code to be hashed and decrypted, and thus a higher cost. It is also possible to link the hashing itself to other code by using a keyed hash function, such as HMAC. Other proposals for hash-like functions and encryption routines are constructions based on T-functions, introduced by Shamir et al. [11]. These light-weight functions are popular as they have a direct equivalent available in both software and hardware. Nevertheless, it is still unclear whether constructions based on T-function are cryptographically secure.

As software tamper resistance is typically defined as techniques that make tampering with code harder, we can illustrate that our crypto guards offer protection against tampering. Namely, using code of a to decrypt (i.e. deriving a decryption key from a's code) could be seen as an implicit way of creating tamper resistance; modifying a will result in an incorrect hash value (i.e. encryption key), and consequently incorrect decryption of $\bar{b}$.

Furthermore, changing $\bar{b}$ will result in one or more changes to b; in case of an additive stream cipher a bit change in the ciphertext will correspond to a bit change the plaintext at the same location. However, if this plaintext itself is used as key material in a later stage (e.g, to derive decryption keys for its callees), this will result in incorrect code. Furthermore, due to the brittleness of binary code and the denseness of the IA32 instruction set, a single bit flip in the clear code might change the opcode of an instruction, resulting in an incorrect instruction to be executed, but also in desynchronizing the next instructions [12], which most likely will lead to a crashing program.

Another advantage of this scheme is that the key is computed at run time, which means the key is not hard-coded in the binary and therefore hard to find through static analysis (e.g., entropy scanning [17]). The main disadvantage is performance: loading a fixed-length cryptographic key is usually more compact and faster than computing one at run time, which in our case may involve computing a hash value.

Although we believe that cryptographic hash functions and ciphers are more secure, we used a simpler XOR-based scheme – which satisfies our two properties – to minimize the performance cost in speed and size after embedding the crypto guards. We therefore do not claim that our encrypted code is cryptographically secure, but rather sufficiently masked to resist analysis and tampering attacks in a white-box environment, where the attacker has full privileges.

4.2 A Network of Crypto Guards

With *crypto guards* as building blocks we can construct a network of code dependencies that make it harder to analyze or modify code statically or dynamically.

A first requirement is protection against static analysis. Therefore, all functions in the binary image, except for the entry function, are encrypted with unique dynamic keys. We opted to decrypt the functions just before they are called and to re-encrypt them after they have returned. In this case, only functions on the call stack will be in the clear.

Secondly, as the key for decryption should be fixed, regardless of how the function was reached, we need to know in advance the state of the code from which the key is derived (encrypted or in the clear). Many functions have multiple potential callers. Therefore, we cannot always use the code of the caller to derive the key. The solution is to use a dominator in the call graph. As a dominator is by definition on the call stack when the function is called, it is guaranteed to be in the clear. We have chosen to use the immediate dominator to derive the key.

Note that it is also possible to derive the key of other functions, allowing one to create schemes which offer delayed failure upon malicious tampering [20]. On the one hand, this may allow a tampered application to run longer, on the other hand this does not correlate the moment of failure to the embedded checking or reaction mechanism.

Thus, a good mode of operation for the encryption (i.e. with error propagation) in combination with our dependency scheme, will propagate bit flips (triggered by tampering):

– through the modified function due to the mode of operation,
– inheritably from caller to callee according to the call graph due to the dependency scheme.

The latter, however, does not validate for multiple callers due to our relaxation (using the dominator's code instead of caller's to derive the key) or to functions with no callees. In theory this could be solved by using authenticated encryption

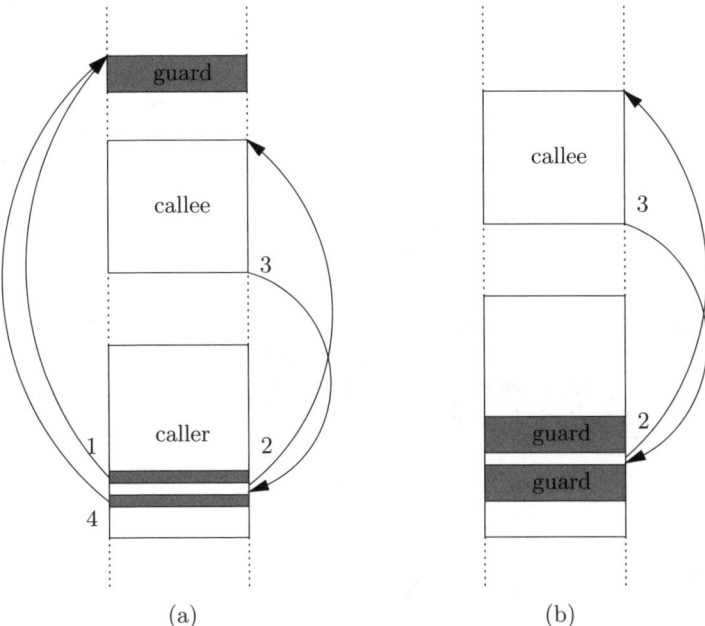

Fig. 1. (a) Memory layout of function call with calls to a crypto guard prior to the actual call and after its corresponding return. (b) After inlining the guard code. Note that the caller will increase in size depending on the size of the guard code.

modes, such as EAX [2] or the more efficient OCB [16]. These modes aim to efficiently offer confidentiality and integrity.

The operation of a function call is illustrated in Fig. 1. It consists of the following steps:

1. the caller calls a guard to decrypt the callee;
   (a) the guard computes a checksum of the immediate dominator of the callee;
   (b) the callee is decrypted with the checksum as key;
   (c) the guard returns;
2. the caller calls the callee;
3. the callee returns;
4. the caller calls the guard to encrypt the callee;
   (a) the guard computes a checksum of the immediate dominator of the callee;
   (b) the callee is encrypted with the checksum as key;
   (c) the guard returns;

5 Numerical Evaluation

In our experiments we tested 5 benchmark programs out of the SPEC CPU2006 Test Suite [19] on an AMD Sempron 1200 MHz, running GNU/Linux with 1 GB of RAM. We first measure the impact of bulk encryption. Subsequently, we apply our on-demand encryption scheme where we protect a maximal number of functions, such that our scheme can offer tamper-resistance according to the properties mentioned in Section 4. To insert the guard code we used Diablo [7], a link-time binary rewriter, allowing us to patch binary code, insert extra encryption functionality, and perform dominator analysis on either the control flow graph or the function call graph. As we are generating self-modifying code, we mark all code segments to be readable and writable.

Our current implementation only handles functions which respect the call-return conventions. Recursive functions (denoted by cycles in the function call graph) are protected by decrypting ahead, i.e. just before entering a recursive cycle, one decrypts all functions part of that cycle.

To report the performance cost we define the *time cost* C_t for a program P and its protected version $\bar{P}$ as follows:

$$C_t(P, \bar{P}) = \frac{T(\bar{P})}{T(P)}$$

where $T(X)$ is the execution time of program X.

5.1 Bulk Decryption

For the bulk decryption we added a decryption routine that is executed prior to transferring control to the entry point of the program. For simplicity, we encrypted the entire code section of the binary (including library functions as Diablo works on statically compiled binaries). The resulting overhead in execution time is less than 1%.

5.2 On-demand Decryption

On-demand decryption protects functions by decrypting them just before they are called and reencrypting them after they have returned. This limits their exposure in memory. Despite the simplicity of this scheme, a number of issues need to be addressed. An overview is given below.

Loops. A scheme considering only decryption should not be nested in a loop (unless it tests for the state – cleartext or ciphertext). Bulk decryption for example should happen only once. However, the sooner this decryption is performed, the longer code will be exposed. As our scheme operates on a function level and a corresponding function call graph, we do not posses information on loops, unless derived from further analysis (e.g., via profile information).

Recursion. If a function calls itself (pure recursive call), it should – according to our scheme definitions – decrypt itself, although it might be in clear already. Therefore, we suggest decrypting a recursive function only once: namely when

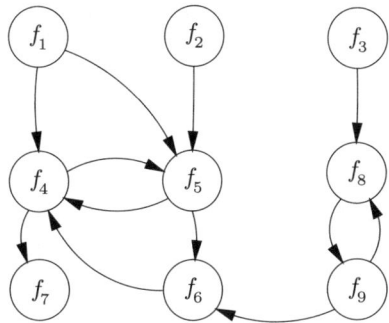

Fig. 2. A partial function call graph containing recursive cycles: $\{f_4, f_5\}$, $\{f_4, f_5, f_6\}$, and $\{f_8, f_9\}$. Functions f_1, f_2, and f_3 are the functions giving control to the recursive cycles after decrypting all functions in the reachable cycles.

it gets called by another function. We can extend this to recursive cycles, where a group of functions together form a recursion. In this case, all functions in the recursive cycle should be decrypted before entering the recursive cycle. Figure 2 illustrates this. For example, before giving control to f_8 (via f_3), cycles $\{f_8, f_9\}$ and $\{f_4, f_5, f_6\}$ have to be decrypted. Function f_7 can be decrypted (before calling) in f_4 as it will always be re-encrypted (after returning) before f_4 calls it a second time (e.g., in another iteration of the recursion).

Multiple callers. In order to propagate errors through the whole call graph according to the call stack, decryption of a callee should depend on the integrity of all callers. This is not straightforward as we defined our scheme to rely on cleartext code, but only one of the callers has to be in clear. Cappaert et al. [3] is possible to decrypt the cleartext code of each caller. However, this requires $O(nd)$ decryptions (via a guard) where n represents the number of callers and d the difference in the call graph depth of each encrypted caller relative to the actual caller. To overcome this overhead we propose to apply a similar strategy as proposed for recursion, namely to decrypt ahead of the call to the callee. Thus, to decrypt a function b with multiple callers a_i we can decrypt the code of b before entering one its callers a_i. This would only result in $O(n)$ guards but expose f_b's code a little longer.

In our implementation we rely on the immediate dominator instead of the actual callers, but we only decrypt the code of b when it is called from one of its callers a_i. The reason is that the dominator is always on the call stack, and thus in the clear, when a function is reached. This only requires $O(n)$ guards.

Table 1 shows the time cost after applying our on-demand encryption scheme to 5 benchmark programs out of the SPEC CPU2006 suite. It is clear that, depending on the nature of the program (number of calls, function size, etc.), the impact of our scheme is moderate for some, while expensive for others.

Table 1. Time cost for on-demand encryption, using our tamper resistance scheme. This table shows the total number of functions, functions protected with the on-demand encryption scheme, the time cost, and the number of guard pairs (D and E) in the binary.

Program name	Functions total	on-demand	Speed cost C_t	Number of guard pairs
mcf	22	20	1.09	28
milc	159	146	8.17	543
hmmer	234	184	3.20	873
lbm	19	12	1.00	20
sphinx_livepretend	210	192	6.65	1277

5.3 Combined Scheme

To address the trade-off between performance and protection we propose a combined scheme. This scheme combines the merits of bulk encryption and the tamper-resistant properties of our on-demand decryption scheme. To decide whether a function is a good candidate for on-demand decryption, we define a heuristic *hotness* that is correlated to the frequency a function is called, namely:

Definition 1. *A function is **hot** when it is part of the set of most frequently called functions that together contribute to $K\%$ of all function calls.*

The call information was collected by analyzing dynamic profile information gathered by Diablo. This definition can be expressed by the following formula:

$$f \text{ is hot} \leftrightarrow calls(f) \geq threshold$$

with

$$threshold = calls(f_i) \mid \sum_{j=1}^{i} calls(f_i) > K \sum_{j=1}^{n} calls(f_i)$$

assuming n functions, ordered descending according to the number of times a function f_i is called, i.e. $calls(f_i)$.

When a function is hot, it is not selected for on demand encryption but protected by bulk encryption. Table 2 contains the time costs of the same benchmark programs tested when we apply the combined scheme. It is clear that defining a *hot* threshold reduces the overhead introduced by our guards. We believe that further fine-tuning of our threshold (e.g., increasing the K factor) will improve the performance of all programs.

Furthermore, we also would like to stress that we are aiming to protect all functions at all times, while most other software protection techniques focus on the critical parts only, or all functions but not at all times (e.g., bulk encryption).

Table 2. Time cost for our combined scheme, combining on-demand encryption with bulk encryption for $K = 0.90$

Program name	Functions total	on-demand	Speed cost C_t	Number of guard pairs
mcf	22	19	1.04	24
milc	159	135	1.95	486
hmmer	234	183	1.15	862
lbm	19	8	1.00	17
sphinx_livepretend	210	181	1.72	1257

6 Attacks and Improvements

6.1 White-Box Attacks

Our guards, which modify code depending on other code, offer several advantages over the software guards proposed by Chang and Attalah [4] and the those from Horne et al. [9]:

Confidentiality. As long as code remains encrypted in memory it is protected against dynamic analysis attacks. With a good scheme it is feasible to ensure only a minimal number of code blocks are present in memory in decrypted form;

Tamper resistance. Together with a good dependency scheme, our guards offer protection against any tampering attempt. If a function is tampered with statically or even dynamically, the program will generate corrupted code at a later stage and thus will it most likely eventually crash due to illegal instructions. Furthermore, if the modification generates executable code, this change will be propagated to other functions, resulting in erroneous code.

Resistance to a hardware-assisted circumvention attack. This attack, proposed by van Oorschot et al. [22], exploits differences between data reads and instruction fetches to bypass self-checksumming code. The attack consists of duplicating each memory page, one page containing the original code, while another contains tampered code. A modified kernel intercepts every data read and redirects it to the page containing the original code, while the code that gets executed is the modified one. However, more recent work of Giffin et al. [8] illustrates that self-modifying code can detect such an attack and thus protect against it. As our work focusses on self-encrypting code, a type of self-modifying code, these results also apply to our techniques.

Nevertheless, in a white-box environment, an attacker has full privileges. For example, he or she can debug and emulate the program at will. This implies that our dynamically computed keys will be visible at some moment in time. The same counts for addresses of the decryption areas, etc. Therefore, we propose to protect guards in a diversified manner by obfuscation techniques [24] such that not all of them can be broken in an automated way. Another option is hardware support, such as cryptographic co-processors [21]. However, this usually comes a a higher cost.

6.2 Inlining Guard Code

Embedding a single decryption routine in a binary is not a secure stand-alone protection technique. It should always be combined with other techniques such as obfuscation or self-checking code. The strength of our scheme is a direct consequence of its distributed nature, i.e. a network of guards (as explained in Section 4.2). If implementation of the dependency scheme consists of a single instance of the guard code and numerous calls to it, an attacker can modify the guard or crypto code to write all decrypted content to another file or memory region. To avoid that an attacker only needs to attack this single instance of the guard code, inlining the entire guard could preclude this attack and force an attacker to modify all instances of the guard code at run time, as all nested guard code will initially be encrypted. This has been illustrated in Figure 1(b). However, a disadvantage of this inlining is code expansion. Compact encryption routines might keep the spacial cost relatively low, but implementations of secure cryptographic functions are not always small.

Even though our initial results illustrated in Table 1 and Table 2 were performed by inlining calls, we expect similar performance results as our guard code in its most compact form does not exceed 40 bytes, while the calls we used for testing are 47 bytes long (pushing and popping arguments included).

6.3 Increasing Granularity and Scheme Extensions

Our scheme is built on top of static call graph information and therefore uses functions as building blocks. If one increases the granularity, and encrypts parts of functions, the guards can be integrated into the program's control flow which will further complicate analyzing the network of guards especially when inlined. However, we believe that such a fine-grained structure will induce much more overhead. The code blocks to be encrypted will be much smaller than the added code. Furthermore, more guards will be required to cover the whole program code. Hence it is important to trade-off the use of these guards, focusing instead on critical parts of the program and avoiding 'hot spots' such as frequently executed code.

As implied by Figure 1, the caller remains in cleartext as long as it is part of the call stack. Another extension involves encrypting the caller of a callee when the callee executes. This corresponds to protecting functions on the call stack. As such, only the executing function will be in cleartext. This extension would double the number of guards per original function call inducing considerable overhead, see also [3]. However, using dedicated heuristics, such as *hotness*, would help us make a better trade-off between on-demand encryption and bulk encryption.

7 Conclusions

This paper presents a new type of software guards which are able to encipher code at run time, relying on other code as key information. This technique offers confidentiality of code, a property that previously proposed software guards did not offer yet. As code is used as a key to decrypt other code, it becomes possible to create code dependencies which make the program more tamper-resistant. We propose a scheme that makes code depending on one of its dominators. We compare our approach to the less secure bulk encryption. We introduce a heuristic based on the frequency that a particular function is called to reduce overhead. To validate our claims we implemented our scheme with Diablo, a binary rewriter, and applied it on 5 programs of the SPEC CPU2006 benchmarks suite.

Acknowledgements

This work was supported in part by the Research Foundation - Flanders (FWO Vlaanderen), the Institute for the Promotion of Innovation through Science and Technology in Flanders (IWT Vlaanderen), the Concerted Research Action (GOA) Ambiorics 2005/11 of the Flemish Government, and by the BCRYPT Interuniversity Attraction Pole (IAP VI/26) programme of the Belgian government. We would also like to thank Elena Andreeva for her contributions.

References

1. Aucsmith, D.: Tamper resistant software: an implementation. In: Anderson, R. (ed.) IH 1996. LNCS, vol. 1174, pp. 317–333. Springer, Heidelberg (1996)
2. Bellare, M., Rogaway, P., Wagner, D.: The eax mode of operation: A two-pass authenticated-encryption scheme optimized for simplicity and efficiency. In: Roy, B., Meier, W. (eds.) FSE 2004. LNCS, vol. 3017, pp. 389–407. Springer, Heidelberg (2004)
3. Cappaert, J., Kisserli, N., Schellekens, D., Preneel, B.: Self-encrypting code to protect against analysis and tampering. In: 1st Benelux Workshop on Information and System Security (WISSec 2006) (2006)
4. Chang, H., Atallah, M.J.: Protecting software codes by guards. In: Sander, T. (ed.) DRM 2001. LNCS, vol. 2320, pp. 160–175. Springer, Heidelberg (2002)
5. Chen, Y., Venkatesan, R., Cary, M., Pang, R., Sinha, S., Jakubowski, M.: Oblivious hashing: a stealthy software integrity verification primitive. In: Petitcolas, F.A.P. (ed.) IH 2002. LNCS, vol. 2578, pp. 400–414. Springer, Heidelberg (2003)
6. Collberg, C., Thomborson, C., Low, D.: A taxonomy of obfuscating transformations. Technical Report #148, Department of Computer Science, The University of Auckland (1997)
7. De Sutter, B., Van Put, L., Chanet, D., De Bus, B., De Bosschere, K.: Link-time compaction and optimization of arm executables. ACM Transactions on Embedded Computing Systems 6(1) (2007)
8. Giffin, J.T., Christodorescu, M., Kruger, L.: Strengthening software self-checksumming via self-modifying code. In: Proceedings of the 21st Annual Computer Security Applications Conference (ACSA 2005), pp. 23–32. IEEE Computer Society Press, Los Alamitos (2005)

9. Horne, B., Matheson, L.R., Sheehan, C., Tarjan, R.E.: Dynamic Self-Checking Techniques for Improved Tamper Resistance 2320, 141–159 (2001)
10. Howard, M., LeBlanc, D.C.: Writing Secure Code, 2nd edn. Microsoft Press (2002)
11. Klimov, A., Shamir, A.: Cryptographic applications of T-functions. In: Matsui, M., Zuccherato, R.J. (eds.) SAC 2003. LNCS, vol. 3006, pp. 248–261. Springer, Heidelberg (2004)
12. Linn, C., Debray, S.: Obfuscation of executable code to improve resistance to static disassembly. In: CCS 2003: Proceedings of the 10th ACM conference on Computer and communications security, pp. 290–299 (2003)
13. Low, D.: Java Control Flow Obfuscation. Master's thesis, University of Auckland, New Zealand (1998)
14. Mehta, N., Clowes, S.: Shiva – ELF Executable Encryptor. Secure Reality, http://www.securereality.com.au/
15. Menez, A.J., van Oorschot, P.C., Vanstone, S.A.: Handbook of Applied Cryptography. CRC Press, Boca Raton (1997)
16. Rogaway, P., Bellare, M., Black, J.: Ocb: A block-cipher mode of operation for efficient authenticated encryption. ACM Transactions on Information and System Security (TISSEC) 6(3), 365–403 (2003)
17. Shamir, A., van Someren, N.: Playing "Hide and Seek" with Stored Keys. In: Franklin, M.K. (ed.) FC 1999. LNCS, vol. 1648, pp. 118–124. Springer, Heidelberg (1999)
18. Song, Y., Locasto, M.E., Stavrou, A., Keromytis, A.D., Stolfo, S.J.: On the infeasibility of modeling polymorphic shellcode. In: Proceedings of the 14th ACM conference on Computer and communications security (CCS 2007), pp. 541–551. ACM Press, New York (2007)
19. SPEC – Standard Performance Evaluation Corporation. SPEC CPU (2006), http://www.spec.org/cpu2006/
20. Tan, G., Chen, Y., Jakubowski, M.H.: Delayed and controlled failures in tamper-resistant software. In: Camenisch, J.L., Collberg, C.S., Johnson, N.F., Sallee, P. (eds.) IH 2006. LNCS, vol. 4437, pp. 216–231. Springer, Heidelberg (2007)
21. Tygar, J.D., Yee, B.: Dyad: A system for using physically secure coprocessors. In: IP Workshop Proceedings (1994)
22. van Oorschot, P.C., Somayaji, A., Wurster, G.: Hardware-assisted circumvention of self-hashing software tamper resistance. IEEE Transactions on Dependable and Secure Computing 2(2), 82–92 (2005)
23. Viega, J., Messier, M.: Secure Programming Cookbook for C and C++. O'Reilly Media, Inc (2003)
24. Wroblewski, G.: General Method of Program Code Obfuscation. PhD thesis, Wroclaw University of Technology, Institute of Engineering Cybernetics (2002)

A New Public Key Broadcast Encryption Using Boneh-Boyen-Goh's HIBE Scheme*

Jong Hwan Park and Dong Hoon Lee

Center for Information Security Technologies(CIST),
Korea University, Seoul, Korea
{decartian, donghlee}@korea.ac.kr

Abstract. We offer an alternative Public Key Broadcast Encryption (PKBE) scheme which is fully collusion-secure. Our construction is based on the method for generating private keys in the Boneh, Boyen and Goh's hierarchical identity-based encryption scheme. Our scheme provides a trade-off between ciphertext size and public key size. With appropriate parametrization we achieve a PKBE scheme where both ciphertexts and private keys are sublinear size for any subset of receivers. Private keys shrink as revoked users increase, and public key size is more reduced than other PKBE schemes. We extend our scheme to obtain chosen ciphertext security by using hash-based method.

Keywords: Public Key Broadcast Encryption, Full Collusion-Security.

1 Introduction

Broadcast encryption scheme [11] allows a sender to securely distribute messages to a dynamically changing set of users over an insecure channel. In general, broadcast encryption schemes are used to support a hybrid (KEM-DEM) encryption paradigm where a ciphertext encrypts a message encryption key used to encrypt the messages under a symmetric key cipher. The sender can broadcast the ciphertext to any receiver set S of his choice. Any user in S then decrypts the ciphertext and revoked users (i.e., any user not in S) should obtain no information about the messages.

Basically, the broadcast encryption scheme should provide a mechanism to handle revocation of users. Since revoked users could collude, the scheme must be secure against collusion attack of the revoked users. When the broadcast encryption scheme is secure against any number of colluders, we say that the scheme is fully collusion-secure. Broadcast encryption schemes are motivated by applications such as pay-TV systems and the distribution of copyrighted materials. In this paper, we mainly focus on the broadcast encryption scheme with large number of users.

---

* This research was supported by the MIC(Ministry of Information and Communication), Korea, under the ITRC(Information Technology Research Center) support program supervised by the IITA(Institute of Information Technology Advancement) (IITA-2008-(C1090-0801-0025)).

There are two kinds of settings of broadcast encryption in the literature. In the private key setting [11,15,14,13], only the trusted center generates all the private keys and broadcasts messages to some set of users. The best known schemes [15,14,13] in this setting achieve $O(r)$ ciphertexts and $O(\log n)$ private keys, where r is the number of revoked users and n is the number of total users. In the public key setting [16,8,9,4,10] any user can encrypt to some set of users under a public key initialized at system setup. It overcomes a shortcoming of the private key setting, which is that the center may be a single point of failure. By the work of Dodis and Fazio [9], some broadcast encryption schemes in the private key setting could be transformed into schemes in the public key setting (i.e., Public Key Broadcast Encryption (PKBE) scheme), using the Hierarchical Identity-Based Encryption (HIBE) scheme [12]. Their method was further improved by applying the HIBE scheme suggested by Boneh, Boyen and Goh [2], which results in PKBE schemes with $O(r)$ ciphertexts and $O(\log^2 n)$ private keys.

Recently, Boneh, Gentry and Waters [4] proposed an efficient PKBE scheme for large n users. In the BGW scheme, with appropriate parametrization both ciphertexts and private keys are of $O(\sqrt{n})$ size (or $O(\sqrt{n})$ ciphertexts and $O(1)$ private keys when public key elements required to decrypt are transmitted together with ciphertexts). More recently, Delerablee, Paillier and Pointcheval [10] suggested a new PKBE scheme that features $O(r)$ ciphertexts and $O(1)$ private keys at the expense of computation cost upon decryption and public key size. In terms of transmission cost, the DPP scheme is attractive when r is small (i.e., $r < \sqrt{n}$), but when $r > \sqrt{n}$ the BGW scheme provides a better solution than the DPP scheme. These schemes [4,10] are fully collusion-secure, unlike the previous PKBE schemes [16,8,9] where the number of colluders is restricted to some fixed $t < n$.

Our Results. In this paper we suggest an alternative PKBE solution which is fully collusion-secure. Our construction makes use of an efficiently computable bilinear map (i.e., pairing). Our scheme provides a trade-off between ciphertexts size and public key size as in the BGW scheme [4]. When $n(=ab)$ users are partitioned into a equal size subsets $S_1, \ldots, S_a$, our scheme has $O(\sqrt{n})$ ciphertexts and $O(\sqrt{n} - \tilde{r})$ private keys, where $\tilde{r}$ is the minimum value (as the worst case) among the number of revoked users in each subset S_i. The $O(\sqrt{n} - \tilde{r})$ means that private keys in our scheme shrink as the revoked set becomes large. Also, decryption procedure requires the same amount of computation as the BGW scheme does, which is more efficient than the DPP scheme [10]. Another feature is that the public key size is more shortened than the BGW and DPP schemes. In particular, in comparison to the BGW scheme which is considered as the most efficient one, our scheme is more preferable than the BGW scheme in applications where transmission is an important factor (a precise comparison is given in Section 4).

The idea behind our construction is based on the method used to generate user's private key in the BBG HIBE scheme [2]. Briefly speaking, in the b-level BBG scheme, the key generation algorithm outputs a private key d_{ID} for an identity $\mathsf{ID} = \mathsf{I}_1$ of depth 1 as

$$\left(g_2^\alpha \cdot (g_3 \cdot h_1^{\mathsf{I}_1})^r,\ g^r,\ h_2^r, \ldots,\ h_b^r \right)$$

for a random $r \in \mathbb{Z}_p$. After excluding g_3 we add to the public key a more elements $x_1, \ldots, x_a$, which are representative of the subsets $\mathsf{S}_1, \ldots, \mathsf{S}_a$ respectively. We then compute the private key d_i for a user $i \in \{1, \ldots, n\}$ such that $i = (u-1)b+v$ as

$$\left(g_2^\alpha \cdot (x_u \cdot h_v)^r,\ g^r,\ h_1^r, \ldots,\ h_{v-1}^r,\ h_{v+1}^r, \ldots, h_b^r \right).$$

This modification leads to our PKBE scheme which can accommodate $n(=ab)$ users in total, and provides ours with the trade-off between ciphertext size and public key size. We prove security of our proposed PKBE scheme under the Bilinear Diffie-Hellman Exponent (BDHE) assumption, which was already used to prove security of the BGW scheme [4].

Outline. Section 2 describes our security model for PKBE and the complexity assumption. In Section 3 we present our scheme and prove its security, and in Section 4 we give a performance comparison between the different PKBE schemes. In Section 5 we show how our scheme can be extended to obtain chosen ciphertext security by applying the hash-based method of [6].

2 Preliminaries

2.1 Public Key Broadcast Encryption

Following [4], we define public key broadcast encryption (PKBE) as below.

Setup(n) takes as input the number of receivers n. and outputs a public key PK and n private keys $d_1, \ldots, d_n$.

Encrypt$(\mathsf{S}, \mathsf{PK})$ takes a subset $\mathsf{S} \subseteq \{1, \ldots, n\}$ and a public key PK as input, and outputs a pair (Hdr, K) where Hdr is the header and $K \in \mathcal{K}$ is a message encryption key, often called the broadcast ciphertext.

Let M be a message to be broadcast to the set S and let C_M be the encryption of M under the symmetric key K. A broadcast message is $(\mathsf{S}, \mathsf{Hdr}, C_M)$, where the pair $(\mathsf{S}, \mathsf{Hdr})$ is often called the full header and C_M is often called the broadcast body.

Decrypt$(d_i, \mathsf{S}, \mathsf{Hdr}, \mathsf{PK})$ takes as input the private key d_i for user i, a subset $\mathsf{S} \subseteq \{1, \ldots, n\}$, a header Hdr, and the public key PK. If user i is in S, the algorithm outputs the message encryption key $K \in \mathcal{K}$, which is used to decrypt C_M and obtain the message M.

We require that for all $\mathsf{S} \subseteq \{1, \ldots, n\}$ and $i \in \mathsf{S}$, if $(\mathsf{PK}, (d_1, \ldots, d_n)) \xleftarrow{R} \mathtt{Setup}(n)$ and $(\mathsf{Hdr}, K) \xleftarrow{R} \mathtt{Encrypt}(\mathsf{S}, \mathsf{PK})$ then $\mathtt{Decrypt}(d_i, \mathsf{S}, \mathsf{Hdr}, \mathsf{PK}) = K$.

To describe the chosen ciphertext security for PKBE, we define the following game between an attacker $\mathcal{A}$ and a challenger $\mathcal{C}$ as in [4]. Both $\mathcal{C}$ and $\mathcal{A}$ are provided with n, the total number of users, as input.

Init: Attacker $\mathcal{A}$ outputs a set $\mathsf{S}^* \subseteq \{1, \ldots, n\}$ of receivers that it intends to attack.

Setup: Challenger $\mathcal{C}$ runs $\mathtt{Setup}(n)$ to obtain a public key PK and private keys $d_1, \ldots, d_n$. It gives $\mathcal{A}$ the public key PK and all private keys d_j for $j \notin \mathsf{S}^*$.

Query Phase 1: $\mathcal{A}$ adaptively issues decryption queries $q_1, \ldots, q_m$ where a decryption query consists of the triple $(i, \mathsf{S}, \mathsf{Hdr})$ where $\mathsf{S} \subseteq \mathsf{S}^*$ and $i \in \mathsf{S}$. $\mathcal{C}$ responds with $\mathtt{Decrypt}(d_i, \mathsf{S}, \mathsf{Hdr}, \mathsf{PK})$.

Challenge: $\mathcal{C}$ runs algorithm $\mathtt{Encrypt}(\mathsf{S}^*, \mathsf{PK})$ to obtain (Hdr^*, K) where $K \in \mathcal{K}$. Next, the challenger picks a random $b \in \{0, 1\}$. If $b = 1$, it sets $K^* = K$. Otherwise, it sets K^* to a random string of length equal to $|K|$. $\mathcal{C}$ gives a *challenge* ciphertext (Hdr^*, K^*) to $\mathcal{A}$.

Query Phase 2: $\mathcal{A}$ adaptively issues decryption queries $q_{m+1}, \ldots, q_{q_D}$ where a decryption query consists of $(i, \mathsf{S}, \mathsf{Hdr})$ with $\mathsf{S} \subseteq \mathsf{S}^*$ and $i \in \mathsf{S}$. $\mathcal{A}$ cannot issue a decryption query such that $\mathsf{Hdr} = \mathsf{Hdr}^*$. $\mathcal{C}$ responds as in **Query Phase 1**.

Guess: Attacker $\mathcal{A}$ outputs a guess $b' \in \{0, 1\}$. $\mathcal{A}$ wins if $b' = b$.

The advantage of $\mathcal{A}$ in breaking a public key broadcast encryption scheme is defined as
$$\mathsf{Adv}_{\mathcal{A},n}^{\mathsf{PKBE}} = \left| \Pr[b = b'] - \frac{1}{2} \right|$$
where n is given to both the $\mathcal{C}$ and $\mathcal{A}$ as input.

Definition 1. *We say that a public key broadcast encryption scheme is (t, ϵ, n, q_D)-CCA secure if for all t-time attackers $\mathcal{A}$ who make q_D decryption queries, we have that $\mathsf{Adv}_{\mathcal{A},n}^{\mathsf{PKBE}} < \epsilon$.*

This game above models an attack where all users not in the set S^* collude to try and expose a broadcast message intended only for users in S^*. The attacker in this model is static as in [4]. That is, it chooses S^* and obtains the keys for users outside of S^*, before it sees the public key PK.

The game above can be used to define semantic security for a broadcast encryption scheme if the attacker is not permitted to issue decryption queries. We say that a public key broadcast encryption scheme is (t, ϵ, n)-semantically secure if it is $(t, \epsilon, n, 0)$-CCA secure.

2.2 Bilinear Pairing and Complexity Assumption

We briefly summarize the bilinear pairings and define the $(b+1)$-Bilinear Diffie-Hellman Exponent (BDHE) assumption.

Bilinear Pairing: We follow the notation in [3,1]. Let $\mathbb{G}$ and $\mathbb{G}_T$ be two (multiplicative) cyclic groups of prime order p. We assume that g is a generator of $\mathbb{G}$. Let $e: \mathbb{G} \times \mathbb{G} \to \mathbb{G}_T$ be a function that has the following properties:

1. Bilinear: for all $u, v \in \mathbb{G}$ and $a, b \in \mathbb{Z}$, we have $e(u^a, v^b) = e(u, v)^{ab}$.
2. Non-degenerate: $e(g, g) \neq 1$.
3. Computable: there is an efficient algorithm to compute the map e.

Then, we say that $\mathbb{G}$ is a bilinear group and the map e is a bilinear pairing in $\mathbb{G}$. Note that $e(,)$ is symmetric since $e(g^a, g^b) = e(g,g)^{ab} = e(g^b, g^a)$.

The Bilinear Diffie-Hellman Exponent Assumption: The $(b+1)$-BDHE problem in $\mathbb{G}$ is defined as follows: given a $(2b+2)$-tuple $(z, g, g^\alpha, \ldots, g^{\alpha^b}, g^{\alpha^{b+2}}, \ldots, g^{\alpha^{2b}}) \in \mathbb{G}^{2b+2}$ as input, compute $e(z,g)^{\alpha^{b+1}} \in \mathbb{G}_T$. An algorithm $\mathcal{A}$ has advantage ϵ in solving $(b+1)$-BDHE in $\mathbb{G}$ if

$$\Pr\left[\mathcal{A}(z, g, g^\alpha, \ldots, g^{\alpha^b}, g^{\alpha^{b+2}}, \ldots, g^{\alpha^{2b}}) = e(z,g)^{\alpha^{b+1}}\right] \geq \epsilon$$

where the probability is over the random choice of α in $\mathbb{Z}_p$, the random choice of $z \in \mathbb{G}$, and the random bits of $\mathcal{A}$. Let $g_i = g^{(\alpha^i)}$ and let $\vec{g}_{\alpha,b} = (g_1, \ldots, g_b, g_{b+2}, \ldots, g_{2b})$. Similarly, we say that an algorithm $\mathcal{B}$ that outputs $b \in \{0,1\}$ has advantage ϵ in solving the *decision* $(b+1)$-BDHE problem in $\mathbb{G}$ if

$$\left|\Pr[\mathcal{B}(z, g, \vec{g}_{\alpha,b}, e(z, g_{b+1})) = 0] - \Pr[\mathcal{B}(z, g, \vec{g}_{\alpha,b}, T) = 0]\right| \geq \epsilon$$

where the probability is over the random choice of α in $\mathbb{Z}_p$, the random choice of $z \in \mathbb{G}$, the random choice of $T \in \mathbb{G}_T$, and the random bits of $\mathcal{B}$.

Definition 2. *We say that the (decision) $(t, \epsilon, b+1)$-BDHE assumption holds in $\mathbb{G}$ if no t-time algorithm has advantage at least ϵ in solving the (decision) $(b+1)$-BDHE problem in $\mathbb{G}$.*

3 Chosen Plaintext Secure Construction

We first present a new PKBE scheme that is secure against chosen plaintext secure. We show how to build the new PKBE scheme via a simple variation of the HIBE scheme of Boneh, Boyen, and Goh [2]. To obtain a generalized PKBE scheme which provides a trade-off between the public key and private key and the ciphertext sizes, we use the idea of [4]. For a positive integer b dividing $n(=ab)$, the number of total users, we denote the proposed scheme by b-PKBE scheme. The choice of b would depend on the concrete application.

3.1 Scheme

Let $\mathbb{G}$ and $\mathbb{G}_T$ be groups of prime order p, and let $e : \mathbb{G} \times \mathbb{G} \to \mathbb{G}_T$ be the bilinear map. Note that the Decrypt algorithm does not require any public key elements as input.

Setup($1^k, n$): To generate b-PKBE parameters, the algorithm picks a random generator $g \in \mathbb{G}$. It selects a random $\alpha \in \mathbb{Z}_p^*$ and sets $g_1 = g^\alpha$. Next, it picks random elements $h, x_1, \ldots, x_a, y_1, \ldots, y_b \in \mathbb{G}$. The public key PK (with the description of $(\mathbb{G}, \mathbb{G}_T, e, p)$) is given by

$$\mathsf{PK} = (g, g_1, h, x_1, \ldots, x_a, y_1, \ldots, y_b) \in \mathbb{G}^{a+b+3}.$$

The private key for user $i \in \{1, \ldots, n\}$ is computed as follows: find two values u, v (where $1 \leq u \leq a$ and $1 \leq v \leq b$) such that $i = (u-1)b + v$. It means user i is assigned to index v within a subset S_u. Then, pick a random $r \in \mathbb{Z}_p$ and set the private key for user i as

$$d_i = \left(h^\alpha \cdot (x_u \cdot y_v)^r,\ g^r,\ y_1^r, \ldots, y_{v-1}^r, y_{v+1}^r, \ldots, y_b^r \right) \in \mathbb{G}^{b+1}.$$

The algorithm outputs the public key PK and the n private keys $d_1, \ldots, d_n$.

Encrypt(S, PK): A sender chooses a random $s \in \mathbb{Z}_p$ and set $K = e(h, g_1)^s \in \mathbb{G}_T$. Wlog, assume that the set S is divided into subsets $\mathsf{S}_1, \ldots, \mathsf{S}_a$. Next, compute

$$\mathsf{Hdr} = \left(\left(x_1 \cdot \prod_{j \in \mathsf{S}_1} y_j\right)^s, \ldots, \left(x_a \cdot \prod_{j \in \mathsf{S}_a} y_j\right)^s,\ g^s \right) \in \mathbb{G}^{a+1}.$$

The algorithm outputs the pair (Hdr, K). The sender broadcasts $(\mathsf{S}, \mathsf{Hdr}, C_M)$, where C_M is an encrypted message under the K using a symmetric key cipher.

Decrypt(d_i, S, Hdr): Assume user i is assigned to index v within the subset S_u, and decrypts the Hdr using his private key $d_i = (d_{i,1}, d_{i,2}, k_{i,1}, \ldots, k_{i,v-1}, k_{i,v+1}, \ldots, k_{i,b})$. Let $\mathsf{Hdr} = (A_1, \ldots, A_a, B)$. Then, output

$$K = e(d_{i,1} \cdot \prod_{\substack{j \in \mathsf{S}_u \\ j \neq v}} k_{i,j},\ B)\ /\ e(A_u,\ d_{i,2}).$$

3.2 Correctness

We verify that K is correctly derived from the well-formed Hdr. Assuming user i belongs to S_u with index v, then it decrypts as follows:

$$K = e(d_{i,1} \cdot \prod_{\substack{j \in \mathsf{S}_u \\ j \neq v}} k_{i,j},\ B)\ /\ e(A_u,\ d_{i,2})$$

$$= e(h^\alpha \cdot (x_u \cdot y_v)^r \cdot \prod_{\substack{j \in \mathsf{S}_u \\ j \neq v}} y_j^r,\ g^s)\ /\ e((x_u \cdot \prod_{j \in \mathsf{S}_u} y_j)^s,\ g^r)$$

$$= e(h^\alpha \cdot (x_u \cdot \prod_{j \in \mathsf{S}_u} y_j)^r,\ g^s)\ /\ e((x_u \cdot \prod_{j \in \mathsf{S}_u} y_j)^s,\ g^r)$$

$$= e(h, g_1)^s.$$

3.3 Security

The semantic security of the b-PKBE scheme above is proven under the decision $(b+1)$-BDHE assumption.

Theorem 1. *Suppose that the decision $(t, \epsilon, b+1)$-BDHE assumption holds in $\mathbb{G}$. Then the previous b-PKBE scheme is (t', ϵ, n)-semantically secure for any positive integers n, b and $t' < t - \Theta(\tau bn)$, where τ is the maximum time for an exponentiation in $\mathbb{G}$.*

Proof. Suppose there exists an adversary $\mathcal{A}$ which has advantage ϵ in attacking the b-PKBE scheme. We want to construct an algorithm $\mathcal{B}$ that uses $\mathcal{A}$ to solve the decision $(b + 1)$-BDHE problem in $\mathbb{G}$. For a generator $g \in \mathbb{G}$ and $\alpha \in \mathbb{Z}_p$, let $g_i = g^{(\alpha^i)} \in \mathbb{G}$. On input $(z, g, g_1, \ldots, g_b, g_{b+2}, \ldots, g_{2b}, T)$, $\mathcal{B}$ outputs 1 if $T = e(z, g_{b+1})$ and 0 otherwise. $\mathcal{B}$ works by interacting with $\mathcal{A}$ as follows:

Init: $\mathcal{A}$ outputs a set S^* that it intends to attack.

Setup: $\mathcal{B}$ first divides the challenge set S^* into subsets $\mathsf{S}_1^*, \ldots, \mathsf{S}_a^*$. To generate a public key PP, $\mathcal{B}$ selects a random $\rho \in \mathbb{Z}_p$ and set $h = g_b \cdot g^\rho$. Next, it picks random $\gamma_1, \ldots, \gamma_b, \delta_1, \ldots, \delta_a \in \mathbb{Z}_p$. It sets $y_i = g^{\gamma_i} g_i$ for $i = 1, \ldots, b$ and sets $x_j = g^{\delta_j} \cdot \left(\prod_{k \in \mathsf{S}_j^*} g_k \right)^{-1}$ for $j = 1, \ldots, a$. Finally, $\mathcal{B}$ gives $\mathcal{A}$ the public key

$$\mathsf{PK} = (g, g_1, h, x_1, \ldots, x_a, y_1, \ldots, y_b).$$

Since $\rho, \{\gamma_i\}$, and $\{\delta_j\}$ values are chosen uniformly at random, this public key has an identical distribution to that in the actual construction.

Next, $\mathcal{B}$ needs to generate private keys d_i for $i \notin \mathsf{S}^*$. Consider a private key for user i such that $i = (u - 1)b + v$ for some $1 \leq u \leq a$ and $1 \leq v \leq b$. $\mathcal{B}$ picks a random $r \in \mathbb{Z}_p$. Let $\tilde{r} = r - \alpha^{(b+1-v)}$. $\mathcal{B}$ generates the private key d_i for user i as

$$\left(h^\alpha \cdot (x_u \cdot y_v)^{\tilde{r}},\ g^{\tilde{r}},\ y_1^{\tilde{r}}, \ldots, y_{v-1}^{\tilde{r}},\ y_{v+1}^{\tilde{r}}, \ldots, y_b^{\tilde{r}} \right)$$

which is a properly distributed private key for user i. We show that $\mathcal{B}$ can compute all elements of this private key given the values that it knows. To generate the first component of the private key, observe that

$$(x_u \cdot y_v)^{\tilde{r}}$$

$$= \left(g^{\delta_u} \cdot (\prod_{k \in \mathsf{S}_u^*} g_k)^{-1} \cdot g^{\gamma_v} g_v \right)^{\tilde{r}}$$

$$= \left(g^{\delta_u} \cdot (\prod_{k \in \mathsf{S}_u^*} g_k)^{-1} \cdot g^{\gamma_v} g_v \right)^r \left(g^{\delta_u} \cdot (\prod_{k \in \mathsf{S}_u^*} g_k)^{-1} \cdot g^{\gamma_v} g_v \right)^{-\alpha^{b+1-v}}$$

$$= \left(g^{\delta_u} \cdot (\prod_{k \in \mathsf{S}_u^*} g_k)^{-1} \cdot g^{\gamma_v} g_v \right)^r \left(g_{b+1-v}^{\delta_u} \cdot (\prod_{k \in \mathsf{S}_u^*} g_{b+1-v+k})^{-1} \cdot g_{b+1-v}^{\gamma_v} \right)^{-1} g_{b+1}^{-1}.$$

Note that since $i \notin \mathsf{S}^*$, we see that $v \notin \mathsf{S}_u^*$ and then $k - v \neq 0$ for $k \in \mathsf{S}_u^*$. Since $h^\alpha = g_{b+1} \cdot g_1^\rho$, the first component in the private key can be computed as

$$g_1^\rho \cdot \left(g^{\delta_u} \cdot (\prod_{k \in \mathsf{S}_u^*} g_k)^{-1} \cdot g^{\gamma_v} g_v \right)^r \cdot \left(g_{b+1-v}^{\delta_u} \cdot (\prod_{k \in \mathsf{S}_u^*} g_{b+1-v+k})^{-1} \cdot g_{b+1-v}^{\gamma_v} \right)^{-1}$$

where the unknown term g_{b+1} is canceled out. The other terms $g^{\tilde{r}}$ and $y_i^{\tilde{r}}$ are computable since $g^{\tilde{r}} = g^r \cdot g_{b+1-v}^{-1}$ and $y_i^{\tilde{r}} = (g^{\gamma_i} \cdot g_i)^r \cdot (g_{b+1-v}^{\gamma_i} \cdot g_{b+1-v+i})^{-1}$ for $i = 1, \ldots, v-1, v+1, \ldots, b$. Since $i \neq v$, these values do not require knowledge of g_{b+1}.

Challenge: To generate a challenge (Hdr^*, K^*) under the receiver set S^*, $\mathcal{B}$ sets $\mathsf{Hdr}^* = \left(z^{\delta_1 + \sum_{k \in \mathsf{S}_1^*} \gamma_k}, \ldots, z^{\delta_a + \sum_{k \in \mathsf{S}_a^*} \gamma_k}, z\right)$ and $K^* = T \cdot e(g_1, z^\rho)$, where z and T are input values given to $\mathcal{B}$. Observe that if $z = g^c$ for some (unknown) $c \in \mathbb{Z}_p$, then

$$z^{\delta_i + \sum_{k \in \mathsf{S}_i^*} \gamma_k} = \left(g^{\delta_i} \cdot (\prod_{k \in \mathsf{S}_i^*} g_k)^{-1} \cdot \prod_{k \in \mathsf{S}_i^*} g^{\gamma_k} g_k\right)^c = \left(x_i \cdot \prod_{k \in \mathsf{S}_i^*} y_j\right)^c$$

for $i = 1, \ldots, a$. If $T = e(z, g_{b+1})$ then $K^* = e(h, g_1)^c$ and thus (Hdr^*, K^*) is a valid challenge to $\mathcal{A}$ for the receiver set S^*. On the other hand, when T is uniform and independent in $\mathbb{G}_T$, then Hdr^* is independent of K^* in the adversary's view.

Guess: $\mathcal{A}$ outputs a guess $b' \in \{0, 1\}$. If $b' = 1$ then it indicates $T = e(z, g_{b+1})$. Otherwise, it indicates $T \neq e(z, g_{b+1})$.

When T is random in $\mathbb{G}_T$ then $\Pr[\mathcal{B}(z, g, \vec{g}_{\alpha,b}, T) = 0] = 1/2$. When $T = e(z, g_{b+1})$, $\mathcal{B}$ replied with a valid challenge (Hdr^*, K^*). Then $|\Pr[b = b'] - 1/2| \geq \epsilon$. Therefore, $\mathcal{B}$ has that

$$\left|\Pr[\mathcal{B}(z, g, \vec{g}_{\alpha,b}, e(z, g_{b+1})) = 0] - \Pr[\mathcal{B}(z, g, \vec{g}_{\alpha,b}, T) = 0]\right| \geq \epsilon.$$

This completes the proof of Theorem 1. □

4 Performance Analysis

Let n be the total number of users the PKBE scheme can handle, and let n users be divided into a subsets in which each set has at most b users. Let R be the set of revoked users with $\mathbf{r} = |\mathsf{R}|$. As in the BGW scheme [4], when $\mathbf{r} \ll n$, the sender can broadcast $(\mathsf{R}, \mathsf{Hdr}, C_M)$ to the set S instead of $(\mathsf{S}, \mathsf{Hdr}, C_M)$, where the Hdr is still constructed under the set S. In that case, the private key for user i is computed as

$$d_i = \left(h^\alpha \cdot (x_u \cdot y_v)^r \cdot \Big(\prod_{\substack{j=1 \\ j \neq v}}^{b} y_j\Big)^r, g^r, y_1^r, \ldots, y_{v-1}^r, y_{v+1}^r, \ldots, y_b^r\right) \in \mathbb{G}^{b+1}.$$

Let R be split into $\mathsf{R}_1, \ldots, \mathsf{R}_a$ subsets. For the revoked set R_u, during the decryption procedure, the value $\prod_{j \in \mathsf{R}_u} y_j^r$ is removed from the first component in the private key and thereafter $\{y_j^r\}_{j \in \mathsf{R}_u}$ can be discarded. Thus, as the size of the set R_u increases the private key becomes shortened. More precisely, all the private keys d_i for $i \in \mathsf{S}_u$ have $(b + 1 - \mathbf{r}_u)$ elements in $\mathbb{G}$ where $\mathbf{r}_u = |\mathsf{R}_u|$. Note that remaining users, for example, in S_u, do not need to store the information of

Table 1. Performance Comparison of the PKBE schemes for $n = ab$

	Transmission Cost	User Storage Cost	Computation Cost	PK Size
BGW-1	$(a+2b)$ G $+$ r l_{id}	1 G	2 p $+ \widehat{\mathtt{r}}$ m	$(a+2b)$ G
BGW-2	$(a+1)$ G$+$ r l_{id}	$(2b+1)$ G	2 p $+ \widehat{\mathtt{r}}$ m	$(a+2b)$ G
DPP-1	$(\mathtt{r}+2)$ G $+$ r $\mathbb{Z}_p$	2 G $+$ 1 $\mathbb{Z}_p$	2 p $+$ r $\cdot$ (e $+$ m)†	$(n+2)$ G $+$ $(n+1)$ G$_T$ $+$ n $\mathbb{Z}_p$
DPP-2	2 G $+$ r l_{id}	$(n+1)$ G $+$ n $\mathbb{Z}_p$	2 p $+$ r²/2 $\cdot$ (e $+$ m)‡	same as above
Ours	$(a+1)$ G$+$ r l_{id}	$(b+1-\widetilde{\mathtt{r}})$ G	2 p $+ \widehat{\mathtt{r}}$ m	$(a+b+3)$ G

G; element in $\mathbb{G}$,   G$_T$; element in $\mathbb{G}_T$, $\mathbb{Z}_p$; element in $\mathbb{Z}_p$
p; pairing in $\mathbb{G}$,   m; multiplication (or division) in $\mathbb{G}$,   e; exponentiation in $\mathbb{G}$
$\widehat{\mathtt{r}} = \max\{\mathtt{r}_1, \ldots, \mathtt{r}_a\}$ $\widetilde{\mathtt{r}} = \min\{\mathtt{r}_1, \ldots, \mathtt{r}_a\}$ $l_{id} = \log_2 n$
†, ‡; extra calculation to perform about r (or r²/2) inversions in $\mathbb{Z}_p$ is more required.

the revoked set R_u. For some new revoked set R'_u, the receiver firstly compares the remaining elements $\{y_j^r\}_{j \in \mathsf{S}_u \setminus \mathsf{R}_u}$ with the set R'_u, and then identifies the set of elements $\{y_j^r\}_{j \in (\mathsf{S}_u \setminus \mathsf{R}_u) \cap \mathsf{R}'_u}$ to be removed.

Performance Comparison of PKBE Schemes: Before we compare our scheme with the previous PKBE schemes, we consider two cases in regard to the BGW scheme; 1) when the PK elements required to decrypt are transmitted along with the Hdr (BGW-1), 2) when the PK elements needed by decryption procedure are included into the private key (BGW-2). The reason why we consider these two cases is that in the BGW scheme, the Decrypt algorithm needs some of the public key elements for decryption and thus each receiver should obtain these elements. Basically, these elements may be stored into each user's device from the beginning. Also, these elements can be transmitted along with the Hdr, because these elements are not required to be kept secret. Regarding the DPP scheme [10], the authors suggested two kinds of PKBE constructions to provide tradeoffs between ciphertext size and public key size. We refer to the two PKBE constructions in [10] as DPP-1 and 2 (for more details, see [10]).

The efficiency of broadcast encryptions is mostly measured by transmission, user storage, and computation costs at a user device. Here, the user storage cost means the size of user's private key needed to decrypt. In light of these aspects, Table 1 shows the performances of the previous and our PKBE schemes in terms of transmission cost, user storage cost, computation cost (in decryption), and the public key size. For simplicity, we consider the case when the bilinear map e is symmetric. Note that the DPP scheme does not provide such a generalized version that the BGW and our schemes do for $n = ab$. Instead, the DPP scheme is 'dynamic' in the sense that the system setup is fully independent from the expected number n of users. We also note that the schemes [4,10] including ours are all fully collusion-secure.

With the appropriate parametrization, we can show that our PKBE scheme has $O(\sqrt{n})$ ciphertexts and $O(\sqrt{n}-\tilde{\mathbf{r}})$ private keys where $\tilde{\mathbf{r}} = \min\{\mathbf{r}_1, \ldots, \mathbf{r}_a\}$ as the worst case. We see that the DPP-1 achieves $O(r)$ ciphertexts and $O(1)$ private keys at the expense of computation cost and PK size. In terms of transmission cost (excluding the set information $\mathbf{r}\ l_{id}$ or $\mathbf{r}\ \mathsf{Z_p}$), the DPP-1 is more appealing than the BGW-2 and our PKBE scheme when about $r < \sqrt{n}$, and vice versa when about $r > \sqrt{n}$. Among the PKBE schemes above, our scheme has the shortest PK size for n users, and the computation time for decryption is as efficient as the BGW schemes.

In comparison to the BGW scheme which is considered as the most efficient one, our scheme is located as an intermediate one. For example, in applications where the transmission cost is an important factor, our scheme is more preferable than the BGW-2 since the user storage cost of ours is more reduced than the BGW-2. However, in some settings where user device has a very limited storage capacity, then the BGW-1 is more favorable than ours.

Joinging and Revoking of Users: Like other PKBE schemes [8,9,4,10], our scheme has an advantage over broadcast encryption schemes [11,15,14,13] in the private key setting, which can avoid complex and costly re-keying procedures to handle joining and revoking of users.

First, in order to deal with the incremental addition of new users, the Setup algorithm may select value n (and a, b) large enough to accommodate expected users. If users become larger than the initial value n, the Setup algorithm only adds necessary (and random) values $(x_{a+1}, \ldots, x_{a+\delta})$ to the public keys, which enables the scheme to deal with new $b\delta$ users. In this procedure, each element $x_{a+i} \in \mathbb{G}$ covers new b users respectively, and the preexisting user's private key remains the same. This is the same result as in the BGW scheme. In contrast, whenever a new user joins the scheme the DPP scheme is required to add three more elements (one in $\mathbb{Z}_p$, one in $\mathbb{G}_T$, and one in $\mathbb{G}$) to the public key (although the DPP scheme is dynamic). Second, whenever the sender wants to exclude or newly construct a set of receivers, he has only to reconstruct the identity set S' of receivers and compute a header under the new receiver set S'.

5 Chosen Ciphertext Secure Construction

In this section we propose a CCA secure PKBE scheme by applying the ideas of hash-based method (so called "BMW transformation") in [6] to our semantically secure construction. Unlike the signature-based method [7] and message authentication code (MAC)-based method [5], the BMW transformation does not need to attach a one-time signature or a MAC to a ciphertext so that it has shorter ciphertexts than both the signature and MAC-based methods. To employ the BMW transformation, we need a family of collision resistant hash functions $H_k : \mathbb{G} \to \mathbb{Z}_p$ indexed by $k \in \mathcal{K}$. We say that a family of hash functions is (t, ϵ)-collision resistant if no t-time adversary is able to find two distinct values x, y such that $H_k(x) = H_k(y)$ with probability at least ϵ. As in the previous section, we denote our construction by the b-PKBE scheme for a positive integer b such that $n = ab$.

5.1 Scheme

Setup($1^k, n$): To generate b-PKBE parameters, the algorithm picks a random generator $g \in \mathbb{G}$. It selects a random $\alpha \in \mathbb{Z}_p^*$ and sets $g_1 = g^\alpha$. Next, it picks random elements $h_1, h_2, x_1, \ldots, x_a, y_1, \ldots, y_b \in \mathbb{G}$. The algorithm additionally picks a random hash key $k \in \mathcal{K}$ for hash function H. The public key PK (with the description of $(\mathbb{G}, \mathbb{G}_T, e, p, H)$) is given by

$$\mathsf{PK} = (g, g_1, h_1, h_2, x_1, \ldots, x_a, y_1, \ldots, y_b) \in \mathbb{G}^{a+b+4}.$$

The private key for user $i \in \{1, \ldots, n\}$ is computed as follows: as before, find two values u, v (where $1 \le u \le a$ and $1 \le v \le b$) such that $i = (u-1)b + v$. Pick a random $r \in \mathbb{Z}_p$ and set the private key for user i as

$$d_i = \left(h_1^\alpha \cdot (x_u \cdot y_v)^r,\ h_2^r,\ g^r,\ y_1^r, \ldots, y_{v-1}^r, y_{v+1}^r, \ldots, y_b^r \right) \in \mathbb{G}^{b+2}.$$

The algorithm outputs the public key PK and the n private keys $d_1, \ldots, d_n$.

Encrypt(S, PK): A sender chooses a random $s \in \mathbb{Z}_p$ and set $K = e(h_1, g_1)^s \in \mathbb{G}_T$. Next, the sender computes g^s and $\mu = H_k(g^s)$. A header (Hdr) is generated as

$$\mathsf{Hdr} = \left(\ (x_1 \cdot h_2^\mu \cdot \prod_{j \in S_1} y_j)^s, \ldots, (x_a \cdot h_2^\mu \cdot \prod_{j \in S_a} y_j)^s,\ g^s\ \right) \in \mathbb{G}^{a+1}.$$

The algorithm outputs the pair (Hdr, K).

Decrypt(d_i, S, Hdr, PK): Assume user i is assigned to index v within the subset S_u, and decrypts the Hdr using his private key $d_i = (d_{i,1}, d_{i,2}, d_{i,3}, k_{i,1}, \ldots, k_{i,v-1}, k_{i,v+1}, \ldots, k_{i,b})$. Let Hdr $= (A_1, \ldots, A_a, B)$. Compute $\mu' = H_k(B)$ and check that the following equality

$$e(A_u,\ g) = e(x_u \cdot h_2^{\mu'} \cdot \prod_{j \in S_u} y_j,\ B)$$

holds. If not, output $\perp$. Otherwise, output

$$K = e(d_{i,1} \cdot d_{i,2}^{\mu'} \cdot \prod_{\substack{j \in S_u \\ j \ne v}} k_{i,j},\ B)\ /\ e(A_u,\ d_{i,3}).$$

Note that the pair $\left(d_{i,1} \cdot d_{i,2}^{\mu'} \cdot \prod_{\substack{j \in S_u \\ j \ne v}} k_{i,j},\ d_{i,3}\right)$ is chosen from the following distribution

$$\left(\ h_1^\alpha \cdot (x_u \cdot h_2^{\mu'} \cdot \prod_{j \in S_u} y_j)^{\tilde r},\ g^{\tilde r}\ \right)$$

where $\tilde r$ is uniform in $\mathbb{Z}_p$. Next, the correctness of decryption algorithm is checked by the similar calculation to the one in Section 3.1.

5.2 Security

As opposed to the $(b+1)$-BDHE assumption for the semantic security in Section 3, the CCA security of the above b-PKBE scheme is based on the $(b+2)$-BDHE assumption.

Theorem 2. *Suppose that the decision $(t_1, \epsilon_1, b+2)$-BDHE assumption holds in $\mathbb{G}$ and the family of hash function $\{H_k\}$ is (t_2, ϵ_2)-collision resistant. Then the previous b-PKBE scheme is $(t_3, \epsilon_3, n, q_D)$-CCA secure for $t_3 < t_1 - \Theta(\tau b n)$ and $\epsilon_1 + \epsilon_2 \geq \epsilon_3$, where τ is the maximum time for an exponentiation in $\mathbb{G}$.*

Proof. Suppose there exists an adversary $\mathcal{A}$ which has advantage ϵ_3 in attacking the b-PKBE scheme. We build an algorithm $\mathcal{B}$ that uses $\mathcal{A}$ to solve the decision $(b+2)$-BDHE problem in $\mathbb{G}$. For a generator $g \in \mathbb{G}$ and $\alpha \in \mathbb{Z}_p$, let $g_i = g^{(\alpha^i)} \in \mathbb{G}$. On input $(z, g, g_1, \ldots, g_{b+1}, g_{b+3}, \ldots, g_{2b+2}, T)$, $\mathcal{B}$ outputs 1 if $T = e(z, g_{b+2})$ and 0 otherwise. $\mathcal{B}$ works by interacting with $\mathcal{A}$ as follows:

Init: $\mathcal{A}$ outputs a set S^* that it intends to attack.
Setup: $\mathcal{B}$ first divides the challenge set S^* into subsets $\mathsf{S}_1^*, \ldots, \mathsf{S}_a^*$. To generate a public key PK, $\mathcal{B}$ first computes $\mu^* = H_k(z)$ and selects two random $\rho, \tau \in \mathbb{Z}_p$. It sets $h_1 = g_{b+1} \cdot g^\rho$ and $h_2 = g_{b+1} \cdot g^\tau$. Next, it picks random $\gamma_1, \ldots, \gamma_b, \delta_1, \ldots, \delta_a \in \mathbb{Z}_p$. It sets $y_i = g^{\gamma_i} g_i$ for $i = 1, \ldots, b$ and sets $x_j = g^{\delta_j} \cdot (\prod_{k \in \mathsf{S}_j^*} g_k)^{-1} \cdot g_{b+1}^{-\mu^*}$ for $j = 1, \ldots, a$. Finally, $\mathcal{B}$ gives $\mathcal{A}$ the public key

$$\mathsf{PK} = (g, g_1, h_1, h_2, x_1, \ldots, x_a, y_1, \ldots, y_b).$$

Since $\rho, \tau, \{\gamma_i\}$, and $\{\delta_j\}$ values are chosen uniformly at random, this public key has an identical distribution to that in the actual construction.

Next, $\mathcal{B}$ needs to generate private keys d_i for $i \notin \mathsf{S}^*$. Consider a private key for user i such that $i = (u-1)b + v$ for some $1 \leq u \leq a$ and $1 \leq v \leq b$. $\mathcal{B}$ picks a random $r \in \mathbb{Z}_p$. Let $\tilde{r} = r - \alpha^{(b+2-v)}$. $\mathcal{B}$ generates the private key d_i for user i as

$$\left(h_1^\alpha \cdot (x_u \cdot y_v)^{\tilde{r}}, \, h_2^{\tilde{r}}, \, g^{\tilde{r}}, \, y_1^{\tilde{r}}, \ldots, y_{v-1}^{\tilde{r}}, \ldots, y_{v+1}^{\tilde{r}}, \ldots, y_b^{\tilde{r}} \right)$$

which is a properly distributed private key for user i. By the similar calculation to that in Section 3, we can show that $\mathcal{B}$ is able to compute all elements of this private key given the input values, except $h_2^{\tilde{r}}$. The term $h_2^{\tilde{r}}$ becomes

$$h_2^{\tilde{r}} = (g_{b+1} \cdot g^\tau)^r \cdot (g_{2b+3-v} \cdot g_{b+2-v}^\tau)^{-1}.$$

Since $1 \leq v \leq b$, the unknown value g_{b+2} is not required to compute $h_2^{\tilde{r}}$.
Query Phase 1: Let $(i, \mathsf{S}, \mathsf{Hdr})$ be a decryption query where $\mathsf{S} \subseteq \mathsf{S}^*$ and $i \in \mathsf{S}$. Let $\mathsf{Hdr} = (A_1, \ldots, A_a, B)$. Wlog, let $i = (u-1)b + v$. When we divide S into subsets $(\mathsf{S}_1, \ldots, \mathsf{S}_a)$, we have that $i \in \mathsf{S}_u \subseteq \mathsf{S}_u^*$. To decrypt the queried ciphertext, $\mathcal{B}$ does as follows:

1. Compute $\mu' = H_k(B)$ and check if the components (A_u, B) in the Hdr are of the valid form, using the following equation
$$e(A_u, g) = e(x_u \cdot h_2^{\mu'} \cdot \prod_{k \in S_u} y_k, B).$$
   If the equality does not hold, $\mathcal{B}$ responds with $\bot$.

2. Otherwise, check that $\mu' = \mu^*$. If the equality holds, $\mathcal{B}$ outputs a random bit $b \in \{0,1\}$ and aborts the simulation (in this case, the collision of hash function H_k occurs).

3. Otherwise, from the equation above, $\mathcal{B}$ has that $A_u = (x_u \cdot h_2^{\mu'} \cdot \prod_{k \in S_u} y_k)^s$ for some (unknown) $s \in \mathbb{Z}_p$ such that $B = g^s$. Plugging in the values of x_u, h_2, and y_k, the A_u becomes

$$A_u = \left(g^{\delta_u} \cdot \left(\prod_{k \in S_u^*} g_k\right)^{-1} \cdot g_{b+1}^{-\mu^*} \cdot (g_{b+1} g^{\tau})^{\mu'} \cdot \prod_{k \in S_u} g^{\gamma_k} g_k\right)^s$$
$$= \left(g_{b+1}^{(\mu' - \mu^*)} \cdot g^{\eta} \cdot \prod_{k \in S_u^* \setminus S_u} g_k\right)^s$$

where $\eta = \delta_u + \tau \mu' + \Sigma_{k \in S_u} \gamma_k$. $\mathcal{B}$ computes

$$\tilde{d}_{i,1} = g_1^{-\eta/(\mu' - \mu^*)} \cdot A_u \cdot \left(\prod_{k \in S_u^* \setminus S_u} g_{k+1}\right)^{-1/(\mu' - \mu^*)}, \quad \tilde{d}_{i,3} = B \cdot g_1^{-1/(\mu' - \mu^*)}.$$

Since $1 \leq k \leq b$, $\mathcal{B}$ does not require knowledge of g_{b+2} and then is able to compute $\tilde{d}_{i,1}$ with input values. Let $\tilde{r} = s - \alpha/(\mu' - \mu^*)$. Then,

$$\tilde{d}_{i,1} = g_1^{-\eta/(\mu' - \mu^*)} \left(g_{b+1}^{(\mu' - \mu^*)} \cdot g^{\eta} \cdot \prod_{k \in S_u^* \setminus S_u} g_k\right)^s \left(\prod_{k \in S_u^* \setminus S_u} g_{k+1}\right)^{-1/(\mu' - \mu^*)}$$
$$= g_{b+2} \cdot \left(g_{b+1}^{(\mu' - \mu^*)} \cdot g^{\eta} \cdot \prod_{k \in S_u^* \setminus S_u} g_k\right)^{\tilde{r}}$$
$$= g_{b+2} \cdot \left(x_u \cdot h_2^{\mu'} \cdot \prod_{k \in S_u} y_k\right)^{\tilde{r}},$$
$$\tilde{d}_{i,3} = g^s \cdot g_1^{-1/(\mu' - \mu^*)} = g^{\tilde{r}}.$$

Recall that $h_1^{\alpha} = g_{b+2} \cdot g_1^{\rho}$. For the re-randomization, $\mathcal{B}$ selects a random $r' \in \mathbb{Z}_p$ and computes $\tilde{d}'_{i,1} = \tilde{d}_{i,1} \cdot g_1^{\rho} \cdot (x_u \cdot h_2^{\mu'} \cdot \prod_{k \in S_u} y_k)^{r'}$ and $\tilde{d}'_{i,3} = \tilde{d}_{i,3} \cdot g^{r'}$. For some (unknown) $\tilde{r}' = \tilde{r} + r'$,

$$\tilde{d}'_{i,1} = h_1^{\alpha} \cdot \left(x_u \cdot h_2^{\mu'} \cdot \prod_{k \in S_u} y_k\right)^{\tilde{r}'}, \quad \tilde{d}'_{i,3} = g^{\tilde{r}'}.$$

$\mathcal{B}$ responds with $e(\tilde{d}'_{i,1}, B)/e(A_u, \tilde{d}'_{i,3})$. This response is identical to the Decrypt algorithm in a real attack, because r' (and $\tilde{r}'$) is uniform in $\mathbb{Z}_p$.

Challenge: $\mathcal{B}$ computes Hdr^* as $(z^{\delta_1+\tau\mu^*+\sum_{k\in\mathsf{S}_1^*}\gamma_k}, \ldots, z^{\delta_a+\tau\mu^*+\sum_{k\in\mathsf{S}_a^*}\gamma_k}, z)$ and $K^* = T \cdot e(g_1, z^\rho)$, where z and T are input values given to $\mathcal{B}$. Recall that $\mu^* = H_k(z)$. As before, if $z = g^c$ for some (unknown) $c \in \mathbb{Z}_p$, then

$$z^{\delta_i+\tau\mu^*+\sum_{k\in\mathsf{S}_i^*}\gamma_k} = \left(g^{\delta_i} \cdot \left(\prod_{k\in\mathsf{S}_i^*} g_k\right)^{-1} \cdot g_{b+1}^{-\mu^*} \cdot (g_{b+1}g^\tau)^{\mu^*} \cdot \prod_{k\in\mathsf{S}_i^*} g^{\gamma_k} g_k\right)^c$$

$$= \left(x_i \cdot h_2^{\mu^*} \cdot \prod_{k\in\mathsf{S}_i^*} y_j\right)^c$$

for $i = 1, \ldots, a$. If $T = e(z, g_{b+2})$ then $K^* = e(h_1, g_1)^c$ and thus (Hdr^*, K^*) is a valid challenge to $\mathcal{A}$ for the receiver set S^*. On the other hand, when T is uniform and independent in $\mathbb{G}_T$, then Hdr^* is independent of K^* in the adversary's view.

Query Phase 2: $\mathcal{A}$ issues more decryption queries. $\mathcal{B}$ responds as in query phase 1.

Guess: $\mathcal{A}$ outputs a guess $b' \in \{0,1\}$. If $b = b'$ then $\mathcal{B}$ outputs 1, indicating $T = e(z, g_{b+2})$. Otherwise, it outputs 0, indicating $T \neq e(z, g_{b+2})$.

When T is random in $\mathbb{G}_T$ then $\Pr[\mathcal{B}(z, g, \vec{g}_{\alpha,b+1}, T) = 0] = 1/2$. Let Collision denote the event that $\mathcal{A}$ submits a valid header $\mathsf{Hdr} = (A_1, \ldots, A_a, B)$ such that $\mu^* = H_k(B)$ as a decryption query. In the case of Collision, $\mathcal{B}$ cannot reply to the decryption query and aborts the simulation. When $T = e(z, g_{b+2})$, $\mathcal{B}$ replied with a valid message encryption key unless event Collision occurs. Then, $\mathcal{B}$ has

$$\left|\Pr[\mathcal{B}(z, g, \vec{g}_{\alpha,b+1}, T) = 0] - \frac{1}{2}\right| \geq \left|\Pr[b = b' \wedge \overline{\mathsf{Collision}}] - \frac{1}{2}\right| - \Pr[\mathsf{Collision}].$$

Since $\mathcal{B}$ provided $\mathcal{A}$ with perfect simulation when event Collision did not occur, $|\Pr[b = b' \wedge \overline{\mathsf{Collision}}] - 1/2| \geq \epsilon_3$. Also, note that $\Pr[\mathsf{Collision}]$ is negligible. This means that $\Pr[\mathsf{Collision}] < \epsilon_2$ since otherwise $\mathcal{B}$ finds two values z, B such that $H_k(z) = H_k(B)$, which is contradiction to the definition of H. Therefore,

$$\left|\Pr[\mathcal{B}(z, g, \vec{g}_{\alpha,b+1}, e(z, g_{b+2})) = 0] - \Pr[\mathcal{B}(z, g, \vec{g}_{\alpha,b+1}, T) = 0]\right| \geq \epsilon_3 - \epsilon_2.$$

This completes the proof of Theorem 2. □

6 Conclusion

We presented an alternative PKBE scheme which is fully collusion-secure, based on the idea of generating private keys in the BBG HIBE scheme [2]. Our construction shows that a HIBE scheme can be another primitive for building a PKBE scheme. Our resulting scheme provided a trade-off between ciphertext size and public key size as in the BGW scheme [4]. With the appropriate parametrization we achieved a new PKBE scheme which has $O(\sqrt{n})$ ciphertexts and $O(\sqrt{n} - \tilde{r})$ private keys, where $\tilde{r}$ is the minimum number of revoked users in divided subsets. The public key size can be more shortened than the BGW and DPP schemes [10], and decryption time is as efficient as in the BGW scheme.

References

1. Boneh, D., Boyen, X.: Efficient selective-ID secure identity based encryption without random oracles. In: Cachin, C., Camenisch, J.L. (eds.) EUROCRYPT 2004. LNCS, vol. 3027, pp. 223–238. Springer, Heidelberg (2004)
2. Boneh, D., Boyen, X., Goh, E.: Hierarchical identity based encryption with constant size ciphertext. In: Cramer, R.J.F. (ed.) EUROCRYPT 2005. LNCS, vol. 3494, pp. 440–456. Springer, Heidelberg (2005)
3. Boneh, D., Franklin, M.: Identity-based encryption from the Weil pairing. In: Kilian, J. (ed.) CRYPTO 2001. LNCS, vol. 2139, pp. 213–229. Springer, Heidelberg (2001)
4. Boneh, D., Gentry, C., Waters, B.: Collusion resistant broadcast encryption with short ciphertexts and private keys. In: Shoup, V. (ed.) CRYPTO 2005. LNCS, vol. 3621, pp. 258–275. Springer, Heidelberg (2005)
5. Boneh, D., Katz, J.: Improved efficiency for CCA-secure cryptosystems built using identity-based encryption. In: Menezes, A. (ed.) CT-RSA 2005. LNCS, vol. 3376, pp. 87–103. Springer, Heidelberg (2005)
6. Boyen, X., Mei, Q., Waters, B.: Direct chosen ciphertext security from identity-based techniques. In: ACM Conference on Computer and Communications Security - CCS 2005, pp. 320–329. ACM Press, New-York (2005)
7. Canetti, C., Halevi, S., Katz, J.: Chosen ciphertext security from identity-based encryption. In: Cachin, C., Camenisch, J.L. (eds.) EUROCRYPT 2004. LNCS, vol. 3027, pp. 207–222. Springer, Heidelberg (2004)
8. Dodis, Y., Fazio, N.: Public key broadcast encryption for stateless receivers. In: Feigenbaum, J. (ed.) DRM 2002. LNCS, vol. 2696, pp. 61–80. Springer, Heidelberg (2003)
9. Dodis, Y., Fazio, N.: Public key broadcast encryption secure against adaptive chosen ciphertext attack. In: Desmedt, Y.G. (ed.) PKC 2003. LNCS, vol. 2567, pp. 100–115. Springer, Heidelberg (2002)
10. Delerablee, C., Paillier, P., Pointcheval, D.: Fully collusion secure dynamic broadcast encryption with constant-size ciphertexts or decryption keys. In: Takagi, T., Okamoto, T., Okamoto, E., Okamoto, T. (eds.) Pairing 2007. LNCS, vol. 4575, pp. 39–59. Springer, Heidelberg (2007)
11. Fiat, A., Naor, M.: Broadcast encryption. In: Stinson, D.R. (ed.) CRYPTO 1993. LNCS, vol. 773, pp. 480–491. Springer, Heidelberg (1994)
12. Gentry, C., Silverberg, A.: Hierarchical ID-based cryptography. In: Zheng, Y. (ed.) ASIACRYPT 2002. LNCS, vol. 2501, pp. 548–566. Springer, Heidelberg (2002)
13. Goodrich, M.T., Sun, J.Z., Tamassia, R.: Efficient tree-based revocation in groups of low-state devices. In: Franklin, M. (ed.) CRYPTO 2004. LNCS, vol. 3152, pp. 511–527. Springer, Heidelberg (2004)
14. Halevi, D., Shamir, A.: The lsd broadcast encryption scheme. In: Yung, M. (ed.) CRYPTO 2002. LNCS, vol. 2442, pp. 47–60. Springer, Heidelberg (2002)
15. Naor, D., Naor, M., Lotspiech, J.: Revocation and tracing schemes for stateless receivers. In: Kilian, J. (ed.) CRYPTO 2001. LNCS, vol. 2139, pp. 41–62. Springer, Heidelberg (2001)
16. Naor, M., Pinkas, B.: Efficient trace and revoke schemes. In: Frankel, Y. (ed.) FC 2000. LNCS, vol. 1962, pp. 1–20. Springer, Heidelberg (2001)

RSA Moduli with a Predetermined Portion: Techniques and Applications

Marc Joye

Thomson R&D France
Technology Group, Corporate Research, Security Laboratory
1 avenue Belle Fontaine, 35576 Cesson-Sévigné Cedex, France
marc.joye@thomson.net
http://www.geocities.com/MarcJoye/

Abstract. This paper discusses methods for generating RSA moduli with a predetermined portion. Predetermining a portion enables to represent RSA moduli in a compressed way, which gives rise to reduced transmission- and storage requirements. The first method described in this paper achieves the compression rate of known methods but is fully compatible with the fastest prime generation algorithms available on constrained devices. This is useful for devising a key escrow mechanism when RSA keys are generated on-board by tamper-resistant devices like smart cards. The second method in this paper is a compression technique yielding a compression rate of about 2/3 instead of 1/2. This results in higher savings in both transmission and storage of RSA moduli. In a typical application, a 2048-bit RSA modulus can fit on only 86 bytes (instead of 256 bytes for the regular representation). Of independent interest, the methods for prescribing bits in RSA moduli can be used to reduce the computational burden in a variety of cryptosystems.

Keywords: RSA-type cryptosystems, RSA moduli, RSA key lengths, diminished-radix moduli, key compression, key generation, key transport, key storage, key transmission, key escrow, tamper-resistant devices, smart cards, kleptography, setup.

1 Introduction

In 1976, Diffie and Hellman introduced the concept of public-key cryptography [11]. Soon after Rivest, Shamir, and Adleman proposed a concrete realization that works for encryption as well as for digital signatures: the so-called RSA algorithm [26]. RSA has withstood years of extensive cryptanalysis (see e.g. [4]) and is still the most widely deployed and used public-key cryptosystem.

The security of RSA relies on the problem of factoring large numbers, or more exactly, on the problem of computing roots modulo a large composite number. The largest factored RSA modulus is RSA-200 (663 bits), whose factorization was reported by a team of German researchers on May 2005 [28]. Current RSA-based applications typically use 1024-bit RSA moduli but we observe a trend to push for larger moduli like 2048 bits or 4096 bits. It is meaningless to define a threshold value for the key length separating security from insecurity. Security is defined relatively to a security model: the adversarial goal and the adversary's resources. Further, it is highly dependent on the implementation. There is no need for strong cryptographic algorithms if they are poorly implemented. Clearly, selecting the "appropriate" key length for a given application is a touchy problem. A recent list of recommended key lengths and guidelines is provided in [12].

At first glance, the safe approach would be to increase the key length to (hopefully) increase the security level. Amdahl's law applied to security says that strengthening a secure part (in this case using larger keys) does not help much [16]. A system is as secure as its weakest point and cryptography is rarely the weakest point. More importantly, the use of larger keys comes at a cost. First, it affects the performance in terms of speed. Second, larger keys consume more bandwidth. Third, larger keys imply more memory requirements for their storage. This last point is particularly relevant for constrained devices whose price is mainly dictated by the size of their different memories.

This paper is aimed at mitigating the impacts resulting from the use of larger RSA keys. We develop simple methods to reduce considerably the transmission and storage requirements of RSA moduli. We show how to construct RSA moduli where many bits can be prescribed. Furthermore, such RSA moduli can give rise to substantial speed improvements.

Let n denote the bit length of an RSA modulus and t the number of prescribed bits. If the prescribed portion of the RSA moduli is shared among a group of users, only $(n-t)$ bits are needed to represent the RSA modulus of each user together with a single copy of the t bits used by the entire group. Another scenario is to use t bits of an RSA modulus to represent the user's identity and other publicly available information. In this case, there is no need to store or to transmit the value of those t bits and an RSA modulus can be encoded with only $(n-t)$ bits. Alternatively, one can imagine that a string of t bits is constructed by applying a public function to some seed σ. An RSA modulus is then represented by σ and $(n-t)$ bits; the so-obtained representation is particularly advantageous for short σ's. Yet another application is to make use of t bits of an RSA modulus to convey certain information. This information may appear in clear or in an encrypted form. An example of the first case is presented in [22] where the representation of a DSA prime, $p = \alpha q + 1$, embeds the value of prime divisor q and a certificate of proper generation. The second case (namely, encrypted form) can be helpful for key-escrow purposes. For example, t bits of public modulus N can be used to encode the encryption of the corresponding private key or a part thereof.

A modulus N is called a diminished-radix (DR) modulus if it has the special form $N = 2^n - \mu$ for some $\mu < 2^{n-t}$. DR moduli are attractive for implementing the RSA (see, e.g., [21,24,34]) because they greatly simplify the modular reductions, which can be computed with only shifts, additions and single-precision multiplications. RSA moduli N can also be constructed under a sparse form, that is, with a reduced Hamming weight. This can be useful for the Paillier cryptosystem [25] and its derivatives where one computes N^{th} powers.

1.1 Related Work

In [33], Vanstone and Zuccherato described several methods for generating RSA moduli with a predetermined portion. Typically, for a n-bit RSA modulus, they were able to specify up to $n/2$ bits but in a rather inefficient way. They also proposed a faster method for specifying up to $n/4$ bits, as well as mixed methods of intermediate efficiency for specifying between $n/4$ and $n/2$ bits. A much simpler yet more secure method for specifying up to $n/2$ bits was later presented at ASIACRYPT '98 by Lenstra. This method appears to have being reinvented many times (see [18] and the references therein). It is similar to the method given in [17] for producing RSA moduli with many leading 1-bits and further discussed in [20]. More recently, Shparlinski [29] considered an alternative approach and derived a method with a rigorous analysis for specifying about $n/4$ bits. In [2] (see also [3]), Bernstein reports an unpublished result by Coppersmith for specifying up to $2n/3$ bits using lattice reduction.

Methods for prescribing part of the public key are also found in key-escrow systems: authorities want decryption keys to be escrowed for law enforcement purposes. Pairs of public/private keys are generated using a setup (secretly embedded trapdoor with universal protection) mechanism [35,36] by trusted third parties or tamper-resistant devices. The notion of setup is related to that of subliminal channel due to Simmons [30] (see also [10]). The setup allows the secure leakage of the private key from the corresponding public key. For RSA cryptosystem, RSA modulus $N = pq$ (and/or public exponent e) is used to secretly embed a representation of secret factor p [35] (see also [10]) or private RSA exponent d [9].

1.2 Our Contribution

A simple yet efficient method for constructing RSA moduli with a predetermined portion referred to as 'folklore method' is given in [18]. This method enables to specify about half the bits of an RSA modulus. This paper presents other methods for generating such moduli and discusses associated applications.

The first method is a simple variation of the folklore method. It generates an RSA modulus $N = pq$ with a predetermined portion (up to its half) by randomly generating prime p and then prime q from a *prescribed interval*. The folklore method proceeds similarly except that prime q is constructed incrementally, which may result in prohibitively too long running times for constrained devices like smart cards. We note that the fastest smart-card implementations of prime generation algorithms [14] (see also [15]) require primes p and q to be chosen in a prescribed interval. Efficient generation of RSA moduli with a predetermined portion on smart cards is particularly relevant for key-escrow purposes as this additional feature is often implemented through tamper resistance.

The second method makes use of an extended version of Euclid's algorithm and enables to generate RSA moduli where about the *two thirds* can be prescribed. Prescribing more than one half is for example very useful to ensure the interoperability of RSA-enabled devices with different key lengths. There are still programs and/or devices designed in a way such that they cannot accommodate

RSA moduli larger than 1024 bits whereas many applications are now requiring at least 2048-bit RSA moduli. Using the folklore method, a 2048-bit RSA modulus can be represented in compact form with 1024 bits *plus* the seed needed to recover the predetermined portion and so will not fit in a 1024-bit memory buffer. If now the two thirds can be predetermined, this is possible since only 683 bits plus the seed are needed to represent a 2048-bit RSA modulus. More generally, achieving a higher compression rate is always useful because this leads to more savings in both storage and bandwidth.

The rest of this paper is organized as follows. In the next section, we provide some necessary definitions and notation. We also review the folklore method for generating RSA moduli with a predetermined portion. In Section 3 and 4, we improve on it and present relevant applications. Section 3 describes an efficient escrow mechanism for RSA keys well suited for constrained tamper-resistant devices like smart cards. Section 4 presents highly compact representations of RSA keys which greatly reduce the storage and transmission requirements. Finally, we conclude in Section 5.

2 Preliminaries and Notation

We first introduce some notation. The concatenation of two bit strings X_0 and X_1 is denoted by $X_0 \| X_1$. To ease the presentation, we do not make the distinction between an integer and its representation. For an integer X, we denote by $|X|_2$ the bit length of X. By an ℓ-bit integer, we mean an integer X such that $2^{\ell-1} \leqslant X < 2^\ell$, that is, $|X|_2 = \ell$.

Throughout this paper and unless otherwise specified, we consider a n-bit RSA modulus $N = pq$ which is the product of two large primes where p is a $(n-n_0)$-bit prime and q is a n_0-bit prime, for some $1 < n_0 < n$. Without loss of generality, we assume that $|p|_2 \leqslant |q|_2$, or equivalently, that $2n_0 \geqslant n$.

2.1 RSA Primitive

For a public exponent e with $\gcd(e, \lambda(N)) = 1$, the corresponding private exponent d satisfies the relation

$$ed \equiv 1 \pmod{\lambda(N)},$$

where λ is Carmichael's function. For $N = pq$, we have $\lambda(N) = \operatorname{lcm}(p-1, q-1)$. Given $x < N$, the public operation (e.g., message encryption or signature verification) consists in raising x to the e-th power modulo N, i.e., in computing $y = x^e \bmod N$. Then, given y, the corresponding private operation (e.g., decryption of a ciphertext or signature generation) consists in computing $y^d \bmod N$. From the definition of e and d, it readily follows that $y^d \equiv x \pmod{N}$. The private operation can also be carried out at higher speed through Chinese remaindering (CRT mode). Computations are then independently performed modulo p and q and then recombined.

To sum up, a n-bit RSA modulus $N = pq$ is the product of two large prime integers p and q such that $|p|_2 = n - n_0$, $|q|_2 = n_0$, and $\gcd(p-1,e) = \gcd(q-1,e) = 1$. For security reasons, so-called 'balanced' RSA moduli are generally preferred, which means $n = 2n_0$.

2.2 Folklore Method

We review a simple yet efficient method for fixing the leading bits of N. The goal is to construct an RSA modulus N of the form $N = N_H \| N_L$ and where the leading portion, N_H, is predetermined.

Letting t the bit length of N_H, we can write

$$N = N_H\, 2^{n-t} + N_L \quad \text{for some } 0 < N_L < 2^{n-t} \;. \tag{1}$$

We follow the presentation of [18]. For some integer $t' \leqslant t$, pick at random a $(n-t')$-bit prime p such that $\gcd(p-1,e) = 1$. Define $N' = N_H\, 2^{n-t}$ and upper round it to the nearest multiple of p to get $q' = \lceil \frac{N'}{p} \rceil$. Find the smallest nonnegative integer m such that $q = q' + m$ is prime and $\gcd(q-1,e) = 1$. If $N = pq$ satisfies Eq. (1) then return $\{N_L, p, q\}$; otherwise re-iterate the process.

We note that several variations of the previous method can be found in [18].

3 Escrowing RSA Keys

Key escrow allows one to get access to the decryption keys. This can be helpful in certain situations. For example, if an employee leaves her company without returning her private key, a key-escrow mechanism enables to ensure that data intended to this employee is not lost. A key-escrow mechanism can also be used by a manager to read all data of employees within her organization.

In the case of an RSA modulus $N = pq$, the knowledge of about half the bits of p suffices to recover the private key using lattice reduction techniques [6] (see also [5,7,8]). Therefore if about half the bits of p are encrypted under some secret key K and embedded in the representation of public RSA modulus N then, from N, an 'authority' knowing key K can reconstruct p and thus compute the corresponding private RSA key. Alternative techniques are described in [9].

Remark 1. When RSA key generation is performed on-board in smart cards, it is desirable that secret key K is not shared by all smart cards. It is much better that each employee Id — where Id is a unique identifier (e.g., email address, badge number, ...) — has a different secret key, say K_{Id}, embedded in the tamper-resistant memory of her smart card. To facilitate the key management, the key-escrow authority may hold a master secret key K from which the employees' keys, K_{Id}'s, can be derived.

The folklore method can be adapted to this end. We present a solution in Algorithm 1. It requires a secure length-preserving symmetric cipher $\mathcal{E}$ that on input a plaintext x and a key K_{Id} returns the ciphertext $c = \mathcal{E}_{K_{Id}}(x)$.

Algorithm 1. Given key lengths n, n_0 and public exponent e, this algorithm outputs an *escrowed* n-bit RSA modulus $N = pq$ with $|p|_2 = n - n_0$ and $|q|_2 = n_0$, and private exponent d.

1. [Prime p] Generate a random prime $p \in [2^{n-n_0-1}+1, 2^{n-n_0}-1]$ such that $\gcd(p-1,e) = 1$.
2. [SETUP] Let p_h denote the κ high-order bits of p,
$$p_h = \left\lfloor \frac{p}{2^{n-n_0-\kappa}} \right\rfloor \quad \text{with } \kappa = \lceil (n-1)/4 \rceil \ .$$
Define
$$N_H = 1 \| \mathcal{E}_{\mathsf{K}_{\mathsf{ld}}}(p_h) \quad \text{and} \quad \kappa' = |N_H|_2 = \kappa + 1 \ .$$
3. [Prime q] Generate a random prime
$$q \in \left[\left\lfloor \frac{2^{n-\kappa'} N_H}{p} \right\rfloor + 1, \left\lfloor \frac{2^{n-\kappa'}(N_H+1)-1}{p} \right\rfloor \right] \quad (2)$$
such that $\gcd(q-1,e) = 1$.
4. [Output] Return $N = pq$ and $d = e^{-1} \bmod (p-1)(q-1)$.

3.1 Analysis

In contrast with the folklore method, the two primes in the RSA key generation of Algorithm 1 lie in a prescribed interval. Their generation can therefore fully benefit from the fast prime generation techniques in [14] (see also [15]).

Suppose we have to generate a prime $q \in [q_{\min}, q_{\max}]$. Basically, define Π as the product of many primes so that $\Pi \leqslant q_{\max} - q_{\min}$ and $\phi(\Pi)/\Pi$ is as small as possible (and thus contains a maximum number of small primes).[1,2] Define also an element $a \in (\mathbb{Z}/\Pi\mathbb{Z})^*$. Next, for a random element $k \in (\mathbb{Z}/\Pi\mathbb{Z})^*$ and a random $T \in [q_{\min}, q_{\max}+1-\Pi]$, find the smallest nonnegative integer i such that
$$q = [(a^i k - T) \bmod \Pi] + T \quad (3)$$
is prime. This method presents the advantage that all candidates tested for primality are by construction already coprime to Π: $q \equiv a^i k \pmod{\Pi} \in (\mathbb{Z}/\Pi\mathbb{Z})^*$. The expected number of candidates to be tried heuristically amounts to
$$n_0 \ln 2 \, \frac{\phi(\Pi)}{\Pi} \quad (4)$$
where $n_0 = |q|_2$ (cf. [14, Section 2.3]).

The next proposition shows that the interval $[q_{\min}, q_{\max}]$ in Step 3 of Algorithm 1 is optimal w.r.t. the above prime generation (Eq. (3)).

---
[1] ϕ denotes Euler's totient function; $\phi(\Pi) = \#(\mathbb{Z}/\Pi\mathbb{Z})^*$.
[2] In smart card implementations, parameter Π is predetermined before compile time and hard-coded in the prime generation routine. As a consequence, since the values of $q_{\min}$ and $q_{\max}$ depend on p and so change at each execution, parameter Π should be chosen as the largest possible value so that the relation $\Pi \leqslant q_{\max} - q_{\min}$ will always be satisfied.

Proposition 1. *The integer interval q is chosen from is maximal and contains (at least) $2^{n_0-\kappa'}$ elements.*

Proof. Define $q_{\min} = \lfloor \frac{2^{n-\kappa'} N_H}{p} \rfloor + 1$ and $q_{\max} = \lfloor \frac{2^{n-\kappa'}(N_H+1)-1}{p} \rfloor$. We have

$$p\, q_{\min} = p \left\lfloor \frac{2^{n-\kappa'} N_H}{p} \right\rfloor + p$$
$$= 2^{n-\kappa'} N_H + p - (2^{n-\kappa'} N_H \bmod p) = N_H \| N_L^{(\min)}$$

with $1 \leqslant N_L^{(\min)} = p - (2^{n-\kappa'} N_H \bmod p) \leqslant p$. Therefore, since the least significant bit of N_L must be 1, we see that $p\,(q_{\min} - 1)$ cannot be of the required form. Likewise, we have

$$p\, q_{\max} = p \left\lfloor \frac{2^{n-\kappa'}(N_H+1) - 1}{p} \right\rfloor$$
$$= 2^{n-\kappa'} N_H + 2^{n-\kappa'} - 1 - ([2^{n-\kappa'}(N_H+1) - 1] \bmod p) = N_H \| N_L^{(\max)}$$

with $2^{n-\kappa'} - p \leqslant N_L^{(\max)} = 2^{n-\kappa'} - 1 - ([2^{n-\kappa'}(N_H+1) - 1] \bmod p) \leqslant 2^{n-\kappa'} - 1$, and $p\,(q_{\max} + 1)$ cannot be of the required form. Consequently, the interval is maximal.

For the second part of the proposition, we have

$$q_{\max} = \left\lfloor \frac{2^{n-\kappa'}(N_H+1) - 1}{p} \right\rfloor \geqslant \left\lfloor \frac{2^{n-\kappa'} N_H}{p} \right\rfloor + \left\lfloor \frac{2^{n-\kappa'} - 1}{p} \right\rfloor \,.$$

So, we get

$$q_{\max} - q_{\min} \geqslant \left\lfloor \frac{2^{n-\kappa'} - 1}{p} \right\rfloor - 1 \geqslant \left\lfloor \frac{2^{n-\kappa'} - 1}{2^{n-n_0} - 1} \right\rfloor - 1 \geqslant 2^{n_0 - \kappa'} - 1$$

since $n - \kappa' = n - (1 + \lceil (n-1)/4 \rceil) \geqslant n - (1 + \lceil (2n_0 - 1)/4 \rceil) \geqslant n - n_0$, which concludes the proof. □

The worst case for the generation of q appears for balanced RSA moduli (i.e., $n = 2n_0$), in which case the length of Π is halved compared to the regular prime generation (i.e., without key escrow). Hence, from Eq. (4) and using the figures given in [15, Fig. 7], we get:

Table 1. Heuristic expected number of primality tests to generate a balanced n-bit RSA moduli with and without key escrow

n	1024	1536	2048
With key escrow	70.73	99.14	126.56
Without key escrow	66.58	93.80	119.96

From this, we conclude that embedding the key-escrow mechanism described in this section has little impact on the overall performance of the RSA key generation. We refer the reader to [18] for security considerations.

3.2 Recovering the Private Key

It remains to explain how to recover a private RSA key corresponding to a given RSA modulus. The technique is based on a powerful result making use of the LLL reduction algorithm [19].

Theorem 1 (Coppersmith). *Let $\mathscr{P}(x,y)$ be an irreducible polynomial in two variables over $\mathbb{Z}$, of maximum degree δ in each variable separately. Let X, Y be bounds on the desired solutions x_0, y_0. Define $\widetilde{\mathscr{P}}(x,y) = \mathscr{P}(xX, yY)$ and let W be the absolute value of the largest coefficient of $\widetilde{\mathscr{P}}$. If*

$$X \cdot Y \leqslant W^{2/(3\delta)}$$

then in time polynomial in $(\log W, 2^\delta)$, we can find all integer pairs (x_0, y_0) with $\mathscr{P}(x_0, y_0) = 0$, $|x_0| < X$, and $|y_0| < Y$.

Proof. See [6, Corollary 2]. □

Let N_H denote the κ' leading bits of n-bit RSA modulus N and let N'_H denote N_H without its most significant bit: $N'_H = N_H \bmod 2^{\kappa'-1}$. Using corresponding secret key K_ld, the key-escrow authority can recover $p_h = \mathcal{E}_{\mathsf{K}_\mathsf{ld}}^{-1}(N'_H)$. For completeness, we show below that if $|p_h|_2 \geqslant \lceil (n-1)/4 \rceil$ then the knowledge of p_h suffices to recover the whole value of p (and thus the corresponding private key). This is an application of Coppersmith's theorem.

Write

$$p = \bar{p} + x_0 \quad \text{and} \quad q = \bar{q} + y_0$$

for some unknown integers x_0 and y_0, and where $\bar{p}$ and $\bar{q}$ are defined by

$$\bar{p} = 2^{n-n_0-\kappa-1}(2p_h + 1) \quad \text{and} \quad \bar{q} = \left\lfloor \frac{N}{\bar{p}} \right\rfloor.$$

It is easily verified that respective bounds X and Y on $|x_0|$ and $|y_0|$ are given by

$$|x_0| < 2^{n-n_0-\kappa-1} = X \quad \text{and} \quad |y_0| < 2^{n_0-\kappa} = Y.$$

Now, define the bivariate polynomial

$$\mathscr{P}(x,y) = (\bar{p}+x)(\bar{q}+y) - N = \bar{q}x + \bar{p}y + xy + (\bar{p}\bar{q} - N),$$

an integer solution of which is (x_0, y_0): $\mathscr{P}(x_0, y_0) = 0$. Corresponding polynomial $\widetilde{\mathscr{P}}$ is given by $\widetilde{\mathscr{P}}(x,y) = \bar{q}X\,x + \bar{p}Y\,y + XY\,xy + (\bar{p}\bar{q} - N)$. Hence, it follows that

$$W := \max\{\bar{q}X, \bar{p}Y, XY, |\bar{p}\bar{q} - N|\} = \bar{p}Y = 2^{n-2\kappa-1}(2p_h + 1)$$
$$\geqslant 2^{n-2\kappa-1}(2^\kappa + 1) > 2^{n-\kappa-1}.$$

Noting that $n - 1 \leqslant 4\kappa$, this yields

$$X \cdot Y = 2^{n-2\kappa-1} \leqslant (2^{n-\kappa-1})^{2/3} < W^{2/3}.$$

Consequently, the conditions of Theorem 1 are satisfied and so the key-escrow authority can recover (x_0, y_0) and thus the two secret factors of RSA modulus N, $p = \bar{p} + x_0$ and $q = \bar{q} + y_0$. The private RSA exponent is then recovered as $d = e^{-1} \bmod (p-1)(q-1)$.

3.3 Variants

Analogously to [33,18], it is possible to fix the trailing bits of modulus N rather than the leading bits. The SETUP phase then defines $N_L = \mathcal{E}_{\mathsf{K}_{\mathsf{Id}}}(p_h)\|1$ and prime q is generated as $q = C + q'\, 2^{\kappa'}$ with $C = N_L/p \bmod 2^{\kappa'}$ for some random q' in

$$\left[\left\lceil \frac{2^{n-1}+1-Cp}{2^{\kappa'}p} \right\rceil, \left\lfloor \frac{2^n - Cp}{2^{\kappa'}p} \right\rfloor\right] .$$

More generally, it is possible to fix some leading bits and some trailing bits of N.

The proposed method can also be adapted to support RSA moduli that are made of more than two factors, for example, 3-prime RSA moduli or RSA moduli of the form $N = p^r\, q$ [31].

4 Compressing RSA Keys

Compressing RSA moduli leads to substantial reductions in storage and transmission requirements. This is even more true as standard bodies and organizations are pushing for increasingly longer RSA keys. In particular, storage requirements can be critical for constrained devices for which RSA moduli are typically stored in EEPROM-like memory, which is expensive. Halving the representation of a 2048-bit modulus already frees 128 bytes in memory. In this section, we will present a method that enables to compress a 2048-bit on only 86 bytes.

As exemplified in the introduction, the techniques of this section can also used to reduce the computational requirements.

We require a mask generating function (MGF). A practical implementation can be found in [1, Appendix A]. The MGF takes on input a seed s_0 and expands it into a binary string of κ' bits. Moreover, we force the leading to 1 so as to obtain a κ'-bit integer, $N_H = 2^{\kappa'-1} \vee \mathtt{MGF}(s_0)$. Primes p and q are then generated so that the κ' leading bits of $N = pq$ represent N_H. The compressed RSA modulus is given by the $(n - \kappa')$ bits of N, N_L. If seed s_0 is not public (or cannot be publicly recovered), it should be returned together with N_L.

Here is the detailed algorithm.

Algorithm 2. Given key lengths n, n_0, public exponent e and compression parameter κ', this algorithm outputs (the representation of) a *compressed* n-bit RSA modulus $N = pq$ with $|p|_2 = n - n_0$ and $|q|_2 = n_0$, $\widetilde{N}$, and private exponent d.

1. [Fixing N_H] Produce a κ'-bit integer N_H from a seed s_0:

$$N_H := 2^{\kappa'-1} \vee \mathtt{MGF}(s_0) \in [2^{\kappa'-1}, 2^{\kappa'} - 1] .$$

2. [Primes p and q] Generate random primes p and q with $\gcd(p-1, e) = \gcd(q-1, e) = 1$, $|p|_2 = n - n_0$, $|q|_2 = n_0$, and such that

$$pq = N_H \| N_L \quad \text{for some } 1 \leqslant N_L < 2^{n-\kappa'} .$$

3. [Output] Return $\widetilde{N} = \{N_L\,[,s_0]\}$ and $d = e^{-1} \bmod (p-1)(q-1)$.

Given the representation $\widetilde{N} = \{N_L\,[,s_0]\}$, anyone can recover the corresponding n-bit RSA modulus N as $N_H \| N_L$ with $N_H = 2^{\kappa'-1} \vee \mathtt{MGF}(s_0)$. We note that decompressing $\widetilde{N}$ to recover N is very fast.

Remark 2. Clearly, Algorithm 1 can be used to generate primes p and q in the previous algorithm. From Eq. (2), we see however that if $2^{n-\kappa'} \leqslant p$ then the interval q is chosen from may be empty and thus κ' should be at most n_0. Therefore, the method of Algorithm 1 can compress at best n-bit RSA moduli up to n_0 bits. For balanced RSA moduli (i.e., $n = 2n_0$), this yields a compression rate of $1/2$.

4.1 Beyond the 1/2 Compression Rate

We consider now higher compression rates, that is, $\kappa' \geqslant n_0 + 1$. From the description of Algorithm 2, we have $N = pq = N_H \| N_L = N_H\, 2^{n-\kappa'} + N_L$, which implies that $N_L = -N_H\, 2^{n-\kappa'} \bmod p$ since $N_L < 2^{n-\kappa'} \leqslant 2^{n-n_0-1} < p$.

Consequently, achieving higher compression rates translates into the problem of finding an $(n - n_0)$-bit prime p such that

$$(-N_H\, 2^{n-\kappa'} \bmod p) < 2^{n-\kappa'}\ .$$

Indeed, letting

$$q = \left\lfloor \frac{N_H\, 2^{n-\kappa'}}{p} \right\rfloor + 1$$

and, provided that it is prime, we obtain

$$pq = N_H\, 2^{n-\kappa'} + \underbrace{p - (N_H\, 2^{n-\kappa'} \bmod p)}_{= N_L < 2^{n-\kappa'}}$$

as required.

The following algorithm derived from Okamoto-Shiraishi's paper [23] (see also [13]) seeks a solution to the above problem.

Algorithm 3. Given key lengths n, n_0, compression parameter κ' and κ'-bit predetermined portion N_H, this algorithm outputs the lower portion N_L of n-bit RSA modulus $N = N_H \| N_L = pq$ with $|p|_2 = n - n_0$ and $|q|_2 = n_0$.

1. [Initialization] Choose a random $(n - n_0)$-bit integer p_0 and define

$$q_0 = \left\lfloor \frac{N_H\, 2^{n-\kappa'}}{p_0} \right\rfloor\ .$$

2. [Euclidean step] Form the list $\mathcal{L}$ of pairs (x_i, y_i) verifying

$$|z_i - x_i\, y_i| < 2^{n-\kappa'-1} \qquad (5)$$

where (x_i, y_i, z_i) are defined as

$$\begin{cases} (z_0, x_0, y_0) = \left((N_H 2^{n-\kappa'} \bmod p_0) + 2^{n-\kappa'-1},\ 0,\ 0\right) \\ (z_i, x_i, y_i) = \left(z_{i-1} \bmod d_i,\ x_{i-1} + \left\lfloor \frac{z_{i-1}}{d_i} \right\rfloor u_i,\ y_{i-1} + \left\lfloor \frac{z_{i-1}}{d_i} \right\rfloor v_i\right) \end{cases}$$

and

$$\begin{cases} (d_0, u_0, v_0) = (p_0,\ 0,\ 1),\quad (d_{-1}, u_{-1}, v_{-1}) = (q_0,\ 1,\ 0) \\ (d_i, u_i, v_i) = \left(d_{i-2} \bmod d_{i-1},\ u_{i-2} - \left\lfloor \frac{d_{i-2}}{d_{i-1}} \right\rfloor u_{i-1},\ v_{i-2} - \left\lfloor \frac{d_{i-2}}{d_{i-1}} \right\rfloor v_{i-1}\right) \end{cases}.$$

3. [Finished?] Find a pair $(x_i, y_i) \in \mathcal{L}$ such that $p = p_0 + x_i$ and $q = q_0 + y_i$ are prime. If no such pair is found, go to Step 1.
4. [Output] Compute $N = (p_0 + x_i)(q_0 + y_i)$ and return $N_L = N \bmod 2^{n-\kappa'}$.

The next proposition shows that a solution returned by the algorithm is of the correct form.

Proposition 2. *Using the notations of Algorithm 2 and provided that $|z_i - x_i y_i| < 2^{n-\kappa'-1}$, any pair (x_i, y_i) verifies*

$$(p_0 + x_i)(q_0 + y_i) = N_H\, 2^{n-\kappa'} + N_L$$

for some $1 \leqslant N_L < 2^{n-\kappa'}$.

Proof. Let $N_L := 2^{n-\kappa'-1} + x_i y_i - z_i$. Since at Step 4, $(x_i, y_i) \in \mathcal{L}$, it follows that (z_i, x_i, y_i) satisfies Eq. (5) and thus $1 \leqslant N_L \leqslant 2^{n-\kappa'} - 1$, as desired.

From this definition of N_L, we also get $z_i = x_i y_i + 2^{n-\kappa'-1} - N_L$, which in turn implies

$$\begin{aligned} q_0 x_i + p_0 y_i + z_i &= q_0 x_i + p_0 y_i + x_i y_i + 2^{n-\kappa'-1} - N_L \\ &= (p_0 + x_i)(q_0 + y_i) - p_0 q_0 + 2^{n-\kappa'-1} - N_L \\ &= N_H\, 2^{n-\kappa'} - p_0 q_0 + 2^{n-\kappa'-1} \\ &= (N_H\, 2^{n-\kappa'} \bmod p_0) + 2^{n-\kappa'-1} \end{aligned} \quad (\dagger)$$

by noting that $p_0 q_0 = p_0 \lfloor N_H 2^{n-\kappa'}/p_0 \rfloor = N_H 2^{n-\kappa'} - (N_H 2^{n-\kappa'} \bmod p_0)$. Moreover, any tuple of (z_i, x_i, y_i) verifies the property

$$q_0 x_i + p_0 y_i + z_i = z_0\ .$$

This easily follows by construction:

$$\begin{aligned} q_0 x_i + p_0 y_i + z_i &= q_0 x_{i-1} + p_0 y_{i-1} + \left\lfloor \tfrac{z_{i-1}}{d_i} \right\rfloor (q_0 u_i + p_0 v_i) + z_i \\ &= q_0 x_{i-1} + p_0 y_{i-1} + \left\lfloor \tfrac{z_{i-1}}{d_i} \right\rfloor d_i + z_i \\ &= q_0 x_{i-1} + p_0 y_{i-1} + z_{i-1} = z_0\ . \end{aligned}$$

Comparing with $(\dagger)$, we see that $\left((N_H 2^{n-\kappa'} \bmod p_0) + 2^{n-\kappa'-1}, 0, 0\right)$ is a valid choice for (z_0, x_0, y_0). □

4.2 Analysis

Clearly, the sequences $\{u_i\}$, $\{v_i\}$ and $\{d_i\}$ defined in Algorithm 3 are those given by extended Euclid's algorithm: $q_0 u_i + p_0 v_i = d_i$. The sequence $|z_i - x_i y_i|$ is decreasing and then increasing. This gives a condition break in the construction of list $\mathcal{L}$ in Algorithm 3. For small compression parameters κ', the algorithm finds many pairs $(x_i, y_i) \in \mathcal{L}$. When κ' increases, the number of pairs decreases.

In the balanced case (that is, the worst case), we observed that list $\mathcal{L}$ is always nonempty for $\kappa' \lessapprox 2n/3$. We conducted numerous experiments to assess this. For each tested predetermined portion N_H, a pair of matching primes p and q was found. We give below one such pair of primes (p, q) when N_H was set as the 1360 leading bits of the RSA-2048 challenge [27].

RSA2048 = c7970ceedcc3b075 4490201a7aa613cd 73911081c790f5f1 a8726f463550bb5b
7ff0db8e1ea1189e c72f93d1650011bd 721aeeacc2acde32 a04107f0648c2813
a31f5b0b7765ff8b 44b4b6ffc93384b6 46eb09c7cf5e8592 d40ea33c80039f35
b4f14a04b51f7bfd 781be4d1673164ba 8eb991c2c4d730bb be35f592bdef524a
f7e8daefd26c66fc 02c479af89d64d37 3f442709439de66c eb955f3ea37d5159
f6135809f85334b5 cb1813addc80cd05 609f10ac6a95ad65 872c909525bdad32
bc729592642920f2 4c61dc5b3c3b7923 e56b16a4d9d373d8 721f24a3fc0f1b31
31f55615172866bc cc30f95054c824e7 33a5eb6817f7bc16 399d48c6361cc7e5

$p =$ f2cbf408c0712b00 bb40d1ff5ef0d42b 981ba43a174da647 a474918aea017483
e8406e140d522a09 da65cb960a912c3f 5bf031af675b7907 5f5eb2151ad9c0ff
7bd518dd0f01bdc2 ac68f8b8edd30426 7b58d3317ab47072 4a04313d85be7d88
f63fe405a7628b12 3b34217ca4d45e42 97b5d728c2f74cd9 7fa673e6483804f5

$q =$ d2719ab388ad9e05 e9f46df9ce8c822e de61d36a7ce61b6c a4d3b4a3b41a8f42
0935eec7ce1a57c1 2e15bfaf4873e2d2 095297c6fd8d49d9 8ef44b955a983ba9
75f9f1be4f1730fb 2e9834e075988ed0 9229cb1514998172 7c1b58d2e20932d5
25a06de1111311af 5a88ae25f3e27e3d c2c44e9b51ffae50 2ed18dd903907931

$p \cdot q =$ c7970ceedcc3b075 4490201a7aa613cd 73911081c790f5f1 a8726f463550bb5b
7ff0db8e1ea1189e c72f93d1650011bd 721aeeacc2acde32 a04107f0648c2813
a31f5b0b7765ff8b 44b4b6ffc93384b6 46eb09c7cf5e8592 d40ea33c80039f35
b4f14a04b51f7bfd 781be4d1673164ba 8eb991c2c4d730bb be35f592bdef524a
f7e8daefd26c66fc 02c479af89d64d37 3f442709439de66c eb955f3ea37d5159
f6135809f85334b5 cb18fd5b056dbd78 01de0bb2fd1e7b5a b4d33205ac4c9a71
800cbfe76ac1424a 90121c232d945edc 6e7d34038e271b4c 92b620e5ddf836da
62eede67b33ab2b4 ae58d531cf27f090 6034201bf753711e 24417374f5e0bfe5

4.3 Variants

As in Section 3, the methods of this section are subject to numerous variants. For example, it is possible to fix the trailing bits of N, or some leading bits and some trailing bits of N.

To achieve higher compression rates, multi-prime RSA moduli can be used (as suggested in [32]) or RSA moduli of the form $p^r q$ [31]. Unbalanced RSA moduli (i.e., $n \lneq 2n_0$) always offer better compression rates.

5 Conclusions

We have presented enhancements to the folklore method for generating RSA moduli with a predetermined portion and pointed out relevant applications. We have shown how to efficiently implement a key escrow mechanism. Special care was taken to make it compatible with the fastest smart-card prime generation algorithms and to optimally benefit from them to only mildly affect the global performance. We have also presented a compression technique that enables to represent RSA moduli with about three times fewer bits.

Acknowledgments. I thank Igor Shparlinski for sending a copy of [29], and Alain Durand and Mohamed Karroumi for stimulating discussions. I also thank the anonymous referees for useful comments.

References

1. Bellare, M., Rogaway, P.: The exact security of digital signatures. In: Maurer, U.M. (ed.) EUROCRYPT 1996. LNCS, vol. 1070, pp. 399–416. Springer, Heidelberg (1996)
2. Bernstein, D.J.: Stop overestimating RSA bandwidth! Rump session of CRYPTO 2004, Santa Barbara, CA, USA (August 17, 2004), http://cr.yp.to/talks/2004.08.17/slides.pdf
3. Bernstein, D.J.: Compressing RSA/Rabin keys. Invited talk, Number Theory Inspired By Cryptography (NTIBC 2005), Bannf Centre, Alberta, Canada, (November 6, 2005), http://cr.yp.to/talks/2005.11.06/slides.pdf
4. Boneh, D.: Twenty years of attacks on the RSA cryptosystem. Notices of the American Mathematical Society (AMS) 46(2), 203–213 (1999)
5. Coppersmith, D.: Finding a small root of a bivariate integer equation; factoring with high bits known. In: Maurer, U.M. (ed.) EUROCRYPT 1996. LNCS, vol. 1070, pp. 155–165. Springer, Heidelberg (1996)
6. Coppersmith, D.: Small solutions to polynomial equations, and low exponent RSA vulnerabilities. Journal of Cryptology 10(4), 233–260 (1997)
7. Coron, J.-S.: Finding small roots of bivariate integer polynomial equations revisited. In: Cachin, C., Camenisch, J.L. (eds.) EUROCRYPT 2004. LNCS, vol. 3027, pp. 492–505. Springer, Heidelberg (2004)
8. Coron, J.-S.: Finding small roots of bivariate integer polynomial equations: A direct approach. In: Menezes, A. (ed.) CRYPTO 2007. LNCS, vol. 4622, pp. 379–394. Springer, Heidelberg (2007)
9. Crépeau, C., Slakmon, A.: Simple backdoors for RSA key generation. In: Joye, M. (ed.) CT-RSA 2003. LNCS, vol. 2612, pp. 403–416. Springer, Heidelberg (2003)
10. Desmedt, Y.: Abuses in cryptography and how to fight them. In: Goldwasser, S. (ed.) CRYPTO 1988. LNCS, vol. 403, pp. 375–389. Springer, Heidelberg (1990)

11. Diffie, W., Hellman, M.E.: New directions in cryptography. IEEE Transactions on Information Theory IT-22(6), 644–654 (1976)
12. Gehrmann, C., Näslund, M., (eds.): ECRYPT yearly report on algorithms and keysizes. ECRYPT Report, D.SPA.16, Revision 1.0 (January 2006), http://www.ecrypt.eu.org/documents/D.SPA.16-1.0.pdf
13. Girault, M., Misarski, J.-F.: Selective forgery of RSA signatures using redundancy. In: Fumy, W. (ed.) EUROCRYPT 1997. LNCS, vol. 1233, pp. 495–507. Springer, Heidelberg (1997)
14. Joye, M., Paillier, P.: Fast generation of prime numbers on portable devices: An update. In: Goubin, L., Matsui, M. (eds.) CHES 2006. LNCS, vol. 4249, pp. 160–173. Springer, Heidelberg (2006)
15. Joye, M., Paillier, P., Vaudenay, S.: Efficient generation of prime numbers. In: Paar, C., Koç, Ç.K. (eds.) CHES 2000. LNCS, vol. 1965, pp. 340–354. Springer, Heidelberg (2000)
16. Juels, A.: Provable security: Some caveats. Panel discussion, 6th ACM Conference on Computer and Communications Security (ACM CCS 1999), Singapore (November 1–4, 1999)
17. Knobloch, H.-J.: A smart card implementation of the Fiat-Shamir identification scheme. In: Günther, C.G. (ed.) EUROCRYPT 1988. LNCS, vol. 330, pp. 87–95. Springer, Heidelberg (1988)
18. Lenstra, A.K.: Generating RSA moduli with a predetermined portion. In: Ohta, K., Pei, D. (eds.) ASIACRYPT 1998. LNCS, vol. 1514, pp. 1–10. Springer, Heidelberg (1998)
19. Lenstra, A.K., Lenstra Jr., H.W., Lovász, L.: Factoring polynomials with rational coefficients. Mathematische Annalen 261, 515–534 (1982)
20. Meister, G.: On an implementation of the Mohan-Adiga algorithm. In: Damgård, I.B. (ed.) EUROCRYPT 1990. LNCS, vol. 473, pp. 496–500. Springer, Heidelberg (1991)
21. Mohan, S.B., Adiga, B.S.: Fast algorithms for implementing RSA public key cryptosystems. Electronics Letters 21(7), 761 (1985)
22. Naccache, D., M'Raïhi, D., Vaudenay, S., Raphaeli, D.: Can D.S.A. be improved? Complexity trade-offs with the digital signature standard. In: De Santis, A. (ed.) EUROCRYPT 1994. LNCS, vol. 950, pp. 77–85. Springer, Heidelberg (1995)
23. Okamoto, T., Shiraishi, A.: A fast signature scheme based on quadratic inequalities. In: 1985 IEEE Symposium on Security and Privacy, pp. 123–133. IEEE Computer Society Press, Los Alamitos (1985)
24. Orton, G., Peppard, L., Tavares, S.: A design of a fast pipelined modular multiplier based on a diminished-radix algorithm. Journal of Cryptology 6(4), 183–208 (1993)
25. Paillier, P.: Public-key cryptosystems based on composite degree residuosity classes. In: Stern, J. (ed.) EUROCRYPT 1999. LNCS, vol. 1592, pp. 223–238. Springer, Heidelberg (1999)
26. Rivest, R.L., Shamir, A., Adleman, L.M.: A method for obtaining digital signatures and public-key cryptosystems. Communications of the ACM 21(2), 120–126 (1978)
27. RSA Laboratories. The RSA challenge numbers, http://www.rsa.com/rsalabs/node.asp?id=2093
28. RSA Laboratories. RSA-200 is factored! (May 2005), http://www.rsa.com/rsalabs/node.asp?id=2879
29. Shparlinski, I.E.: On RSA moduli with prescribed bit patterns. Designs, Codes and Cryptography 39(1), 113–122 (2006)

30. Simmons, G.J.: The subliminal channel and digital signatures. In: Beth, T., Cot, N., Ingemarsson, I. (eds.) EUROCRYPT 1984. LNCS, vol. 209, pp. 364–368. Springer, Heidelberg (1985)
31. Takagi, T.: Fast RSA-type cryptosystem modulo $p^k q$. In: Krawczyk, H. (ed.) CRYPTO 1998. LNCS, vol. 1462, pp. 318–326. Springer, Heidelberg (1998)
32. Vanstone, S.A., Zuccherato, R.J.: Using four-prime RSA in which some of the bits are specified. Electronics Letters 30(25), 2118–2119 (1994)
33. Vanstone, S.A., Zuccherato, R.J.: Short RSA keys and their generation. Journal of Cryptology 8(2), 101–114 (1995)
34. Walter, C.D.: Faster modular multiplication by operand scaling. In: Feigenbaum, J. (ed.) CRYPTO 1991. LNCS, vol. 576, pp. 313–323. Springer, Heidelberg (1992)
35. Young, A., Yung, M.: The dark side of "black-box" cryptography, or: Should we trust Capstone? In: Koblitz, N. (ed.) CRYPTO 1996. LNCS, vol. 1109, pp. 89–103. Springer, Heidelberg (1996)
36. Young, A., Yung, M.: Kleptography: Using cryptography against cryptography. In: Fumy, W. (ed.) EUROCRYPT 1997. LNCS, vol. 1233, pp. 62–74. Springer, Heidelberg (1997)

Variants of the Distinguished Point Method for Cryptanalytic Time Memory Trade-Offs*

Jin Hong, Kyung Chul Jeong, Eun Young Kwon,
In-Sok Lee**, and Daegun Ma**

Department of Mathematical Sciences and ISaC-RIM,
Seoul National University, Seoul, 151-747, Korea
{jinhong,white483,madgun7}@snu.ac.kr,
{jeongkc,islee}@math.snu.ac.kr

Abstract. The time memory trade-off (TMTO) algorithm, first introduced by Hellman, is a method for quickly inverting a one-way function, using pre-computed tables. The distinguished point method (DP) is a technique that reduces the number of table lookups performed by Hellman's algorithm.

In this paper we propose a new variant of the DP technique, named variable DP (VDP), having properties very different from DP. It has an effect on the amount of memory required to store the pre-computed tables. We also show how to combine variable chain length techniques like DP and VDP with a more recent trade-off algorithm called the rainbow table method.

Keywords: time memory trade-off, Hellman trade-off, distinguished points, rainbow table.

1 Introduction

In many cases, cryptanalysis of a cryptographic system can be interpreted as the process of inverting a one-way function. Unlike most approaches that depend on the specific target system, time memory trade-off (TMTO) is a generic approach that can be used on any one-way function.

Let $f : \mathcal{X} \to \mathcal{Y}$ be any one-way function. For example, this could be a map sending a key to the encryption of a specific fixed plaintext. A way to efficiently invert this map would imply total breakdown of the encryption system. There are two trivial ways to invert f that do not involve the inner workings of f. Given a target $y \in \mathcal{Y}$ to invert, one may go about the time consuming process of computing $f(x)$ for every $x \in \mathcal{X}$, until a match $f(x) = y$ is found. The other method is to do this exhaustive process in a pre-computation phase and to store the resulting pairs $(x, f(x))$ in a table, sorted according to the second components. Then, when a target $y \in \mathcal{Y}$ is given, it can be searched for in the

---

* All authors are supported in part by BK 21.
** Partially supported by KRF Grant ♯2005-070-C00004.

table among the second components and the corresponding first component is simply read off as the answer. Whereas the exhaustive search method takes a long time, the table lookup method requires a large storage space. TMTO is a method that comes between these two extremes and can invert a one-way function in time shorter than the exhaustive search method using memory smaller than the table lookup method.

Cryptanalytic TMTO was firstly introduced by Hellman [11]. If the one-way function f to be inverted is defined on a set of size N, under typical parameters, the pre-computation phase of his algorithm takes time $\mathcal{O}(N)$ in creating certain one-way chains, after which a *digest* of this exhaustive computation is stored in a table of size $\mathcal{O}(N^{\frac{2}{3}})$. This table is used during the online phase to recover the pre-image x of a given target $f(x)$ in time $\mathcal{O}(N^{\frac{2}{3}})$. Soon after Hellman's work, the idea of distinguished points (DP), attributed to Rivest in [9], was introduced. When applied to Hellman's algorithm, it reduces the number of table lookups required during the online phase. This is useful when the table is so large that table lookups become expensive. More recently, Oechslin [15] suggested a different way of creating the one-way chain. It is called the rainbow table method and a reduction in online time by a factor of two was claimed. It is known that, asymptotically, these algorithms are the best one can hope for if the structure of f is not to be used [5].

The contributions of this paper are two-folds. The first is the introduction of a new technique which we shall call *variable DP* (VDP). As with the original DP idea, VDP is a technique that can be used with the Hellman method and also with the multi-target versions of the trade-off algorithms [3,10,6,13]. Simply put, a DP is a point in the one-way chain that satisfies a preset condition. Whereas the original DP idea had this condition fixed for all chains, VDP allows this condition to depend on the chain's starting point.

While VDP is a variant of the original DP, the two methods show very different characteristics. The simple idea of allowing the chain stopping condition to vary with the chains brings about unexpected consequences. It leads to the removal of the sorting procedure that was needed in the Hellman method's pre-computation phase. Another surprising characteristic is that, whereas all previous trade-off algorithms stored both ends of the one-way chains in the table, our method completely removes the need to store the starting point. This is because the chain end contains information about the chain beginning.

The second contribution of this paper is in successfully applying the DP (and VDP) idea to the rainbow table method. A combination of the DP technique with a variant of the rainbow table method was suggested in [5,4], but there is a natural barrier to its combination with the original rainbow table method. The one-way chain created during the pre-computation phase is re-traced in the online phase in the opposite direction, and with rainbow tables, this is not possible unless the chain length is known. So techniques like DP that disturb the length of chains were thought to be incompatible with the rainbow table method. We have overcome this difficulty by employing a sorting that takes the chain lengths into account. Our new technique VDP can also be combined with the rainbow table method in a similar way.

The rest of the paper is organized as follows. We start by briefly reviewing some of the previous TMTO works. Then, in Section 3, the new VDP technique is presented. In Section 4, we show how to apply the DP and VDP ideas to rainbow table method. This is followed by Section 5, giving a rough comparison between various TMTO methods and explaining the issues involved in such a comparison. We summarize this paper in Section 6.

2 Previous Works

In this section we will quickly review the theory of the time memory trade-offs, recalling the basic concepts and fixing notation. Readers new to the trade-off technique should refer to the original papers. For example, we shall not explain matters related to the success probability of these methods [11,14,15].

Throughout this paper, we fix a finite set $\mathbf{Z}_N = \{0, 1, \ldots, N-1\}$ of size N and we shall use $f : \mathbf{Z}_N \to \mathbf{Z}_N$ to denote the target one-way function that is to be inverted. The amount of memory needed to store a digest of the pre-computation is denoted by M and the online attack time is denoted by T.

All trade-off algorithms will involve parameters $t, m \in \mathbf{Z}_N$, satisfying $mt^2 = N$, known as the *matrix stopping rule*. We shall not be concerned with the exact choice of these numbers, which depends on the resources available to the attacker and also on his needs. All trade-off algorithms will involve a family of permutations, $r_i : \mathbf{Z}_N \to \mathbf{Z}_N$, called the *reduction functions*. The range of i will vary with each trade-off algorithm. Each of these defines an *iterating function* $f_i : \mathbf{Z}_N \to \mathbf{Z}_N$ through the equation $f_i(x) = r_i \circ f(x)$.

All trade-off algorithms consist of a pre-computation phase, in which tables are prepared, and an online phase. In the online phase, an inversion target $f(x_0)$ is given, to which the trade-off algorithm will return an X such that $f(X) = f(x_0)$. As f is not injective, there is no guarantee that $X = x_0$, and this has to be checked outside the trade-off algorithm. If X is found to be an unsatisfactory answer, a situation referred to as a *false alarm*, the trade-off algorithm is simply resumed.

2.1 Hellman Trade-Off

Hellman's original work [11] was presented as an attack on block ciphers, but we shall describe his trade-off algorithm as a generic inversion technique, applicable to any one-way function.

Pre-computation Phase. What is explained below shall be repeated t times, once for each i in the range $0 \le i < t$, to build t tables. We start by choosing, preferably distinct, m starting points, labeled $\text{SP}_0^i, \text{SP}_1^i, \ldots, \text{SP}_{m-1}^i$. For each $0 \le j < m$, we set $X_{j,0}^i = \text{SP}_j^i$ and compute

$$X_{j,k}^i = f_i(X_{j,k-1}^i) \quad (1 \le k \le t),$$

recursively. This is said to be the *Hellman chain*. The ending point is written as EP_j^i, so that $EP_j^i = f_i^t(SP_j^i)$. All intermediate points of the Hellman chains are discarded and just the ordered pairs $\{(SP_j^i, EP_j^i)\}_{j=0}^{m-1}$ are stored as the i-th *Hellman table* HT_i, after they have been sorted with respect to the ending points. A set of Hellman chains that was used to create a single table is referred to as the *Hellman matrix*. Note that we have t tables, each containing m entries, so that the total storage cost is $M = mt$.

Online Phase. Given a target point $f(x_0)$, the process below is repeated for each i. We first compute $Y_0^i = r_i(f(x_0)) = f_i(x_0)$ and check if this appears as an ending point in the i-th Hellman table HT_i. This table lookup is done for each recursively computed $Y_k^i = f_i(Y_{k-1}^i)$, where $k = 1, 2, \ldots, t-1$. To distinguish this chain from the Hellman chain, in this paper, we shall refer to this Y_k^i-chain as the i-th *online chain*.

Whenever a match $Y_k^i = EP_j^i$ is found, we compute $X = X_{j,t-k-1}^i = f_i^{t-k-1}(SP_j^i)$. Since

$$f_i^k(f_i(X)) = f_i^{k+1}(X) = f_i^t(SP_j^i) = EP_j^i = Y_k^i = f_i^k(Y_0^i),$$

there is a large chance that $f_i(X) = Y_0^i$, which is equivalent to $f(X) = f(x_0)$, due to r_i being injective. In such a case, the algorithm returns X. But, as f_i^k is not injective, there could be a merge between the Hellman and online chains, and it is possible to have $f(X) \neq f(x_0)$. This is also referred to as a *false alarm*, in which case the next k is processed. Disregarding the time taken to process false alarms, it takes t iterations of f_i to process each of the t tables, so the online time is $T = t^2$.

Application of the matrix stopping rule to the online time $T = t^2$ and storage size $M = mt$ brings out the *Hellman trade-off curve* $TM^2 = N^2$. Conversely, any T and M satisfying the trade-off curve lead to parameters m and t appropriate for the Hellman trade-off algorithm.

2.2 Distinguished Points

The distinguished point method was suggested by Rivest and issues concerning its practical use were investigated in [8,16]. Rather than fixing the length of each Hellman chain, the iteration $X_{j,k}^i = f_i(X_{j,k-1}^i)$ is continued until an $X_{j,k}^i$ satisfying a certain condition is found, and we obtain chains of varying lengths. For example, if one wants the average chain length to be $t = 2^d$, DP are typically defined to be points whose first d bits are all zero.

In practice, some of the chains created in this way could be too long for practical use, and some chains may even fall into a loop and never reach a DP. So we throw away chains longer than a preset $\hat{t} = t_{\max}$. If needed, the shortened average length can be adjusted by discarding chains shorter than a preset $\check{t} = t_{\min}$. The effects of $\hat{t}$ and $\check{t}$ are discussed in more detail in [16]. The length of each chain is usually recorded in the Hellman table so that they can be used when resolving false alarms.

The main advantage of using the DP method is in the reduction of table lookups made during the online phase. The generated point $Y_k^i = f_i^k(Y_0^i)$ can appear as an endpoint in the Hellman table only if it is a DP. So it suffices to do a search of the table only when the online chain reaches a DP, and the number of table lookups is reduced by a factor of 2^d.

As the ending point is the only DP in any Hellman chain, when a certain Y_k^i is found to be a DP, but not in HT_i, the target cannot be in the i-th Hellman matrix, and one can move onto the next table. So the average length of chains generated online is expected to be about 2^d. In this paper, we shall refer to this trade-off method as Hellman+DP.

2.3 Rainbow Table

The rainbow table method was introduced by Oechslin [15]. Instead of using a single reduction function for each table, t different reduction functions are sequentially used in each chain of length t to generate a single table. Explicitly, the j-th *rainbow chain* is generated by iterating $X_{j,k+1} = f_{k+1}(X_{j,k})$, and we allow j to run in the range[1] $0 \le j < mt$. As with the Hellman method, $\{(\text{SP}_j, \text{EP}_j)\}$ is stored in the rainbow table RT, after sorting.

In the online phase, for each $0 \le k < t$, the k-th online chain

$$r_{t-k}(f(x_0)) \xrightarrow{f_{t-k+1}} \circ \xrightarrow{f_{t-k+2}} \cdots \cdots \circ \xrightarrow{f_{t-1}} \circ \xrightarrow{f_t} Y^k$$

is computed and Y^k is searched for among the second component of the rainbow table. Thus the online time of the rainbow table method is $T = \frac{1}{2}t^2$, and this is one half of the original Hellman method, when the two are storing the same number of entries. The rainbow table contains $M = mt$ entries, and the rainbow trade-off curve is given by $TM^2 = \frac{1}{2}N^2$.

2.4 Checkpoints

Experiments show that a considerable fraction of the online time is spent in resolving false alarms. The checkpoint method [2] was introduced to solve this problem. It allows recognition of false alarms without the costly regeneration of the Hellman/rainbow chains. The checkpoint method is applicable to all three trade-off algorithms we have described.

3 Variable Distinguished Points

In this section, we propose a new technique, named the *variable distinguished point* (VDP) method, which is a variant of the DP method, but with very different properties.

---

[1] This is non-restrictive choice that allows a direct comparison between Hellman and rainbow methods.

3.1 The Basic Idea

As with the original DP method, our VDP method terminates a Hellman chain when a point satisfying a certain relation is reached. The crucial difference is that, unlike DP, we allow this condition to depend on the starting point of the chain. This results in the ending point containing information about the starting point, so that by using information which is common to the table, one may be able to recover the starting point from the ending point.

While the main objective of the original DP method was to reduce the number of table searches, the VDP method aims to eliminate the need to store the starting points so as to lessen storage requirements.

3.2 Applying VDP to Hellman Trade-Offs

Let us show how we may apply the VDP technique to the original Hellman trade-off algorithm. To simplify our discussion, we shall restrict to the typical parameters $m = t = N^{\frac{1}{3}}$ and set $d = \frac{1}{3}\log_2 N$. Ways to use more general parameters will be dealt with in Section 3.4.

When creating the j-th Hellman chain of the i-th table, we take our starting point to be

$$\text{SP}_j^i = (0 \,\|\, i \,\|\, j),$$

where each of the three concatenated components are of d bits. The Hellman chain is created as usual through iterated computation of $X_{j,k}^i = f_i(X_{j,k-1}^i)$, starting from $X_{j,0}^i = \text{SP}_j^i$, but it is terminated only when the most significant d bits of some $X_{j,k}^i$ is found to be j. Chains longer than a preset $\hat{t} = t_{\max}$ are discarded. The ending point EP_j^i we have reached in the j-th chain is stored at $\text{HT}_i[\text{j}]$, the j-th position of the i-th Hellman table. There is no table sorting involved. Since the chain length is variable, storing chain length information would reduce online time spent dealing with false alarms, but this is not mandatory. We remark that if we take the first d bits of an ending point as its hash[2] value, then the Hellman+VDP table we have created can be seen as a perfect hash table.

Notice that since the storage position index j is equal to the first d bits of EP_j^i and also to the most meaningful part of SP_j^i, neither the starting point nor the first d bits of the ending point need to be stored. The pre-computation phase of Hellman trade-off with VDP, under restricted parameters $m = t = N^{\frac{1}{3}}$, is summarized in Algorithm 1..

The online phase of the simplified version of VDP is given in Algorithm 2.. When we want to check whether a point from the online chain is an ending point, we can look up the table entry at the position given by the point's first d bits. There is no searching involved. If we find a match, the corresponding starting point can be recovered using the table number and the position index.

---

[2] We are referring to the data structuring method and not to cryptographic hash functions.

Algorithm 1. Pre-computation Phase of Hellman+VDP

Require:
  (1) parameters m, t, and $\hat{t} = t_{\max}$.
  (2) functions $f_i = r_i \circ f$ ($i = 0, \ldots, t-1$).
  (3) empty tables $\text{HT}_0, \text{HT}_1, \cdots, \text{HT}_{t-1}$.

Ensure:
  (1) $m = t = N^{\frac{1}{3}} = 2^d$.

1: **for** $i = 0, \ldots, t-1$ and $j = 0, \ldots, m-1$ **do**
2:     $X \leftarrow (0 \,\|\, i \,\|\, j)$ ▷ $X = \text{SP}_j^i$
3:     **for** $k = 1$ to $\hat{t}$ **do**
4:        $X \leftarrow f_i(X)$ ▷ iterate Hellman chain
5:        **if** $j ==$ (significant d bits of X) **then**   ▷ check for DP
6:           $\text{HT}_i[j] \leftarrow$ (less significant $(n-d)$ bits of X)$\|k$
                                                                         ▷ $\text{HT}_i[j] =$ (lower part of EP_j^i)$\|$(chain length)
7:           break   ▷ process next chain if DP is reached
8:        **end if**
9:     **end for**   ▷ leave $\text{HT}_i[j]$ empty if $\hat{t}$ is reach before a DP
10: **end for**
11: **return** $\text{HT}_0, \text{HT}_1, \cdots, \text{HT}_{t-1}$.

Algorithm 2. Online Phase of Hellman+VDP

Require:
  (1) target $f(x_0)$
  (2) parameters t, $\hat{t} = t_{\max}$ and functions $f_i = r_i \circ f$ ($i = 0, \ldots, t-1$)
  (3) pre-computed Hellman+VDP tables $\text{HT}_0, \text{HT}_1, \cdots, \text{HT}_{t-1}$

Ensure:
  (1) $m = t = N^{\frac{1}{3}} = 2^d$.

1: **for** $i = 0, \ldots, t-1$ **do**
2:     $Y \leftarrow r_i(f(x_0))$
3:     **for** $k = 1$ to $\hat{t}$ **do**
4:        $j \leftarrow$ (significant d bits of Y)
5:        $\text{EP} \,\|\, l \leftarrow \text{HT}_i[j]$ ▷ $\text{HT}_i[j] =$ (lower bits of EP_j^i)$\|$(chain length)
6:        **if** $k < l$ and $\text{EP} ==$ (less significant $(n-d)$ bits of Y) **then**
7:           $X \leftarrow f_i^{l-k-1}(0 \,\|\, i \,\|\, j)$ ▷ $X = f_i^{l-k-1}(\text{SP}_j^i)$
8:           **if** $f(X) == f(x_0)$ **then**   ▷ check for false alarm
9:              **return** X   ▷ return pre-image of $f(x_0)$
10:          **end if**
11:        **end if**
12:        $Y \leftarrow f_i(Y)$ ▷ iterate online chain
13:     **end for**
14: **end for**
15: **return** 'failure'

3.3 Technical Details of Hellman+VDP

To maintain the success probability provided by the original Hellman tradeoff, we need to ensure that our Hellman+VDP method results in average chain length of approximately $t = 2^d$ and that not too many of the Hellman table entries are left empty.

When the VDP is defined using d bits, the average chain length would naturally become $t = 2^d$, except that we are throwing away some of the longer chains. The first issue can be approached, as with the original Hellman+DP method, by setting an appropriate lower bound $\check{t} = t_{\min}$ in addition to the upper bound $\hat{t} = t_{\max}$ for chain lengths. But whereas the DP method may simply throw away chains not falling within these bounds and generate more chains from other starting point, with the VDP method, there are no other starting points that can be used, and every discarded chain would imply an empty Hellman table entry.

A solution to the empty table entry problem is to use starting points of the form
$$\text{SP}_j^i = \tau \,\|\, i \,\|\, j,$$
where τ is a counter that is incremented every time creation of the j-th chain fails. Now, for reconstruction of SP_j^i during the online phase to be possible, the τ value will need to be stored, so we place a restriction on the size of τ. We allow at most 2^s trials to be done for the j-th chain, and if all trials fail, we use the longest chain among those shorter than $\check{t}$. The entry $\text{HT}_i\text{[j]}$ is left empty only if all the 2^s chains were longer than $\hat{t}$.

For the parameters $t = 2^d$ and $\hat{t} = c \cdot t$, the probability of generating a chain longer than $\hat{t}$ is
$$\left(1 - \frac{1}{2^d}\right)^{\hat{t}} \approx \exp\left(-\frac{\hat{t}}{2^d}\right) = \exp(-c).$$
With the use of s-many extra bits per table entry, the probability of a table position $\text{HT}_i\text{[j]}$ being left empty would become as small as $\exp(-c \cdot 2^s)$. When $m = N^{\frac{1}{3}}$ chains are used for each Hellman table, by choosing s to satisfy $m \cdot \exp(-c \cdot 2^s) < 1$, or equivalently,
$$\frac{\log \log N - \log 3c}{\log 2} < s,$$
we can expect to find less than a single empty entry from each table, resulting in a minimal perfect hash table. Note that the above bound on s is certainly small and asymptotically negligible when compared to the number of bits needed for the other major parts. Also, the attacker may choose to use an even smaller s according to his needs.

The small number of empty entries can be marked by writing zero as the chain length, or through use of one additional bit, when the chain length is not recorded. One may even choose to fill it with random value and let it generate false alarms at the worst. A typical Hellman+VDP table is depicted in Figure 1.

Note that the ending point is the only DP within that chain. So if an online chain reaches a DP for the j-th Hellman chain and EP_j^i is found to be a non-match, the inversion target $f(x_0)$ cannot belong to the j-th Hellman chain. There is no reason to refer to the j-th chain any further, even if the online chain reaches another DP for the same chain. So by keeping track of which ending points have

$$\text{SP}_0^i = (\tau_0 \,\|\, i \,\|\, 0) \xrightarrow{f_i^{l_0}} (0 \,\|\, \mathcal{R}_0) = \text{EP}_0^i \rightsquigarrow \quad \text{HT}_i[0] = \{\mathcal{R}_0, \tau_0, l_0\}$$

$$\text{SP}_1^i = (\tau_1 \,\|\, i \,\|\, 1) \xrightarrow{f_i^{l_1}} (1 \,\|\, \mathcal{R}_1) = \text{EP}_1^i \rightsquigarrow \quad \text{HT}_i[1] = \{\mathcal{R}_1, \tau_1, l_1\}$$

$$\vdots \qquad\qquad\qquad\qquad\qquad \vdots$$

$$(\text{EP}_j^i \text{ generation failure}) \rightsquigarrow \quad \text{HT}_i[j] = \{-, -, 0\}$$

$$\vdots \qquad\qquad\qquad\qquad\qquad \vdots$$

$$\text{SP}_{m-1}^i = (\tau_{m-1} \,\|\, i \,\|\, m-1) \xrightarrow{f_i^{l_{m-1}}} (m-1 \,\|\, \mathcal{R}_{m-1}) = \text{EP}_{m-1}^i \rightsquigarrow \quad \text{HT}_i[\text{m-1}] = \{\mathcal{R}_{m-1}, \tau_{m-1}, l_{m-1}\}$$

Fig. 1. Typical i-th Hellman Table for Hellman+VDP

been processed, one may reduce the number of table lookups and the chance of false alarms.

One undesirable property of the VDP method concerns its online time. We need to go through t tables with each table costing $\hat{t}$ iterations of f_i, so that the online time is $T = t \cdot \hat{t}$. Hence, one would wish to choose $\hat{t}$ to be as small as possible. But reducing $\hat{t}$ must be paired with an increase in $\check{t}$, and this has the effect of increasing the pre-computation time, if the success probability is to be maintained.

There is one trick that can be used to reduce online time, with no change given to the pre-computation phase, and at a very small cost in success probability. One can simply move onto the next Hellman table a little before the online chain length reaches $\hat{t}$. The effect of this on the inversion success probability will be small due to two reasons. As was mentioned before, after the first lookup of the ending point EP_j^i, the whole j-th chain may be disregarded. The second reason is that all chains shorter than the online chain generated so far may be disregarded. So, only the long chains that have not yet been referred to has any chance of containing the inversion target. Even for these chains, points that are closer to the ending point than the length of currently generated online chain cannot be the target of our inversion. Thus once the online chain reaches a certain length, most of the Hellman matrix has already been searched for and skipping the rest should have only a small effect on the success probability.

The above argument shows that the online phase of Hellman+VDP is much more efficient at the start of each table processing than at the end. This is somewhat similar to a characteristic of the rainbow table method and can be very advantageous when the online phase of Hellman+VDP is carefully scheduled.

3.4 Using General Parameters

So far, we have only worked with parameters $m = t = N^{\frac{1}{3}}$. Even though the average length of the Hellman chains can be slightly adjusted by changing the bounds $\check{t} = t_{\max}$ and $\hat{t} = t_{\min}$, other measures are needed when we want parameters m and t to differ by a large factor.

Suppose the parameters m and t obtained from the matrix stopping rule $mt^2 = N$ satisfy $t = 2^r m$. To explain how to use these parameters, let us write $m = 2^d$ and $t = 2^{d+r}$. As before, we can set $\text{SP}_j^i = (0 \, \| \, i \, \| \, j)$ for the i-th table, where 0 and i are of $d + r$ bits and j is of d bits. It only remains to bring the average chain length to $t = 2^{d+r}$. This is easily done by defining the DP for the j-th chain to be those points starting with $j\|0$, where j is of d bits and 0 is of r bits. In a way, this can be seen as a combination of the DP and VDP methods.

We next consider the opposite $m = 2^r t$ case. Let us write $m = 2^{d+r}$ and $t = 2^d$. The starting point for the j-th chain in the i-th table is set to $\text{SP}_j^i = (0 \, \| \, i \, \| \, j)$, where 0 and i are of d bits and j is of $d + r$ bits. A point in the j-th chain is regarded as a DP if its most significant d bits are equal to the most significant d bits of j. Since this *distinguisher* does not contain enough information to fully distinguish between the possible j, ending points corresponding to the same significant j parts are sorted before storage, and r bits of the starting point are also stored. This is not as satisfactory as the previous case, but still reasonable unless r is large. In any case, this can be seen as having placed more of the original Hellman flavor back into Hellman+VDP.

To deal with m and t that are not powers of 2, one can use their closest powers and also utilize $\hat{t}$ and $\check{t}$ for fine adjustments.

4 Applying DP and VDP to the Rainbow Table Method

The rainbow table method applies a different function f_i to every column in its chain creation. During the online phase, creation of the online chain proceeds in a backward direction, and having a fixed chain length is crucial in knowing which f_i to use. In this section, we show that by sorting the table in a slightly different way, it is possible to use rainbow chains of variable lengths.

4.1 Rainbow+DP

As with the Hellman+DP situation, we can use $\hat{t} = t_{\max}$ and $\check{t} = t_{\min}$ to adjust the average chain length. With these numbers fixed, we choose $\hat{t}$ reduction functions defining the iterating functions f_i. The rainbow chains are generated as with the original rainbow table method, setting $X_{j,0} = \text{SP}_j$ and iteratively computing $X_{j,k} = f_k(X_{j,k-1})$. The chain is terminated when a DP is reached, and the starting point, the ending point, and the chain length are stored. So far, we have simply combined the rainbow table method with the DP technique.

Now, the rainbow table is sorted first with respect to chain lengths and then with respect to the ending points within those chains of same length. If collisions are found among those of the same length, one may optionally discarding all but one of them and generating more chains to take their places. Note that collision of ending points between chains of different lengths have minimal effect as they do not correspond to collision within a rainbow matrix column. Also, no collision within a rainbow matrix column is undetected, since any such colliding chains would end at the same length.

$$
\begin{array}{c}
\text{RT}_{\check{t}} \left|
\begin{array}{l}
\text{SP}_{\check{t},0} \xrightarrow{f_1} \circ \xrightarrow{f_2} \cdots \cdots \circ \xrightarrow{f_{\check{t}}} \text{EP}_{\check{t},0} \\
\text{SP}_{\check{t},1} \xrightarrow{f_1} \circ \xrightarrow{f_2} \cdots \cdots \circ \xrightarrow{f_{\check{t}}} \text{EP}_{\check{t},1} \\
\vdots
\end{array}
\right. \\[2em]

\vdots \qquad \vdots \qquad \ddots \\[1em]

\text{RT}_{\hat{t}-1} \left|
\begin{array}{l}
\text{SP}_{\hat{t}-1,0} \xrightarrow{f_1} \circ \xrightarrow{f_2} \cdots \circ \xrightarrow{f_{\check{t}}} \cdots \circ \xrightarrow{f_{\hat{t}-1}} \text{EP}_{\hat{t}-1,0} \\
\text{SP}_{\hat{t}-1,1} \xrightarrow{f_1} \circ \xrightarrow{f_2} \cdots \circ \xrightarrow{f_{\check{t}}} \cdots \circ \xrightarrow{f_{\hat{t}-1}} \text{EP}_{\hat{t}-1,1} \\
\vdots
\end{array}
\right. \\[2em]

\text{RT}_{\hat{t}} \left|
\begin{array}{l}
\text{SP}_{\hat{t},0} \xrightarrow{f_1} \circ \xrightarrow{f_2} \cdots \circ \xrightarrow{f_{\check{t}}} \cdots \circ \xrightarrow{f_{\hat{t}-1}} \circ \xrightarrow{f_{\hat{t}}} \text{EP}_{\hat{t},0} \\
\text{SP}_{\hat{t},1} \xrightarrow{f_1} \circ \xrightarrow{f_2} \cdots \circ \xrightarrow{f_{\check{t}}} \cdots \circ \xrightarrow{f_{\hat{t}-1}} \circ \xrightarrow{f_{\hat{t}}} \text{EP}_{\hat{t},1} \\
\vdots
\end{array}
\right.
\end{array}
$$

Fig. 2. Sorted Rainbow Matrix for Rainbow+DP

The sorted data is stored in separate tables $\text{RT}_{\check{t}}$, $\text{RT}_{\check{t}+1}$, ..., $\text{RT}_{\hat{t}}$, indexed by the length of chains they correspond to and the length data within each entry are discarded. It is also possible to store the whole data as one table together with an index file containing the starting positions for each length. The resulting rainbow+DP matrix of sorted rainbow chains is depicted in Figure 2.

During the online phase, we search through this matrix from right to left, and, within each column, from top to bottom. Given a target $f(x_0)$, we first compute $Y_{\hat{t}}^1 = r_{\hat{t}}(f(x_0))$. If this is a DP, it is searched for among the ending points of $\text{RT}_{\hat{t}}$. In the next step, we search for $Y_{\hat{t}-1}^2 = r_{\hat{t}-1}(f(x_0))$ and $Y_{\hat{t}}^2 = f_{\hat{t}}(Y_{\hat{t}-1}^2)$ in $\text{RT}_{\hat{t}-1}$ and $\text{RT}_{\hat{t}}$, respectively, if any of them are DP.

In the j-th iteration, starting from $Y_{\hat{t}-j+1}^j = r_{\hat{t}-j+1}(f(x_0))$, the online chain

$$Y_{\hat{t}-j+1}^j \xrightarrow{f_{\hat{t}-j+2}} Y_{\hat{t}-j+2}^j \xrightarrow{f_{\hat{t}-j+3}} \cdots \cdots \xrightarrow{f_{\hat{t}-1}} Y_{\hat{t}-1}^j \xrightarrow{f_{\hat{t}}} Y_{\hat{t}}^j$$

is computed. While computing, if we come across a $Y_{\hat{t}-j+k}^j$, which is a DP and we have $\hat{t} - j + k \geq \check{t}$, it is searched for among the ending points of $\text{RT}_{\hat{t}-j+k}$. Whenever a DP is reached, the rest of that online chain is skipped and we proceed with the next iteration.

Our j-th iteration requires $j-1$ function iterations at the worst, and we go through $\hat{t}$ iterations. So the worst case online time is approximately $T = \frac{\hat{t}^2}{2}$ and the number of table searches will be $\hat{t}$ at the most. On average, for $\hat{t} = c \cdot t$, we can expect $\hat{t} - (1 - \frac{1}{e^c})t$ table searches and online time of $t \cdot (\hat{t} - (1 - \frac{1}{e^c})t)$. This is explained in the full version of this paper [12].

4.2 Rainbow+VDP

To simplify discussion, we take parameters $m = t = 2^d = N^{\frac{1}{3}}$. We fix $\check{t}$ and $\hat{t}$, and choose $\hat{t}$ reduction functions. We take $mt = N^{\frac{2}{3}}$ starting points of the form $\text{SP}_{i,j} = (0 \,\|\, i \,\|\, j)$, where both i and j run over all d-bit values. The distinguished points for the $\text{SP}_{i,j}$-chain are defined to be points with most significant d bits equal to i. So, chains can be split into groups of size 2^d according to their definition of DP.

Sorting is done within each DP group with respect to chain lengths.[3] We write them in 2^d tables indexed by their DP definition, which is also equal to the center d bits of the starting points they contain and also to the first d bits of ending points. Unlike rainbow+DP, the chain length may not be discarded.

The online phase proceeds as with rainbow+DP, except that every computed Y_k^j is now a DP for some definition of DP. So after each computation of Y_k^j, the corresponding table is checked for a chain of correct length and matching ending point. The worst case online time of rainbow+VDP is about $\frac{\hat{t}^2}{2}$ and this is also the number of table searches needed.

5 Trade-Off Curves and Storage Issues

In this section, we make a very rough comparison of the various trade-off algorithms and look into some storage optimization techniques, which can complicate any serious attempt at comparison.

5.1 Trade-Off Curves

Let us make a very rough comparison of the trade-off algorithms we have discussed in this paper. The relevant facts are summarized in Table 1.

Table 1. Comparison of trade-off algorithms ($mt^2 = N$, $\hat{t} = c \cdot t$)

	table entries (M)	table lookups	function evaluations (T)	trade-off curve
Hellman	mt	t^2	t^2	$TM^2 = N^2$
Rainbow	mt	t	$\frac{1}{2}t^2$	$TM^2 = \frac{1}{2}N^2$
Hellman+DP	mt	t	t^2	$TM^2 = N^2$
Hellman+VDP	mt	$t \cdot \hat{t}$	$t \cdot \hat{t}$	$TM^2 = cN^2$
Rainbow+DP	mt	$\hat{t}$	$\frac{1}{2}\hat{t}^2$	$TM^2 = \frac{c^2}{2}N^2$
Rainbow+VDP	mt	$\frac{1}{2}\hat{t}^2$	$\frac{1}{2}\hat{t}^2$	$TM^2 = \frac{c^2}{2}N^2$

---

[3] It is also possible to sort exactly as with rainbow+DP and obtain similar results.

The table assumes that the parameters m and t satisfy the matrix stopping rule and that we have $\hat{t} = t_{\max} = c \cdot t$. We have listed the total number of pre-computed table entries M and the number of online f_i iterations T. The presented time complexity T disregards false alarms, and corresponds to the worst case, rather than the average case. In any real world use of a trade-off algorithm, there is a practical limit to how much can be loaded onto fast memory, and with bigger tables, access speed of the cheaper and slower storage becomes an important factor of the online time. So we have also given the number of online table searches.

The last column contains the trade-off curves satisfied by T and M. A hasty conclusion from this column alone would be that the rainbow method is the best and that the three algorithms we have introduced are inferior. But this does not seem to be the correct picture. For example, it is argued in [5] that each entry of a rainbow table demands about twice as many bits than that of a Hellman table. So, with equal amount of storage, the Hellman method would be faster by a factor of two, contrary to the naïve interpretation. This shows that finding the optimum number of bits to use for each table entry is crucial in comparing these algorithms.

Another issue in interpreting the above table concerns success probability, which is believed to be somewhat higher than 50% for all of the above algorithms. There are arguments giving lower bounds or expected values for the success rate, but this is not a very well understood subject, and a fair comparison of the algorithms should compare them at the same success rate. A related issue is how much pre-computation is needed to achieve this success rate.

For now, we can only state that the algorithms we have suggested are roughly the same in performance to the previous trade-off algorithms. There will be situations where one of the above algorithms is more suitable than the others, but any difference of performance between them will be by a small multiplicative factor.

Deferring a more exact and fair comparison between trade-off algorithms to a future work, in the next subsection, we will take a closer look into the complexity of finding the optimum number of bits to be allocated to a single entry.

5.2 Table Optimization

When using the Hellman trade-off, by setting the starting point to $(0 \,\|\, i \,\|\, j)$, one may store just j, and not i, which is common to HT$_i$. There are many other techniques for reducing storage that need to be considered. But, as these have side effects, such as more false alarms, their use is not simple.

We have tested some of the techniques discussed below, using Hellman+VDP, and the result is given in the full version of this paper [12]. Although the tests are not conclusive about the optimum choice, it shows that the following techniques should be considered.

Hash Table. Hash table is a way of structuring data in such a way that table searches take constant time. The idea is to use a simple function of the data as the address in which to store a given data. As explained in [7] and [2], this can also make ending point storage more efficient. One can save up to $\log(m)$ bits per entry from a table containing m entries. When seen as a hash table, our VDP method reaches this limit.

Ending Point Truncation. If a table contains m entries, we need at least $\log(m)$ bits to distinguish between the entries. If we expect to do l table lookups, we would want $\log(l)$ additional bits to filter out most of the accidental matches. Hence, simply leaving only $\log(ml)$ bits from the ending point could be an option. Depending on the trade-off algorithm, this method may or may not give additional savings, when used in conjunction with the hash table savings.

Storing Chain Lengths. With trade-off algorithms producing chains of variable length, as indicated in [16], storage of chain lengths reduces effort spent on false alarms. On the other hand, this requires $\log(t_{\max} - t_{\min})$ additional bits per table entry and we believe this may not be as cost effective as believed.

By storing only a few significant bits of the lengths or by simply not storing the lengths, we may increase the time spent on each false alarm, but the saved memory could be used to hold more (SP, EP) pairs and lead to smaller online f_i iterations. Moreover, proper use of the checkpoint method [2] may resolve the false alarm issue with just few extra bits per entry.

6 Conclusion

In this paper we suggested a new time memory trade-off technique named variable distinguished points (VDP), and showed how to combine the rainbow table method with the DP and VDP ideas.

The original Hellman trade-off terminated a pre-computation chain when it reached a certain fixed length, whereas chain termination in the DP method was taken when a chain element satisfied some preset condition. Our VDP method generalizes DP by allowing the termination condition itself to vary with each chain. The properties of VDP are very different from those of DP, requiring no sorting and aiming to reduce storage, rather than the number of table lookups.

Our combination of the rainbow method and DP or VDP, though simple, is also a nontrivial result. The changing reduction function of the rainbow method and varying chain length of the DP method presented a barrier to this combination, and the only known successful attempt [5,4] was on a rainbow variant that uses repeating patterns of reduction functions. We have shown that it is possible to overcome this barrier through a different sorting.

The performance of our algorithms is on a par with that of the previous trade-off algorithms, and thus there are more candidates to be considered with time memory trade-offs, than what was known before.

References

1. 3GPP TS 35.202 V7.0.0, Kasumi specification (2007-06), http://www.3gpp.org
2. Avoine, G., Junod, P., Oechslin, P.: Time-Memory Trade-Offs: False Alarm Detection Using Checkpoints. In: Maitra, S., Veni Madhavan, C.E., Venkatesan, R. (eds.) INDOCRYPT 2005. LNCS, vol. 3797, pp. 183–196. Springer, Heidelberg (2005)
3. Babbage, S.: Improved "Exhaustive Search" Attacks on Stream Ciphers. In: European Convention on Security and Detection, Conference publication, vol. 408, pp. 161–166, IEEE (1995)
4. Barkan, E.: Cryptanalysis of Ciphers and Protocols, Ph. D. Thesis. (2006), http://www.cs.technion.ac.il/users/wwwb/cgi-bin/tr-info.cgi?2006/PHD/PHD-2006-04
5. Barkan, E., Biham, E., Shamir, A.: Rigorous Bounds on Cryptanalytic Time/Memory Tradeoffs. In: Dwork, C. (ed.) CRYPTO 2006. LNCS, vol. 4117, pp. 1–21. Springer, Heidelberg (2006)
6. Biryukov, A., Shamir, A.: Cryptanalytic Time/Memory/Data Tradeoffs for Stream Ciphers. In: Okamoto, T. (ed.) ASIACRYPT 2000. LNCS, vol. 1976, pp. 1–13. Springer, Heidelberg (2000)
7. Biryukov, A., Shamir, A., Wagner, D.: Real Time Cryptanalysis of A5/1 on a PC. In: Schneier, B. (ed.) FSE 2000. LNCS, vol. 1978, pp. 1–18. Springer, Heidelberg (2001)
8. Borst, J., Preneel, B., Vandewalle, J.: On the Time-Memory Tradeoff Between Exhaustive Key Search and Table Precomputation. In: Proceedings of the 19th Symposium in Information Theory in the Benelux, WIC, pp. 111–118 (1998)
9. Denning, D.E.: Cryptography and Data Security, p. 100. Addison-Wesley, Reading (1982)
10. Golic, J.D.: Cryptanalysis of Alleged A5 Stream Cipher. In: Fumy, W. (ed.) EUROCRYPT 1997. LNCS, vol. 1233, pp. 239–255. Springer, Heidelberg (1997)
11. Hellman, M.E.: A Cryptanalytic Time-Memory Trade-Off. IEEE Transactions on Information Theory IT-26(4), 401–406 (1980)
12. Hong, J., Jeong, K.C., Kwon, E.Y., Lee, I.-S., Ma, D.: Variants of the Distinguished Point Method for Cryptanalytic Time Memory Trade-offs (Full version). Cryptology ePrint Archive, Report 2008/054 (2008), http://eprint.iacr.org/2008/054
13. Hong, J., Sarkar, P.: New Applications of Time Memory Data Tradeoffs. In: Roy, B. (ed.) ASIACRYPT 2005. LNCS, vol. 3788, pp. 353–372. Springer, Heidelberg (2005)
14. Kim, I.-J., Matsumoto, T.: Achieving Higher Success Probability in Time-Memory Trade-Off Cryptanalysis without Increasing Memory Size. IEICE Transactions on Fundamentals E82-A(1), 123–129 (1999)
15. Oechslin, P.: Making a Faster Cryptanalytic Time-Memory Trade-Off. In: Boneh, D. (ed.) CRYPTO 2003. LNCS, vol. 2729, pp. 617–630. Springer, Heidelberg (2003)
16. Standaert, F.-X., Rouvroy, G., Quisquater, J.-J., Legat, J.-D.: A Time-Memory Tradeoff Using Distinguished Points: New Analysis & FPGA Results. In: Kaliski Jr., B.S., Koç, Ç.K., Paar, C. (eds.) CHES 2002. LNCS, vol. 2523, pp. 593–609. Springer, Heidelberg (2003)

Secure Cryptographic Precomputation with Insecure Memory*

Patrick P. Tsang and Sean W. Smith

Department of Computer Science
Dartmouth College
Hanover, NH 03755, USA
{patrick,sws}@cs.dartmouth.edu

Abstract. We propose a solution that provides secure storage for cryptographic precomputation using insecure memory that is susceptible to eavesdropping and tampering. Specifically, we design a small tamper-resistant hardware module, the *Queue Security Proxy (QSP)*, that situates transparently on the data-path between the processor and the insecure memory. Our analysis shows that our design is secure and flexible, and yet efficient and inexpensive. In particular, both the timing overhead and the hardware cost of our solution are independent of the storage size.

1 Introduction

1.1 Precomputation

Precomputation is an optimization technique that reduces an algorithm's execution latency by performing some of its operations before knowing the input to the algorithm. The intermediate result produced by precomputation is stored and later used, when the input arrives, to compute the final output of the algorithm. As only the *post-computation*, i.e., the remaining computation that has not been precomputed, needs to be done to produce the output upon the input's arrival, execution latency is reduced.

Cryptographic Precomputation. In cryptography, precomputation is an old and well-known technique. For example, fixed-base modular exponentiation, which is an operation fundamental to almost all public-key cryptographic algorithms, can be sped up by precomputing a set of related exponentiations [6]. As another example, it has been widely observed that DSA signatures, as well as ElGamal and Schnorr signatures, can be precomputed [6]. More generally, all signature schemes converted from Σ-protocols [15] using the Fiat-Shamir transformation [4], which include many group signatures and anonymous credential

---

* This work was supported in part by the U.S. Department of Homeland Security under Grant Award Number 2006-CS-001-000001, the Institute for Security Technology Studies, under Grant number 2005-DD-BX-1091 awarded by the Bureau of Justice Assistance, and the National Science Foundation, under grant CNS-0524695. The views and conclusions do not necessarily represent those of the sponsors.

systems such as [5,7,29], can benefit from precomputation quite significantly, as most of the heavyweight operations, namely group exponentiation, can be precomputed in these schemes. Finally, precomputing homomorphic encryption can speed up mix-nets [8], as recently suggested in [1].

Reusable and Consumable Precomputation. Precomputation can be *reusable*, i.e., a single precomputation can be reused in multiple algorithm executions, or *consumable*, i.e., a new precomputation is needed per execution. Speeding up modular exponentiation using the sliding window method [31] is an example of reusable precomputation: any modular exponentiation with the same base can be sped up by one-time precomputing a set of values for that base. On the other hand, the precomputation of DSA signatures is consumable: the group generator must be exponentiated with a new exponent for every signature to be signed.

Consumable precomputation poses a bigger challenge than reusable precomputation does when it comes to efficiently securing it against hardware attacks. Precomputation, in general, requires *integrity* of the precomputation results. Consumable precomputation usually requires *confidentiality* and *protection against replay* as well. Finally, the storage space necessary for consumable precomputation grows with the rate and burstiness of the execution of an algorithm, while it is a constant in reusable precomputation.

In this paper, we are interested in overcoming the bigger challenge, i.e., how to efficiently secure consumable precomputation. In what follows, we refer to consumable precomputation as precomputation, for simplicity's sake.

1.2 The Challenge

Precomputation is capable of reducing the execution latency of an algorithm only if a precomputed result is available upon an input's arrival. In situations where an algorithm is routinely being executed over time, computing and storing only a single precomputation result would not sustain a low latency throughout the executions; to sustain a low latency, one must therefore buffer up precomputation results, i.e., precompute those results in advance and store them in such a way that they are readily available when needed.

The Need for Secure Storage. It is therefore of paramount importance to ensure that no security breach is introduced to a cryptographic algorithm by precomputing it. The safest approach when handling the precomputation results is to treat them as internal states of the entity executing the algorithm, thereby effectively assuming them to be unobservable and unmodifiable by anyone else. Consequences could be devastating should such an assumption cease to hold. For example, when precomputing DSA signatures, allowing an adversary to eavesdrop, overwrite, or replay even only one precomputation result would leak the private signing key.

As storing multiple precomputation results requires significantly larger memory than storing only the internal states needed for a single execution, it is unrealistic to assume that the whole storage would fit in a tamper-resistant

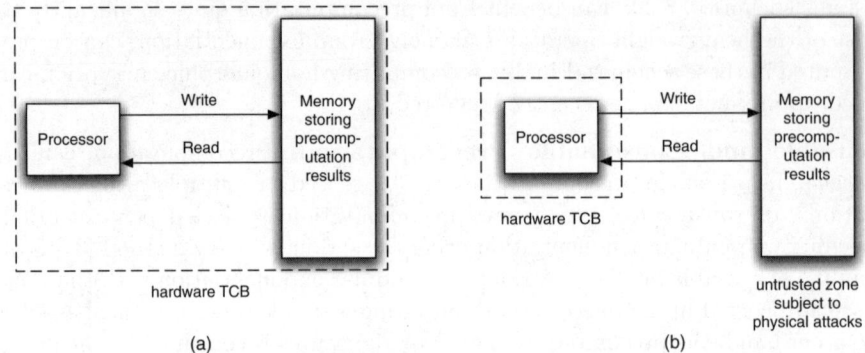

Fig. 1. (a) Keeping the storage inside the hardware TCB is unrealistic; (b) putting the storage outside the hardware TCB exposes us to attacks

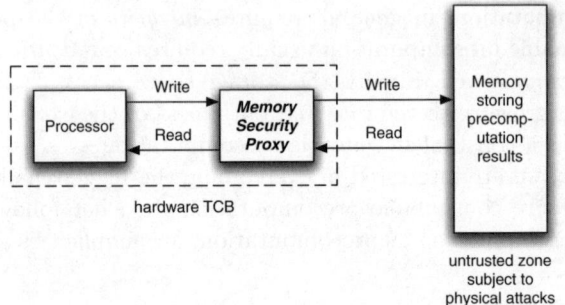

Fig. 2. In our model, we keep the hardware TCB small by leaving the storage outside, but adding a small Memory Security Proxy

module such as a hardened CPU (see Figure 1(a)). Leaving the memory outside (see Figure 1(b)) exposes us to the attacks discussed above. In this paper, we design a small tamper-resistant hardware module that effectively turns insecure memory into one that is secure for storing precomputation results—see Figure 2.

1.3 Our Contributions

We make the following contributions in this paper:

- We motivate that, to sustain the reduced execution latency of cryptographic algorithms made possible by precomputation, one needs to store a pool of readily available precomputation results; and that the security of such storage is critical to the security of the cryptographic algorithms.
- We design an architecture that transparently turns untrusted memory into one that is secure for storing precomputation results. The design is very efficient and has hardware and timing costs independent of the size of the memory. Our analysis shows that the architecture we propose is secure.

The rest of this paper is organized as follows. In Section 2, we provide some background on hardware-based security and review the necessary cryptography. In Section 3, we describe our approach to overcome the posed challenge. We present our solution in detail in Section 4, and analyze its security and efficiency in Section 5. We discuss several research directions that are worth exploring in Section 6, and conclude the paper in Section 7.

2 Background

2.1 Hardware-Based Security

Designing hardware-based security mechanisms into the computing architecture is important as software security solutions are incapable of defending against hardware attacks and many software attacks. There are mechanisms that provide security against physical tampering through means such as tamper resistance, tamper evidence, and tamper detection and response. Deploying a hardware-based security mechanism could be very expensive; different trade-offs between security and cost can lead to radically different solution paradigms.

The IBM 4756 Approach. The IBM 4758/4764 cryptographic coprocessors [25,12] are secure crypto processors implemented on a programmable PCI board, on which components such as a microprocessor, memory, and a random number generator are housed within a tamper-responding environment. They are general-purpose x86 computers with a very high security assurance against physical attacks. While they find applications in the commerce sector such as securing bank ATMs, their high costs prevent most end-users from benefiting from them.

The Hardened-CPU Approach. A more realistic approach to secure general-purpose computers such as today's PCs against software and even certain hardware attacks is by assuming that only CPUs are hardened. In their *Oblivious RAM (ORAM)* work, Goldreich and Ostrovsky [14] formalized a general approach to protecting the contents of exposed memory, including hiding access patterns. However, ORAM is too inefficient to use in practice. Lie et al.'s *eXecute-Only Memory (XOM)* [18] architecture built hardened-CPU prototypes but is vulnerable to replay attacks. Suh et al. later proposed *AEGIS* [26], which is immune to replay attacks and uses techniques such as Merkle-trees [20] for better efficiency. Other advances include using AES in the Counter mode to reduce memory-write latencies [27,30], prediction techniques to hide the memory-read latencies in [22,24], and on-chip caches [13] and incremental multi-set hashes [9] to reduce latency incurred by memory integrity checking.

The architecture we are going to propose in this paper falls under the hardened-CPU approach. Rather than arbitrary software, however, our architecture deals only with precomputation. We note that although architectures like AEGIS can provide the same functionality as ours, ours is simpler and more efficient due to the exploitation of properties of precomputation. In fact, while AEGIS aims to provide a secure execution environment for general-purpose computers such as x86 PCs, we gear our architecture towards a coprocessor for embedded devices.

The TCG's TPM Approach. The *Trusted Computing Group (TCG)* is a consortium that works towards increasing the security of standard commodity platforms. The group proposed a specification of an inexpensive micro-controller chip called the *Trusted Platform Module (TPM)* [28] to be mounted on the motherboard of commodity computing devices such as PCs. In the last few years, major vendors of computer systems have been shipping machines that have included TPMs, with associated BIOS support.

A TPM provides cryptographic functions, e.g., encryption, digital signature and hardware-based random number generation, and internal storage space for storing, e.g., cryptographic keys. TPMs act as a hardware-based root of trust and can be used to attest the initial configuration of the underlying computing platform (*attestation*), as well as to seal and bind data to a specific platform configuration (*unsealing* or *unwrapping*). The aspiration is that if the adversary compromises neither the TPM nor the BIOS, then the TPM's promises of trusted computing will be achieved. The reality is murkier: attacks on the OS can still subvert protections; recent work (e.g., [17]) is starting to demonstrate some external hardware integration flaws; and the long history of low-cost physical attacks on low-cost devices (e.g., [2]) hasn't caught up with the TPM yet.

2.2 Cryptographic Tools

Various symmetric and asymmetric cryptographic techniques provide security guarantees such as confidentiality, authentication and integrity. For example, AES is a block cipher that provides confidentiality of data, whereas HMAC is a message authentication scheme that provides both message authentication and integrity. Here we review a relatively recent cryptographic tool called *authenticated encryption*, which effectively combines the functionality of AES and HMAC. Our solution makes use of it.

Modes of Operation. A block cipher is a function that operates on blocklength bit strings based on a key; each key determines some way of mapping block-length strings to block-length strings. Since using a block cipher on its own leads to many problems—for example, what to do with messages that are longer than a single block—*modes of operation* have been developed that describe how to extend a cipher to a secure encryption scheme.

Standard modes of operation include *Electronic Code Book (ECB)*, *Cipher-Block Chaining (CBC)*, and the *Counter (CTR)* mode. Different modes have different properties. For instance, decryption is faster than encryption under the CBC mode, which is preferable when decryption is on the critical path. The CTR mode can potentially further reduce both encryption and decryption latency by taking the AES operations away from the critical path.

Authenticated Encryption. Encryption constructed from block ciphers such as AES operating under any of the modes aforementioned provides data confidentiality but no data authenticity or integrity. The past decade has seen the emergence of modes of operation that efficiently provide both. When operating under these modes, a block cipher effectively becomes authenticated encryption [3], rather than just encryption alone. Among these modes, the *Counter with CBC-MAC (CCM)* mode and the *Galois/Counter (GC)* mode are particularly attractive because authentication is done without any feedback of datablocks. This means that both authentication and encryption can be parallelized to achieve extremely high throughput. We use AES under GC mode (AES-GCM) in our solution.

AES-GCM has two operations, authenticated encryption AEnc and authenticated decryption ADec. AEnc takes four inputs: (i) a *secret key K* appropriate for the underlying AES, (ii) an *initialization vector IV*, (iii) a *plaintext P*, and (iv) an *additional authenticated data (AAD) A*. Both the plaintext and the AAD will be authenticated; however, only the plaintext will be encrypted as well. AEnc outputs (i) a *ciphertext C* whose length is the same as that of P and (ii) an *authentication tag T*. The authentication tag is essentially the cryptographic checksum of the message. ADec takes five inputs: K, IV, C, A and T. It outputs either P or a special symbol that indicates failure, i.e., the inputs are not authentic. We refer the readers to [19,11] for details regarding the specification, performance and security of AES-GCM.

3 Our Approach

We now return to the challenge we discussed in Section 1: how to cost-effectively provide a secure storage for cryptographic precomputation so that it can provide a sustainable benefit without breaking the security. We introduce in this section our approach to overcome such a challenge.

3.1 Memory Security Proxy

Since putting memory within the hardware TCB would not meet our design goal of being cost-effective, in our solution insecure memory will be used. To account for the fact that insecure memory can be eavesdropped and tampered with, we augment its use with security measures enforced by a small tamper-proof hardware module through cryptographic techniques. We call such a module the *Memory Security Proxy (MSP)*. The MSP must be efficient in both space and computation: its size (e.g., in terms of gate-count) and the timing overhead it incurs should grow as slowly as possible with—or even better, be independent of—the size of the insecure memory it is securing.

In our solution, the MSP situates between the insecure memory and the processor, the latter of which executes (the pre- and post-computation of) the cryptographic algorithm. The MSP effectively turns the insecure memory into a secure one by instrumenting the processor's read and write accesses. This means that the MSP will incur timing overhead on these accesses, but should otherwise be transparent to the processor: the processor is oblivious to whether it is accessing insecure memory without protection whatsoever, memory secured through hardware tamper-proof mechanisms, or our MSP. This is an attractive property, as it simplifies designs and allows better interoperability and upgradability.

In a threat model where adversary is physically present and capable of launching hardware attacks against the computing devices, the processor that executes the cryptographic operations must be trusted to behave securely regardless of those attacks. Similarly, we rely on the MSP to be as trustworthy as the main processor. This is a realistic assumption because any satisfactory MSP design is going to have a very small physical size, most likely just a small fraction of the size of the processor. Figure 2 depicts our architectural model.

We point out that the above model is not a new one; rather, all architectures we reviewed in Section 2 that take the hardened-CPU approach follow this model. However, all those architectures focus on securing general-purpose computers such as PCs, in which the insecure memory being protected is randomly-accessible. It has been proven in these works that it is very difficult to efficiently secure insecure RAM. However, we only need to protect a storage of precomputed results. As we will show next, we can exploit the properties of cryptographic precomputation to avoid some of the difficulties and thus achieve better performance results.

3.2 Data Structure for Precomputation Storage

Applying precomputation to a cryptographic algorithm turns the algorithm's execution into a process that follows the *producer-consumer model*. Under such a model, the producer produces, through precomputation, the goods (i.e., the precomputation results) that are later consumed by the consumer, through postcomputation, upon the arrival of algorithmic inputs. The asynchronous communication channel between the producer and the consumer may be implemented using data structures such as stacks, *First-In-First-Out (FIFO)* queues, register arrays (a.k.a. RAM), depending on the desired order of the goods being consumed (relative to them being produced).

We make the observation that using precomputation results in the same order as they were produced always yields a correct execution of the cryptographic algorithms. In fact, in many cases precomputation results are statistically uncorrelated to one another, and one may thus even use them in arbitrary order. The precomputation of DSA signatures is one example. Consequently, data structures such as RAM and FIFO queues are legitimate candidates for storing cryptographic precomputation results. In our design to be presented in the next section, we use FIFO queues rather than RAM because of the following reasons:

– Securing insecure RAM efficiently has been proven to be difficult. On the contrary, as we will see, our securing insecure FIFO queues is very efficient.
– Insecure FIFO queues can be efficiently implemented using insecure RAM (in both software and hardware) but not the other way round. Hence, our solution requires only the "weaker" data structure.

From now on, we abbreviate FIFO queues as queues. Also, we call the Memory Security Proxy we are going to build the *Queue Security Proxy (QSP)*, as it is specialized for protecting queues. Next, we provide some formalism of queues, which is necessary to reason about the correctness and security of our design.

Queues. A queue is a data structure that implements a First-In, First-Out (FIFO) policy by supporting two operations, namely Enqueue and Dequeue, which inserts and deletes elements from the data structure respectively. Such a policy can be more rigorously specified using the axiomatic approach of Larch [16], in which an object's sequential history is summarized by a value that reflects the object's state at the end of the history. A queue implementation is said to be *correct* if the policy is satisfied. For simplicity's sake, we also use the following verbal definition of correctness: A queue is correct if the i-th item dequeued has the same value as the i-th item enqueued for all $i \in \mathbb{N}$. Note that correctness is defined assuming the absence of an adversary.

3.3 Threat Model

We now define the security requirements of the QSP and the threat model under which these requirements must be met. To attack the security of the QSP, a computationally bounded but physically present adversary may launch physical attacks on the untrusted zone of the architecture, as illustrated in Figure 2. Such an adversary may also probe the input-output relationship of the QSP as follows. She may arbitrarily and adaptively ask the processor to produce a precomputation result and enqueue it to the QSP, as well as to dequeue a precomputation result from the QSP and reveal it to her. Note that in reality a precomputation result is never directly revealed to anybody. We give such a capability to the adversary so that the security of the QSP can be agnostic to the cryptographic algorithm being precomputed. Such a modeling provides a confidentiality guarantee at least as strong as needed.

We regard a QSP design as secure if it has correctness, confidentiality and integrity, defined as follows.

Correctness. If the underlying queue that a QSP is protecting is correct, then the QSP behaves correctly as a queue in the absence of an adversary.

Confidentiality. We hinted earlier that the safest strategy to take when securing precomputation storage is to assume the entire precomputation result to be as private as any algorithmic internal states. In certain scenarios, however, part of the precomputation result can be made public. One such scenario is when that part will eventually appear in the final algorithmic output, and its release prior to the arrival of the input does not lead to security breaches. Not having to encrypt the whole result improves efficiency.

As an example, the precomputation result of DSA signing is of the form (r, k^{-1}) (as defined in [21]). The knowledge of r alone, which will eventually be a part of the output signature, does not give any extra information to any computationally bounded adversary, whereas knowing k^{-1} would allow the extraction of the secret key and thus lead to universal compromise.

If we denote a precomputation result to be enqueued as a data object $D = (A, P)$, where confidentiality is necessary for P, but not A, then a QSP design has confidentiality if no adversary, whose capabilities are as described above, can learn, with non-negligible probability, any information about the P in any D that the adversary did not ask the processor to reveal.

Integrity. Roughly speaking, a QSP with integrity is one that either responds to accesses correctly as a queue, or signals an error when having been tampered with. Note that this definition of integrity implies both authenticity and freshness of precomputation results. Specifically, if an adversary can modify a precomputation result, say the i-th one enqueued, without the QSP being able to detect it no latter than it is being dequeued, then the QSP would not be correct as what is dequeued at the i-th time is different from what was enqueued at the i-th time. Similarly, the ability to replay an old result leads to the same violation of integrity.

More formally, an adversary is successful in attacking the integrity of a QSP when there exists an $i \in \mathbb{N}$ such that the precomputation results enqueued at the i-th time differs from what is dequeued at the i-th time. A QSP design has integrity if no adversary with capabilities described above can succeed with non-negligible probability.

4 Our QSP Design

We first give the solution idea behind our QSP design. We then present the actual design, first in the form of software pseudo-code to facilitate understanding of the design and reasoning about its correctness and security, then in the form of a hardware architectural design.

4.1 Solution Idea

The use of authenticated encryption makes our QSP design very simple. Precomputation results (*Data_in*) generated by the processor are fed to the QSP. The QSP encrypts these results with AES-GCM, incrementing the initialization vector (*IV_out*) per encryption. Incrementing the IV serves two purposes. First, for AES-GCM to be secure, the IV should never be reused under the same key. Second, the IV serves as a counter that gives a sequential and consecutive ordering to the precomputation results being operated on, and hence helps defending against replay attacks. The output of the AES-GCM encryption (*SecData_out*) can then be enqueued into an insecure queue.

When the processor asks for a precomputation result from storage, the QSP dequeues an entry from the insecure queue and decrypts that entry using AES-GCM. Again, the initialization vector (*IV_in*) increments per decryption. As long as *IV_in* and *IV_out* are set to the same value (e.g. zero) during start-up before any enqueue or dequeue operations, the precomputation result encrypted with an IV value will eventually be decrypted with the same IV value.

4.2 The Construction

System Parameters. Keys in the QSP may remain constant throughout the lifetime of the QSP, or be randomly generated during boot-time. Using a new set of keys effectively means all the old precomputation results are flushed. The two IVs are set to zero during start-up. We chose AES-128 for AES-GCM. This means a key size of 128-bit. The size of the IVs has to be such that the IVs never overflow. We used 80-bit IVs. Finally we selected 96-bit as the size of the Tag.

Software Construction. Without loss of generality, we assume that the underlying insecure queue, denoted by Q, provides an interface for querying whether it is full or not, and empty or not. Algorithms below show the software implementation of the enqueue and dequeue operations performed by the QSP.

Algorithm QSP.Enqueue($Data_{in}$)
private input: K, IV_{out}, Q
1: if Q.isFull() then
2:    return error
3: $\langle P_{in}, A_{in} \rangle \leftarrow Data_{in}$
4: $\langle C_{out}, T_{out} \rangle \leftarrow$ AEnc($K, IV_{out}, P_{in}, A_{in}$)
5: $IV_{out} \leftarrow IV_{out} + 1$
6: $SecData_{out} \leftarrow \langle A_{in}, C_{out}, T_{out} \rangle$
7: Q.enqueue($SecData_{out}$)

Algorithm QSP.Dequeue()
private input: K, IV_{in}, Q
1: if Q.isEmpty() then
2:    return error
3: $SecData_{in} \leftarrow Q$.dequeue()
4: $\langle A_{out}, C_{in}, T_{in} \rangle \leftarrow SecData_{in}$
5: $res \leftarrow$ ADec($K, IV_{in}, C_{in}, A_{out}, T_{in}$)
6: if $res =$ **failure** then
7:    return error
8: else
9:    $IV_{in} \leftarrow IV_{in} + 1$
10:   $P_{out} \leftarrow res$
11:   return $Data_{out} \leftarrow \langle P_{out}, A_{out} \rangle$

Hardware Construction. Figure 3 shows the architectural design of our QSP. $Data\_in$ and $Data\_out$ are connected to the processor, while $SecData\_in$ and $SecData\_out$ are connected to the insecure queue. We assume that the insecure queue is asynchronous, i.e., it supports asynchronous enqueuing and dequeuing. It is straightforward to modify the design if a synchronous queue is used instead.

Notice that the authenticated encryption of a precomputation result is bigger in size than the result itself. One may replace the data-bus for $SecData$ (both in and out) with a wider one. Another possibility is to change the software that implements the cryptographic algorithm so that precomputation results do not use up the whole bus-width and that they still fit in the bus after the expansion. However, both approaches require modification to the existing hardware and/or software and thus lack transparency and interoperability.

Our recommended approach is to have the QSP split up every incoming precomputation result into two halves and enqueue each half as if it was a single precomputation result. Splitting into two halves works as long as precomputation results are greater than tags in size, which is practical always the case (recall that tags are 96-bit long). Similarly, when being dequeued, the QSP dequeues

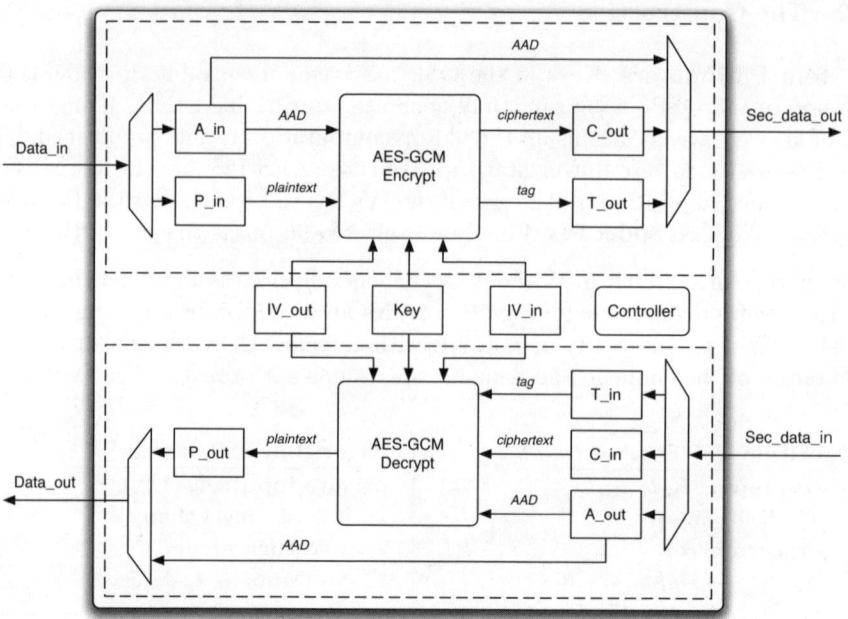

Fig. 3. The architectural design of our QSP. The upper region contributes to the QSP.Enqueue logic; the lower region contributes to the QSP.Dequeue logic. Control signals are omitted for clarity.

the insecure queue twice and combine the two items into a single precomputation result. It is easy to see that a secure QSP remains secure with this splitting mechanism in place.

5 Solution Analysis

5.1 Security

Correctness of our QSP design is a straightforward consequence of AES-GCM's correctness. It is also trivial to see that the confidentiality of AES-GCM implies that our QSP design has confidentiality.

Our QSP design has integrity as well. We argue why below. Assume the contrary that our QSP has no integrity, then there exists an adversary whose capabilities are as described in Section 3.3 such that he, during an attack, was successful in causing the QSP to return a precomputation result D' at the i-th dequeue for some i, where D' is different from the precomputation result D given to the QSP during the i-th enqueue. If i is not unique, let i be the minimum value. Now since AES-GCM decryption did not return failure during that particular dequeue of QSP, the security of AES-GCM implies that $D = D'$, which contradicts to $D \neq D'$. Therefore our QSP has integrity.

5.2 Efficiency

Let n be the maximum number of precomputation results the insecure memory will store. Let the bit-lengths of the key K, the IVs IV_{in} and IV_{out}, the plaintext P, the AAD A and the tag T be ℓ_K, ℓ_{IV}, ℓ_P, ℓ_A and ℓ_T respectively. The bit-length of a precomputation result ℓ_D is thus $\ell_A + \ell_P$.

Space Complexity. Our QSP requires a trusted storage of constant size independent of the size of the storage for precomputation results; it has a untrusted storage overhead of $\frac{\ell_T}{\ell_D}$. In case of DSA precomputation, $\ell_D = 320$ and the overhead is thus 30% (recall that we picked $\ell_T = 96$). Space overhead is generally not a problem as insecure memory is inexpensive. Moreover, the figure would be a lot smaller for many group signatures, as they can easily have precomputation results comprised of 10 or more 160-bit elements.

Time Complexity. The latency incurred by our QSP during an enqueue operation is the time it takes to do one—or two, if precomputation results are split into halves as previously discussed—AES-GCM encryption. As discussed, we chose AES-GCM to implement the authenticated encryption because of its extremely low latency independent of ℓ_D, which is made possible by parallelization. The actual throughput and latency of AES-GCM operations depend on the hardware implementation. Some performance figures can be found in [19,23]. In [23], AES-GCM achieves 102 Gbps throughout with 979 Kgates using 0.13-μm CMOS standard cell library.

The latency incurred by our QSP during a dequeue operation can be argued similarly. However, we would like to highlight that enqueue latency is usually not a concern as this operation, like precomputation itself, is not on the critical path of the algorithmic execution. Therefore, one might not even care about speeding up the QSP's enqueue operation. For example, in case of a hardware implementation, one could save cost by using less or even no parallelization, at the expense of slower enqueuing.

Table 1. Many existing approaches can be used to secure insecure memory for storing precomputation results, but their complexities grow with n, the number of precomputation results to be stored; our QSP requires constant trusted storage size, and incurs constant total latency when reading or writing precomputation results. (The $\log^4 n$ ORAM algorithm only becomes more efficient when $n > 2^{20}$.)

	Trusted Storage Size	Write Latency	Read Latency
Hardened RAM	$O(n)$	$O(1)$	$O(1)$
Oblivious RAM [14]	$O(\log n)$	$O(\sqrt{n}\log n)$, $O(\log^4 n)$	$O(\sqrt{n}\log n)$, $O(\log^4 n)$
AEGIS [26]	$O(1)$	$O(\log n)$	$O(\log n)$
AEGIS with prediction and caching [24,22,13]	$O(1)$	$O(\log n)$	$O(\log n)$ total, $O(1)$ non-hideable
Our QSP	$O(1)$	$O(1)$	$O(1)$

On the other hand, since QSP dequeuing is usually on the critical path, dequeuing latency is a concern. To dequeue more quickly, we suggest slightly changing the QSP design to pre-fetch and pre-decrypt the next precomputation result stored in the insecure queue. (If splitting is employed, the next two results are pre-fetched and pre-decrypted instead.) This way, precomputation results become readily available to be dequeued at the QSP when the processor wants them. Hence, our QSP provides all its security guarantees with virtually zero timing overhead during dequeuing.

Table 1 compares the efficiency of our QSP with other approaches.

6 Discussion

A DSA Signing Coprocessor. One can build a cost-effective low-latency DSA signature signing secure coprocessor by using our QSP to securely store DSA precomputation. Such a coprocessor can be used to secure the communications in critical infrastructures, especially those that impose stringent timing requirements on tolerable latency of message delivery such as some Supervisory Control And Data Acquisition (SCADA) systems in the power grid.

Generalizing the Producer-Consumer Model. We have assumed that the producer and the consumer of precomputation results are the same entity, namely the processor. Alternatively, they can be two separated entities such that the insecure queue through which precomputation results are piped is the only communication channel between them. This allows dynamic pairing between the producers and the consumers.

More interestingly, the number of producers and that of consumers can differ. For example, multiple consumers may be coupled with only a single producer trusted by the consumers. Consider a scenario where people carry electronic devices. For security reasons, each device signs DSA signatures on its outgoing messages when communicating with devices carried by other people and therefore requires a DSA signing engine. However, if a person has a single DSA precomputation module shared and trusted by all devices he carries, then those devices need only to do the post-computation. The hardware saving is huge since the circuitry for DSA postcomputation is a lot simpler than that for precomputation. Similar scenarios include communications among sensors installed in cars, among household electrical appliances, as well as among sensors and actuators in power substations.

MSPs for Other Data Structures. In this paper, we have focused on building a Memory Security Proxy for FIFO queues as they fit naturally for cryptographic precomputation. Some other works have looked at ways to secure RAM for general-purpose computing. MSPs for other data structures, e.g., stacks, sets and dictionaries, may also be useful. For instance, resource-limited devices such as smart cards and set-top boxes may offload implementations of data structures on to hostile platforms. As an example, Devanbu et al. [10] have proposed how to protect the integrity (but not confidentiality) of stacks and queues.

7 Conclusions

In this paper, we have motivated the need for a secure storage for cryptographic precomputation to provide sustainable benefits securely. Our solution to the challenge of how to construct such a storage is a small tamper-resistant module called the *Queue Security Proxy (QSP)*. We have demonstrated how our design can guarantee the necessary security despite hardware attacks. We have also shown, via analysis, that our proposed design provides these security benefits without impacting performance.

In the future, we plan to prototype our QSP solution using FPGA to gain empirical figures on its performance (in terms of throughput and latency) and hardware costs (in terms of gate counts), and compare these figures with other approaches.

References

1. Adida, B., Wikström, D.: Offline/Online Mixing. In: Arge, L., Cachin, C., Jurdziński, T., Tarlecki, A. (eds.) ICALP 2007. LNCS, vol. 4596, pp. 484–495. Springer, Heidelberg (2007)
2. Anderson, R., Kuhn, M.: Tamper Resistance—A Cautionary Note. In: Proceedings of the 2nd USENIX Workshop on Electronic Commerce, pp. 1–11 (1996)
3. Bellare, M., Namprempre, C.: Authenticated Encryption: Relations among Notions and Analysis of the Generic Composition Paradigm. In: Okamoto, T. (ed.) ASIACRYPT 2000. LNCS, vol. 1976, pp. 531–545. Springer, Heidelberg (2000)
4. Bellare, M., Rogaway, P.: Random Oracles are Practical: A Paradigm for Designing Efficient Protocols. In: Proceedings of the 1st ACM conference on Computer and communications security, pp. 62–73. ACM Press, New York (1993)
5. Boneh, D., Boyen, X., Shacham, H.: Short Group Signatures. In: Franklin, M. (ed.) CRYPTO 2004. LNCS, vol. 3152, pp. 41–55. Springer, Heidelberg (2004)
6. Brickell, E.F., Gordon, D.M., McCurley, K.S., Wilson, D.B.: Fast Exponentiation with Precomputation (Extended Abstract). In: Rueppel, R.A. (ed.) EUROCRYPT 1992. LNCS, vol. 658, pp. 200–207. Springer, Heidelberg (1993)
7. Camenisch, J., Lysyanskaya, A.: An Efficient System for Non-transferable Anonymous Credentials with Optional Anonymity Revocation. In: Pfitzmann, B. (ed.) EUROCRYPT 2001. LNCS, vol. 2045, pp. 93–118. Springer, Heidelberg (2001)
8. Chaum, D.: Untraceable Electronic Mail, Return Addresses, and Digital Pseudonyms. Communications of the ACM 4(2) (February 1981)
9. Clarke, D.E., Devadas, S., van Dijk, M., Gassend, B., Suh, G.E.: Incremental Multiset Hash Functions and Their Application to Memory Integrity Checking. In: Laih, C.-S. (ed.) ASIACRYPT 2003. LNCS, vol. 2894, pp. 188–207. Springer, Heidelberg (2003)
10. Devanbu, P.T., Stubblebine, S.G.: Stack and Queue Integrity on Hostile Platforms. IEEE Trans. Software Eng. 28(1), 100–108 (2002)
11. Dworkin, M.: Recommendation for Block Cipher Modes of Operation: Galois/Counter Mode (GCM) and GMAC (June 2007)
12. Dyer, J.G., Lindemann, M., Perez, R., Sailer, R., van Doorn, L., Smith, S.W., Weingart, S.: Building the IBM 4758 Secure Coprocessor. IEEE Computer 34(10), 57–66 (2001)

13. Gassend, B., Suh, G.E., Clarke, D.E., van Dijk, M., Devadas, S.: Caches and Hash Trees for Efficient Memory Integrity. In: HPCA, pp. 295–306 (2003)
14. Goldreich, O., Ostrovsky, R.: Software Protection and Simulation on Oblivious RAMs. Journal of the ACM 43(3), 431–473 (1996)
15. Goldwasser, S., Micali, S., Rackoff, C.: The Knowledge Complexity of Interactive Proof Systems. SIAM J. Comput. 18(1), 186–208 (1989)
16. Guttag, J.V., Horning, J.J.: Larch: Languages and Tools for Formal Specification. Springer, New York (1993)
17. Kauer, B.: OSLO: Improving the Security of Trusted Computing. In: USENIX Security Symposium, USENIX, pp. 229–237 (2007)
18. Lie, D., Thekkath, C.A., Mitchell, M., Lincoln, P., Boneh, D., Mitchell, J.C., Horowitz, M.: Architectural Support for Copy and Tamper Resistant Software. In: ASPLOS, pp. 168–177 (2000)
19. McGrew, D.A., Viega, J.: The Security and Performance of the Galois/Counter Mode (GCM) of Operation. In: Canteaut, A., Viswanathan, K. (eds.) INDOCRYPT 2004. LNCS, vol. 3348, pp. 343–355. Springer, Heidelberg (2004)
20. Merkle, R.C.: Protocols for Public Key Cryptosystems. In: IEEE Symposium on Security and Privacy, pp. 122–134 (1980)
21. NIST. FIPS 186-2: Digital Signature Standard (DSS). Technical report, National Institute of Standards and Technology (NIST) (2000)
22. Rogers, B., Solihin, Y., Prvulovic, M.: Memory Predecryption: Hiding the Latency Overhead of Memory Encryption. SIGARCH Computer Architecture News 33(1), 27–33 (2005)
23. Satoh, A.: High-Speed Parallel Hardware Architecture for Galois Counter Mode. In: ISCAS, pp. 1863–1866. IEEE Computer Society Press, Los Alamitos (2007)
24. Shi, W., Lee, H.-H.S., Ghosh, M., Lu, C., Boldyreva, A.: High Efficiency Counter Mode Security Architecture via Prediction and Precomputation. In: ISCA, pp. 14–24. IEEE Computer Society Press, Los Alamitos (2005)
25. Smith, S.W., Weingart, S.: Building a High-performance, Programmable Secure Coprocessor. Computer Networks 31(8), 831–860 (1999)
26. Suh, G.E., Clarke, D.E., Gassend, B., van Dijk, M., Devadas, S.: AEGIS: Architecture for tamper-evident and tamper-resistant processing. In: ICS, pp. 160–171. ACM Press, New York (2003)
27. Suh, G.E., Clarke, D.E., Gassend, B., van Dijk, M., Devadas, S.: Efficient Memory Integrity Verification and Encryption for Secure Processors. In: MICRO, pp. 339–350. ACM/IEEE (2003)
28. TPM Work Group. TCG TPM Specification Version 1.2 Revision 103. Technical report, Trusted Computing Group (2007)
29. Tsang, P.P., Au, M.H., Kapadia, A., Smith, S.W.: Blacklistable Anonymous Credentials: Blocking Misbehaving Users without TTPs. In: CCS 2007: Proceedings of the 14th ACM conference on Computer and communications security, pp. 72–81. ACM, New York (2007)
30. Yang, J., Zhang, Y., Gao, L.: Fast Secure Processor for Inhibiting Software Piracy and Tampering. In: MICRO, pp. 351–360. ACM/IEEE (2003)
31. Yen, S.-M., Laih, C.-S., Lenstra, A.K.: Multi-Exponentiation. In: IEEE Proc. Computers and Digital Techniques, vol. 141, pp. 325–326 (1994)

Securing Peer-to-Peer Distributions for Mobile Devices

André Osterhues[1], Ahmad-Reza Sadeghi[1], Marko Wolf[1], Christian Stüble[2], and N. Asokan[3]

[1] Horst Görtz Institute for IT Security, Ruhr-University Bochum, Germany
andre.osterhues@rub.de, ahmad.sadeghi@trust.rub.de, mwolf@crypto.rub.de
[2] Sirrix AG Security Technologies, Bochum, Germany
stueble@sirrix.com
[3] Nokia Research Center, Helsinki, Finland
n.asokan@nokia.com

Abstract. Peer-to-peer (P2P) architectures offer a flexible and user-friendly way to distribute digital content (e.g., sharing, rental, or superdistribution). However, the parties involved have different interests (e.g., user privacy vs. license enforcement) that should be reflected in the P2P security architecture.

We identify characteristic P2P scenarios and demonstrate how these can be realized by applying a few basic licensing operations. We present a security architecture to realize these basic license operations (i) in a generalized fashion and (ii) employing the ARM TrustZone technology, which is popular for embedded systems. Lastly, we extend existing superdistribution schemes for offline application, allowing a mobile peer to access superdistributed content without the need to first contact the actual licensor.

Keywords: Trusted Computing, security architectures, peer-to-peer, superdistribution, TrustZone.

1 Introduction

In contrast to traditional client-server software distribution architectures, a party in a peer-to-peer (P2P) distribution architecture is both client and server at the same time, since it can both acquire and (re-)distribute content. Since no central server is required, P2P architectures enable flexible, efficient, and user-friendly means of distributing digital content such as lending, sharing, transfer of ownership, and superdistribution. To attain wide acceptance and become deployed in commercial applications, P2P content distribution architectures need to carry out adequate measures to preserve the security of *all* parties involved (e.g., user privacy vs. license enforcement). Up to now, most content distribution systems rely on traditional client-server architectures with a trusted server and a client that connects to the corresponding server to acquire certain content. While the server can be protected by various effective security mechanisms, the corresponding client devices can hardly be verified for a proper configuration. Particularly, since clients are often devices that are logically and physically under the control of their owners, client users can attack and circumvent even the most sophisticated protection mechanisms by running exploits, re-configuring the underlying operating system, or mounting even simple hardware attacks. Faced with these difficulties, providers tend to impose inflexible usage conditions on their users that, for instance, prevent users from transferring content between devices, lending or selling it to others or, even worse, blindly prevent the copying of protected content at all.

Main Contribution. In this work, we present a generic security architecture that is able to securely realize existing P2P distribution scenarios, even for mobile devices that are completely under the control of their owners. To demonstrate this, we first identify available P2P use cases and show how they can be implemented by applying a few basic license operations. We show the technical feasibility of securely realizing these license operations and propose an example implementation applicable particularly to mobile devices based on the TrustZone technology from ARM [1]. Further, we extend existing superdistribution schemes for *offline* application, allowing a mobile peer to access superdistributed content immediately without having to contact the actual licensor before.

Outline. Following this introductory discussion, in Section 2 we identify various P2P use cases and define a small set of basic license operations sufficient to realize all these P2P use cases. In Section 3, we present a generic security architecture that is able to realize these basic license operations and the corresponding security requirements. To demonstrate that the described architecture is suitable also for mobile devices, in Section 4 we propose an exemplary implementation based on ARM TrustZone technology [1].

Related Work. Superdistribution was devised by Ryoichi Mori in 1983. The first implementation [7] is targeted at software rather than multimedia content and uses a tamper-resistant hardware extension called S-Box, which contains a microprocessor, RAM, ROM and a real-time clock. A software program distributed via superdistribution communicates with the S-Box in order to monitor usage information. Thus, the software program has to include code to support the S-Box. Also, the S-Box hardware has only been implemented as a prototype, therefore being complex and expensive. However, the authors conclude that future versions could be designed on a single chip attached to the bus.

More recently, the Open Mobile Alliance (OMA) included superdistribution into the OMA DRM 2.0 standard [9], which defines the requirements and architecture for superdistribution, but not how it should be implemented. However, a lot of today's mobile phones already support OMA DRM 2.0.

Sandhu and Zhang [11] present an architecture that provides access control (which can be used to enable stateful licenses) using Trusted Computing technology. Their architecture features a trusted hardware component such as a TPM, a secure kernel, sealed storage, and a trusted reference monitor that interacts with applications through secure channels. However, the authors only give a high-level description of the distribution protocol, thus neglecting replay attacks.

In [10], the authors present a security architecture based on Trusted Computing technology as proposed by the Trusted Computing Group (TCG). This approach, which is based on virtualization, a small security kernel and a TCG Trusted Platform Module (TPM), provides protection on the client side, where only authorized platforms with authorized configurations are able to access the protected content. Moreover, it realizes the basic security functionality allowing applications to securely manage and enforce stateful licenses, which maintain state information about past usage. However, TPMs are not available in mobile devices and thus, in this paper, we propose a generic approach based on some core functionalities that have to be provided by the underlying generic hardware.

The authors of [8] propose a system for redistribution of digital content that requires the following hardware functionalities: SHA-1, RSA, AES, secure storage, secure RAM, and a secure content decoder. Thus, their system could be implemented using both a TPM-based or TrustZone-based system. To secure their system against replay attacks, for each content file a hash of the license and the associated content is stored in secure non-volatile memory. Thus, the memory requirements grow linear in the number of content files, in contrast to our method which only requires a small constant amount of non-volatile memory.

Recently, the TCG published the Mobile Trusted Module (MTM) specification [17], which can be seen as an extension of a TPM, adapted for mobile devices. A MTM can be implemented in various ways, either by using an additional hardware chip or by integrating some functionalities in the CPU core, complemented by software. The latter option can be realized using a TrustZone-based system. Although a full MTM implementation is more complex than required by our security architecture, it could be used to realize our security architecture.

Prior to the TCG, there have been several approaches to run secure software using secure hardware [5,13,18,19,20]. All of them have in common the concept of a tamper-resistant module that runs security-critical applications. In contrast to these systems, which require (expensive and specialized) custom secure coprocessors, our proposed architecture is based on cheap and easily available commercial off-the-shelf (COTS) hardware (TPM or TrustZone).

2 Peer-to-Peer Distribution

In this section, various P2P use cases are identified before the basic license operations, which are used to realize all use cases, are defined.

2.1 Identification of Use Cases

The use cases involve content *providers* (licensors) and various *peers* (licensees resp. users). We consider a provider as the representative party for rights-holders, whereas the peer represents the consumer of digital content. These parties have only limited trust in each other. The provider distributes digital content (e.g., software, media files) together with the corresponding *license*, which defines the *usage rights* (e.g., play, print) and *alteration rights* (e.g., loan, share) applicable to the content. The peer consumes the content according to the license. Possible compensations (e.g., payments, subscriptions, gifts) can be negotiated independently between the involved peers [3].

Transfer. A peer (*sender*) moves a content to another peer (*receiver*) while invalidating the license on the sender's site.

Sharing. A peer (*sharer*) copies a content to another peer (*co-partner*) that is also entitled to use the content. Hence, in contrast to a transfer, the content remains available on the sharer's site.

Rental. A peer (*lender*) copies a content to another peer (*borrower*) while disabling the content on the lender's site during the loan period. After the loan period, the content becomes inaccessible on the borrower's platform and available again on the lender's platform (i.e., if sufficient rights are left). We distinguish between an *active rental*, where the borrower has to return his lending actively to the lender, and a *passive rental*, which ends automatically after a previously defined period, without having the borrower to actively return his lending.

Preview. A peer (*promoter*) copies a limited copy of a content to another peer (*tester*) as a sample. The tester can try out the corresponding content in a (temporally or quantitative) limited manner without revealing his identity and without giving any inherent commitments for the promoter or for the tester. Once the previews are spent, the tester can convert the preview into a fully legitimate content by reporting it to the promoter. Otherwise, the content trial becomes inaccessible for the tester.

Superdistribution. A peer (*superdistributor*) copies a content to another peer (*sublicensee*) while keeping the content completely available on the superdistributor's site. In contrast to the sharing use case, the sublicensee is required to contact the superdistributor for necessary compensations before being able to use the content. In this context, we introduce the idea of *offline superdistribution*, where the superdistributed copy can be used immediately without a prior authorization (and thus involvement) of the initial content provider. Instead, the sublicensee (or the superdistributor) is allowed to report (and compensate) the additional copy to the initial content provider later (i.e., according to the individual license conditions).

2.2 Basic License Operations

As noted in the previous section, the license defines the rights (e.g., usage, alteration) applicable to the corresponding digital content. In the following, we define six basic operations on licenses that suffice to realize all P2P use cases described above. We therefore describe the respective license operations together with the corresponding security objectives required by the involved users and providers.

Store and **Load** are used to save a license to and retrieve a license from persistent storage. Thus, both operations have to ensure that unauthorized alterations of licenses (*integrity*), unauthorized disclosures (*confidentiality*), and replay attacks (*freshness*) are infeasible. Hence, a license being retrieved using **Load** is always exactly the same as it has been saved using the last **Store** operation.

Transform conveys an input license into a set of new output licenses such that the rights of the output licenses add up to the rights of the original input license. Therefore, Transform ensures that unauthorized alterations of licenses are infeasible and that it is impossible to gain unauthorized rights by applying arbitrary license transformations (*logical integrity*).

Invalidate irrevocably deactivates a license and all corresponding rights, ensuring that replay attacks on invalidated licenses (*freshness*) and unauthorized reactivations via modifications (*integrity*) are infeasible.

Transfer is used to copy a license from one device to another while ensuring license *integrity*, *freshness*, and *confidentiality* with regard to other parties not involved. Transfer further ensures that the copied license has appropriate transfer rights and that the hardware and software configuration of the destination device meets the demands of the copied license and thus of the initial licensor.

Report allows to contact the lender in order to return actively borrowed rights (cf. Section 2.1), or to contact the initial licensor in order to acquire new rights or to extend existing rights. Report does not handle possible compensations. However, in case of superdistribution, Report ensures that it is infeasible to gain more than a previously defined amount of new/extended rights without contacting the initial licensor. Thus, the amount of unreported (pending) rights stated in the license is individually defined by the licensor and can range from zero (i.e., immediate contact required) to infinity (i.e., no contact is required).

2.3 Use Case Realizations Using Basic License Operations

We now show how the P2P use cases identified in Section 2.1 are realized using only the few basic license operations defined in the previous Section 2.2. The basic operations are provided by an application called distribution controller (DC) that runs on top of our security architecture (cf. Section 3). All realizations assume that licenses are securely read from (and written to) persistent storage using the basic license operations Load and Store respectively.

Transfer. As shown in Figure 1, DC_S first changes the owner of the transferred license to the identity of the receiver using Transform. Then, the license is copied to the receiver DC_D using Transfer and invalidated at the source DC_S using Invalidate at the same time (i.e., atomically).

Sharing. As shown in Figure 2, DC_S of the sharer first uses Transform to split the original license into two sublicenses, one for the initial sharer and one for the

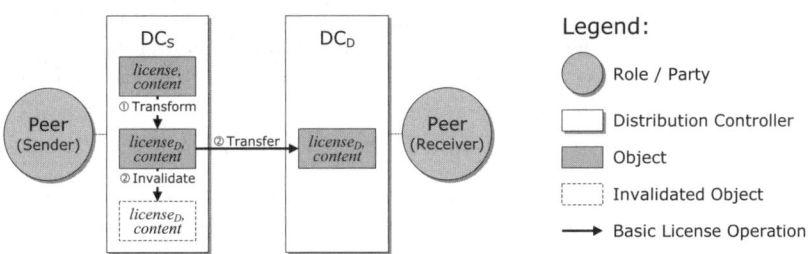

Fig. 1. Transfer of Ownership

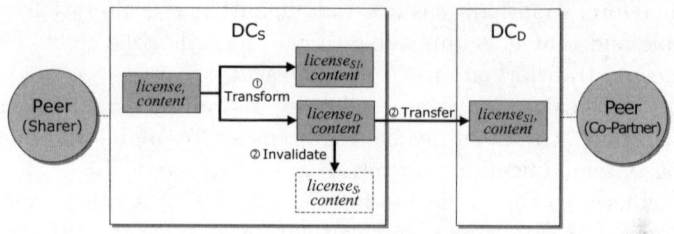

Fig. 2. Sharing of Ownership

new co-partner(s)[1]. Finally, the license of the co-partner is moved from DC_S to DC_D using Transfer and Invalidate atomically.

Rental. The rental use case is quite similar to the sharing use case. DC_S uses Transform to divide the original license of the lender into two new licenses such that the rights of the two new licenses again add up to the rights of the original license. Afterwards, DC_S uses Transfer and Invalidate to securely move the borrower's license to DC_D. However, in case of a passive timed rental, the license for DC_D is valid only for the loan period, whereas the license for DC_S remains invalid during the loan period[2]. In case of an active rental, the license for DC_D remains valid (and hence the license for DC_S invalid) until DC_D actively returns the license back to DC_S using Report.

Preview. The preview use case is also quite similar to the sharing use case. DC_S uses Transform to create an additional anonymous (stateful) license including only some restricted (temporally[3] or quantitative) usage rights according to the preview policy of the original license. Note that a preview license includes only preview rights, so the original license is not modified. DC_S then uses Transfer and Invalidate to securely move the preview license to DC_D. Once the free previews are used, DC_D can offer the tester to convert the preview license into a full license by contacting the initial licensor via Report. Alternatively, DC_D "remembers" the expired preview for a certain period (according the corresponding preview conditions of the license) via Store to prevent immediate preview replays.

Superdistribution. The realization of the superdistribution use case is depicted in Figure 3. DC_S first uses Transform to create a copy of the original license with the identity of the sublicensee together with an authorization commitment, whereas the original license remains unaffected and fully enabled. The authorization commitment is used to report the respective transaction to the corresponding content provider. It contains a reference to the original license and the required compensation agreement (e.g., a payment obligation). A commitment can be *sender-reported* or *receiver-reported*. In the first case, DC_S is required to report the new license to the initial licensor, otherwise DC_D has to do so. Both

---

[1] The original license must already include the usage rights for the sharer and its co-partner(s), such that the rights of all new sublicenses add up to the rights of the original license.
[2] The realization of this use case requires the availability of a secure timer.
[3] A temporally restricted usage right also requires the availability of a secure timer.

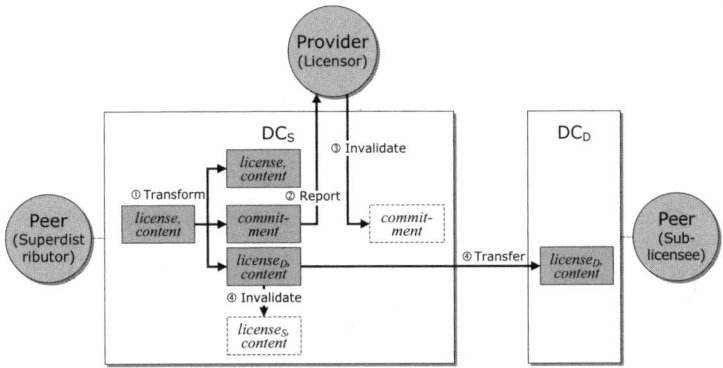

Fig. 3. Sender-reported superdistribution

DC_S and DC_D use Report to settle a commitment and hence to legitimate the superdistributed license. Once the license has been successfully reported, DC_S (or DC_D) apply Invalidate to securely remove the respective commitment and enable the usage of the corresponding content. Figure 3, for instance, depicts a sender-reported superdistribution, where DC_S settles the commitment before it moves the new license to the sublicensee using Transfer and Invalidate.

However, using this approach, a superdistributed copy cannot be used until DC_S or DC_D have reported the new license to the initial licensor. This requires a direct connection to the licensor, which may not always be available, particularly not in mobile environments. Thus, our approach for an *offline superdistribution* allows that a superdistributed copy can be used immediately without a prior authorization by the initial licensors; the sublicensee (or the superdistributor) is allowed to report (and compensate) the new copy to the actual licensor later. However, each additional license created during a superdistribution has to be reported once to fulfill the security objectives on Report (cf. Section 2.2).

Our basic idea for such an offline superdistribution scheme is that DC internally saves all unreported commitments cm in a set of unreported commitments CM, with $cm \in CM$. DC additionally manages licensor-specific unreported commitments counters c_{cm}—one for each licensor P. The set of all counters $\overrightarrow{c_{cm}}$ and the set of all unreported commitments CM are persistently stored (and retrieved) using Store and Load. To limit the number of unreported commitments c_{cm} for a certain licensor P, once c_{cm} reaches a specific limit, DC (i) refuses to accept further commitments for that licensor until some pending commitments are reported, and (ii) may limit the usage of the corresponding content according to the respective licensor policy. To settle an unreported commitment via Report, the content provider sends a *proof of compensation* p_{cm} that can be verified by DC to remove the corresponding commitment cm from CM, the set of report-pending commitments, and decreases the corresponding counter in $\overrightarrow{c_{cm}}$. The two protocols involved are described in detail in the following. It is assumed that,

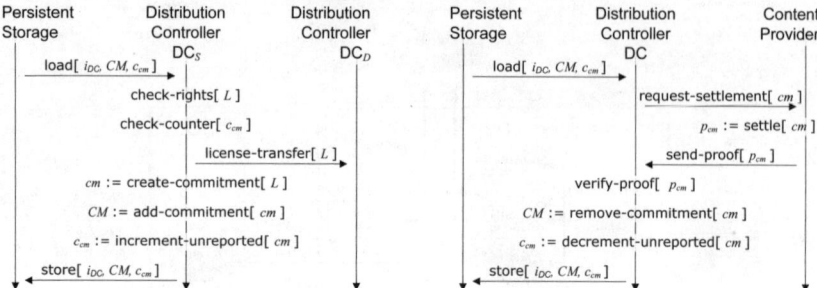

Fig. 4. Sender-reported distribution protocol   **Fig. 5.** Reporting protocol

on startup, DC uses Load to load its current index i_{DC} that indexes all available licenses and content, the set of unreported commitments CM, and the set of report-pending counters $\overrightarrow{c_{cm}}$.

Offline Superdistribution Distribution Protocol. The distribution protocols (Figure 4 shows the sender-reported variant) work as follows. To *distribute* a license L (and corresponding content) to DC_D, DC_S first loads L and checks if all conditions for the corresponding transfer-right are fulfilled, and asks for a sender-reported or receiver-reported superdistribution. In case of sender-reported superdistribution, DC_S also checks whether the corresponding $c_{cm} \in \overrightarrow{c_{cm}}$ has reached its limit. Second, DC_S uses Transfer to verify that DC_D's configuration conforms to the security policy of L. Third, on successful examination, DC_S creates a new commitment cm and sends L (and the corresponding content) to DC_D via Transfer. Finally, in case of (i) a sender-reported superdistribution, DC_S adds the new commitment cm to CM, increments the corresponding counter in $\overrightarrow{c_{cm}}$ while synchronizing both with the values stored in persistent storage via Store. In case of (ii) a receiver-reported superdistribution, on DC_D's acceptance, that means after a successful license verification and verification of the corresponding c_{cm}, DC_D updates its corresponding CM and $\overrightarrow{c_{cm}}$.

Offline Superdistribution Reporting Protocol. To *report* a pending commitment from DC to a provider P (cf. Figure 5), DC first uses Report to send all user-selected pending commitments $cm \in CM$ to P and requests the proofs of compensation p_{cm}. Second, if P is the legitimate licensor of the commitments and the compensations have been settled, P creates and returns p_{cm} to DC. Finally, on successful verification of p_{cm}, DC removes the commitments from CM, decreases the counter in $\overrightarrow{c_{cm}}$ and stores both using Store.

3 Generic Security Architecture

In this section, we introduce a generic security architecture which provides two high-level security abstractions, namely *Trusted Storage* and *Trusted Channels*, that allow to securely realize all basic license operations. We then define essential (mostly hardware-based) low-level platform security functionalities and show

how the security abstractions can be securely implemented based on the generic security architecture and the platform security functionalities.

3.1 Security Kernel Architecture

We assume a layered system structure running multiple (independent) processes in parallel on top of a security kernel, which serves as a central control entity, located between the hardware layer and the application layer. To enable the security kernel to run in a trusted environment, the hardware includes a Trusted Computing component, such as TrustZone or a TPM[4].

Our application layer is able to execute several OS instances and individual applications (e.g., DC) independently and in parallel, while being *strongly isolated* from each other. In this context, strong isolation ensures that it is impossible for separated subsystems, components, or even individual applications to access (i.e., data, functionality) or even affect (e.g., performance) each other. A process that is strongly isolated from other processes is called a *compartment* henceforth.

To enable DC to realize the basic license operations, our security kernel provides two high-level *security abstractions* named Trusted Storage and Trusted Channels. The security kernel in turn employs several low-level *platform security functionalities* such as verifiable bootstrapping, secure non-volatile memory, and random numbers to securely implement the two security abstractions.

3.2 Security Abstractions

In the following we describe the two security abstractions Trusted Storage and Trusted Channels and show how they can be used to securely realize the basic license operations identified in Section 2.2. In the context of security abstractions, we introduce the terms *configuration* and *measurement*. The *configuration* of a compartment unambiguously describes the compartment's I/O behavior, while the term *measurement* refers to the process of deriving the configuration of a certain compartment (cf. Section 3.3).

Trusted Storage. The Trusted Storage abstraction provides persistent storage preserving integrity, confidentiality, authenticity (by binding data to the compartment configuration and/or user secrets), and freshness of the stored data. Since a complete tamper-resistant storage unit would be very costly and inflexible, we employ untrusted storage (e.g., external flash memory) with the help of the platform security functionalities (cf. Section 3.4).

Trusted Channels. A Trusted Channel [14] is a secure channel[5] that is *bound* to the configuration of the respective communication endpoint. Therefore, a Trusted Channel additionally allows each endpoint compartment to (i) validate the configuration of the other endpoint compartment and (ii) to bind data to

---

[4] A trusted environment has to be based on hardware components, as software-only environments could be easily circumvented.

[5] We define a secure channel to ensure confidentiality, integrity, and authenticity of the communicated data.

the configuration of the endpoint compartment such that only this compartment with this specific configuration can access the data. To prevent replay attacks, the Trusted Channel abstraction further has to provide freshness detection.

Based on the security architecture providing Trusted Storage and Trusted Channels, all basic license operations can be implemented as follows.

Load, Store, and Invalidate require a persistent storage location to securely save, retrieve, or deactivate/delete a license, while ensuring the integrity, confidentiality, and freshness of the handled licenses. Trusted Storage is able to enforce all these security requirements and thus can be employed to realize Load, Store, and Invalidate. However, since DC represents the communication endpoint for our Trusted Storage abstraction, it has to be ensured that solely and exclusively a correctly configured DC can access its Trusted Storage location. By further employing a (local) Trusted Channel to access the Trusted Storage, DC is (i) securely authenticated and (ii) its corresponding data (e.g., licenses) is bound to the configuration of DC.

Transform requires logical license integrity such that unauthorized alterations of licenses are infeasible. All license transformations are done inside of DC by an internal protocol engine, which can be verified for correctness by an involved peer each time before it sends a new license (and corresponding content) using a Trusted Channel. The strong isolation capability provided by our security architecture prevents runtime modifications of DC and its protocol engine. Finally, our Trusted Storage security abstraction assures that even offline modifications of DC cannot affect the correctness of DC's license transformations, as a (unauthorized) modified DC would not longer be able to access its data, since the functionality of Load, Store, and Invalidate are mandatory bound the (correct) configuration of DC.

Transfer and Report are used to securely communicate with authenticated peers (e.g., other users, content providers) while requiring confidentiality, integrity, and freshness for transferred data. The Trusted Channel security abstraction is able to fulfill these communication security requirements by enforcing confidentiality, integrity, and freshness of communicated data and securely authenticating involved communication endpoints (by validating their configurations and binding the corresponding channel solely and exclusively to that verified configuration). Trusted Channels together with the Trusted Storage abstraction further enforce the correctness of DC regarding the internal management of transfer rights and commitments, while preventing unauthorized online and offline manipulations.

3.3 Platform Security Functionalities

The implementation of our high-level security abstractions relies on the availability of several low-level platform security functionalities, which in turn can only be implemented in combination with appropriate hardware (extensions). Before describing possible realizations for Trusted Storage and Trusted Channels in Section 3.4, we first describe the necessary security functionalities of the platform, which form the basis for the security abstractions.

The platform security functionalities can be implemented in various ways, for instance (i) by using virtualization technology and a TCG TPM chip [16], (ii) by using ARM's TrustZone technology [1] (optionally in combination with virtualization technology), or (iii) by using a combination of hard- and software that allows to securely implement the following set of security functionalities (e.g., a smartcard/software combination or using a tamper-resistant cover).

Verifiable Bootstrapping. For a verifiable initialization of the security kernel and DC, a secure chain of measurements that is anchored in tamper-resistant hardware has to be established, using functions that measure[6] all security kernel binaries (i.e., system kernel, legacy OS, and compartments like DC) prior to executing them. The functions to be provided are (i) init_measurement that acts as root of trust and initializes the chain of measurements by measuring the bootloader, (ii) extend_measurement to extend the chain of measurements with a new measurement *value* (e.g., a hash value), and (iii) read_measurement to read the current measurement value. After booting has completed, a (remote) party can verify the integrity of the security kernel by comparing the measurement values with "known good" references that are conform to its security policy.

Secure Non-Volatile Memory. To securely store at least one symmetric key and a freshness detection value, the platform has to provide a small amount of non-volatile secure memory with read and write access. The symmetric key serves as the root key of a hierarchy of keys, used for example to securely employ external storage, whereas the freshness detection value refers to potential freshness detection mechanisms such as monotonic counters or hash trees. The secure memory interface consists of two functions, write_to_sm to store data into secure memory and read_from_sm to retrieve data from secure memory.

Using this interface, a *monotonic counter* can be realized, providing the functions create_counter to create the counter (using write_to_sm), read_counter to read the current counter value (using read_from_sm), and increment_counter to increment the counter value (using write_to_sm[read_from_sm[] + 1] in an atomic operation). To prevent premature overflow, the counter should be sufficiently large (at least 32-bit). Multiple monotonic counters can be realized in software by employing virtual monotonic counters [12] on top of one physical counter.

True Random Number Generator. To securely implement various cryptographic schemes, the security kernel has to provide a function rand that generates *true random numbers* from an unpredictable source (physical process).

Strong Isolation. The security kernel has to implement a strong isolation for applications, based either on hardware measures [1,15] or virtualization approaches [2,6], which permits the reutilization of legacy operating systems and existing applications, e.g. by using (para-)virtualization techniques.

3.4 Realizing the Security Abstractions

In the following, we describe how the security abstractions can be realized using just the platform security functionalities of Section 3.3.

---

[6] Measuring can be done by computing the cryptographic hash of the software binary.

Trusted Storage. As persistent storage is untrusted in our model, we employ the generic platform security functions of Section 3.3 to implement Trusted Storage (similar to the approach in [10]). To ensure confidentiality and integrity, data to be stored is first hashed and then encrypted using a symmetric root key that is generated at initial installation using rand and bound to the configuration of the Trusted Storage compartment derived during the verifiable bootstrapping. It is stored in secure non-volatile memory using write_to_sm with a predefined reference ref_{TS} that exclusively identifies the Trusted Storage compartment and its actual configuration. Freshness can be detected by employing a monotonic counter: Before writing data to untrusted storage, the counter is incremented and the counter value is stored together with the data. After reading the data, the stored counter value is compared to the current counter value, which must be the same if the data is fresh.

Trusted Channels. To allow an endpoint compartment to validate the other endpoint's configuration and thus provide authenticity, a slightly modified version of the protocol in [14] is employed. It uses binding of local keys and remote attestation, which in turn is based on verifiable bootstrapping in combination with a cryptographic protocol. The nonces and keys used in the protocol are generated using the rand function. To detect replay attacks and hence provide freshness, monotonic counters are used. Further, strong isolation ensures integrity and confidentiality of the internal state of the Trusted Channels compartment.

4 ARM TrustZone-Based Implementation Proposal

ARM TrustZone [1] is a security technology for single-chip embedded processors, which are called *system-on-a-chip* (SoC). For example, the Texas Instruments OMAP platform (www.ti.com/omap) implements TrustZone on a SoC. As shown in Figure 6, a TrustZone-based SoC includes a CPU with an ARMv6 core, cryptographic hardware (SHA-1, AES, TRNG), a few write-once (hardware fuse) keys, RAM, ROM, non-volatile memory, and a memory/bus controller for external devices (normal and secure) and external memory (flash and SDRAM).

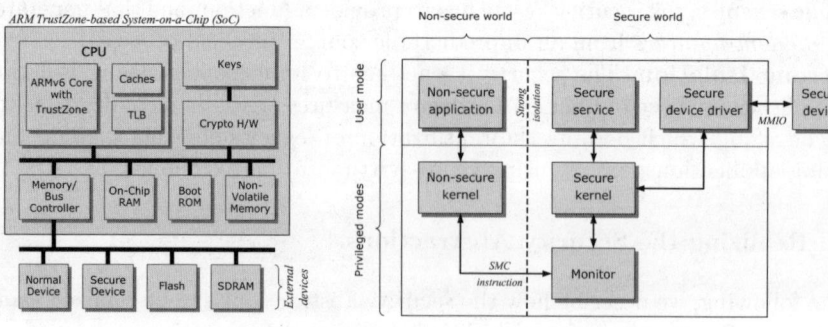

Fig. 6. A TrustZone-based SoC   **Fig. 7.** The TrustZone model

The TrustZone model depicted in Figure 7 splits the computing environment into two isolated worlds, the *secure world* and the *non-secure world*, that are linked by a software *monitor* running in the secure world. Communication between the two worlds is only possible by calling the privileged *Secure Monitor Call* (SMC) instruction from the non-secure kernel, which transfers execution to the monitor. Throughout this section, we use the term *trusted software* to refer to software running in the secure world.

4.1 Realizing the Platform Security Functionalities

In the following we explain how to implement the platform security functionalities defined in Section 3.3 using TrustZone-based hardware.

Strong Isolation. To provide *strong isolation* between the two worlds, the CPU provides an additional status bit called non-secure (NS) bit, which determines in which world the program executes. To switch back to the non-secure world, the secure kernel sets the NS status bit, which is located in the CPU's Secure Configuration Register. When switching between the two worlds, the current world's processor context including registers is saved and the other world's context is restored. Cache lines and memory pages are also tagged as either secure or non-secure by setting the appropriate NS bit, which can only be done by code running in privileged mode in the secure world. Further, devices attached to the bus can also be marked as secure or non-secure. A secure device (e.g., external flash memory) can only be controlled by a driver running in the secure world.[7] Thus, the TrustZone model provides *strong isolation* between the secure world and the non-secure world. The two worlds have separate logical address spaces, inter-process communication (IPC) is carried out by SMC calls, and access control of hardware resources is implemented by secure device drivers. The security-critical compartments run on top of a virtualization layer (the secure kernel in Figure 7) in the secure world while the legacy OS and noncritical applications run in the non-secure world.

Verifiable Bootstrapping. At reset, the TrustZone core executes bootstrap code (8-12 kB) in the secure world. The code is located in the on-chip boot ROM and considered to be tamper-resistant, since a modification would require significant effort. As the boot ROM is limited in size, external (untrusted) flash memory is used to store the binaries of the security kernel and DC. The bootstrap code loads these binaries from external memory into secure on-chip RAM, where they are then measured using init_measurement and extend_measurement, which access the hardware SHA-1 hash function. The measurements are stored in secure on-chip RAM, where they can be read out later by using read_measurement in order to report the platform configuration to an external party.

Secure Non-Volatile Memory. The SoC's non-volatile memory is assumed to be secure, as tampering would require to manipulate the hardware chip.

---

[7] On ARM, devices are addressed by memory-mapped I/O (MMIO). A device's physical memory is mapped to secure or non-secure logical addresses by the MMU.

4.2 Comparison of TrustZone- and TPM-Based Approaches

A prototype of the security architecture proposed in Section 3.1 based on a TCG TPM 1.2 [16] and COTS hardware has been implemented in the EMSCB project (www.emscb.org), where the platform security functionalities were realized using a TPM (verifiable bootstrapping, secure non-volatile memory, true random number generation) and a microkernel (strong isolation).

For embedded and mobile devices, however, a full-fledged TPM chip would cause additional costs. A TrustZone-based system, in contrast, can be efficiently integrated on a single chip (SoC). Further, as the crypto engine is directly attached to the CPU, cryptographic operations can be carried out faster and more secure [4] than in a TPM-based system, where the communication is done using the vulnerable LPC bus. On the other hand, using today's technology, non-volatile memory can be hard/expensive to integrate on a SoC. Also, the migration of secrets in case of a SoC failure remains an open question.

5 Conclusion and Future Work

We recapitulatory sketch that the defined platform security functionalities are sufficient to satisfy the overall security objectives for all P2P distribution scenarios identified in Section 2.1. As shown in Section 2.3, all existing P2P scenarios can be securely realized by the distribution controller (DC) using only the few basic license operations defined in Section 2.2. DC and its basic license operations in turn can be securely realized by the two security abstractions Trusted Storage and Trusted Channels as shown in Section 3.2. Lastly, Section 3.4 describes how these two security abstractions can be securely implemented based on our generic security architecture and the platform security functionalities as defined Section 3.1 and Section 3.3 respectively. Thus, with the help of DC in combination with our security architecture, the platform security functionalities implement the two security abstractions Trusted Storage and Trusted Channels, which realize the basic license operations, which again realize all P2P scenarios.

Due to the generic interfaces to the underlying platform, our security architecture can be implemented on top of any hardware that provides the defined platform security functionalities, including Trusted Computing platforms such as the TPM and the MTM. However, since neither TPMs nor MTMs are currently available for mobile devices, we proposed an exemplary implementation based on ARM TrustZone technology, which is popular for embedded systems. While the ARM TrustZone implementation is currently work-in-progress, we further currently try to adapt our approach also for the OpenMoko project (www.openmoko.org).

Acknowledgements

We thank Jan-Erik Ekberg for his contributions in jointly developing the concept of and protocols for offline superdistribution.

References

1. ARM Ltd. ARM TrustZone. www.arm.com/products/esd/trustzone_home.html
2. Dragovic, B., Fraser, K., Hand, S., Harris, T., Ho, A., Pratt, I., Warfield, A., Barham, P., Neugebauer, R.: Xen and the Art of Virtualization. In: SOSP 2003: Proceedings of the ACM Symposium on Operating Systems Principles (October 2003)
3. Ginzboorg, P., Ekberg, J.-E., Laitinen, P., Ylä-Jääski, A.: Charging for Broadband Access. In: ICTEC'98: Proceedings of the 1st International Conference on Telecommunications and Electronic Commerce (November 1998)
4. Kauer, B.: OSLO: Improving the Security of Trusted Computing. In: Proceedings of the 16th USENIX Security Symposium, pp. 229–237 (August 2007)
5. Kent, S.T.: Protecting Externally Supplied Software in Small Computers. PhD thesis, Massachusetts Institute of Technology (1980)
6. Liedtke, J.: Towards Real Microkernels. Communications of the ACM 39(9), 70–77 (1996)
7. Mori, R., Kawahara, M.: Superdistribution: The Concept and the Architecture. Transactions of the IEICE E 73(7), 1133–1146 (1990)
8. Nair, S.K., Popescu, B.C., Gamage, C., Crispo, B., Tanenbaum, A.S.: Enabling DRM-preserving Digital Content Redistribution. In: Proceedings of the 7th International IEEE Conference on E-Commerce Technology (July 2005)
9. Open Mobile Alliance. OMA DRM Version 2.0 (March 2006), http://www.openmobilealliance.org
10. Sadeghi, A.-R., Wolf, M., Stüble, C., Asokan, N., Ekberg, J.-E.: Enabling Fairer Digital Rights Management with Trusted Computing. In: Garay, J.A., Lenstra, A.K., Mambo, M., Peralta, R. (eds.) ISC 2007. LNCS, vol. 4779, Springer, Heidelberg (2007)
11. Sandhu, R., Zhang, X.: Peer-to-Peer Access Control Architecture Using Trusted Computing Technology. In: SACMAT 2005, Stockholm, Sweden (June 2005)
12. Sarmenta, L.F.G., van Dijk, M., O'Donnell, C.W., Rhodes, J., Devadas, S.: Virtual monotonic counters and count-limited objects using a TPM without a trusted OS. In: STC 2006: Proceedings of the 1st ACM Workshop on Scalable Trusted Computing, pp. 27–42 (2006)
13. Smith, S.W.: Secure Coprocessing Applications and Research Issues. Los Alamos Unclassified Release LA-UR-96-2805, Los Alamos National Laboratory (1996)
14. Stewin, P., Sadeghi, A.-R., Unger, M., Gasmi, Y., Asokan, N.: Beyond Secure Channels. In: STC 2007: Proceedings of the 2nd ACM Workshop on Scalable Trusted Computing (2007)
15. Suh, G., Clarke, D., Gassend, B., van Dijk, M., Devadas, S.: AEGIS: Architecture for Tamper-evident and Tamper-resistant Processing. In: Proceedings of the Annual USENIX Technical Conference (2003)
16. Trusted Computing Group. TPM Main Specification. Technical Report Version 1.2 Revision 94 (2006)
17. Trusted Computing Group. TCG Mobile Trusted Module Specification (June 2007)
18. Tygar, J.D., Yee, B.S.: Strongbox: A System for Self-Securing Programs. In: CMU Computer Science: A 25th Anniversary Commemorative, pp. 163–197. Addison-Wesley, Reading (1991)
19. Tygar, J.D., Yee, B.S.: Dyad: A System for Using Physically Secure Coprocessors. In: Proceedings of the IP Workshop (1994)
20. White, S.R., Comerford, L.D.: ABYSS: A Trusted Architecture for Software Protection. In: Proceedings of the IEEE Symposium on Security and Privacy (1987)

Unified Rate Limiting in Broadband Access Networks for Defeating Internet Worms and DDoS Attacks

Keun Park, Dongwon Seo, Jaewon Yoo, Heejo Lee*, and Hyogon Kim

Division of Computer and Communication Engineering
Korea University, Seoul 136-713, Korea
{aerosmiz,heejo,hyogon}@korea.ac.kr

Abstract. Internet worms and DDoS attacks are considered the two most menacing attacks on today's Internet. The traditional wisdom is that they are different beasts, and they should be dealt with independently. In this paper, however, we show that a unified rate limiting algorithm is possible, which effectively works on both Internet worms and DDoS attacks. The unified approach leads to higher worm traffic reduction performance than that of existing rate limiting schemes geared toward worm mitigation, in addition to the added advantage of dropping most DDoS attack packets. In our experiments with attack traffics generated by attacking tools, the unified rate limiting scheme drops 80.7% worm packets and 93% DDoS packets, while 69.2% worms and 3.4% DDoS packets are dropped at maximum by previous worm scan rate limiting schemes. Also, the proposed scheme requires less computing resources, and has higher accuracy for dropping attack packets but not dropping legitimate packets.

1 Introduction

Internet worms and DDoS attacks are considered two main threats in today's Internet. The majority of Internet Service Providers (ISPs) view Distributed Denial of Service (DDoS) attack as the most significant operational security issue of today [1], while future worm epidemics are predicted to spread at yet unprecedented rates [2].

As the broadband access technologies such as Fiber To The Node (FTTN) and Fiber To The Home (FTTH) make their way to customer premises, the problem aggravates, as higher "fire power" is given to the potential attackers. It has even become possible for an attacker to launch an attack at such high speed as 100Mbps or higher, from home. With "botnets" that can mobilize up to a few hundred thousands of these high-speed agents [3], the collective attack intensity becomes formidable. Therefore, the emergence of broadband access networks raises the pressing need to monitor, and possibly control, the attack traffic near the sources.

---

* To whom all correspondence should be addressed.

In this paper, we focus on *rate limiting* for the specific defense mechanism to deploy in the access networks near attack sources. Rate limiting has been used in many defense mechanisms against worm and DDoS attacks. It controls the rate of traffic so that the traffic under the specified rate is allowed, whereas the traffic exceeding the rate is dropped or delayed.

Prior works in this field such as the rate limiting applications [4] and network-side rate limiting against DDoS attacks have also been studied in various ways. Pushback [5] uses the rate limiting to drop malicious packets and notify upstream routers to drop such packets. Pushback works best against DDoS flooding-style attacks, but it could sacrifice normal packets since it does not have distinction standard between normal and malicious packets except traffic quantity. Secure Overlay Services(SOS) [6] represents a private enterprise network for the rate limiting. It offers resilience to node failure, as surviving nodes assume the role of failed nodes, plus the resilience against denial of service on the system itself. But it is designed to work with private services only, as it requires changes in client software and an extensive overlay infrastructure. D-WARD [7] is another inline system that collects two-way traffic statistics from the border router at the source network and compares them to the network traffic models built upon the specification of application and transport protocols. However, it should set up and maintain complicated procedures to apply rate limiting. A study has shown how to protect e-commerce networks with the application of D-WARD [8]. MUlti-Level Tree for Online Packet Statistics(MULTOPS) [9] is proposed as an efficient data structure against DDoS which can be used for rate limiting. MULTOPS is a tree of nodes that contains packet rate statistics for subnet prefixes at different aggregation levels. MULTOPS dynamically adapts its configuration to reflect the changes in packet rates, and can avoid memory exhaustion attack. However, the authors said, given the structure of the MULTOPS tree, the size of a table (1040 bytes), the size of a record (28 bytes), a packet size of 34 bytes, and a threshold of 1000 packets per second, an attacker is able to lead the memory exhaustion to neutralize MULTOPS.

For preventing worms, a few rate limiting defense mechanisms have been developed recently [10,11,12,13,14]. IP throttling [10] limits the sending rate at an infected end host. Failed-connection-based scheme [11] and credit-based rate limiting [12] concentrate on the fact that worm scanning activities produce high number of failed connections. DNS-based rate limiting [13,14] investigates using DNS behavior as a basis for the rate limiting. These worm rate limiting defense mechanisms focus on the deployment of a host side or an edge router mechanism, performing the distinction between worms and DDoS attacks. These mechanisms will be discussed in detail in the next section, as we design our scheme coping efficiently with worm and DDoS simultaneously.

The main contribution of this paper is the introduction of the *unified* rate limiting scheme for the defending against both Internet worms and DDoS attacks, which could be put as "killing two birds with one stone." That is, while it is generally thought that worm and DDoS defense are separately considered due to their different attack behaviors, we attempt to effectively defend these two attacks using a single algorithm. We will demonstrate that its worm detection accuracy is higher than that of the existing worm defense schemes, and that it fares nicely in detecting DDoS attack packets. Furthermore, the overhead in terms of CPU and memory usage is shown to be affordable for end hosts and edge routers.

The remainder of this paper is organized as follows. Section 2 describes the design of a unified rate limiting scheme as well as the analysis of the traditional rate limiting schemes. Section 3 explains the implementation details of the scheme, and Sect. 4 presents the performance evaluation and comparison with other conventional rate limiting schemes. Lastly, Sect. 5 concludes the paper.

2 The Design of the Unified Rate Limiting Scheme

2.1 The Problems of Existing Scan Rate Limiting Schemes

As rate limiting against worm is usually performed close to the attack sources, we build our unified rate limiting scheme around it, adding the components necessary for DDoS rate limiting. A major observation of the existing rate limiting schemes listed above is that rate limiting decisions are always based on worm's aggressive connection attempts. For instance, they concentrate on the worm behavior that incurs a great number of TCP connections in a short period of time. We term these schemes as *scan rate limiting schemes*. While they work for even unknown worms, a drawback is that they are useless to defend against DDoS attacks, as discussed below.

Scan rate limiting schemes bring about three major problems for it to be used against DDoS attacks as well. The first is that they typically use a whitelist policy. In the whitelist policy, once a flow (such as a TCP connection) is verified as valid, then there would be no further examination so the subsequent packets in the flow bypass the rate limiter. Thus the rate limiter is incapable of preventing DDoS attacks flooding packets in an acceptable connection. The second problem is due to the lack of IP spoofing prevention. Many attackers forge, or "spoof", the IP source address of each packet they send to conceal their location, thereby forestalling an effective response [15]. The third problem is in the precision of detecting attack packets. The information used in the scan rate limiting schemes, such as TCP connection information, credit value and DNS record, is insufficient to identify DDoS attacks. See [16] for an empirical study.

2.2 The Design Principles of Unified Rate Limiting Scheme

Now we design a rate limiting scheme, with two objectives. The first is to cover both worm and DDoS attack as mentioned above. The second is to make our rate limiting algorithm fast and light-weight so that it does not interfere with the normal services.

Our unified rate limiting scheme consists of five modules to defense against Internet worms and DDoS attacks simultaneously. The five modules are shown in Fig. 1 and described as follows.

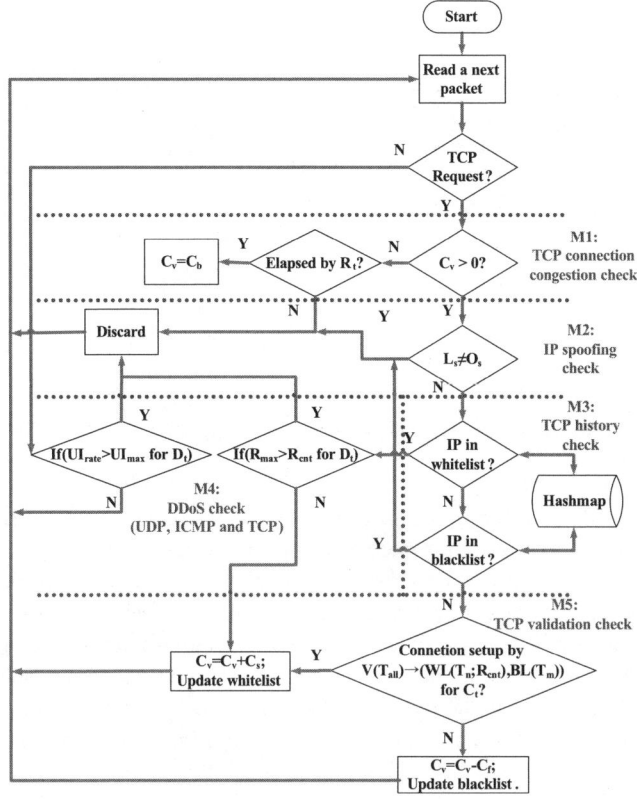

Fig. 1. Unified rate limiting algorithm

- **TCP connection congestion check(M1):** monitoring whether connection failures excessively occurred.
- **IP spoofing check(M2):** checking source address spoofing to discard suspicious packets as many as possible before establishing a connection.
- **TCP history check(M3):** utilizing black and white lists to reduce the execution time of rate limiter through the reuse of the existing lists.
- **DDoS check(M4):** allowing a connection only if the transmission rate does not exceed the predefined threshold.
- **TCP validation check(M5):** updating connection information such as ACK response time and request count, and deciding which list the IP should belong to; whitelist or blacklist.

Using these five modules, it is possible to screen excessive traffic which is caused by Internet worms and DDoS attack.

Even though the scheme prevents those attacks very well, it is useless if the algorithm overhead is unaffordable. Figure 2 shows the reason why we set the module order like Fig. 1. In Fig. 2, our scheme examines credit value first that

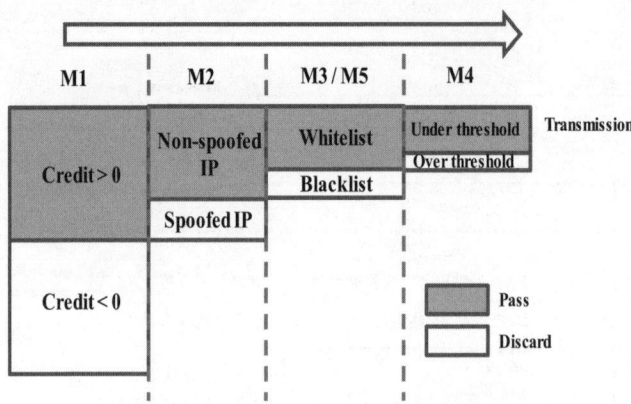

Fig. 2. Unified rate limiting policy order

holds the largest number of packets to decide whether the packet should be passed or blocked. IP spoofing check module handles second largest number of packets. After that, only if a packet is in whitelist, we check the packet transmission rate of the connection. From this order of module execution, we are able to consume the smallest computation on the average for handling one packet.

Unified rate limiting scheme can be deployed in the various places such as client PC's, NAT boxes and edge routers. In Sect. 4, we will show that the unified scheme has higher attack packet dropping ratio and lower false detection than the existing rate limiting schemes.

2.3 The Details of Unified Rate Limiting Scheme

- **M1(TCP connection congestion check):** When a new TCP connection setup request is made, we first check the "congestion" status of TCP connections by the credit value C_v. A TCP packet is allowed to pass if $C_v > 0$. We compute C_v as follows. We initialize $C_v = C_b$ at the beginning, and bound the maximum value of C_v to C_{max}. C_b is a default credit value which is normally set to small positive integer like 5. If the initiated TCP connection fails to set up, C_v is subtracted by C_f. Therefore, if a worm generates a number of failed connections, we eventually have $C_v < 0$. Then further connection attempts are blocked. As soon as we reach a negative value of C_v, we run a timer, and the connection setup blocking is enforced until the timer reaches R_t, when the credit value is reinitiated to C_b. If the three-way handshake succeeds on the other hand, C_v is incremented by C_s. $C_v > 0$ upon the connection attempt means that there are not too many failed or ongoing connection attempts, so we allow new attempts.
- **M2(IP spoofing check):** for the allowed connection attempt, we validate the source address for forgery. We check the local address L_s against the source address of an outgoing packet O_s, and if $L_s \neq O_s$, we drop the packet.

- **M3(TCP history check):** two lists are used for the faster processing of subsequent packets. If a TCP packet is transmitted, we check if the destination address of the packet is recorded in $WL(T_n, R_{cnt})$ or $BL(T_m)$. If former, it is allowed to pass and R_{cnt} is incremented. If latter, the packet is immediately dropped. The packet belonging to the blacklist should not be dropped permanently so that the blacklist is reset in BL_t, blacklist timeout.
- **M4(DDoS check):** If R_{cnt} above exceeds a predefined rate R_{max} within time D_t, it means that an excessive number of connections are made to the destination of T_n in $WL(T_n, R_{cnt})$, *i.e.* a TCP flooding attack. Then, the packets are dropped. In case of UDP or ICMP, we need to compare the current sending rate UI_{rate} to the predefined maximum rate UI_{max}. If $UI_{rate} > UI_{max}$ within D_t, packets will be dropped. After passing P_t time period, UI_{rate} is reset to 0. To reduce the false positives incurred by lots of legitimate retransmissions, D_t can be defined as a small period, e.g. 1 or 2 seconds. Thus, it is not possible that a legitimate user retransmitting packets is regarded as an attacker.
- **M5(TCP validation check):** If not listed in neither the whitelist nor the blacklist, the TCP packet should be validated to be registered in either list. In case that the source address is validated and the outgoing TCP connection attempt is allowed to pass the filter, we check if it gets an ACK within the time C_t. Depending on the result of the check, all outgoing TCP packets T_{all} are classified into two groups – normal group T_n or malicious group T_m. T_n and T_m are stored with the request counter R_{cnt} in the whitelist $WL(T_n, R_{cnt})$ and the blacklist $BL(T_m)$, respectively. This is depicted in Fig. 1 as $V(T_{all}) \rightarrow \{T_n, T_m\}$ for C_t.

3 Prototype Implementation

3.1 Packet Filter Driver and Application

To evaluate the performance of the unified rate limiting, we have implemented a prototype as an application program based on the algorithm[1]. The program takes control of packets in the user and the kernel mode in Microsoft Windows system.

We implemented the packet filter driver with filter hook driver provided by Windows Driver Development Kit (DDK). For the implementation, we let the functions in filter driver use a number of control codes which determines to call appropriate functions.

3.2 Network Simulator

We developed a network simulator in order to measure the possible impact of the proposed algorithm on the Internet under partial deployment, and to find an

---

[1] The application program and the network simulator developed are available at http://ccs.korea.ac.kr/URL

effective deployment strategy for a better performance. We utilize the Internet AS connectivity graph of year 2006 obtained from the RouteView project [17] as a network topology, which consists of 21,211 nodes. Even though the AS graph represents the connectivity between AS's instead of routers or computers, we use it since it is closer to the real Internet topology than any artificially generated graphs. The network simulator does not consider asymmetric routing that exists in the real network because the routing path does not take any effect on the proposed mechanism. The reason is that our mechanism only controls the rate limiting of outgoing packets at the edge of network. Among 21,211 nodes, 21,022 terminal nodes are regarded as clients and 189 central nodes are considered routers.

The inputs to the worm attack scenarios are scanning speed, the ratio of infection success, and attack strategy. Attack strategy can be categorized as random or local. In the random strategy, infection targets are chosen randomly. In the local strategy, 50% of the targets are chosen randomly, whereas the other 50% of the targets are chosen in the local subnet where the infected node resides. As to the DDoS attack scenario, attack packets per second, the number of attack nodes, and attack strategy (random or local) are given as input. Meanwhile, the defense configurations have the following elements – deployment ratio of a rate limiting algorithm, deployment strategy (random or local), false positive and negative rate of a rate limiting algorithm with respect to the worm and DDoS attacks. In particular, the local deployment strategy represents a rate limiting algorithm fully installed in a specific subnetwork (deployment ratio of 100%). On the other hand, the random deployment strategy is to install the rate limiters randomly.

The output of the network simulator includes a network graph with the infection status of each node, a sequence of infection steps for animating the progress of infection on a network. In our experiments, statistics are collected for 10 minutes simulation in each case of worm and DDoS attacks. The working example and sample output of the simulator is shown in Fig. 3.

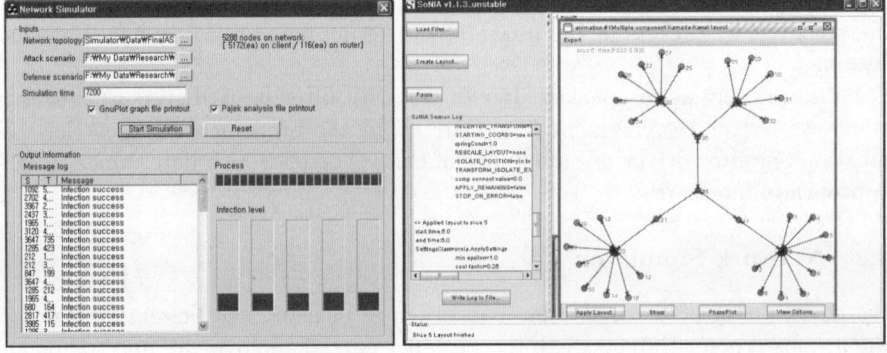

Fig. 3. Network simulation: (left) the operation of the network simulator, (right) the output of a network infection animation file

4 Evaluation

4.1 Experimental Setup

We use the malicious worms such as Blaster, CodeRed, Sasser and Welchia. As to DDoS attack traffic, we generate TCP, UDP, ICMP packets by the use of publicly available attacking tools. The experimental system is equipped with Pentium4 CPU running at 3.0GHz, 512MB main memory, on Microsoft Windows XP. Additionally, we also run the network simulator with the results from the experimental system as the input values, in order to measure the effect on network.

We use the following settings for each rate limiting schemes in our experiment. IP throttling has a five-address working set and a delay queue length of 100 [10]. Credit-based connection rate limiting is configured with its original setting in the reference [12]. DNS-based rate limiting scheme is implemented with 100,000 DNS lists and the rest is the same as in the previous work [13]. Our unified rate limiting scheme has the following configuration: $C_b = 20$, $C_o = -1$, $C_s = +3$, $C_f = -1$, $C_t = 1\text{sec}$, $D_t = 1\text{sec}$, $P_t = 10\text{sec}$, $BL_t = 10\text{sec}$, $C_{max} = 100$, $R_{max} = 500$, and $UI_{max} = 1,000$. This is not necessarily an optimal setting, which can be acquired by further tests. For the whitelist and the blacklist, hashmap [18] is used in our experiments, since it performs well to record and retrieve IP address and the request counter. The hashmap has dynamic size depending on the number of connection, and its searching time guarantees $O(1)$.

In the experiments, we consider four performance metrics. The first metric is the dropping ratio of attack packets. This metric allows us to see defense performance when we adopt a rate limiting scheme. Another performance metric is false alarm rates - false positive and false negative. This shows the precision of a rate limiting scheme. The third metric is the effectiveness of deployment strategy such as local deployment or random deployment. The fourth metric is the overhead.

4.2 Simulation Results

In the first place, we measure the attack packet dropping ratio and the detection accuracy, *i.e.*, false positive and negative. Figure 4 shows the results for the worm attack, with rate limiting schemes[2], at the end host.

As shown in the figure, the unified rate limiting scheme has the highest attack packet dropping ratio. On the other hand, it shows the lowest false rates. In Fig. 4 (right), the curves represent the sum of false positive and false negative ratios. The increased accuracy in the unified rate limiting is owing to the two validation checks, *i.e.*, with IP address and the credit value.

For the DDoS attack, we measured the attack packet dropping ratio and the detection accuracy as well. The DDoS attack packets were comprised of 25%

---

[2] IP_RL: IP Throttling Rate Limiting, CB_RL: Credit Based Rate Limiting, DNS_RL: DNS based Rate Limiting and UNI_RL: Unified Rate Limiting (our proposed scheme).

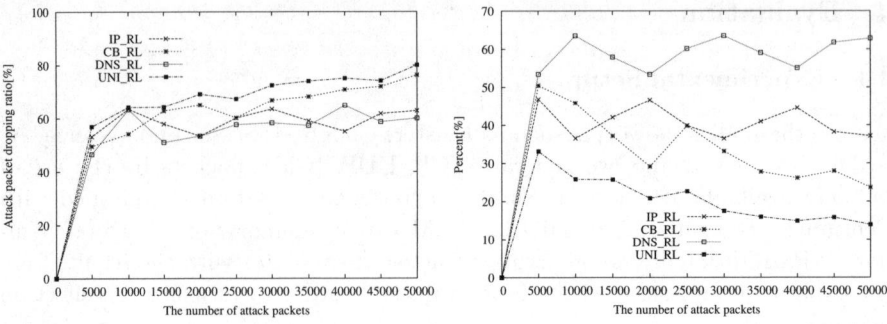

Fig. 4. Simulation results for rate limiting schemes on worm attack in local environment: (left) attack packet dropping ratio, (right) sum of false positive and false negative ratio

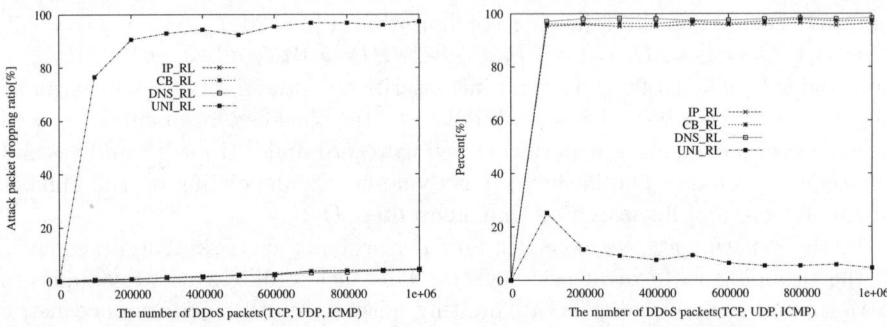

Fig. 5. Simulation results for rate limiting schemes on DDoS attack in local environment: (left) attack packet dropping ratio, (right) sum of false positive and false negative ratio

IP-spoofed TCP packet, 25% normal TCP packet, 25% UDP packet, and 25% ICMP packet.

Figure 5 shows that the unified rate limiting scheme is highly effective for dropping DDoS attack packets in both measures. Namely, most IP-spoofed TCP packets are detected and prevented from going out into the network. In particular, the blacklist helps drop excessively requested IPs. In contrast, the existing worm scan rate limiting schemes are quite ineffective, as only 5% packets are dropped at maximum. This demonstrates the advantage of the unified limiting scheme.

To measure the performance of a rate limiting algorithm and deployment strategy in broadband access networks, we obtained the results as shown in Fig. 6. Figure 6 shows the attack packet dropping ratio in various rate limiting schemes with respect to the deployment ratio. In the figure, the unified rate limiting scheme shows a strong detection capability, not only for worm attacks

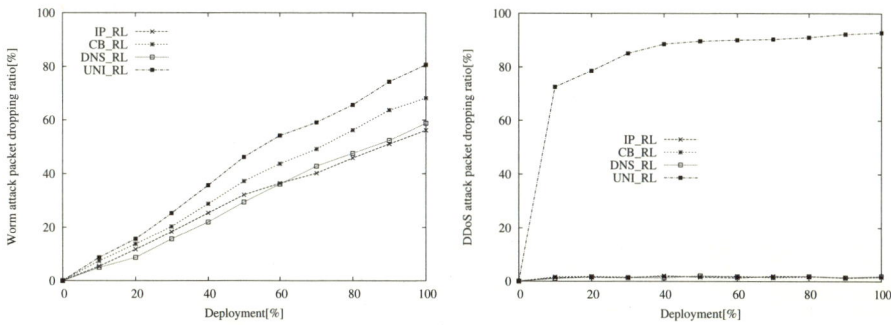

Fig. 6. Simulation of attack packet dropping ratio of rate limiting schemes with respect to deployment ratio: (left) worm attack, (right) DDoS attack

but also for DDoS attacks. The unified rate limiting scheme drops 80.7% worm scanning packets and 93% DDoS packets at the full deployment, while at most 69.2% worm scanning packets and 3.4% DDoS packets are dropped by existing rate limiting schemes.

To show the effectiveness of the rate limiting schemes with respect to the deployment strategy and the deployment ratio for worm and DDoS attack, we make an experiment with 21,022 nodes in subnetworks measured for identifying worm and DDoS attack. In the local deployment scenario of worm attack, worm infection is more mitigated than in the random deployment. This implies the installation of a rate limiting scheme in subnetwork can be effective for reducing worm traffic. However, the wider the deployment goes, the less the performance difference between local and random strategy results.

In addition, we notice that worm scan rate limiting schemes have virtually no DDoS detection capability, and that they record more than 20,000 DDoS attack nodes even though 100% deployment is provided, regardless of the deployment strategy. However, the unified rate limiting scheme takes effect both in the local and random deployment. Unlike in the worm attack scenario, the deployment strategy has no significant impact on the performance.

4.3 Overhead Analysis

For each rate limiting scheme considered in this paper, its time and space complexity is summarized in Table 1. Q represents the length of the queue for IP throttling and DNS-based rate limiting scheme. L represents the length of the DNS list in DNS-based rate limiting scheme. M and N represent the length of the blacklist and whitelist of unified rate limiting scheme respectively. In terms of the time complexity, IP throttling complexity includes the search time of the queue and the whitelist. The complexity for the DNS-based rate limiting includes the DNS list search time along with the queue and whitelist search time. Credit-based rate limiting searches the whitelist when $C_v < 0$, which costs

Table 1. Comparison of complexities and CPU usages of rate limiting algorithms

Rate limiting algorithms	Complexity		CPU usages	
	Time	Space	Worm(5,000 TCP packets)	DDoS(10,000 TCP packets)
IP_RL	O(N)	O(Q+N)	6%	2.5%
DNS_RL	O(N+L)	O(Q+N+L)	3.2%	2.4%
CB_RL	O(N)	O(N)	7.5%	2.3%
UNI_RL	O(N+M)	O(N+M)	4.7%	2.7%

$O(N)$. The unified rate limiting searches the whitelist and the blacklist so that the complexity becomes $O(N + M)$.

During the experiments, the overhead is measured as shown in CPU usages of Table 1. We notice that CPU usage is tightly coupled with time complexity. But even if 5,000 IP addresses should be simultaneously searched, it consumes only 3.2–7.5% of the CPU cycles in the hashmap data structure. Moreover, in case of the credit-based rate limiting and the unified rate limiting scheme, there is no need for the search with respect to the value of C_v. It drastically reduces the CPU usage. In terms of the memory usage, all rate limiting schemes consume 6.5MB of memory, which is readily affordable on the modern computers.

5 Conclusion

As the broadband access technology brings high-speed pipes to the customers, it also raises a security concern because the attackers can exploit the increased bandwidth to mount stronger attacks. Thus the attack mitigation strategy that places defense mechanisms close to the potential attack sources becomes important in the Internet with emerging broadband access networks. The unified rate limiting scheme that we propose in this paper works close to the attack sources, and deals with the two most threatening attacks, Internet worms and DDoS attacks. Unlike existing rate limiting schemes, it is effective to both, and the performance from the unified monitoring is also higher than any existing rater limiters. In particular, it sharply contrasts with the existing rate limiting schemes by drastically reducing DDoS attack packets. Through extensive simulations, we show that the unified approach drops more worm packets than any other rate limiting schemes, with less false alarm. We also show that the unified rate limiting scheme is most effective in the locally and highly deployed networks. As being exploited unknowingly in the worm propagation or DDoS attacks is an unpleasant experience to anybody, we believe that ISPs can include the unified rate limiting scheme in their distribution packages to deploy on subscriber PCs. Or, the ISPs can deploy the scheme in the ingress routers as the pipes which are not too thick, thereby rendering the deployment cost low. Since a single piece of software can deal with both worms and DDoS, separate installation is not necessary. As for the deployment cost, the proposed unified scheme also operates with affordable CPU and memory overhead, making it easily integrable into existing networks elements.

Acknowledgments

This work was supported in part by KT (Korea Telecom), Defense Acquisition Program Administration and Agency for Defense Development under the contract UD060048AD. Additionally supported by the ITRC program of the Korea Ministry of Information & Communications.

References

1. Arbor Networks: Worldwide Infrastructure Security Report (September 2007)
2. Chen, T.M., Robert, J.-M.: Worm Epidemics in High-Speed Networks. IEEE Computer 37(6), 48–53 (2004)
3. Yaneza, J., Sancho, D.: The trend of threats today: 2005 annual roundup and 2006 forecast. Trend Micro White Paper (2005)
4. CISCO SYSTEMS: ONS 15327 Multi-Service Provisioning Platform (November 2002)
5. Mahajan, R., Bellovin, S.M., Floyd, S., Ioannidis, J., Paxson, V., Shenker, S.: Controlling High Bandwidth Aggregates in the Network. ACM SIGCOMM Computer Communications Review 32(3), 62–73 (2006)
6. Keromytis, A., Misra, V., Rubenstein, D.: SOS: Secure Overlay Services. In: Proc. of ACM SIGCOMM, pp. 61–72 (August 2002)
7. Mirkovic, J., Prier, G., Reiher, P.: Attacking DDoS at the source. In: Proc. of 10th IEEE International Conference on Network Protocols (November 2002)
8. Kang, J., Zhang, Z., Ju, J.: Protect e-commerce against DDoS attacks with improved D-WARD system. In: Proc. of the e-Technology, e-Commerce and e-Service conference, March 2005, pp. 100–105 (2005)
9. Gil, T., Poletto, M.: MULTOPS: a data-structure for bandwidth attack detection. In: Proc. of 10th Usenix Security Symposium (August 2001)
10. Williamson, M.M.: Throttling Viruses: Restricting propagation to defeat malicious mobile code. In: Proc. of the 18th Annual Computer Security Applications Conference (ACSAC) (June 2002)
11. Chen, S., Tang, Y.: Slowing Down Internet Worms. In: Proc. of the 24th International Conference on Distributed Computing and Systems (ICDCS) (March 2004)
12. Schechter, S.E., Jung, J., Berger, A.W.: Fast Detection of Scanning Worm Infections. In: Jonsson, E., Valdes, A., Almgren, M. (eds.) RAID 2004. LNCS, vol. 3224, pp. 59–81. Springer, Heidelberg (2004)
13. Whyte, D., Kranakis, E., van Oorschot, P.C.: DNS-based detection of scanning worms in an enterprise network. In: Proc. of the 12th ISOC Symposium on Network and Distributed Systems Security(NDSS) (February 2005)
14. Granger, G., Economou, G., Bielski, S.: Self-securing network interfaces: What, why and how. Technical report, Carnegie Mellon University, CMU-CS-02-144 (May 2002)
15. Moore, D., Voelker, G.M., Savage, S.: Inferring Internet Denial-of-Service Activity. ACM Transactions on Computer Systems (TOCS) 24(2), 115–139 (2006)
16. Wong, C., Bielski, S., Studer, A., Wang, C.: Empirical Analysis of Rate Limiting Mechanisms. In: Valdes, A., Zamboni, D. (eds.) RAID 2005. LNCS, vol. 3858, pp. 22–42. Springer, Heidelberg (2006)
17. Meyer, D.: University of Oregon Route Views archive project (2006), http://archive.routeviews.org
18. SGI: Standard Template Library Programmer's Guide; hashmap containers, http://www.sgi.com/tech/stl/hash_map.html

Combating Spam and Denial-of-Service Attacks with Trusted Puzzle Solvers*

Patrick P. Tsang and Sean W. Smith

Department of Computer Science
Dartmouth College
Hanover, NH 03755, USA
{patrick,sws}@cs.dartmouth.edu

Abstract. Cryptographic puzzles can be used to mitigate spam and denial-of-service (DoS) attacks, as well as to implement timed-release cryptography. However, existing crypto puzzles are impractical because: (1) solving them wastes computing resources and/or human time, (2) the time it takes to solve them can vary dramatically across computing platforms, and/or (3) applications become non-interoperable due to competition for resources when solving them.

We propose the use of *Trusted Computing* in constructing crypto puzzles. Our puzzle constructions have *none* of the drawbacks above and only require each client machine to be equipped with a small tamper-resistant *Trusted Puzzle Solver (TPS)*, which may be realized using the prevalent Trusted Platform Module (TPM) with minimal modifications.

1 Introduction

1.1 Cryptographic Puzzles

Cryptographic puzzles are problems that require a designated amount of time and/or resources to solve. Since 1978 when Merkle first proposed them for securing key agreement [23], crypto puzzles have been used to overcome a range of security challenges.

Proof-of-Work Puzzles. Spammers try to send as many spam emails (i.e., unsolicited bulk emails) as possible to maximize their profits; attackers can take down a web server by requesting many webpages within a short period of time. Unfortunately, although it is well-known that charging fees on service accesses would provide the necessary disincentive for abuses as such, there is no practical way to charge money in the electronic world today. One major use of crypto

---

* This work was supported in part by the U.S. Department of Homeland Security under Grant Award Number 2006-CS-001-000001, the Institute for Security Technology Studies, under Grant number 2005-DD-BX-1091 awarded by the Bureau of Justice Assistance, and the National Science Foundation, under grant CNS-0524695. The views and conclusions do not necessarily represent those of the sponsors.

puzzles is to impose costs on the clients by forcing them to do some work per service access (and hence the name "Proof-of-Work" [17]), thereby consuming their resources, e.g., CPU cycles.

Proof-of-Work puzzles are also known as *Client Puzzles* [2,18,31], especially when they are used to mitigate denial-of-service (DoS) attacks at the lower layers of the communication protocol stack such as the network layer and the transport layer. Client Puzzles have the additional property that their generation, as well as the verification of their solution must be done efficiently because otherwise these two operations would become new DoS attack surfaces.

There are scenarios when having the ability to obtain and solve Proof-of-Work puzzles before the actual service accesses is desirable. For example, allowing the puzzles to be "presolved" hides from the user the latency of solving the puzzles when trying to access web servers for webpages, and can still rate-limit accesses from the user. However, presolvable client puzzles are less effective in mitigating DoS attacks because the adversary can accumulate enough puzzle solutions and use all of them at the same time.

Dwork and Naor were the first to propose the use of crypto puzzles for fighting spam [13]. Back independently invented "hashcash" [3]. Other applications of Proof-of-Work puzzles include metering visits to websites [15], providing incentives in peer-to-peer systems [27], mitigating (distributed) DoS attacks [21,2,12], rate-limiting TCP connections [18] and defending against Sybil attacks [7]. Finally, Roman et al. [26] proposed a scheme that uses pre-challenges to fight spam, in which the pre-challenges can range from, e.g., security questions to micro-payments to CAPTCHAs [30]. While our work focuses on constructing better crypto puzzles, their work provides insights on several compatibility and usability issues when one deploys our solution on existing email infrastructures.

Time-Lock Puzzles. May [22] first discussed the idea of sending information into the future, i.e., encrypting a message so that no one can decrypt it until a predetermined time. Rivest et al. [25] later formally proposed *Timed-Release Cryptography (TRC)* and *Time-Lock puzzles*—crypto puzzles that can be solved only after a predetermined time—and their use to realize TRC.

The algorithm for solving Time-Lock puzzles must be non-parallelizable, i.e., a Timed-Lock puzzle with multiple machines won't be any faster than solving it with a single machine. For instance, puzzles that ask for the preimage of hash values are bad Time-Lock puzzles because computing hash preimages can be parallelized. Rivest et al.'s Time-Lock puzzles [25] ask for a series of modular squarings, the computation of which no one knows how to parallelize.

Applications of TRC and hence some Time-Lock puzzles include sealed-bid auctions [25], encapsulated key escrow [25,4], digital time capsule [24], and timed release of digital signatures [16] and commitments [6]. Chan and Blake proposed a timed-release encryption scheme that provides user anonymity [11] but requires a passive server. Some other timed-release constructions are [9,10].

1.2 Problems with Existing Crypto Puzzles

Existing crypto puzzles fail to effectively combat spams and DoS attacks, as they all suffer from one or more of the drawbacks below. As we will see, our design of crypto puzzles to be presented later in this paper has *none* of these drawbacks.

Impreciseness. A problem faced by all existing crypto puzzles is that it is extremely difficult to precisely specify the time and/or resources required to solve a puzzle, mostly due to the heterogeneity of computing devices available today. For instance, solving a crypto puzzle that requires 1 minute to solve on a Desktop PC could take an hour on a PDA.

For Proof-of-Work puzzles, this impreciseness adds complication to, if not rendering it entirely infeasible, their use for defeating service abuse. For example, if one sets the difficulty of solving the puzzles assuming the presence of resourceful spammers, then legitimate users will probably be practically unable to send emails on their PDAs, or PCs they bought three years ago. The situation gets no better for Time-Lock puzzles: timed-release cryptography becomes insecure if Time-Lock puzzles can be solved faster than the puzzle creator expected. In Internet-based contests, for example, a more resourceful candidate can decrypt the test questions earlier, resulting in unfairness.

Environmental and User Unfriendliness. Solving crypto puzzles consumes resources in the computing devices. Most existing constructions of crypto puzzles are computationally intensive and exhaust CPU cycles for a continuous period of time before their solutions can be computed. Unfortunately, the computation involved in solving these puzzles does not result in any other useful output.

Worse still, crypto puzzles can waste human time, which could have a much higher value than CPU cycles. For example, if a website limits users' accesses to webpages by giving out crypto puzzles that require 10s to solve per webpage download, then users will experience a delay of 10s for every page they see. To help cease this problem, some Proof-of-Work puzzles are designed so that they can be pre-solved; by pre-fetching these puzzles and solving them before actual service requests, the latency incurred can be hidden from the users.

Non-Interoperability. If a machine has two or more crypto puzzles to solve, all of which require a common resources, then the machine can only solve them one at a time. For example, if a mail server decides that a honest client machine will only send at most one email per minute on average and thus gives out puzzles that require one minute to solve, and a website thinks a honest client machine will only get at most one webpage per minute on average and thus also gives out puzzles that require one minute to solve, then a honest client machine won't be able to *both* send 1 email and visit 1 page per minute! By similar arguments, users can only participate in one Internet-based contest at a time.

1.3 Trusted Computing

The term "trusted computing" has come to denote work in the spirit of the *Trusted Computing Group* (TCG) consortium [29]: increasing the security of standard commodity platforms by adding a small amount of physical hardware and careful integration of software support for it.

In the TCG approach, this hardware takes the form of a *trusted platform module* (TPM) [28], which is an inexpensive chip on the motherboard that participates in the boot process. The TPM maintains a set of *platform configuration registers* (PCRs) that indicate the hardware and software configuration of the platform, and provides services both to release secrets to the platform only if the PCRs show the right values ("unsealing" or "unwrapping"), as well as to prove to remote parties what the current platform configuration is ("attestation").

This notion of trusted computing thus embodies two security design principles. One is the modern notion of cost-benefit tradeoff: the goal is to improve security without spending too much money. Consequently, one adds a small chip, rather than armoring the entire machine. Another is the classical notion of minimizing the *trusted computing base* (TCB). Although the TPM's promises of trusted computing initially rest on the assumption that the adversary compromises neither the TPM nor the BIOS, the reality is murkier: attacks on the OS can still subvert protection, and low-cost and highly-effective physical attacks have begin to emerge (e.g., [20]).

1.4 Our Contributions

We present an alternative vision for trusted computing: using *Trusted Puzzle Solvers* to construct crypto puzzles with many desirable properties missing from existing constructions. Our solution is secure and efficient, and yet only requires each client to be equipped with minimal tamper-resistant hardware.

Paper Organization. We explain in Section 2 the details of Trusted Puzzle Solvers, the vital piece of trusted hardware that enables our constructions of crypto puzzles, which are presented in Section 3 and Section 4. We discuss the implications of our design in Section 5 before we conclude the paper in Section 6.

2 Trusted Puzzle Solvers

In our design of crypto puzzles to be presented in the next two sections, all client machines are equipped with a hardware module that we call the *Trusted Puzzle Solver*, or *TPS*. We make the assumption that all the functionality provided by these modules are correct and secure, even when subject to certain hardware attacks, such as probing, launched by adversaries in physical proximity. In other words, these modules are the *Trusted Computing Base (TCB)* of our constructions. It is therefore important to minimize their size, in terms of physical volume, circuitry complexity, codebase, and etc, so that we can manufacture them at low costs and yet with high assurance of them meeting our trust assumptions.

Every TPS has a distinct asymmetric key pair (a private key sk and a public key pk),[1] generated and installed by its vendor during manufacturing. The

---

[1] As will become clear, the key pair is for digital signature in our Proof-of-Work puzzles and for public-key encryption in our Time-Lock puzzles.

private key *sk* resides in, and never leaves, the tamper-proof storage of the TPSs. The public key *pk* is certified by one or more Certification Authorities (CAs), such as the TPS vendors, which all servers recognize and trust. Client machines know the public key and the associated certificate *cert* of the TPS they are equipped with. Servers know the public keys of the CAs for certificate signing and thus can verify the correctness of the public keys of the TPS modules.

TPSs also contain several other components within their tamper-resistance boundaries. One such component is a clock. The clocks in the TPSs need not be synchronized to a global clock and may be reset at power-on, as long as they all are ticking at the same and reasonably precise frequency. Other components include several registers for storing key materials and internal states, some simple logic for arithmetics and control, and a cryptographically secure random number generator (RNG). Finally, as we will explain in detail in the next section, TPSs further contain the necessary circuit to perform cryptographic operations such as computing HMACs, digital signature signing and public-key decryption.

3 Our Proposed Proof-of-Work Puzzles

Recall that the ultimate goal of having clients solve Proof-of-Work puzzles is to rate-limit their service accesses. While existing constructions of Proof-of-Work puzzles achieve this goal by imposing a computational cost on each access, our design relies on the TPS of the client to do the policing: only TPSs know how to solve the puzzles, and TPSs will only solve puzzles up to a certain rate.

More concretely, a puzzle consists of a nonce and a fee. The nonce prevents the clients from replaying puzzle solutions. The fee is a parameter that *precisely* specifies the time it takes to solve the puzzle. A valid solution to a puzzle is a signature signed by a TPS on the puzzle. Thus only TPSs can solve the puzzles.

It suffices to make sure the TPS modules don't solve the puzzles too quickly. Each TPS has a register named `balance`, the value of which is incremented periodically. In our construction, it is incremented by 1 every millisecond. TPSs leave their factories with `balance` initialized to zero. The value stored in `balance` may be persistent across up-times or set to zero upon reset. Given a puzzle with a fee, a TPS solves it only if the current balance is no less than the fee, in which case the TPS also deducts the fee from the balance.

3.1 Protocol Description

We now describe our proposed protocol executed between a server and a client, during which the server would like the client to solve a Proof-of-Work puzzle before granting a service request made by the client. We name the client Alice and the server Bob.

We have also included a diagrammatic description of the protocol in Figure 1.

1. Alice → Bob : ⟨request⟩
   Alice requests Bob for his service.

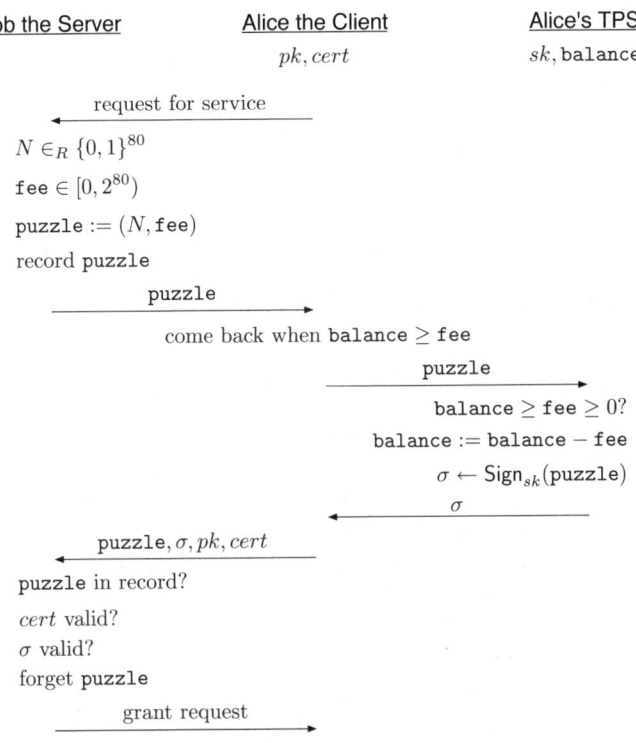

Fig. 1. Diagrammatic Protocol Description of Our Proof-of-Work Puzzles

2. Bob → Alice : ⟨puzzle⟩
   Bob challenges Alice to solve puzzle $= (N, \text{fee})$, where N is a 80-bit random nonce and fee is a 80-bit non-negative integer. The fee may be a constant or a function of the current load of the server, and/or even the identity of the client. Bob records puzzle.
3. Alice examines the fee in the puzzle. If her TPS doesn't have enough balance to pay for the fee at the moment, she comes back later when balance has become sufficient. In the meantime, she can do something meaningful instead of busy-waiting or stalling. Alice knows when to come back by keeping track of the time and her TPS usage. Alternatively, if Alice thinks that the fee is too expensive, she may refrain from accessing Bob's service by terminating the protocol.
4. Alice → TPS : ⟨puzzle⟩
   Alice relays puzzle to her TPS.
5. TPS → Alice : ⟨σ⟩
   Alice's TPS aborts if the current balance is less than fee. Otherwise, the TPS deducts fee from balance, signs puzzle with its private key sk, resulting in a signature $\sigma = \text{Sign}_{sk}(\text{puzzle})$. The TPS returns σ to Alice.
6. Alice → Bob : ⟨soln⟩
   Alice answers Bob's challenge with soln $= (\text{puzzle}, \sigma, pk, cert)$.

7. Alice's soln = (puzzle, $\sigma, pk, cert$) is valid *if and only if cert* is a valid certificate on the pk, σ is a valid signature on puzzle under pk, and puzzle appears in Bob's record. If soln is valid, Bob grants Alice's service request and removes puzzle from his record. He declines the request otherwise.

3.2 Analysis

Properties. Our construction has *none* of the drawbacks we discussed in Section 1.2. First, the time it takes to solve a puzzle is as precise as the clock in the TPS, and thus a PDA can solve as many puzzles as a resourceful desktop PC. Also, there is no need to waste any resources such as CPU cycles on the client machine, or human time waiting for puzzles to be solved as long as there is enough balance in the TPS.

By having the TPS keep a separate balance for each application, our construction allows multiple applications to solve their own puzzles in parallel. The cost per application is only one extra register (for storing the balance). Notice that these extra registers need not be tamper-proof; one can store the balance values in insecure memory outside the TPS by using techniques similar to "sealing" in TCG's TPMs. Thus, our TPS construction allows interoperability among any number of applications requiring Proof-of-Work puzzles and yet requires only a constant amount of trusted storage.

Parameters. We have chosen RSASSA-PKCS1-v1.5 [19, §8.1] using SHA-1 as the digital signature scheme used by the TPS because all TPMs that are compliant to the TCG's TPM v1.2 specification [28] must support it. Nonces are 80-bit and hence picking them uniformly at random prevents nonce reuse. We allow the fee of a puzzle to be any 80-bit non-negative integer. A puzzle is thus only 20 bytes in size. The tamper-resistant register balance is 80-bit in size, which will never overflow in practice at the rate of incrementing by 1 per millisecond. In fact, one might want to set a much smaller upper bound for it so as to limit the module's ability to presolve puzzles.

Efficiency. The client has nothing to do except relaying a few messages at the right time; the TPS signs one signature on the puzzle. Like any other Proof-of-Work puzzle schemes, there are 4 rounds of communication between the server and the client. Generating a puzzle is efficient, as it involves only picking a random nonce and deciding on the fee of the puzzle. Verifying the solution of a puzzle involves two digital signature verification. For each service request pending for a puzzle solution, the server needs to remember a 20-byte puzzle only.

Security. A client in possession of a TPS for t milliseconds has a balance of at most t at any time instant during the period of the possession. Assume the contrary that the construction is insecure, then the client has been able to correctly solve puzzles such that the sum of their fees exceeds t during the same time period. Hence there exists at least one correctly solved puzzle that was not solved by the TPS. Since all puzzles are distinct (due to the nonces in them), the solution to the one puzzle that was not solved by the TPS contains a forged signature, which contradicts to the unforgeability of the digital signature scheme.

4 Our Proposed Time-Lock Puzzles

The traditional means of ensuring a puzzle to be solvable only after a predetermined time by requiring the client to go through some tedious operation suffers from all the drawbacks we listed in Section 1.2. Our solution relies on the TPSs present in the client machines as trusted time servers: the TPSs make sure that sufficient time has elapsed before they help the clients solve the puzzles.

Specifically, when a client machine receives a puzzle from the server, it relays the puzzle to its TPS. In a naive solution, the TPS would wait for enough time and then return the solution to the client machine. However, this is undesirable since either the TPS is incapable of concurrently solving concurrent but independent time-lock puzzles, or the TPS must keep in its tamper-resistant memory states of size linear to the number of puzzles allowed to be solved at a time. Rather, in our design, the TPS time-stamps the puzzle, thus witnessing that the client machine has obtained the puzzle at a particular time. When the client machine later comes back with the time-stamped puzzle after sufficient time has elapsed, the TPS will solve the puzzle for the client machine.

We highlight that although our solution requires each machine to have a TPS, we do *not* rely on the uniformity of the computational resources these TPSs possess. In fact, we envision that as trusted hardware modules, be them TPSs or TCG's TPMs, become more and more prevalent, vendors will manufacture these modules with different processing power and capability, much like any other components in custody PCs we see nowadays. Our design is secure so long as the TPS hardware satisfies certain basic requirements such as possessing a trusted clock, some trusted circuitry and a few trusted storage.

4.1 Protocol Description

We now describe our proposed protocol executed between a server and a client when the client requests a Time-Lock puzzle from the server. Again we name the client Alice and the server Bob.

Figure 2 shows a diagrammatic description of the protocol.

1. Alice $\rightarrow$ Bob : $\langle pk, cert \rangle$
   Alice requests Bob for a Time-Lock puzzle by sending him her TPS's public key pk and its certificate $cert$.
2. Bob $\rightarrow$ Alice : $\langle \texttt{puzzle} \rangle$
   Bob aborts if $cert$ is not a valid certificate for pk. Otherwise, he returns Alice with $\texttt{puzzle} = (\tilde{N}, \texttt{delay})$, where $\texttt{delay}$ is a 80-bit non-negative integer that denotes the time (in ms) necessary for solving the puzzle and $\tilde{N}$ is the encryption of a 80-bit random nonce N concatenated with $\texttt{delay}$ under the TPS's public key pk, i.e. $\tilde{N} = \mathsf{Enc}_{pk}(N || \texttt{delay})$.
3. Alice $\rightarrow$ TPS : $\langle \tilde{N} \rangle$
   Alice relays the $\tilde{N}$ to her TPS.
4. TPS $\rightarrow$ Alice : $\langle t_0, \texttt{tstamp} \rangle$
   Let the current time be t_0. The TPS returns t_0 and $\texttt{tstamp}$ to Alice, where

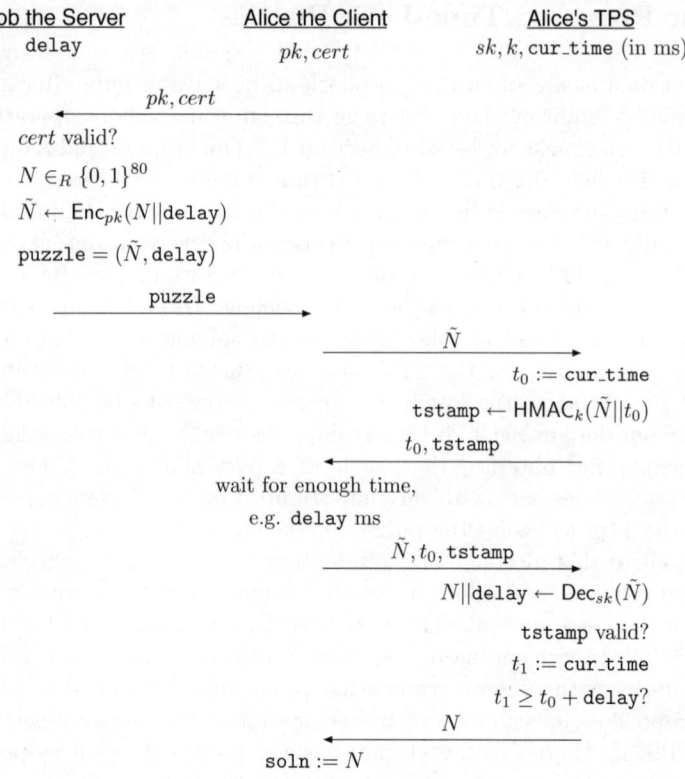

Fig. 2. Diagrammatic Protocol Description of Our Time-Lock Puzzles

tstamp is the time-stamp on $\tilde{N}$ at time t_0 under the TPS's secret HMAC key k, i.e. $\texttt{tstamp} = \mathsf{HMAC}_k(\tilde{N}||t_0)$.

5. Alice comes back after sufficient time, i.e. after delay ms or more. Again, she is free to do anything in the meantime, rather than busy-waiting or stalling.
6. Alice $\rightarrow$ TPS : $\langle \tilde{N}, t_0, \texttt{tstamp} \rangle$
   Alice sends to her TPS $\tilde{N}$, t_0 and tstamp.
7. TPS $\rightarrow$ Alice : $\langle N \rangle$
   Given $\tilde{N}$, t_0 and tstamp, Alice's TPS proceeds as follows. It first decrypts $\tilde{N}$ into $N||\texttt{delay}$ using its private key sk, i.e. $N||\texttt{delay} = \mathsf{Dec}_{sk}(\tilde{N})$. If tstamp is valid, i.e. $\texttt{tstamp} = \mathsf{HMAC}_k(\tilde{N}||t_0)$, and $t_1 \geq t_0 + \texttt{delay}$, where t_1 is the current time, the TPS returns N to Alice. The TPS aborts otherwise.
8. The solution to the puzzle is $\texttt{soln} = N$.

4.2 Analysis

Properties. Our proposed Time-Lock puzzles have all properties we have desired. The puzzles have a solving time as precise as the clock in the TPSs. They are environmental friendly because virtually no resources is wasted by the client in solving them. Finally, one client machine can solve multiple time-lock puzzles concurrently, without any slowdown in solving any of them.

Parameters. We have picked RSA-ES-OAEP [19, §7.1] using SHA-1 as the asymmetric encryption and HMAC-SHA-1 as the message authentication scheme. Again the support of these functions is required by TPM specification v1.2 [28]. cur_time is a 80-bit register that stores the current time in millisecond (relative to, e.g., the time the TPS was last reset) and will never overflow in practice.

Efficiency. To create a puzzle, Bob needs to do one asymmetric encryption of a one-block plaintext. The TPS has to do two HMACs and one asymmetric decryption of a one-block ciphertext. Alice does not need to do any computation.

Neither the client nor the TPS has to stall when handling a Time-Lock puzzle and thus practically any number of Time-Lock puzzles can be solved concurrently. Also, the TPSs needs not keep any state for each pending puzzle.

Security. A secure time-lock puzzle cannot be solved earlier than the specified time. We argue in the following that this requirement holds in our construction. Assuming the contrary that a client machine can solve a puzzle without having waited for the specified delay after obtaining the puzzle, then the client must have successfully decrypted the ciphertext in the puzzle before the predetermined time (i.e., the time the machine received the puzzle plus the delay specified in the puzzle). The TPS could not have decrypted the ciphertext as it would imply a forgery of a time-stamp on the puzzle with a time earlier than the time the machine obtained the puzzle, contradicting to the security of the HMAC. As a result, the fact that the client was able to decrypt the ciphertext violates the security guarantee of the encryption, which leads to a contradiction.

It is also crucial for time-lock puzzles to be solvable at the specified time (rather than some time much later). For example, this property is necessary to guarantee fairness in applications such as sealed-bid auctions and Internet-based contests. It is easy to see that our construction of time-lock puzzles enjoys this property. In fact, our construction enjoys it at a stricter sense—even when some client machines are solving more than one time-lock puzzle at the same time.

4.3 Realizing Timed-Release Encryption

How to use the Time-Lock puzzles we just proposed is application-dependent. Here, we give an example of using our puzzles to realize Timed-Release Encryption, for applications such as Internet-based contests.

We will need in addition a secure symmetric encryption scheme and a secure cryptographic hash function. Let ℓ denote the length of the symmetric key used in the encryption scheme, $\mathcal{E}$ and $\mathcal{D}$ denote the encryption and decryption algorithms respectively, and $H : \{0,1\}^* \rightarrow \{0,1\}^\ell$ denote the cryptographic hash function. We can implement the symmetric encryption scheme using AES operating under Counter Mode [14] with 128-bit key, i.e. $\ell = 128$. We can implement H using SHA-1 with proper encoding.

To perform timed-release encryption, i.e., to encrypt a plaintext P so that the resulting ciphertext can't be decrypted by a client Alice until a release-time predetermined by a server Bob, Bob does the following:

1. Create a Time-Lock puzzle for Alice with delay equal to the difference between the release-time and the current time in millisecond, according to the protocol we described in Section 4.1.
2. Generate a symmetric encryption key s by hashing the nonce N in the puzzle, i.e. $s \leftarrow H(N)$.
3. Encrypt the plaintext P under the symmetric encryption key s, resulting in a ciphertext C, i.e. $C = \mathcal{E}_s(P)$.
4. Return C to Alice along with the Time-Lock puzzle.

Consequently, by the time Alice has solved the puzzle, she can reconstruct the symmetric encryption key s, decrypt the ciphertext C, and recover the original plaintext P, i.e. $P = \mathcal{D}_s(C)$.

Security. To see why such a Timed-Release Encryption is secure given that the underlying Time-Lock puzzle is secure, consider the following arguments. Assume the contrary that the above Timed-Release Encryption is insecure, then the adversary can learn information about the plaintext from the ciphertext prior to the predetermined release-time. Since the underlying Time-Lock puzzle is secure, the puzzle leaks no information about the solution to the puzzle to any computationally bounded adversary at the time when the adversary learned the information. Now the security of the cryptographic hash function implies that the symmetric key was picked uniformly at random in the computational sense. Therefore, the adversary's ability to learn information about the plaintext from the ciphertext contradicts the security of the symmetric encryption scheme.

5 Discussion

Feasibility. The use of trusted hardware has been conceived by some as waving a magic wand: like invoking magic, it's just unrealistic. We have different opinions. All cryptographic security measures require, at the very least, the secure execution of the cryptographic algorithms and a secure storage of the keys; it is assumed, implicitly or explicitly, that some type of computing engine and storage lies beyond the reach of the adversary. Using trusted hardware simply makes this assumption explicit; designing it requires explicitly thinking about the types of physical attacks an adversary might mount. Deploying it in the real world requires considering trade-offs between strength of the tamper protections, robustness, cost, and computational power. At one extreme, a powerful piece of trusted hardware such as an IBM 4758 or 4764 secure coprocessor can securely host a (small) application in its entirety but is very expensive; at the other end, a resource-constrained piece of trusted hardware such as a TPM chip is inexpensive but does little beyond several primitive cryptographic operations. (We note that both these devices exist in the real world—and that TPMs now are ubiquitous in nearly all new desktop and laptop platforms.)

The real challenge when designing a solution to a security problem is how to cost-effectively provide sufficient security with confidence through intelligently minimizing the TCB. Thus, one of our goals when designing the TPS was to make its wide deployment feasible by minimizing the functionality requirements on them. We aimed for something the size of a TPM. In fact, most of the functionality needed by a TPS, such as HMAC-SHA1 and RSA operations, is already present in TCG's TPMs in their current specification, with the exception of a trusted clock. One could therefore expect that the cost of a TPS is comparable to, if not less than, that of a TPM (assuming that TPS manufacturing enjoys the same economy of scale that TPM manufacturing does).

TPS Compromises. Given that it is not impossible to circumvent the tamper-resistance of TPSs, it is worth looking at the security implications when tampering happens. In both of our puzzle constructions, if an adversary can read the registers, he learns the private signing/decryption key, and can then solve puzzles at any rate. If the adversary can write to the registers or make the clock tick faster, then he can increase the balance in case of Proof-of-Work puzzles, or fast-forward the current time in case of Time-Lock puzzles. In both cases, the adversary can solve puzzles faster than he should have been able to.

As a defensive mechanism, servers should audit TPS activities, become suspicious if they see some TPSs solving puzzles too quickly and eventually declare those TPSs to have been compromised. Servers should revoke all compromised TPSs by, e.g., using Certificate Revocation-Lists (CRLs) in X.509 [1], which is a revocation mechanism currently also used by TCG's TPMs.

Bot-nets. Nowadays spammers seldom use their own machines for spamming. Rather, they take over machines on the network through the use of, e.g. worms and malware, and "steal" resources, e.g., computational power, electrical power, email addresses and IP addresses, from these "zombies" machines to send unsolicited bulk emails. Conventional Proof-of-Work puzzles become ineffective when spammers can summon their can zombies to solve puzzles for them. The problem here is that these puzzles are solver-anonymous: anyone can solve a puzzle and the solution contains no trail of who produced it. Our proposed Proof-of-Work puzzles are more resilient to bot-nets than conventional puzzles because the solution to a puzzle contains the identity of the solver's TPS. This provides some clues to the server whether the solving of the puzzles has been outsourced—and can potentially be addressed by revocation.

User Anonymity. As discussed, being able to identify the TPSs helps revoke compromised TPSs and resist bot-nets. However, this implies that our proposed puzzles do not protect the anonymity of the user. In the case of Proof-of-Work puzzles, the server knows which TPS has solved the puzzle by looking at the digital signature; in the case of Time-Lock puzzles, the client must reveal the public key of her TPS to the server when obtaining a puzzle.

Our proposed Proof-of-Work puzzles can be modified to provide user anonymity as follows. TPSs sign a group signature [5] instead of a digital signature to hide their identity among the set of all TPSs. Since TPM v1.2 implements *Direct*

Anonymous Attestation (DAA) [8], v1.2 TPMs already have the necessary circuitry to implement TPSs with user anonymity. We point out that the use of group signatures makes puzzle solution verification more computationally intensive. Augmenting user anonymity to our proposed Time-Lock puzzles in an efficient way seems to be a lot more complicated. We thus leave it as future work.

Isn't the TPS PKI Enough? Since each TPS possesses a certified key pair, a wide deployment of TPS modules implies a global Public-Key Infrastructure (PKI) as well. One might think that the mere existence of a global PKI would suffice to mitigate spam and DoS attacks and thus using TPS to do the same would be redundant. We believe this is not the case, for several reasons.

For PKI to be effective in deterring attacks, the certificates need to meaningfully bind a client to a key pair. Large-scale PKIs that do this have proven an elusive and expensive proposition. However, the TPS PKI merely needs to assert a key pair belongs a genuine TPS; as with the TPM PKI, already in existence, it omits the expensive part.

Furthermore, a PKI alone won't solve the problem. Even if we had a global PKI, using it to fight spam and DoS attacks would still require us to ensure the integrity of the client software and to isolate malware from the private keys; these tasks rely on the security of the operating system and the hardware. This almost dictates us to put the entire computing platform into the TCB, which is not only costly but also infeasible. In our solution, the TCB only consists of a small and simple hardware module.

By similar arguments, requiring authentication at the client side using, e.g. TLS, during web browsing does not mitigate DoS attacks. In fact, the extra communications and cryptographic computation required by TLS might actually open up a new DoS attack surface.

Puzzle Pricing. Regardless of whether real currencies, traditional computation-based crypto puzzles or our TPS-based puzzles are used, pricing the service accesses right is the key to the effective mitigation of spam and DoS attacks without adversely impacting the honest users. For instance, a web server may want to hand out puzzles that are more difficult to solve as its load increases. Similarly, some have suggested that the price for emailing to a mailing list should be function of how big and commercial the list is.

Our TPS-based puzzles facilitate correct pricing better than existing puzzles for a number of reasons. First, the fee of a puzzle can be set at a very fine-grained level. Second, the effort to generate a puzzle and verify its solution is independent of its fee. Third, the time it takes to solve a puzzle is very precise.

6 Conclusions

We have proposed the use of trusted computing in designing two types of crypto puzzles, namely Proof-of-Work puzzles and Time-lock puzzles. In particular, we have presented how to construct these puzzles by assuming that each client machine is equipped a *Trusted Puzzle Solver*, or *TPS*, which is a small tamper-resistant hardware module. Our proposed crypto puzzles are the first that achieve all the aforementioned desirable properties simultaneously, and can thus be used to effectively combat spam and DoS attacks. Our analysis has shown that our designs are secure and efficient.

TPSs are cost-effective and trustworthy because of their simplicity. Almost all the necessary functionality is already present in TCG's TPM architecture today. These factors make it feasible for TPSs to be widely deployed.

Acknowledgment

We would like to thank Jianying Zhou and the anonymous reviewers for their helpful comments.

References

1. Adams, C., Farrell, S.: Internet X.509 Public Key Infrastructure Certificate Management Protocols. Internet Engineering Task Force: RFC 2510 (1999)
2. Aura, T., Nikander, P., Leiwo, J.: DOS-Resistant Authentication with Client Puzzles. In: Christianson, B., Crispo, B., Malcolm, J.A., Roe, M. (eds.) Security Protocols 2000. LNCS, vol. 2133, pp. 170–177. Springer, Heidelberg (2001)
3. Back, A.: Hashcash (1997), http://hashcash.org
4. Bellare, M., Goldwasser, S.: Encapsulated Key Escrow. Technical report, Massachusetts Institute of Technology, Cambridge, MA, USA (1996)
5. Bellare, M., Shi, H., Zhang, C.: Foundations of Group Signatures: The Case of Dynamic Groups. In: Menezes, A. (ed.) CT-RSA 2005. LNCS, vol. 3376, pp. 136–153. Springer, Heidelberg (2005)
6. Boneh, D., Naor, M.: Timed Commitments. In: Bellare, M. (ed.) CRYPTO 2000. LNCS, vol. 1880, pp. 236–254. Springer, Heidelberg (2000)
7. Borisov, N.: Computational Puzzles as Sybil Defenses. In: Peer-to-Peer Computing, pp. 171–176. IEEE Computer Society Press, Los Alamitos (2006)
8. Brickell, E.F., Camenisch, J., Chen, L.: Direct Anonymous Attestation. In: ACM Conference on Computer and Communications Security, pp. 132–145. ACM Press, New York (2004)
9. Cathalo, J., Libert, B., Quisquater, J.-J.: Efficient and Non-interactive Timed-Release Encryption. In: Qing, S., Mao, W., López, J., Wang, G. (eds.) ICICS 2005. LNCS, vol. 3783, pp. 291–303. Springer, Heidelberg (2005)
10. Chalkias, K., Stephanides, G.: Timed Release Cryptography from Bilinear Pairings Using Hash Chains. In: Leitold, H., Markatos, E.P. (eds.) CMS 2006. LNCS, vol. 4237, pp. 130–140. Springer, Heidelberg (2006)
11. Chan, A.C.-F., Blake, I.F.: Scalable, Server-Passive, User-Anonymous Timed Release Cryptography. In: ICDCS, pp. 504–513. IEEE Computer Society Press, Los Alamitos (2005)
12. Dean, D., Stubblefield, A.: Using Client Puzzles to Protect TLS. In: SSYM: Proceedings of the 10th conference on USENIX Security Symposium, Berkeley, CA, USA, 2001. USENIX Association, p. 1 (2001)
13. Dwork, C., Naor, M.: Pricing via Processing or Combatting Junk Mail. In: Brickell, E.F. (ed.) CRYPTO 1992. LNCS, vol. 740, pp. 139–147. Springer, Heidelberg (1993)

14. Dworkin, M.: Recommendation for Block Cipher Modes of Operations–Methods and Techniques. Technical report, National Institute of Standards and Technology (NIST) (December 2001),
    http://csrc.nist.gov/publications/nistpubs/800-38a/sp800-38a.pdf
15. Franklin, M.K., Malkhi, D.: Auditable Metering with Lightweight Security. In: Hirschfeld, R. (ed.) FC 1997. LNCS, vol. 1318, pp. 151–160. Springer, Heidelberg (1997)
16. Garay, J.A., Jakobsson, M.: Timed Release of Standard Digital Signatures. In: Blaze, M. (ed.) FC 2002. LNCS, vol. 2357, pp. 168–182. Springer, Heidelberg (2003)
17. Jakobsson, M., Juels, A.: Proofs of Work and Bread Pudding Protocols. In: CMS 1999: Proceedings of the IFIP TC6/TC11 Joint Working Conference on Secure Information Networks, Deventer, The Netherlands, pp. 258–272. Kluwer Academic Publishers, Dordrecht (1999)
18. Juels, A., Brainard, J.G.: Client Puzzles: A Cryptographic Countermeasure Against Connection Depletion Attacks. In: NDSS. The Internet Society (1999)
19. Kaliski, B., Staddon, J.: PKCS #1: RSA Cryptography Specifications Version 2.0 (1998)
20. Kauer, B.: OSLO: Improving the Security of Trusted Computing. In: USENIX Security Symposium, pp. 229–237. USENIX (2007)
21. Mankins, D., Krishnan, R., Boyd, C., Zao, J., Frentz, M.: Mitigating Distributed Denial of Service Attacks with Dynamic Resource Pricing. In: ACSAC 2001: Proceedings of the 17th Annual Computer Security Applications Conference, p. 411. IEEE Computer Society, Los Alamitos (2001)
22. May, T.: Time-release Crypto. Manuscript (February 1993)
23. Merkle, R.C.: Secure Communications Over Insecure Channels. Commun. ACM 21(4), 294–299 (1978)
24. Rivest, R.L.: Description of the LCS35 Time Capsule Crypto-Puzzle (April 1999),
    http://www.lcs.mit.edu/about/tcapintro041299
25. Rivest, R.L., Shamir, A., Wagner, D.A.: Time-lock Puzzles and Timed-release Crypto. Manuscript,
    http://theory.lcs.mit.edu/~rivest/RivestShamirWagner-timelock.ps
26. Roman, R., Zhou, J., Lopez, J.: Protection Against Spam Using Pre-Challenges. In: SEC, pp. 281–294. Springer, Heidelberg (2005)
27. Serjantov, A., Lewis, S.: Puzzles in P2P systems. In: 8th Cabernet Radicals Workshop (October 2003)
28. TPM Work Group. TCG TPM Specification Version 1.2 Revision 103. Technical report, Trusted Computing Group (2007)
29. Trusted Computing Group. TCG Specification Architecture Overview Revision 1.4. Technical report, Trusted Computing Group (2007)
30. von Ahn, L., Blum, M., Hopper, N.J., Langford, J.: CAPTCHA: Using Hard AI Problems for Security. In: Biham, E. (ed.) EUROCRYPT 2003. LNCS, vol. 2656, pp. 294–311. Springer, Heidelberg (2003)
31. Waters, B., Juels, A., Halderman, J.A., Felten, E.W.: New Client Puzzle Outsourcing Techniques for DoS Resistance. In: ACM Conference on Computer and Communications Security, pp. 246–256. ACM Press, New York (2004)

PROBE: A Process Behavior-Based Host Intrusion Prevention System

Minjin Kwon, Kyoochang Jeong, and Heejo Lee

Department of Computer Science and Engineering,
Korea University, Seoul 136-713, Korea
{mjkwon,kyoochang,heejo}@korea.ac.kr

Abstract. Attacks using vulnerabilities are considered nowadays a severe threat. Thus, a host needs a device that monitors system activities for malicious behaviors and blocks those activities to protect itself. In this paper, we introduce PROcess BEhavior (PROBE), which monitors processes running on a host to identify abnormal process behaviors. PROBE makes a process tree using only process creation relationship, and then it measures each edge weight to determine whether the invocation of each child process causes an abnormal behavior. PROBE has low processing overhead when compared with existing intrusion detections which use sequences of system calls. In the evaluation on a representative set of critical security vulnerabilities, PROBE shows desirable and practical intrusion prevention capabilities estimating that only 5% false-positive and 5% false-negative. Therefore, PROBE is a heuristic approach that can also detect unknown attacks, and it is not only light-weight but also accurate.

1 Introduction

According to a variety of attacks, security is a substantial issue in today's networks. Malicious users are attempting enormous methods to successfully disrupt a target system. Against them, many technologies such as firewalls, anti-virus programs, and intrusion detection systems (IDSs) have been used to keep networks and hosts safe. However, according to the advent of sophisticated attacks, we nowadays need a new method based on intrusion prevention systems (IPSs) to protect systems. Even though network-based IPS can block malicious traffic, some can pass through it [1]. Thus, host-based IPS plays an important role in the last line of defense.

To defend these attacks, we propose PROcess BEhavior (PROBE) which is a host-based intrusion prevention system that investigates system processes to identify abnormal process behaviors. By using it, intrusions which use remote exploits to infiltrate a system are detected because an attack is behaved out of common behavior. We present a novel characterization for process sequences of a system. This characterization is based on two observations: a process is always executed when a user wants to execute a program, and a process on an operating system runs in sequence. The previous researches [2,3,4] detect anomalous behavior of system programs by inspecting different system call sequences in comparison with normal patterns of short sequences of system calls. The approaches to the solutions are not practical for preventing the vulnerabilities in the real world because of system call monitoring complexity. On the other hand, PROBE is designed to detect major security violations by monitoring just several process behaviors without tracing every system call triggered by running processes.

This paper's main contribution lies in detecting unknown attacks and advancing a practical mechanism for intrusion detection. Our approach detects any novel intrusions different from normal procedures without prior knowledge of the attack mechanism. We represent processes' relationship as a tree, and then perceive the execution of an abnormal process just by examining a process's parent process and its child process. Thus, PROBE has low process monitoring overhead and it is appropriate for adoption to protect a host from intrusions.

2   Related Work

Intrusion Detection Systems (IDSs) are designed to detect unwanted attack or manipulation of a computer system. However, they cannot stop traffic, only identify an attack as it occurs. On the contrary, Intrusion Prevention Systems (IPSs) not only detect an attack, but also block the attack. Thus, it is considered as a combination of both an IDS which has the power of detecting attacks and a firewall which has the power of filtering attacks. Researchers have followed two main directions in the investigation of techniques to identify attacks: anomaly detection based IDS and misuse detection based IDS.

Anomaly detection based IDS generates an alert when a behavior deviates far from the predefined normal behavior. There were studies of intrusion detection for anomaly detection[2,3,4] using short sequences of system calls of running processes. While this technique can detect unknown attacks, it unfortunately generates false-positive[1] problem. Thus, most IDS products in the market today use misuse detection instead of anomaly detection[1].

Misuse detection based IDS contains signature database which has typical patterns of exploits used by attackers. If the attack signature matches any of some predefined set of signatures, IDS raises an alarm. Autograph[5] is a Internet worm signature monitoring system. However, its main drawback is that one must know the signature of attack to detect intrusion, so it is difficult to detect unknown, novel attack. Polygraph[6] is a study about the automatic generation of signatures that match polymorphic worms and the detection of them. To evade the problem of signature database maintenance, the techniques which detect malware on the basis of its behaviors are being studied.

Behavior-based Spyware Detection[7] is one of the typical behavior-based malware detection techniques. While this technique can detect obfuscation transformations which can easily be evaded by signature-based techniques, it has high false-positive and false-negative[2] as compared with signature-based detection.

---

[1] False-positive represents a legitimate behavior that is incorrectly identified as a malicious behavior.
[2] False-negative denotes an abnormal behavior that is incorrectly identified as a legitimate behavior.

These detection techniques of IDSs focus on how an attack works, so it detects attacks after a system is already infected by malwares. To stop malicious behavior before it causes any harm, IPSs, in contrast, focus on what an attack does—its behavior[1]. Thus, we propose a dynamic detection system, PROBE, that uses normal and abnormal characteristics of process connection. PROBE does not require signatures for attacks as with misuse detection, nor monitoring every system calls as previous system call trace studies. Thus, we instead concentrate on the behavior of the system processes.

3 The PROBE Mechanism

Since it is difficult to find out all vulnerabilities of operating systems and to patch them, we need a technique that can control abnormal access to a system by discovering characteristics of process creation. Before we get down to details of a technique that is based on the characterization of process behavior, we should examine the execution procedure of normal boot processes closely to use a control technique which can regulate an abnormal access within boot processes. The majority of the actual intrusions do not follow normal system operations no matter which exploit was used [8]. Thus, we will investigate from boot processes running during the operating system startup, then explain a principle and control procedures of abnormal processes.

3.1 Windows NT Boot Process

A process is a container for a set of resources used when executing an instance of a program. As with other operating systems, Microsoft Windows system goes through an elaborate boot up process. The boot process has a series of sequential steps since the computer is powered on. By understanding the details of the boot processes, we can diagnose problems that can arise during a boot. Our objective is to make our host system safe against any intrusions since the host starts up. The tracing abnormal behavior of system processes can achieve an execution of safe system booting and correct booting procedure. Thus, we show the execution steps of boot support files and the information on what some of the system files are for. We can represent process execution sequences of an operating system as a tree design. Figure 1 illustrates process execution sequences of Microsoft Windows NT system. The sequence of Windows boot processes is all arranged beforehand until application programs are executed. Application processes will be corresponded to a leaf node which is a node that has zero child nodes. When considering the process sequence tree, we can see that the path from a root node to a leaf node has a regular pattern. If an unauthorized user accesses to a system using a system's vulnerabilities, the executed process sequence by the attacker has a different characteristic from the normal process execution sequence. Thus, we propose a model which can detect an abnormal execution of a process by analyzing process execution relationship from a root node to a leaf node using a process tree.

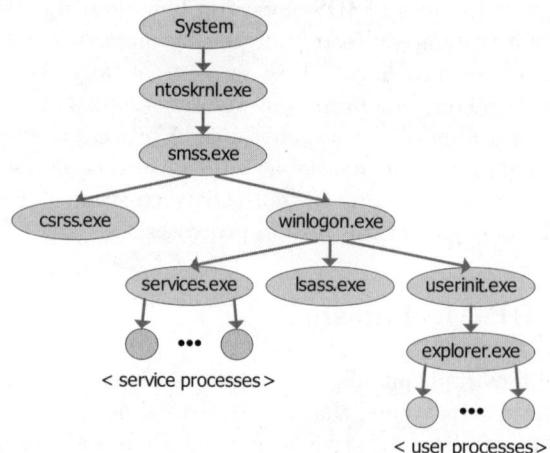

Fig. 1. The process tree of Microsoft Windows NT system

3.2 Design

The boot processes are executed in sequence during the booting steps of an operating system. However, it is possible that an adversary is able to exploit a system using specific bugs or vulnerabilities such as overflows during a boot. Since an attacker executes at least one process to invoke an abnormal behavior to overwhelm a system, a check of whether a process is executed by the operating system came from a normal process or a non-related process helps prevent attacks such as an overflowed buffer exploit. Thus, we design a host-based intrusion prevention system beginning with boot processes to execute the system securely. Our system, PROBE, takes a closer and deeper look at the activity of processes run on the host, calculates three weights on each edge based on relationship between a parent process and a child process, and determines acceptance or rejection of a process using the three weights. Therefore, PROBE protects desktops or servers by keeping operating systems securely from intrusions.

Process Information. To build a process tree and obtain the characteristics of each path, we need some information related to processes. PROBE utilizes the information which is provided by the operating system related to the processes. A number of tools for viewing processes and process information are available[9]: the tools included within Windows itself, Windows resource kits, and etc. The most widely used tool to examine process activity is Task Manager. We arranged these information into the six categories in Fig. 2.

3.3 Three-Phase PROBE Mechanism

PROBE inspects and detects abnormal behaviors by looking at processes within a host. To facilitate the understanding the relationship of processes, we present a process tree that shows parent and child connection between processes. For

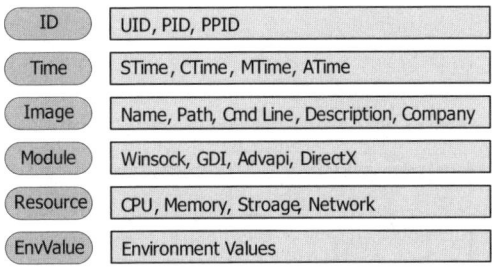

Fig. 2. Process Information which presents a unique process characteristic that can be gained from Windows

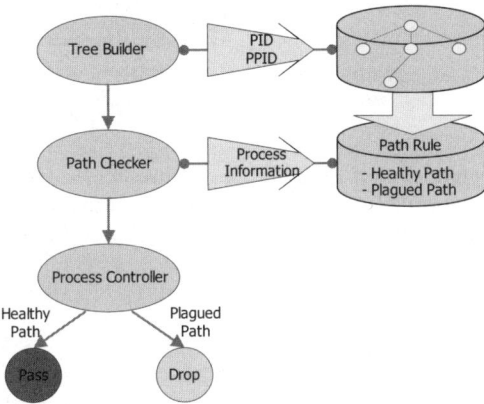

Fig. 3. The architecture of PBOBE that consists of three phases: Tree Builder, Path Checker, and Process Controller

doing this, PROBE works according to following three phases: *Tree Builder, Path Checker,* and *Process Controller.* We schematized the architecture of PROBE in Fig. 3.

A process behavior-based host intrusion prevention system starts from creating a tree structure. Tree Builder creates a process tree using PID and PPID of a process. After the process tree is created, Path Checker analyzes each tree path based on Healthy Path Rule and Plagued Path Rule. First, if the path is not determined as a Leaf-Node path which is a Plagued Path Rule, the process is a healthy path. Otherwise it is a suspicious process, so it needs additional steps. If there is a path which is decided as a healthy path by Healthy Path Rule among plagued paths, it becomes also a healthy path. Finally, Process Controller manages the process according to the prejudged decision. Healthy paths are executed and plagued paths are dropped in this phase. This procedure is illustrated in Fig. 4.

Tree Builder. Tree Builder monitors processes of a system, then creates a process tree from running processes on an operating system. A node in a tree is a

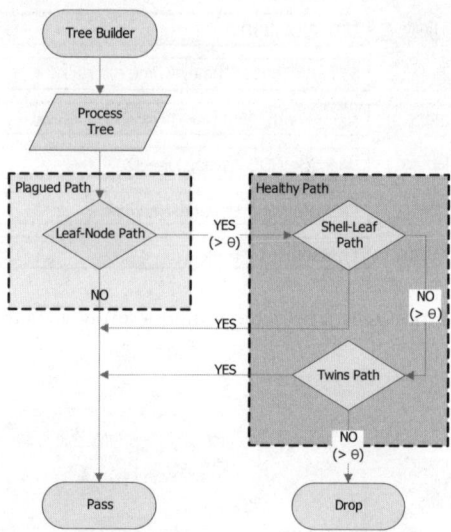

Fig. 4. The general algorithm of PBOBE. The θ threshold value represents a discriminator to distinguish a normal process and an abnormal process. Thus, the value of θ should be feasible for discriminating between a usual process and a unusual process. We set the value as 0.7 in our simulation.

running process and it has references to other nodes. To construct a tree, we use a process identifier which is a number used by an operating system kernel to uniquely identify one specific process. Using two process identifiers, one for a process's PID (Process ID) and the other for a process's PPID (Parent Process ID), it can create a tree based on a relationship between a parent process and a child process. The tree is created by first running system process with both child pointers null. Thus, the root node of a tree is the node with no parents. After the following process begins according to process steps required to boot a system, the additional node is created and inserted into the root node as child node to build a larger tree. Thus, a process which has a PID of a newly launched process creates a node. After checking its PPID, the process becomes a child node of its parent process node. The procedure of Tree Builder is described in Fig. 5.

Path Checker. Path Checker analyzes each directed edge of a tree which was made at Tree Builder phase and detects if something abnormal occurs according to Healthy Path Rule and Plagued Path Rule. For this, we use important information from operating system about system objects—attributes, modification time, etc. This Process Information is later used for checking the processes whether they are under the rule of Healthy Path or Plagued Path. Path Checker uses this Process Information to attempt to determine the intent of a process by catching the relationship with a parent process and a child process. PROBE can detect abnormal process execution just only examining local tree information of

```
Input: Process List
Output: Process Tree T = (V, E) where V is the set of vertices and E is the set of edges

Tree Builder Algorithm
1  V ← ∅;
2  E ← ∅;
3  WHILE EnumProcess()
4      PID ← GetProcessID(); // PID of current process
5      PPID ← GetParentProcessID(); // PID of current process's parent
6      IF (V ∩ Node(PID) == ∅
7          V ← V ∪ Node(PID);
8          E ← E ∪ Edge(PPID , PID);
9      END IF
10 END WHILE
END of Algorithm
```

Fig. 5. The first phase of PROBE: Tree Builder

an edge between a parent node and a child node, which was connected by the creation procedure of a process, not all tree information.

- **Plagued Path:** Abnormal path. It defines the edge in the process tree which is constructed through Tree Builder phase when the process is executed by a suspicious behavior. We assigned Leaf-Node Path into the plagued path which has a probability of something abnormal behavior happening.
- **Healthy Path:** Normal path. It defines the edge in the process tree which is constructed through Tree Builder phase when the process is executed by an ordinary behavior. We assigned Shell-Leaf Path, the parent process serves as a shell process, and Twins Path, two related processes triggered from one program execution, into the healthy path.

Leaf-Node Path. Leaf-Node Path checks if the child process is an application process node. Each downward path from a root node to a leaf node is unique. In principle, processes from application programs are dangled at the bottommost level of the tree. Typically, most of application processes do not create any child processes except a process that carries out a function as a shell program. Leaf node application processes are only executed by a particular parent process such as a shell program. Figure 6 describes an algorithm that measures weight of Leaf-node path. Thus, if it is perceived that both a parent process and a child process are processes derived from any application programs, there might be a possibility that something abnormal such as execution of exploits using buffer overflow is happening. That is, it is considered as a doubtful activity that application process creates another application process.

Shell-Leaf Path. Shell-Leaf Path checks if the parent node which executes a child process node is a shell program process. A shell denotes not only the system-defined shell, Explorer.exe, but also a program which serves as a shell process. The way to determine normal behavior would be to monitor process relationships in execution. Figure 7 shows these relationships. To identify a shell process, sibling processes created from a same parent process are influenced to weight a value of Shell-Leaf Path.

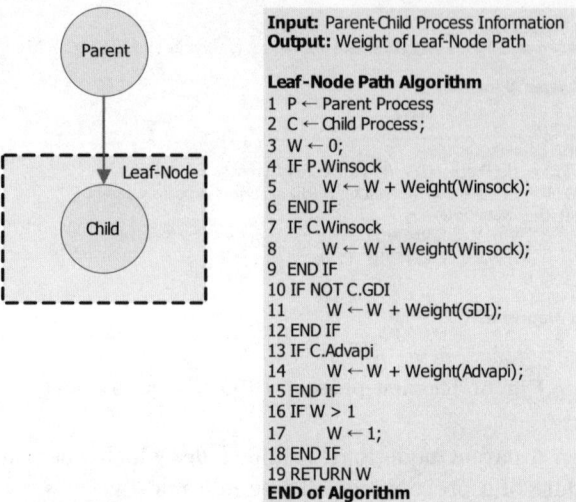

```
Input: Parent-Child Process Information
Output: Weight of Leaf-Node Path

Leaf-Node Path Algorithm
1  P ← Parent Process
2  C ← Child Process;
3  W ← 0;
4  IF P.Winsock
5      W ← W + Weight(Winsock);
6  END IF
7  IF C.Winsock
8      W ← W + Weight(Winsock);
9  END IF
10 IF NOT C.GDI
11     W ← W + Weight(GDI);
12 END IF
13 IF C.Advapi
14     W ← W + Weight(Advapi);
15 END IF
16 IF W > 1
17     W ← 1;
18 END IF
19 RETURN W
END of Algorithm
```

Fig. 6. Leaf-Node Path, which is a plagued path, is considered to be a security risk if the behavior of process is related to any of intrusion's behaviors we defined as follows: 1) the parent process uses network services, 2) the child process uses network services, 3) the child process is not associated with Windows graphics, or 4) the child process utilizes advanced Windows API's.

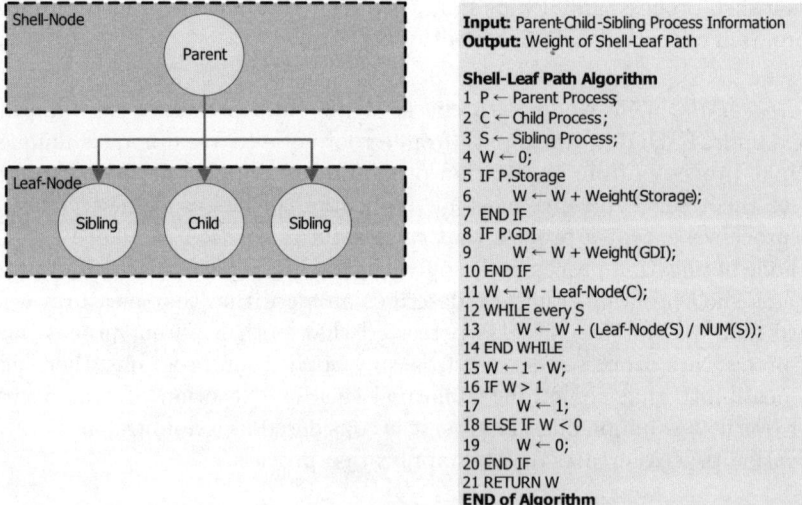

```
Input: Parent-Child-Sibling Process Information
Output: Weight of Shell-Leaf Path

Shell-Leaf Path Algorithm
1  P ← Parent Process
2  C ← Child Process;
3  S ← Sibling Process;
4  W ← 0;
5  IF P.Storage
6      W ← W + Weight(Storage);
7  END IF
8  IF P.GDI
9      W ← W + Weight(GDI);
10 END IF
11 W ← W - Leaf-Node(C);
12 WHILE every S
13     W ← W + (Leaf-Node(S) / NUM(S));
14 END WHILE
15 W ← 1 - W;
16 IF W > 1
17     W ← 1;
18 ELSE IF W < 0
19     W ← 0;
20 END IF
21 RETURN W
END of Algorithm
```

Fig. 7. Shell-Leaf Path which is a healthy path to check the parent process fills the role of characteristics of Windows shell

Twins Path. Twins Path checks a characteristic of closeness between two nodes. We named it Twins Path that a path between a parent process and a child

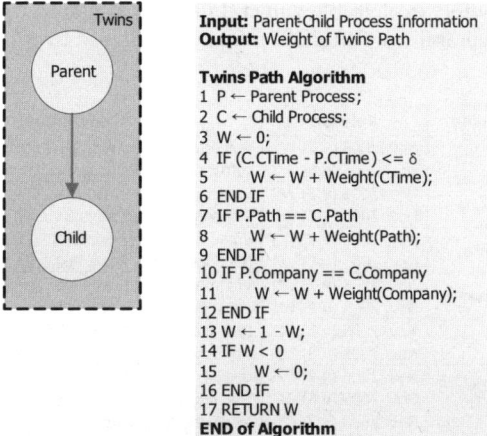

Fig. 8. Twins Path which is a healthy path to measure how much the parent process and the child process are related. The δ threshold value denotes time interval to measure the creation time difference of a parent process and a child process within a certain span.

process has a similar characteristic. When there is a similarity between processes, an application process can execute another application process. Thus, a process not owned by the requesting process will be blocked by this phase. This is a signal that an abnormal behavior is happening. To measure the similarity between a parent process and a child process, we use the Process Information such as process image creation time and company to reflect weight of similarity into Twins Path as shown in Fig. 8.

Process Controller. Process Controller regulates process execution according to whether the process path is healthy path or plagued path. When the process behavior of a system deviates far from the Path Rule, alerts are generated and the process cannot be executed.

4 Evaluation

Today attacks are often taking advantage of multiple vulnerabilities. In order to measure the effectiveness of PROBE, we need to develop a means to produce an accurate model of today's Internet security vulnerabilities. It has been tested using SANS Top-20 lists[10] released in recent two years, November 2006 and November 2005. SANS announces critical vulnerabilities, the most often exploited Internet security flaws, that led to worms like Blaster, Slammer, and Code Red every year since 2000. Among 40 vulnerabilities released in 2006 and 2005, there are 28 vulnerabilities (13 in 2006 and 15 in 2005) which are applicable to Windows system. Out of 28, we selected 16 remotely exploitable vulnerabilities

Table 1. The 16 remotely exploitable vulnerabilities in Windows system among critical Internet security vulnerabilities (SANS Top-20 lists) released by SANS Institute in 2006 and 2005

No.	Vulnerability	Release	Description
1	Internet Explorer	Nov. 2006 (v.7) W1 Nov. 2005 (v.6) W2	Vulnerabilities in ActiveX controls installed by software. Remote code execution
2	Windows Libraries	Nov. 2006 (v.7) W2 Nov. 2005 (v.6) W3	Vulnerabilities in Windows libraries. A remote attacker executes arbitrary code
3	Microsoft Office	Nov. 2006 (v.7) W3 Nov. 2005 (v.6) W4	Vulnerabilities in Microsoft Office applications (Outlook, Word, PowerPoint, Excel, Visio, Etc.)
4	Windows Services	Nov. 2006 (v.7) W4 Nov. 2005 (v.6) W1	Vulnerabilities in a wide variety of services. networking methods and technologies
5	Web Applications	Nov. 2006 (v.7) C1 Nov. 2005 (v.6) C3	PHP remote file include, SQL injection, cross-site scripting (XSS), cross-site request forgeries
6	Database Software	Nov. 2006 (v.7) C2 Nov. 2005 (v.6) C4	Use of default configurations, buffer overflows, SQL injection, use of weak passwords
7	P2P File Sharing Applications	Nov. 2006 (v.7) C3 Nov. 2005 (v.6) C5	Modifying legitimate files with malware, seeding malware files into shared directories
8	Media Players	Nov. 2006 (v.7) C5 Nov. 2005 (v.6) C7	A malicious webpage or a media file to compromise a user's system without interaction

on Windows system except for vulnerabilities overlapped or applied to a specific application. We assumed that 16 vulnerabilities to be arisen in our system. Those are shown in Table 1.

We simulated PROBE using vulnerability information on Microsoft Windows XP Professional SP2. Figure 9 presents a system process tree that shows processes used in our simulation. We need weight of Process Information such as Winsock, GDI, Advapi, Storage, CTime, Path, and Company to calculate weight of each edge between a parent process and a child process. We use these weights to calculate Leaf-Node Path, Shell-Leaf Path, and Twins Path in PROBE's 3 phases. In each phase, the weights of Process Information have a same value within its phase. By using these weights of Process Information, each process calculates three edge weights. The first one is Leaf-Node value. If its value is close to 1, the process has a high possibility that it is an abnormal process. The second value is Shell-Leaf. If a process relationship is Shell-Leaf, the value is close to 0. It means that an abnormal behavior of a process has 1. The third value is Twins. It checks how much the two processes are similar. If they are totally different, it has a value close to 1. Thus, if all three weight values exceed a predefined threshold, the process is regarded as an abnormal process. We can see the results of PROBE simulation in Fig. 10. All attacks were detected except for "attack 4" and it shows false-negative. This happens because the process used vulnerabilities in "services.exe". PROBE does not detect an intrusion in case of an attack which uses a vulnerability of a known shell. Also, there is a false-positive case. Because yahoo widget is not known as a process which roles as a shell, it causes a false alarm.

Therefore, PROBE detects most of intrusions which utilize remotely exploitable vulnerabilities except for attacks via normal processes. Thus, PROBE shows desirable host-based intrusion prevention capabilities. By investigating

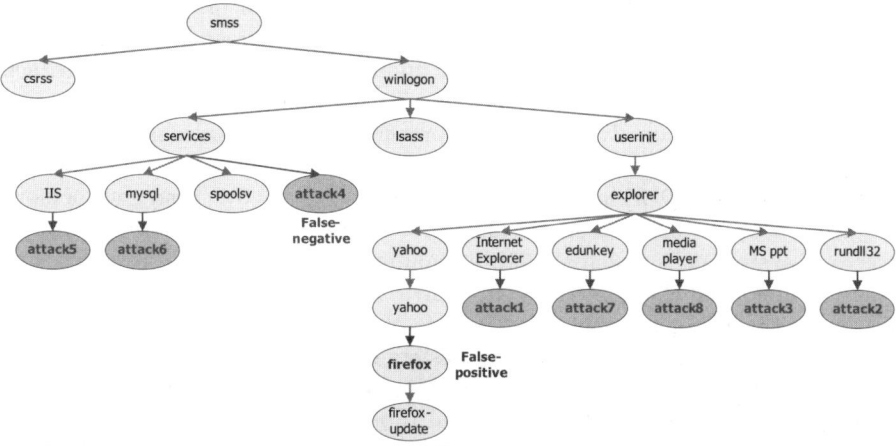

Fig. 9. A system process tree that shows process relationships used in our simulation

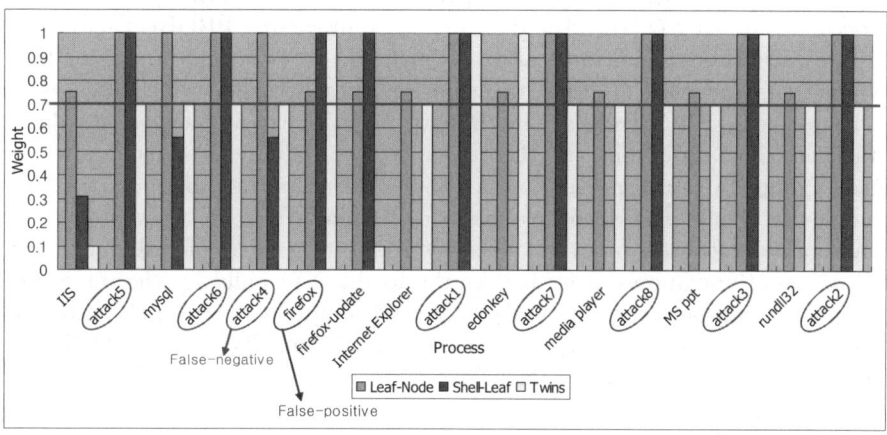

Fig. 10. The result of our simulation. Among 8 attack cases, 7 attacks are detected. There happened one false-negative case and one false-positive case.

more Healthy Path Rule to strengthen PROBE, we will be able to reduce false-positive and false-negative rate, and achieve a much better result than now.

5 Discussion

5.1 Benefits of PROBE

When an unauthorized user wants to have access to a system, the user utilizes bugs or design flaws in the system. The flaw or weakness in the system makes an opportunity to force it to conduct unintended operations by malicious users and vandals. Especially, the unknown attacks occur when prevalent signatures of attacks are not able to identify the attacks. It takes a great deal of time until patches to be applied and signatures to be updated. Fighting the unknown attack is one of the greatest challenges facing the security industry today[11]. Thus, we need to adopt an anomaly detection approach to reduce a false-negative effect against unknown attacks.

Additionally, PROBE has very low process monitoring overhead and memory requirements. The existing studies[2,3,4] for anomaly detection need enormous traces of system calls which should be monitored to discriminate between normal and abnormal characteristics. In contrast to the earlier approach based on system call behavior (normal database size of sendmail-1318, lpr-198, and ftpd-1017, which is the unique sequence of system calls for each of the process to be stored in each process database)[4], we only use 7 process information to determine a normal process and an abnormal process. Thus, it is light-weight and practical solution for intrusion prevention. Also, Fig. 11 shows the PROBE's elapsed time of API calls in comparison with existing mechanisms. We can see that PROBE has the highest efficiency in processing by comparing the elapsed time of API calls. Our evaluation of PROBE demonstrates that it exhibits low process monitoring overhead and memory requirements. PROBE rapidly and efficiently detects novel attacks at exceedingly low memory and processing time. When compared with existing intrusion detection methods which use system call sequences, PROBE differs in that we use a much simpler way to detect intrusions. For a program, the theoretical sets of system call sequences will be huge. Complete attack prevention is not realistically attainable due to system complexity. Thus, we rely on examples of normal system process runs rather than normal databases of all unique sequences during traces of system calls. An advantage of our approach is that we do not have to build up the set of normal system call patterns for the database. We simply compare with predefined process creation rules by tracing processes of a system. Therefore, PROBE is an efficient solution for detecting intrusions.

5.2 PROBE Limitations and Future Work

PROBE is a network-based intrusion prevention system that uses system processes to detect attacks which use security vulnerabilities by looking for intrusions performing programs without passing through legal process creation procedure. System damage due to an attack is caused by running programs that execute system processes. Thus, we restrict our attention to running system processes. Intrusions are detected when a process behaves out of its characteristics of normal system processes. The Path Rule between processes is defined to represent the ongoing behavior of the process creation.

It is important that intrusion detection systems are capable of detecting attacks against the Windows NT operating systems because of its growing importance in government and commercial environments[12]. There are lists of Windows NT attacks developed for the 1999 DARPA Intrusion Detection Evaluation[12]. These attacks categorize with groupings of the possible attack

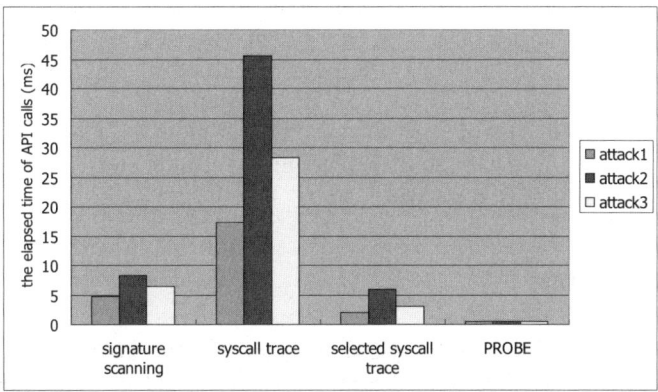

Fig. 11. We measured the elapsed time of API calls (milliseconds). PROBE is compared with existing intrusion detection mechanisms: signature scanning (misuse detection), syscall trace (system call traces), and selected syscall trace (partial system call traces). We tested under 3 attack environments: attack1 (Remote-to-User attack which establishes backdoors), attack2 (Remote-to-User attack which is a trojan horse that allows a remote attacker to control a system), and attack3 (Remote-to-User attack which uses a buffer overrun vulnerability). Under these attacks, we can see that PROBE executes intrusion detection at a low processing time.

types: Denial-of-Service, Remote-to-User, and User-to-Super-user. Table 2 shows a description of each attack category and document the individual Windows NT attacks in each category. These attacks spawn processes which deviate from normal process execution. PROBE can detect intrusions which use system or software bugs or exploits such as vulnerabilities in the victim computer or trojan programs to establish backdoors on the victim system. Most attacks create a new process which deviates from normal process behavior even in case of adding a user to penetrate into the system by exploiting a vulnerability on a system. Thus, it does not pass through normal process creation procedure.

The major problem is that system's behaviors change with time. As a result, the system's behavior can deviate more from the Path Rule initially determined. To solve the problem of false-negative by the unknown attacks, we followed anomaly detection approach. However, it has a limitation to discriminate between attack and non-attack. To protect against newly discovered attacks, we

Table 2. Windows NT Attacks Developed for the 1999 DARPA Intrusion Detection Evaluation

Attack Category	Attack Name
Denial-of-Service	CrashIIS, DoSNuke
Remote-to-User	Netbus, NetCat, PPMacro
User-to-Super-user	CaseSen, NTFSDOS, SecHole, Yaga

need more Path Rule to evolve. Certain intrusions which can only be detectable by examining other aspects of a process's behavior, and so we might need to consider them later. Future work will focus on extending PROBE to find other abuses of privilege and to find an error in configuration of a system. Also, we intend to expand our base of intrusions and gather more data for more processes running in real environments, so we can get more realistic and accurate estimates of false-positive and false-negative.

6 Conclusions

Our system, PROBE is a host-based intrusion prevention system which is installed on a particular host and detect attacks targeted to that host only. For the purpose of protecting a system against host-based attacks, we proposed process behavior-based protection approach. PROBE is designed to detect security vulnerabilities in a host without monitoring every system calls. It only finds out the characteristics of process relationship between a parent process and a child process. Thus, it can detect unknown attacks by judging a behavior of process creation relationship. Also, it is a light-weight solution, and shows practical and accurate result for intrusion prevention. Our approach was evaluated on a test set of SANS Top-20 Internet Security Attack Targets. The results demonstrate that our approach can effectively identify the behavior of abnormal processes. Future work will focus on extending PROBE to reduce false-positive by analyzing process relationships and find out more accurate results. By using PROBE, we expect to secure our systems against unknown system vulnerabilities of new kinds of exploits.

Acknowledgments

This work was supported by Defense Acquisition Program Administration and Agency for Defense Development under the contract UD060048AD and the ITRC program of the Korea Ministry of Information & Communications.

References

1. Sequeira, D.: Intrusion Prevention Systems: Security's Silver Bullet? In: Business Communications Review (March 2003)
2. Forrest, S., Longstaff, T.A.: A Sense of Self for Unix Processes. In: IEEE Symposium on Security and Privacy, pp. 120–128 (1996)
3. Forrest, S., Hofmeyr, S.A., Somayaji, A.: Computer Immunology. Communications of the ACM 40, 88–96 (1997)
4. Hofmeyr, S.A., Forrest, S., Somayaji, A.: Intrusion Detection using Sequences of System Calls. Journal of Computer Security 6, 151–180 (1998)
5. Kim, H.A., Karp, B.: Autograph: Toward Automated, Distributed Worm Signature Detection. In: Proceedings of the 13th Usenix Security Symposium (August 2004)

6. Newsome, J., Karp, B., Song, D.: Polygraph: Automatically Generating Signatures for Polymorphic Worms. In: IEEE Security and Privacy Symposium (May 2005)
7. Kirda, E., Kruegel, C., Banks, G., Vigna, G., Kemmerer, R.A.: Behavior-based Spyware Detection. In: 15th Usenix Security Symposium (August 2006)
8. Cunningham, R.K., Lippmann, R.P., Webster, S.E.: Detecting and Displaying Novel Computer Attacks with Macroscope. IEEE Transactions on Systems, Man and Cybernetics (July 2001)
9. Russinovich, M.E., Solomon, D.A.: Microsoft Windows Internals. 4 edn., Microsoft Press (December 2004)
10. SANS: SANS Top20 Lists (November 2006), http://www.sans.org/top20/
11. Henry, P.A.: Day zero threat mitigation, Seminar: Fighting the Unknown Attack (May 2006), http://www.pisa.org.hk/event/fighting-unknown-attack.htm
12. Korba, J.: Windows NT Attacks for the Evaluation of Intrusion Detection Systems (June 2000)

Towards the World-Wide Quantum Network

Quoc-Cuong Le[1], Patrick Bellot[1], and Akim Demaille[2]

[1] Institut TELECOM, Telecom ParisTech, Paris, France
[2] EPITA Research and Developpement Laboratory (LRDE), Paris, France

Abstract. QKD networks are of much interest due to their capacity of providing extremely high security keys to network participants. Most QKD network studies so far focus on trusted models where all the network nodes are assumed to be perfectly secured. This restricts QKD networks to be small. In this paper, we first develop a novel model dedicated to large-scale QKD networks, some of whose nodes could be eavesdropped secretely. Then, we investigate the key transmission problem in the new model by an approach based on percolation theory and stochastic routing. Analyses show that under computable conditions large-scale QKD networks could protect secret keys with an extremely high probability. Simulations validate our results.

1 Introduction

The problem of transmitting a secret key from an origin to a destination over the network was considered for a long time. The current solution in most Internet applications is using Public Key Infrastructure (PKI). PKI relies on plausible but unproven assumptions about the computation power of eavesdroppers and the non-existence of effective algorithms for certain mathematical hard problems. As a result, PKI cannot meet the highest security level, also called *unconditional security*. Quantum Key Distribution (QKD) technology is a prominent alternative [1]. It was proven that QKD can provide unconditional security [2,3,4]. It is successfully implemented in realistic applications [5,6,7,8]. However, QKD only supports point-to-point connections and intrinsically causes serious limits on throughput and range [5,9]. A long-distance QKD transmission needs intermediate nodes to relay the key. In realistic scenarios, some of these nodes could be eavesdropped without the others knowing it. In consequence, the security of key will be compromised. Larger networks are more vulnerable.

This paper studies a partially compromised QKD network model that allows any member pair establishing securely a common key with almost certainty. The contributions are (i) a model of partially compromised QKD networks, (ii) the use of percolation theory techniques to find where almost-certainty can be achieved, (iii) stochastic routing proposals capable of achieving a given secrecy level.

The remainder is organized as follows. Section 2 introduces the QKD network's context and proposes a novel model of the world-wide QKD network. Section 3 presents related works. Section 4 seeks for the necessary condition to achieve a given high secrecy of key transmissions. Section 5 presents our adaptive stochastic routing algorithms and analyzes their performances. We conclude in Section 6. The proofs of the theorems are given in Appendix.

2 A Proposal for the World-Wide Quantum Network

Preliminary. QKD networks present two types of links: classical and QKD. Classical links are easy to implement, capable of providing high-speed but low-confidentiality communications. By contrast, QKD links aim at *unconditional security*. This causes undesirable limits of rate and range [5, 9]. The ultimate goal of QKD networks is unconditional security. QKD networks rather sustain QKD's restrictions to reach this goal. As such, there is no need to consider classical links in studying QKD network prototypes. In the following we will simply write links instead of QKD links.

The feasibly-implemented model of QKD networks so far is the trusted network model. Its representers are SECOQC and DARPA networks [10, 6, 11, 12]. This model assumes that all the network nodes are perfectly secured. This assumption is too strong in large-scale scenarios. Actually, eavesdroppers can ingeniously attack a proportion of nodes without leaving any trace in large-scale networks. Consequently, security may be compromised.

Restricted by a modest length of link, QKD networks don't present many choices of topology. Meshed topology would suit QKD networks [12]. Besides, distributed architecture is considered to be good. This paper follows these ideas. However we focus on the world-wide quantum network that is very different from small-scale quantum networks like DARPA and SECOQC. For simplicity, we choose the 4-connected grid topology. Nodes are represented by squares. Links have no representation because they have no effect on security analysis (see Fig. 1).

In QKD networks, intermediate nodes are vulnerable. Attacks are either detectable or undetectable. In principle, if an attack is detectable then we can find solutions to fix it. Undetectable attacks are very dangerous. We cannot detect them until great damage has been done. We take into account such attacks. Assume that each node sustains a probability p_e being eavesdropped without knowledge of the others. For simplicity, we focus only on cases where p_e is the same for all the nodes. Note that p_e should be small unless eavesdropper resources are much larger than those of legitimate users.

Modeling the World-Wide QKD Network Problem. Consider a 4-connected grid lattice network (see Fig. 1). The network is large enough so that we can ignore its borders. Nodes are represented by squares. Each node is connected with its four neighbors. Links however are not represented since they do not affect the security analysis. In graph theory our network is described as follows. Network is the set of vertices $V = Z^2$. A vertex is *safe* if it is not eavesdropped. Otherwise, it is called *unsafe*. Each vertex is eavesdropped *without any trace* with probability $p_e \in [0, 1]$. As mentioned above, we focus only on the cases where p_e is the same for all the vertices. The probability that a vertex is safe is $p_s = 1 - p_e$.

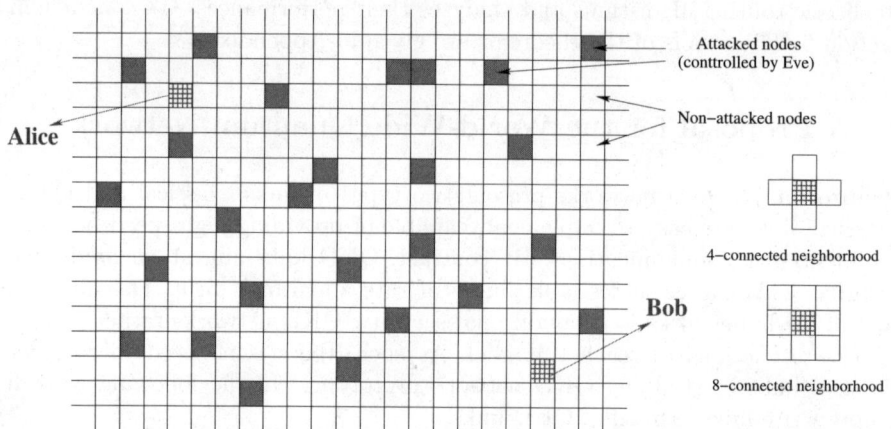

Fig. 1. Two dimensional lattice network

Alice and Bob are represented by vertices v_A and v_B. Alice wants to convey a secret key K to Bob. We study the secrecy probability Σ that K is not revealed to the eavesdropper Eve. If v_A and v_B are adjacent then K certainly is safe, i.e. $\Sigma = 1$. Otherwise, K must pass over l intermediate vertices $v_1, v_2, .., v_l$ whose task is to relay K. The sequence $\pi = v_A, v_1, v_2, .., v_l, v_B$ is a path from v_A to v_B. A path is *safe* if all its nodes are safe.

We define the *length* of path as the number of intermediate vertices. Since K is transmitted in π, we have $\Sigma(K) = p_s^l$. This implies that Σ is dramatically decreased with respect to (w.r.t) the length l. We focus on a simple way to improve Σ: sending a number of sub-keys $K_1, K_2, .., K_N$ by different paths $\pi_1, \pi_2, .., \pi_N$. K is computed by a bitwise XOR operation over $K_1, K_2, .., K_N$. As such, K is safe unless Eve intercepts *all* $\pi_1, \pi_2, .., \pi_N$. If the graph presents safe paths then with a larger N, K is more likley to be safe. The following questions are basic:

1. When are all the safe vertices almost certainly connected? In other words, find the condition on p_s such that $\forall \Delta \in [0,1] : \Sigma_\infty = \lim_{N \to \infty}(\Sigma) \geq 1 - \Delta$.
2. Assume that $\Sigma_\infty \geq 1 - \Delta$. Given a pair of vertices (v_A, v_B), consider a set of N paths $\pi_1, \pi_2, .., \pi_N$ from v_A to v_B generated by a proposed routing algorithm. Let $\lambda(N)$ be the secrecy probability of the final key if N sub-keys are sent by $\pi_1, \pi_2, .., \pi_N$. Find N_0 such that for any small $\epsilon \geq \Delta$, $\epsilon \in [0,1]$, we have: $\forall N \geq N_0 : \lambda(N) \geq 1 - \epsilon$.

3 Related Work

Percolation Theory. This theory investigates the transition phase from the non-existence to the existence of the giant wetted cluster when we pour water at the center of a graph [13,14,15]. The 2-dimensional site percolation model can be roughly described as follows. Let $G = (V, E)$ be a graph with vertices set V and

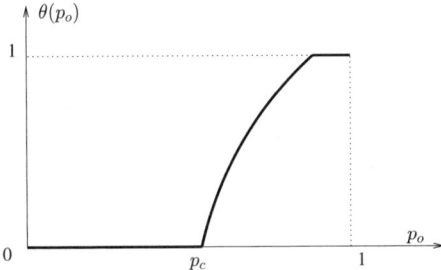

Fig. 2. The percolation probability $\theta(p_o)$

edges set E. Vertices and edges are either *open* or *closed*. In the open status, they allow water to pass through and water make them become wetted. Otherwise, they do not allow the passage of water. All the edges are open. Each vertex is open with *open probability* $p_o \in [0,1]$. Let $\theta(p)$ be the *percolation probability* that measures the proportion of wetted vertices to open vertices. Fig. 2 roughly shows the behavior of θ w.r.t p_o. The value p_c, the *critical probability*, is the minimum p_o such that $\theta(p_o) > 0$.

The 2-dimensional site percolation's framework is similar to our network model's one. The open probability p_o and the safe probability p_s play an equivalent role. If we set $p_s = p_o$ and assume that v_A sends to v_B an infinite set of sub-keys $K_1, K_2, ..$ by an infinite set of different paths $\pi_1, \pi_2, ..$, then the secrecy probability Σ of the final key K is identical to the probability existing a safe path between v_A and v_B. However this probability is equivalent to the probability θ that almost open vertices belong to the infinite open cluster. We can apply to Σ two important properties of θ [15]:

1. θ is a non-decreasing and continuous function in the right of p_c (see Fig. 2).
2. The number of infinite open clusters is either 0 or 1 for $\theta = 0$ or $\theta > 0$, respectively.

Stochastic Routing Algorithms. Traditional routing algorithms, such as those used on the Internet, are mostly deterministic. Tailored to be efficient, they are guessable, which is not a good property for our purpose. By contrast, stochastic routing algorithms seem to be better. The basic idea is sending randomly a packet to one of possible routes, not necessarily the "best" one. When the message holder forwards a packet, the choice of next-hop is random, following a next-hop probability distribution. The main challenge is how to determine the best next-hop probabilities that optimize a given specific goal. Previous works on stochastic routing [16,17,18] focus on performance metrics (latency, throughput, acceptance rate, etc.) which are not of major importance to QKD networks whose priority is security. Besides, the 4-connected grid topology also makes previous optimizations on stochastic routing useless. We need to build our own stochastic routing algorithms.

4 Condition on p_s for $\Sigma \geq 1 - \Delta$

Safe Connectivity Function. Two vertices v_A and v_B are safely connected if there exists a safe path between them. In the percolation literature, $\Sigma_\infty(v_A, v_B)$ can be interpreted as the connectivity function $\tau(v_A, v_B)$. We can use the following approximation from [13]:

$$\Sigma_\infty(v_A, v_B) = \tau(v_A, v_B) \sim \theta^2 \tag{1}$$

Given a non-negative small value Δ, we must find out the critical p_c such that $\forall p_s : p_c \leq p_s \leq 1$, we have $\Sigma_\infty \geq 1 - \Delta$. Here, we propose a heuristic method and use simulations to validate our method.

It is well known that the critical probability for the 2-dimensional lattice percolation is about 0.6. From this value to 1, the percolation probability θ is greater than zero, non-decreasingly and continuously tends to 1. Let ξ be the probability that a given vertex is encircled by unsafe vertices, we have $\theta = 1 - \xi$. From Approximation 1 we can derive the condition on ξ w.r.t a given Δ as follows:

$$\xi \leq 1 - \sqrt{1 - \Delta}$$

Our task now turns into studying ξ in the region close to 0. The trivial case where the given vertex is encircled by its four unsafe neighbors gives the lower bound of ξ, or:

$$\xi \geq (1 - p_s)^4 \quad \text{(equality i.i.f } p_s = 1\text{)} \tag{2}$$

If we set $p_s = 0.8$ then from (2) we have $\xi > 1.6 \times 10^{-3}$. It is small enough to temporarily set $p_c = 0.8$ in order to incrementally study ξ in its low-value region.

We first study ξ in the one-dimensional case. To distinguish ξ in the one-dimensional and two-dimensional cases we denote by $\xi^{(1)}$ and $\xi^{(2)}$, respectively. We measure $\xi^{(1)}$ for a given radius r (see Fig. 3.A).

$$\xi^{(1)} = \big(\Pr(\text{At least one unsafe vertex in the left})\big) \times \\ \big(\Pr(\text{At least one unsafe vertex in the right})\big) = (1 - p_s^r)^2 \tag{3}$$

We now extend to $\xi^{(2)}$ from $\xi^{(1)}$. Assume that we are focusing on the vertex O in the two-dimensional lattice. Let $R(r)$ be the set of vertices of distance r from O. We study unsafe circuits inside $R(r)$. Denote by (see Fig. 3.C and Fig. 3.B):

- $G(r)$: the event that there are unsafe circuits that encircle the vertex O and do not exceed $R(r)$.
- $G_{LR}(r)$: the event that there are unsafe vertices at both the left and the right of the vertex O. These unsafe vertices are inside the radius r from O.
- $G_{UD(r)}$: the event that are unsafe vertices both above and below the vertex O. These unsafe vertices are inside the radius r from O.

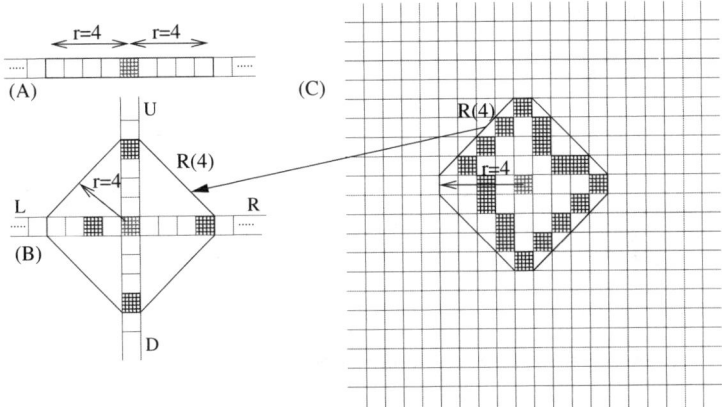

Fig. 3. Unsafe circuits in the one-dimensional and two-dimensional cases

Obviously, $\Pr\bigl(G(r)\bigr) \leq \Pr\bigl(G_{LR}(r)\bigr) \times \Pr\bigl(G_{UD}(r)\bigr)$. That means

$$\xi(r) = \xi^{(2)}(r) \leq \bigl(\xi^{(1)}(r)\bigr)^2 \tag{4}$$

By applying (3) to (4), we have:

$$\xi(r) \leq (1 - p_s^r)^4 \tag{5}$$

Based on $G(r)$ we define the event $G(r_1, r_2)$ is an event that there is no unsafe circuit inside the inferior $R(r_1)$ but there is an unsafe circuit inside the exterior $R(r_2)$. Let $\xi(r_1, r_2)$ be the probability that the event $G(r_1, r_2)$ appears. We have:

$$\xi(r_2) = \xi(r_1, r_2) + \xi(r_1)$$

Let r_2 tend to infinity and set $r_1 = r$, we have:

$$\xi = \xi(\infty) = \xi(r) + \xi(r, \infty) \tag{6}$$

The upper bound of ξ is estimated by applying (5) to (6):

$$\xi = \xi(\infty) \leq (1 - p_s^r)^4 + \xi(r, \infty) \tag{7}$$

If a circuit belongs to the set $G(r, \infty)$ then its length must be equal or greater than $2r$. As such, the minimum degree of p_e in the function $\xi(r, \infty)$ is $2r$ or $\xi(r, \infty) = O(p_e^{2r}) = O\bigl((1 - p_s)^{2r}\bigr)$.

We consider the ratio between ξ and $(1 - p_s)^{2r}$. From (2),

$$\lim_{r \to \infty} \frac{\xi}{(1 - p_s)^{2r}} \geq \lim_{r \to \infty} \frac{(1 - p_s)^4}{(1 - p_s)^{2r}} = \infty$$

This is to say $\xi \gg (1 - p_s)^{2r} \sim \xi(r, \infty)$, or $\xi \gg \xi(r, \infty)$ as $r \to \infty$. Fig. 4 shows the ratio between two quantities $(1 - p_s)^4$ and $(1 - p_s)^{2r}$ with values of

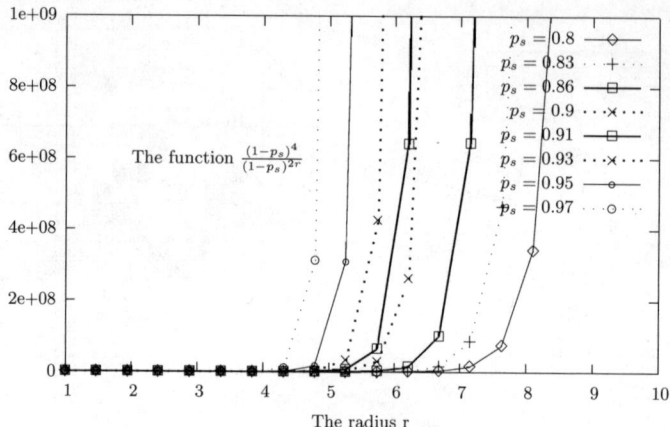

Fig. 4. The ratio between $(1-p_s)^4$ and $(1-p_s)^{2r}$

p_s in $[0.8:1]$. We realize that in order to get a great ratio about 10^8, we can choose $r = 8$ for $p_s \in [0.8:0.9]$ and $r = 6$ for $p_s \in [0.9:1]$. With these choices of r, we can ignore $\xi(r, \infty)$ in the formula of the upper bound of ξ. We derive from (7) to the following approximation:

$$\xi \leq \begin{cases} (1-p_s^8)^4, & \text{if } 0.8 \leq p_s < 0.9 \\ (1-p_s^6)^4, & \text{if } 0.9 \leq p_s \leq 1 \end{cases}$$

Simulations. We first determined the possible size of the world-wide quantum network according to our proposed model. The Earth's surface is 510,065,600 square kilometers. The optimal length of QKD links so far is believed to be approximately 40 km long [11]. Thus, the network size is approximatively of 600×600.

Simulation was done in the 2-dimensional grid lattice 600×600. For each experiment, we randomly generated an untrusted network w.r.t a given p_s. Then, we used the spreading algorithm to find the greatest connected safe cluster. We calculate the probability ξ_{si} that a safe vertex does not belong to the greatest safe cluster as follows:

$$\xi_{si} = 1 - \frac{\text{The number of nodes belonging to the greatest safe cluster.}}{\text{The number of all the safe nodes.}}$$

We executed 10^4 experiments for each p_s. Table 1 shows theoretic values and simulation results. We realize that as p_s increases the mean of ξ_{si} gets closer to its lower bound, and both tends to 0. For $p_s \in [0.8:0.9]$, the upper bound of ξ is important in comparison with $p_e = 1 - p_s$. This implies that the probability that the final key is eavesdropped in its transmission is greater than that of the final key being eavesdropped at the transmitter. This is out of our interest. By contrast, for $p_s \in [0.93:1]$ the upper probability of ξ is approximate or less than the probability of this vertex itself being unsafe. This seems more interesting. Table 1 also suggests that $\xi \sim \xi_{lb} = (1-p_s)^4$ for $p_s \in [0.93:1]$.

Table 1. Lower bound ξ_{lb}, mean of simulations $E(\xi_{si})$ and upper bound ξ_{ub}

p_s	ξ_{lb}	$E(\xi_{si})$	ξ_{ub}
0.8	1.6×10^{-3}	2.14×10^{-3}	4.79×10^{-1}
0.83	8.35×10^{-4}	1.03×10^{-3}	3.6×10^{-1}
0.86	3.84×10^{-4}	4.47×10^{-4}	2.4×10^{-1}
0.9	1×10^{-4}	1.12×10^{-4}	4.82×10^{-2}
0.93	2.4×10^{-5}	2.7×10^{-5}	1.55×10^{-2}
0.95	6.25×10^{-6}	7×10^{-6}	4.92×10^{-3}
0.97	8.1×10^{-7}	1×10^{-6}	7.78×10^{-4}

5 Applying Stochastic Routing Algorithms

5.1 Some Proposed Routing Algorithms

An Adaptive Drunkard's Routing Algorithm (ADRA). In the classic drunkard's walk problem, the next-hop probability distribution is unbiased. We propose an adaptive drunkard's routing algorithm, named ADRA, that is biased. The idea is to give a bigger chance for the vertex that is closer to the destination vertex. Assume that the vertex v_A wants to send a message to the vertex v_B. The vertex v_A computes next-hop probabilities for its neighbors. This computation is based on the coordinate correlations between neighbors and v_B. The higher probability is given to the vertex that is closer to v_B. Then the vertex v_A randomly chooses one of its neighbors to forward the message, but according to the probability distribution that has been computed. Anyone that subsequently receives the message would do the same thing and the chain of communication would continue to reach to v_B.

A Constant-Length Stochastic Routing Algorithm (l-SRA). The *length* of a path is the number of the vertices belonging to the path. A vertex may be counted as many times as the path runs through this vertex. The *distance* between two vertices is the length of the shortest path between these vertices.

Our *constant-length stochastic routing algorithm*, called l-SRA(l) or l-SRA for short, is a stochastic routing algorithm that takes a value l as input and tries to transmit a message by a random path of length l.

Assume that there are some different paths $\pi_1, \ldots, \pi_m$ that hold $l_{(\pi_1)} = \ldots = l_{(\pi_m)} = l$. Note that in the 4-connected grid lattice, it must $l = d + 2 \times k, k \geq 0$. When sending a message l-SRA will choose randomly a path π_i among $\pi_1, \ldots, \pi_m$ according to a probability distribution that holds two following conditions:

1. $\forall i, 1 \leq i \leq m : 0 \leq \Pr(l\text{-SRA}(l) \text{ takes } \pi_i) \leq 1$
2.
$$\sum_{i=1}^{m} \Pr(l\text{-SRA}(l) \text{ takes } \pi_i) = 1 \qquad (8)$$

Theorem 1. *The probability that l-SRA(l) chooses successfully a safe path to send one message depends only on the safe probability p and the length l, not on the distance d between Alice and Bob:*

$$\Pr(1, p, d, l\text{-}SRA(l)) = p^l$$

A Parameterized-Length Stochastic Routing Algorithm (k-SRA). This algorithm takes an input parameter $k > 1$, and tries to transmit the message by a path of length $l \leq k \times d$. We call this algorithm k-SRA(k) or k-SRA for short. It is built based on l-SRA. The idea is as follows. When k-SRA(k) receives the input $k > 1$, it considers the paths of length $l \leq k \times d$. Note that the difference between the length and the distance cannot be an odd number. Therefore, the possible lengths are $d, (d+2), \ldots, (d + 2 \times \lfloor \frac{(k-1) \times d}{2} \rfloor)$. When sending a message k-SRA(k) chooses randomly for l a value among $d, (d+2), \ldots, (d+2 \times \lfloor \frac{(k-1) \times d}{2} \rfloor)$ according to the uniform distribution, i.e:

$$\forall i, 0 \leq i \leq u = \lfloor \frac{(k-1) \times d}{2} \rfloor : \Pr\Big((d + 2 \times i) \text{ is taken for } l\Big) = \frac{1}{(k+1) \times d}$$

Once l was chosen, k-SRA uses l-SRA to send the message. This implies that the message will take a random path that has the length l.

Theorem 2. *The probability that k-SRA(k) chooses successfully a safe path to send one message depends on the safe probability p, the input parameter k, and also the distance d between Alice and Bob:*

$$\lambda = \Pr(1, p, d, k\text{-}SRA(k)) = \frac{p^d \times (1 - p^{2 \times (u+1)})}{(u+1) \times (1 - p^2)} \tag{9}$$

5.2 Our Proposed Routing Algorithms in Some Attack Strategies

We consider two attack strategies of Eve:

1. Dynamic attack: To catch a set of N messages Eve frequently re-chooses nodes being attacked.
2. Static attack: Eve keeps her choice of the nodes being attacked until all N messages have been sent.

Because the algorithm ADRA is based on random walk, it does not give rigorous mathematical results. Its performance is estimated by experimental statistics. The algorithm l-SRA is not a real routing solution. This algorithm only executes one sub-task of the algorithm k-SRA. The algorithm k-SRA presents some rigorous bounds.

Theorem 3. *If Eve executes a dynamic attack, then the probability that there is at least one safe path in N routings of k-SRA(k) depends on N, the safe probability p, the input parameter k, and the distance d between Alice and Bob:*

$$\Pr(N, p, d, k\text{-}SRA(k)) = 1 - (1 - \lambda)^N$$

Where λ is evaluated in (9).

We have a lemma derived directly from the theorem 3.

Lemma 1. *If Eve executes a dynamic attack, given ϵ and k-SRA(k), then we have the threshold N_0 responding to the second question stated in Section 2:*

$$N_0 = \frac{\lg(\epsilon)}{1 - \lg(\lambda)}$$

Where λ is evaluated in (9).

Theorem 4. *If Eve executes a static attack, then the upper bound of the probability that there is at least one safe path in N routings of k-SRA(k) depends on N, the safe probability p, the input parameter k, and the distance d between Alice and Bob:*

$$\Pr(N, p, d, k\text{-}SRA(k)) \leq 1 - (1 - \lambda)^N$$

Where λ is evaluated in (9). The equality is possible when $N \leq 4$.

We have a lemma derived directly from the theorem 4.

Lemma 2. *If Eve executes a static attack, given ϵ and k-SRA(k), we have the threshold N_0 responding to the second question stated in Section 2:*

$$N_0 \geq \frac{\lg(\epsilon)}{1 - \lg(\lambda)}$$

Where λ is evaluated in (9). The equality is possible when $N_0 \leq 4$.

5.3 Simulations

ADRA's Simulations. The next-hop probabilities computation can vary to result in many ADRA's variants. Here we reused the next-hop probabilities computation presented in [19]. Then, we ran simulations in the lattice 600 × 600, in varying the safety probability $p_s \in [0.93 : 1]$ and the distance d_{AB} between Alice and Bob [19, 20]. For each p_s, we generated a network with randomly spread eave-droppers. For each distance d_{AB}, we generated 400 (Alice, Bob) pairs. For each such pair, we ran 400 experiments. In each one we generated stochastic routes from Alice to Bob until we find a safe one (i.e., a route with no Eve). For each 400 experiments we gathered the largest number of messages that were needed. To avoid sending an infinite number of messages, we set the maximum effort to 10^4 messages.

Table 2 presents simulation results. This suggests that there exists a threshold of the number of sending messages above which we can be almost certain that there exists at least one safe message.

k-SRA's Simulations. Simulations were implemented in the lattice 600 × 600. We ran 10^4 experiments. The table 3 shows the lower bounds, the simulation values, and the upper bounds for the case of $k = 2$ and $d = 10$ with $p_s = 0,93; 0.95; 0.97; 0.99$. Note that the lower bound holds if N messages have taken

Table 2. Worst cases's experiment results. Symbol × stands for more than 10,000.

d	\multicolumn{7}{c}{p_s}	d	\multicolumn{7}{c}{p_s}
	0.99	0.98	0.97	0.96	0.95	0.94	0.93		0.99	0.98	0.97	0.96	0.95	0.94	0.93
1	8	12	12	22	14	12	14	10	149	169	340	1267	3731	1267	2854
2	44	105	122	68	82	425	106	20	127	338	829	9300	×	×	×
3	87	51	273	99	122	233	439	30	315	1987	2908	×	×	×	×
4	95	171	160	408	244	1125	476	40	386	4111	×	×	×	×	×
5	66	61	186	917	286	967	2149	50	437	×	×	×	×	×	×
6	34	397	356	377	644	583	921	60	656	×	×	×	×	×	×
7	43	194	155	395	625	420	2102	70	1911	×	×	×	×	×	×
8	72	1645	224	414	936	773	1663	80	3117	×	×	×	×	×	×
9	53	185	477	386	585	717	2794	90	7039	×	×	×	×	×	×
10	149	169	340	1267	3731	1267	2854	100	4117	×	×	×	×	×	×
								110	×	×	×	×	×	×	×

Table 3. Lower bound, experimental results, upper bound of the key secrecy for $p_s = 0.93; 0.95; 0.97; 0.99$. λ_{si} is the percentage in 10^4 experiments done.

	$p_s = 0.93$				$p_s = 0.97$		
N	$\lambda_{lb}(\%)$	$\lambda_{si}(\%)$	$\lambda_{ub}(\%)$	N	$\lambda_{lb}(\%)$	$\lambda_{si}(\%)$	$\lambda_{ub}(\%)$
1	34.71	42.54	34.71	1	63.66	69.99	63.66
10	34.71	80.57	98.59	10	63.66	93.84	98.59
100	34.71	95.36	100	100	63.66	98.94	100
1000	34.71	99.52	100	1000	63.66	99.94	100
10000	34.71	99.96	100	10000	63.66	100	100
	$p_s = 0.95$				$p_s = 0.99$		
N	$\lambda_{lb}(\%)$	$\lambda_{si}(\%)$	$\lambda_{ub}(\%)$	N	$\lambda_{lb}(\%)$	$\lambda_{si}(\%)$	$\lambda_{ub}(\%)$
1	47.04	54.31	47.04	1	86.05	88.75	86.05
10	47.04	87.96	98.59	10	86.05	98.40	100
100	47.04	97.59	100	100	86.05	99.81	100
1000	47.04	99.84	100	1000	86.05	99.99	100
10000	47.04	100	100	10000	86.05	100	100

the only possible path. The convergence of the experimental results to their upper bound is significant. We realize that the secrecy probability of the final key is a non-decreasing function. As the number of sent messages increases, this probability converges to its upper bound. Moreover, both tend to 1 as $N \to \infty$.

6 Conclusions

We investigated constraints of quantum networks, in particularly, the ineluctable probability that some nodes are compromised. Given the distance between source and destination, we proposed routing algorithms and estimated the number of pieces that the message must be divided into with respect to the distance and the compromising probability distribution imposed over nodes. The principle result of our work is that it opens another door allowing to investigate QKD networks using percolation theory and stochastic routing.

A lot of work remains to be done in the future. For example, we need to take into account key authentication to complete our key exchange scheme. The eavesdropping distribution was uniform in this paper. More complex probability distributions seem more interesting. Studying other topologies will be of significance, grids are only the first step. We also aim at finding rigorous and tight formulas. Besides, we must improve our stochastic routing proposals, e.g. hiding routing information as onion routing. We attach importance to throughput and computational overhead in practice. We plan to carry out a cost estimation with respect to today's QKD technology.

Acknowledgements. We thank Steve Frank and Daniela Becker for their proofreading. All the mistakes are ours.

References

1. Bennett, C., Brassard, G.: Quantum cryptography: Public key distribution and coin tossing. In: Proc. of IEEE Int. Conf. on Computers, Systems, and Signal Processing, Bangalore, India, pp. 175–179 (December 1984)
2. Mayer, D.: Unconditional security in quantum cryptography. Journal of the ACM 48, 351–406 (2001)
3. Lo, H.K.: A simple proof of the unconditional security of quantum key distribution. Journal of Physics A 34, 6957–6967 (2001)
4. Chau, H.: Practical scheme to share a secret key through an up to 27.6% bit error rate quantum channel. Phys. Rev. A 66, 060302 (2002)
5. Elliott, C., Pearson, D., Troxel, G.: Quantum cryptography in practice. In: Proc. of the Conf. on Applications, Technologies, Architectures, and Protocols for Computer Communications, Karlsruhe, Germany, pp. 227–238 (August 2003)
6. Elliott, C., Colvin, A., Pearson, D., Pikalo, O., Schlafer, J., Yeh, H.: Current status of the DARPA quantum network (March 2005),
  http://arxiv.org/abs/quant-ph/0503058v2
7. Bellot, P., Gallion, P., Guilley, S., Danger, J.L.: The hqnet project (2006),
  http://hqnet.enst.fr
8. Qing, X., Costa e Silva, M.B., Danger, J., Guilley, S., Gallion, P., Bellot, P., Mendieta, F.: Towards Quantum key distribution System using Homodyne Detection with Differential Time-multiplexed Reference. In: Proc. of the 5th Int. Conf. on Computer Sciences, Research Innovation and Vision for the Futur, Hanoi, Vietnam, pp. 158–165 (March 2007)
9. Kimura, T., Nambu, Y., Hatanaka, T., Tomita, A., Kosaka, H., Nakamura, K.: Single-photon interference over 150-km transmission using silica-based integrated-optic interferometers for quantum cryptography criterion. Japanese Journal of Applied Physics 43, L1217–L1219 (2004)
10. Elliott, C.: Building the quantum network. New Journal of Physics 4, 46.1–46.12 (2002)
11. Alléaume, R., Roueff, F., Maurhart, O., Luthenhaus, N.: Architecture, Security and Topology of a global Quantum key distribution Network. In: IEEE/LEOS Summer Topical Meeting on Quantum Communications in Telecom Networks, Quebec (July 2006)

12. Alléaume, R., et al.: Secoqc white paper on quantum key distribution and cryptography (January 2007), http://arxiv.org/abs/quant-ph/0701168
13. Grimmett, G.: Percolation, 2nd edn. Springer, Heidelberg (1999)
14. Hughes, B.D.: Random walks and random environments, vol. 1. Oxford University Press, Oxford (1995)
15. Hughes, B.D.: Random walks and random environments, vol. 2. Oxford University Press, Oxford (1995)
16. Bohacek, S., Hespanha, J.P., Lee, J., Lim, C., Obraczka, K.: Game theoretic stochastic routing for fault tolerance and security on computer networks. IEEE Transactions on Parallel and Distributed Systems 18, 1227–1240 (2007)
17. Hespanha, J., Bohacek, S.: Preminilary results in routing games. In: American Control Conference, Arlington, Virginia, USA, vol. 3, pp. 1904–1909 (June 2001)
18. Bohacek, S., Hespanha, J.P., Obraczka, K., Lee, J., Lim, C.: Enhancing security via stochastic routing. In: Proc. 11th Int. Conf. on Computer Communication and Networks, Miami, Florida, USA, pp. 58–62 (October 2002)
19. Le, Q.C., Bellot, P., Demaille, A.: Stochastic Routing in Large Grid Shaped Quantum Networks. In: Proc. of the 5th Int. Conf. on Computer Sciences, Research Innovation and Vision for the Futur, Hanoi, Vietnam, pp. 166–174 (March 2007)
20. Le, Q.C., Bellot, P., Demaille, A.: On the security of Quantum Networks: A proposal framework ans its capacity. In: Proc. of the Int. Conf. on New Technologies, Mobility, and Security, Paris, France, pp. 385–396 (May 2007)

Appendix

Proof of theorem 1. $\Pr\big(1,p,d,l\text{-SRA}(1)\big)$

$$= \sum_{i=1}^{k} \Big(\Pr\big(l\text{-SRA}(1) \text{ takes } \pi_i\big) \times \Pr(\pi_i \text{ is safe}) \Big) = \sum_{i=1}^{k} \Big(\Pr\big(l\text{-SRA}(1) \text{ takes } \pi_i\big) \times p^l \Big)$$

$$= \Big(\sum_{i=1}^{k} \Pr\big(l\text{-SRA}(1) \text{ takes } \pi_i\big) \Big) \times p^l = p^l \quad (\text{ from } (8))$$

Proof of theorem 2. $\lambda = \Pr\big(1,p,d,k\text{-SRA}(k)\big)$

$$= \sum_{l=d,..,d+2u} \Big(\Pr\big(k\text{-SRA}(k) \text{ takes } l\big) \times \Pr\big(l\text{-SRA}(l) \text{ takes a safe path}\big) \Big)$$

$$= \sum_{l=d,..,d+2u} \Big(\frac{1}{(u+1)} \times \Big(\Pr\big(1,p,d,l\text{-SRA}(1)\big) \Big) \Big)$$

$$= \frac{1}{(u+1)} \times \Big(\sum_{l=d,..,d+2u} \Big(\Pr\big(1,p,d,l\text{-SRA}(1)\big) \Big) \Big)$$

$$= \frac{1}{(u+1)} \times \Big(\sum_{l=d,..,d+2u} p^{(l)} \Big) = \frac{p^d \times (1-p^{2(u+1)})}{(u+1) \times (1-p^2)}$$

Proof of theorem 3. It is a memoryless system. From (9),

$$\Pr(\text{All the N trials are failed}) = \big(1 - \Pr(\text{A trial is successful})\big)^N = (1-\lambda)^N$$
$$\to \Pr(N, p, d, k\text{-SRA}(k)) = \Pr(\text{At least one of N trials is successful})$$
$$= 1 - \Pr(\text{All the N trials are failed}) = 1 - (1-\lambda)^N.$$

Proof of theorem 4. We must take into account the path dependence of N paths taken by N messages sent. The probability that k-SRA(k) takes an unsafe path for each trial is:

$$\overline{\Pr(1,p,d,k\text{-SRA}(k))} = \sum_{d \leq l \leq k \times d} \Big(\Pr\big(k\text{-SRA}(k) \text{ takes } l\big) \times \Pr\big(l\text{-SRA}(l) \text{ takes an unsafe path}\big)\Big) = 1 - \lambda \quad (10)$$

The probability of N messages being intercepted is:

$$\overline{\Pr(N,p,d,k\text{-SRA}(k))} = \sum_{\substack{d \leq l_1 \leq k \times d \\ \vdots \\ d \leq l_N \leq k \times d}} \Bigg(\Pr\big(k\text{-SRA}(k) \text{ takes } (l_1,\ldots,l_N)\big) \times$$
$$\Bigg(\sum_{\substack{l_{\pi_1} = l_1, \\ \vdots \\ l_{\pi_N} = l_N}} \Big(\Pr(l\text{-SRA takes } \pi_1\ldots\pi_N) \times \big(\Pr(\pi_1\ldots\pi_N \text{ are failed})\big)\Big)\Bigg)\Bigg) \quad (11)$$

For a given path set $(\pi_1,\ldots,\pi_N)$, we can prove the following inequality:

$$\Pr(\pi_1,\ldots,\pi_N \text{ are failed}) \geq \prod_{i=1}^{N} \Pr(\pi_i \text{ is failed}) \quad (12)$$

Where the equality holds i.i.f $\pi_1,\ldots,\pi_N$ are independent.

We first prove with $N=2$. Assume that π_1, π_2 have the length l_1, l_2 respectively, and have l common nodes $(0 \leq l \leq \min(l_1, l_2))$. We have:

$$\Pr(\pi_1, \pi_2 \text{ are failed}) = p^l \times (1 - p^{(l_1-l)}) \times (1 - p^{(l_2-l)}) + (1 - p^l)$$
$$= (1 - p^{(l_1)}) \times (1 - p^{(l_2)}) + (p^{(l_1+l_2-l)} - p^{(l_1+l_2)})$$
$$\geq (1 - p^{(l_1)}) \times (1 - p^{(l_2)}) = \Pr(\pi_1 \text{ is failed}) \times \Pr(\pi_2 \text{ is failed})$$

Inequality (12) was proven with $N = 2$. We iterate this to obtain (12) for $\forall N$. Note that the equality holds iff $\pi_1\ldots\pi_N$ are separated. In the square 4-connected lattice there are maximum 4 separated paths between Alice and Bob. Thus, if $N > 4$, the equality for (12) cannot appear. By applying (12) to (11), we have:

$$\overline{\Pr(N,p,d,k\text{-SRA(k)})} > \sum_{\substack{d \leq l_1 \leq k \times d \\ \vdots \\ d \leq l_N \leq k \times d}} \left(\left(\prod_{i=1}^{N} \Pr\left(k\text{-SRA(k) takes } l_i\right) \right) \times \right.$$

$$\left. \left(\sum_{\substack{l_{\pi_1}=l_1, \\ \vdots \\ l_{\pi_N}=l_N}} \left(\prod_{i=1}^{N} \Pr(l\text{-SRA takes } \pi_i) \right) \times \left(\prod_{i=1}^{N} \Pr(\pi_i \text{ is failed}) \right) \right) \right)$$

$$= \sum_{\substack{d \leq l_1 \leq k \times d \\ \vdots \\ d \leq l_N \leq k \times d)}} \left(\left(\prod_{i=1}^{N} \Pr\left(k\text{-SRA(k) takes } l_i\right) \right) \times \right.$$

$$\left. \left(\prod_{l_j=l_1}^{l_N} \left(\sum_{l_{\pi_i}=l_j} \left(\Pr(l\text{-SRA takes } \pi_i) \times \Pr(\pi_i \text{ is failed}) \right) \right) \right) \right)$$

$$= \sum_{\substack{d \leq l_1 \leq k \times d \\ \vdots \\ d \leq l_N \leq k \times d)}} \left(\prod_{i=1}^{N} \Pr\left(k\text{-SRA(k) takes } l_i\right) \times \prod_{l_j=l_1}^{l_N} \Pr\left(l\text{-SRA}(l_j) \text{ takes an unsafe path}\right) \right)$$

$$= \sum_{\substack{d \leq l_1 \leq k \times d \\ \vdots \\ d \leq l_N \leq k \times d)}} \left(\left(\prod_{i=1}^{N} \Pr\left(k\text{-SRA(k) takes } l_i\right) \times \Pr\left(l\text{-SRA}(l_j) \text{ takes an unsafe path}\right) \right) \right)$$

$$= \prod_{i=1}^{N} \left(\left(\sum_{d \leq l_i \leq k \times d} \Pr\left(k\text{-SRA(k) takes } l_i\right) \times \Pr\left(l\text{-SRA}(l_i) \text{ takes an unsafe path}\right) \right) \right)$$

$$= \prod_{i=1}^{N} \left(\Pr\left(k\text{-SRA(k) takes an unsafe path}\right) \right) = (1-\lambda)^N \text{ (from (10))}$$

Thus,

$$\Pr(N,p,d,k\text{-SRA(k)}) = 1 - \overline{\Pr(N,p,d,k\text{-SRA(k)})} = 1 - (1-\lambda)^N.$$

Synthesising Monitors from High-Level Policies for the Safe Execution of Untrusted Software

Andrew Brown and Mark Ryan

School of Computer Science, University of Birmingham
Edgbaston, Birmingham, UK. B15 2TT
A.J.Brown@cs.bham.ac.uk, M.D.Ryan@cs.bham.ac.uk

Abstract. Preventing malware from causing damage to its host system has become a topic of increasing importance over the past decade, as the frequency and impact of malware infections have continued to rise. Most existing approaches to malware defence cannot guarantee complete protection against the threats posed. Execution monitors can be used to defend against malware: they enable a target program's execution to be analysed and can prevent any deviation from its intended behaviour, recovering from such deviations where necessary. They are, however, difficult for the end-user to define or modify.

This paper describes a high-level policy language in which users can express a priori judgments about program behavior, which are compiled into execution monitors. We show how this approach can defend against previously unseen malware and software vulnerability exploits.

1 Introduction

Malware is software designed to penetrate or damage a computer system without a user's awareness or consent. It is written by a programmer with malicious intent to purposefully compromise the confidentiality, integrity or availability of a user's data, services or devices. Defective software can cause similar problems: it has a legitimate purpose but contains 'bugs' which may allow such harmful behaviour. For these reasons it is difficult for a user to trust any executable they use. A program may contain features the user requires but may also invoke unwanted behaviour, which its user is generally unaware of.

1.1 Execution Monitoring

Execution monitoring is a technique which can be used to defend against malicious or defective software. An execution monitor is a co-routine that executes in parallel with a third-party application in order to fully regulate that program's interaction with its host machine, enabling harmful behavior to be prevented and recovered from in real-time. By analysing the system calls a program makes, or by viewing the calls it makes to some application programming interface (API), an execution monitor affords the host a fine-grained view of a program behavior. Monitoring at the system call level can be problematic: it is often difficult to attribute a sequence of system calls to a program event. Further, one may wish to analyse an action which does not involve the target program making a system call [8,11].

API calls are give a more abstract representation of program behaviour, allowing policies to reason about advanced behaviour with lower policy development effort. Monitoring executions in this way presents new opportunities for defending against malware. However, authoring the policies which define an execution monitor usually requires programming ability: even monitoring a program at the API call level requires the policy author to predict the sequences of calls that a target program will make to an API.

End-users and system administrators require a mechanism for translating their own high-level requirements of a program's execution into low-level representations, like those which define an execution monitor.

BMSL [13] is a user-friendly policy language for reasoning about program execution. It provides constructs for expressing high-level policies, though an author must still forecast the type and order of any events which indicate a policy violation. Where a policy is violated, its author must define a sequence of events to recover from this violation. Both these requirements are infeasible expectations of most end-users. BMSL's enforcement engine is also unsuitable for monitoring program execution: it was designed as an intrusion detection and prevention system, so does not have access to as much information about program state as other monitoring systems do.

1.2 Objectives

To allow end-users to access the benefits of execution monitoring, we address these problems. Our work:

– Extends the BMSL language, to allow high-level requirements of a program's execution to be expressed simply in a policy.
– Develops an enforcement mechanism for our extended version of BMSL. Our mechanism works by translating a BMSL policy into a policy enforcement language called Polymer [3].

Polymer [3] is a fully-implemented language for specifying execution monitors for Java programs. Its enforcement engine monitors the API calls a program makes and responds to a policy violation by suggesting a bytecode insertion.

In this paper we assume that target programs are written in Java. The principles we establish are not restricted to Java: they can be used with C programs too, in which case, a policy would reason about system calls and enforce a policy at that level.

1.3 Related Work

The foundations of execution monitoring are described by Schneider in [12], where a formal treatment is given to techniques which analyse the actions of a target program and terminate it where it violates a policy. This process is modelled by the *security automaton*. Schneider shows that this class of execution monitor can only enforce safety properties.

Execution monitoring was first implemented by PoET (Policy Enforcement Toolkit) which performed 'in-line' monitoring[1] of a program binary using policies expressed in declarative language called PSLang (Policy Specification Language) [6]. PSLang cannot capture or store the values of arguments to events, making it difficult to express the context in which an event occurs. Naccio [7] is another 'in-line' monitoring system, whose main advancement was the ability for policies to contain abstract resource specifications. However, its policy language can only check invariant properties on these specifications and is difficult for a non-technical user to comprehend.

Ligatti [1,9] defined a more powerful model of an execution monitor that could suppress or insert program actions, superseding Schneider's model. This class of monitor is modelled by the *edit automaton*, which is implemented by the Polymer framework [3,2]. It defines policies as logical operations on a set of security-relevant program points which are separate to the target program. Its policies are easy to maintain, re-use, or compose into a hierarchy of policies. The execution monitors it defines observe the principles of soundness[2] and transparency[3], allowing correctness guarantees to be made. Polymer's policy language is imperative: it has high expressive power but is difficult for end-users to use or comprehend; a realistic policy is around 1500-2000 lines of code.

Full paper. Due to space limitations, this version of our paper does not include all details of the approach we have developed to compute an enforcement mechanism from a high-level policy. A full version of this paper is available at http://www.cs.bham.ac.uk/~ajb/files/ispec.pdf.

2 High-Level Security Policies

In order to bring execution monitors to a user-deployable level, we have extended BMSL [13]: a high-level language for specifying policies which reason about arbitrary program events. Our intention is for end-users to express policies textually (as a system administrator in an organisation might) or by means of a graphical user interface (as an individual end-user would).

2.1 Behaviour Modelling Specification Language (BMSL)

BMSL is a policy specification language designed to reason about application behavior using arbitrary events. Appendix A gives its BNF description.

A BMSL policy consists of a set of rules, or a set of variables followed by a set of rules. Variable declaration may be *local* or *global*: a local variable's scope

---

[1] **In-line monitoring** generates new system libraries that include the checking code necessary to enforce a policy.
[2] **Soundness:** All observable outputs of a policy obey that policy.
[3] **Transparency:** The semantics of an execution that already obeys a policy are always preserved.

is limited to a single rule, whereas a global variable applies to the whole policy. A history, H, models the target program's instruction stream and is expressed by a pattern over a sequence of events: pat. A pat can measure event *occurrence, non-occurrence, sequencing, alternation* and *repetition* to determine the temporal properties of a target program's behavior. This gives BMSL higher expressive power than alternative mechanisms for specifying temporal properties [4].

A rule is of the form pat → action, where pat denotes a pattern over a sequence of actions and action denotes a response action where this pattern is matched. Only if the sequence of actions a program invokes precisely matches pat will the responsive steps in action be initiated. Atomic events are of the form $e(x_1, x_2, ..., x_n)|cond$, where e is a program action (a system call or a call to some API), x is an argument to that action, and cond is a boolean-valued expression on that action's arguments. A condition can make use of the arithmetic, comparison and logical operators, enabling precise identification of the context in which an event occurs.

A response action associated with the rule pat → action is launched where a suffix of the event history matches pat. A response action can be an assignment to a global variable, the invocation of a further sequence of recovery events, or a call to an external support function, written in C. BMSL has the following advantages over other policy specification languages [7,6,3,5]:

- It extends regular expressions to model events that are characterised by argument values as well as by name.
- Response actions can be associated to patterns, which allow sequencing, alternation, and repetition. A response is automatically launched when the implementing system observes a match for the pattern.
- Variables give BMSL specifications more expressive power than regular expressions alone. Its policies are comparable to attribute grammars in terms of what they can express.

2.2 Limitations

BMSL includes a number of intricacies that do not lend it to end-user policy specification. Its limitations can be summarised as:

1. **Specifying Event Histories:** BMSL requires the policy author to explicitly state the sequence of events which a policy reasons about. The author must populate a policy with system calls and their arguments, whose temporal order must be accurately stated. This is an infeasible requirement of most end-users, who do not have extensive knowledge about how programs execute. The language does provide the abstract event construct, E, to which events can be concatenated to form an execution trace. However, unless this work is done on behalf of the user, their policies are likely to contain vulnerabilities or redundancies.
2. **Specifying Recovery Events:** In a similar manner to event history specification, the policy author must specify a sequence of events (or abstract events (E)) which should be invoked to recover from a policy violation. The end-user is unlikely to be able to reason about recovering from a violation

without having in-depth knowledge about how the target program executes. Inaccurate specification of a recovery event sequence could introduce vulnerabilities to the target system or may cause undesirable effects on dependent processes.
3. **Strong vs. Weak Temporal Order:** BMSL does not make a clear distinction between strong and weak temporal order. Its default sequencing construct assumes that strong temporal order is expressed. This representation is not suitable for many models of program execution where events may happen simultaneously or housekeeping operations are performed between events. Weak ordering of events is more suitable for most policies (where events which a policy does not reason about can occur in between those which it does reason about). The concept can be expressed by a BMSL policy, but only by calling an external function.
4. **Counting Event Occurrence:** Counting the number of occurrences of an event can be important when monitoring a target program to enforce some high-level requirement (e.g., *a program may attempt to authenticate with a service a maximum 'n' times in a time period, 't'*). BMSL does not provide a mechanism for measuring event occurrence.
5. **Comparison Operators:** Only the operators =, :=, and ∈ are made available by the language for comparison within a condition, **cond**. When monitoring a program with respect to a high-level requirement, more expressive operators are required (e.g., to monitor whether a URL which a program connects to starts with a particular substring).

2.3 Extensions

To address these limitations, we provide the following additions to BMSL:

1. **Specifying Event Histories:** Atomic events can be composed to form abstract events using the construct, E, which is a non-empty set. An abstract event allows the policy author to represent the actions that a program may perform in a high-level way (e.g., *read from a local file, send an e-mail on a network port, receive an IMAP e-mail*). We build upon this ability with an abstract event referencing system which allows clear mapping of abstract events to the APIs they refer to: our mechanism uses the abstract constructs **zone**, **resource** and **action**, to allow the user to refer to the **zone** a program may interact with (e.g., **internet**, **lan**, **localhost**), the resources within a zone it may access, and the actions which it may perform on those resources. The events which are referenced using this scheme exist as part of a pre-specified event library, whose elements are Java classes of type `AbstractAction`. These classes collect together the atomic event constructors, method calls, and their arguments to which an abstract event reference refers. Policy 1 illustrates this with some example specifications of this kind.
2. **Specifying Recovery Events:** We introduce a construct H → cond to enable the policy author to specify their requirements of program execution in a purely declarative manner. We consider this specification technique to

Policy 1 Example abstract event specifications using our BMSL extension

- internet.service.Connect():
  Target program (P) initiates a connection event to an unspecified Internet service.
- internet.data.Send(HttpRequest r):
  P invokes a send event, which sends an HTTP request to a remote URL.
- lan.device.Print(Printer p)|p.name()="picasso":
  P invokes a print event to a network printer whose name is "picasso".
- localhost.localdisk.Write(File f)|f.extension()=".txt":
  P invokes a write event to the local disk, of a file whose extension is ".txt".

  be more user-friendly as it does not require the user to enumerate the events which should occur in response to a policy violation. Whenever the target program's execution history satisfies H, the condition cond is evaluated. If cond evaluates to *true*, the program's execution is allowed to continue. If, however, cond evaluates to *false*, then a sequence of recovery actions derived from cond at compile-time are executed through bytecode re-writing. If cond is ⊥, program execution is aborted.
3. **Strong vs. Weak Temporal Order:** Our extensions to BMSL denote strong temporal order by separating events with a semi-colon (';'), and weak temporal order with a double semi-colon (';;').
4. **Counting Event Occurrence:** We have added a modifier in order to count event occurrences. An event pattern, pat can be an event E, one of a number of events ($E_1 \vee E_2 \vee ... \vee E_n$), or an event with our occurrence modifier following it. This modifier allows the number of occurrences of an event to be compared to an integer or to the number of occurrences of another event. This feature is lacking from many declarative policy languages [7,6,5].
5. **Comparison Operators:** To enhance the expressive power of conditions we add operators such as contains, startsWith, endsWith, and intersects. This enables more advanced reasoning about the conditions of an event occurrence: for example, whether some argument to an event contains a particular substring.

3   Monitoring Program Execution

Polymer [3] is a Java-based system which enables the security practitioner to enforce first-class policies on untrusted Java programs by monitoring a target program's behaviour at execution time. The centralised nature of its policies ensures that access control checks are not scattered throughout libraries and binaries, as in [5,6,7]. Polymer policies can therefore be enforced on logically separate components of a system. In the case of malware, Polymer can be used to monitor a previously unseen binary, which could be obfuscated.

3.1   The Polymer Framework

Polymer is composed of two main tools. The first is a policy compiler that compiles execution monitors defined in Polymer's language into Java source code and then into Java bytecode. The second tool is a bytecode rewriter that processes bytecode in order to insert calls to an execution monitor in all necessary places. This implementation ensures that every security-sensitive method is monitored every time it is called by the target, guaranteeing soundness. The policy language has well defined formal semantics, in [3], and can apply all Java's conditional constructs, primitive data types and logical operators. Expressive, fine-grained policies can therefore be composed.

To construct a policy, the policy author extends Polymer's `Policy` class. Each `Policy` object contains three main elements: a security state which keeps track of program activity during execution; a decision procedure which reacts to security-sensitive program events; and, methods to update a policy's state each time the monitored application exhibits some behavior which the policy reasons about. Each of these procedures are specified by overriding a `Policy`'s `query()` method.

A decision procedure is achieved by overriding a `Policy`'s `query()` method. This uses method signatures (e.g., `<public void java.sql.*.<init>(String s, ..)>` – any constructor in the `java.sql` package whose first argument is of type `String`) to reference atomic events, or may use a composition of many events, encapsulated by an `Action` object. An `AbstractAction` is a Java bean which collects together `Actions` in order to express high-level program operations. This assists the policy author in reducing redundant events and minimises the risk of then neglecting critical events.

When a policy's decision procedure is evaluated, one of six types of object can be returned in order to suggest how the policy should be enforced at the bytecode level. These objects are referred to as `Suggestions`, since they do not guarantee that a policy will have an effectful reaction (e.g., where it is composed in a hierarchy containing other policies). Example suggestions include `OKSug` (that event can be invoked); `InsSug` (that event should be re-evaluated after some additional code is inserted); and, `ReplSug` (that event's return value should be replaced with some pre-computed value). A `HaltSug` suggests that the target application is terminated.

Imperative languages like Polymer often provide multiple constructs which can achieve similar results in reasoning: it may be unclear to the author how some policies might be expressed. This can impact on the accuracy, readability and complexity of the policies a user specifies, or in the worst case, mean that a user simply cannot write a policy. This motivates the need for a succinct high-level language, like BMSL.

3.2 Our Use of Polymer

We bring the execution monitoring abilities of Polymer to a user-operable level by creating a compiler (Section 5) between our extended version of BMSL and Polymer. Our work creates a 'layer' between the target program in execution and the Java Virtual Machine (JVM). Figure 1 shows an overview of how our system operates. Most of the behaviour a target program invokes cannot be secured against by the JVM – an execution monitor is required to achieve full regulation of the

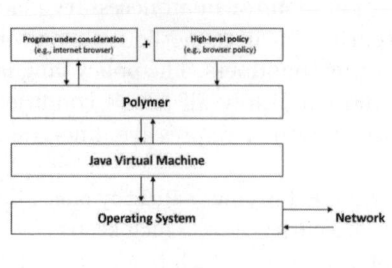 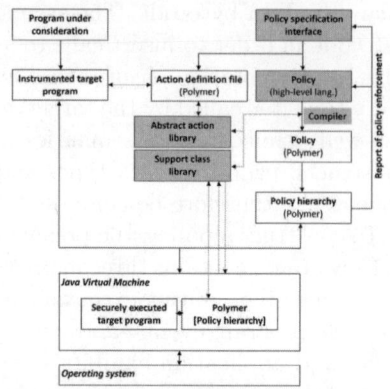

Fig. 1. System overview: Integration of Polymer with the JVM

Fig. 2. System architecture: our enforcement model showing how we extend Polymer (shaded)

target's interface with the JVM's resources. The monitor passes all events it sees directly to the JVM, except those which are explicitly reasoned about by a policy.

Figure 2 shows how an untrusted program can be translated into a securely executed target program by our work. It indicates the target and a Polymer monitor executing in parallel on the JVM. A BMSL policy is given as an argument to our compiler, which computes a Polymer `Policy` class from it. In doing so, our compiler refers to a library of abstract program events which are expressed as `AbstractActions`.

To determine the context in which an atomic event (e) occurs, one can populate a set of arguments. An abstract event (E) can also refer to some abstract data object, O. An O is a member of a set of data abstraction classes (cf. support class library) and enables an abstract event's meaning to be identified more precisely, giving an execution monitor greater knowledge of the status of that event's invocation. For example, where a policy reasons about an program which sends an HTTP response, an object is constructed to represent this response: it contains that response's header (e.g., status code, date, server, content-type), body (e.g., HTML, XML) and a reference to the HTTP request which invoked it. Our event abstraction mechanism expands on the capabilities of previous works [7,6].

4 Securing an Untrusted Internet Browser

For many users, the Internet browser is arguably their most commonly used application. Browsers are becoming increasingly important in everyday computing, providing a user with access to many remote services, some of which operate solely inside the browser and negate the need for stand-alone desktop software. Modern browser platforms (e.g., Microsoft Internet Explorer, Mozilla Firefox, and Opera) support extensions and plug-ins which give the browser such additional functionality but which are a potential source of malware. This section illustrates how one might construct policies for a malicious Internet browser which preserve as much of that program's legitimate behaviour as possible.

4.1 Attacks

Cookies play a central role in ensuring that the multiple interactions a browser makes with a remote service can be traced. They allow frequently required data to be stored for the user, preventing them authenticating with a service on each use, for example. Through the addition of a malicious extension to a browser, or through a vulnerability within that browser, cookie data can compromise a user's privacy, confidentiality and data integrity in various ways.

We show how our work may assist in constructing a monitor for an untrusted browser to prevent it executing malicious code which uses cookie data to compromise user privacy. Such attacks require a more interesting class of execution monitor: one which must consider the data an event sequence uses in order to prevent sensitive information being leaked.

1. **Cookie Theft Using Session Hijacking:** During normal operation, the browser sends cookies to and from server (or a group of servers in the same domain). Since cookies may contain sensitive information (a username, or a token used for authentication), their values should not be accessible to other hosts. Cookie theft is the act of cookies being intercepted by a third party, usually via packet sniffing.
2. **Cross-Site Cooking:** Each site the browser accesses should only have permission to read its own cookies: a site *www.malicious.com* should not be able to read, alter or set cookies for another site, *www.good.com*. Cross-site cooking vulnerabilities in web browsers allow malicious sites to break this rule; the attacker exploits non-malicious users with vulnerable browsers instead of attacking a site directly. The goal of such an attack may be *session fixation*: the attacker attempts to authenticate with a site by setting the user's session identifier (SID) himself.
3. **Monitoring Browsing History Using Cookies:** Even where a policy enforces that a cookie should only be sent to the server which set it, a web page may contain images or other components stored on a server in another domain. Cookies that are set during retrieval of these components are called third-party cookies. A malicious advertising company might use these to trace a user's interaction with multiple sites where it has placed a common component which reads from a cookie (e.g., a banner advert). Knowledge of the user's browsing history allows the malicious party to target them with marketing based on their presumed preferences.

4.2 Policy Construction

The user requires the use of cookies, but they do not trust their Internet browser or some of the remote sites they access. They can construct policies using BMSL with our extensions to defend against the attacks they are aware of which involve cookie data.

Cookie Theft Using Session Hijacking: To prevent against Attack 1, the browser should send any cookie that is likely to contain sensitive data using a secure network protocol (e.g., HTTPS). The user wishes a policy to be enforced whereby if the browser does not send cookie data using a secure protocol, the event which sends that data should be prevented. Policy 2 illustrates how the user might construct such a policy.

Policy 2 Policy to defend against cookie theft through session hijacking

Policy (English)	The target program may send a cookie to the network only if that cookie is sent using a secure network connection. A network connection is assumed to be a secure connection where it uses the HTTPS protocol.
Policy format	zone.resource.Action(Object)|cond → cond
Policy (BMSL)	internet.data.Send(HttpRequest r)|r.hasCookie() → r.hasProtocol("https");
Policy meaning	Any network send request which contains data that matches the definition of a cookie may only be sent to the network where the protocol on which this data is to be sent is HTTPS.
Abstract actions	internet.data.Send(HttpRequest r)
Abstract conditions	r.hasCookie()
	r.hasProtocol("https")

The table shows an interpretation of the attack written in plain English: such a sentence may be formulated by the end-user when considering how to prevent Attack 1. The policy the user constructs is a purely declarative statement which uses our addition to BMSL for specifying event histories, H → cond (section 2.3). If the conclusion of this policy is not satisfied at the point at which a cookie is sent, *any* action which relates to sending an HTTP request which contains cookie data is prevented. The abstract event internet.data.Send(HttpRequest r) relates to the low-level actions that are used to send a cookie, which Polymer monitors. Our policy enforcement model constructs an HttpRequest object when this abstract event is triggered. This abstraction encapsulates the data being sent or received by the untrusted browser.

Cross-Site Cooking: To prevent against Attack 2, one must compare the content of the cookie's path variable to the foremost characters contained within the URL of the page previously loaded. Our additions to BMSL prove useful here: the startsWith operator can compare the start of the URL string which was last loaded by the browser to the content of the cookie's path. The URL's protocol reference (e.g., http://) must be removed from the URL string for this to work.

Policy 3's format is a result of our additions to BMSL and reads as: *"an event(x) such that condition(c) may happen iff an event(y) such that condition(d) has already occurred"*. Here, the invocation of internet.data.Send(HttpRequest r) requires the event internet.data.Open(Url u) to have already occurred. For policies of the form H → cond, cond can itself be a reference to an abstract event, E. This policy clearly indicates how event context is expressed: its conclusion only refers to Open events to a URL which starts with the value of the global variable path, and its premise only refers to Send events which contain an HTTP request that includes a cookie, whose path variable is equal to path. This declarative structure

Policy 3 Policy to defend against cross-site cooking

Policy (English)	*The target may send a cookie to the network only if the URL of the page previously loaded starts with a value equal to the path variable of the cookie being sent.*
Policy format	zone.resource.Action(Object)|cond → zone.resource.Action(Object)|cond
Policy (BMSL)	internet.data.Send(HttpRequest r)|r.hasCookie(path) → internet.data.Open(Url u)|u.startsWith(path);
Policy meaning	Any network send request that contains a cookie may only be sent to the network where the URL of the page previously loaded starts with the path defined by that cookie's **path** variable.
Abstract actions	internet.data.Send(HttpRequest r) internet.data.Open(Url u)
Abstract conditions	r.hasCookie(path) u.contains(path)

enables the user to precisely mitigate program behaviour, ensuring they are not required to specify an event sequence to enforce a policy sanction.

Browser History Monitoring Using Cookies: One can prevent against Attack 3 by refining Policy 3 (specified for Attack 2). Policy 4 shows these revisions, adding an extra condition to the policy's conclusion.

In order to prevent a web-page component sending cookies to a different domain, one must analyse both the URL of the page previously loaded and the path defined by the cookie's **path** variable. Where these two values match the domain to which the **Send** action will send the cookie, program execution can continue. If, however, either of these conditions evaluates to false, then a sequence of recovery actions derived from **cond** at compile-time are invoked. In this case, the **Send** event would be suppressed by raising a Polymer **Suggestion** of type **ExnSug**: the browser's execution would proceed without that cookie being sent.

4.3 Restricting Information Flow

Our model of policy enforcement enables a class of policies to be enforced which prevent malicious programs from leaking sensitive information. We ensure that if an information flow constraint cannot be mitigated, the events which cause it are denied.

Policy 4 Policy to defend against browser history monitoring using cookies

Policy (English)	*The target program may send a cookie to the network only if the URL requesting that cookie starts with that cookie's path variable and contains the URL of the page header previously loaded.*
Policy format	zone.resource.Action(Object)|cond → zone.resource.Action(Object)|cond ∧ cond
Policy (BMSL)	internet.data.Send(HttpRequest r)|r.hasCookie(path) → internet.data.Open(Url u)|u.startsWith(path) ∧ r.contains(u)
Policy meaning	Any network send request that contains a cookie may only be sent to the network where the URL requesting that cookie starts with the path defined by that cookie's **path** variable AND where the URL of the page previously loaded contains the the domain of the site requesting the cookie.
Abstract actions	internet.data.Send(HttpRequest r) internet.data.Open(Url u)
Abstract conditions	r.hasCookie(path), u.contains(path), r.contains(u)

Execution monitoring cannot capture all cases of information flow [12]: full information flow analysis is required to achieve this [10]. The approach reasons about the program's internal structure and whether a trace of variable assignments results in the target program leaking information. The difference between our language and core BMSL [13] when considering information flow is its ability to specify abstract data objects as arguments to abstract events. This provides the monitor with a more fine-grained data representation than core BMSL does.

5 Synthesising Execution Monitors

Our work implements a compiler between BMSL and Polymer. This is designed to operate in a just-in-time manner, allowing users to modify or refine policies whilst the target program is being monitored. They may do this to weaken a policy where it denies some program behaviour they wish to permit, or strengthen it where they learn of some security-relevant vulnerability in the target program. Our extensions to BMSL enable policy refinement in a manageable way: Policy 5 in Section 4.2 gives an example of this.

Our compiler integrates with Polymer as shown in Figure 2. It takes a BMSL policy as input and translates this to output a Polymer `Policy` class. For details of how to translate a BMSL specification to a `Policy` class, and illustrations showing the contents of such a class, please refer to the full version of this paper[4].

5.1 Results

We have tested our compiler and our extensions to BMSL using the examples given in Section 4. BMSL was originally unsuitable for specifying attacks like those described. It could not reason about a program's usage of cookie data, for example, as it monitored events at the system call level where it was not possible specify precisely which event sequence performed such an operation. We have extended BMSL to monitor calls to an API and to express event and data abstractions.

Whereas core BMSL requires one to specify the sequence of actions required to recover from a policy violation, users of our work can simply specify policies declaratively, using conditions which must become true before a triggering event can occur. Our experiments have shown that our compiler can correctly compute suggested recovery actions from these conditions alone.

In order to enforce policies 3, 4, and 5 and to mitigate the attacks we present which use cookies, our policy compiler output 115 lines of Polymer policy code, in three `Policy` classes. Equivalent policies can be expressed in BMSL (with our extensions) using 7 lines of code: a policy name declaration, global variable declarations and three lines of rules – one per attack. These policies are readable and understandable by the non-technical user, who may also construct them given a specification of the commands that can be used for their construction.

---

[4] A full version of this paper is available at:
http://www.cs.bham.ac.uk/~ajb/files/ispec.pdf

Our tests have shown that our policies successfully prevented the attacks we defined. In all cases, program execution was allowed to continue once a policy violation had been dealt with. We tested our work using a network packet sniffer: when monitoring with the policies presented in Section 4.2 we did not see any HTTP requests or responses which contained cookie data where the target program did not adhere to a policy's conditions.

6 Conclusion

Our work provides the basis for a user-operable sandboxing technique in which execution monitors prevent and recover from an untrusted program's invoking of malicious behaviour.

6.1 Summary of Contributions

We have designed a high-level language, a policy enforcement model, and an implementing system that:

- Uses purely declarative constructs to simplify policy specification and make it feasible for end-users without programming knowledge to express policies as direct translations of their own requirements.
- Is more expressive than other policy languages, without requiring imperative constructs.
- Is able to associate atomic program actions and program data into suitable abstractions, such that program behaviour can be specified at a user-comprehensible level. This reduces policy vulnerabilities and redundancies.
- Builds upon Polymer, which is fully implemented execution monitoring scheme in which more powerful execution monitors can be expressed than in previous schemes. Guarantees can be made about Polymer's enforcement of a policy.

6.2 Future Work

Our future work will prove that the policies we compute are at least as strong as the BMSL policies which specified them, when enforced by our model. This proof will enable users to place guarantees in our work, making it suitable for deployment in the domains for which it is intended. We also intend to generalise our work to enforce policies on programs written in languages other than Java: most anti-malware solutions require the ability to monitor programs written in other languages; C/C++, for example.

Our policies currently only reason about the execution of a single program, on a single host. Managers in organisations may wish to specify and enforce a policy on many programs or many hosts simultaneously: to do so they will require an extended policy format in which policies can be composed using meta-policies.

References

1. Bauer, L., Ligatti, J., Walker, D.: More enforceable security policies. In: Cervesato, I. (ed.) Foundations of Computer Security: Proceedings of the FLoC 2002 workshop on Foundations of Computer Security, Copenhagen, Denmark, DIKU Technical Report, July 25–26, pp. 95–104 (2002)
2. Bauer, L., Ligatti, J., Walker, D.: A language and system for composing security policies. Technical Report TR-699-04, Princeton University (January 2004)
3. Bauer, L., Ligatti, J., Walker, D.: Composing security policies with Polymer. In: PLDI 2005: Proceedings of the 2005 ACM SIGPLAN conference on Programming language design and implementation, New York, NY, USA, pp. 305–314. ACM, New York (2005)
4. Dwyer, M.B., Avrunin, G.S., Corbett, J.C.: Patterns in property specifications for finite-state verification. In: ICSE 1999: Proceedings of the 21st international conference on Software engineering, Los Alamitos, CA, USA, pp. 411–420. IEEE Computer Society Press, Los Alamitos (1999)
5. Edjlali, G., Acharya, A., Chaudhary, V.: History-based access-control for mobile code. Technical report, University of California at Santa Barbara, Santa Barbara, CA, USA (1998)
6. Erlingsson, U., Schneider, F.B.: IRM enforcement of Java stack inspection. In: Proceedings of the 2000 IEEE Symposium on Security and Privacy (SP 2000), Washington, DC, USA, p. 246. IEEE Computer Society, Los Alamitos (2000)
7. Evans, D., Twyman, A.: Flexible policy-directed code safety. In: IEEE Symposium on Security and Privacy, pp. 32–45. IEEE Computer Society Press, Los Alamitos (1999)
8. Farmer, D., Venema, W.: Forensic Discovery. Professional Computing Series. Addison-Wesley, Reading (2004)
9. Ligatti, J., Bauer, L., Walker, D.: Edit automata: Enforcement mechanisms for run-time security policies. International Journal of Information Security 4(1–2), 2–16 (2005)
10. Myers, A.C., Liskov, B.: Protecting privacy using the decentralized label model. ACM Transactions on Software Engineering Methodology 9(4), 410–442 (2000)
11. Provos, N.: Improving host security with system call policies. In: Paxson, V. (ed.) Proceedings of 12th USENIX Security Symposium, Washington, DC, USENIX, pp. 128–146 (August 2003)
12. Schneider, F.B.: Enforceable security policies. ACM Trans. Inf. Syst. Secur. 3(1), 30–50 (2000)
13. Sekar, R., Uppuluri, P.: Synthesizing fast intrusion prevention/detection systems from high-level specifications. In: SSYM 1999: Proceedings of the 8th conference on USENIX Security Symposium, Berkeley, CA, USA, p. 6. USENIX Association (1999)

A High-Level Policy Language

policy ::= policy* | name = {policy} | policy[name] | rule | var$_1$; var$_2$; ...; var$_n$; rule;
rule ::= H → R
H ::= pat | pat* | pat$_1$; pat$_2$; ...; pat$_n$ | pat$_1$;; pat$_2$;; ...;; pat$_n$ | pat$_1$ ∨ pat$_2$ ∨ ... ∨ pat$_n$
R ::= E | cond | ⊥
pat ::= E | E$_1$ ∨ E$_2$ ∨ ... ∨ E$_n$ | ¬(E$_1$ ∨ E$_2$ ∨ ... ∨ E$_n$) | E occ
E ::= E* | E(..) | E(O$_1$, O$_2$, ..., O$_n$) | action | zone.resource.action
O ::= O name | O(value$_1$, value$_2$, ..., value$_n$) name
zone ::= $internet$ | lan | $localhost$
resource ::= $data$ | $service$ | $device$
action ::= e(value$_1$, value$_2$, ..., value$_n$)|cond | name
cond ::= ϵ | ¬cond | exp | (exp$_1$ ∨ exp$_2$ ∨ ... ∨ exp$_n$) | (exp$_1$ ∧ exp$_2$ ∧ ... ∧ exp$_n$)
occ ::= ATMOST times | ATLEAST times | MORETHAN times | LESSTHAN times
times ::= n | E
exp ::= var oper var | var oper value
var ::= name := value | name.$const$ | name.action
oper ::= ¬oper | = | := | ∈ | startsWith | endsWith | contains | intersects | returns |...

E : Action | AbstractAction
O : AbstractDataObject
value : char | int | double | float | byte | long | bool | String
name : String
n ∈ ℕ

Fig. 3. BMSL policy language with our additions, expressed in BNF

Mediator-Free Secure Policy Interoperation of Exclusively-Trusted Multiple Domains

Xingang Wang*, Dengguo Feng, Zhen Xu, and Honggang Hu

State Key Laboratory of Information Security,
Institute of Software, Chinese Academy of Sciences
100080 Beijing, China
{wangxg, feng, xu, hghu}@is.iscas.ac.cn

Abstract. The current schemes for security policy interoperation in multi-domain environments are based on a centralized mediator, where the mediator may be a bottleneck for maintaining the policies and mediating cross-domain resource access control. In this paper, we present a mediator-free scheme for secure policy interoperation. In our scheme, policy interoperation is performed by the individual domains, for which, a distributed multi-domain policy model is proposed, and distributed algorithms are given to create such cross-domain policies. Specially, the policies are distributed to each domain, and we ensure that the policies are consistent and each domain keeps the complete policies it shall know.

Keywords: Secure Policy Interoperation, Multi-Domain, RBAC.

1 Introduction

With the rapid development of internet and related technologies, interoperations in multi-domain environments become more and more popular. Interoperations bring feasibility to the resource sharing of domains and thus to their collaboration, but also bring security problems at the same time. One problem is the access control of resources across multiple domains. Access control of resources across multiple domains needs secure interoperation among the interoperating domains, and the point is security policy interoperation.

The existing works [1,12,3,2,10,5,7,14,8] proposed to address security policy interoperation are mainly oriented to control resource sharing with the following characters.

1. It is with a considerable scale. Groups of resources are provided by individual domains, groups of entities belonging to different domains access them, and sometimes some resources such as computing services become entities to access other resources. It is of this state for a considerably long time, such as a collaboration between two or more organizations lasting one year or longer. Besides, it is certain-degree-coupled, which makes entities be able to access resources provided by the domains they belong to in a cross-domain manner. And resources mostly contain data or information.

* Corresponding author.

2. It is in a domain-to-domain way. Each domain decides sharing which resources to which domain or which entities of another domain. This is distinguished from the popular peer-to-peer way in the open distributed environments, where a peer is an entity with some attributes such as age and job — part or all or none of the attributes probably are issued by many domains, and resources sharing is among the entities (the concept of domain is weaken or none) and controlled based on the attributes.
3. It is in relatively closed environments — the domains involved in it are certain at any time.

These existing works are all based on a mediator, where policy interoperation is performed mainly as follows.

- There exists a mediator and a global policy for cross-domain resource access control. The mediator maintains the global policy: first it creates a global policy that maybe violates the security of individual domains, and then it detects and removes security violation.
- The mediator makes or aids in cross-domain resource access decision according to the global policy.

However, the mediator may be a bottleneck for maintaining cross-domain policies and mediating cross-domain resource access control.

We present a mediator-free scheme for secure policy interoperation. Our scheme assumes RBAC policies [4, 6], and policy interoperation is achieved by inter-domain role mapping. Besides, we assume that each domain in the collaboration trust other domains. How to establish or manage trust relationship between or among domains is out of the range of this paper.

In our scheme, there is no such mediator and global policy as in the mediator-based schemes, and policy interoperation is performed only by the individual domains. The details are as follows.

- It is the responsibility of all the domains in the collaboration to create and maintain cross-domain policies. Because there is no more a mediator for policy management, the policies are kept in the domains in a distributed way.
- The cross-domain policies may also violate the security of the domains in the collaboration. Any security violation to any domain can be detected by the domain itself and each domain finding security violation to it inducts a negotiation among domains to remove the security violation.
- Each domain is responsible for making the access decisions when entities from other domains access resources kept in it. Corresponding to this responsibility, the cross-domain policies kept in each domain is complete for the domain to make the decisions. (We will give the precise meaning of "completeness" in Section 3.)

First, we give a multi-domain distributed graph-based policy model for cross-domain policies free of security violation, with each domain maintaining two interoperation policy graphs, which have two characters of consistency (or soundness or being free of violation of individual domains' security) and completeness (each domain keeps the complete policies it shall know) and can be used to make cross-domain resource access decisions. Then we give a distributed algorithm for creating the interoperation policy graphs of each domain.

This paper is organized as follows. In Section 2, we give some necessary preliminaries. We propose our distributed multi-domain policy model in Section 3. We give the distributed algorithms for creating cross-domain policies in Section 4. Section 5 discusses related work. Finally Section 6 concludes this paper.

2 Preliminaries

First, we give the concept of domains and roles[1]:

Definition 1. *D is the set of domains. R is the set of roles. There is a set of roles specific for each domain. A domain is related with any role specific for it through a pair $(r, domain)$, and RD is the set of these pairs. For any role $r \in R$, there exists one and only one domain d such that $(r, d) \in RD$, and d is also denoted by $Domain(r)$.*

In practice, roles are identified by relating domain names (or id) with globally unique role names. Role names can be made globally unique by a common vocabulary.

Each domain maintains a domain policy graph defined as follows.

Definition 2. *Domain Policy Graph. For a domain $domain_n \in D$, $G_n = (V_n, E_n)$ is its policy graph, which is an acyclic directed graph. $V(G_n^D)$ is the set of roles specific for $domain_n$, $V(G_n^D) = \{r | (r, domain_n) \in RD\}$, $E(G_n^D)$ is a set of role pairs (r_1, r_2), where $r_1 \in V(G_n^D)$, $r_2 \in V(G_n^D)$, r_1 is authorized to r_2 (r_1 is a junior role of r_2), and for any $r_i, r_j \in V(G_n)$, if there exists a directed path from r_i to r_j, then r_i is authorized to r_j (r_i is a junior role of r_j).*

We restrict this policy graph as Osborn etc. have done on their role graph model [22]: in any domain policy graph, there exists no redundant edges, i.e. for any domain $domain_i \in D$, and for any two vertices $v_m, v_n \in E(G_i^D)$, if there exists a path with the length greater than 1 from v_m to v_n, then there exists no edge from v_m to v_n. Besides, we give another restriction that for any domain policy graph there exists no self-loop.

The policy interoperation is based on single-directional role mapping. The following is the definition of role map.

Definition 3. *Role map. $Map \subseteq R \times R$ is a set of role maps. A role map is a pair $(role, role)$. The roles in a role map must belong to different domains, i.e. for any role map $(r_1, r_2) \in Map$, there exists $Domain(r_1) \neq Domain(r_2)$. For any role map $(r_1, r_2) \in Map$, if an entity such as a user is authorized to r_2, it is authorized to r_1 too. For any role map $(r_1, r_2) \in Map$, it is a role-link-out of $Domain(r_1)$ to $Domain(r_2)$, and is also a role-link-in of $Domain(r_2)$ from $Domain(r_1)$.*

For domains' autonomy in cross-domain authorization and for simplicity, we assume that each domain can directly create or remove a role map that is from one of its roles to one of the roles of another domain. Given domain policy graphs and role maps between domains, we let each domain maintain an extended domain policy graph as follows.

---

[1] A role is a collection of permissions; the description of permission is omitted here, for such a description is not necessary for presenting our scheme. For further information, refer to [4,6].

Definition 4. *Extended Domain Policy Graph. For each domain $domain_i \in D$, G_i^e is its extended policy graph, which is a directed graph and is extended from G_i^D, and the extension is made by adding the role maps for which $domain_i$ is link-in-domain or link-out-domain as edges to G_i^D. Formally, first let $V(G_i^e) = V(G_i^D)$ and let $E(G_i^e) = E(G_i^D)$, then for any role-link-in (r_1, r_2), let $r_1 \in V(G_i^e)$ and $(r_1, r_2) \in E(G_i^e)$, and for any role-link-out (r_1, r_2), let $r_2 \in V(G_i^e)$ and $(r_1, r_2) \in E(G_i^e)$.*

We model cross-domain authorization as follows.

Definition 5. *Let G denote the union of the extended policy graphs of all the domains. For any two vertices $v_i, v_j \in V(G)$, if there exists a directed path from v_i to v_j, then the entities authorized to v_j are also authorized to v_i.*

Policy interoperation may bring security violation. With respect to the policies our scheme assumes, two kinds of security violation shall be considered.

Violation of Least Privilege. Some domains may adhere to the principle of least privilege strictly; the principle states that an entity should be given only those privileges that it needs in order to complete its task. Policy interoperation may violate this principle to be adhered to in the individual domains involved in the interoperation. In detail, suppose for a $domain_n \in D$, and for $r_i, r_j \in V(G_n^D)$, there exists no directed path from r_i to r_j or from r_j to r_i in G_n^D (r_i and r_j is incomparable in $domain_n$), and there exists a directed path p from r_i to r_j in G. Then r_j is authorized to r_i unnecessarily by policy interoperation.

Role Cycle. If a cycle exists in the policy graph G, security policies of some related domains are violated, with an exception that the cycles with the length of 2 like the following one will not violate any domain's security: $r_i \xrightarrow{(r_i, r_j)} r_j \xrightarrow{(r_j, r_i)} r_i$, $Domain(r_i) \neq Domain(r_j)$. Moreover, the cycles composed of these kinds of cycles do not violate any domain's security either. We assume there is no cycle if there is no interoperation. Then we need not to consider the following case: given a cycle $r_1 \xrightarrow{(r_1, r_2)} r_2 \xrightarrow{(r_2, r_3)} r_3, ..., r_n \xrightarrow{(r_n, r_1)} r_1$, for any $r_i, r_j \in \{r_1, r_2, ..., r_n\}$, there exists $Domain(r_i) = Domain(r_j)$.

In policy interoperation, security violation shall be removed.

Definition 6 (Consistent Policy Interoperation). *We policy interoperation being consistent if G is free of cycle and violation of least privilege principle of the domains adhering to the principle strictly. Such G is denoted by Sec_G.*

3 Multi-domain Distributed Policy Model

The requirements of policy interoperation of domains can be seen as providing policies for controlling cross-domain resource access. In the mediator-based scheme, a global policy like G is created by the mediator and satisfies the requirements. In our scheme, G is not created and maintained physically, and we just let each domain keep the policies related with mediating access of its resources.

Definition 7 (Policy Graph). *Any subgraph of G is a policy graph and we call any subgraph of Sec_G a consistent policy graph.*

Graph algorithms on edge traversal [11] are fundamental for our work. Informally, given a policy graph G' and a vertex v_1 in it,

- by "forward traverse edges in G' from v_1" we mean traversing all the edges for whose start-vertex there is a directed path from v_1 to it;
- by "backward traverse edges in G' from v_1" we mean traversing all the edges for whose end-vertex there is a directed path from it to v_1.

Definition 8 (Interoperation Policy Graph 1). *For any $domain_i \in D$, G_i^{IOP-1} is its Interoperation Policy Graph 1, $V(G_i^{IOP-1})$ is the set of roles, $E(G_i^{IOP-1})$ is the set of role pairs, it consists of all the policy for $domain_i$ to know which inner-domain roles can be accessed by which roles of other domains. Then Interoperation Policy Graph 1 of $domain_i$ shall be equal to the policy graph obtained as follows.*

- *For each role-link-out (r_1, r_2) of $domain_i$ in Sec_G, forward traverse all the edges from r_2 in Sec_G, and backward traverse all the edges from r_1 in G_i^e. Then compose G_i^{IOP-1} of all the traversed edges.*

Definition 9 (Interoperation Policy Graph 2). *For any $domain_i \in D$, G_i^{IOP-2} is its interoperation policy graph 2, $V(G_i^{IOP-2})$ is the set of roles, $E(G_i^{IOP-2})$ is the set of role pairs. $E(G_i^{IOP-2})$ consists of all the policies for $domain_i$ to know which roles of other domains can be accessed by which roles of its own. Interoperation Policy Graph 1 of $domain_i$ shall be equal to the policy graph obtained as follows.*

- *For each role-link-in (r_1, r_2) of $domain_i$ in Sec_G, forward traverse all the edges from r_2 in G_i^e, and backward traverse all the edges from r_1 in Sec_G. Then compose G_i^{IOP-2} of all the traversed edges.*

There are two characters of Interoperation Policy Graphs.

- Consistency. Interoperation Policy graphs are sub policy graphs of Sec_G, so they are consistent — they do not violate the security of individual domains.
- Completeness. For any $domain_m \in D$, if in Sec_G, there exists a directed path from v_i to v_j where $Domain(v_i) = domain_m$ and $Domain(v_j) \neq domain_m$, then there must exist the same path in G_m^{IOP-1}. For any $domain_m \in D$, if in Sec_G, there exists a directed path from v_i to v_j where $Domain(v_j) = domain_m$ and $Domain(v_i) \neq domain_m$, then there must exist the same path in G_m^{IOP-2}. Thus with respect to the authorization effect, for any $domain_m \in D$, G_m^{IOP-1} is the same as Sec_G in making $domain_m$ know which roles of it are authorized to which roles of other domains, and G_m^{IOP-2} is the same as Sec_G in making $domain_m$ know which roles of other domains are authorized to which roles of it.

About Cross-Domain Resource Access Decision. With the presence of interoperation policy graphs, cross-domain resource access can be controlled in the following way. When entities attaching roles in other domains access resources of a domain such as $domain_i \in D$, $domain_i$ can convert the roles attached to the entities into roles of $domain_i$ and make access decision according to the inner-domain roles: Given G_i^{IOP-1} and a role r_1 from another domain, find the vertex r_1 in G_i^{IOP-1}, and find all the paths to this vertex, then convert r_1 into all the roles that are in the found paths and belong to $domain_i$.

4 Creation of Cross-Domain Policies

From our model described in Section 3, the point of policy interoperation is to create and maintain interoperation policy graphs for any domain joining the collaboration. In this section, we describe the protocols or distributed algorithms for creating the policy graphs for all the domains joining the collaboration. Note that G is not maintained physically in our scheme as the global policy in the mediator-based schemes.

As a preparation, we have a definition of active joining.

Definition 10. *For each domain $domain_i \in D$, if it has any role-link-out to any other domain, we call this domain joining the collaboration actively.*

The domains' active joining is dealt with domain by domain — dealing with one domain's active joining is a subprocess. After all of the subprocesses, the initial collaboration among domains is established.

First, each new domain $domain_i$ puts its domain policy graph as the origin of both G_i^{IOP-1} and G_i^{IOP-2}.

For simplicity of description, we call two domains between which there exist role maps as neighbor domains. In the whole process, domains keep sending policy graphs to neighbor domains for updating their interoperation policy graphs. Suppose $domain_n$ is a neighbor domain of $domain_m$, we use G_{m-n}^{IOP-1} to denote the policies sent by $domain_m$ to $domain_n$ for updating G_n^{IOP-1}, and G_{m-n}^{IOP-2} for updating G_n^{IOP-2}.

The process of dealing with the active joining of one domain such as $domain_i \in D$ is as follows.

1. For each $domain_j$ of its neighbor domains, $domain_i$ sends a message msg_{i-j} to $domain_j$ for G_{j-i}^{IOP-1} and G_{j-i}^{IOP-2}. msg_{i-j} is with the role-link-outs from $domain_i$ to $domain_j$.
2. Each $domain_j$ of the domains receiving msg_{i-j} computes G_{j-i}^{IOP-1} (as in Procedure 1.1) and sends them to $domain_i$ by a reply message msg_{i-j}^r.
3. After $domain_i$ receives all the reply messages, it updates its interoperation policy graph 1 G_i^{IOP-1} as the union of G_i^{IOP-1} and all the received policy graphs.
4. For each $domain_j$ of its neighbor domains, $domain_i$ computes G_{i-j}^{IOP-1} and G_{i-j}^{IOP-2} (as in Procedure 1.2), and sends them to $domain_j$.
5. Each $domain_j$ of the neighbor domains updates its interoperation policy graphs: compose a new and maybe insecure G_j^{IOP-1}/G_j^{IOP-2} of the original G_j^{IOP-1}/G_j^{IOP-2} and $G_{i-j}^{IOP-1}/G_{i-j}^{IOP-2}$ (by computing the union of them).

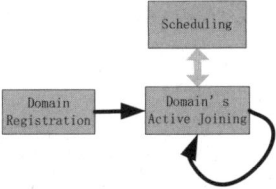

Fig. 1. Creation of Cross-Domain Policies

6. Each domain updating its interoperation policy graphs detects security violation to it. (This will be described in Subsection 4.1.)
7. Each domain whose security is violated inducts a negotiation among domains to remove the security violation to it. (This will be described in Subsection 4.1.)

Procedure 1 *Procedures for Local Algorithms in Creation of Cross-Domain Policies*
1. *Compute_Requested_Policies*
   Input *Role_Link_In, the set of role-link-ins from $domain_i$; G_j^{IOP-1}; G_j^{IOP-2}*
   Output G_{j-i}^{IOP-1}
   Variable G_1, *a policy graph*
   a. $G_1 = G_j^{IOP-1} \cup G_j^{IOP-2}$
   b. *For each role-link-in $(r_1, r_2) \in Role\_Link\_In$*
      $Forward\_Traverse(G_{j-i}^{IOP-1}, v_2, G_1)$
2. *Compute_Neighbor–Needed_Policies*
   Input G_i^{IOP-1}
   Output G_{i-j}^{IOP-1} *and* G_{i-j}^{IOP-2}
   a. *Let* $V(G_{i-j}^{IOP-1}) = \emptyset$ *and* $E(G_{i-j}^{IOP-1}) = \emptyset$
   b. *Let* $V(G_{i-j}^{IOP-2}) = \emptyset$ *and* $E(G_{i-j}^{IOP-2}) = \emptyset$
   c. *For each role-link-out (r_1, r_2) of $domain_j$ in G_i^{IOP-1},*
      $Forward\_Traverse(G_i^{IOP-1}, r_2, G_{i-j}^{IOP-1})$
   d. *For each role-link-in (r_1, r_2) of $domain_j$ in G_i^{IOP-1},*
      $Backward\_Traverse(G_i^{IOP-2}, r_1, G_{i-j}^{IOP-2})$
3. *Subroutine $Forward\_Traverse(G_1, v_1, G_2)$*
   Input G_1, G_2: *policy graphs; v_1, a vertex in G_1.*
   a. *For each vertex $v \in V(G_1)$, mark v unvisited.*
   b. *$forward\_traverse(v_1)$.*
   c. *Procedure $forward\_traverse(v)$*
      For each edge $(v, v') \in E(G_1)$,
         if v' is marked unvisited,
            let $v' \in V(G_2)$ and $(v, v') \in E(G_2)$, mark v' visited,
            and $forward\_traverse(v')$.
4. *Subroutine $Backward\_Traverse(G_1, v_1, G_2)$*
   Input G_1, G_2: *policy graphs; v_1, a vertex in G_1.*
   a. *For each vertex $v \in V(G_1)$, mark v unvisited.*
   b. *$backward\_traverse(v_1)$.*
   c. *Procedure $backward\_traverse(v)$*
      For each edge $(v, v') \in E(G_1)$,
         if v' is unvisited,
            let $v' \in V(G_2)$ and $(v, v') \in E(G_2)$, mark v' visited,
            and $backward\_traverse(v')$.

Next we give the algorithms or protocols used in the above algorithm to detect and remove security violation, i.e. the algorithms or protocols used to make cross-domain policies consistent.

4.1 Detecting and Removing Security Violation

In the mediator-based scheme, a global policy like G is held by the mediator. Then the mediator can detect role cycles and induct a negotiation among domains to break them, and detect violation of least privilege principle with respect to some domains, thus making policies free of role cycle and making certain domains strictly adhering to the principle of least privilege. In our scheme, although the authorization effects of G does exist — the effects of interoperation policy graphs, G does not physically exist and is not held by a certain site. Then we have a lemma aiding in security violation detection and removal in our scheme.

As a preparation, recall that the domain policy graph of each of the domains to join the collaboration is the origin of its two interoperation policy graphs. According to our assumption, the domain policy graphs are consistent; then before domains' active joining is dealt with, there exists no security violation. The lemma is as follows.

Lemma 1. *In dealing with each of the active joining, such as $domain_i$'s active joining, assume that there exists no security violation before dealing with it. Then,*

- *after the neighbor domains of $domain_i$ update their two interoperation policy graphs, for each $domain_j$ of them, the union of G_j^{IOP-1} and G_j^{IOP-1} includes all the policies for detecting if $domain_i$'s active joining brings any role cycle to violate $domain_j$'s security, and includes all the policies for detecting if $domain_i$'s active joining brings violation of least privilege principle with respect to $domain_j$.*

Thus, with respect to each active joining, each of the neighbor domains can finds all the security violation to itself. Then all the security violation brought by each active joining can be found. If all the security violation is removed, the domains establish consistent secure interoperation after the process of creation of cross-domain policies.

4.1.1 Detecting Security Violation

According to the above analysis, detection of role cycle can be performed by the domain joining the collaboration actively. Detection of violation of the least privilege principle of each of the related domains can be performed by the domain itself.

An algorithm was given for finding out all the simple cycles in a finite directed graph in [15]. We use this algorithm for each of the domains joining the collaboration actively to find simple cycles in the union of its updated interoperation policy graphs. Cycles are composed of simple cycles. If all the simple cycles (except the cycles with the length of 2) in the global policy graph are found and broken, then there are no cycles (except the cycles with the length of 2) any more. In the remainder of this paper the term "cycle", when not otherwise modified, will be used only to refer to simple cycles with the length greater than 2.

At the same time of detecting and breaking role cycles, detection and removal of violation of least privilege principle are performed. Suppose one domain $domain_i$ needs to adhere to the least privilege principle. Then violation of this principle to $domain_i$ can be detected by the following algorithm.

1. Compute all the vertex pairs from $V(G_i^D)$ where between the two vertices there exist no directed paths in G_i^D.

2. For each vertex pair r_p, r_q obtained above, find all the simple directed paths from r_p to r_q in the union of the two interoperation policy graphs of $domain_i$ if there exists no directed path from r_q to r_p in the union, or find all the simple directed paths from r_q to r_p in the union if there exists no directed path from r_p to r_q in it. If there exists any path found, the path brings violation of least privilege to $domain_i$.

Furthermore, the paths causing the security violation are included in a sub policy graph of the union; this graph is acquired by deleting all the vertices that are not connected to any link-out-point or to which no link-in-point is connected to from the union. Moreover, the vertex pairs needed to be considered can be further restricted to the pairs that are in this sub policy graph and satisfy: between one of the two vertices and one of the link-in-points (or link-out-points) there exists a directed path and the other one of the two vertices is connected to one of the link-in-points.

An algorithm presented by Kleene for solving general path problems [23] can compute all the paths between any two vertices in a direct graph in polynomial time. We apply this algorithm to find the simple paths in the above algorithm.

Besides, an algorithm with a worst-case time complexity of $O(m)$ can be created to find whether there exists a directed path between two vertices in a finite directed graph.

4.1.2 Removing Security Violation by Concurrent Negotiation

After security violation detection, cycles or simple path(s) will be found if there exists indeed secure violation. To remove the violations, all the cycles and paths shall be broken, i.e. one edge in each of them shall be removed.

We present a concurrent negotiation protocol to break the cycles and paths. With respect to the role cycles, the domain finding them inducts the negotiation among the domains related with the cycles, deciding the edge(s) to remove. Similarly, with respect to each of the paths, the domain finding it inducts a negotiation among all the domains related with the path, and decides the edge(s) to remove. All the negotiations are performed in a concurrent way.

Obviously, it does not further bring role cycle to remove any edge. If role pairs in domain policy graphs are removed, this may violate the least privilege principle of the domain removing the inheritance pairs, and can only bring this violation. For simplicity the removed edges are only the ones whose removal does not cause violation of the least privilege principle with respect to the related domains strictly adhering to it.

The following is the negotiation protocol.

There are six kinds of messages: $Msg_{induction-1}$, for a domain whose security is violated to induct a negotiation among domains to remove security violation for the first time; $Msg_{induction-2}$, for a domain whose security is violated to induct a negotiation for the second time — this is because the negotiation process it inducted for the first time cannot remove the security violation to it; $Msg_{induction-1-reply}$ and $Msg_{induction-2-reply}$, the reply messages of $Msg_{induction-1}$ and $Msg_{induction-2}$ respectively, attaching the edges which domains volunteer to remove; $Msg_{negotiaiton-end}$, for domains which have inducted a negotiation to inform the related domains of this negotiation being ended and of the edge(s) to be removed; $Msg_{Edge\_Removed}$, it is for a domain volunteering to remove edge(s) to inform related domains that they shall update their policy graphs, and this is after the domain inducting the negotiation informs it that the edge(s) is indeed selected to remove, and this message is with the edges removed.

For each $domain_n$ of the domains whose security is violated, it starts its actions as follows.

- If no message received, it decides if the security violation can be removed by just removing one or more edges from its policy graph. If so, it sends a message of the kind $Msg_{Edge\_Removed}$ to each of the domains needing to update its policies ($domain_n$ can decide the domains by only its interoperation policy graphs as in Procedure 2); otherwise, it acts as follows.
  1. It sends a message of the kind $Msg_{induction-1}$ to each of the related domains one or more of whose edges are in the path(s) or cycle(s).
  2. It waits for messages of the kind $Msg_{induction-1-reply}$, and waits for messages of the kind $Msg_{Edge\_Removed}$ from other negotiation(s).
- Otherwise, if one or more messages of the kind $Msg_{Edge\_Removed}$ has been received from other domains, it finds if the edges removed in the messages plus the edges it decides to remove from its domain policy graph are enough for removing the security violation it found. If so, it updates its interoperation policy graphs according to the removed edges (removing the edges in the policy graphs) and sends a message $Msg_{Edge\_Removed}$ to each of the domains needing to update policies with the edges it removed from its policy graphs. Otherwise, it acts as in Sub Item 1 and Sub Item 2 of the last item.

For each of the domains whose security is violated, after its sending messages of the kind of $Msg_{induction-1}$, it follows the following actions upon different kinds of messages.

- Upon one or more messages of the kind of $Msg_{Edge\_Removed}$ from other negotiation(s) received, it checks if all the edges informed of their removal by these received messages and all the received messages of the kind $Msg_{induction-1-reply}$ are enough for removing violation of its security. If so, it sends a message of the kind $Msg_{negotiation\_end}$ to each domain in the negotiation it inducted. Then it updates its interoperation policy graphs according to the removed edges. Otherwise,
  • if there already exist replying messages from part of the other domains in the negotiation, which is with the edges the replying domains volunteer to remove, then it checks if all these edges plus the edges just referred are enough for removing violation of its security. If so, it sends a message of the kind $Msg_{negotiation\_end}$ to each domain in the negotiation it inducted, with the edges selected from the ones in the replying messages to remove. Otherwise, it waits for the messages from the domains whose replying messages are not received yet, and for the messages of the kind of $Msg_{Edge\_Removed}$ from other negotiations.
  • if replying messages from all the other domains in the negotiation have been received, then it checks if all these edges plus the edges just referred are enough for removing violation of its security. If so, it sends a message of the kind $Msg_{negotiation\_end}$ to each domain in the negotiation it inducted, with the edges selected from the ones in the replying messages to remove. Otherwise, it

sends a message of the kind $Msg_{induction-2}$ to the domains in the negotiation, with the paths and cycles not yet broken.
- Upon one or more messages of the kind $Msg_{induction-1-reply}$ received, it checks if all the edges informed of their removal by these received messages and the received messages $Msg_{Edge\_Removed}$ are enough for removing violation of its security. If so, it sends a message of the kind $Msg_{negotiation\_end}$ to each domain in the negotiation it inducted. Then it updates its interoperation policy graphs according to the removed edges. Otherwise, it acts following the actions in the first or the second sub item of the above item.

For each $domain_n$ of the domains whose security is violated, after its sending messages of the kind of $Msg_{induction-2}$, it follows the following actions upon different kinds of messages.

- Upon one or more messages of the kind $Msg_{induction-2-reply}$ received, it checks if all the edges in the received messages plus the edges in the received messages of the kind $Msg_{Edge\_Removed}$ are enough for removing violation of its security. And if so, it selects the edges to remove, and sends a message of the kind $Msg_{negotiation\_end}$ to each of the domains in the negotiation, with the edges attached in the messages. Otherwise,
    - if messages of the kind $Msg_{induction-2-reply}$ from all the domains in the negotiation have been received, it removes a role-link-out to ensure its security.
    - otherwise, it waits for messages of the kind $Msg_{induction-1-reply}$, and waits for messages of the kind $Msg_{Edge\_Removed}$ from other negotiation(s).
- Upon one or more messages of the kind $Msg_{Edge\_Removed}$ received, it checks if all the edges in all the received messages (including those received before) plus the edges in the replying messages are enough for removing violation of its security. And if so, it selects the edges to remove, and sends a message of the kind $Msg_{negotiation\_end}$ to each of the domains in the negotiation, with the edges attached in the messages. Otherwise, it waits for messages of the kind $Msg_{induction-1-reply}$, and waits for messages of the kind $Msg_{Edge\_Removed}$ from other negotiation(s).

For each $domain_n$ of the domains receiving a message of the kind $Msg_{induciton-1}$ or $Msg_{induction-2}$ from a domain $domain_m$, it selects the edges to remove from G_i^e (excluding role-link-ins) and sends them to $domain_m$. The set of the edges can be null.

For each $domain_n$ of the domains receiving a message $Msg_{induction-end}$ from $domain_m$, it follows the following actions. If this message is received before it sends the replying message $Msg_{induction-1-reply}$ or $Msg_{induction-2-reply}$ in the negotiation, it ends dealing with the message $Msg_{induciton-1}$ or $Msg_{induction-2}$. Otherwise,

1. it updates its interoperation policy graphs according to the removed edges.
2. if there exists edge(s) in G_n^e to be removed, then it finds the related domains needing to update their policy graphs according to the removed edges and sends a message $Msg_{Edge\_Removed}$ with the removed edges to the domains.

For each $domain_n$ of the domains receiving a message of the kind $Msg_{Edge\_Removed}$, if this domain has inducted one or more negotiations, the actions it shall follow have been given above; otherwise it just updates its interoperation policy graphs according to the removed edges.

Procedure 2 *Domains_Related_with_Edge_Removal*
Input G_n^{IOP-1} and G_n^{IOP-2}, *temporarily insecure Interoperation policy graphs of $domain_n$; edges_removed, set of edges removed by $domain_n$; D', set of the domains which $domain_n$ knows — roles of the domains are in the policy graphs of $domain_n$.*
Var G_1 and G_2, *policy graphs.*
Output D_1, *set of the domains needing to update their interoperation policy graphs because of edge removal; Edges_Removed$_{1'}$, Edges_Removed$_{2'}$, ... , Edges_Removed$_{|D_1|'}$, sets of edges to be removed from view policy graphs of domains (in D_1) $domain_{1'}$, $domain_{2'}$,..., $domain_{|D_1|'}$ respectively as a result of edges removal.*
1. If $edges\_removed \neq \emptyset$,
 (a). Let $G_1 = G_n^{IOP-1} \cup G_n^{IOP-1}$
 (b). For each $(r_i, r_j) \in edges\_removed$,
  A. let $V(G_2) = \emptyset$ and $E(G_2) = \emptyset$
  B. $Forward\_Traverse(G^g, r_j, G_1)$ and $Backward\_Traverse(G^g, r_i, G_1)$,
  C. let $r_i, r_j \in V(G_1)$ and $(r_i, r_j) \in E(G_1)$.
  D. For each $domain_m \in D'$,
   for each vertex $v \in V(G_1)$
    if $Domain(v) = domain_m$,
    let $(r_i, r_j) \in Edges\_Removed_m$ and let $domain_m \in D_1$
    break;

Besides, when a role pair in the domain policy graphs is removed and part of the authorization effects of the corresponding edge shall be kept, some edge(s) can be added without any security violation. For this, we have the following lemma.

Lemma 2. *Suppose an edge (r_1, r_2) is added, and (r_1, r_2) is in the transition closure of the former secure domain policy graph (before dealing with this active joining). Then adding (r_1, r_2) will bring no security violation.*

4.2 Remarks

We have the following claim about our distributed algorithms for creating cross-domain policies.

Claim. By our distributed algorithms for creating cross-domain policies, the interoperation policy graphs are got, with two characters: consistency and completeness.

We do not give its proof here, because it is trivial.

Assume that n domains join the collaboration, then the worst communication complexity of the distributed algorithm for the process of creating cross-domain policies is $O(n^3)$. The following is a detailed description. Each domain has role-link-outs to at most $n-1$ domains; so for each domain, it sends messages for policies to at most $n-1$ different domains. In the dealing with each domain's active joining, each domain's security may be violated in the worst case, and each of these domains inducts a negotiation that maybe involves all the other $n-1$ domains — sends and receives messages from $n-1$ domains for a constant number of times.

5 Related Works

There are many works dealing with security interoperation in a way that a third party or a centralized mediator creates or maintains cross-domain policies. De Capitani di Vimercati, Samarati, Dawson, et al. gave a series of works [3, 10, 2] on authorization and access control in federated systems — a collection of cooperating database systems or information systems. They presented many issues and ideas for access control or authorization in federated systems, especially presented a modeling and architectural solution to the problem of providing security and interoperation of heterogeneous systems based on the use of wrappers and a mediator. Gong and Qian [1] studied the complexity of secure interoperation of multiple domains employing access control lists. Bonatti, Sapino and Subrahmanian [12] presented efficient approaches to merging multiple heterogeneous security orderings. The above works all did not consider RBAC policies. There are also some other works (of mediator-based security interoperation) assuming RBAC policies. Pan, Mitra and Liu [14]presented semantic interoperation of RBAC policies. Du and Joshi [7] analyzed hybrid RBAC in the interoperation. Smithi and Joshi [8] introduced time into the interoperation of RBAC policies. Basit, et al. [5] proposed a policy integration framework for merging heterogeneous RBAC policies of multiple domains into a global policy.

Shehab, Bertino and Ghafoor [9, 17] presented a decentralized scheme for cross-domain resource access control. They presented the idea of secure access path. A set of role maps between the domains are maintained, and the role map in the access path must be selected from the set. The set cannot ensure security of domains, i.e. there is no security analysis on this set. Users can ask for single access paths, and after evaluation according to some rules, they can get a single secure access path, by which he can access some resources. However, single secure path cannot achieve the scale of the cross-domain policies needed by secure interoperation. Their scheme is not qualified for secure interoperation of multiple domains, and is just for cross-domain resource access control of small-scale. Moreover, there still exists a problem in their scheme, i.e. the composition of multiple single secure paths may be insecure (A secure path forms upon a path request), and this composition is possible.

Moreover, there are many works [16, 13, 19, 20, 21, 18] presenting credential-based access control schemes for distributed environments. In these works, service providers can issue credentials telling which entities or principals with which name, with which properties or with which attributes can access which services they provide. These works are most intended to perform authorization and access control in loose-coupled multi-domain environments or open environments, where the scale of cross-domain policies between any two domains is small and the concept of domain is weak or even none (peer to peer). Besides, violation of security policies of individual domains are more oriented to be less considered in these works.

6 Conclusion

In this paper we deal with secure policy interoperation of multiple domains without a centralized mediator. In our scheme, cross-domain policies are created and maintained by the individual domains; access decision for cross-domain resource access can be made in individual domains locally. Thus, our scheme is more appropriate for large-scale secure interoperation than the mediator-based schemes, where the mediator may be a bottleneck, and suitable for the situation where domains cannot get a centralized mediator. Besides, in secure interoperation of multiple domains, there are three cases of policy evolutions [5]: evolution of collaborating domains' access control policies, addition of new domains in the collaborative system and removal of domains from collaborations. We have a gradual policy evolution scheme and will present it in another paper.

References

1. Gong, L., Qian, X.: Computational Issues in Secure Interoperation. IEEE Trans. Software Eng. 22(1) (January 1996)
2. De Capitani di Vimercati, S., Samarati, P.: Authorization specification and enforcement in federated database systems. Journal of Computer Security 5(2), 155–188 (1997)
3. Dawson, S., Qian, S., Samarati, P.: Providing Security and Interoperation of Heterogeneous Systems. Distrib. Parallel Databases 8(1), 119–145 (2000)
4. Sandhu, R.S., et al.: Role-Based Access Control Models. IEEE Computer 29(2), 38–47 (1996)
5. Shafiq, B., Joshi, J.B.D., Bertino, E., Ghafoor, A.: Secure Interoperation in a Multidomain Environment Employing RBAC Policies. IEEE Transactions on Knowledge and Data Engineering 17(11), 1557–1577 (2005)
6. Ferraiolo, D.F., Kuhn, D.R., Chandramouli, R.: Role-Based Access Control. Artech House, Inc., Norwood, MA (2003)
7. Du, S., Joshi, J.B.: Supporting authorization query and inter-domain role mapping in presence of hybrid role hierarchy. In: Proceedings of the Eleventh ACM Symposium on Access Control Models and Technologies, SACMAT 2006, Lake Tahoe, California, USA, June 07–09, pp. 228–236. ACM Press, New York (2006)
8. Piromruen, S., Joshi, J.B.D.: An RBAC Frame-work for Time Constrained Secure Interoperation in Multi-domain Environments. In: Proceedings of the 10th IEEE International Workshop on Object-Oriented Real-Time Dependable Systems, February 02–04, pp. 36–48 (2005)
9. Shehab, M., Bertino, E., Ghafoor, A.: SERAT: SEcure role mApping technique for decentralized secure interoperability. In: Proceedings of the Tenth ACM Symposium on Access Control Models and Technologies, SACMAT 2005, Stock-holm, Sweden, June 01–03, 2005, pp. 159–167. ACM Press, New York (2005)
10. De Capitani di Vimercati, S., Samarati, P.: Access control in federated systems. In: Proceedings of the 1996 Workshop on New Security Paradigms, NSPW 1996, Lake Arrowhead, California, United States, September 17–20, 1996, pp. 87–99. ACM Press, New York (1996)
11. Corman, T.H., Leiserson, C.E., Rivest, R.L.: Introduction to Algorithms, pp. 525–700. The MIT Press, Cambridge (1990)
12. Bonatti, P.A., Sapino, M.L., Subrahmanian, V.S.: Merging heterogenous security orderings. J. Comput. Secur. 5(1), 3–29 (1997)
13. Herzberg, A., Mass, Y.: Relying Party Credentials Framework. Electronic Commerce Research 4(1–2), 23–39 (2004)
14. Pan, C., Mitra, P., Liu, P.: Semantic access control for information interoperation. In: Proceedings of the Eleventh ACM Symposium on Access Control Models and Technologies, SACMAT 2006, Lake Tahoe, California, USA, June 07-09, 2006, pp. 237–246. ACM Press, New York (2006)

15. Weinblatt, H.: A New Search Algorithm for Finding the Simple Cycles of a Finite Directed Graph. J. ACM 19(1), 43–56 (1972)
16. Ellison, C., Frantz, B., Lampson, B., Rivest, R., Thomas, B., Ylonen, T.: SPKI Certificate Theory. IETF RFC 2693 (September 1999)
17. Shehab, M., Bertino, E., Ghafoor, A.: Secure collaboration in mediator-free environments. In: Proceedings of the 12th ACM Conference on Computer and Communications Security, CCS 2005, Alexandria, VA, USA, November 07–11, 2005, pp. 58–67. ACM Press, New York (2005)
18. Chaum, D.: Security without identification: transaction systems to make big brother obsolete. Commun. ACM 28(10), 1030–1044 (1985)
19. Li, N., Mitchell, J.C., Winsborough, W.H.: Design of a Role-Based Trust-Management Framework. In: Proceedings of the 2002 IEEE Symposium on Security and Privacy, Washington, DC, May 12 - 15, 2002, SP, p. 114. IEEE Computer Society, Los Alamitos (2002)
20. Biskup, J., Wortmann, S.: Towards a credential-based implementation of compound access control policies. In: Proceedings of the Ninth ACM Symposium on Access Control Models and Technologies, SACMAT 2004, Yorktown Heights, New York, USA, June 02–04, 2004, pp. 31–40. ACM, New York (2004)
21. Yu, T., Winslett, M., Seamons, K.E.: Supporting structured credentials and sensitive policies through interoperable strategies for automated trust negotiation. ACM Trans. Inf. Syst. Secur. 6(1), 1–42 (2003)
22. Nyanchama, M., Osborn, S.: The role graph model and conflict of interest. ACM Trans. Inf. Syst. Secur. 2(1), 3–33 (1999)
23. Mehlhorn, K.: Data structures and Algorithms 2: Graph algorithms and NP-Completeness, pp. 133–139. Springer, Heidelberg (1984)

Privacy of Recent RFID Authentication Protocols

Khaled Ouafi[1] and Raphael C.-W. Phan[2],*

[1] Laboratoire de sécurité et de cryptographie (LASEC),
Ecole Polytechnique Fédérale de Lausanne (EPFL), CH-1015, Switzerland
khaled.ouafi@epfl.ch
[2] Electronic & Electrical Engineering,
Loughborough University, LE11 3TU, Leics, United Kingdom
r.phan@lboro.ac.uk

Abstract. Privacy is a major concern in RFID systems, especially with widespread deployment of wireless-enabled interconnected personal devices e.g. PDAs and mobile phones, credit cards, e-passports, even clothing and tires. An RFID authentication protocol should not only allow a legitimate reader to authenticate a tag but it should also protect the privacy of the tag against unauthorized tracing: an adversary should not be able to get any useful information about the tag for tracking or discovering the tag's identity. In this paper, we analyze the privacy of some recently proposed RFID authentication protocols (2006 and 2007) and show attacks on them that compromise their privacy. Our attacks consider the simplest adversaries that do not corrupt nor open the tags. We describe our attacks against a general untraceability model; from experience we view this endeavour as a good practice to keep in mind when designing and analyzing security protocols.

Keywords: RFID, authentication protocols, privacy, untraceability, provably secure.

1 Introduction

RFIDs are widely used in inventory control and supply chain management [1,7,18,19,25], in e-passports [12,6,11,15,20] e.g. for US' visa waiver policies, in contactless credit cards [10]. Thus the daily dealings of the present day individual is in fact a wireless interconnected network involving interactions both within his connected personal area network (PAN) among the things carried in his bag or pocket, and between the PAN and the servers providing the services and connectivitiy to those things. Among the things that the individual is carrying on him would include those that are RFID enabled i.e. items he bought from a retail chain, the credit cards in his wallet that he uses to purchase the items, and his e-passport to identify himself to authorities.

---

* Work done while the author was with LASEC, EPFL.

Privacy, both in terms of tag *anonymity* and tag *untraceability* (or unlinkability), is a significant concern that needs to be addressed if RFIDs are to be as widely deployed as conceived by proponents. To date, a rigorous treatment of privacy for RFID models is still being developed, notably the work of Avoine [2], Juels and Weis [13], Le, Burmester and de Medeiros [16]; and Vaudenay [27,28]. These models differ mainly in their treatment of the adversary's ability to corrupt tags. In fact, the recent privacy models [13,27,16,28] define privacy in the untraceability sense. This is intuitive since untraceabile privacy (UPriv) is a strictly stronger notion (i.e. it implies) than anonymous privacy (APriv). To see this, note that if there exists an adversary breaking APriv then he can easily also break UPriv; while the converse is not necessarily true.

In this paper, we analyze the privacy issues of recently (in 2006 and 2007) proposed RFID protocols, namely [8,14,24,4,9]. Our attacks do not even need the strong requirement of corrupting tags [26,13,27,17,16,28,22]. To the best of our knowledge, attacks presented here are the first known analyses of ProbIP [8], MARP [14], Auth2 [24], YA-TRAP+ [4], O-TRAP [4] and RIPP-FS [9].

2 RFID Privacy Models

We describe for completeness, the general untraceable privacy (UPriv) model that will be the setting in which we use in later sections to demonstrate how to trace tags and thus show that the schemes do not achieve the notion of untraceable privacy. It is also good practice to design and analyze security protocols with reference to a clearly-defined model [23].

We do not claim to define a new model, for our emphasis in this paper is instead on the analysis of the privacy and security issues of recent RFID protocols. In fact, the model defined herein can be seen as an alternative definition of the Juels-Weis model [13] with some differences e.g. in constraints put on the adversary (see the discussion in section 6.1) in a style that is more in line with the Bellare et al. [3] models for authenticated key exchange (AKE) protocols, for which RFID protocols have close relationship with.

A protocol party is a $\mathcal{T} \in Tags$ or $\mathcal{R} \in Readers$ interacting in protocol sessions as per the protocol specifications until the end of the session upon which each party outputs Accept if it feels the protocol has been normally executed with the correct parties. Adversary $\mathcal{A}$ controls the communications between all protocol parties (tag and reader) by interacting with them as defined by the protocol, formally captured by $\mathcal{A}$'s ability to issue queries of the following form:

Execute($\mathcal{R}, \mathcal{T}, i$) **query.** This models *passive* attacks, where adversary $\mathcal{A}$ gets access to an honest execution of the protocol session i between $\mathcal{R}$ and $\mathcal{T}$ by eavesdropping.

Send(U_1, U_2, i, m) **query.** This query models *active* attacks by allowing the adversary $\mathcal{A}$ to impersonate some reader $U_1 \in Readers$ (resp. tag $U_1 \in Tags$) in some protocol session i and send a message m of its choice to an instance of some tag $U_2 \in Tags$ (resp. reader $U_2 \in Readers$). This query subsumes the

TagInit and ReaderInit queries as well as challenge and response messages in the Juels-Weis model.

Corrupt$(\mathcal{T}, K)$ **query.** This query allows the adversary $\mathcal{A}$ to learn the stored secret K' of the tag $\mathcal{T} \in Tags$, and which further sets the stored secret to K. It captures the notion of *forward security* or *forward privacy* and the extent of the damage caused by the compromise of the tag's stored secret. This is the analog of the SetKey query of the Juels-Weis model.

Test$_{\text{UPriv}}(U, i)$ **query.** This query is the only query that does not correspond to any of $\mathcal{A}$'s abilities or any real-world event. This query allows to define the indistinguishability-based notion of *untraceable privacy* (UPriv). If the party has accepted and is being asked a Test query, then depending on a randomly chosen bit $b \in \{0, 1\}$, $\mathcal{A}$ is given $\mathcal{T}_b$ from the set $\{\mathcal{T}_0, \mathcal{T}_1\}$. Informally, $\mathcal{A}$ succeeds if it can guess the bit b. In order for the notion to be meaningful, a Test session must be *fresh* in the sense of Definition 2.

Definition 1 (Partnership & Session Completion). *A reader instance $\mathcal{R}_j$ and a tag instance $\mathcal{T}_i$ are partners if, and only if, both have output Accept$(\mathcal{T}_i)$ and Accept$(\mathcal{R}_j)$ respectively, signifying the completion of the protocol session.*

Definition 2 (Freshness). *A party instance is fresh at the end of execution if, and only if,*

1. *it has output Accept with or without a partner instance,*
2. *both the instance and its partner instance (if such a partner exists) have not been sent a Corrupt query.*

Definition 3 (Untraceable Privacy (UPriv)). *Untraceable privacy (UPriv) is defined using the game $\mathcal{G}$ played between a malicious adversary $\mathcal{A}$ and a collection of reader and tag instances. $\mathcal{A}$ runs the game $\mathcal{G}$ whose setting is as follows.*

Phase 1 (Learning): $\mathcal{A}$ is able to send any Execute, Send, and Corrupt queries at will.

Phase 2 (Challenge)
1. At some point during $\mathcal{G}$, $\mathcal{A}$ will choose a fresh session on which to be tested and send a Test query corresponding to the test session. Note that the test session chosen must be fresh in the sense of Definition 2. Depending on a randomly chosen bit $b \in \{0, 1\}$, $\mathcal{A}$ is given a tag $\mathcal{T}_b$ from the set $\{\mathcal{T}_0, \mathcal{T}_1\}$.
2. $\mathcal{A}$ continues making any Execute, Send, and Corrupt queries at will, subjected to the restrictions that the definition of freshness described in Definition 2 is not violated.

Phase 3 (Guess): Eventually, $\mathcal{A}$ terminates the game simulation and outputs a bit b', which is its guess of the value of b.

The success of $\mathcal{A}$ in winning $\mathcal{G}$ and thus breaking the notion of UPriv is quantified in terms of $\mathcal{A}$'s advantage in distinguishing whether $\mathcal{A}$ received $\mathcal{T}_0$ or $\mathcal{T}_1$, i.e. it correctly guessing b. This is denoted by $\text{Adv}_{\mathcal{A}}^{\text{UPriv}}(k)$ where k is the security parameter.

It remains to remark on the models other than Juels-Weis, namely the Le-Burmester-de Medeiros (LBdM) model and the Vaudenay model. The LBdM model similarly allows the corruption of tags. Nevertheless, proof of security is in the universal composability (UC) model [5].

The Vaudenay model [27,28] is stronger than both the Juels-Weis and Le-Burmester-de Medeiros models in terms of the adversary's corruption ability. In more detail, it is stronger than the Juels-Weis model in the sense that it allows corruption even of the two tags used in the challenge phase. It is stronger than the Le-Burmester-de Medeiros model in the sense that it considers all its privacy notions even for corrupted tags, in contrast to the Le-Burmester-de Medeiros model that only considers corruption for its forward privacy notion.

Our choice to describe our tracing attacks in later sections with reference to a defined model is for more uniformity between similar attacks on different RFID protocols, and for better clarity to illustrate how an adversary can circumvent the protocols using precise types of interactions that he exploits, as captured by his oracle queries. This will facilitate the task of a designer when an attempt is made to redesign an attacked protocol.

3 ProbIP

At RFIDSec '07, Castellucia and Soos [8] proposed an RFID protocol (ProbIP) that allows tag identification by legitimate readers. Its security is based on the SAT problem, which is proven to be in the $\mathcal{NP}$ class of complexity. See Fig. 1, where the symbols in **bold** beneath each device denotes the stored state, and $K[a_i]$ represents the a_i-th bit of the ℓ-bit length secret K. The authors of ProbIP gave arguments [8] for its security in the Juels-Weis model.

For simplicity, we assume, and for the rest of this paper, that the reader and backend database server (if it exists) are one entity. This is sound since it is commonly assumed by RFID protocol designers that the channel between the reader and server are secure.

Reader   **Tag**
Database: $\{\ldots, (\text{ID}, K), \ldots\}$ **Shared Secret:** K

$$\xrightarrow{\text{HELLO}}$$

Do P times:
generate a_i, b_i for $i = 1 \ldots L$ s.t.

Find (ID, K) s.t. $\xleftarrow{a_1, b_1, \ldots, a_L, b_L}$ $\sum_{i=1}^{L} K[a_i] \oplus b_i = \frac{L}{2}$.
K satisfies all the equations

Fig. 1. The ProIP protocol

3.1 Violation of Anonymous Privacy

We first start by two remarks:

1. The tag does not update its secret key so at each authentication, some information is leaked from the *same* key.

2. The tag does not check the authenticity of the reader, i.e. an adversary can query the tag as many times as he likes.

From an information-theoretic point of view, a severe consequence of these two statements is that at one point an adversary will gather enough information to extract the key K from the responses of the tag.

Let us consider an adversary that will keep sending HELLO messages via Send queries to the tag until he gets ℓ equations. Since at each request tags generate P equations, an adversary would need to query the tag $\frac{n}{P}$ times. After that, she obtains the following system in which v_i^j denotes a boolean variable that is set to 1 if the $K[i]$-th bit of K is present in the j-th equation:

$$\begin{cases} \sum_{i=1}^{L} v_i^1 (K[i] \oplus b_i^1) &= \frac{L}{2} \\ \sum_{i=1}^{L} v_i^2 (K[i] \oplus b_i^2) &= \frac{L}{2} \\ \cdots \\ \sum_{i=1}^{L} v_i^\ell (K[i] \oplus b_i^\ell) &= \frac{L}{2} \end{cases} \quad (1)$$

As for any boolean v we can write $v + \bar{v} = 1$, we replace any $\bar{K}[i]$ by the value $1 - K[i]$. As a consequence we can deduce that there are as many as 3^n possible equations because every variable $K[i]$ can have three coefficients: $0, 1, -1$.

This way, the adversary gets a linear system of n equations and n variables that can be solved using standard methods such as the Gaussian elimination method. In the case where the n equations are not linearly independant, the adversary can still can obtain more equations from the tag by sending HELLO messages until she gets enough equations.

3.2 Countermeasure

The weakness of this authentication protocol comes from the fact that each round the advesary gets some information from the same key. So a quick way to counter our attack is to include a key-updating mechanism similar to OSK[21] at the end of the protocol using a one-way function.

In this case, adversaries do not get more than P equations for each key so that the security proof and reduction to the SAT problem become sound. The resulting protocol is even forward-private providing that adversaries do not get side-channel information from the reader [28].

4 MARP

MARP is proposed by Kim et al. [14] at CARDIS '06. They first describe a scheme consisting of separate phases, and then describe a more integrated one. For lack of better names, we denote these as MARP-1 and MARP-2, respectively. Here, a MARP is like a PDA to which several tags could be attached. The channels between reader and MARP, and between MARP and tag, are assumed by Kim et al. to be insecure.

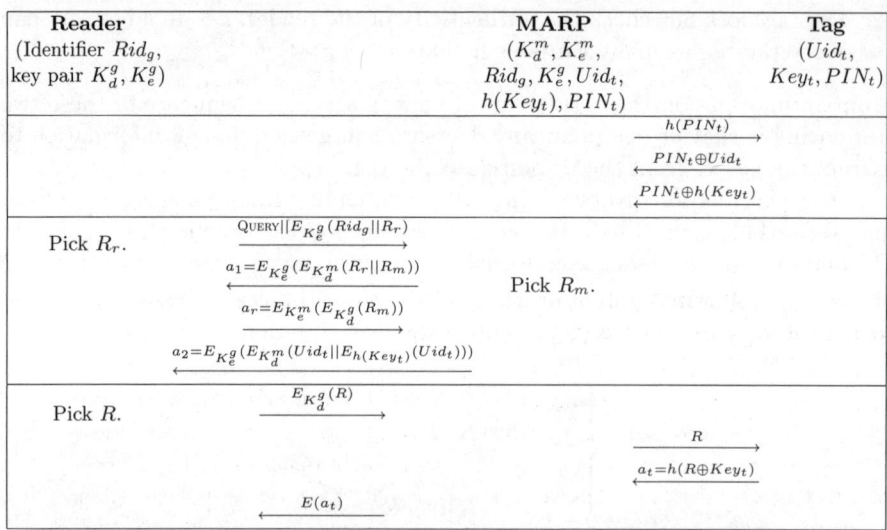

Fig. 2. The MARP-1 protocol, comprising 3 phases: setup, privacy protection, and authentication

Reader $(Rid_g,$ $K_d^g, K_e^g)$		MARP $(K_d^m, K_e^m,$ $Rid_g, K_e^g, Uid_t,$ $h(Key_t), PIN_t)$		Tag $(Uid_t,$ $Key_t, PIN_t)$
Pick R_r.	$\xrightarrow{\text{QUERY}\|\|E_{K_d^g}(Rid_g\|\|R_r)}$			
	$\xleftarrow{a_1 = E_{K_e^g}(E_{K_d^m}(R_r\|\|R_d))}$	Pick R_d.		
	$\xrightarrow{a_r = E_{K_e^m}(E_{K_d^g}(R_d))}$			
	$\xleftarrow{a_2 = E_{K_e^g}(E_{K_d^m}(Uid_t\|\|E_{h(Key_t)}(Uid_t)))}$			
Pick R_s.	$\xrightarrow{h(Key_t) \oplus R_s}$			
			$\xrightarrow{a_s = R_d\|\|h(R_d \oplus h(PIN_t))\|\|h(PIN_t) \oplus R_s}$	
			$\xleftarrow{a_3 = h(Key_t \oplus R_s)}$	
	$\xleftarrow{a_3}$			

Fig. 3. The MARP-2 protocol, comprising 2 phases: MARP authentication and tag authentication

We summarize these schemes in Figs. 2 and 3, which show only the bare minimal detail for understanding of our attacks. It suffices to note that $\langle K_d^g, K_e^g \rangle$ (resp. $\langle K_d^m, K_e^m \rangle$) is the private-public key pair of the reader (resp. MARP). Key_t and PIN_t are stored secrets of the tag. The reader is referred to [14] for more detailed descriptions.

4.1 Cryptanalysis of MARP-1

Tracing. Note that a_2 is fixed per tag, being a function of a particular tag T_t's unique identifier Uid_t and secret key Key_t. As the channel between the reader and the MARP is not confidential, an adversary via Execute queries (i.e. eavesdropping) can easily track the movement of T_t by checking for matches of a_2 with previously captured values, as long as the encryption is deterministic. Alternatively, the adversary can replay an old R from MARP to the tag via Send queries, and check if the response a_t matches the old value of a_t corresponding to the replayed R.

We remark that these attacks have less requirement than the ones performed by Juels and Weis [13] on some other older RFID protocols that require Corrupt queries.

Violating the Anonymous Privacy. Note that the initial setup messages allow to compute

$$z = [PIN_t \oplus Uid_t] \oplus [PIN_t \oplus h(Key_t)]$$
$$= Uid_t \oplus h(Key_t).$$

Then the adversary simply issues Execute queries to be able to compute z, and then issues a Send query to replace the message R from MARP to the tag with $R' = 0$, and so the tag responds with $a_t = h(Key_t)$. This allows to compute:

$$z \oplus a_t = [Uid_t \oplus h(Key_t)] \oplus h(Key_t)$$
$$= Uid_t,$$

and so reveals a potential unique identifier of the tag, which can be cross-checked against the possible list of identifiers for a match.

4.2 Tracing MARP-2

MARP-2 also allows tracing. By eavesdropping both messages via Execute queries between the reader and the MARP and between the MARP and the tag, an adversary gets $h(key_t) \oplus R_s$ and $h(PIN_t) \oplus R_s$. By XOR-ing these two values, the adversary gets $h(PIN_t) \oplus h(key_t)$ which does not depend on the session parameters and can be used to trace a tag.

This scheme is also vulnerable to a replay attack since the response of the tag does only depend on the parameters sent by the MARP. So if an adversary sends twice the same message a_s via Send queries, she will get the same response a_3 which can also be used for tracing.

5 Auth2

At PerCom '07, Tan et al. [24] proposed two RFID protocols. We are interested here in the second protocol, and more exactly to the first variant described therein. For lack of better names we simply call it Auth2, see Fig. 4 for a complete description of the protocol, where r_j is a unique identifier of the reader, f and h are two collisions-resistant hash functions and $h(.)_m$ denotes the function that truncates the output of h to its m first bits.

```
            Reader R_j                                                    Tag T_i
Database: {..., (ID_i, t_i, f(r_j||t_i)), ...}                       Shared secret: t_i
                                      ─── REQUEST ──→
                                      ←──── n_i ─────      Pick n_i.
                    Pick n_j.  ──── n_j, r_i ───→          h_1 = h(f(r_j||t_i)).
Check ∃t_i s.t. h(f(r_j||t_i))_m = h_1.  ←── h_1, h_2 ──   h_2 = h(f(r_j||t_i)||n_j||n_i) ⊕ ID_i.
Compute ID_i = h_2 ⊕ h(f(r_j||t_i)||n_j||n_i).
```

Fig. 4. The Auth2 protocol

5.1 Cryptanalysis of Auth2

Definite Tracing. It was noted by Auth2 designers that indefinite tracing is possible but not a concern since many tags could result in the same $h(f(r_j||t_i))_m$ value. We show how this tracing can be made definite, i.e. it can precisely track a unique tag, not just a group of them that have the same $h(f(r_j||t_i))_m$.

1. **Learning:** The adversary eavesdrops via Execute queries for a short period during the protocol sessions involving tag T_0 and two readers R_1, R_2 to obtain $\langle r_1, h(f(r_1||t_0))_m \rangle$ and $\langle r_2, h(f(r_2||t_0))_m \rangle$.
2. **Challenge:** Some time later, when the adversary wishes to track the tag T_0, he starts a session with the challenge tag $T_b \in \{T_0, T_1\}$ replaying r_1 via a Send query and checks the response from the tag for a match on the first message component with $h(f(r_1||t_0))_m$. He starts another session replaying r_2 via a Send query and checks the response from the tag for a match on the first message component with $h(f(r_2||t_0))_m$. With both matches, it is highly likely that this is the same tag whose session he had initially eavesdropped on, i.e. $T_b = T_0$. Else $T_b = T_1$.

Violating the Anonymous Privacy. When analyzing the anonymous privacy of their Auth2 scheme, the authors [24] assume that the adversary has access to the reader's list L of data corresponding to targeted tags, i.e. each entry in L is of the form $\langle ID_i, f(r_j||t_i) \rangle$.

The adversary only needs two entries in L corresponding to the targeted tag T_i, i.e. $\langle ID_i, f(r_1||t_i) \rangle$ and $\langle ID_i, f(r_2||t_i) \rangle$.

Issue a Send query with r_1 in a session, and then another Send query with r_2 in another session to T_i. Check if both responses match $f(r_1||t_i)$ and $f(r_2||t_i)$ respectively.

6 YA-TRAP, YA-TRAP+ and O-TRAP

At SecureComm '06, Burmester et al. [4] proposed two RFID protocols with formal proofs of security in the universal composability model [5], namely YA-TRAP+ and O-TRAP. These were inspired by YA-TRAP proposed at PerCom '06 by Tsudik [26].

Reader $\mathcal{R}_j$ **Tag** $\mathcal{T}_i$
Database $L: \{\ldots,(t_j,\mathrm{HMAC}_{K_i}(t_j)),\ldots\}$ **Shared secret:** K_i, t_0, t_i, t_{max}

$$\xrightarrow{t_j}$$

$$\text{if } (t_j < t_i) \text{ or } (t_j > t_{max})$$
$$h_j = \mathrm{PRNG}_i^j.$$
$$\text{else}$$
$$h_j = \mathrm{HMAC}_{K_i}(t_j) \text{ and}$$
$$\xleftarrow{h_j} \quad \text{update } t_i \leftarrow t_j.$$

check $\exists t_j$ s.t. $(t_j, h_j) \in L$.

Fig. 5. The YA-TRAP protocol

6.1 YA-TRAP

The steps of YA-TRAP [26] are given in Fig. 5, where HMAC is a message authentication code and PRNG is a pseudo-random number generator. It works as follows: a tag is initialized with an initial timestamp t_0 and the top timestamp value t_{max}, as well as with a unique secret value K_i. Tags are also assumed to be able to compute a PRNG, where PRNG_i^j denotes the jth invocation by the tag $\mathcal{T}_i$ of its own PRNG.

The main goal of YA-TRAP's design was to achieve untraceable privacy (UPriv) with adversaries assumed to be able to corrupt tags.

Two operating modes were proposed [26] for YA-TRAP, namely *real-time* and *batch*. The difference is that for batch mode, responses from tags are collected by the reader in batches for later communication to the server for offline processing and identification. This latter mode is suited for settings e.g. inventory control where tags are assumed honest, since they will only be authenticated later in batches rather than online. Thus, this mode is not suitable for applications where feedback is required on the spot, e.g. library check-outs, or retail outlets for both tags in purchased items as well as tags in credit cards.

Tsudik observed that it was possible for denial of service (DoS) attacks to be launched towards YA-TRAP, and remarks that DoS resistance is not among the key goals of YA-TRAP.

What is more subtle, however, is the fact that a denial-of-service kind of attack could lead to an adversary being able to track a tag in the YA-TRAP protocol.

Tracing Tags in Real Time. In the YA-TRAP specification, it was suggested [26] that the top value t_{max} of a tag's timestamp need not be unique but could instead be shared by a batch of tags.

Consider a scenario where tags have different t_{max}, operating in real-time mode. Indeed, acknowledging the fact that tags are produced by different manufacturers for diverse applications, it seems inevitable that some tags will have differing t_{max}. An adversary can trace a tag, i.e. distinguish between two tags (corresponding to a break of the privacy notion in the Juels-Weis model [13] and the UPriv notion we described in Section 2), as follows. For simplicity, assume two tags $\mathcal{T}_0$ and $\mathcal{T}_1$ with respective t_{max0} and t_{max1}, where $t_{max0} < t_{max1}$.

1. **Learning:** Issue a Send query with $t_j = t_{max0}$ to a tag $\mathcal{T} \in \{\mathcal{T}_0, \mathcal{T}_1\}$. Since t_{max0} is much into the future than current t_i value, a response $h_j = \text{HMAC}_{K_i}(t_j)$ is expected, irrespective of which tag it is. Furthermore, the tag will update its local time counter as $t_i = t_{max0}$. This action serves to send the tag into the future by marking it for future tracing.
2. **Challenge:** Some time later, when it is desired to trace the tag, issue a Send query with t_j for $t_{max0} < t_j < t_{max1}$. If $\mathcal{T} = \mathcal{T}_0$, it will respond $h_j = \text{PRNG}_i^j$ and will not successfully pass the validation check by the reader. If $\mathcal{T} = \mathcal{T}_1$, it will respond $h_j = \text{HMAC}_{K_i}(t_j)$ and will successfully pass the validation check. Thus by observing the reader-tag interaction via Execute queries, an adversary can distinguish between $\mathcal{T}_0$ and $\mathcal{T}_1$ and win the privacy game.

Juels and Weis [13] gave two tracing attacks on YA-TRAP that are valid in their privacy model, thus showing YA-TRAP does not meet their definition of strong privacy. Nevertheless, their tracing attacks would no longer apply in a weaker privacy model, and in fact one which better models the practical setting, where the adversary is further restricted by limiting its access to the TAGINIT message [13] as follows: when the TAGINIT message is issued to its two selected tags $\mathcal{T}_0$ and $\mathcal{T}_1$ used during the challenge phase, the adversary does not know which one of them was issued the message. This better models the practical privacy setting as the adversary is unaware during the learning phase which tag it has queried.

In contrast, our attack still applies in this weakened-adversary setting, and thus our result shows that setting a common t_{max} for tags offers more advantage over having individual t_{max} for each tag.

YA-TRAP was designed to specifically output a random response even if the tag does not want to be validated by the reader, such that an adversary is unable to distinguish between that random response and a proper response. Yet, by observing the output of the reader-tag interaction, i.e. seeing if the tag passes the validation or not, still allows the distinguishing. In this sense, using the YA-TRAP approach of generating random responses by itself is not sufficient to prevent tracing.

To reiterate, our attack can be prevented if the adversary is unable to observe the output of the reader-tag interaction, i.e. it does not know if the tag successfully passes the reader's validation check. This inability in fact corresponds to the *narrow* adversary model defined in Vaudenay's privacy model [28]. One example setting that fits this narrow model is the batch mode suggested by Tsudik [26] for YA-TRAP. Nevertheless, it is worth recalling here that batch mode is not relevant for applications where immediate feedback is required e.g. retail and library check-outs, and furthermore is only meaningful in the setting where tags are assumed to be honest (not usually the case) since they are not authenticated on the spot but later.

Cloning. An adversary can issue Send queries to the tag with arbitrarily many values of t_j and obtain the corresponding responses h_j. These values allow the

Reader $\mathcal{R}_j$ **Tag** $\mathcal{T}_i$
Database L: $\{\ldots,(t_j,\mathrm{HMAC}_{K_i}(t_j)),\ldots\}$ **Shared secret**: K_i, t_0, t_i

$$\xrightarrow{t, r_t}$$

Pick r_i.
if $(t > t_i)$
   $h_1 = H_{K_i}(00 || t || r_t)$
else
$$\xleftarrow{r_i, h_1}$$
   $h_1 = H_{K_i}(01 || r_i || r_t)$ if $(t \le t_i)$.

[*] Calculate $h_2 = H_{K_i}(10 || r_i || t)$ $\xrightarrow{[*]\ r_i, h_2}$
check $\exists (t_j, \mathrm{HMAC}_{K_i}(t_j)) \in L$ s.t.   [*]check $h_2 = H_{K_i}(10 || r_i || t)$.
    $h_1 = H_{K_i}(00 || t || r_t)$,   if $(t > t_i)$
or $h_1 = H_{K_i}(01 || r_i || r_t)$.   Update $t_i \leftarrow t$.

Fig. 6. The YA-TRAP+ protocol

tag to be cloned so that when the cloned tag is queried a particular t_j value, it will reply with the captured response h_j. The problem here stems from the fact that tag responses h_j are pre-computable only with the presence of the tag and not the reader since the supposed reader-supplied challenge is a predictable monotonically increasing timestamp t_j.

6.2 Tracing YA-TRAP+ with Second Pass

The steps of YA-TRAP+ are shown in Fig. 6, where $H_K(\cdot)$ denotes a keyed hash function and the steps preceeded by [*] are optional, and only meant to be used by the reader if it is felt that DoS attacks are rampant. Legitimate readers share with the tags their secret keys K_i.

It turns out that the tracing attack of subsection 6.1 is simpler when applied to YA-TRAP+ if its optional second pass (preceeded in Fig. 6 by [*]) is made compulsory.

1. **Learning:** An adversary first issues Send queries to the tag $\mathcal{T}_0$ with some r_t and a value t that is predictably much larger than the tag's t_i, obtaining the response $r_i, h_1 = H_K(00 || t || r_t)$. It then intentionally modifies via a Send query the message h_2 from reader to tag such that the tag does not successfully authenticate the reader and thus the tag does not update its internal time counter t_i to t.
2. **Challenge:** Issue a Send query to the tag in future (i.e. let the challenge tag $\mathcal{T}_b \in \{\mathcal{T}_0, \mathcal{T}_1\}$ during the challenge phase) with the same r_t and t. Since $t > t_i$, it will return the response $r'_i, h_1 = H_K(00 || t || r_t)$ for which h_1 is the same if the challenge tag $\mathcal{T}_b = \mathcal{T}_0$. Otherwise, the adversary knows $\mathcal{T}_b = \mathcal{T}_1$. This allows to track the tag and win the privacy game.

Note that YA-TRAP+ was specifically designed to resist the kind of tracing attack on its predecessor YA-TRAP that we mounted in subsection 6.1, and yet this result shows that the optional second pass of YA-TRAP+ that requires to check h_2 before updating the stored secret, although meant to provide additional security to resist denial of service attacks, will in fact cause the protocol to fall to tracing.

```
         Reader  R_j                                    Tag T_i
    Database L: {..., (r_i, K_i), ...}            Shared secret: r_i, K_i
                                    r_t
                              ─────────────→
                                   r_i, h
                              ←─────────────  Compute h = H_{K_i}(r_t, r_i).
      check ∃(r_i, K_i) in DB: s.t.              Update r_i ← H_{K_i}(r_i).
   h = H_{K_i}(r_t, r_i) or h = H_{K_i}(r_t, r_i).
      Update r_i ← H_{K_i}(r_i) ∈ L.
```

Fig. 7. The O-TRAP protocol

6.3 Tracing O-TRAP

The steps of O-TRAP are shown in Fig. 7. The reader contains a hash table indexed by r_i with entries $\langle r_i, K_i \rangle$ where r_i and K_i correspond to secrets of tags to which it has legitimate access.

1. **Learning:** An adversary can issue a Send query to the tag T_0 with random values r_t repeatedly, causing the tag to update its r_i each time such that it is way into the future compared to its synchronization with the reader.
2. **Challenge:** The adversary observes the future interaction between a tag $T_b \in \{T_0, T_1\}$ and a reader via Execute queries to see if the reader accepts the tag as valid. If not, then the adversary knows this was the tag that it marked during the learning phase, i.e. $T_b = T_0$. Else, $T_b = T_1$.

Note that this kind of attack has been independently applied by Juels and Weis [13] to a couple of other older RFID protocols. Yet what is interesting as has been demonstrated here, is that recent provably secure protocols like YA-TRAP+ and O-TRAP in some sense still allow for tracing.

7 RIPP-FS

RIPP-FS was proposed by Conti et al. [9] at PerCom '07. The steps of RIPP-FS are given in Fig. 8.

Each tag T_i is initialized with a tag key $K_{T_i}^0$ that it shares with the reader, as well as the initial value-pair (K_0, t_0) generated by the reader, where K_0 is the last value in a hash chain

$$K_\ell = w$$
$$K_i = H(K_{i+1}) = H^{\ell-1}(w), i = 0, \ldots, \ell - 1$$

for w a seed, and t_j $(j = 0, \ldots, \ell)$ is a time interval counter.

A tag is also assumed to be able to compute a pseudo-random number generator (PRNG), where PRNG_i^j denotes the jth invocation by the tag T_i of its own PRNG.

One of the goals of RIPP-FS's design was to achieve untraceable privacy (UPriv) against adersaries able to corrupt tgs, and it is claimed to offer more security properties than YA-TRAP, YA-TRAP+ and O-TRAP.

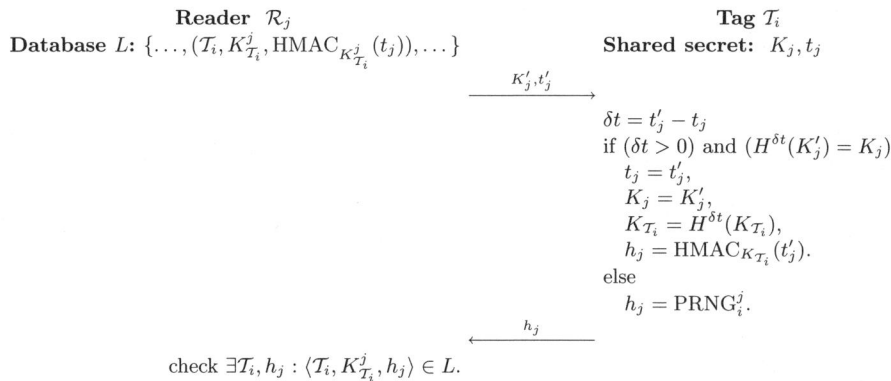

Fig. 8. The RIPP-FS protocol

7.1 Tracing Tags

We show how to trace tags in the RIPP-FS protocol.

1. **Learning**
   (a) Query Send to the reader to initiate two protocol sessions, obtaining (K'_j, t'_j) and (K'_{j+1}, t'_{j+1}), where $t'_{j+1} > t'_j$, and $K'_j = H(K'_{j+1})$.
   (b) Make a Send query to a tag $\mathcal{T}_0$ with the value (K'_{j+1}, t'_{j+1}). Since this is a valid message generated from the reader, a response $h_j = \text{HMAC}_{K_{\mathcal{T}_i}}(t'_{j+1})$ is expected. More importantly, the tag will update its time interval counter as $t_j = t'_{j+1}$, as well as the other secrets $K_j = K'_{j+1}$ and $K_{\mathcal{T}_i} = H^{t'_{j+1} - t_j}(K_{\mathcal{T}_i})$.
2. **Challenge:** Some time later, when it is desired to trace the tag, issue a Send query with (K'_j, t'_j) to the challenge tag $\mathcal{T}_b$, and pass the response h_{j+1} to the reader. If $\mathcal{T}_b = \mathcal{T}_0$, it will respond $h_{j+1} = \text{PRNG}_i^j$ and will not successfully pass the validation check by the reader. If $\mathcal{T}_b = \mathcal{T}_1$, it will respond $h_{j+1} = \text{HMAC}_{K_i}(t'_j)$ and will successfully pass the validation check. Thus by observing the reader-tag interaction via Execute queries, an adversary can distinguish between $\mathcal{T}_0$ and $\mathcal{T}_1$ and win the privacy game.

8 Concluding Remarks

We first provided an alternative description of privacy models that captures the notion of untraceable privacy (UPriv) and discussed its relation to existing models. This was to pave the way for our analysis results in later sections. We showed how the notion of UPriv cannot be achieved by some recent RFID protocols.

Our emphasis in this paper was to analyze the level of untraceable privacy offered by the protocols. We only discussed reasons why our attacks worked and intentionally did not propose any tweaks nor fixes on the protocols; mainly because there are already many available in literature, and so we feel this was not necessary unless there is a serious void of well designed provably secure RFID protocols.

Final remarks: while a uniformly accepted privacy model for RFID protocols is still being developed by the community, the results here serve to strengthen the need for such a standard model to facilitate better design of RFID protocols that offer both privacy and security. This has to be fulfilled if RFIDs are ever to be widely used by each individual within his network space of interconnected things.

References

1. Albertsons Announces Mandate, RFID Journal (March 5, 2004), http://www.rfidjournal.com/article/articleview/819/1/1/
2. Avoine, G.: Adversarial Model for Radio Frequency Identification, Cryptology ePrint Archive, report 2005/049 (February 20, 2005), http://eprint.iacr.org/2005/049
3. Bellare, M., Pointcheval, D., Rogaway, P.: Authenticated Key Exchange Secure against Dictionary Attacks. In: Preneel, B. (ed.) EUROCRYPT 2000. LNCS, vol. 1807, pp. 139–155. Springer, Heidelberg (2000)
4. Burmester, M., Le, T.V., de Medeiros, B.: Provably Secure Ubiquitous Systems: Universally Composable RFID Authentication Protocols. In: Proceedings of Securecomm 2006, pp. 1–9 (last revised December 5, 2006), full version available at IACR ePrint Archive, http://eprint.iacr.org/2006/448
5. Canetti, R.: Universally Composable Security: A New Paradigm for Cryptographic Protocols. In: Proc. IEEE FOCS 2001, pp. 136–145 (2001), (last revised December 13, 2005), full version available at IACR ePrint Archive, http://eprint.iacr.org/2000/067
6. Carluccio, D., Lemke, K., Paar, C.: E-Passport: The Global Traceability or How to Feel Like a UPS Package. In: Lee, J.K., Yi, O., Yung, M. (eds.) WISA 2006. LNCS, vol. 4298, pp. 391–404. Springer, Heidelberg (2007)
7. CASPIAN, Boycott Benetton (accessed September 19, 2007), http://www.boycottbenetton.com
8. Castelluccia, C., Soos, M.: Secret Shuffling: A Novel Approach to RFID Private Identification. In: Proceedings of RFIDSec 2007, pp. 169–180 (2007)
9. Conti, M., Di Petro, R., Mancini, L.V., Spognardi, A.: RIPP-FS: An RFID Identification, Privacy Preserving Protocol with Forward Secrecy. In: Proceedings of PerCom 2007, pp. 229–234 (2007)
10. Heydt-Benjamin, T.S., Bailey, D.V., Fu, K., Juels, A., O'Hare, T.: Vulnerabilities in First-Generation RFID-enabled Credit Cards. In: FC 2007. LNCS, vol. 4535, Springer, Heidelberg (2008)
11. Hoepman, J.-H., Hubbers, E., Jacobs, B., Oostdijk, M., Schreur, R.W.: Crossing Borders: Security and Privacy Issues of the European e-Passport. In: Yoshiura, H., Sakurai, K., Rannenberg, K., Murayama, Y., Kawamura, S.-i. (eds.) IWSEC 2006. LNCS, vol. 4266, pp. 152–167. Springer, Heidelberg (2006)
12. Juels, A., Molnar, D., Wagner, D.: Security and Privacy Issues in E-Passports. In: Proceedings of SecureComm 2005, pp. 74–88 (2005) (last revised September 18, 2007), full version available at IACR ePrint Archive, http://eprint.iacr.org/2005/095

13. Juels, A., Weis, S.A.: Defining Strong Privacy for RFID. In: Proceedings of PerCom 2007, pp. 342–347 (2007) (April 7, 2006), http://eprint.iacr.org/2006/137
14. Kim, S.-C., Yeo, S.-S., Kim, S.K.: MARP: Mobile Agent for RFID Privacy Protection. In: Domingo-Ferrer, J., Posegga, J., Schreckling, D. (eds.) CARDIS 2006. LNCS, vol. 3928, pp. 300–312. Springer, Heidelberg (2006)
15. Kosta, E., Meints, M., Hansen, M., Gasson, M.: An Analysis of Security and Privacy Issues Relating to RFID Enabled ePassports. In: Venter, H., Eloff, M., Labuschagne, L., Eloff, J., von Solms, R. (eds.) IFIP International Federation for Information Processing, New Approaches for Security, Privacy and Trust in Complex Environments, vol. 232, pp. 467–472. Springer, Boston (to appear, 2007)
16. Le, T.V., Burmester, M., de Medeiros, B.: Universally Composable and Forward-Secure RFID Authentication and Authenticated Key Exchange. In: Proceedings of ASIACCS 2007, pp. 242–252 (2007) (February 14, 2007), http://eprint.iacr.org/2007/051
17. Lim, C.H., Kwon, T.: Strong and Robust RFID Authentication Enabling Perfect Ownership Transfer. In: Ning, P., Qing, S., Li, N. (eds.) ICICS 2006. LNCS, vol. 4307, pp. 1–20. Springer, Heidelberg (2006)
18. Michelin Embeds RFID Tags in Tires, RFID Journal (January 17, 2003), http://www.rfidjournal.com/article/articleview/269/1/1/
19. Mitsubishi Electric Asia Switches on RFID, RFID Journal (September 11, 2006), http://www.rfidjournal.com/article/articleview/2644/
20. Monnerat, J., Vaudenay, S., Vuagnoux, M.: About Machine-Readable Travel Documents: Privacy Enhancement using (Weakly) Non-Transferable Data Authentication. In: Proceedings of RFIDSec 2007, pp. 15–28 (2007)
21. Ohkubo, M., Suzuki, K., Kinoshita, S.: RFID Privacy Issues and Technical Challenges. Communications of the ACM 48(9), 66–71 (2005)
22. Paise, R.-I., Vaudenay, S.: Mutual Authentication in RFID: Security and Privacy. In: Proceedings of AsiaCCS (2008) (to appear)
23. Rogaway, P.: On the Role Definitions in and Beyond Cryptography. In: Maher, M.J. (ed.) ASIAN 2004. LNCS, vol. 3321, pp. 13–32. Springer, Heidelberg (2004)
24. Tan, C.C., Sheng, B., Li, Q.: Serverless Search and Authentication Protocols for RFID. In: Proceedings of PerCom 2007, pp. 3–12 (2007)
25. Target, Wal-Mart Share EPC Data, RFID Journal (October 17, 2005), http://www.rfidjournal.com/article/articleview/642/1/1/
26. Tsudik, G.: YA-TRAP: Yet Another Trivial RFID Authentication Protocol. In: Proceedings of PerCom 2006, pp. 640–643 (2006)
27. Vaudenay, S.: RFID Privacy based on Public-Key Cryptography. In: Rhee, M.S., Lee, B. (eds.) ICISC 2006. LNCS, vol. 4296, pp. 1–6. Springer, Heidelberg (2006)
28. Vaudenay, S.: On Privacy Models for RFID. In: Kurosawa, K. (ed.) ASIACRYPT 2007. LNCS, vol. 4833, pp. 68–87. Springer, Heidelberg (2007)

A New Hash-Based RFID Mutual Authentication Protocol Providing Enhanced User Privacy Protection[*]

Jihwan Lim[1], Heekuck Oh[1], and Sangjin Kim[2]

[1] Hanyang University, Department of Computer Science and Engineering,
Republic of Korea
jhlim@cse.hanyang.ac.kr, hkoh@hanyang.ac.kr
[2] Korea University of Technology and Education,
School of Information and Media Engineering, Republic of Korea
sangjin@kut.ac.kr

Abstract. The recently proposed Radio Frequency Identification (RFID) authentication protocol based on a hashing function can be divided into two types according to the type of information used for authentication between a reader and a tag: either a value fixed or one updated dynamically in a tag. In this study we classify the RFID authentication protocol into a static ID-based and a dynamic-ID based protocol and then analyze their respective strengths and weaknesses and the previous protocols in the static/dynamic ID-based perspectives. Also, we define four security requirements that must be considered in designing the RFID authentication protocol including mutual authentication, confidentiality, indistinguishability and forward security. Based on these requirements, we suggest a secure and efficient mutual authentication protocol. The proposed protocol is a dynamic ID-based mutual authentication protocol designed to meet requirements of both indistinguishability and forward security by ensuring the unlinkability of tag responses among sessions. Thus, the protocol can provide more strengthened user privacy compared to previous protocols and recognizes a tag efficiently in terms of the operation quantity of tags and database.

Keywords: RFID, Authentication, User Privacy.

1 Introduction

An RFID system is an automatic cognition technology that can read individual information remotely with a RF telecommunication that with a wireless interface. In general, an RFID system is composed of three components: an RFID tag, an RFID reader and a host system, each of which plays a role as a transponder, a transceiver and a back-end server system (hereinafter referred to as a 'tag', a 'reader' and a 'database'). An RFID system purposes to recognize an entity attached with a tag. Normally, tags transmit their identity to the reader in response to a reader's wireless probe. This unique identity of a

---

[*] This research was supported by the MIC (Ministry of Information and Communication), Korea, under the HNRC (Home Network Research Center) - ITRC (Information Technology Research Center) support program supervised by the IITA (Institute of Information Technology Assessment).

tag is sometimes referred as EPC (Electronic Product Code). However, as the tag and the reader communicate through an insecure channel using a wireless interface, the tag sends its own information responding to a signal of the reader without authenticating if the reader is valid. Since this property of the RFID operation allows an attacker impersonating a legal reader or a third party around a reader to obtain the user's purchase history and location information with ease, a user privacy problem can occur. The RFID privacy protection schemes are widely classified into three types: hash-based approach, re-encryption-based approach, and a XOR-based approach. Then, the hash-based RFID mutual authentication protocol can be divided into static or dynamic ID-based protocols according to whether information saved in a tag, which is used for authentication between a reader and a tag, is fixed or updated for saving. In this paper, we analyze the previous hash-based authentication protocols from the perspectives of static/dynamic IDs and propose a new protocol that improves their security and efficiency. The proposed protocol is a dynamic-ID based RFID mutual authentication protocol that updates a tag's ID information continuously using a one-way property of hash functions.

The remainder of this paper is organized as follows. In section 2, we review protocol design issues and security requirements that should be considered for a secure and efficient RFID system. In section 3 and 4, we provide analysis of the previous protocols in the perspective of the design issues discussed in section 2 and propose a new protocol based on the analysis. Section 5 analyzes security and efficiency of the proposed protocol and finally conclusions are continued at Section 6.

2 RFID Protocol Design Issues and Security Requirements

2.1 Considerations for Efficiency and Security of the RFID System

Like other research fields, the RFID system has a trade-off between efficiency and security; the efficiency may be lowered to obtain security. In other words, a more efficient protocol can be designed by excluding any security threat or an attack model. However, it is not a right approach in the study to design mutual authentication protocol to provide secure RFID service.

In this section, we will discuss the core research issues to be considered to design a secure and efficient RFID protocol based on previous research results about a hash-based RFID mutual authentication protocols.

Static/Dynamic ID-Based Mutual Authentication Protocol. As mentioned above, the current hash-based RFID mutual authentication protocols can be divided into two types; a static ID-based mutual authentication protocol [4] and a dynamic ID-based protocol [1,2,3,5]. The two types of mutual authentication protocols have unique merits and demerits of their own, which should be considered in designing a protocol according to a RFID system application.

First of all, in a static-ID based mutual authentication protocol, a tag responds to a query of a reader with a fixed ID value (authentication/identification information). This means that the response value changes by using a random value for every session, while its own ID, which is saved in the tag, is always the same. The static ID-based mutual authentication protocol has an advantage in implementing a global database because it can keeping the same ID for distributed database as it can keep the fixed ID. However, the database requires operations proportional to the number of tags it maintains to identify a tag because the tag hashes its ID with random number for ever response. In addition, because it is not realistic for a tag to have a tamper resistant function, an attacker can trace a tag user's past behaviors using static ID information saved in a tag so the forward security cannot be satisfied.

In a dynamic ID-based mutual authentication protocol, a tag updates an ID of a previous session for every session to change a response to a query of a reader. Normally a protocol can recognize a tag directly by searching an ID saved in a database using a synchronized ID and also ensure forward security by using a one-way function in updating an ID. To do so, however the database and the tag should keep the ID and authentication information synchronized. In particular the database needs to perform additional operations for resynchronization when the synchronization is broken. Because a fixed ID cannot be kept in several databases, it is difficult to implement a distributed database.

To design a mutual authentication protocol using a dynamic ID, we focus on protecting a user's privacy by ensuring forward security rather than by implementing a global database.

Synchronization Problem between a Database and a Tag and Operation Quantity of the Database. As mentioned above, mutual authentication protocols designed based on a dynamic ID have to keep a updated ID and authentication information synchronized by both a database and a tag. Asynchronization between the database and the tag may occur when a session cannot be normally completed because of an unusual transmission error caused by an attacker in a wireless channel of the reader-tag section. For resynchronization and control of it, the database process protocol becomes complicated and needs additional operation. Because there are many easier physical ways of attacks that incapacitate a tag, Dimitriou [1] suggested a mutual authentication protocol without considering that an attack can cause asynchronization Although attacks causing asynchronization have less possibility to occur [1] , they can make it impossible to 'recognize a tag', which is the fundamental intent of the RFID system, if the asynchronous problem happens in a protocol that does not consider synchronization.

The study here considers ensuring security of the RFID system more important rather than considering additional costs of resynchronization. Thus, a protocol is designed focusing on the purpose to reduce additional burdens of the database while considering control of asynchronous problems and resynchronization.

User Location Privacy and Operation Quantity of the Database. To control asynchronization and the problem of resynchronization to the database, authentication information and IDs of a current session and a previous one can be kept in the database [2,3]. Lee [2] et al. suggested a protocol that can recognize a tag without additional data operation in an asynchronous situation by keeping IDs of a current session and a previous one as well as their hash values of the IDs in the database. Despite the efficiency of the scheme, the tag cannot update the current ID with a new one and then transmits the same ID and authentication information when an attacker blocks the last message of a session in transmission from a reader to a tag. As a result, the location of the user bearing the tag can be traced.

The study thus designs a protocol to ensure a user's location privacy as well as to reduce database operation quantity by updating ID values unconditionally regardless of closing status while keeping previous and current values in authentication fields only so that an ID and authentication of a tag can be differentially updated according to a session closing condition.

2.2 RFID Security Requirements

To protect a user's privacy in the RFID system, it should be robust against forgery attacks in order to pass an authentication process using unjust tags such as a replay attack or a spoofing attack. This requirement should include the following security problems.

- Data Privacy: In the RFID system, a tag responds to a query of a ready unconditionally. Thus, transmitting a tag's information to an unidentified reader without protection through an insecure channel may cause a data privacy problem. An attacker also can easily recognize a specific medication history and or possession of a drug or expensive personal items of a RFID user.
- Location Privacy: Even when data privacy is protected, if an attacker can trace a response message of a tag that is transmitted at every session, a user's location privacy problem may occur. In other words, transmitting authentication information with the same value or distinguishable value according to a query of a reader may cause a user's mobile path to be exposed.

To solve the security problems above, the following security requirements should be considered.

- Mutual Authentication: A tag and a reader should be able to confirm that an entity communicating with is a just tag.
  - A reader's tag authentication: A reader should be able to verify a just tag to authenticate and identify a tag safely from a replay attack or a spoofing attack.
  - A tag's reader authentication: A tag should be able to confirm that a just reader is communicating with it. By using an assumption that only a just reader can access a database, reader authentication by a tag can be excluded from consideration.
- Confidentiality: An attacker should be able neither to analogize or calculate a certain value through all tag messages transmitted through an insecure channel nor infer a tag's own ID.
- Indistinguishability: An output value of a tag should be neither distinguished from a random number nor connected to a tag ID. If possible to find out values of a certain tag from a random tag message, he can distinguish the certain tag and trace a user's location.
- Forward Security: Even when confidential tag information is disclosed to an attacker, the information should not be available to know a message or confidential information of a previously calculated tag. If an attacker can figure out and calculate past responses when it is possible to know current status and ID information of a target tag obtained in a physical way, they could breach a user's data and location privacy based on knowledge about the user's past behaviors.

3 Related Work

3.1 Terminologies

The notation in Table 1 is used in related research and the proposed protocol.

3.2 CRAP Scheme by Rhee et al.

Challenge-Response based Authentication Protocol (CRAP) [4] proposed by Rhee et al. is a static ID-based mutual authentication protocol that changes a tag response using a hash function and the random number. A tag changes its response by hashing the random number received from a reader and its own random number along with its static ID value kept in the tag. CRAP guarantees mutual authentication, confidentiality and indistinguishability among the four security requirements but not forward security. To identify a tag, a database has to perform hash operation equal to the number of saved tags ($O(n)$) every time.

3.3 LCAP Scheme by Lee et al.

Low-Cost Authentication Protocol (LCAP) [2] proposed by Lee et al. is a mutual authentication protocol that improves database operation quantity for resynchronization efficiently while solving an asynchronous problem between a tag and a database that can occur in a dynamic ID-based mutual authentication protocol. A database keeps a current ID, an ID-hashed value, a previous ID and its hashed value to control an asynchronous status. A tag ID is updated through XOR with the random number received from a reader, while a database can identify a tag only by searching a tag list without additional operation. However, the protocol cannot provide forward security as it uses the XOR operation to update an ID. Also, if an attacker intentionally blocks the last message, the same value is given as a response to a query of a reader so as not to satisfy indistinguishability and allow location tracing.

Table 1. Notation

D, R, T	Database, Reader, Tag
K	Symmetric key kept by a tag and a database
N_X	Nonce of a participating entity X
$M_1 \| M_2$	Concatenation of message M_1 and M_2
G, H	An one-way hash function with 1 as a length of an output value and $0, 1^*0, 1^l$
$H(K, M)$	A value after hashing the one-way hash function H with a key K and a message M
	$H_L(K, M), H_R(K, M)$ are the left half and the right half of a hash function for each

Fig. 1. CRAP by Rhee et al.

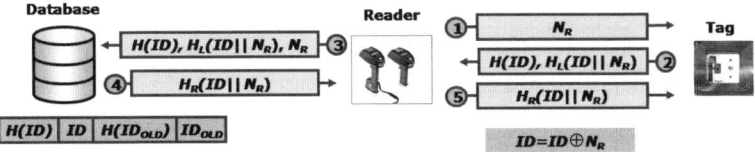

Fig. 2. LCAP by Lee et al.

3.4 LTC Scheme by Dimitriou et al.

Dimitriou et al. suggested a Lightweight RFID protocol to protect against Traceability and Cloning attacks (LTC) [1] protocol that can ensure forward security by updating a tag ID using an one-way hash function. The LTC, a dynamic ID-based mutual authentication protocol, updates a tag ID by hashing a previous session ID with an one-way function. However, as this protocol keeps a current tag ID only, a database needs additional hash operations as many as the number of saved tags every time to identify a tag. In addition, despite its design based on a dynamic ID, a database cannot distinguish a tag when the last message is blocked by an attacker, because it does not consider control of asynchronous status and resynchronization.

3.5 Hash Chain Scheme by Ohkubo et al.

The hash chain method [5] suggested by Ohkubo et al. is a dynamic ID-based authentication protocol that changes a tag ID with two one-way hash functions and creates authentication information. A tag uses the following two hash functions, $G, H : 0, 1^* \rightarrow 0, 1^l$ Using a confidential value $S_{t,i}$ for a query of a reader, a tag creates $S_{t,i+1} = H(S_{t,i})$ and then creates $a_{t,i} = G(S_{t,i})$ with a G hash function. A tag creates and transmits $S_{t,i+1} = H(S_{t,i})$ and $a_{t,i} = G(S_{t,i})$ whenever a reader queries. Among the four RFID security requirements, this scheme can satisfy confidentiality, indistinguishability and forward security but can still allow a spoofing attack and a reply attack as mutual authentication cannot be done. In addition, a database requires too many operation to find out a tag responding to a transmitted value because it has to figure out the seed value $S_{t,i}$ that produces $a'_{t,i}$ which is consistent with $a_{t,i}$ received from a reader by calculating seed values for all has changes $S_{t,i}(1 \leq t \leq n)$ and $a'_{t,i} = G(H^{i-1}(S_{t,i}))(1 \leq i \leq m)$ for all hash chains. This means that, when n is the number of tags saved in the database and m is the maximum length of a hash chain that

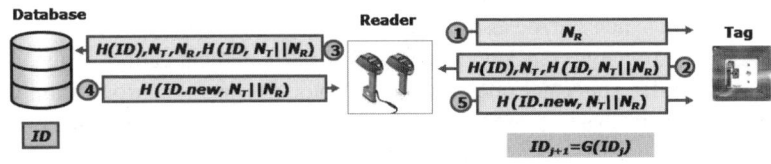

Fig. 3. LTC by Dimitriou et al.

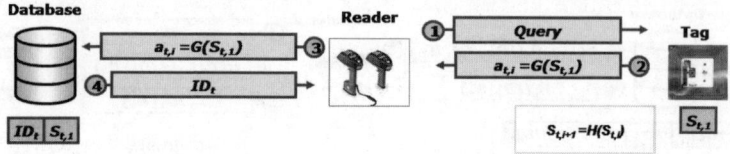

Fig. 4. Hash Chain Scheme by Ohkubo et al.

represents the maximum number of times to read a tag, the database should perform hash operations equal to $O(nm)$ times.

4 Proposed Protocol

In this paper, we propose an RFID mutual authentication protocol that meets all RFID security requirements including mutual authentication, confidentiality, indistinguishability and forward security as mentioned in 2.1 and 2.2 above. It is also effective in terms of database operation quantity. The proposed protocol is composed of two stages: initialization and execution.

4.1 Initialization

In the proposed RFID system, a tag T_i that keeps the following information can be distinguished only by EPC_i.

- K_i: A symmetric key between a tag and a database. The symmetric key of each tag is calculated as $K_i = H(K_D, EPC_i)$ from the master key of a database K_D.
- ID_j: The jth dynamic ID of a tag, calculated as $ID_j = H(K_i, ID_{j-1})$. Here the first tag ID ID_0 is assumed as being shared between a tag and a database.
- N_k: A tag creates and uses a random number N_k to make a different response for each query of a reader. Considering operation capacity of a tag, the random number is calculated as $N_k = H(K_i, N_{k-1})$. Here the first random number N_0 is assumed to be saved in a tag when it is created.

A database keeps a master key K_D and the following information.

- EPC_i: The only identification code of a tag T_i
- ID_j: The jth dynamic tag ID synchronized with a tag
- C_Key: A current tag key value to be used when the tag is authenticated at the next session. Under a normal operation of the protocol, key values of a tag and a database are synchronized as the C_Key value.
- P_Key: A previous tag key value used for tag authentication at the previous session. Under abnormal operation of a protocol|when synchronization between a tag and a database is broken|the database can identify a tag using the P_Key value.

4.2 Execution

In the execution stage of the proposed protocol, a tag, a reader and a database send and receive the following message as shown in Figure 5 and operates as follows.

- Step 1: A reader creates and transmits a random number N_R to prevent a reply or a spoofing attack by ensuring message freshness for a tag response.
- Step 2: A tag calculates $H_L(K_i, N_R||N_k)$ with N_R received from a reader, its key number and a random number and sends it to a reader. Then the tag updates the current ID ID_j as $ID_{j+1} = H(K_i, ID_j)$. A tag ID is updated regardless of normal completion of a session. A tag updates its current ID after responding to a query of a reader. A reader then sends its random number N_R and a message received from a tag to a database.
- Step 3: The database received the message at Step 2 searches for the same ID on the tag list saved as a received value ID_j. When the received ID and a saved ID is coincident, the database regards the tag as just and calculates $H_L(K_i, N_R||N_k)$ with C_Key of the tag to confirm synchronization status and update a key. If the calculated value is coincident with the received value, it updates a current tag ID, a current key value and a key value of a previous session. If $H_L(K_i, N_R||N_k)$ is not same with the value calculated with C_Key, the current tag key K_i are synchronized with P_Key. Thus, the database does not update a key value but an ID only. When the database received the message of Step 2 cannot search for a tag with the received ID, it finds out a value coincident with a received value by calculating $H_L(K_i, N_R||N_k)$ with all saved C_Key values. When the value is found, the database updates a current key value and one of the previous session as well as the current ID using the ID value of a received message. Step 3 may have many exceptions caused by an attacker, which will be described in Section 5.
- Step 4: After tag identification, the database transmits a tag EPC and the authentication value $H_R(K_i, N_R||N_k)$ to a reader. Then, a reader sends the authentication value $H_R(K_i, N_R||N_k)$ to a tag, while the tag verifies it. If $H_R(K_i, N_R||N_k)$ is authenticated in a right way, the tag updates and saves the current key as $K_{i+1} = H(K_i||N_R)$. If not, or when the message of Step 4 itself cannot be received, the tag does not update the key value.

5 Analysis

This Section shows that the proposed protocol operates always normally and analyzes stability of the security requirements defined in Section 2. Furthermore, efficiency of the protocol is analyzed through comparing database and tag operation quantity with precedent studies.

5.1 Attack Model and System Assumption

The proposed system assumes that an attacker has the following capabilities.

- An attacker can wiretap all messages in the reader-tag session, which is an insecure channel, and has all messages of the previous session.

	Database [ID, C_Key, P_Key, EPC]		Reader		Tag [ID_j, K_i, N_k]
1			N_R	$\rightarrow$	
2				$\leftarrow$	$ID_j, N_k, H_L(K_i, N_R \| N_k)$
		$\leftarrow$	add N_R		

3	if($storedID=receivedID_j$){
	　compute $H'_L=H_L$(C_Key, $N_R\|N_k$)
	　if($received\ H_L==H'_L$){
	　　update C_Key: $K_{i+1}=H(K_i\|N_R)$
	　　update P_Key: K_i
	　}
	　update $ID_{j+1}=H(K_i, ID_j)$
	}else{
	　for all C_Key
	　compute $H'_L=H_L$(?, $N_R\|N_k$)
	　if($received\ H_L==H'_L$)){
	　　update C_Key: $K_{i+1}=H(K_i\|N_R)$
	　　update P_Key: K_i
	　　update $ID_{j+1}=H(K_i, received\ ID_j)$
	　}else {
	　　for all P_Key
	　　compute $H'_L=H_L$(?, $N_R\|N_k$)
	　　if($received\ H_L==H'_L$){
	　　　update $ID_{j+1}=H(K_i, received\ ID_j)$
	　　}
	　}
	}
					update
					$ID_{j+1}=H(K_i, ID_j)$

4	EPC, $H_R(K_i, N_R\|N_k)$	$\rightarrow$			
			$H_R(K_i, N_R\|N_k)$	$\rightarrow$	

5					if($H_R==receivedH_R$){
					　($updateK_{i+1}=H(K_i\|N_R)$)
					}

Fig. 5. Proposed Protocol

– A communication channel between a reader and a database is regarded as secure. Thus, an attacker cannot send a message to a database as if he is a just reader. This means that an attacker can perform a reply attack to a just reader disguising as a tag and communicate with a tag as if a reader. However, only a legal reader can access to the database and obtain tag information.

5.2 Analysis of Protocol Completeness

This section shows that the proposed protocol can authenticate a tag normally and resynchronize it even when synchronization between a tag and a database is broken by an attacker's intervention. Figure 6 show tag synchronization and resynchronization process between a tag and a database according to session progress. Database-tag synchronization status can be divided into 5 types (see top-left table of Figure 6).

[Synchronized Statues of Tag and Database]

Status	ID Synch.	Key Synch.
0	O	Current Key
1	O	Previous Key
2	X	Current Key
3	X	Previous Key
4	X	X

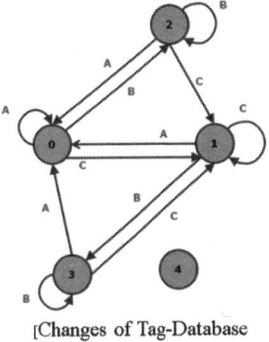

[Changes of Tag-Database Synchronization]

[Progress of a Protocol Session - Intervention by an Attacker]

Action	Step 2	Step 4	Remark
A	O	O	Normal Session
B	X	·	Message block at Step 2
C	O	X	Message block at Step 4

Fig. 6. Synchronization statues of Tag and Database

Here we assume that an attacker can control a session by delivering a message like that in bottom-left Table of Figure 6 to intervene normal protocol progress and break synchronization.

Figure 7 shows changes of ID and key synchronization status of a tag and a database according to session progress through an example. Top-left table of Figure 7 presents how the ID synchronization (see Figure 6) is broken and changes to a synchronized status between a previous key value of a tag saved in a database and the current key value, after a session begins at tag-database synchronization (status 0) and ends by a message block of Step 2. As shown at top-left table of Figure 7, the proposed protocol can resynchronize IDs and keys when a session progresses in the Status 2 normally without message blocks of Step 2 and 4. As the above results show, the proposed protocol can keep synchronization between a database and a tag regardless of attack attempts (see state diagram of Figure 6). Also, when key or ID synchronization is partially broken, resynchronization can be normally done so that the database can always identify a just tag.

Step 2 Message Blocked at Normal Status

Action	Database			Tag		Sync. Status
	ID	C_Key	P_Key	ID	Key	
	ID_i	K_i	K_{i-1}	ID_i	K_i	0
B	ID_i	K_i	K_{i-1}	ID_{i+1}	K_i	2
A	ID_{i+1}	K_{i+1}	K_i	ID_{i+2}	K_{i+1}	0

Step 4 Message Blocked at Normal Status

Action	Database			Tag		Sync. Status
	ID	C_Key	P_Key	ID	Key	
	ID_{i+2}	K_{i+1}	K_i	ID_{i+2}	K_{i+1}	0
C	ID_{i+3}	K_{i+2}	K_{i+1}	ID_{i+3}	K_{i+1}	1
A	ID_{i+4}	K_{i+2}	K_{i+1}	ID_{i+4}	K_{i+2}	0

Sequential Blocks of Step 4 and 2 Messages

Action	Database			Tag		Sync. Status
	ID	C_Key	P_Key	ID	Key	
	ID_{i+4}	K_{i+2}	K_{i+1}	ID_{i+4}	K_{i+2}	0
C	ID_{i+5}	K_{i+3}	K_{i+2}	ID_{i+5}	K_{i+2}	1
B	ID_{i+5}	K_{i+3}	K_{i+2}	ID_{i+6}	K_{i+2}	3
A	ID_{i+7}	K_{i+3}	K_{i+2}	ID_{i+7}	K_{i+3}	0

Sequential Blocks of Step 2 and 4 Messages

Action	Database			Tag		Sync. Status
	ID	C_Key	P_Key	ID	Key	
	ID_{i+7}	K_{i+3}	K_{i+2}	ID_{i+7}	K_{i+3}	0
B	ID_{i+7}	K_{i+3}	K_{i+2}	ID_{i+8}	K_{i+3}	2
C	ID_{i+9}	K_{i+4}	K_{i+3}	ID_{i+9}	K_{i+3}	1
A	ID_{i+10}	K_{i+4}	K_{i+3}	ID_{i+10}	K_{i+4}	0

Fig. 7. Intervention by an Attacker

5.3 Security Analysis

This section shows that the proposed protocol meets the four RFID security requirements defined at Section 2 and can protect a user's data and location privacy.

- Mutual Authentication: In the proposed protocol, the database can authenticate a tag through a synchronized ID value, which is updated at every session and created by a secret key shared by both a database and a tag. Thus, an attacker without knowing the key cannot calculate it. Even when ID synchronization is broken, the database can confirm if a tag knows a secret key K_i by calculating the received value, $H_L(K_i, N_R||N_k)$. Meanwhile, the tag authenticates a just database and renews a key value only it is identified by receiving the last message $H_R(K_i, N_R||N_k)$ of Step 4.
- Confidentiality: What the RFID system protects for data privacy is a tag's EPC information. All messages transmitted in the proposed protocol do not include EPC information and cannot be connected even when an attacker has collected dynamically updated IDs. Thus, he cannot figure out which RFID tags the RFID user possesses.
- Indistinguishability: The proposed protocol responds to a query of a reader with a different value for each session by updating an ID dynamically. As the ID value calculated with an one-way hash function uses a key value shared with database, an attacker cannot calculate an ID for a next session from the current ID without knowing the key value. Also, the $H_L(K_i, N_R||N_k)$ sent along with the ID changes by associating with new random numbers of every session regardless of an attacker's intervention. Thus, an attacker who does not know a key value cannot associate two different messages each other.
- Forward Security: The proposed protocol updates an ID and a key value every session using an one-way hash function. Even when an attacker has obtained the last key value of a tag through capturing a tag in a physical way, they cannot calculate a key value of a previous session due to the one-way property of hash functions and therefore cannot restore a message of a previous session to know or trace a user's past behaviors.

5.4 Efficiency Analysis

The proposed protocol is a dynamic ID-based mutual authentication protocol using an one-way hash function. Figure 8 compares security and efficiency of protocols suggested in the past. The Proposed protocol can identify a tag only with database searching cost during ID synchronization and should perform a hash operation proportionate to the number of tags saved in a database when the ID synchronization is broken. Also, the proposed protocol needs a $O(2n)$ database operation in the worst case, which occurs only when the Step 4 message is blocked and the Step 2 message is sequentially blocked in the next session by an attacker. However, when assuming that the attacks occur infrequently, the proposed protocol can ensure a user's privacy strengthened compared to past protocols with same or excellent efficiency in the perspective of database operation quantity.

	Dynamic /static ID	Mutual Authen.	Confi.	Indisting.	Forward Security	Database Operation Quantity		Tag operation quantity	Remark
						normal	worst		
Rhee	Static	O	O	O	X	$O(n)$	$O(n)$	2H+R*	
Lee	Dynamic	O	O	X	X	$O(\log n)$**	$O(\log n)$	2H	Location tracing possible
Dimit.	Dynamic	O	O	O	X	$O(n)$	$O(n)$	4H+R	Unable to identify a tag upon an asynchronous attack
Ohkubo	Dynamic	X	O	O	O	$O(n \times m)$***	$O(n \times m))$	2H	Reply attack possible
Ours	Dynamic	O	O	O	O	$O(\log n)$	$O(2n)$	4H	

*: R is an operation to create a random number.
**: n means the number of tags saved in a database, while $O(\log n)$ a database search cost.
***: m presents the maximum number of times to be able to read a tag as a length of a hash chain of a tag.

Fig. 8. Security and Efficiency of Protocols Suggested by Related Studies

6 Conclusion

In this paper, we proposed a dynamic ID-based RFID mutual authentication protocol to guarantee a RFID user's data and location privacy. Furthermore, we reviewed RFID design issues that should be considered to design a secure and efficient RFID authentication protocol. Then, the four security requirements were defined including mutual authentication, confidentiality, indistinguishability and forward security related to a RFID privacy infringement threat. The proposed protocol can meet the all four RFID security requirements, provide strengthened privacy protection compared to past studies and is effective in terms of database operation quantity.

References

1. Dimitiriou, T.: A Lightweight RFID protocol to protect against traceability and cloning attack. In: Proc. of the SecureComm 2005, pp. 59–66 (2005)
2. Lee, S., Hwang, Y.: Efficient authentication for low-cost RFID systems. In: Gervasi, O., Gavrilova, M.L., Kumar, V., Laganá, A., Lee, H.P., Mun, Y., Taniar, D., Tan, C.J.K. (eds.) ICCSA 2005. LNCS, vol. 3480, pp. 619–629. Springer, Heidelberg (2005)
3. Henrici, D., Muller, P.: Hash-based enhancement of location privacy for radio-frequency identification devices using varying identifiers. In: Proc. of the PERCOMW 2004, pp. 149–153. IEEE Computer Society Press, Los Alamitos (2004)
4. Rhee, K., Kwak, J., Kim, S., Won, D.: Challenge-response based RFID authentication protocol for distributed database environment. In: Hutter, D., Ullmann, M. (eds.) SPC 2005. LNCS, vol. 3450, pp. 70–84. Springer, Heidelberg (2005)
5. Ohkubo, M., Suzuki, K., Kinoshita, S.: Efficient hash-chain based RFID privacy protection scheme. In: Int. Conf. on Ubiquitous Computing, Workshop Privacy: Current Status and Future Directions (2004)

An Efficient Countermeasure against Side Channel Attacks for Pairing Computation

Masaaki Shirase[1], Tsuyoshi Takagi[1], and Eiji Okamoto[2]

[1] Future University Hakodate, Japan
[2] University of Tsukuba, Japan

Abstract. Pairing-based cryptosystems have been widely researched, and several efficient hardware implementations of pairings have also been proposed. However, side channel attacks (SCAs) are serious attacks on hardware implementations. Whelan et al. pointed out that pairings except the η_T pairing might not be vulnerable against SCAs by setting the secret point to the first parameter [25]. This paper deals with SCAs for the η_T pairing over $\mathbb{F}_{3^n}$. To our knowledge, the randomized-projective-coordinate method has the smallest overhead among all countermeasures against SCAs for the η_T pairing. The cost of that overhead is $3nM$, where M is the cost of a multiplication in $\mathbb{F}_{3^n}$. In this paper, we propose another countermeasure based on random value additions $(x_p + \lambda)$ and $(y_p + \lambda)$, where $P = (x_p, y_p)$ is the input point, and λ is a random value in $\mathbb{F}_{3^n}$. The countermeasure using the random value addition was relatively slow in the case of the scalar multiplication of elliptic curve cryptosystems. However, in the case of the η_T pairing, we can construct an efficient countermeasure due to the form of the function $g_P(x, y) = y_p^3 y - (x_p^3 + x - 1)^2$ for a point $P = (x_p, y_p)$. The overhead of our proposed scheme is just $0.5nM$, which is a reduction of more than 75% compared with the randomized-projective-coordinate method.

Keywords: η_T pairing, Tate pairing, side channel attacks, random value addition.

1 Introduction

Pairings over elliptic curves are functions from two points on an elliptic curve to an element over finite fields that exhibit bilinearity and non-degeneracy. Tate pairing is a popular pairing and the Miller algorithm is the first efficient algorithm for computing Tate pairing [18]. Barreto et al. improved the Miller algorithm by denominator elimination, which is called the BKLS algorithm in this paper [1]. Moreover, the η_T pairing [2] and Ate pairing [10] are efficient algorithms for computing the Tate pairing for supersingular curves and ordinary curves, respectively. The Ate pairing is a variation of the BKLS algorithm. However, the η_T pairing requires a special algorithm that arises from the function $g_P(x, y) = y_p^3 y - (x_p^3 + x - 1)^2$ for a point $P = (x_p, y_p)$.

There have been many research studies on software and hardware implementations of pairings. Indeed, pairings have implemented on FPGAs [7,12,23,20,3] and smart cards [22]. On the other hand, side channel attacks (SCAs) reveal secret data on hardware devices by monitoring side channel information such as power consumption and timing [15,16]. Therefore, hardware devices executing cryptographic algorithms with secret data need countermeasures against SCAs.

Countermeasures for pairing devices have recently been investigated [21,19,25] [13,26]. Let $e(P,Q)$ be a pairing for two points $P = (x_p, y_p)$, $Q = (x_q, y_q)$ on the underlying elliptic curve. Scott proposed the method of randomizing the intermediate value [21]. This method multiplies a random value in the finite field by a Miller variable. The overhead of this method is $3.5nM$ for the η_T pairing over $\mathbb{F}_{3^n}$ according to our estimation. On the other hand, Coron proposed some countermeasures against SCAs on the scalar multiplication over an elliptic curve cryptosystem (ECC) [6]. Page et al. applied Coron's countermeasures to the pairing, and proposed two countermeasures [19]. The first countermeasure is the scalar multiplication and bilinearity method that computes $e(\alpha P, \beta Q)^{1/\alpha\beta}$ for randomized integers α and β instead of $e(P,Q)$, and its overhead is about $18nM$ for the η_T pairing over $\mathbb{F}_{3^n}$. The second countermeasure is the point-blinding method that computes $e(P, Q+R)/e(P,R)$ for randomized point R, and its overhead is about $7.5nM$ for the η_T pairing over $\mathbb{F}_{3^n}$. Kim et al. evaluated their efficiency for the η_T pairing over $\mathbb{F}_{2^n}$. Moreover, they proposed the randomized-projective-coordinate method [13]. In this method, settings $X_p \leftarrow \lambda x_p$, $Y_p \leftarrow \lambda y_p$, and $Z_p \leftarrow \lambda$ are performed, and its overhead is $3nM$ for the η_T pairing over $\mathbb{F}_{3^n}$. Whelan et al. also considered SCAs against pairings [25,26]. They concluded that pairings using the BKLS algorithm (such as Ate pairing) might not be vulnerable against SCAs by setting the secret point P to the first parameter of $e(P,Q)$. However, a countermeasure is needed for the η_T pairing algorithm due to its symmetric structure.

In this paper, we provide an improved η_T pairing algorithm over characteristic three, which is secure against SCAs. The proposed scheme is based on random value additions $(x_p + \lambda)$ and $(y_p + \lambda)$, where $P = (x_p, y_p)$ is the input point and λ is a random value of $\mathbb{F}_{3^n}^*$. The overhead of the proposed countermeasure is just $0.5nM$ for the η_T pairing over $\mathbb{F}_{3^n}$. This method is similar to the randomized linearly transformed coordinate (RLC) method for ECC [11,17] although RLC is a relatively slow countermeasure against SCAs. However, our method is a very efficient countermeasure for the η_T pairing. That is an interesting result. We noted that changing "$r_0 \leftarrow x_p + x_q + d$" to "$r_0 \leftarrow (x_p + \lambda) + (x_q - \lambda) + d$" using a random element λ at Step 5 in Algorithm 1 described in Section 2 fixes r_0. Although we have to randomize the y-coordinate, the resulting cost is not large. Therefore, randomizations "$x_p \leftarrow x_p + \lambda$, $y_p \leftarrow y_p + \lambda$, $x_q \leftarrow x_q - \lambda$, and $y_q \leftarrow y_q - \lambda$" in Algorithm 1 can be used to derive an efficient countermeasure against SCAs.

The remainder of this paper is organized as follows. In Section 2, we explain pairings and computational cost of some computations used in this paper. In Section 3, we briefly review SCAs against hardware implementations of the η_T pairing. Then, we describe existing countermeasures against SCAs for the η_T

pairing. In Section 4, we propose an efficient countermeasure based on the random value addition. In Section 5, we conclude this paper.

2 η_T Pairing and Computational Cost

In this section, we first explain the η_T pairing, which is one of the most efficient pairings proposed by Barreto et al. [2]. Second, we discuss the costs of the multiplication in $\mathbb{F}_{3^{6n}}$ and the scalar multiplication on the supersingular elliptic curve over $\mathbb{F}_{3^n}$. These cost estimations are applied to the comparison among various countermeasures against SCAs for the η_T pairing.

2.1 η_T Pairing

Let $\mathbb{F}_{3^n}$ be an extension field of extension degree n over $\mathbb{F}_3$. Let E^b be a supersingular elliptic curve defined by

$$E^b : y^2 = x^3 - x + b \text{ with } b \in \{1, -1\}. \tag{1}$$

All supersingular curves are isomorphic to this curve. All points in E^b with the point at infinity $\mathcal{O}$ are denoted by

$$E^b(\mathbb{F}_{3^n}) = \{(x, y) \in \mathbb{F}_{3^n} \times \mathbb{F}_{3^n} : y^2 = x^3 - x + b\} \cup \{\mathcal{O}\}.$$

Then, $E^b(\mathbb{F}_{3^n})$ forms a group, and the summation $P + Q \in E^b(\mathbb{F}_{3^n})$ for any $P, Q \in E^b(\mathbb{F}_{3^n})$ is computed by an explicit formula [9,24]. For $P \in E^b(\mathbb{F}_{3^n})$ and an integer $m (\neq 0)$, the operation

$$mP = P + P + \cdots + P \text{ (summation of } m \text{ terms)}$$

is called the *scalar multiplication*.

The extension degree n satisfies $gcd(n, 6) = 1$ because n is chosen to be a prime [2]. Then, n satisfies $n \equiv 1, 5, 7, 11 \pmod{12}$.

Denote the number of elements in the set S by $\#S$. Then, we know that

$$\#E^b(\mathbb{F}_{3^n}) = 3^n + 1 + b' 3^{(n+1)/2},$$

where b' is defined by the following equation:

$$b' = \begin{cases} b & \text{if } n \equiv 1, 11 \pmod{12}, \\ -b & \text{if } n \equiv 5, 7 \pmod{12}. \end{cases}$$

The distortion map ψ is defined by

$$\psi(x, y) = (\rho - x, y\sigma) \tag{2}$$

with $\sigma^2 = -1$ and $\rho^3 = \rho + b$.

Let $l_{3P', b'P}$ be a function of a line going through $3P'$ and $b'P$, and let

$$g_R(x, y) = y_r^3 y - (x_r^3 + x - b)^2$$

Algorithm 1: Computation of η_T pairing for $n \equiv 1 \pmod{12}$
input: $P = (x_p, y_p), Q = (x_q, y_q) \in E^b(\mathbb{F}_{3^n})$
output: $(\eta_T(P,Q)^{3^{(n+1)/2}})^W \in \mathbb{F}_{3^{6n}}^*$

1. **if** $b' = 1$ **then** $y_p \leftarrow -y_p$
2. $R_0 \leftarrow -y_p(x_p + x_q + b) + y_q\sigma + y_p\rho$
3. $d \leftarrow b$
4. **for** $i \leftarrow 0$ **to** $(n-1)/2$ **do**
5. $\quad r_0 \leftarrow x_p + x_q + d$
6. $\quad R_1 \leftarrow -r_0^2 + y_p y_q \sigma - r_0 \rho - \rho^2$
7. $\quad R_0 \leftarrow R_0 R_1$
8. $\quad y_p \leftarrow -y_p$
9. $\quad x_q \leftarrow x_q^9,\ y_q \leftarrow y_q^9$
10. $\quad R_0 \leftarrow R_0^3$
11. $\quad d \leftarrow d - b \pmod 3$
12. **end for**
13. **return** R_0^W

be a function whose divisor is $(g_R) = 3(R) + (-3R) - 4(\mathcal{O})$ for $R = (x_r, y_r)$. The η_T pairing,

$$\eta_T : E^b(\mathbb{F}_{3^n}) \times E^b(\mathbb{F}_{3^n}) \to \mathbb{F}_{3^{6n}}^*$$

is defined by

$$\eta_T(P,Q) = l_{3P', b'P}(\psi(Q)) \prod_{j=0}^{(n-1)/2} g_{3^{-j}P'}(\psi(Q))^{3^j}, \quad (3)$$

where $P, Q \in E^b(\mathbb{F}_{3^n})$ and $P' = 3^{(n-1)/2}P$. Note that g_R only has such a simple form for supersingular elliptic curve $E^b(\mathbb{F}_{3^n})$. To obtain the bilinearity of the η_T pairing, we need a powering by

$$W = (3^{3n} - 1)(3^n + 1)(3^n + 1 - b'(3^{(n+1)/2})) \,(= (3^{6n} - 1)/\#E^b(\mathbb{F}_{3^n})). \quad (4)$$

Then, $\eta_T(aP, Q)^W = \eta_T(P, aQ)^W = (\eta_T(P, Q)^W)^a$ holds for any non-zero integer a. This powering by W is called the *final exponentiation*.

Next, we explain a relationship between the η_T pairing and Tate pairing[1] $e : E^b(\mathbb{F}_{3^n}) \times E^b(\mathbb{F}_{3^n}) \to \mathbb{F}_{3^{6n}}^*$, which is often used in practice. Then, there is a relationship between the η_T pairing and Tate pairing,

$$(\eta_T(P,Q)^W)^{3T^2} = e(P,Q)^Z,$$

where T and Z are integers defined by

$$T = 3^{(n+1)/2} + b',\ Z = -b' 3^{(n+3)/2}.$$

Eq. (3) provides Algorithm 1 for computing the η_T pairing over $\mathbb{F}_{3^n}$, which is the no-cube-root version proposed by Beuchat et al. [3].

---
[1] More precisely e is the *modified Tate pairing*.

2.2 Cost of Some Computations

In this section, we describe computational costs of a multiplication in $\mathbb{F}_{3^{6n}}$, Algorithm 1, and a point addition and a scalar multiplication of a point on $E^b(\mathbb{F}_{3^n})$. These descriptions are required to compare the cost of our countermeasure with other existing countermeasures.

Some notations about the computational costs in $\mathbb{F}_{3^n}$ are defined as follows: M, C, I, A, and As are computational costs of a multiplication, a cubing, an inversion, an addition/subtraction, and some additions/subtractions in $\mathbb{F}_{3^n}$, respectively. We know that the cost of cubing in $\mathbb{F}_{3^{6n}}$ is $6M + As$.

We use the basis $\{1, \sigma, \rho, \sigma\rho, \rho^2, \sigma\rho^2\}$ for the extension field $\mathbb{F}_{3^{6n}}$, where σ and ρ are defined for the distortion map (Eq. (2)). For simplicity, $a_0 + a_1\sigma + a_2\rho + a_3\sigma\rho + a_4\rho^2 + a_5\sigma\rho^2 \in \mathbb{F}_{3^{6n}}$ is represented as $(a_0, a_1, a_2, a_3, a_4, a_5)$.

We have the following computational costs of some multiplications with special constant coefficients in $\mathbb{F}_{3^{6n}}$. Note that Step 7 in Algorithm 1 is computed by (ii) (not (i)).

Property 1. Multiplications in $\mathbb{F}_{3^{6n}}$ are computed by the Karatsuba method [14] with the following costs:

(i) $18M + As$ for multiplication $(a_0, a_1, a_2, a_3, a_4, a_5) \times (b_0, b_1, b_2, b_3, b_4, b_5)$ [12],
(ii) $13M + As$ for multiplication $(a_0, a_1, a_2, a_3, a_4, a_5) \times (b_0, b_1, b_2, 0, -1, 0)$ [8],
(iii) $15M + As$ for multiplication $(a_0, a_1, a_2, a_3, a_4, a_5) \times (b_0, b_1, b_2, 0, b_4, 0)$.

Proof. Refer to Appendix A for the proof of (iii). □

The cost of Algorithm 1 except the final exponentiation (Step 13) is estimated using Property 1. Note that a multiplication of Step 7, $R_0 R_1$, costs $13M + As$ according to Property 1. Thus, Steps 2, 5, 6, 7, 8, 9, and 10 cost M, As, $2M$, $13M + As$, As, $4C$, and $6C + As$, respectively. Therefore, the total cost of Algorithm 1 except the final exponentiation is $M + ((n+1)/2) \cdot (As + 2M + 13M + As + As + 4C + 6C + As) = (7.5n + 8.5)M + (5n + 5)C + As$.

A scalar multiplication on $E^b(\mathbb{F}_{3^n})$ is efficiently performed with the tripling-and-addition method because a computation of tripling the point is very efficient. Indeed, a tripling point and a point addition using a projective coordinate system cost $M + 6C$ and $12M + 4C$, respectively. Then, a computation of scalar multiplication of mP costs

$$(9 \log_3 m)M + (8.7 \log_3 m)C + 2I \qquad (5)$$

on average because $\log_3 m$ point triplings and $2/3 \cdot \log_3 m$ point additions on average and two inversions for restoring a point to the affine coordinate are required [9].

3 Previous Countermeasures against SCAs

In this section, we review previously known SCAs on pairing and countermeasures against them.

SCAs try to reveal the secret information on hardware devices by selectively inputting data into the device and monitoring the side channel information such as power consumption and timing while the device executes a cryptographic algorithm [15,16].

Scott first pointed out that SCAs can be used against pairing devices when P is public and Q is secret for the input of pairing $e(P,Q)$ [21]. For example, such a situation appears in Boneh and Franklin's identity-based encryption [4]. Moreover, Scott proposed two countermeasures, namely the *scalar multiplication and bilinearity method* and the *method of randomizing the intermediate value*. Page et al. [19] showed that SCAs can reveal secret data by monitoring a multiplication of the secret data by public data. They also proposed two countermeasures against these attacks, the *improved scalar multiplication and bilinearity method* and the *point-blinding method*. Kim et al. [13] showed that a computation of $\alpha \cdot (\beta + \gamma)$ can also be a subject of differential power analysis (DPA) attacks, where α and β are secret, and γ is public. They proposed a countermeasure, the *randomized-projective-coordinate method*, and that was improved by Choi et al. [5].

Whelan et al. [25] explained that a multiplication of secret data by public data, and squaring and square-root computations of secret data became subjects of SCAs if we use the pairing over finite fields of characteristic two. Moreover, they discuss that one input point Q of pairing $e(P,Q)$ is fixed (never changed) during computation of the BKLS algorithm. Thus, one might resist SCAs by setting the secret data to the updating point P. On the contrary, one needs a countermeasure in the case of the η_T pairing due to its symmetric structure.

Let $P = (x_p, y_p)$ and $Q = (x_q, y_q)$ be points input into Algorithm 1. If P is a secret point, the target operations of SCA are $y_p(x_p + x_q + b)$ in Step 2, r_0^2 in Step 6, $y_p y_q$ in Step 6, or $R_0 R_1$ in Step 7. Moreover, if Q is a secret point, then x_q^9 or y_q^9 in Step 9 could also be the target of the attack.

In the remainder of this section, we explain details of the above countermeasures and estimate their costs when using the η_T pairing over $\mathbb{F}_{3^n}$.

3.1 Scalar Multiplication and Bilinearity Method [19]

In the scalar multiplication and bilinearity method, an integer α with $0 \leq \alpha < l$ is selected at random by a device, and another integer $\beta = (\alpha^{-1} \bmod l)$ is computed, where l is the largest prime factor of the order of the points. The device then computes
$$\eta_T(\alpha P, \beta Q)^W,$$
which is equal to $\eta_T(P,Q)^W$ because $\eta_T(\alpha P, \beta Q)^W = (\eta_T(P,Q)^W)^{\alpha\beta} = \eta_T(P,Q)^W$ due to the bilinearity of the η_T pairing. Even if point Q is selected by the attacker, it is changed to βQ by the device, and the attacker cannot know βQ. Therefore, this method provides a secure computation method for the η_T pairing against SCAs. The overhead is two scalar multiplications on the elliptic curve, which is $18nM + 17.4nC + 2I$ on average according to Eq. (5) because α and $\beta \approx 3^n$ and $\log_3 \alpha \approx \log_3 \beta \approx n$. Now, the costs of the computation of β and additions/subtractions is ignored.

3.2 Point-Blinding Method [19]

The point-blinding method computes

$$(\eta_T(P, Q + R) \cdot \eta_T(P, -R))^W,$$

where point R is selected by the device at random, and thus, the attacker cannot control R. Note that this value is equal to $\eta_T(P,Q)^W$ because $(\eta_T(P,Q + R) \cdot \eta_T(P, -R))^W = \eta_T(P, Q + R)^W \cdot \eta_T(P, -R)^W = \eta_T(P,Q)^W \cdot \eta_T(P,R)^W \cdot (\eta_T(P,R)^W)^{-1} = \eta_T(P,Q)^W$ due to the bilinearity of the η_T pairing. The overhead is a point addition on the elliptic curve ($12M + 2I$) ($2I$ is needed for conversion of coordinates), a computation of the η_T pairing without final exponentiation (($7.5n + 8.5)M + (5n + 5)C$), and a multiplication in $\mathbb{F}_{3^{6n}}$ ($18M$). Note that there is no cost for the computation of $-R$ because $-R = (x_r, -y_r)$ for $R = (x_r, y_r)$. Then, the overhead cost is $(7.5n + 38.5)M + (5n + 5)C + 2I$.

3.3 Method of Randomizing Intermediate Value [21]

In the method of randomizing the intermediate value proposed by Scott, randomizations are performed for intermediate values related to Q and R_0 in loops of the pairing algorithm. Then, Steps 2, 5, and 6 in Algorithm 1 are modified as follows:

2. $R_0 \leftarrow -\lambda \cdot y_p(x_p + x_q + b) + \lambda \cdot y_q\sigma + \lambda \cdot y_p\rho$
5. $r_0 \leftarrow \lambda \cdot x_p + \lambda \cdot x_q + \lambda \cdot d$
6. $R_1 \leftarrow -\lambda \cdot r_0^2 + \lambda \cdot y_py_q\sigma - \lambda \cdot r_0\rho - \lambda \cdot \rho^2$

where λ is a random value in $\mathbb{F}_{3^n}^*$ selected by the device. Denote by Algorithm 1' the modified Algorithm 1. Then, (R_0 in Step 12 of Algorithm 1) $= \lambda'(R_0$ in Step 12 of Algorithm 1') for some $\lambda' \in \mathbb{F}_{3^n}^*$. However, the effect of λ' is removed by the final exponentiation, namely $(\lambda' \cdot \eta_T(P,Q))^W = \eta_T(P,Q)^W$ for W of Eq. (4). Indeed, for $r \in \mathbb{F}_{3^{3n}}^*$ or $r \in \mathbb{F}_{3^n}^*$

$$r^W = 1 \qquad (6)$$

is in general satisfied because

$$r^W = r^{(3^{3n}-1)(3^n+1)(3^n+1-b'(3^{(n+1)}))} = 1^{(3^n+1)(3^n+1-b'(3^{(n+1)}))} = 1.$$

Scott recommends to multiply intermediate values by λ not at once but one by one for security. Then, the overheads of Steps 2, 5, and 6 are $3M$, $3M$, and $3M$, respectively. Note that Step 7 also creates an overhead because R_1 has the form of $(b_0, b_1, b_2, 0, b_4, 0)$ not $(b_0, b_1, b_2, 0, -1, 0)$. Then, Step 7 takes $15M$ not $13M$ according to Property 1; namely, the overhead of Step 7 is $2M$. Therefore, the total overhead of this method is $(3.5n + 6.5)M$.

3.4 Randomized-Projective-Coordinate Method

Kim et al. proposed a randomized-projective-coordinate method for the η_T pairing algorithm over characteristic two [13].

Algorithm 2: Computation of the η_t pairing with the randomized projective coordinate method for $n \equiv 1 \pmod{12}$

input: $P = (x_p, y_p), Q = (x_q, y_q) \in E^b(\mathbb{F}_{3^n})$
output: $(\eta_T(P,Q)^{3^{(n+1)/2}})^W \in \mathbb{F}_{3^{6n}}^*$

	randomizing P		randomizing Q
0.	$(X_p, Y_p, Z_p) \leftarrow (\lambda x_p, \lambda y_p, \lambda)$	0.	$(X_q, Y_q, Z_q) \leftarrow (\lambda x_q, \lambda y_q, \lambda)$
	(λ is a random value in $\mathbb{F}_{3^n}^*$)		(λ is a random value in $\mathbb{F}_{3^n}^*$)
1.	if $b' = 1$ then $Y_p \leftarrow -Y_p$	1.	if $b' = 1$ then $y_p \leftarrow -y_p$
2.	$R_0 \leftarrow -Y_p(X_p + Z_p(x_q + b))$	2.	$R_0 \leftarrow -y_p(Z_q(x_p + b) + X_q)$
	$+Z_p^2 y_q \sigma + Z_p Y_p \rho$		$+y_q\sigma + Z_q y_p \rho$
3.	$d \leftarrow b$	3.	$d \leftarrow b$
4.	for $i \leftarrow 0$ to $(n-1)/2$ do	4.	for $i \leftarrow 0$ to $(n-1)/2$ do
5.	$r_0 \leftarrow X_p + Z_p(x_q + d)$	5.	$r_0 \leftarrow Z_q(x_q + d) + X_q$
6.	$R_1 \leftarrow -r_0^2 + Z_p Y_p y_q \sigma$	6.	$R_1 \leftarrow -r_0^2 + Z_q y_p Y_q \sigma$
	$-Z_p r_0 \rho - Z_p^2 \rho^2$		$-Z_q r_0 \rho - Z_q^2 \rho^2$
7.	$R_0 \leftarrow R_0 R_1$	7.	$R_0 \leftarrow R_0 R_1$
8.	$Y_p \leftarrow -Y_p$	8.	$y_p \leftarrow -y_p$
9.	$x_q \leftarrow x_q^9, y_q \leftarrow y_q^9$	9.	$X_q \leftarrow X_q^9, Y_q \leftarrow Y_q^9, Z_q \leftarrow Z_q^9$
10.	$R_0 \leftarrow R_0^3$	10.	$R_0 \leftarrow R_0^3$
11.	$d \leftarrow d - b \pmod 3$	11.	$d \leftarrow d - b \pmod 3$
12.	end for	12.	end for
13.	return R_0^W	13.	return R_0^W

This paper gives a characteristic three version of the randomized-projective-coordinate algorithm (Algorithm 2), where the left side uses the projective coordinate for P, and the right side does that for Q. Although $R_0 = \lambda' \eta_T(P,Q)^{3^{(n+1)/2}}$ holds for some $\lambda' \in \mathbb{F}_{3^n}^*$ at Step 12 in both sides of Algorithm 2, the effect of λ' is removed by the final exponentiation as well as the method of randomizing the intermediate value. Note that like the method of randomizing the intermediate value, the cost of Step 7 in each side of Algorithm 2 is $15M$; namely, the overhead is $2M$ for each side. The cost of the left side of Algorithm 2 is $(10.5 + 17.5)M + (5n + 5)C + As$. Then, the overhead is $(3n+9)M$. The cost of the right side is $(10.5 + 15.5)M + (6n + 6)C$. Then, the overhead is $(3n+7)M + (n+1)C$. When $2M > (n+1)C$, for example, when $C = 0$ using a normal basis of $\mathbb{F}_{3^n}$ over $\mathbb{F}_3$, the left side is more efficient than the right side. In other cases, the right side is more efficient than the left side.

4 Proposed Countermeasure

In this section, we propose an efficient countermeasure against SCAs for the computation of η_T pairing over $\mathbb{F}_{3^n}$. The basic strategy is as follows: (1) The point (x_p, y_p) input into the η_T pairing is randomized by the random value

Algorithm 3: Proposed secure η_T pairing algorithm against SCAs for $n \equiv 1 \pmod{12}$

input: $P = (x_p, y_p), Q = (x_q, y_q) \in E^b(\mathbb{F}_{3^n})$
output: $(\eta_T(P,Q))^{3^{(n+1)/2}} \in \mathbb{F}_{3^{6n}}^*$

1-1. **if** $b' = 1$ **then** $y_p \leftarrow -y_p$
1-2. $Y_p \leftarrow \lambda' y_p$, $Y_q \leftarrow \lambda' y_q$ (λ' is a random value in $\mathbb{F}_{3^n}^*$)
1-3. $x_p \leftarrow x_p + \lambda$, $y_p \leftarrow y_p + \lambda$, $x_q \leftarrow x_q - \lambda$, $y_q \leftarrow y_q - \lambda$, $\lambda'' \leftarrow \lambda^2$
   (λ is a random value in $\mathbb{F}_{3^n}^*$, $\lambda = \lambda'$ is possible)
2. $R_0 \leftarrow -Y_p(x_p + x_q + b) + Y_q \sigma + Y_p \rho$
3. $d \leftarrow b$
4. **for** $i \leftarrow 0$ **to** $(n-1)/2$ **do**
5. $r_0 \leftarrow x_p + x_q + d$
6. $R_1 \leftarrow -(r_0 + \lambda)(r_0 - \lambda) - \lambda'' + (y_p y_q + \lambda(y_p - y_q - \lambda))\sigma - r_0 \rho - \rho^2$
7. $R_0 \leftarrow R_0 R_1$
8. $x_p \leftarrow x_p - \lambda + \lambda^9$, $y_p \leftarrow -y_p + \lambda + \lambda^9$
9. $x_q \leftarrow x_q^9$, $y_q \leftarrow y_q^9$, $\lambda \leftarrow \lambda^9$, $\lambda'' \leftarrow \lambda''^9$
10. $R_0 \leftarrow R_0^3$
11. $d \leftarrow d - b \pmod{3}$
12. **end for**
13. **return** R_0^W

additions $(x_p + \lambda)$ and $(y_p + \lambda)$, where λ is a random value in $\mathbb{F}_{3^n}^*$. (2) The effects of the random additions are removed at some steps in the algorithm. The proposed algorithm is represented as Algorithm 3.

4.1 Correctness of Algorithm 3

In the following, we prove that Algorithm 3 outputs the correct value of the η_T pairing over $\mathbb{F}_{3^n}$.

We try to investigate the differences between Algorithms 1 and 3. To distinguish the values in Algorithm 1 from those in Algorithm 3, each variable is denoted by suffix "$_1$" or "$_3$", respectively. For example, x_{p1} is denoted by x_p in Algorithm 1. Without of generality we can assume $\lambda' = 1$ due to Eq. (6). Then, we can prove the following lemma.

Lemma 1. *Suppose $\lambda' = 1$, then we have the following relationships*

$$x_{p3} = x_{p1} + \lambda^{9^i}, y_{p3} = y_{p1} + \lambda^{9^i}, x_{q3} = x_{q1} - \lambda^{9^i}, \text{ and } y_{q3} = y_{q1} - \lambda^{9^i} \quad (7)$$

at the beginning of the i-th iteration of Algorithms 1 and 3.

Proof. We prove the lemma by induction. We can easily see that Eq. (7) is satisfied for $i = 0$ at Step 1-3 of Algorithm 3. Next, suppose that at the i-th iteration Eq. (7) is correct. In Algorithm 1, x_{p1}, y_{p1}, x_{q1}, and y_{q1} are updated as

$x_{p1}, -y_{p1}, x_{q1}^9$, and y_{q1}^9, respectively. At Step 8 of the i-th iteration in Algorithm 3, x_{p3} is updated as

$$x_{p3} \leftarrow x_{p3} - \lambda^{9^i} + \lambda^{9^{i+1}} = (x_{p1} + \lambda^{9^i}) - \lambda^{9^i} + \lambda^{9^{i+1}} = x_{p1} + \lambda^{9^{i+1}},$$

and y_{p3} is updated as

$$y_{p3} \leftarrow -y_{p3} + \lambda^{9^i} + \lambda^{9^{i+1}} = -(y_{p1} + \lambda^{9^i}) + \lambda^{9^i} + \lambda^{9^{i+1}} = -y_{p1} + \lambda^{9^{i+1}}.$$

At Step 9 of the i-th iteration in Algorithm 3, x_{q3} and y_{q3} are updated as

$$x_{q3} \leftarrow x_{q3}^9 = (x_{q1} - \lambda^{9^i})^9 = x_{q1}^9 - \lambda^{9^{i+1}}, \text{ and } y_{q3} \leftarrow y_{q3}^9 = (y_{q1} - \lambda^{9^i})^9 = y_{q1}^9 - \lambda^{9^{i+1}},$$

respectively. Therefore, Eq. (7) is satisfied at the beginning of every $(i+1)$-th iteration. □

To prove the correctness of Algorithm 3, showing that

$$r_{03} = r_{01} \text{ and } R_{13} = R_{11}$$

are satisfied at every i-th iteration under the assumption $\lambda' = 1$ is sufficient. Indeed, at every i-th iteration we have the relationship

$$r_{03} = x_{p3} + x_{q3} + d = (x_{p1} + \lambda^{9^i}) + (x_{q1} - \lambda^{9^i}) + d = x_{p1} + x_{q1} + d = r_{01} \quad (8)$$

and

$$\begin{aligned}R_{13} &= -(r_{03} + \lambda)(r_{03} - \lambda) - \lambda'' + (y_{p3}y_{q3} + \lambda(y_{p3} - y_{q3} - \lambda))\sigma - r_0\rho - \rho^2 \\ &= -r_{03}^2 + \lambda^2 - \lambda'' + (y_{p3}y_{q3} + \lambda(y_{p3} - y_{q3} - \lambda))\sigma - r_0\rho - \rho^2 \\ &= -r_{01}^2 + y_{p1}y_{q1}\sigma - r_{01}\rho - \rho^2 \\ &= R_{11}\end{aligned}$$

from Eqs. (7) and (8) because $\lambda'' = \lambda^2$ holds in every i-th iteration. Therefore, we proved the correctness of Algorithm 3.

4.2 Security

We discuss the security of Algorithm 3 against SCAs. The attacker targets Steps 2, 5, 6, and 7 in Algorithm 3. However, all values are randomized by random values λ and λ'' for Steps 2, 5, and 6. Step 7 is also secure because, although R_1 is not randomized, R_0 is randomized by λ' at Step 1-2. An explanation may be needed for Step 6. Note that

$$-(r_0 + \lambda)(r_0 - \lambda) - \lambda'' = -r_0^2$$

because λ'' is equal to λ^2, as noted above. However, we need the computation of "$-(r_0 + \lambda)(r_0 - \lambda) - \lambda'''$" (not r_0^2) because r_0 is unchangeable either with the randomization at Step 1-3 or without it. Therefore, if this process is not performed, then the attacker may guess r_0^2.

Table 1. Comparison of overheads for countermeasure against SCAs

Countermeasure method	Additional Cost
Point Multiplication and Bilinearity Method [19]	$18nM + 17.4nC + 2I$
Point-Blinding Method [19]	$(7.5n + 38.5)M + (5n + 5)C + 2I$
Method of Randomizing the Intermediate Value [21]	$(3.5n + 6.5)M$
Left Side of Algorithm 2*	$(3n + 9)M$
Right Side of Algorithm 2*	$(3n + 7)M + (n + 1)C$
The Proposed Method (Algorithm 3)	$\mathbf{(0.5n + 3.5)M + (3n + 3)C}$

* Algorithm 2 is the characteristic three version of the randomized-projective-coordinate method [13].

4.3 Comparison with Other Methods

We estimate the computational cost of the proposed scheme and compare it with the previously known methods described in Section 3. Now, we suppose that the cost of a squaring is equal to that of a multiplication.

Here, we ignore the costs of additions/subtractions. Step 7 in Algorithm 3 requires $13M$ as well as Algorithm 1 because R_1 in Algorithm 3 has the form of $(b_0, b_1, b_2, 0, -1, 0)$ due to Property 1. Note that this sparse multiplication can be applied to neither Algorithm 2 nor the method of randomizing the intermediate value. Steps 1-2, 2, 6, 7, 8, 9, and 10 in Algorithm 3 cost $3M$, M, $3M$, $13M$, $2C$, $6C$, and $6C$, respectively. Therefore, the total cost of Algorithm 3 except the final exponentiation is $3M + M + ((n+1)/2) \cdot (3M + 13M + 2C + 6C + 6C) = (8n + 12)M + (7n + 7)C$. Then, the overhead is $(0.5n + 3.5)M + (3n + 3C)$.

A comparison of the proposed countermeasure with existing countermeasures is shown in Table 1. Note that the extension degree should satisfy $n \geq 97$ for security reasons. We estimate the cost of cubing to be $C = 0.07M$ for the polynomial basis [8,20] and $C = 0$ for the normal basis on hardware. The overhead of the proposed method is $72.58M$ for $C = 0.07M$ and $n = 97$ and that of the left side of Algorithm 2 is $300M$, which is the smallest of any algorithm. Then, the overhead cost is reduced by 76%. When we choose a sufficiently large n, then the overhead of the proposed method and Algorithm 2 becomes $0.5nM$ and $3nM$, respectively, for $C = 0$. In this case, the overhead is reduced by 83%.

5 Conclusion

In this paper, we proposed a variation of the η_T pairing over $\mathbb{F}_{3^n}$ that is secure against SCAs. The randomization technique in the proposed scheme uses the random value additions $x_p + \lambda$ and $y_p + \lambda$ for the input point $P = (x_p, y_p)$ and a random value $\lambda \in \mathbb{F}_{3^n}^*$. Interestingly, the symmetric structure of the η_T pairing provides a simple algebraic equation with a random value of λ in the main loop. Therefore, the proposed scheme has the smallest overhead of the randomization secure against SCAs, which is just $0.5nM$ for the η_T pairing over $\mathbb{F}_{3^n}$. That is reduced by more than 75% compared with the randomized-projective-coordinate method. The method of this paper is applied to the Duursma-Lee algorithm due to its similarity with the η_T pairing algorithm.

Acknowledgments

This work was supported by the New Energy and Industrial Technology Development Organization (NEDO), Japan.

References

1. Barreto, P., Kim, H., Lynn, B., Scott, M.: Efficient algorithms for pairing-based cryptosystems. In: Yung, M. (ed.) CRYPTO 2002. LNCS, vol. 2442, pp. 354–368. Springer, Heidelberg (2002)
2. Barreto, P., Galbraith, S., ÓhÉigeartaigh, C., Scott, M.: Efficient pairing computation on supersingular abelian varieties. In: Designs, Codes and Cryptography, vol. 42(3), pp. 239–271. Springer, Heidelberg (2007)
3. Beuchat, J.-L., Shirase, M., Takagi, T., Okamoto, E.: An algorithm for the η_T pairing calculation in characteristic three and its hardware implementation. In: 18th IEEE International Symposium on Computer Arithmetic, ARITH-18, pp. 97–104 (2007)
4. Boneh, D., Franklin, M.: Identity based encryption from the Weil pairing. SIAM Journal of Computing 32(3), 586–615 (2003)
5. Choi, D.H., Han, D.-G., Kim, H.W.: Construction of efficient and secure pairing algorithm and its application. Cryptology ePrint Archive, Report 2007/296 (2007)
6. Coron, J.-S.: Resistance against differential power analysis for elliptic curve cryptosystems. In: Koç, Ç.K., Paar, C. (eds.) CHES 1999. LNCS, vol. 1717, pp. 292–302. Springer, Heidelberg (1999)
7. Grabher, P., Page, D.: Hardware acceleration of the Tate pairing in characteristic three. In: Rao, J.R., Sunar, B. (eds.) CHES 2005. LNCS, vol. 3659, pp. 398–411. Springer, Heidelberg (2005)
8. Granger, R., Page, D., Stam, M.: Hardware and software normal basis arithmetic for pairing-based cryptography in characteristic three. IEEE Transactions on Computers 54(7), 852–860 (2005)
9. Harrison, K., Page, D., Smart, N.P.: Software implementation of finite fields of characteristic three. LMS JCM 5, 181–193 (2002)
10. Hess, F., Smart, N.P., Vercauteren, F.: The Eta pairing revisited. IEEE Transactions on Information Theory 52, 4595–4602 (2006)
11. Itoh, K., Izu, T., Takenaka, M.: Efficient countermeasures against power analysis for elliptic curve. In: CARDIS 2004, pp. 99–114 (2004)
12. Kerins, T., Marnane, W., Popovici, E., Barreto, P.: Efficient hardware for the Tate pairing calculation in characteristic three. In: Rao, J.R., Sunar, B. (eds.) CHES 2005. LNCS, vol. 3659, pp. 412–426. Springer, Heidelberg (2005)
13. Kim, T.H., Takagi, T., Han, D.-G., Kim, H.W., Lim, J.: gPower analysis attacks and countermeasures on η_T pairing over binary fields. ETRI Journal 30(1), 68–80 (2008)
14. Knuth, D.E.: Seminumerical algorithms. Addison-Wesley, Reading (1981)
15. Kocher, P.: Timing attacks on implementations of Diffie-Hellman, RSA, DSS, and other systems. In: Koblitz, N. (ed.) CRYPTO 1996. LNCS, vol. 1109, pp. 104–113. Springer, Heidelberg (1996)
16. Kocher, P., Jaffe, J., Jun, B.: Differential power analysis. In: Wiener, M.J. (ed.) CRYPTO 1999. LNCS, vol. 1666, pp. 388–397. Springer, Heidelberg (1999)

17. Mamiya, H., Miyaji, A., Morimoto, H.: Secure elliptic curve exponentiation against RPA, ZRA, DPA, and SPA. IEICE Transactions on Fundamentals E90-A(1), 22–28 (2006)
18. Miller, V.: The Weil pairing, and its efficient calculation. Journal of Cryptology 17(4), 235–261 (2004)
19. Page, D., Vercauteren, F.: A fault attack on pairing based cryptography. IEEE Transactions on Computers 55(9), 1075–1080 (2006)
20. Ronan, R., ÓhÉigeartaigh, C., Murphy, C., Kerins, T., Barreto, P.: A reconfigurable processor for the cryptographic η_T pairing in characteristic 3. In: Information Technology: New Generations, ITNG 2007, pp. 11–16. IEEE Computer Society, Los Alamitos (2007)
21. Scott, M.: Computing the Tate pairing. In: Menezes, A. (ed.) CT-RSA 2005. LNCS, vol. 3376, pp. 293–304. Springer, Heidelberg (2005)
22. Scott, M., Costigan, N., Abdulwahab, W.: Implementing cryptographic pairings on smartcards. In: Goubin, L., Matsui, M. (eds.) CHES 2006. LNCS, vol. 4249, pp. 134–147. Springer, Heidelberg (2006)
23. Shu, C., Kwon, S., Gaj, K.: FPGA accelerated Tate pairing based cryptosystems over binary fields. Cryptology ePrint Archive, Report 2006/179 (2006)
24. Silverman, J.: The arithmetic of elliptic curves. Springer, Heidelberg (1986)
25. Whelan, C., Scott, M.: Side channel analysis of practical pairing implementations: Which path is more secure? In: Nguyên, P.Q. (ed.) VIETCRYPT 2006. LNCS, vol. 4341, pp. 81–98. Springer, Heidelberg (2006)
26. Whelan, C., Scott, M.: The importance of the final exponentiation in pairings when considering fault attacks. In: Takagi, T., Okamoto, T., Okamoto, E., Okamoto, T. (eds.) Pairing 2007. LNCS, vol. 4575, pp. 225–246. Springer, Heidelberg (2007)

A Proof of Property 1

Property 1. Multiplications in $\mathbb{F}_{36^n}$ are computed by the Karatsuba method [14] with the following cost:

(i) $18M + As$ for multiplication $(a_0, a_1, a_2, a_3, a_4, a_5) \times (b_0, b_1, b_2, b_3, b_4, b_5)$ [12],
(ii) $13M + As$ for multiplication $(a_0, a_1, a_2, a_3, a_4, a_5) \times (b_0, b_1, b_2, 0, -1, 0)$ [8],
(iii) $15M + As$ for multiplication $(a_0, a_1, a_2, a_3, a_4, a_5) \times (b_0, b_1, b_2, 0, b_4, 0)$.

Proof. (i) and (ii) are known results. However, we provide proofs of all cases because an explanation of (i) is needed to show (iii), and there may not be an explicit proof of (ii). First, consider a multiplication in $\mathbb{F}_{3^{2n}}$

$$(a_0 + a_1\sigma) \times (b_0 + b_1\sigma) = (a_0b_0 - a_1b_1) + (a_0b_1 + a_1b_0)\sigma.$$

Using the Karatsuba method costs $3M + As$. Indeed, $(a_0b_1 - a_1b_0)$ can be computed as $(a_0b_1 - a_1b_0) = (a_0 + a_1)(b_0 + b_1) - a_0b_0 - a_1b_1$. Then, three multiplications, a_0b_0, a_1b_1, and $(a_0 + a_1)(b_0 + b_1)$ are needed to compute $(a_0 + a_1\sigma) \times (b_0 + b_1\sigma)$.

(i) Suppose that $(a_0, a_1, a_2, a_3, a_4, a_5) \times (b_0, b_1, b_2, b_3, b_4, b_5) = (c_0, c_1, c_2, c_3, c_4, c_5)$. Let $\tilde{a}_{i(i+1)}, \tilde{b}_{i(i+1)},$ and $\tilde{c}_{i(i+1)}$ be elements in $\mathbb{F}_{3^{2n}}$ defined by $a_i + a_{i+1}\sigma, b_i + b_{i+1}\sigma,$

and $c_i + c_{i+1}\sigma$, respectively, for $i = 0, 2, 4$. For example, $(a_0, a_1, a_2, a_3, a_4, a_5)$ is represented as $\tilde{a}_{01} + \tilde{a}_{23}\rho + \tilde{a}_{45}\rho^2$. Then, $(a_0, a_1, a_2, a_3, a_4, a_5) \times (b_0, b_1, b_2, b_3, b_4, b_5)$ is computed as follows:

$$\begin{aligned}
\tilde{d}_0 &= \tilde{a}_{01}\tilde{b}_{01}, \\
\tilde{d}_1 &= (\tilde{a}_{01} + \tilde{a}_{23})(\tilde{b}_{01} + \tilde{b}_{23}) - \tilde{a}_{01}\tilde{b}_{01} - \tilde{a}_{23}\tilde{b}_{23}, \\
\tilde{d}_2 &= (\tilde{a}_{01} + \tilde{a}_{45})(\tilde{b}_{01} + \tilde{b}_{45}) + \tilde{a}_{23}\tilde{b}_{23} - \tilde{a}_{01}\tilde{b}_{01} - \tilde{a}_{45}\tilde{b}_{45}, \\
\tilde{d}_3 &= (\tilde{a}_{23} + \tilde{a}_{45})(\tilde{b}_{23} + \tilde{b}_{45}) - \tilde{a}_{23}\tilde{b}_{23} - \tilde{a}_{45}\tilde{b}_{45}, \\
\tilde{d}_4 &= \tilde{a}_{45}\tilde{b}_{45},
\end{aligned} \qquad (9)$$

and

$$\begin{aligned}
\tilde{c}_{01} &= \tilde{d}_0 + b\tilde{d}_3, \\
\tilde{c}_{23} &= \tilde{d}_1 + \tilde{d}_3 + b\tilde{d}_4, \\
\tilde{c}_{45} &= \tilde{d}_2 + \tilde{d}_4,
\end{aligned}$$

where $b = 1$ or -1 defined by Eq. (1). Therefore, a multiplication in $\mathbb{F}_{3^{6n}}$ takes 6 multiplications,

$$\tilde{a}_{01}\tilde{b}_{01},\ \tilde{a}_{23}\tilde{b}_{23},\ \tilde{a}_{45}\tilde{b}_{45},\ (\tilde{a}_{01}+\tilde{a}_{23})(\tilde{b}_{01}+\tilde{b}_{23}),\ (\tilde{a}_{01}+\tilde{a}_{45})(\tilde{b}_{01}+\tilde{b}_{45}),$$
$$\text{and } (\tilde{a}_{23}+\tilde{a}_{45})(\tilde{b}_{23}+\tilde{b}_{45}),$$

and some additions/subtractions in $\mathbb{F}_{3^{2n}}$. Then a multiplication in $\mathbb{F}_{3^{6n}}$ takes $18M + As$.

(ii) In this case, $\tilde{b}_{23} = b_2$ and $\tilde{b}_{45} = -1$ in Eq. (9). Each of $\tilde{a}_{01}\tilde{b}_{01}$, $(\tilde{a}_{01}+\tilde{a}_{23})(\tilde{b}_{01}+\tilde{b}_{23})$, and $(\tilde{a}_{01}+\tilde{a}_{45})(\tilde{b}_{01}+\tilde{b}_{45})$ takes $3M+As$, but each of the other multiplications takes a smaller cost. Indeed, $\tilde{a}_{23}\tilde{b}_{23} = a_2b_2 + a_3b_2\sigma$ takes $2M + As$, $\tilde{a}_{45}\tilde{b}_{45} = -a_4 - a_5\sigma$ takes no cost, and $(\tilde{a}_{23} + \tilde{a}_{45})(\tilde{b}_{23} + \tilde{b}_{45}) = (a_2 + a_4)(b_2 - 1) + (a_3 + a_5)(b_2-1)\sigma$ takes $2M+As$. Therefore, $(a_0, a_1, a_2, a_3, a_4, a_5) \times (b_0, b_1, b_2, 0, -1, 0)$ takes $13(= 3 \times 3 + 2 + 0 + 2)M + As$.

(iii) In this case $\tilde{b}_{23} = b_2$ and $\tilde{b}_{45} = b_4$ in Eq. (9). Each of $\tilde{a}_{01}\tilde{b}_{01}$, $(\tilde{a}_{01}+\tilde{a}_{23})(\tilde{b}_{01}+\tilde{b}_{23})$ and $(\tilde{a}_{01} + \tilde{a}_{45})(\tilde{b}_{01} + \tilde{b}_{45})$ takes $3M + As$ as well as (ii). On the other hand, each of the other multiplications takes $2M + As$ because $\tilde{a}_{23}\tilde{b}_{23} = a_2b_2 + a_3b_2\sigma$, $\tilde{a}_{45}\tilde{b}_{45} = a_4b_4 + a_5b_4\sigma$, and $(\tilde{a}_{23} + \tilde{a}_{45})(\tilde{b}_{23} + \tilde{b}_{45}) = (a_2 + a_4)(b_2 + b_4) + (a_3 + a_5)(b_2 + b_4)\sigma$. Therefore, $(a_0, a_1, a_2, a_3, a_4, a_5) \times (b_0, b_1, b_2, 0, b_4, 0)$ takes $15(= 3 \times 3 + 3 \times 2)M + As$. □

Efficient Arithmetic on Subfield Elliptic Curves over Small Finite Fields of Odd Characteristic

Keisuke Hakuta[1], Hisayoshi Sato[1], and Tsuyoshi Takagi[2]

[1] Hitachi, Ltd., Systems Development Laboratory,
1099, Ohzenji, Asao-ku, Kawasaki, 215-0013, Japan
{keisuke.hakuta.cw, hisayoshi.sato.th}@hitachi.com
[2] Future University - Hakodate,
School of Systems Information Science,
116-2, Kamedanakano-cho, Hakodate, 041-8655, Japan
takagi@fun.ac.jp

Abstract. In elliptic curve cryptosystems, scalar multiplications performed on the curves have much effect on the efficiency of the schemes, and many efficient methods have been proposed. In particular, recoding methods of the scalars play an important role in the performance of the algorithm used. For integer radices, the non-adjacent form (NAF) [21] and its generalizations (e.g., the generalized non-adjacent form (GNAF) [6] and the radix-r non-adjacent form (rNAF) [28]) have been proposed for minimizing the non-zero densities in the representations of the scalars. On the other hand, for subfield elliptic curves, the Frobenius expansions of the scalars can be used for improving efficiency [25]. Unfortunately, there are only a few methods apply the techniques of NAF or its analogue to the Frobenius expansion, namely τ-adic NAF techniques on Koblitz curves [16,27,3] and hyperelliptic Koblitz curves [10]. In this paper, we try to combine these techniques, namely recoding methods for reducing non-zero density and the Frobenius expansion, and propose two new efficient recoding methods of scalars on more general family of subfield elliptic curves in odd characteristic. We also prove that the non-zero densities for the new methods are same as those for the original GNAF and rNAF. As a result, the speed of the proposed methods improve between 8% and 50% over that for the Frobenius expansion method.

Keywords: Elliptic Curves, Non-Adjacent Form (NAF), Frobenius Expansions, τ-adic NAF (τ-NAF), ϕ-adic NAF (ϕ-NAF).

1 Introduction

Elliptic curve cryptosystems (ECC) were proposed in 1985 independently by Victor Miller [19] and by Neal Koblitz [14]. Since ECC provide many advantages, for example, shorter key length and faster computation speed than those of RSA cryptosystems, ECC have been the focus of much attention. In ECC, each protocol such as ECDH, EC-ElGamal, and ECDSA involves scalar multiplications for given points on an elliptic curve by positive integers. These multiplications have much effect on the efficiency of the schemes, and many efficient methods have been proposed.

As one such method, the use of subfield elliptic curves (i.e. elliptic curves over finite fields which are actually defined over some subfield [4]) is especially attractive because by using the Frobenius maps, which is efficiently computed, scalar multiplication on subfield elliptic curves can be performed much faster than that on curves over prime fields. Koblitz [15] suggested anomalous binary curves, and Müller [18] extended Koblitz's idea to achieve the Frobenius expansions over small fields of characteristic two. Smart [25] generalized Müller's result to elliptic curves over small fields of odd characteristic. Indeed, Smart [25] shows that every element $d \in \mathbb{Z}[\phi]$ can be written as $d = \sum_{i=0}^{\ell-1} d_i \phi^i$, where $d_i \in \{0, \pm 1, \cdots, \pm(q-1)/2\}$, q is the order of the defining field of an $\mathbb{F}_q$-subfield elliptic curve E, ϕ is the q-th power Frobenius map on E, t is the trace of ϕ, and $(q, t) \neq (5, \pm 4), (7, \pm 5)$. Therefore, scalar multiplication method using ϕ in place of doublings can be deployed on subfield elliptic curves. Note that neither of these methods can be applied in the case of curves over prime fields (the case in which the group of prime field rational points is used for the cryptosystem). In [11], the authors proposed efficiently computable endomorphisms other than Frobenius endomorphisms that can be used for fast scalar multiplication. Moreover, in [20], the authors proposed two kinds of endomorphisms from [11] that can be used together for a certain class of curves, and they also presented a new expansion method.

In addition, the recoding method of the scalars also plays an important role in the performance. In general, smaller non-zero densities in the representations of scalars improve the efficiency. The non-adjacent form (NAF) [21] and its generalizations such as the generalized non-adjacent form (GNAF) [6] and the radix-r non-adjacent form (rNAF) [28], are methods used for minimizing the non-zero densities. So as to achieve further improvement, it has been tried to combine the subfield curve method with the recoding methods. In [27], Solinas proposed an efficient method of scalar multiplication on binary Koblitz curves, namely τ-adic NAF (τ-NAF), and [16] proposed τ-adic NAF on some supersingular elliptic curves defined over the prime field of characteristic three using the Frobenius endomorphism of the curves. In addition, [10] proposed a generalization of τ-adic NAF on hyperelliptic Koblitz curves. Recently, in [3], the authors proposed the radix-τ width-w NAF for every integer in all Euclidean quadratic imaginary fields. But, only a few curves are available for the above methods so far. Since the choice of curves can seriously affect the security and efficiency of ECC, it is highly unlikely that only binary Koblitz curves will be used as subfield elliptic curves for cryptographic usage. There might be demand for subfield elliptic curves other than binary Koblitz curves. From this reason, to find suitable subfield elliptic curves and to develop efficient scalar multiplication algorithms on those curves is a very important matter. However, in [1], the authors say that "The study [18,25] is not as detailed as Solinas' "(pp.367). This means that no method combining Frobenius expansions and NAF or its analogue on the curves in [18,25] is known yet.

1.1 Contribution of This Paper

The contribution of this paper is to propose two generalizations of τ-NAF, that is, two classes of ϕ-adic NAF (ϕ-GNAF and ϕ-rNAF) using the techniques of GNAF and rNAF, respectively, which can be applied to a family of subfield elliptic curves defined over finite fields of odd characteristic. The digit set of NAF is $\{0, \pm 1\}$ and the digit set of the Frobenius expansion is $\{0, \pm 1, \cdots, \pm(q-1)/2\}$. We may well not be able to directly apply the technique of NAF to the Frobenius expansions except for τ-NAF on binary Koblitz curves because of the narrowness of the digit set of NAF. Thus as a natural development, we apply the GNAF and rNAF techniques, which are the generalizations of the ordinary NAF, to apply τ-NAF to elliptic curves in odd characteristic. For the resulting recoding methods, ϕ-GNAF and ϕ-rNAF, if the radix is small (e.g., 3, 5), the difference between the computational costs for the precomputation tables of ϕ-GNAF and ϕ-rNAF is relatively small (a few elliptic additions). But, if the radix is significantly large, the computational cost for the precomputation table of ϕ-rNAF is quite large compared to that for ϕ-GNAF. However the non-zero density for ϕ-rNAF is significantly smaller than that for ϕ-GNAF. Thus, these two generalizations are complementary. The speed of the proposed methods improve between 8% and 50% over that for the Frobenius expansion method. In this paper, as the first step in the generalizations of ϕ-NAF, we concentrate on investigating only ϕ-GNAF and ϕ-rNAF, and we do not deal with the width-w versions of these. The family of subfield elliptic curves is a natural generalization of binary Koblitz curves and some examples of the curves with a large prime divisor in the group order are listed in [25]. These curves are considered to be very useful for ECC.

This paper is organized as follows. Section 2 reviews the ordinary GNAF, rNAF, and τ-adic NAF on binary Koblitz curves. Section 3 shows how to generalize τ-NAF on binary Koblitz curves to two classes of ϕ-adic NAF on a family of subfield elliptic curves and proves some properties of ϕ-GNAF and ϕ-rNAF. Section 4 compares the total computational costs of several previous methods and the proposed methods.

2 Preliminaries

In this paper, in general, for any complex number $\psi(\neq 0)$, we denote ψ-expansion $\sum_{i=0}^{\ell-1} c_i \psi^i$ with $c_i \in \mathbb{Z}$ by $(c_{\ell-1}, \cdots, c_0)_\psi$. The Hamming weight of $(c_{\ell-1}, \cdots, c_0)_\psi$ is defined by the number of non-zero c_i's. According to convention, we denote $-a$ by $\bar{a}$ for any natural number a. We denote $\mathbb{Z}_{>0} = \{x \in \mathbb{Z} | x > 0\}$.

2.1 GNAF, rNAF

In this section, we review the ordinary GNAF and rNAF. Let r, α be relatively prime positive integers. We denote $D_{r,\alpha}$ a set defined as follows.

$$D_{r,\alpha} := \begin{cases} \{0, \pm 1, \cdots, \pm \alpha\} & \text{if } \alpha < r, \\ \{0, \pm 1, \cdots, \pm \alpha\} \setminus \{\pm r, \pm 2r, \cdots, \pm \lfloor \alpha/r \rfloor r\} & \text{otherwise.} \end{cases}$$

For an integer radix $r \geq 2$, GNAF and rNAF have been proposed for minimizing the numbers of non-zero densities in the representations of integer scalars. In [6] and [28], the authors calculate the non-zero densities using Markov chains. In this paper, we regard non-zero densities of some representations as average densities of non-zero digits of the representations (See Section 3 for precise definitions).

Definition 1. [GNAF [6]] *A radix-r generalized non-adjacent form (GNAF) of a positive integer d is a representation $d = \sum_{i=0}^{\ell-1} e_i r^i$ where $e_i \in D_{r,r-1}, e_{\ell-1} \neq 0$*

and for each i, one of the following holds : (1) $e_{i+1}e_i = 0$, (2) if $e_{i+1}e_i > 0$, then $|e_{i+1} + e_i| < r$, (3) if $e_{i+1}e_i < 0$, then $|e_{i+1}| > |e_i|$. The length of the GNAF is ℓ. For $a, b \in D_{r,r-1}$, if a, b satisfy one of the followings : (1) $ab = 0$, (2) if $ab > 0$, then $|a + b| < r$, (3) if $ab < 0$, then $|a| > |b|$, then we call a pair (a, b) radix-r admissible pair, and otherwise, we call (a, b) radix-r non-admissible pair.

Definition 2. [r**NAF** [28]] *A radix-r non-adjacent form (rNAF) of a positive integer d is a representation $d = \sum_{i=0}^{\ell-1} e_i r^i$ where $e_i \in D_{r,(r^2-1)/2}$, $e_{\ell-1} \neq 0$ and for each i, it satisfies $e_{i+1}e_i = 0$ where we define $e_\ell = 0$. The length of the rNAF is ℓ. For $a, b \in D_{r,(r^2-1)/2}$, if $ab = 0$, then we call a pair (a, b) radix-r non-adjacent pair, and otherwise, we call (a, b) radix-r adjacent pair.*

In the above definitions, note that for the radix $r = 2$, GNAF and rNAF coincide, and in this case, we call these recoding method "NAF"([28], pp.104). It can be seen that GNAF and rNAF have some interesting properties. For details, consult [6] for GNAF, and [28] for rNAF.

Proposition 1. [**Properties of GNAF (*resp.* rNAF) [6,28]**]
(1) *Every positive integer d has a unique GNAF (resp. rNAF).*
(2) *GNAF (resp. rNAF) of d has the smallest Hamming weight among all signed representations of d with digit set $D_{r,r-1}$ (resp. $D_{r,(r^2-1)/2}$).*
(3) *The average non-zero density of GNAF (resp. rNAF) is asymptotically $(r-1)/(r+1)$ (resp. $(r-1)/(2r-1)$).*

2.2 Subfield Elliptic Curves, Frobenius Expansion, and Scalar Multiplication

We briefly review subfield elliptic curves, the Frobenius expansion on subfield elliptic curves, and scalar multiplication on subfield elliptic curves. For detail, refer to [25], [4] and [24].

Definition 3. [$\mathbb{F}_q$**-subfield elliptic curves [25]**] *Let p be a prime, $q = p^r$ a power of p, and $\mathbb{F}_q$ the finite field with q-elements. An elliptic curve defined over $\mathbb{F}_q$ is called an "$\mathbb{F}_q$-subfield elliptic curve" if for some cryptographic usage, we focus on the group of $\mathbb{F}_{q^n}$-rational points $E(\mathbb{F}_{q^n})$ for some $n \geq 2$. An $\mathbb{F}_q$-subfield elliptic curve E is given by a Weierstrass equation*

$$y^2 + a_1 xy + a_3 y = x^3 + a_2 x^2 + a_4 x + a_6,$$

where $a_i \in \mathbb{F}_q$, and if $q \geqslant 5$, then an $\mathbb{F}_q$-subfield elliptic curve E is given by a short Weierstrass equation

$$y^2 = x^3 + ax + b,$$

where $a, b \in \mathbb{F}_q$. Let us denote ϕ the qth-power Frobenius map on E.

$$\phi : E \to E, \quad (x, y) \mapsto (x^q, y^q),$$

and set $t_n := q^n + 1 - \#E(\mathbb{F}_{q^n})$, $t := t_1$, where $E(\mathbb{F}_{q^n})$ means the set of $\mathbb{F}_{q^n}$-rational points on E. We can regard ϕ as a complex number which satisfies the following characteristic equation : $\phi^2 - t\phi + q = 0$.

Scalar multiplication is the operation of computing dP for given P on an elliptic curve by positive integer d. We describe a scalar multiplication algorithm using window w-NAF method in [12] (Algorithm 3.36, pp.100). The computational cost of Algorithm 1. is approximately

$$\left[\mathcal{D}_\mathcal{P} + (2^{w-2} - 1)\mathcal{A}_\mathcal{P}\right] + \left[\frac{\ell}{w+1}\mathcal{A}_\mathcal{S} + \ell\mathcal{D}_\mathcal{S}\right],$$

where $\mathcal{A}_\mathcal{P}, \mathcal{D}_\mathcal{P}$ (resp. $\mathcal{A}_\mathcal{S}, \mathcal{D}_\mathcal{S}$) stand for the computational cost of the point addition, point doubling in the precomputational step (resp. scalar multiplication step), respectively.

Algorithm 1. Scalar multiplication (window w-NAF) [12]	**Algorithm 2.** Scalar multiplication (Frobenius expansion)
Input: $d = (d_{\ell-1}, \cdots, d_0)_{w\text{-NAF}} \in \mathbb{Z}_{>0}$, $d_i \in D_{w\text{-NAF}}$ $= \{0, \pm 1, \pm 3, \cdots, \pm(2^{w-1}-1)\}$, $\ell \leqslant \lceil \log_2(d) \rceil + 1$, $P \in E(\mathbb{F}_{q^n})$	**Input:** $d = (d_{\ell-1}, \cdots, d_0)_\phi \in \mathbb{Z}_{>0}$, $d_i \in D_\phi$ $= \{0, \pm 1, \pm 2, \cdots, \pm \alpha\}$, $\ell \leqslant \lceil 2\log_q 2\sqrt{N_{\mathbb{Z}[\phi]/\mathbb{Z}}(d)} \rceil + 4$, $P \in E(\mathbb{F}_{q^n})$
Output: dP	**Output:** dP
1: Compute $P_i = iP$ for $i \in \{1, 3, 5, \cdots, 2^{w-1} - 1\}$	1: Compute $P_i = iP$ for $i \in \{1, 2, \cdots, \alpha\}$
2: $Q \leftarrow \mathcal{O}$	2: $Q \leftarrow \mathcal{O}$
3: **for** i from $\ell - 1$ downto 0 **do**	3: **for** i from $\ell - 1$ downto 0 **do**
4: $\quad Q \leftarrow 2Q$	4: $\quad Q \leftarrow \phi(Q)$
5: $\quad Q \leftarrow Q + P_{d_i}$	5: $\quad Q \leftarrow Q + P_{d_i}$
6: **end for**	6: **end for**
7: **return** Q	7: **return** Q

It is well-known that the cost of the Frobenius map ϕ is almost free in normal basis representation. In [25], Smart shows that every element $d \in \mathbb{Z}[\phi]$ has a ϕ-adic representation with some digit set. More precisely, they show the followings.

Theorem 1. [Frobenius expansion on subfield elliptic curves [25]] *Let E be an elliptic curve over $\mathbb{F}_q$, ϕ be its qth-power Frobenius map of E, t is the trace of ϕ. We assume that $(q, t) \neq (5, \pm 4), (7, \pm 5)$. Let $d \in \mathbb{Z}[\phi]$, then we can write $d = \sum_{i=0}^{\ell-1} c_i \phi^i$, where $c_i \in \{0, \pm 1, \cdots, \pm(q-1)/2\}$ and $\ell \leqslant \lceil 2\log_q 2\sqrt{N_{\mathbb{Z}[\phi]/\mathbb{Z}}(d)} \rceil + 4$. We denote $\ell_{\phi\text{-EXP}}(d)$ the length of ϕ-adic expansion of $d \in \mathbb{Z}[\phi]$.*

From theorem 1, we can compute dP efficiently using a precomputation table $\left\{iP \middle| i = 1, 2, \cdots, \frac{q-1}{2}\right\}$ and Horner's method;

$$dP = \left(\sum_{i=0}^{\ell-1} c_i \phi^i\right) P = \phi(\cdots \phi(c_{\ell-1}\phi(P) + c_{\ell-2}P) + \cdots + c_1 P) + c_0 P.$$

We describe a scalar multiplication algorithm using Horner's method based on Frobenius expansion with digit set $D_\phi = \{0, \pm 1, \pm 2, \cdots, \pm \alpha\}$. The computational cost of Horner's method using Smart's Frobenius expansion method (Algorithm 2. with $\alpha = (q-1)/2$, digit set $D_\phi = D_{q,(q-1)/2}$) is approximately

$$\left[\frac{q-1}{q}\ell \mathcal{A_S} + \ell \mathcal{F_S}\right](q=3), \left[\mathcal{D_P} + \frac{q-5}{2}\mathcal{A_P}\right] + \left[\frac{q-1}{q}\ell \mathcal{A_S} + \ell \mathcal{F_S}\right](q \geqslant 5),$$

where $\mathcal{F_S}$ stand for the computational cost of the Frobenius map in the scalar multiplication step. In step 5 of Algorithm 1. and Algorithm 2., if $d_i < 0$, we compute $Q \leftarrow Q - P_{-d_i}(= Q + P_{d_i})$ and if $d_i = 0$, we do not need to compute $Q \leftarrow Q + P_{d_i}$. This is the reason that smaller non-zero densities in the representations of the scalars improve the efficiency.

In [27], Solinas proposed τ-NAF which is a combining techniques of NAF and the Frobenius expansion on binary Koblitz curves $E_a/\mathbb{F}_2 : y^2 + xy = x^3 + ax^2 + 1 (a = 0$ or $1)$ for reducing the non-zero density of the Frobenius expansion. Because of space limitation, we omit an explanation about τ-NAF (See [27,2,1] for details). It is unknown whether any analogue of τ-NAF exists on another subfield elliptic curves except for binary Koblitz curves and ellipitc curves in [3]. But, only a few curves are available for the above methods so far. Our goal is to develop efficient scalar multiplication algorithms on a more general family of subfield elliptic curves. However, because of the narrowness of the digit set of NAF, we may well not be able to directly apply the technique of NAF to the Frobenius expansions except for τ-NAF on binary Koblitz curves. So as to reduce the non-zero densities of the Frobenius expansion, we use redundant digit sets instead of the digit set of NAF. In these cases, it is necessary to know the non-zero densities and the maximum lengths of the proposed methods. In the next section, we will propose two classes of ϕ-NAF on a family of subfield elliptic curves. In the following, we call these two classes of ϕ-NAF ϕ-GNAF and ϕ-rNAF, respectively.

3 Proposed Methods (Two Classes of ϕ-NAF)

In this section, we investigate how to expand two classes of ϕ-NAF on a family of subfield elliptic curves. Let $SEC_t[\mathbb{F}_q]$ be the set of $\mathbb{F}_q$-subfield elliptic curves with the trace of the qth-power Frobenius map t. In the following, **we focus on the case $t = 1$** and consider a scalar multiplication for a given integer d and for a given point $P \in E (\in SEC_1[\mathbb{F}_q])$. In this case, it satisfies that

$$\phi^2 - \phi + q = 0 \; ((1, -1, q)_\phi = 0),$$

and by easy calculation, we have

$$\phi^3 + (q-1)\phi^2 + q^2 = 0 \; ((1, q-1, 0, q^2)_\phi = 0).$$

The property of being anomalous depends on the base field. If E is anomalous over $\mathbb{F}_q$, it is not necessarily anomalous over any $\mathbb{F}_{q^n}$ for $n \geqslant 2$. For details, refer to [30]. Weil descent attack (or GHS attack) in the case of odd characteristic [5] is presented in [8,9], etc. In order to keep the security, we should avoid the extension degree in [8,9,1], etc. For details, refer to [1].

For all $P \in E(\mathbb{F}_{q^n})$, $(\phi^n - 1)P = \mathcal{O}$ is satisfied. Hence $dP = (d \bmod (\phi^n - 1))P$ for any integer scalar d. From [25], there exist $Q, d' \in \mathbb{Z}[\phi]$ such that $d = Q(\phi^n - 1) + d'$ with $d' = 0$ or $\Psi(d') < \lambda \Psi(\phi^n - 1)$, where Ψ is a multiplicative function. Note that this provides a 50% improvement in the performance thanks to a shorter length of the Frobenius expansions of d. In this paper, "the Frobenius expansion" means the expansion in [25].

3.1 The First ϕ-NAF (ϕ-GNAF)

At first, we show how to expand the multiplication by d map on $E(\mathbb{F}_{q^n})$ in terms of ϕ-GNAF and prove some properties of this. We begin with the definition of ϕ-GNAF on every subfield elliptic curves, and give two algorithms which compute ϕ-GNAF for a given $d \in \mathbb{Z}[\phi]$. Algorithm 3. computes the ϕ-GNAF for a given $d \in \mathbb{Z}[\phi]$ by the conversion of the Frobenius expansions to ϕ-GNAF. Algorithm 4. computes the ϕ-GNAF for a given $d \in \mathbb{Z}[\phi]$ without the calculation of the Frobenius expansions and reduces the memory consumption to compute the ϕ-GNAF compared to Algorithm 3.

Definition 4. [ϕ-GNAF] *Let $E \in SEC_t[\mathbb{F}_q]$ and $d \in \mathbb{Z}[\phi]$. A ϕ-adic GNAF (ϕ-GNAF) of d on E is a representation $d = \sum_{i=0}^{\ell-1} e_i \phi^i$ where $e_i \in D_{q,q-1}$ for each i, $e_{\ell-1} \neq 0$, and one of the followings holds : (1) $e_{i+1}e_i = 0$, (2) if $e_{i+1}e_i > 0$, then $|e_{i+1} + e_i| < q$, (3) if $e_{i+1}e_i < 0$, then $|e_{i+1}| > |e_i|$. Let $a, b \in D_{q,q-1}$. If a, b satisfy one of the followings : (1) $ab = 0$, (2) if $ab > 0$, then $|a + b| < r$, (3) if $ab < 0$, then $|a| > |b|$, then we call a pair $(a, b)_\phi$ ϕ-admissible pair follow the lead of [29]. Otherwise, we call $(a, b)_\phi$ ϕ-non-admissible pair. We denote $\ell_{\phi\text{-}GNAF}(d)$ the length of ϕ-GNAF of $d \in \mathbb{Z}[\phi]$.*

The following lemma and theorem show the correctness of Algorithm 3. and Algorithm 4., thus the existence of ϕ-GNAF. From the lemma, for any given the Frobenius expansion, we can have a sequence with digits in $D_{q,q-1}$ such that any adjacent digits are ϕ-admissible. Moreover, the theorem below gives the finiteness of the sequence (hence ϕ-GNAF) and evaluates the upper bound of the length of ϕ-GNAF. For the proof of the lemma, it is easily seen that the proof of Theorem 12.2.3 in [29] can be applied. For details, refer to [29].

Lemma 1. *Let $b \in D_{q,(q+1)/2}$, $b' \in D_{q,(q-1)/2}$, and $e \in D_{q,q-1}$. We assume that $(b', e)_\phi$ is a ϕ-admissible pair and $(b, b')_\phi$ is a ϕ-non-admissible pair. If we convert*

$$(b, b', e)_\phi \mapsto \begin{cases} (\bar{1}, c, c', e)_\phi := (\bar{1}, b+1, b'-q, e)_\phi & \text{if } b' > 0, \\ (1, c, c', e)_\phi := (1, b-1, b'+q, e)_\phi & \text{otherwise,} \end{cases}$$

then $(c, c')_\phi$, $(c', e)_\phi$ are ϕ-admissible pairs.

Theorem 2. [Maximum length of ϕ-GNAF] *Let $d \in \mathbb{Z}[\phi]$ and $\ell = \ell_{\phi\text{-}EXP}(d)$ be the length of Frobenius expansion of d. Then d has a ϕ-GNAF with digit set $D_{q,q-1}$ such that the length is at most $\ell + 2$.*

Proof. The proof can be found in [13].

Algorithm 3. Generation of ϕ-GNAF on $SEC_1[\mathbb{F}_q]$ with Frobenius expansion	**Algorithm 4.** Generation of ϕ-GNAF on $SEC_1[\mathbb{F}_q]$ without Frobenius expansion
Input: $d \in \mathbb{Z}[\phi]$	**Input:** $d \in \mathbb{Z}[\phi]$
Output: ϕ-GNAF of d	**Output:** ϕ-GNAF of d
1: $d' \leftarrow d \bmod (\phi^n - 1)$	1: $d_0 + d_1\phi \leftarrow d \bmod (\phi^n - 1)$ $(d_0, d_1 \in \mathbb{Z})$
2: $\ell \leftarrow \lceil 2\log_q 2\sqrt{N_{\mathbb{Z}[\phi]/\mathbb{Z}}(d')}\rceil + 4$	2: Set $d' = d_0 + d_1\phi$
3: Compute the Frobenius expansion $(c_{\ell-1}, c_{\ell-2}, \cdots, c_1, c_0)_\phi$ of d'	3: $\ell \leftarrow \lceil 2\log_q 2\sqrt{N_{\mathbb{Z}[\phi]/\mathbb{Z}}(d')}\rceil + 4$
4: $b_0 \leftarrow c_0, b_1 \leftarrow c_1, b_\ell \leftarrow 0, b_{\ell+1} \leftarrow 0$	4: Compute $Q, b \in \mathbb{Z}$ such that $d_0 = Qq + b$ $(b \in D_{q,(q-1)/2})$ (see [25])
5: $i \leftarrow 0$	5: $d_0 \leftarrow Q + d_1, d_1 \leftarrow -Q$
6: **while** $i \leqslant \ell$ **do**	6: $i \leftarrow 1$
7: **if** $b_i \neq 0$ and $b_i \bmod q = 0$ **then**	7: **while** $i \leqslant \ell + 1$ **do**
8: $b_{i+1} \leftarrow b_{i+1} - b_i/q,$ $b_{i+2} \leftarrow c_{i+2} + b_i/q, e_i \leftarrow 0$	8: Compute $Q, a \in \mathbb{Z}$ such that $d_0 = Qq + a$ $(a \in D_{q,(q-1)/2})$
9: **else if** $(b_{i+1}, b_i) : \phi$-admissible pair **then**	9: $d_0 \leftarrow Q + d_1, d_1 \leftarrow -Q$
10: $b_{i+2} \leftarrow c_{i+2}, e_i \leftarrow b_i$	10: **if** $(a, b) : \phi$-admissible pair **then**
11: **else if** $b_i > 0$ **then**	11: $e_{i-1} \leftarrow b, b \leftarrow a$
12: $b_{i+2} \leftarrow c_{i+2} - 1,$ $b_{i+1} \leftarrow b_{i+1} + 1, e_i \leftarrow b_i - q$	12: **else if** $b > 0$ **then**
13: **else**	13: $e_{i-1} \leftarrow b - q, b \leftarrow a + 1,$ $d_0 \leftarrow d_0 - 1$
14: $b_{i+2} \leftarrow c_{i+2} + 1,$ $b_{i+1} \leftarrow b_{i+1} - 1, e_i \leftarrow b_i + q$	14: **else**
15: **end if**	15: $e_{i-1} \leftarrow b + q, b \leftarrow a - 1,$ $d_0 \leftarrow d_0 + q$
16: $i \leftarrow i + 1$	16: **end if**
17: **end while**	17: **end while**
18: **return** $(e_{\ell+1}, e_\ell, \cdots, e_1, e_0)_\phi$	18: **return** $(e_{\ell+1}, e_\ell, \cdots, e_1, e_0)_\phi$

From Lemma 1, we can easily see that step 7, 8 of Algorithm 3. are always skiped in the case of $q \geqslant 7$. However, in the case of $q = 3$ or 5, there is a possibility that b_i is a non-zero multiple of q. If b_i is a non-zero multiple of q (step 7), we convert $(b_{i+1}, b_i)_\phi \mapsto (-b_i/q, b_{i+1} + b_i/q, 0)_\phi$ (step 8). It is easy to show that if b_i is a non-zero multiple of q, then it satisfies that $b_i = \pm q$. Thus for all i, we always have $|b_{i+1}| \leqslant (q+1)/2$, $|b_i| \leqslant (q+3)/2$. Remark that it does not occur that b_{i+1} is a non-zero multiple of q. This shows the correctness of Algorithm 3. and Algorithm 4.

Let ϕ-GNAF$_\ell$ be the set of ϕ-GNAF of length ℓ. We put $A_\ell = \#\phi$-GNAF$_\ell$, $S_\ell = \sum_{d \in \phi\text{-GNAF}_\ell}(\ell - w(d))$, and $C_\ell = \#\{d \in \phi\text{-GNAF}_\ell \mid w(d) = \ell\}$, where $w(d)$ means the Hamming weight of d. In other words, C_ℓ is the number of ϕ-GNAF with length ℓ such that all digits are non-zero. Then the non-zero density of ϕ-GNAF is defined by $1 - \lim_{\ell \to \infty} S_\ell/(\ell A_\ell)$.

ϕ-GNAF has properties same as GNAF. For details, refer to [13].

Proposition 2. [Properties of ϕ-GNAF]
(1) *Every $d \in \mathbb{Z}[\phi]$ has a unique ϕ-GNAF.*

(2) *The average number of non-zero digits for ℓ digits numbers in $\mathbb{Z}[\phi]$ is equal to $((q-1)/(q+1))\ell + 2/(q+1) + O((-1/q)^\ell)$. In particular, the average non-zero density of ϕ-GNAF is asymptotically $(q-1)/(q+1)$.*

If we compute $2P = P+P, (i+1)P = P+iP$ for $1 \leqslant i \leqslant q-2$, the computational cost of Horner's method using ϕ-GNAF (Algorithm 2. based on ϕ-GNAF with $\alpha = q-1$, digit set $D_\phi = D_{q,q-1}$) is approximately

$$\left[\mathcal{D}_P + \frac{q-1}{q+1}\ell\mathcal{A}_S + \ell\mathcal{F}_S\right](q=3), \left[\mathcal{D}_P + (q-3)\mathcal{A}_P + \frac{q-1}{q+1}\ell\mathcal{A}_S + \ell\mathcal{F}_S\right](q \geqslant 5).$$

3.2 The Second ϕ-NAF (ϕ-rNAF)

Next, we show how to expand the multiplication by d map on $E(\mathbb{F}_{q^n})$ in terms of ϕ-adic rNAF and prove some properties of this. As with the previous section, we begin with the definition of ϕ-rNAF on every subfield elliptic curves, and give two algorithms which compute the ϕ-rNAF for a given $d \in \mathbb{Z}[\phi]$. Algorithm 5. computes the ϕ-rNAF for a given $d \in \mathbb{Z}[\phi]$ by the conversion of the Frobenius expansions to ϕ-rNAF. Algorithm 6. computes the ϕ-rNAF for a given $d \in \mathbb{Z}[\phi]$ without the calculation of the Frobenius expansions and reduces the memory consumption to compute the ϕ-rNAF compared to Algorithm 5.

Definition 5. [ϕ-rNAF] *Let $E \in SEC_t[\mathbb{F}_q]$ and $d \in \mathbb{Z}[\phi]$. A ϕ-adic rNAF (ϕ-rNAF) of d on E is a representation $d = \sum_{i=0}^{\ell-1} e_i\phi^i$ such that $e_i \in D_{q,(q^2-1)/2}$, $e_{\ell-1} \neq 0$ and $e_{i+1}e_i = 0$ for each i. Let $a, b \in D_{q,(q^2-1)/2}$. If $ab = 0$, we call $(a,b)_\phi$ ϕ-non-adjacent pair. Otherwise, we call $(a,b)_\phi$ ϕ-adjacent pair. We denote $\ell_{\phi\text{-}r\mathrm{NAF}}(d)$ the length of ϕ-rNAF of $d \in \mathbb{Z}[\phi]$.*

At first sight, it seem that Algorithm 5. is a straightforward combination of the Frobenius expansions and rNAF. But the proof of the correctness of Algorithm 5. is complicated. To prove this, we focus on the fact that in Algorithm 5., the following conversion does not occur:

$$(b_{i+1}, b_i)_\phi \mapsto \begin{cases} (\bar{b}'_i, b_{i+1} + b'_i, 0)_\phi & \text{if } b_i = b'_i q \text{ for some } b'_i \in \mathbb{Z}, \\ (\bar{b}'_{i+1}, b_{i+1}, 0, b_i)_\phi & \text{if } b_{i+1} = b'_{i+1} q \text{ for some } b'_{i+1} \in \mathbb{Z}. \end{cases}$$

In other words, there is no possibility that b_i or b_{i+1} is a non-zero multiple of q when we scan $(b_{i+1}, b_i)_\phi$. More precisely, the following lemma is satisfied. For the proof of the lemma, consult [28].

Lemma 2. *Let $q \geqslant 7$, $c, c', c'' \in D_{q,(q-1)/2}$, $b \in D_{q,(q+1)/2}$, $b' \in D_{q,2q-1}$. We convert $(c, c', c'', b, b')_\phi$ from right-to-left according to the following rule and we denote the result of the conversion $(a, a', e, e', e'', e''')_\phi$.*

The rule: We assume that we scan consecutive two digits $(a, b)_\phi$, then
(Rule 1) If $a \neq 0, b \neq 0$, then convert $(a, b)_\phi$

$$(a,b)_\phi \mapsto \begin{cases} (a, 0, aq+b)_\phi & \text{if } |aq+b| \leqslant (q^2-1)/2, \\ (1, a+(q-1), 0, (aq+b)+q^2)_\phi & \text{else if } aq+b < -(q^2-1)/2, \\ (\bar{1}, a-(q-1), 0, (aq+b)-q^2)_\phi & \text{otherwise.} \end{cases}$$

(Rule 2) If $a \neq 0, b = 0$, then skip the 1-digit b. We scan the next consecutive two digits which include a.
(Rule 3) if $a = 0, b = 0$, then skip the 2-digits a and b. We scan the next consecutive two digits which do not include a.

Then, it always satisfy that $(e, e', e'', e''')_\phi$ is a ϕ-rNAF, $a \in D_{q,(q+1)/2}, a' \in D_{q,2q-1}$. In particular, a and a' are not divisible by q.

Algorithm 5. Generation of ϕ-rNAF on $SEC_1[\mathbb{F}_q]$ with Frobenius expansion

Input: $d \in \mathbb{Z}[\phi]$
Output: ϕ-rNAF of d
1: $d' \leftarrow d \bmod (\phi^n - 1)$
2: $\ell \leftarrow \lceil 2\log_q 2\sqrt{N_{\mathbb{Z}[\phi]/\mathbb{Z}}(d')} \rceil + 4$
3: Compute the Frobenius expansion $(c_{\ell-1}, c_{\ell-2}, \cdots, c_1, c_0)_\phi$ of d'
4: $b_0 \leftarrow c_0, b_1 \leftarrow c_1, b_\ell \leftarrow 0,$
   $b_{\ell+1} \leftarrow 0, b_{\ell+2} \leftarrow 0, b_{\ell+3} \leftarrow 0$
5: $i \leftarrow 0$
6: **while** $i \leqslant \ell + 2$ **do**
7:   **if** $b_i \neq 0$ and $b_i \bmod q = 0$ **then**
8:     $b_{i+1} \leftarrow b_{i+1} - b_i/q,$
       $b_{i+2} \leftarrow c_{i+2} + b_i/q, i \leftarrow i+1$
9:   **end if**
10:   **if** $b_i = 0$ **then**
11:     $b_{i+2} \leftarrow c_{i+2}, e_i \leftarrow 0, i \leftarrow i+1$
12:   **else if** $|b_{i+1}q + b_i| \leqslant (q^2-1)/2$ **then**
13:     $b_{i+3} \leftarrow c_{i+3},$
       $b_{i+2} \leftarrow c_{i+2} + b_{i+1},$
       $e_{i+1} \leftarrow 0, e_i \leftarrow b_{i+1}q + b_i,$
       $i \leftarrow i+2$
14:   **else if** $b_{i+1}q + b_i < -(q^2-1)/2$ **then**
15:     $b_{i+3} \leftarrow c_{i+3} + 1,$
       $b_{i+2} \leftarrow c_{i+2} + b_{i+1} + (q-1),$
       $e_{i+1} \leftarrow 0, e_i \leftarrow b_{i+1}q + b_i + q^2,$
       $i \leftarrow i+2$
16:   **else**
17:     $b_{i+3} \leftarrow c_{i+3} - 1,$
       $b_{i+2} \leftarrow c_{i+2} + b_{i+1} - (q-1),$
       $e_{i+1} \leftarrow 0, e_i \leftarrow b_{i+1}q + b_i - q^2,$
       $i \leftarrow i+2$
18:   **end if**
19: **end while**
20: **return** $(e_{\ell+3}, e_{\ell+2}, \cdots, e_1, e_0)_\phi$

Algorithm 6. Generation of ϕ-rNAF on $SEC_1[\mathbb{F}_q]$ without Frobenius expansion

Input: $d \in \mathbb{Z}[\phi]$
Output: ϕ-rNAF of d
1: $d_0 + d_1\phi \leftarrow d \bmod (\phi^n - 1)(d_0, d_1 \in \mathbb{Z})$
2: Set $d' = d_0 + d_1\phi$
3: $\ell \leftarrow \lceil 2\log_q 2\sqrt{N_{\mathbb{Z}[\phi]/\mathbb{Z}}(d')} \rceil + 4$
4: $i \leftarrow 0$
5: **while** $i \leqslant \ell + 2$ **do**
6:   Compute $Q, b \in \mathbb{Z}$ such that $d_0 = Qq + b$ ($b \in D_{q,(q-1)/2}$) (see [25])
7:   $d_0 \leftarrow Q + d_1, d_1 \leftarrow -Q$
8:   **if** $b = 0$ **then**
9:     $e_i \leftarrow 0, i \leftarrow i+1$
10:   **else**
11:     Compute $Q, a \in \mathbb{Z}$ such that
       $d_0 = Qq + a$ ($a \in D_{q,(q-1)/2}$),
       $d_0 \leftarrow Q + d_1,$
       $d_1 \leftarrow -Q$
12:     **if** $|aq + b| \leqslant (q^2-1)/2$ **then**
13:       $e_i \leftarrow aq + b, e_{i+1} \leftarrow 0,$
         $d_0 \leftarrow a,$
         $d_1 \leftarrow -Q$
14:     **else if** $aq+b < -(q^2-1)/2$ **then**
15:       $e_i \leftarrow aq + b + q^2, e_{i+1} \leftarrow 0,$
         $d_0 \leftarrow a + (q-1),$
         $d_1 \leftarrow -Q + 1$
16:     **else**
17:       $e_i \leftarrow aq + b - q^2, e_{i+1} \leftarrow 0,$
         $d_0 \leftarrow a - (q-1),$
         $d_1 \leftarrow -Q - 1$
18:     **end if**
19:     $i \leftarrow i+2$
20:   **end if**
21: **end while**
22: **return** $(e_{\ell+3}, e_{\ell+2}, \cdots, e_1, e_0)_\phi$

Theorem 3. [Maximum length of ϕ-rNAF] *Let $d \in \mathbb{Z}[\phi]$ and $\ell_{\phi\text{-}EXP}(d)$. Then d has a ϕ-rNAF with digit set $D_{q,(q^2-1)/2}$ such that $\ell_{\phi\text{-}rNAF}(d)$ is at most $\ell + 4$.*

Proof. The proof can be found in [13].

From Lemma 2, we can easily see that step 7,8 of Algorithm 5. are always skiped in the case of $q \geqslant 7$. However, Lemma 2 is not satisfied in the case of $q = 3$ or 5, namely there is the possibility that b_i is a non-zero multiple of q. If b_i is a non-zero multiple of q (step 7), we convert $(b_{i+1}, b_i)_\phi \mapsto (-b_i/q, b_{i+1} + b_i/q, 0)_\phi$ (step 8). It is easy to show that if b_i is a non-zero multiple of q, then it satisfies $b_i = \pm q$. Thus for all i, we always have

$$|b_{i+1}| \leqslant (q-1)/2, |b_i| \leqslant q - 1 \quad \text{or} \quad |b_{i+1}| \leqslant (q+1)/2, |b_i| \leqslant 2q - 1 \ (|b_i| \neq q).$$

Note that it does not occur that b_{i+1} is a non-zero multiple of q. This shows the correctness of Algorithm 5. and Algorithm 6.

Let ϕ-rNAF$_\ell$ be the set of ϕ-rNAF of the length ℓ. We put $B_\ell = \#\phi\text{-rNAF}_\ell$, $T_\ell = \sum_{d \in \phi\text{-rNAF}_\ell}(\ell - w(d))$, where $w(d)$ means the Hamming weight of d. Then as is the case with ϕ-GNAF, the non-zero density of ϕ-rNAF is defined by $1 - \lim_{\ell \to \infty} T_\ell/(\ell B_\ell)$.

For ϕ-rNAF, we also have similar properties. For the proof of the following proposition, refer to [13].

Proposition 3. [Properties of ϕ-rNAF]
(1) *Every $d \in \mathbb{Z}[\phi]$ has a unique ϕ-rNAF.*
(2) *The average number of non-zero digits for ℓ digits numbers in $\mathbb{Z}[\phi]$ is equal to $((q-1)/(2q-1))\ell + q/(2q-1) + O(((1-q)/q)^\ell)$. In particular, the average non-zero density of ϕ-rNAF is asymptotically $(q-1)/(2q-1)$.*

If we compute $2P = P + P, 3P = P + 2P$ $(3P = \phi(P) - \phi^2(P)$ when $q = 3)$, $4P = P + 3P, (q-1)P = P + (q-2)P, (q+1)P = P + (q-1)P$, and so on, the computational cost of Horner's method using ϕ-rNAF (Algorithm 2. based on ϕ-rNAF with $\alpha = (q^2 - 1)/2$, digit set $D_\phi = D_{q,(q^2-1)/2}$) is approximately

$$\left[\mathcal{D}_\mathcal{P} + 2\mathcal{A}_\mathcal{P} + 2\mathcal{F}_\mathcal{P} + \frac{q-1}{2q-1}\ell\mathcal{A}_\mathcal{S} + \ell\mathcal{F}_\mathcal{S}\right](q = 3),$$

$$\left[\mathcal{D}_\mathcal{P} + \frac{q^2 - q - 4}{2}\mathcal{A}_\mathcal{P} + \frac{q-1}{2q-1}\ell\mathcal{A}_\mathcal{S} + \ell\mathcal{F}_\mathcal{S}\right](q \geqslant 5),$$

where $\mathcal{F}_\mathcal{P}$ stands for the computational cost of the Frobenius map in the precomputational step.

Remark. In this paper, we do not discuss the minimality of the Hamming weight of ϕ-GNAF and ϕ-rNAF among various recoding methods with appropriate digit sets. Although the property of minimality is desired, it can be easily seen that for ϕ-GNAF, ϕ-rNAF, conventional proofs (for e.g., GNAF, rNAF, etc.) are not available. It can be considered that these issues are caused by the difference between the rational integer ring and quadratic imaginary integer rings or quadratic order, and we will need some deep observation on number theoretical properties of quadratic integer rings. These issues remain to be discussed.

Table 1. The number of curve operations for each recoding method ($q = 3$)

Method	#Table	$\mathcal{A}_P$	$\mathcal{D}_P$	$\mathcal{F}_P$	$\mathcal{A}_S$	$\mathcal{D}_S$	$\mathcal{F}_S$
w-NAF [27]	2^{w-2}	$(2^{w-2} - 1)$	1	0	$\frac{m_2}{w+1}$	ℓ	0
Frobenius expansion [25]	1	0	0	0	0.67ℓ	0	ℓ
ϕ-GNAF	2	0	1	0	0.5ℓ	0	ℓ
ϕ-rNAF	3	2	1	2	0.4ℓ	0	ℓ

4 Comparisons

We compare several recoding methods for computing scalar multiplications for a point on a subfield elliptic curve with the trace of the Frobenius map 1 using standard left-to-right method (for details, refer to [12]). Let d be a large positive integer and we focus on the group of $\mathbb{F}_{q^n}$-rational points $E(\mathbb{F}_{q^n})$ for sufficient large n which satisfy $d \approx q^n$. Let m_q be the length of the unsigned q-adic expansion of d with digit set $D = \{0, \pm 1, \cdots, \pm(q-1)\}$ and $d_0 = d \bmod (\phi^n - 1)$, respectively.

As $d \approx q^n$, the norm of d will be equal to $d^2 \approx q^{2n}$ and $d_0 \approx q^{n+1}$ (for detail, refer to [25]). So $m_q = \lceil \log_q d \rceil \approx \lceil \log_q q^n \rceil = n$ and $\ell \leqslant \lceil 2\log_q 2\sqrt{N_{\mathbb{Z}[\phi]/\mathbb{Z}}(d_0)} \rceil + 4 \approx \lceil 2\log_q 2q^{(n+1)/2} \rceil + 4 \leqslant n + 6$. To simplify the evaluation of the computational cost, we assume that m_q, $\ell_{\phi\text{-EXP}}(d_0)$, $\ell_{\phi\text{-GNAF}}(d_0)$ and $\ell_{\phi\text{-}r\text{NAF}}(d_0)$ are equal to each other (Strictly speaking, we should analyze each average of $\ell_{\phi\text{-EXP}}(\cdot)$, $\ell_{\phi\text{-GNAF}}(\cdot)$ and $\ell_{\phi\text{-}r\text{NAF}}(\cdot)$ among positive integers in the range $[1, \#E - 1]$ to evaluate the exact computational costs. However, we do not deal with this analysis). In practical meaning, the shift operations are essentially free, thus the cost of Frobenius map on subfield elliptic curves is almost free in normal basis representation.

In the second column, the value #Table equals the number of elements, that have to be precomputed and stored.

Table 2. The number of $\mathbb{F}_{q^n}$-field arithmetic operations (bit length of scalar and $q^n \approx 192$) and total number of multiplications ($S = 0.8M$, $I/M = 8$) for each recoding method

Method	#Table	M	S	I	total number of multiplications
192bit					
w-NAF ($w = 6$)	16	1027.4	850.3	2	$1731.3M$
Frobenius expansion ($q = 3$)	1	658.7	244	1	$855.9M$
ϕ-GNAF ($q = 3$)	2	498	185	2	$656M$
ϕ-rNAF ($q = 3$)	3	404.4	150.4	3	$434.6M$
Frobenius expansion ($q = 5$)	2	541.2	201.2	2	$639M$
ϕ-GNAF ($q = 5$)	4	456.7	170	4	$618.7M$
ϕ-rNAF ($q = 5$)	12	303.1	120.7	10	$491.5M$
Frobenius expansion ($q = 7$)	3	485.3	180.3	3	$602.6M$
ϕ-GNAF ($q = 7$)	6	432	161.3	6	$603M$
ϕ-rNAF ($q = 7$)	24	302.8	119.5	21	$558M$

Table 3. The number of $\mathbb{F}_{q^n}$-field arithmetic operations (bit length of scalar and $q^n \approx 224, 256, 384$) and total number of multiplications ($S = 0.8M, I/M = 8$) for each recoding method

Method	#Table	M	S	I	total number of multiplications
224bit					
w-NAF ($w=6$)	16	1192	1009	2	2009.2
Frobenius expansion ($q=3$)	1	765.3	284	1	994.5
ϕ-GNAF ($q=3$)	2	578	215	2	752
ϕ-rNAF ($q=3$)	3	468.4	174.4	4	609.9
Frobenius expansion ($q=5$)	2	630.8	234.8	2	828.6
ϕ-GNAF ($q=5$)	4	531.3	198	4	715.7
ϕ-rNAF ($q=5$)	12	370.9	139.3	10	556.4
Frobenius expansion ($q=7$)	3	560.6	208.7	3	745.5
ϕ-GNAF ($q=7$)	6	498	186	6	688.8
ϕ-rNAF ($q=7$)	24	343.4	131.8	21	610.8
256bit					
w-NAF ($w=6$)	16	1356.6	1150.7	2	2287.1
Frobenius expansion ($q=3$)	1	872	324	1	1133.2
ϕ-GNAF ($q=3$)	2	658	245	2	856
ϕ-rNAF ($q=3$)	3	532.4	198.4	4	693.1
Frobenius expansion ($q=5$)	2	720.4	268.4	2	945.1
ϕ-GNAF ($q=5$)	4	606	226	4	812.8
ϕ-rNAF ($q=5$)	12	420.7	158	10	621.1
Frobenius expansion ($q=7$)	3	642.9	239.6	3	852.5
ϕ-GNAF ($q=7$)	6	570	213	6	782.4
ϕ-rNAF ($q=7$)	24	387.7	148.4	21	668.4
384bit					
w-NAF ($w=6$)	16	2014.9	1717.6	2	3399
Frobenius expansion ($q=3$)	1	1304	486	1	1694.8
ϕ-GNAF ($q=3$)	2	982	366.5	2	1277.2
ϕ-rNAF ($q=3$)	3	791.6	295.6	4	1030.1
Frobenius expansion ($q=5$)	2	1072.4	400.4	2	1402.7
ϕ-GNAF ($q=5$)	4	899.3	336	4	1194.1
ϕ-rNAF ($q=5$)	12	616.2	231	10	875.3
Frobenius expansion ($q=7$)	3	886.8	330.8	3	1161.4
ϕ-GNAF ($q=7$)	6	840	314.3	6	1133.4
ϕ-rNAF ($q=7$)	24	553.8	210.7	21	884.4

An elementary multiplication in $\mathbb{F}_{q^n}$ (resp. a squaring and an inversion) will be abbreviated by M (resp. S and I), and affine coordinates (resp. Jacobian coordinates) will be abbreviated by $\mathcal{A}$ (resp. $\mathcal{J}$). If we choose

- $\mathcal{A_P} : \mathcal{A} + \mathcal{A} \to \mathcal{A}$ $(2M + S + I)$, $\quad \mathcal{D_P} : 2\mathcal{A} \to \mathcal{A}$ $(2M + 2S + I)$,

- $\mathcal{A_S} : \mathcal{J} + \mathcal{A} \to \mathcal{J}$ $(8M + 3S)$, $\quad \mathcal{D_S} : 2\mathcal{J} \to \mathcal{J}$ $(4M + 4S)$, the total number of M (resp. S and I) to compute scalar multiplication for each method is as follows.

Table 2 shows that the speed of the proposed methods improves between 8% and 50% over that for the Frobenius expansion method.

5 Conclusion

It has been an unsolved problem to generalize τ-NAF techniques on binary Koblitz curves to a more general family of subfield elliptic curves whose endomorphism rings are not necessarily subrings of Euclidean quadratic imaginary number fields. In this paper, we have described two generalized methods on a family of subfield elliptic curves. Those methods are two classes of ϕ-NAF (ϕ-GNAF and ϕ-rNAF). Our proposed methods can be applied to every subfield elliptic curves with the trace of the Frobenius map 1 regardless of whether or not the endomorphism rings are Euclidean. We also prove that these representations have the same non-zero densities as the corresponding original GNAF and rNAF. Because of the high efficiency in computing Frobenius maps, our proposed methods improve the efficiency of scalar multiplication significantly compared to previous methods. The speed of the proposed methods improves between 8% and 50% over that for the Frobenius expansion method. It is an open problem to develop the width-w version of the proposed methods for $w > 2$.

References

1. Avanzi, R., Cohen, H., Doche, C., Frey, G., Lange, T., Nguyen, K., Vercauteren, F.: The Handbook of Elliptic and Hyperelliptic Curve Cryptography. CRC Press, Boca Raton (2005)
2. Avanzi, R.M., Heuberger, C., Prodinger, H.: Minimality of the Hamming Weight of the τ-NAF for Koblitz Curves and Improved Combination with Point Halving. In: Preneel, B., Tavares, S. (eds.) SAC 2005. LNCS, vol. 3897, pp. 332–344. Springer, Heidelberg (2006)
3. Blake, I.F., Murty, V.K., Xu, G.: Nonadjacent radix-τ Expansions of Integers in Euclidean Imaginary Quadratic Number Fields. In: Ganita Laboratory (November 2004), http://www.erin.utoronto.ca/~w3ganita/radix_t.pdf
4. Blake, I., Seroussi, G., Smart, N.P.: Elliptic Curves in Cryptography. LMS Lecture Note Series, vol. 265. Cambridge University Press, Cambridge (1999)
5. Blake, I., Seroussi, G., Smart, N.P. (eds.): Advances in Elliptic Curve Cryptography. LMS Lecture Note Series, vol. 317. Cambridge University Press, Cambridge (2005)
6. Clark, W.E., Liang, J.J.: On arithmetic weight for a general radix representation of integers. IEEE Transactions on Information Theory IT-19, 823–826 (1973)
7. Cohen, H., Miyaji, A., Ono, T.: Efficient elliptic curve exponentiation using mixed coordinates. In: Ohta, K., Pei, D. (eds.) ASIACRYPT 1998. LNCS, vol. 1514, pp. 51–65. Springer, Heidelberg (1998)
8. Diem, C.: A study on theoretical and practical aspects of Weil-restriction of varieties. Ph.D. thesis, Universität Gesamthochschule Essen (2001)
9. Diem, C.: The GHS-attack in odd characteristic. J. Ramanujan Math. Soc. 18, 1–32 (2003)
10. Günther, C., Lange, T., Stein, A.: Speeding up the Arithmetic on Koblitz Curves of Genus Two. In: Stinson, D.R., Tavares, S. (eds.) SAC 2000. LNCS, vol. 2012, pp. 106–117. Springer, Heidelberg (2001)

11. Gallant, R., Lambert, R., Vanstone, S.: Faster Point Multiplication on Elliptic Curves with Efficient Endomorphisms. In: Kilian, J. (ed.) CRYPTO 2001. LNCS, vol. 2139, pp. 190–200. Springer, Heidelberg (2001)
12. Hankerson, D., Menezes, A., Vanstone, S.: Guide to Elliptic Curve Cryptography. Springer, Heidelberg (2004)
13. Hakuta, K., Sato, H., Takagi, T.: Efficient Arithmetic on Subfield Elliptic Curves over Small Finite Fields of Odd Characteristic. Cryptology ePrint Archive, Report 2005/454 (2005), http://eprint.iacr.org/2005/454
14. Koblitz, N.: Elliptic curve cryptosystems. Mathematics of Computation 48, 203–209 (1987)
15. Koblitz, N.: CM-curves with good cryptographic properties. In: Feigenbaum, J. (ed.) CRYPTO 1991. LNCS, vol. 576, pp. 279–287. Springer, Heidelberg (1992)
16. Koblitz, N.: An Elliptic Curve Implementation of the Finite Field Digital Signature Algorithm. In: Krawczyk, H. (ed.) CRYPTO 1998. LNCS, vol. 1462, pp. 327–337. Springer, Heidelberg (1998)
17. Lange, T.: Efficient Arithmetic on Hyperelliptic Koblitz Curves. Ph.D. thesis, University of Essen (2001)
18. Müller, V.: Fast Multiplication on Elliptic Curves over Small Fields of Characteristic Two. Journal of Cryptology 11, 219–234 (1998)
19. Miller, V.: Uses of elliptic curves in cryptography. In: Williams, H.C. (ed.) CRYPTO 1985. LNCS, vol. 218, pp. 417–426. Springer, Heidelberg (1986)
20. Park, T.J., Lee, M.K., Park, K.: New Frobenius Expansions for Elliptic Curves with Efficient Endomorphisms. In: Lee, P.J., Lim, C.H. (eds.) ICISC 2002. LNCS, vol. 2587, pp. 264–282. Springer, Heidelberg (2003)
21. Reitwiesner, G.W.: Binary arithmetic. Advances in Computers 1, 231–308 (1960)
22. Satoh, T., Araki, K.: Fermat quotients and the polynomial time discrete log algorithm for anomalous elliptic curves. Commentarii Mathematici Universitatis Sancti Pauli 47, 81–92 (1998)
23. Semaev, I.A.: Evaluation of discrete logarithms on some elliptic curves. Mathematics of Computation 67, 353–356 (1998)
24. Silverman, J.H.: The Arithmetic of Elliptic Curves. In: GTM 106, Springer, Heidelberg (1986)
25. Smart, N.P.: Elliptic Curve Cryptosystems over Small Fields of Odd Characteristic. Journal of Cryptology 12, 141–151 (1999)
26. Smart, N.P.: The discrete logarithm problem on elliptic curves of trace one. Journal of Cryptology 12, 193–196 (1999)
27. Solinas, J.A.: Efficient Arithmetic on Koblitz Curves. Designs, Codes and Cryptography 19, 195–249 (2000)
28. Takagi, T., Yen, S.M., Wu, B.C.: Radix-r Non-adjacent Form. In: Zhang, K., Zheng, Y. (eds.) ISC 2004. LNCS, vol. 3225, pp. 99–110. Springer, Heidelberg (2004)
29. van Lint, J.H.: Introduction to coding theory. In: GTM 86, Springer, Heidelberg (1982)
30. Washington, L.C.: Elliptic Curves: Number Theory and Cryptography. CRC Press, Boca Raton (2003)

Secure Computation of the Vector Dominance Problem

Jin Yuan[1], Qingsong Ye[1], Huaxiong Wang[1,2], and Josef Pieprzyk[1]

[1] Center for Advanced Computing – Algorithms and Cryptography, Department of Computing, Macquarie University, NSW 2109, Australia
{jyuan, qingsong, hwang, josef}@ics.mq.edu.au
[2] Division of Mathematical Sciences, Nanyang Technological University, Singapore

Abstract. Suppose two parties, holding vectors $A = (a_1, a_2, \ldots, a_n)$ and $B = (b_1, b_2, \ldots, b_n)$ respectively, wish to know whether $a_i > b_i$ for all i, without disclosing any private input. This problem is called the vector dominance problem, and is closely related to the well-studied problem for securely comparing two numbers (Yao's millionaires problem). In this paper, we propose several protocols for this problem, which improve upon existing protocols on round complexity or communication/computation complexity.

1 Introduction

Suppose Alice has a vector $A = (a_1, a_2, \ldots, a_n)$ and Bob has a vector $B = (b_1, b_2, \ldots, b_n)$, where a_i and b_i are natural numbers with bit size at most K. We say that A dominates B if and only if $a_i > b_i$ for all $1 \leq i \leq n$. We define the *dominance predicate* $Dom(A, B) = (A$ dominates $B)$, that is, $Dom(A, B)$ has value 1 if and only if A dominates B, and has value 0 otherwise.

In some applications, Alice and Bob want to participate in a protocol such that one or both of them get to know the value of $Dom(A, B)$, and this should be the only piece of information acquired during the execution of the protocol. This is called the Secure Two-party Vector Dominance (STVD) problem. Solutions of the STVD problem have potential applications in the real life. As an example, in a job advertisement, an employer may stipulate that a successful applicant must meet a minimum requirement for several attributes. For instance, the applicant must hold a bachelor's or higher degree, and must have at least three years work experience. Such requirements can be formulated as an instance of the STVD problem.

The STVD problem can be viewed as a generalization of Yao's millionaires problem, where Alice and Bob are two millionaires who want to know which one is richer without disclosing their respective wealth. A protocol for the millionaires problem is also called a GT (Greater Than) protocol in the literature. Many protocols have been proposed for the millionaires problem [7,11,2,17,13]. In contrast, not much has been done for the vector dominance problem [1,15,16]. For a summary of known results on the vector dominance problem, see Chapter 2 of [15].

Since the vector dominance problem is closely related to the millionaires problem, most known STVD protocols use a (modified) GT protocol as a subroutine. We now overview some interesting techniques used in constructing GT protocols.

The notion of 0-*encodings* was first defined by Lin and Tzeng in [13] for solving the GT problem. Let $s = (s_1 s_2 \cdots s_K)$ be a binary string of length K. The 0-encoding of s is the set S_s^0 of binary strings defined as

$$S_s^0 = \{s_1 s_2 \cdots s_{i-1} 1 \mid s_i = 0 \text{ for } 1 \leq i \leq K\}.$$

The GT protocol in [13] was based on the observation that, for two integers x and y, $x > y$ if and only if S_y^0 contains a prefix of x.

Another approach used to solve the GT problem is as follows. Let x and y be two nonnegative integers with binary representation $x_1 x_2 \ldots x_K$ and $y_1 y_2 \ldots y_K$ respectively, where $x_i, y_i \in \{0, 1\}$, and x_1 and y_1 are the most significant bits. Consider the *bitwise difference* $d_i = x_i - y_i$ for any position i. Then $x > y$ if and only if there exist a position l, such that $d_i = 0$ for all $1 \leq i < l$, and $d_l = 1$. This property was used by Blake and Kolesnikov [2,3] to construct protocols for the GT problem.

Among the known constructions of STVD protocols, the protocol from [1] is not suitable for the malicious model because it uses both symmetric and asymmetric encryption schemes. Sang et al.'s protocols [16,15] are based on properties of 0-encodings, and a protocol for the malicious model is presented in [15].

For the GT problem, the communication complexity of the protocol in [2] was smaller than that of the protocol in [13]. This motivates us to construct STVD protocols based on bitwise differences. In this work, we consider STVD protocols both for the semi-honest model and for the malicious model. In each case, we present a one-round protocol with communication complexity $O(K^n)$, and a K-round protocol with communication complexity $O(nK^2)$. For the K-round protocol, we demonstrate that its computation and communication complexity is lower than that of [15], and in the special case where one of the two parties can perform parallel computation on $K + 1$ platforms, the computation time of our protocols is less than all previously known protocols. We also present a $\lceil \log K \rceil$-round protocol in the semi-honest model.

We will use the following notations throughout this paper. Suppose $0 \leq a_i, b_i < 2^K$ for $1 \leq i \leq n$. Let the binary representation of a_i be $a_{i1} a_{i2} \ldots a_{iK}$, where a_{i1} is the most significant bit. The numbers $b_1, \ldots, b_n$ are represented in the same way.

Now we introduce properties of the homomorphic encryption schemes that will be used later in this paper. A public-key encryption scheme E is *additively homomorphic* if for some operation $\otimes$, $\mathsf{E}(x) \otimes \mathsf{E}(y)$ is an encryption of $x + y$ for any pair (x, y) of plaintext. Thus in such an encryption scheme, given a pair of ciphertexts $\mathsf{E}(x), \mathsf{E}(y)$ and a constant c, one can efficiently calculate $\mathsf{E}(x+y)$ and $\mathsf{E}(cx)$ without knowing x or y.

Now we introduce the additive ElGamal encryption scheme and its (2,2) threshold variant, which will be needed later. Let $\mathbb{G}$ be a cyclic group of prime order q, and let g, f be random generators in $\mathbb{G}$. Let s be a randomly chosen element from $\mathbb{Z}_q$, and $h = g^s$. The public key is the tuple $<\mathbb{G}, q, g, f, h>$, and $s = \log_g h$ is the private key. Given a plaintext $m \in \mathbb{Z}_q$, the encryption algorithm selects r randomly from $\mathbb{Z}_q$, and computes the ciphertext $\mathsf{E}(m) = (g^r, h^r f^m) \in \mathbb{G} \times \mathbb{G}$. When a ciphertext (X, Y) is given, the decryption algorithm calculates $\mathsf{D}(X, Y) = Y/X^s$.

The (2,2) threshold additive ElGamal encryption scheme is similar to the above, with the change that Alice and Bob hold $s_A, s_B \in_R \mathbb{Z}_q$ as their private key respectively, and $h = g^{s_A + s_B}$. Alice and Bob also publishes $h_A = g^{s_A}$ and $h_B = g^{s_B}$ respectively, with a proof of knowledge of the exponent. The encryption algorithm is the same as the basic version, i.e., $\mathsf{E}(m) = (g^r, h^r f^m)$ where $r \in_R \mathbb{Z}_q$. For decryption of a ciphertext (X, Y), Alice and Bob publishes $d_A = X^{s_A}$ and $d_B = X^{s_B}$, with a proof that $\log_X d_A = \log_g h_A$ and $\log_X d_B = \log_g h_B$. Then they calculate $\mathsf{D}(X, Y) = Y/X^{s_A + s_B} = f^m$.

It is easy to verify both encryption schemes above are additively homomorphic, i.e., for any plaintext m, m', $\mathsf{E}(m) \cdot \mathsf{E}(m')$ is an encryption of $m + m'$. Also note that since $\mathsf{D}(\mathsf{E}(m)) = f^m$, an exhaustive search is needed to recover m. However, in this work we only need to test whether m is equal to a particular value (such as 0 or n).

2 The One-Round Protocols

In this section we consider a STVD variant as follows: Alice acts like a client and Bob acts like a server. At the end of the one-round protocol, Alice obtains $Dom(A, B)$ while Bob obtains nothing.

2.1 The One-Round Protocol in the Semi-honest Case

In this subsection, we present the one-round protocol for the STVD problem based on the additive ElGamal cryptosystem. It is shown in Figure 1.

Theorem 1. *In the semi-honest model, the protocol Π_1 in Fig. 1 achieves completeness and soundness for the STVD problem, and is secure under the assumption that the ElGamal encryption is semantically secure. In other words, if A dominates B, the probability of Alice outputting 0 is negligible; if A does not dominate B, the probability of Alice outputting 1 is negligible. Furthermore, the views of semi-honest adversaries in the ideal and real models are computationally indistinguishable.*

Proof. First consider the values $\gamma_{i,j}$ for a fixed i. Note that $\gamma_{i,0} = 0$, and $\gamma_{i,j} = r_{i,j} \gamma_{i,j-1} + d_{i,j}$, where $r_{i,j} \in_R \mathbb{Z}_q$, and $d_{i,j}$ is the bitwise difference $a_{i,j} - b_{i,j}$. We then have the following observation. If A dominates B, then for each i, there exists some $1 \leq j \leq K$ such that $\gamma_{i,j} = 1$. Thus in the final set T, there must be an encryption of n. So Alice outputs 1 with probability 1. If A does not dominate B, then with overwhelming probability, for some $1 \leq i \leq n$, none of the elements $\gamma_{i,j}, 1 \leq j \leq K$ is equal to 1. Thus with overwhelming probability, none of the elements of the final set T is an encryption of n, and so Alice outputs 0.

Protocol Π_1:
Alice's input: $A = (a_1, \ldots, a_n)$; Bob's input: $B = (b_1, \ldots, b_n)$, where $0 \leq a_i, b_i < 2^K$.
Alice's output: $Dom(A, B)$; Bob has no output.

1. Alice runs the setup phase of an additive ElGamal encryption scheme $(\mathbb{G}, q, g, h)$, where $\mathbb{G}$ is a group of order q, g is a generator of $\mathbb{G}$, $h = g^x$, and x is the private key. Alice sends $(pk, \mathsf{E}(a_{1,1}), \mathsf{E}(a_{1,2}) \ldots \mathsf{E}(a_{n,K}))$ to Bob. That is, she sends the public key $(\mathbb{G}, q, g, h)$ and the encryption of all her bits to Bob.
2. Bob receives pk and the $\mathsf{E}(a_{ij})$ for all i and j.
3. For $i = 1 \ldots n$ and for $j = 1 \ldots K$, Bob does the following:
   - calculates $\mathsf{E}(d_{i,j})$, where $d_{i,j} = a_{i,j} - b_{i,j}$, and
   - computes $\mathsf{E}(\gamma_{i,j})$, where $\gamma_{i,0} = 0$, $\gamma_{i,j} = r_{i,j}\gamma_{i,j-1} + d_{i,j}$, and $r_{i,j} \in_R \mathbb{Z}_q$;
4. Bob does the following. Let S be an empty multi-set. For each n-tuple $j_1, j_2, \ldots, j_n \in \{1, 2, \ldots, K\}^n$, Bob puts the value

$$\prod_{1 \leq i \leq n} \mathsf{E}(\gamma_{i,j_i}) = \mathsf{E}\left(\sum_{1 \leq i \leq n} \gamma_{i,j_i}\right)$$

   into S.
5. Bob does the following. Let T be an empty multi-set. For each element $s = \mathsf{E}(x) \in S$, Bob picks an random element $r \in_R \mathbb{Z}_N$ and puts the value $\mathsf{E}(n + r(x - n))$ into T.
6. Bob permutes the elements of T, and sends T to Alice.
7. Alice decrypts all the elements of T. If there exists an element $t \in T$ such that $\mathsf{D}(t) = n$, then she outputs "$Dom(A, B) = 1$", else "$Dom(A, B) = 0$".

Fig. 1. The one-round protocol in the semi-honest case

Then we prove that Π_1 computes the function $Dom(A, B)$ privately. Since this is a two-message protocol and we assume that ElGamal encryption is semantically secure, Bob obtains no knowledge from participating in the protocol. Now we demonstrate a simulator $\mathcal{S}$ such that the input of $\mathcal{S}$ is Alice's private input A and the output of the function $Dom(A, B)$, and the output of $\mathcal{S}$ is computationally indistinguishable from the view of Alice in the protocol. We only need to show that $\mathcal{S}$ can generate a set T' which is computationally indistinguishable from the set T received from Bob. If $Dom(A, B) = 1$, then let T' contain an encryption of $\mathsf{E}(n)$ and $K^n - 1$ encryptions of random elements of $\mathbb{Z}_q$; if $Dom(A, B) = 1$, then let T' contain K^n encryptions of random elements of $\mathbb{Z}_q$. Such a set T' meets the requirement above.

Thus Π_1 computes the function $Dom(A, B)$ securely in the semi-honest model. □

The first part of Bob's computation is based on the following observation. If $a_i > b_i$, with overwhelming probability, exactly one value among $\gamma_{i,1}, \ldots, \gamma_{i,K}$ is 1. This observation was used in the GT-Conditional Encrypted Mapping protocol in [3]. In the next part of Bob's computation, Bob computes a multi-set S. If A dominates B, then with overwhelming probability there is exactly one value in S which is an encryption of n. In the final part, Bob transforms $\mathsf{E}(n)$ to $\mathsf{E}(n)$, and transforms $\mathsf{E}(x)$, where $x \neq n$, to an encryption of a random value.

Remark 1. This protocol can be easily adapted for the following scenario. Alice and Bob respectively send the encryptions of their inputs to a server and obtain the comparison result from the server's output. The server learns nothing about Alice and Bob's inputs. For an example of protocol in this setting, see [3].

Remark 2. This protocol can also be adapted such that both Alice and Bob obtains $Dom(A, B)$ in the end, by using a 2-out-of-2 threshold additive ElGamal encryption scheme.

2.2 A One-Round Protocol in the Malicious-Bob Case

The STVD protocol in Subsection 2.1 cannot be used when Bob is malicious. The reason is that, in the final step, Alice concludes that A dominates B (i.e., $Dom(A, B) = 1$) if and only if the values she received from Bob contain an encryption of n. A malicious Bob can put into T encryptions of $K^n - 1$ random values of $\mathbb{Z}_q$ and one encryption of n. Then Alice will be fooled into concluding that $Dom(A, B) = 1$.

A similar problem appeared in protocols designed for the set-disjointness problem [8,12]. Hohenberger and Weis (HW) introduced a cryptographic primitive called *testable and homomorphic commitment* (THC) to solve this problem [10]. A THC is essentially a BGN (Boneh, Goh and Nissim) encryption [4] set in group $\mathbb{G}$, which has order $n = pq$ where p and q are prime numbers. In this subsection, we will first introduce the properties of THC, and then use THC to construct a STVD protocol secure in the case where Alice is semi-honest, while Bob is malicious.

Informally, a THC scheme should support the following operations [10]:

- Commit: $\mathsf{Com}(m, r)$ is the commitment to message m and randomness r.
- Addition: $\forall m, r, m', r', \mathsf{Com}(m, r) \cdot \mathsf{Com}(m', r') = \mathsf{Com}(m + m', r + r')$.
- Multiplication by a Constant: $\forall m, r, c, \mathsf{Com}(m, r)^c = \mathsf{Com}(cm, cr)$.
- Equality Test: $\mathsf{Test}(\mathsf{Com}(m, r), x)$ returns 1 if $m = x$.

The definition of the HW testable and homomorphic commitment scheme [10] is described in Figure 2.

It was shown in [10] that under the Subgroup Computation Assumption, the HW THC scheme is *computationally hiding* over the distribution of r:

$$\forall m_0, m_1 \in \mathbb{Z}_n^*, \{\mathbb{G}, n, m_0, m_1, \mathsf{Com}(m_0, r)\} \stackrel{c}{\approx} \{\mathbb{G}, n, m_0, m_1, \mathsf{Com}(m_1, r)\}.$$

That is, the two distributions are computationally indistinguishable.

For brevity, when the randomness r is irrelevant, we use $\mathsf{Com}(m)$ in place of $\mathsf{Com}(m, r)$ to denote a testable and homomorphic commitment of message m. The one-round protocol in the malicious-Bob case is given in Fig. 3. Its structure

Testable and Homomorphic Commitment Operations:

1. **Setup:** Let $S(1^k)$ be an algorithm that outputs $(\mathbb{G}, p, q)$ where $\mathbb{G}$ is a group of composite order $n = pq$, and $p < q$ are k-bit primes. Let g, u be random generators of $\mathbb{G}$ and let $h = u^q$. Then h has order p. Publish $(\mathbb{G}, n)$ and keep (p, q, g, h) private.
2. **Commit:** Give m and $r \in \mathbb{Z}_n^*$, compute $\mathsf{Com}(m, r) = g^m h^r$.
3. **Addition:** $\mathsf{Com}(m, r) \cdot \mathsf{Com}(m', r') = g^{m+m'} h^{r+r'} = \mathsf{Com}(m+m', r+r')$.
4. **Multiplication by a Constant:** $\mathsf{Com}(m, r)^c = g^{cm} h^{cr} = \mathsf{Com}(cm, cr)$.
5. **Equality Test:** If $\mathsf{Test}(\mathsf{Com}(m, r), x) = (g^m h^r / g^x)^p = (g^p)^{m-x} = 1$, output 1; else, output 0.

Fig. 2. HW testable and homomorphic commitment scheme

Protocol Π_2:
Alice's input: $A = (a_1, \ldots, a_n)$; Bob's input: $B = (b_1, \ldots, b_n)$, where $0 \leq a_i, b_i < 2^K$.
Alice's output: $Dom(A, B)$; Bob has no output.

1. Alice runs $S(1^k)$ to obtain $(\mathbb{G}, p, q)$, selects random generators g, u in $\mathbb{G}$, and computes $n = pq$ and $h = u^q$. Finally Alice publishes $(\mathbb{G}, n)$.
2. Alice sends $\mathsf{Com}(a_{i,j})$ for all $1 \leq i \leq n$, $1 \leq j \leq K$. That is, she selects randomly $r_{i,j} \in \mathbb{Z}_n^*$ for all $1 \leq i \leq n$, $1 \leq j \leq K$, and sends $(\mathsf{Com}(a_{1,1}, r_{1,1}), \mathsf{Com}(a_{1,2}, r_{1,2}) \ldots \mathsf{Com}(a_{n,K}, r_{n,K}))$ to Bob.
3. Bob receives $\mathsf{Com}(a_{i,j})$ for all i and j.
4. For $i = 1 \ldots n$ and $j = 1 \ldots K$, Bob does the following:
   - calculates $\mathsf{Com}(d_{i,j})$, where $d_{i,j} = a_{i,j} - b_{i,j}$;
   - computes $\mathsf{Com}(\gamma_{i,j})$, where $\gamma_{i,0} = 0$, $\gamma_{i,j} = r_{i,j}\gamma_{i,j-1} + d_{i,j}$, and $r_{i,j} \in_R \mathbb{Z}_N$;
5. Bob does the following. Let S be an empty multi-set. For each n-tuple $j_1, j_2, \ldots, j_n \in \{1, 2, \ldots, K\}^n$, Bob puts the value

$$\prod_{1 \leq i \leq n} \mathsf{Com}(\gamma_{i,j_i}) = \mathsf{Com}\left(\sum_{1 \leq i \leq n} \gamma_{i,j_i}\right)$$

   into S.
6. Bob does the following. Let T be an empty multi-set. For for each element $s = \mathsf{Com}(x) \in S$, Bob picks a random element $r \in_R \mathbb{Z}_N$ and puts the value $\mathsf{Com}(n + r(x - n))$ into T.
7. Bob permutes the elements of T, and sends T to Alice.
8. Alice runs the equality test with n for all the elements of T. If there exists an element $t \in T$ such that $\mathsf{Test}(t, n) = 1$, then she outputs "$Dom(A, B) = 1$", else "$Dom(A, B) = 0$".

Fig. 3. The one-round protocol in the malicious-Bob case

is analogous to that of the protocol in the semi-honest case. The difference is that we use testable and homomorphic commitments instead of encryptions, and in the final step, we use equality tests instead of decryptions.

Theorem 2. *In the malicious-Bob case, the protocol Π_2 in Fig. 3 achieves completeness and soundness for the STVD problem under the assumption that ElGamal encryption is semantically secure. It achieves Malicious-Bob Zero Knowledge and Honest-Alice Perfect Zero Knowledge under the Subgroup Computation Assumption, i.e., a malicious Bob learns nothing about Alice's set A, and a semi-honest Alice learns nothing about Bob's set B beyond $Dom(A, B)$.*

Proof. When both parties follow the protocol, the proof of completeness and soundness is similar to the proof of Theorem 1. The fact that a malicious Bob learns nothing about Alice's set A follows from the computationally hiding property of the THC scheme.

To show that a semi-honest Alice learns nothing about Bob's set B beyond $Dom(A, B)$, we construct a simulator $\mathcal{S}$ such that the input of $\mathcal{S}$ is Alice's private input A and the function $Dom(A, B)$, and the output of $\mathcal{S}$ is computationally indistinguishable from the view of Alice in the protocol. The simulator $\mathcal{S}$ generates a set T' as follows. If $Dom(A, B) = 1$, let T' contain one element $\mathsf{Com}(n)$ and $K^n - 1$ commitments of random elements of $\mathbb{Z}_q$; if $Dom(A, B) = 1$, let T' contain K^n commitments of random elements of $\mathbb{Z}_q$. Then the set T' is computationally indistinguishable from the set T.

Thus Π_1 computes the function $Dom(A, B)$ securely in the malicious-Bob case. $\square$

3 The K-Round Protocols

In this section, we assume that Alice and Bob share the private key of a 2-out-of-2 threshold additive ElGamal encryption scheme.

3.1 A K-Round Protocol in the Semi-honest Case

First, we present a subprotocol for comparing two K-bit numbers a_i and b_i. We wish to achieve the following at the end of the subprotocol: If $a_i > b_i$, both Alice and Bob get $\mathsf{E}(0)$; otherwise, they get $\mathsf{E}(r)$, where r is a random element of $\mathbb{Z}_q$. Note that we cannot directly use the known GT protocols in the literature, since none of them can achieve this.

The idea is as follows: $a_i > b_i$ if and only if there exists a position l such that for any $1 \leq j < l$, $a_{i,j} = b_{i,j}$, while $a_{i,l} = 1$, $b_{i,l} = 0$. This position is called the important position. Note that for any index j and elements $a_{i,j}, b_{i,j} \in \{0, 1\}$, we have $a_{i,j} \oplus b_{i,j} = (a_{i,j} - b_{i,j})^2 = a_{i,j} - 2a_{i,j}b_{i,j} + b_{i,j}$.

Let $r_{i,j} \in_R \mathbb{Z}_q$, and define

$$e_{i,j} = r_{i,j} \cdot \left(\sum_{1 \leq s < j} (a_{i,s} - 2a_{i,s}b_{i,s} + b_{i,s}) \right) + a_{i,j} - b_{i,j} - 1. \qquad (1)$$

Obviously, if $a_i > b_i$ and j is the important position, then $e_{i,j} = 0$, and $e_{i,s} = -1$ for all $1 \leq s < j$; in all other cases, the probability that $e_{i,j} = 0$ is negligible. Thus with overwhelming probability, $a_i > b_i$ if and only if $\prod_{1 \leq j \leq K} e_{i,j} = 0$. For $1 \leq j \leq K$, we define $T_{i,j} = \prod_{1 \leq s \leq j} e_{i,j}$, then with overwhelming probability, $a_i > b_i$ if and only if $T_{i,K} = 0$. Below is a subprotocol for Alice and Bob to compute $\mathsf{E}(T_{i,K})$.

Subprotocol 3. *for comparing a_i and b_i:*

1. Alice sends $\mathsf{E}(a_i) = (\mathsf{E}(a_{i,1}), \ldots, \mathsf{E}(a_{i,K}))$ to Bob.
   Bob computes $\alpha = \mathsf{E}(b_{i,1} - 1) \cdot \mathsf{E}(0)$, and sends $\mathsf{E}(T_{i,1}) = \mathsf{E}(a_{i,1})/\alpha = \mathsf{E}(a_{i,1} - b_{i,1} - 1)$ to Alice.
2. For $j = 2, \ldots, K$,
   (a) Alice computes and sends $(\mathsf{E}(T_{i,j-1})^{a_{i,1}} \cdot \mathsf{E}(0), \ldots, \mathsf{E}(T_{i,j-1})^{a_{i,j}} \cdot \mathsf{E}(0))$ to Bob.
   (b) Using these received values, Bob selects $r_{i,j} \in_R \mathbb{Z}_q^*$, computes $\mathsf{E}(T_{i,j}) = \mathsf{E}(T_{i,j-1})^{e_{i,j}}$, and sends it to Alice. Note that since Bob holds $\mathsf{E}(T_{i,j-1})$ and $\mathsf{E}(T_{i,j-1})^{a_{i,s}} \cdot \mathsf{E}(0)$ for $1 \leq s \leq j$, Bob is able to calculate $\mathsf{E}(T_{i,j})$ according to Equation (1).
3. Finally, they both get $\mathsf{E}(T_{i,K}) = \mathsf{E}(\prod_{1 \leq j \leq K} e_{i,j})$.

The K-round STVD protocol in the semi-honest case is shown in Figure 4.

Theorem 4. *In the semi-honest model, the protocol Π_3 achieves completeness and soundness for the STVD problem, and is secure under the assumption that threshold ElGamal encryption is semantically secure.*

The proof of Theorem 4 is given in Appendix A.

The structure of our protocol is similar to that in [15], in the sense that both protocols use a K-round subprotocol for comparing a pair (a_i, b_i), and the comparison results for all the n pairs are added together. However, in that paper, a structure based on 0-encodings was used in the sub-protocol for comparing a_i and b_i. As we will see, by computing encryptions of the product of $e_{i,j}$ defined in (1), our protocol achieves lower communication and computation complexity than the protocol from [15].

Protocol Π_3:
Alice's input: $A = (a_1, \ldots, a_n)$; Bob's input: $B = (b_1, \ldots, b_n)$, where $0 \leq a_i, b_i < 2^K$.
Alice's and Bob's output: $Dom(A, B)$.

1. For $1 \leq i \leq n$, Alice and Bob runs Subprotocol 3 for comparing a_i and b_i, and they both get $\mathsf{E}(T_{i,K})$.
2. Alice and Bob computes $\mathsf{E}(T) = \sum_{1 \leq i \leq n} \mathsf{E}(T_{i,K})$.
3. Alice and Bob jointly decrypt $\mathsf{E}(T)$. If $T = 0$, they output "$Dom(A, B) = 1$". Otherwise, they output "$Dom(A, B) = 0$".

Fig. 4. The K-round protocol in the semi-honest case

Table 1. Comparison of STVD Solutions

	Computation Cost		Communication Cost
	Serial	$K+1$ Parallel	
Protocol Π_3	$n(K^2+5K-2)$	$4nK$	$[n(K^2+5K-2)]\lambda$
[15]	$n(5K^2+4K-2)+1$	$4nK+2n+1$	$[n(4K^2+2K)+2]\lambda$
[17]	$12nK+25(n-1)$	$12nK+25(n-1)$	$[8nK+12(n-1)]\lambda$
[1]	$48nK+40n$	$48nK+16n+8\lceil\frac{n}{K}\rceil$	$(32nK+16n)\lambda$

Now we analyze the computation and communication resources in Subprotocol 3. In Step 1, Alice computes $2K$ modular exponentiations (mod-exps), and sends $2K$ values to Bob; Bob computes 2 mod-exps and sends 2 values to Alice. In each iteration of Step 2, for a certain j with $2 \leq j \leq K$, Alice computes $2j$ mod-exps and send $2j$ values; Bob computes 2 mod-exps and sends 2 values to Alice. Altogether, in Protocol 3, the total number of mod-exps is $2K + 2 + (2 \cdot 2 + \cdots + 2 \cdot K) + 2(K-1) = K^2 + 5K - 2$, and the number of values exchanged is also $K^2 + 5K - 2$. Thus the total computational cost is $n(K^2 + 5K - 2)$.

Now we consider the case where Alice has $K+1$ platforms for parallel execution while Bob has only one. In practical applications such as multi-commodity bidding, K is usually small and can be set as an integer between 5 and 10, and one of the two parties (e.g. a server) may have larger computing power, so this is a reasonable assumption. In Step 1, Alice computes 2 mod-exps, Bob computes 2 mod-exps. In each iteration of Step 2, Alice computes 2 mod-exps and Bob computes 2 mod-exps. Altogether, in Protocol 3, the total number of mod-exps is $2 + 2 + ((2+2) * (K-1)) = 4K$, so the total computational cost of the protocol Π_3 is $4nK$.

Now we compare the computation and communication costs of Protocol Π_3 and the protocols from [15], [17] and [1] in Table 1. Here λ is a security parameter. When K is small, our protocol compares favorably with the known protocols, and in the case where Alice has $K+1$ platforms, the computational cost of our protocol is smaller than that of the previous protocols.

3.2 A K-Round Protocol in the Malicious Case

In this subsection, we will equip the previous K-round protocol with zero knowledge proofs of knowledge to make it secure against malicious behaviors. For brevity we use the notations similar to those in [15]. For example, we write $ZK\{x|y=g^x\}$ to denote a zero knowledge proof of knowledge of integer x such that $y = g^x$, where y and g are public.

In the sequel, we define $e_{i,j}$ as follows:

$$e_{i,j} = -2 \cdot \left(\sum_{1 \leq s < j} (a_{i,s} - 2a_{i,s}b_{i,s} + b_{i,s}) \right) + a_{i,j} - b_{i,j} - 1. \qquad (2)$$

It is easy to verify that for a pair a_i, b_i, if $a_i > b_i$, then for some j, $e_{i,j}=0$; otherwise, $e_{i,j}$ is nonzero for all j. The reason for the appearance of the constant

-2 in (2) is as follows. Consider the following example: $a_i = 00\cdots$, $b_i = 10\cdots$. Then if we delete -2 from (2), we would have $e_{i,2} = 0$ but $a_i < b_i$.

In our protocol we need the following zero knowledge proofs. In an additive ElGamal cryptosystem, an encryption of message m with randomness r is $\mathsf{E}(m,r) = (g^r, g^m h^r)$, and let $\mathsf{E}(m) = \{\mathsf{E}(m,r) : r \in \mathbb{Z}_q^*\}$.

(1) Proof of knowledge of ElGamal plaintext: Given an ElGamal ciphertext c, the prover P proves to V that he knows plaintext m and randomness r such that $\mathsf{E}(m,r) = c$. This proof comes from Schnorr's protocol for proving knowledge of a discrete logarithm [18] and Fujisaki-Okamoto's protocol for proving knowledge of (m,r) such that $f = g^m h^r$ [9].
(2) Proof that a plaintext is in a two-valued domain: Given an ElGamal ciphertext c and two plaintexts m_0, m_1, the prover P proves to V that $c \in \mathsf{E}(m_0) \cup \mathsf{E}(m_1)$. This comes from the proof of knowledge of ElGamal plaintext (1) above, combined with the OR-composition of proofs of [6]. We denote this proof by $ZK\{c \in \mathsf{E}(m_0) \cup \mathsf{E}(m_1)\}$.
(3) Proof of knowledge of an exponent: $ZK\{r|c_0 = E(x) \wedge c_1 = \mathsf{E}(r) \wedge c_2 = c_0^r \odot \mathsf{E}(0)\}$, where x is unknown to the prover and verifier. This comes from the multiplication protocol in [5].
(4) Proof of computation of a particular form: For a given pair (i,j) where $1 \leq i \leq n$, $2 \leq j \leq K$, suppose the following are public: $\mathsf{E}(T)$, $\mathsf{E}(a_{i,s})$, $\mathsf{E}(b_{i,s})$, $\mathsf{E}(T)^{a_{i,s}}$ for all $1 \leq s \leq j$, and a ciphertext c. The prover P proves to V that $c \in \mathsf{E}(T)^{e_{i,j}}$, where $e_{i,j}$ is defined in (2). It is easy to verify that this proof can be constructed from the three proofs above.

Subprotocol 5. for comparing a_i and b_i:

1. For $1 \leq j \leq K$, Alice computes $\alpha_{i,j} = \mathsf{E}(a_{i,j})$. Alice sends $(\alpha_{i,1}, \ldots, \alpha_{i,K})$ to Bob together with the proof $ZK\{\alpha_{i,j} \in \mathsf{E}(0) \cup \mathsf{E}(1)\}$.
2. For $1 \leq j \leq K$ Bob computes $\beta_{i,j} = \mathsf{E}(b_{i,j})$. Bob sends $(\beta_{i,1}, \ldots, \beta_{i,K})$ to Alice together with the proof $ZK\{\beta_{i,j} \in \mathsf{E}(0) \cup \mathsf{E}(1)\}$.
3. Alice and Bob computes $\mathsf{E}(T_{i,1}) = \mathsf{E}(a_{i,1} - b_{i,1} - 1)$.
4. for $j = 2, \ldots, K$,
   (a) For $1 \leq s \leq j$, Alice computes $\gamma_{i,s} = \mathsf{E}(T_{i,j-1})^{a_{i,s}} \odot \mathsf{E}(0)$, and sends $(\gamma_{i,1}, \ldots, \gamma_{i,j})$ to Bob together with the proof $ZK\{r|c_0 = \mathsf{E}(T_{i,j-1}) \wedge \alpha_{i,s} = \mathsf{E}(r) \wedge \gamma_{i,s} = c_0^r \odot \mathsf{E}(0)\}$ for each $1 \leq s \leq j$.
   (b) Using these received values, Bob computes $\mathsf{E}(T_{i,j}) = \mathsf{E}(T_{i,j-1})^{e_{i,j}}$, and sends it to Alice. Note that according to (2), Bob is able to calculate $\mathsf{E}(T_{i,j})$ based on the above data received from Alice.
5. Finally, they both get $\mathsf{E}(T_{i,K}) = \mathsf{E}(\prod_{1 \leq s \leq K} e_{i,j})$.

The K-round STVD protocol in the malicious case is given in Figure 5.

Theorem 6. *When either Alice or Bob is malicious, Protocol Π_4 achieves completeness and soundness for the STVD problem, and is secure under the assumption that threshold ElGamal encryption is semantically secure.*

> **Protocol Π_4:**
> Alice's input: $A = (a_1,\ldots,a_n)$; Bob's input: $B = (b_1,\ldots,b_n)$, where $0 \leq a_i, b_i < 2^K$.
> Alice's and Bob's output: $Dom(A,B)$.
>
> 1. For $1 \leq i \leq n$, Alice and Bob run Subprotocol 5 for comparing a_i and b_i, and they both get $\mathsf{E}(T_{i,K})$.
> 2. Alice and Bob both compute $\mathsf{E}(T) = \sum_{1 \leq i \leq n} \mathsf{E}(T_{i,K})$.
> 3. Alice selects $r_A \in_R \mathbb{Z}_q$, sends $c_1 = \mathsf{E}(r_A)$, $c_A = \mathsf{E}(T)^{r_A}$ to Bob, together with the proof $PK\{r|c_0 = E(T) \wedge c_1 = \mathsf{E}(r_A) \wedge c_A = c_0^{r_A} \odot \mathsf{E}(0)\}$.
> 4. Bob selects $r_B \in_R \mathbb{Z}_q$, sends $c_1 = \mathsf{E}(r_B)$, $c_B = \mathsf{E}(T)^{r_B}$ to Alice, together with the proof $PK\{r|c_0 = E(T) \wedge c_1 = \mathsf{E}(r_B) \wedge c_A = c_0^{r_B} \odot \mathsf{E}(0)\}$.
> 5. Alice and Bob both compute $\mathsf{E}(S) = c_A \cdot c_B = \mathsf{E}(T)^{r_A + r_B}$, and cooperatively decrypt $\mathsf{E}(S)$. If $S = 0$, they output "$Dom(A,B) = 1$". Otherwise, they output "$Dom(A,B) = 0$".

Fig. 5. The K-round protocol in the malicious case

The proof of Theorem 6 is deferred to Appendix B. Like the semi-honest case, the structure and proof of the our protocol in the malicious case is also similar to those of [15]. However, since our protocol is based on the properties of $e_{i,j}$ of (2) rather than properties of 0-encodings, it has lower communication and computation complexity.

4 The $\lceil \log K \rceil$-Round Protocol in the Semi-honest Model

In this section, we require that at the end of the protocol, only Alice obtains the comparison result. We will use the BGN cryptosystem [4] to improve the round complexity of the protocols in Section 3 to $\lceil \log K \rceil$ in the semi-honest model, at a slight expense of statistical indistinguishability.

4.1 The BGN Cryptosystem

Let $\mathbb{G}$ and $\mathbb{G}_1$ be two cyclic groups of order n. Let g be a generator of $\mathbb{G}$. Let e be a *bilinear map* $e \colon \mathbb{G} \times \mathbb{G} \to \mathbb{G}_1$. In other words, for all $u, v \in \mathbb{G}$ and $a, b \in \mathbb{Z}$, we have $e(u^a, v^b) = e(u,v)^{ab}$.

The BGN public key system is made up of the following three algorithms [4]:

KeyGen(λ): Given a security parameter $\lambda \in \mathbb{Z}^+$, obtain a tuple $(q_1, q_2, \mathbb{G}, \mathbb{G}_1, e)$, where q_1 and q_2 are two random λ-bit primes, $\mathbb{G}$ and $\mathbb{G}_1$ are two cyclic groups of order $n = q_1 q_2$. Let $e : \mathbb{G} \times \mathbb{G} \to \mathbb{G}_1$ be the bilinear map. Let g be a random generator of $\mathbb{G}$. Let h be a random generator of the subgroup of $\mathbb{G}$ of order q_1. The public key is $\mathcal{PK} = (n, \mathbb{G}, \mathbb{G}_1, e, g, h)$. The private key is $\mathcal{SK} = q_1$.

Encrypt($\mathcal{PK}, m$): We assume the message space consists of integers in the set $\{0, 1, \ldots, T\}$ where $T < q_2$. To encrypt a message m using public key $\mathcal{PK}$, pick a random $r \in_R \{0, 1, \ldots, n-1\}$ and compute the ciphertext

$$\mathsf{E}(m) = g^m h^r \in \mathbb{G}. \tag{3}$$

Decrypt($\mathcal{SK}, c$): To decrypt a ciphertext c using the private key $\mathcal{SK} = q_1$, observe that

$$c^{q_1} = (g^m h^r)^{q_1} = (g^{q_1})^m.$$

Let $\hat{g} = g^{q_1}$. To recover m, it suffices to compute the discrete log of c^{q_1} base $\hat{g}$. Since $0 \leq m \leq T$ this takes expected time $\tilde{O}(\sqrt{T})$ using Pollard's lambda method.

It can be seen from Equation (3) that this system is additively homomorphic. Moreover, it is proved in [4] that anyone having the public key can *multiply* two encrypted messages *once* using the bilinear map.

Lemma 1. *[4] Let $c_1 = g^{m_1} h^{r_1}$ and $c_2 = g^{m_2} h^{r_2}$ be encryptions of m_1 and m_2, respectively. Let $h_1 = e(g, h)$. Pick a random $r \in_R \mathbb{Z}_n$. Then $c = e(c_1, c_2) h_1^r \in \mathbb{G}_1$ is a uniformly distributed encryption of $m_1 m_2 \mod n$, but in the group $\mathbb{G}_1$ rather than $\mathbb{G}$.*

We use $E(m)$ and $E_1(m)$ to denote a ciphertext of m in $\mathbb{G}$ and $\mathbb{G}_1$, respectively. Lemma 1 says that from $E(x)$ and $E(y)$, anyone can compute $E_1(xy)$ using only public key. We now construct a procedure which allows to compute $E(xy)$ by interacting with the party holding the private key.

Procedure 7. *Input: Alice has $\mathcal{SK}$; Bob has $\mathcal{PK}$, $E(x)$ and $E(y)$.*
Output: Alice outputs nothing; Bob obtains $E(xy)$.

1. From $E(x)$, $E(y)$, Bob obtains $E_1(xy)$, using the result in Lemma 1.
2. Bob chooses r randomly, computes and sends $c_1 = E_1(xy + r)$ to Alice.
3. Alice decrypts c_1 to obtain $xy + r$, computes and sends $c = E(xy + r)$ to Bob.
4. From $c = E(xy + r)$ and r, Bob computes $E(xy)$.

Subprotocol 8. *Alice's input: a_i and $\mathcal{SK}$; Bob's input: b_i and $\mathcal{PK}$.*
Output: Alice outputs nothing; Bob obtains $\mathsf{E}(T_{i,K}) = \mathsf{E}(\prod_{1 \leq s \leq K} e_{i,j})$.

1. Alice sends $E(a_{i,1}), \ldots, E(a_{i,K})$ to Bob. According to (2), Bob calculates $E(e_{i,1}), E(e_{i,2}), \ldots, E(e_{i,K})$.
2. Bob carries out Procedure 7 with Alice for $K - 1$ times to obtain $\mathsf{E}(T_{i,K}) = \mathsf{E}(\prod_{1 \leq s \leq K} e_{i,j})$. Note that this can be done in $\lceil \log K \rceil$ rounds as follows. For brevity suppose K is a power of two. In the first round Alice and Bob perform $K/2$ executions of Procedure 7 in parallel so that at the end Bob obtains $E(e_{i,1} e_{i,2}), E(e_{i,3} e_{i,4}), \ldots, E(e_{i,K-1} e_{i,K})$. In the second round, Bob obtains $E(e_{i,1} e_{i,2} e_{i,3} e_{i,4}), \ldots, E(e_{i,K-3} e_{i,K-2} e_{i,K-1} e_{i,K})$. This process continues and after $\lceil \log K \rceil$ rounds, Bob obtains $\mathsf{E}(T_{i,K}) = \mathsf{E}(\prod_{1 \leq s \leq K} e_{i,j})$.

The $\lceil \log K \rceil$-round STVD protocol in the semi-honest case is as follows. We omit the proof here since it is similar to that of Theorem 4.

Remark 3. Note that in Step 2 of Procedure 7, we didn't specify from which domain we can choose r. Note that in our application, from Equation (2), we

Protocol Π_5:
Alice's input: $A = (a_1, \ldots, a_n)$ and $\mathcal{SK}$; Bob's input: $B = (b_1, \ldots, b_n)$ and $\mathcal{PK}$, where $0 \leq a_i, b_i < 2^K$.
Alice's output: $Dom(A, B)$; Bob outputs nothing.

1. For $1 \leq i \leq n$, Alice and Bob runs Subprotocol 8 for comparing a_i and b_i, and Bob obtains $\mathsf{E}(T_{i,K})$. Note that this step takes $\lceil \log K \rceil$ rounds, since the executions for all $1 \leq i \leq n$ can be performed in parallel.
2. Bob computes $\mathsf{E}(T) = \sum_{1 \leq i \leq n} \mathsf{E}(T_{i,K})$.
3. Bob selects $r_B \in_R \mathbb{Z}_q$, and sends $c = \mathsf{E}(T)^{r_B} = \mathsf{E}(r_B T)$ to Alice.
4. Alice decrypts c. If the decryption algorithm succeeds and the output is 0, Alices outputs "$Dom(A, B) = 1$". Otherwise, Alice outputs "$Dom(A, B) = 0$".

Fig. 6. The $\lceil \log K \rceil$-round protocol in the semi-honest case

have $-2j \leq e_{i,j} \leq 0$ for all i, j. To ensure that $xy + r \in \{0, \ldots, T\}$, we can choose r randomly from $\{2^K K!, \ldots, T - 2^K K!\}$. Thus the distribution of $E(xy + r)$ is not statistically identical to $E(m)$, where m is a random plaintext. However, the statistical difference is negligible if we choose the parameters T, K with $T \gg K$.

5 Concluding Remarks

In this paper, we proposed five protocols for securely computing the vector dominance relation. We presented a one round and a K-round protocol for the semi-honest and malicious cases, respectively, and demonstrated that the K-round protocols improve on known solutions in communication/computation complexity in certain cases. We also presented a $\lceil \log K \rceil$-round protocol in the semi-honest case, which has the same order of communication/computation complexity as the K-round protocol, at a slight cost of statistical indistinguishability.

Acknowledgements

This work was supported by ARC grants DP0558773 and DP0663452. The research of H. Wang is partially supported by the Ministry of Education of Singapore under grant T206B2204.

References

1. Atallah, M.J., Du, W.: Secure Multi-Party Computational Geometry. In: Dehne, F., Sack, J.-R., Tamassia, R. (eds.) WADS 2001. LNCS, vol. 2125, pp. 165–179. Springer, Heidelberg (2001)
2. Blake, I.F., Kolesnikov, V.: Strong Conditional Oblivious Transfer and Computing on Intervals. In: Lee, P.J. (ed.) ASIACRYPT 2004. LNCS, vol. 3329, pp. 515–529. Springer, Heidelberg (2004)

3. Blake, I.F., Kolesnikov, V.: Conditional Encrypted Mapping and Comparing Encrypted Numbers. In: Di Crescenzo, G., Rubin, A. (eds.) FC 2006. LNCS, vol. 4107, pp. 206–220. Springer, Heidelberg (2006)
4. Boneh, D., Goh, E., Nissim, K.: Evaluating 2-DNF Formulas on Ciphertexts. In: Kilian, J. (ed.) TCC 2005. LNCS, vol. 3378, pp. 325–341. Springer, Heidelberg (2005)
5. Cramer, R., Damgård, I.: Zero-Knowledge Proof for Finite Field Arithmetic, or: Can Zero-Knowledge Be For Free. In: Krawczyk, H. (ed.) CRYPTO 1998. LNCS, vol. 1462, pp. 424–441. Springer, Heidelberg (1998)
6. Cramer, R., Damgård, I., Schoenmakers, B.: Proofs of Partial Knowledge and Simplified Design of Witness Hiding Protocols. In: Desmedt, Y.G. (ed.) CRYPTO 1994. LNCS, vol. 839, pp. 174–187. Springer, Heidelberg (1994)
7. Fischlin, M.: A Cost-Effective Pay-Per-Multiplication Comparison Method for Millionaires. In: Naccache, D. (ed.) CT-RSA 2001. LNCS, vol. 2020, pp. 457–471. Springer, Heidelberg (2001)
8. Freedman, M.J., Nissim, K., Pinkas, B.: Effective Private Matching and Set Interseciton. In: Cachin, C., Camenisch, J.L. (eds.) EUROCRYPT 2004. LNCS, vol. 3027, pp. 1–19. Springer, Heidelberg (2004)
9. Fujisaki., E., Okamoto, T.: Statistical Zero Knowledge Protocols to Prove Modular Polynomial Relations. In: Kaliski Jr., B.S. (ed.) CRYPTO 1997. LNCS, vol. 1294, pp. 16–30. Springer, Heidelberg (1997)
10. Hohenberger, S., Weis, S.A.: Honest-Verifier Private Disjointness Testing Without Random Oracles. In: Danezis, G., Golle, P. (eds.) PET 2006. LNCS, vol. 4258, pp. 277–294. Springer, Heidelberg (2006)
11. Ioannidis., I., Grama, G.: An Efficient Protocol for Yao's Millionaires Problem. In: HICSS 2003, vol. 07(7), p. 205. IEEE, Los Alamitos (2003)
12. Kiayias., A., Mitrofanova, A.: Testing Disjointness of Private Datasets. In: S. Patrick, A., Yung, M. (eds.) FC 2005. LNCS, vol. 3570, pp. 109–124. Springer, Heidelberg (2005)
13. Lin, H.Y., Tzeng, W.G.: An Efficient Solution to the Millionaires Problem Based on Homomorphic Encryption. In: Ioannidis, J., Keromytis, A.D., Yung, M. (eds.) ACNS 2005. LNCS, vol. 3531, pp. 456–466. Springer, Heidelberg (2005)
14. Paillier, P.: Public-Key Cryptosystems Based on Composite Degree Residuosity Classes. In: Stern, J. (ed.) EUROCRYPT 1999. LNCS, vol. 1592, pp. 223–238. Springer, Heidelberg (1999)
15. Sang, Y.: Efficient Solutions to Several Privacy Preserving Computation Problems. Ph.D. thesis, Japan Advanced Institute of Science and Technology (2007)
16. Sang, Y., Shen, H., Zhang, Z.: An Efficient Protocol for the Problem of Secure Two-Party Vector Dominance. In: 6th International Conference on Parallel and Distributed Computing, Applications and Technologies, pp. 488–492. IEEE, Los Alamitos (2005)
17. Schoenmakers, B., Tuyls, P.: Practical Two-Party Computation Based on the Conditional Gate. In: Lee, P.J. (ed.) ASIACRYPT 2004. LNCS, vol. 3329, pp. 119–136. Springer, Heidelberg (2004)
18. Schnorr, C.P.: Efficient Signature Generation by Smart Cards. Journal of Cryptology 4(3), 161–174 (1997)
19. Yao, A.C.: Protocols for Secure Computations. In: 23rd IEEE Symp. on Foundations of Computer Science, pp. 160–164. IEEE Computer Society Press, Los Alamitos (1982)

A Proof of Theorem 4

Proof. In the end of Protocol Π_3, Alice and Bob cooperatively decrypt $\mathsf{E}(T)$ to get $T = \sum_{1 \leq i \leq n} \prod_{1 \leq j \leq K} e_{i,j}$. For each i, if $a_i > b_i$, then $e_{i,j} = 0$ for some $1 \leq j \leq K$; if $a_i \leq b_i$, then with overwhelming probability $e_{i,j} \neq 0$ for all j. Thus Protocol Π_3 achieves completeness and soundness.

Protocol Π_3 is secure because all exchanged data are ciphertexts of the threshold ElGamal encryption, and due to semantic security Alice or Bob alone can obtain no knowledge from these ciphertexts. □

B Proof of Theorem 6

Proof. The proof of completeness and soundness is similar to that of Protocol Π_3. Now let $\overline{M} = (M_1, M_2)$ be a pair of admissible strategies of Alice and Bob respectively in the real model (i.e., at least one of M_1 and M_2 follows the execution prescribed by Π_4). When either Alice or Bob is malicious, we construct a pair of admissible strategies $\overline{\mathcal{M}} = (\mathcal{M}_1, \mathcal{M}_2)$ in the ideal model, and then prove that the view of the two pairs of strategies are computationally indistinguishable.

If Alice is malicious, the execution of $\overline{\mathcal{M}} = (\mathcal{M}_1, \mathcal{M}_2)$ is as follows:

1. For $1 \leq i \leq n$:
   (a) $\mathcal{M}_1$ invokes M_1 for computing $\alpha_{i,j} = \mathsf{E}(a_{i,j})$ and checks $ZK\{\alpha_{i,j} \in \mathsf{E}(0) \cup \mathsf{E}(1)\}$ for $1 \leq j \leq K$. If any proof is incorrect, $\mathcal{M}_1$ aborts; otherwise, $\mathcal{M}_1$ sends the values $\alpha_{i,j}$ to the Trusted Third Party (TTP).
   (b) Bob sends $b_{i,j}$ to the TTP for $1 \leq j \leq K$.
   (c) The TTP computes $\mathsf{E}(T_{i,1}) = \mathsf{E}(a_{i,1} - b_{i,1} - 1)$ and sends $\mathsf{E}(T_{i,1})$ to $\mathcal{M}_1$ and $\mathcal{M}_2$. $\mathcal{M}_1$ sends $\mathsf{E}(T_{i,1})$ to M_1.
   (d) For $j = 2, \ldots, K$,
      i. $\mathcal{M}_1$ invokes M_1 for computing $\gamma_{i,s} = \mathsf{E}(T_{i,j-1})^{a_{i,s}} \odot \mathsf{E}(0)$, and M_1 also sends $(\gamma_{i,1}, \ldots, \gamma_{i,j})$ to $\mathcal{M}_1$ with the proof $ZK\{r|c_0 = \mathsf{E}(T_{i,j-1}) \wedge \alpha_{i,s} = \mathsf{E}(r) \wedge \gamma_{i,s} = c_0^r \odot \mathsf{E}(0)\}$ for each $1 \leq s \leq j$. $\mathcal{M}_1$ checks these proofs. If any proof is incorrect, $\mathcal{M}_1$ aborts.
      ii. $\mathcal{M}_1$ sends $(\gamma_{i,1}, \ldots, \gamma_{i,j})$ to the TTP. The TTP computes $\mathsf{E}(T_{i,j}) = \mathsf{E}(T_{i,j-1})^{e_{i,j}}$, and sends it to $\mathcal{M}_1$ and $\mathcal{M}_2$. $\mathcal{M}_1$ passes it to M_1.
   (e) Finally, $\mathcal{M}_1$ and $\mathcal{M}_2$ get $\mathsf{E}(T_{i,K}) = \mathsf{E}(\prod_{1 \leq s \leq K} e_{i,j})$.
2. $\mathcal{M}_1$ and $\mathcal{M}_2$ both computes $\mathsf{E}(T) = \sum_{1 \leq i \leq n} \mathsf{E}(T_{i,K})$.
3. The TTP selects $r_A, r_B \in_R \mathbb{Z}_q$, computes $c_A = \mathsf{E}(T)^{r_A}$, $c_B = \mathsf{E}(T)^{r_B}$, and sends c_A and c_B to $\mathcal{M}_1$ and $\mathcal{M}_2$ with the proof that c_A was formed correctly. $\mathcal{M}_1$ passes c_A and the proof to M_1.
4. $\mathcal{M}_1$ and $\mathcal{M}_2$ both computes $\mathsf{E}(S) = c_A \cdot c_B = \mathsf{E}(T)^{r_A + r_B}$, and cooperatively decrypt $\mathsf{E}(S)$. If $S = 0$, they output "$Dom(A, B) = 1$". Otherwise, they output "$Dom(A, B) = 0$".

It can be easily verified that due to the property of zero knowledge proofs, the output pair of $\overline{M}$ in the real model and the output pair $\overline{\mathcal{M}}$ in the ideal model are computationally indistinguishable. The case that Bob is malicious can be analyzed similarly. □

Rational Secret Sharing with Repeated Games

Shaik Maleka, Amjed Shareef, and C. Pandu Rangan*

Department of Computer Science and Engineering,
Indian Institute of Technology Madras, Chennai, India
{maleka.smile, amjedshareef}@gmail.com, rangan@cse.iitm.ernet.in

Abstract. This paper introduces the *Repeated Rational Secret Sharing* problem. We borrow the notion of *rational secret sharing* from Halpern and Teague[1], where players prefer to get the secret than not to get the secret and with lower preference, prefer that as few of the other players get the secret. We introduce the concept of repeated games in the rational secret sharing problem for the first time, which enables the possibility of a deterministic protocol for solving this problem. This is the first approach in this direction to the best of our knowledge. We extend the results for the mixed model (synchronous) where at most t players can be malicious. We also propose the first asynchronous protocol for rational secret sharing.

Keywords: Secret sharing, game theory, repeated games, distributed computing.

1 Introduction

Secret sharing is a widely known primitive in modern cryptography. More formally, in a secret sharing scheme there is a unique player called the *dealer* (player 0) who wants to share a secret s among n players, $p_1, \ldots, p_n$. The dealer sends every player a share of the secret in a way that any group of m (threshold value) or more players can together reconstruct the secret but no group of fewer than m players can. Such a system is called an (m, n)-threshold scheme.

Shamir's Secret Sharing Scheme[2] is based on the fact that, it takes m points to define uniquely a polynomial of degree $(m-1)$. The idea is that the dealer who shares the secret among the players, chooses a random $(m-1)$ degree polynomial f, such that $f(0) = s$, and sends the shares to the players such that every player p_i, $i = 1, \ldots, n$ receives the share $f(i)$. Any m players can recover the secret by reconstructing the polynomial through Lagrange's Interpolation. Any subset of players of size less than m cannot reconstruct the polynomial (even if they have infinite computing power).

1.1 Game Theory in Secret Sharing

Game theory provides a clean and effective tool to study and analyze the situations where decision-makers interact in a competitive manner. Game theoretic

---

* Work supported by Microsoft Project No. CSE0506075MICOCPAN on Foundation Research in Cryptology.

reasoning takes into account, which strategy is the best for a player with respect to every other player's strategy. Thus, the goal is to find a solution that is the best for all the players in the game. Every player's decision is based on the decision of every other player in the game and hence, it is possible to reach the equilibrium state corresponding to the global optima.

In distributed computing or secret sharing or multi-party computation, the players are mostly perceived as either honest or malicious players. An honest player follows the protocol perfectly whereas a malicious player behaves in an arbitrary manner. Halpern and Teague[1] introduced the problem of *secret sharing* assuming that the players are rational, which is known as *rational secret sharing*. In rational secret sharing, player's behavior is selfish. They have their own preferences and utility function (the profit they get). They always try to maximize their profits and behave accordingly.

For any player p_i, let w_1, w_2, w_3, w_4 be the payoffs obtained in the following scenarios.

w_1	—	p_i gets the secret, others do not get the secret
w_2	—	p_i gets the secret, others get the secret
w_3	—	p_i does not get the secret, others do not get the secret
w_4	—	p_i does not get the secret, others get the secret

The preferences of p_i is specified by $w_1 > w_2 > w_3 > w_4$. In brief, every player primarily prefers to get the secret than to not get it and secondarily, prefers that the fewer of the other players that get it, the better. The least preferred scenario for p_i is the situation, where he does not get the secret and others get it. A rational player follows the protocol only if it increases his expected utility.

1.2 Related Work

Consider any arbitrary player, say p_i. He needs $(m-1)$ shares from others to compute the secret. If other players (at least $(m-1)$) send him their shares, then he gets the secret, otherwise he cannot. This does not depend on whether he sends his share to others or not, as all the players are assumed to send their shares simultaneously. So, there is no incentive for any player to send his share. Reasoning in a similar way, no player might send his share. This impossibility result is proved by Halpern and Teague[1]. They show that rational secret sharing is not possible with any mechanism that has a fixed running time by iterated deletion of weakly dominated strategies (the strategy of not sending the share weakly dominates the strategy of sending the share). They also proposed a randomized protocol for $n \geq 3$. All these results apply to multi-party computation. Gordon and Katz[3] improved the original protocol and additionally they proposed a protocol for $n = 2$ for rational secret sharing and rational multi-party computation. Abraham *et.al.* [4] analyzed rational secret sharing and rational multi-party computation in an extended setting where players can form coalitions. They use a trusted third party as mediator. Lysyanskaya and Triandopoulos[5] analyzed multi-party computation in mixed behavior model, where players are rational or malicious using a trusted mediator. The malicious adversary can control at most $(\lceil n/2 \rceil - 2)$ players. Recently, Maleka et al.[6]

proposed a deterministic protocol for rational secret sharing by modifying the existing protocol. They did little variation in the model, where dealer instead of sending shares to the players, sends subshares of the shares.

1.3 Practical Applications and Motivation

Game theory has wide range of applications in Political science, Economics, business, Biology and Computer science (online algorithms). By combining game theory and cryptography, we can solve game theoretic problems as shown by Dodis et. al[7] and cryptography can be understood from a different perceptive. Secret sharing has many applications like, need for the secret to keep in distributed environment (arises if the storage is not reliable and there is a high chance that the secret may be lost). Analogously, if the owner of the secret does not trust any single person, there is a threat that the secret may be misused. Hence, the secret needs to be distributed among the members of a group to achieve shared trust. The secret can provide access to important files or critical resources like bank vault, missile launch pad, source code escrow, etc. In short, to all the applications, which need simultaneously achieving secrecy, availability and group trust.

Rational secret sharing has applications in highly competitive real world scenario, where players are modeled selfish. Suppose by obtaining the secret, players start their firm with it (or run online business activity), then they think that, if many persons learn the secret then they will become competitors to him and finally minimize his profit or payoff. A player gets maximum profit if only he runs the firm having the secret and no one else has the secret. So, every player behaves non-cooperatively, i.e., selfishly. We answer this question affirmatively and provide a solution.

In several practical situations, a group of people may wish to share many number of different secrets. Such scenario generally arises in applications where the key (secret) becomes obsolete after a predefined time limit. We model this as a secret sharing game, which is being played many number of times. Hence, this game can be treated as a *repeated game*. In each game, players share only one secret (not multiple secrets as in *multi-secret sharing*[8]). Thus, applying the game theory concepts (rational behavior and repeated games), we extend the work of Halpern and Teague[1] and introduce the *Repeated Rational Secret Sharing (RRSS)* problem.

1.4 Intuition and Contribution

Our intuition is that, the rational players have an incentive to send their share in repeated games by means of punishment strategy. If a player does not cooperate by not sending a share in the current game, then other players adopt the punishment strategy and do not send him the share in the further games. Hence, every player because of the fear of not receiving any share from other players in the further games will cooperate in the current game. Thus, the punishment strategy acts as an incentive for a player to cooperate. The major contribution of our work is that we present the first deterministic protocol for rational secret sharing with repeated games. In an infinitely played repeated game or finitely played repeated game (where players do not know how many times the game will be repeated), we propose a deterministic protocol in both synchronous and asynchronous models. We prove that secret sharing is not possible for finitely played repeated games, where players know how many times the game will be repeated. We extend these results to mixed model (synchronous) where there can be few malicious players.

1.5 Model and Assumptions

We model the secret sharing as a game, denoted by Γ. The players of the game are rational and the game will be repeated for several times. We consider the scenario where m players come together and share the secrets repeatedly. That is, we solve the problem when m players come together to play the secret sharing game Γ repeatedly (the same set of m players). We do not consider the case where every time a new (different) set of players come and repeatedly play the game. Unlike the game defined by Halpern and Teague[1], our model considers both synchronous and asynchronous rational secret sharing and proposes a deterministic protocol. In the synchronous model, the game is finite with respect to time and the starting and ending points are precisely defined. The game proceeds in the following manner. The game starts when the dealer distributes the shares and the players send their shares simultaneously at a predefined synchronized point of time and ends in finite time at another synchronized point of time. Thus, the game has two possible outcomes, either players learn the secret or do not. In short, the game has only one round. On the contrary, in the asynchronous model, the game does not start and end at predefined points of time and has only two possible outcomes as that of the synchronous model.

We assume that all players are connected to each other through secure private channels independently, which ensures that a player can send his share to a selected number of players. Initially, we make an assumption that the underlying network is synchronous and the messages will be delivered in fixed amount of time. Later we consider the asynchronous model. Here, the message delivery time is indefinite. But, in both cases, the communication is guaranteed. In synchronous model, all the players are synchronized with respect to a global clock. Hence, all the players start and end the game at the same time whereas in asynchronous model, there does not exist a global clock. The dealer authenticates the shares, and therefore a player cannot send incorrect value as a share to other players. All the players are assumed to be computationally bounded. There is no trusted mediator and the dealer is assumed to be honest (so, he will not send different messages to different players). We also assume that the players are patient enough and care for their future payoff, hence we assume that the discount factor δ is sufficiently large and closer to 1.

1.6 Paper Outline

In the next section, we briefly explain the basics of Game Theory. Section 3 presents the protocol for the RRSS game, played both infinitely and finitely.

Section 4 discusses the mixed model where few malicious players are also present. Section 5 proposes a protocol for Asynchronous repeated rational secret sharing. Finally, Section 6 concludes the paper and gives an insight on open problems in further direction.

2 Basics of Game Theory

We define some basic terminology of game theory in this section [9].

A *strategy* can be defined as a complete algorithm for playing the game, implicitly listing all moves and counter-moves for every possible situation throughout the game. And a *strategy profile* is a set of strategies for each player which fully specifies all actions in a game. A strategy profile must include one and only one strategy for every player.

Let $\Gamma(N, L, U)$ represents an n persons game, where N is a finite set of n players $(p_1, \ldots p_n)$, $L = \{L_1, \ldots, L_n\}$ is a set of actions for each player p_i, $i \in \{1, \ldots, n\}$ and $U = \{u_1, \ldots, u_n\}$ is a utility function for each player, where $u_i : L \rightarrow R$

Let a_{-i} be a strategy profile of all players except for the player p_i. When each player p_i, $i \in \{1, \ldots, n\}$ chooses strategy $a_i \in L$ resulting in strategy profile $a = \{a_1, \ldots, a_n\}$, then player p_i obtains payoff $u_i(a)$. Note that, the payoff depends on the strategy profile chosen, i.e., on the strategy chosen by player p_i as well as the strategies chosen by all the other players.

Definition 1. (Strict Domination): In a strategic game with ordinal preferences, player $p_i's$ action $a'' \in L_i$ strictly dominates his action $a' \in L_i$ if
$$u_i(a'', a_{-i}) > u_i(a', a_{-i})$$ for every list L_{-i} of the other players' actions.

We say that the action a' is strictly dominated.

Definition 2. (Nash Equilibrium - NE): A strategy profile $a^* \in L$ is a Nash equilibrium (NE) if no unilateral deviation in strategy by any single player is profitable, that is
$$\forall i, u_i(a_i^*, a_{-i}^*) \geq u_i(a_i, a_{-i}^*).$$

2.1 Repeated Games

Repeated games capture the idea that a player can condition his future game's move based on the previous game's outcome. In repeated games, the players interact several number of times $(\Gamma_1, \Gamma_2, \cdots)$. We assume that the players make their moves simultaneously in each game. The set of the past moves of all the players is commonly referred to as the history H of the game. History is uniquely defined at the beginning of each game $(h_1, h_2, \ldots$ and $h_1 = 0)$ and the future move depends on the history. In repeated games, the users typically want to maximize their payoff for all the game they play. Hence, every player p_i tries to maximize his payoff function u_i. But for repeated games, we cannot simply add up the payoffs received at each stage. There is a discount factor $\delta \in (0,1)$ such that the future discounted payoff of player p_i is given by

$$u_i + \delta^1 u_i + \delta^2 u_i + \delta^3 u_i + \cdots$$

In some cases, the objective of the player can be to maximize their payoff only for the current game (which is equivalent to a game, which is played only once). Such game is known as shortsighted game. If the players try to maximize their payoff throughout the repeated game, then it is a long-sighted game. If the game is played finite number of times, then it is a finite repeated game. Otherwise, it is an infinite repeated game.

Definition 3. (Feasible payoff): A payoff profile (payoff vector of n players), say y, is feasible if there exist rational, non-negative values α_a such that for all p_i, we can express y_i (payoff corresponding to p_i) as $\sum_{a \in L} \alpha_a u_i(a)$ with $\sum_{a \in L} \alpha_a = 1$.

Definition 4. (Friedman or Nash folk theorem for infinitely repeated games) [10]: Let Γ be a strategic game in which each player has finitely many actions and $(y_1, y_2, \ldots y_n)$ be a feasible payoff profile of Γ and $(e_1, e_2, \ldots e_n)$ denotes the payoff from a Nash equilibrium of Γ. If $y_i > e_i$ for every player i and if δ is sufficiently close to one, then there exists a Nash equilibrium of infinitely repeated game Γ that achieves $(y_1, y_2, \ldots y_n)$ as the payoff.

3 Protocol for Synchronous Repeated Rational Secret Sharing

We denote our game by $\Gamma(n, m)$, where n is the number of players participating in the game and m is the threshold value of the number of shares to obtain the secret. We consider the scenario where m players come together and share the secrets repeatedly. That is, we solve the problem when m players come together to play the secret sharing game Γ repeatedly (the same set of m players). We do not consider the case where every time a new (different) set of players come and repeatedly play the game. So, exchange of shares is between these m players group, i.e., when a player sends his share to this set (selected players), they intern send their shares, reasoning to this is given below.

For every player, we have two actions namely, sending and not sending. Let us denote the action of sending the share to other $(m-1)$ players by 'A' and not sending by 'B'. Then, the strategy of a player for always not sending is $\{B, B, \ldots\}$ and for always sending is $\{A, A, \ldots\}$. In every game, the strategy profile, strategies chosen by the all players is denoted by n-tuple $(c_1, c_2, \ldots, c_n)$, where $c_i = A$ or $B, i \in \{1, \ldots, n\}$. The Repeated Rational Secret Sharing (RRSS) is similar to the Repeated prisoners' dilemma in many aspects [9].

In the modeled secret sharing game, the strategy which chooses not sending benefits one player and losses the players. We introduce one more punishment strategy known as Limited punishment strategy, which is explained in detail in the section 3.1. We first discuss the strategies of the players, then analyze the cases for both the infinitely and finitely repeated rational secret sharing game.

3.1 Punishment Strategies

1. Grim trigger strategy

- choose A as long as the other players choose A.
- In any game some player chooses not sending (i.e., chooses B), then choose B in every subsequent game.

The grim trigger strategy for a repeated rational secret sharing game is defined as:

$s_i(\phi) = A$ (player p_i chooses A at the start of the game, ϕ denotes initial history), and

$$s_i(h_1,\ldots,h_q) = \begin{cases} A & \text{if } (h_{j1},\ldots,h_{jq}) = (A,\ldots,A) \\ & \text{for every other player } p_j \\ B & \text{otherwise.} \end{cases}$$

That is, player p_i chooses A after any history in which every previous action of every player was A, and B after any other history. Even though the grim trigger strategy is effective in achieving the Nash equilibrium, the cooperating players are also getting the punishment. We propose one more strategy, which punishes only the player who did not send his share and not the other players.

2. Limited Punishment Strategy

- choose A as long as the other players choose A.
- In any game some player chooses not sending (i.e., chooses B), then choose B for k subsequent games.

The intention of this strategy is to punish only the player who did not send his share. If a player p_j does not send his share to a player p_i, then p_i chooses B for k consequent games. p_i will choose A only if p_j keeps sending his share for k consecutive games, even p_i does not send his share. Otherwise p_i will not send share to p_j. This is equivalent to outcast the player who does not send the data from the game for k number of games. The value of k should be such that, the gain obtained by not sending share should be less than loss that occurs in the next k games (as he cannot obtain the secret and others get his share).

In general, both of the strategies discussed here work effectively. But, for the sake of analysis we use only grim trigger strategy.

3.2 Infinitely Repeated Rational Secret Sharing Game

We make an assumption that players are patient enough and care for their future. In other words, the discount factor δ is sufficiently large and close to 1. We first analyze the game and then discuss the Nash equilibrium.

Suppose, a particular player p_j does not send his share to a player p_i, then the player p_i does not get the secret in that particular game. So, the player p_i uses the grim trigger strategy and does not send his share to p_j in further games. Thus, the player p_j will not get the secret from next game onwards. The player p_j realizes that he can no more obtain the secret and so there is no motivation to send his share to other players. Thus, no player learns the secret in further games. Hence, every player, because of the fear of not receiving any share from other players in further games, will cooperate in the current game. This punishment strategy acts as an incentive for a player to cooperate. Therefore, a player p_i's strategy is to always send his share to other players. He stops sending only when he does not receive a share from any other player. In this way every player receives m shares and can get the secret.

Suppose, in k^{th} game a player p_i does not send his share to a player p_j. Then, player p_j chooses grim trigger strategy and henceforth never sends his share to p_i. Thus, player p_i cannot obtain secret from $(k+1)^{th}$ game onwards and his payoff will be $(w_1, w_3, w_3, \ldots)$. If the player p_i always sends his share, then his payoff would be $(w_2, w_2, w_2, \ldots)$. So, for any player the payoff is high if he chooses always sending rather than not sending in any particular game. And every player primarily prefers to get the secret than not to get the secret (players care about future). Hence, every player always chooses to send his share.

But for infinitely repeated games, we cannot simply add up the payoffs received at each stage. The payoff is discounted by a factor, $\delta \in (0,1)$ such that the future discounted payoff of player p_i is given by $\sum_{j=0}^{\infty} \delta^j u_i(\Gamma_j)$. If δ is closer to 0, then the player does not care about his future payoff and concentrates more on the current payoff where as if δ is closer to 1, then the player is very patient and cares much about his future payoff.

Suppose if the player chooses the strategy always send $(A, A, \ldots)$, with payoff $u_i(A) = w_2$, then the overall discounted payoff will be $\sum_{j=0}^{\infty} \delta^j w_2 = \frac{w_2}{(1-\delta)}$.

If the player finks at r^{th} round, then till $(r-1)^{th}$ round the player gets payoff of w_2, at r^{th} round payoff of w_1 and from $(r+1)^{th}$ onwards payoff of w_3.

$$\sum_{j=0}^{\infty} \delta^j u_i(\Gamma_j) = w_2 + \delta w_2 + \delta^2 w_2 + \ldots + \delta^{r-1} w_2 + \delta^r w_1 + \delta^{r+1} w_3 + \delta^{r+2} w_3 + \delta^{r+3} w_3 + \ldots$$
$$= w_2(1 + \delta + \delta^2 + \ldots + \delta^{r-1}) + \delta^r w_1 + \delta^{r+1} w_3 (1 + \delta + \delta^2 + \ldots)$$
$$= w_2() \frac{1-\delta^r}{1-\delta} + \delta^r w_1 + \frac{\delta^{r+1} w_3}{1-\delta}$$
$$= \frac{w_2(1-\delta^r) + \delta^r w_1 + (\delta^{r+1} w_3)}{1-\delta}$$

As δ is close to one,

$$\frac{w_2(1-\delta^r) + \delta^r w_1 + (\delta^{r+1} w_3)}{1-\delta} < \frac{w_2}{1-\delta}$$

So, every player chooses the strategy of always sending $(A, A, \ldots)$.

Theorem 1: *Infinitely Repeated Rational Secret Sharing (RRSS) game, $\Gamma(n, m)$ has a deterministic protocol when a group of m players come together, where n is the number of players and m is the threshold of shares.*

Proof: Given, a player sends his share to $(m-1)$ players and in-turn receives their shares, his payoff would be $(w_2, w_2, \ldots)$. The strategy profile $(A, A, \ldots)$ is a feasible payoff profile of the game and $(B, B, \ldots)$ be the Nash equilibrium of the single game Γ. As the players are patient enough and care for their future payoff, δ is sufficiently closer to one. As payoff corresponding to the strategy A, w_2 is greater than the minmax value, w_3 $(u_i(A) > u_i(B))$, from Nash folk theorem (Definition 4), the strategy profile $(A, A, \ldots)$ is a Nash equilibrium of infinitely repeated game $\Gamma(n, m)$ and the strategy, A is the best strategy for a player provided that every other player also plays his best strategy. In this way, all the players send their shares and thus obtain the secret. Hence, there exists a deterministic protocol for the RRSS game $\Gamma(n, m)$. □

Nash Equilibrium
The strategy $(A, A, \ldots)$ is a Nash equilibrium. Similarly, $(B, B, \ldots)$ is also a Nash equilibrium. But a player prefers to get the secret rather than not getting the secret. Hence, every player prefers to be in the state $(A, A, \ldots)$.

3.3 Finitely Repeated Rational Secret Sharing Game

First we discuss the issue what if the RRSS game is played only once ? Next we propose, in a finitely repeated rational secret sharing game, we have a deterministic protocol if the players are not aware of the last game. If the last game is known in advance, we do not have a solution for the game, $\Gamma(n, m)$.

3.3.1 What if the RRSS Game Is Played only Once?
Before analyzing the cases of infinitely and finitely repeated rational secret sharing game, we make an insight to the RRSS game when played only once (equivalent to a static game). Here, the players do not have a threat of not getting the secret in future games. So, the incentive of sending the share is lost. Lemma 1 proves the impossibility of secret sharing in such a game.

Lemma 1: *Secret Sharing is not possible in an RRSS game $\Gamma(n, m)$ if the game is played only once, where n is the number of players and m is the threshold of shares (considering our model and game $\Gamma(n, m)$).*

Proof: There is no punishment involved in the game, $\Gamma(n, m)$ as it is played only once. If the player p_i gets the secret and everyone else does not get the secret, then the payoff is w_1. If everyone (including p_i) gets the secret, then the payoff is w_2. Thus player p_i can obtain the payoff w_1 by not sending his share and w_2 by sending. As $w_1 > w_2$, the strategy B (not sending) strictly dominates the strategy A (sending). So, every player chooses strictly dominating strategy and no player sends his share. Hence, secret sharing is not possible in an RRSS game $\Gamma(n, m)$ if the game is played only once. □

3.3.2 Players Are Not Aware of the End of the Game
A finitely repeated game can be modeled as an infinitely repeated game, if the players are not aware of the end of the game. Therefore, we can always obtain a solution in this case, which is illustrated in the theorem 2.

Theorem 2: *Finitely Repeated Rational Secret sharing (RRSS) game, $\Gamma(n,m)$ has a deterministic protocol, if the players are not aware of the last game.*

Proof: As players do not know the last game, in every i^{th} game, players are not sure about whether they play the $(i+1)^{th}$ game or not. If a player does not send his share in i^{th} game, he might loss the chance of getting the secret in $(i+1)^{th}$ game onwards (if the game is going to be repeated). The punishment strategy acts as incentive for the players to send their shares. This scenario is similar to that of the infinitely repeated rational secret sharing game. Hence, from theorem 1, every player gets the secret. □

3.3.3 Players Are Aware of the Last Game

When players are aware of the end of the game, we can apply the concept of backward induction because, the game is of complete information (players know the number of times the game will be played). Let us consider the last game. Every player concludes that their dominant strategy is not to send the share of secret to others (i.e., to play 'B'). Given this argument, the best strategy is to play 'B' in the penultimate game. Following the same argument, this technique of backward induction dictates that every player should choose the strategy 'B' in every game. Thus, secret sharing is not possible for the finitely repeated game, given the players are aware of the end of the game. More formal proof is given by the lemma 2 and theorem 3.

Lemma 2: *If the players know that r^{th} game is the last game of finite RRSS game $\Gamma(n,m)$, then secret sharing is not possible in the rth game.*

Proof: Given, the game is going to be played r number of times. As there is no punishment involved for the rth game, there is no incentive for a player to send his share. Thus, this game is equivalent to a game, which is played only once. Hence, from lemma 1, there is no solution for the rth game. □

Theorem 3: *Secret sharing is not possible for the RRSS game $\Gamma(n,m)$, if the players are aware of last game.*

Proof: We prove it by backward induction. Suppose, the game is being played r number of times. Given, the players are aware of the value of r, from the lemma 2, there is no solution for the rth game. That is, no player sends his share in r^{th} game. So, in $(r-1)^{th}$ game, there is no effective punishment strategy, hence there is no incentive for a player to send their share. Hence $(r-1)^{th}$ game is equivalent to a single game. From Lemma 1, there is no solution for the $(r-1)^{th}$ game. Same reasoning applies to $(r-2)^{th}, (r-3)^{th} \ldots 1^{st}$ game. Therefore, in a finitely repeated game where players know the end of the game, repeated rational secret sharing $\Gamma(n,m)$ is not possible. □

Theorem 4: *Repeated Rational Secret Sharing game, $\Gamma(n,m)$ has a deterministic protocol for infinitely repeated games and finite repeated games (where players are not aware of number of times the game is going to be played), where n is the number of players and m is the threshold of shares.*

Proof: Easy observation from theorems 1 and theorem 3. □

3.3.4 Nash Equilibrium

For the finitely repeated rational secret sharing game, we have two cases. One, when players do not know the end of the game. In this case the Nash equilibrium is same as that of an Infinitely repeated game$(A, A, \ldots, A)$. Another, when the players are aware of the last game. In this case the Nash equilibrium is not to send the share, that is $(B, B, \ldots, B)$.

4 Mixed Model

We assume there are at most 't' computationally bounded malicious players. So the malicious players cannot send the wrong shares to other players. According to the protocol, every player distributes his shares to $(m-1)$ players and in-turn obtains their shares. If malicious players are present, then they choose not to send their shares to other players so that, no player learns the secret (even though they do not get the secret). To solve this problem, every player sends his share to $(m+t-1)$ players and in-turn obtains at least $(m-1)$ shares (as at least $(m-1)$ players are honest). If a player p_i did not receive the share of p_j, then player p_i considers p_j as a malicious player and stops sending the shares to p_j alone (sends to every one else).

Theorem 5: *In the presence of at most t malicious players, Repeated Rational Secret Sharing (RRSS) game $\Gamma(n, m)$ has a deterministic protocol for infinitely repeated games and finite repeated games (where players are not aware of number of times the game is going to be played), where n is the number of players and m is the threshold of shares.*

Proof: In mixed model, at most t players can be malicious and every player obtains at least $(m-1)$ shares. Hence, from theorem 4, repeated rational secret sharing (RRSS) game, $\Gamma(n, m)$ with at most t malicious players has a deterministic protocol. □

5 Asynchronous Repeated Rational Secret Sharing

We consider the Asynchronous model of the RRSS game. Here, we do not have a global clock and messages can be indefinitely delayed. For the dealer to know the end of the game and distribute new shares, the players are asked to send a message whenever they obtain the secret. If the dealer receives such messages from all the players, then he will distribute the shares of next secret, thus starting the next game. This protocol followed by the dealer acts as a punishment strategy (players wait indefinitely until every player gets the secret) and creates an incentive for every player to send his share.

Protocol for the Dealer and the Players
1. Protocol for player p_i

1. p_i sends his share to other $(m-1)$ players.

2. In every game, after receiving $(m-1)$ players' shares, calculate the secret and send a message to the dealer that the secret has been obtained mentioning the game.

For e.g., $msg_i =$ " secret obtained in k^{th} game ".

2. Protocol for dealer

1. In the first game, send the shares to all the players $(p_1, p_2, \ldots, p_n)$.
2. After distributing shares in k^{th} game, $k \geq 1$ wait until n number of messages are received, $(msg_1, msg_2, \ldots msg_n)$. If all the messages are received, then distribute the new shares of $(k+1)^{th}$ game to all the players.

Lemma 3: *In Asynchronous model, a player has an incentive to send his share (in every game) to the $(m-1)$ players, in an infinite RRSS game and a finite RRSS game (where players are not aware of the last game).*

Proof: We prove this by contradiction. Assume that there is no incentive for a player p_i to send his share in k^{th} game. So, p_i will not send his share to any player in k^{th} game and no one gets the secret. Now, as per the protocol, the dealer waits indefinitely for the messages from the players and the next game never starts. So, the payoff of p_i from k^{th} game onwards will be $(w_1, w_3, \ldots)$. But, if he sends his share, the payoff would have been $(w_2, w_2, \ldots)$. Given the player does not know about the last game, he prefers $(w_2, w_2, \ldots)$ than $(w_1, w_3, \ldots)$, which is a contradiction. So, there is an incentive for a player to send his share in any given k^{th} game. □

Theorem 6: *Asynchronous Repeated Rational Secret Sharing (RRSS) game, $\Gamma(n, m)$ has a deterministic protocol for infinitely repeated game and finitely repeated game (where players are not aware of the last game), where n is the number of players and m is the threshold of shares.*

Proof: We prove this by contradiction. Assume that there is no incentive for a player p_i to send his share in k^{th} game. So, p_i will not send his share to any player in k^{th} game and no one gets the secret. Now, as per the protocol, the dealer waits indefinitely for the messages from the players and the next game never starts. So, the payoff of p_i from k^{th} game onwards will be $(w_1, w_3, \ldots)$. But, if he sends his share, the payoff would have been $(w_2, w_2, \ldots)$. Given the player does not know about the last game, he prefers $(w_2, w_2, \ldots)$ than $(w_1, w_3, \ldots)$, which is a contradiction. So, there is an incentive for a player to send his share in any given k^{th} game. So, every player sends his share. By considering Theorem 2, it can be observe that the game $\Gamma(n, m)$ finitely repeated games (where players are not aware of last game) is similar to infinitely repeated game. Hence, RRSS game has a deterministic protocol for infinitely repeated games and finitely repeated games (where players are not aware of last game). □

6 Conclusions and Open Problems

We have modeled the secret sharing as a repeated game (the game is played for some r number of times). We analyzed the repeated secret sharing game when

r is both finite and infinite. We propose a deterministic protocol for the infinite repeated game ($r->\infty$) and the finite repeated game (r is a finite number and the players do not know the value of r) in both synchronous and asynchronous models. We proved the impossibility for the finite repeated game when players know the value of r. We extended these results to the mixed model where at most t players are malicious, considering the synchronous model. The main advantage of introducing repeated games is that the players choose the strategy, which is mutually beneficial in terms of long-term gain rather than the one, which gives instantaneous benefit. We expect that the concept of repeated games can be introduced into various other problems of distributed computing (where the players are rational) and the scope for problem solving strategies in asynchronous model can be enhanced.

References

1. Halpern, J., Teague, V.: Rational secret sharing and multiparty computation: extended abstract. In: STOC 2004: Proceedings of the 36th annual ACM Symposium on Theory of Computing, pp. 623–632. ACM, New York, USA (2004)
2. Shamir, A.: How to share a secret. Commun. ACM 22, 612–613 (1979)
3. Gordon, S.D., Katz, J.: Rational secret sharing, revisited. In: De Prisco, R., Yung, M. (eds.) SCN 2006. LNCS, vol. 4116, pp. 229–241. Springer, Heidelberg (2006)
4. Abraham, I., Dolev, D., Gonen, R., Halpern, J.: Distributed computing meets game theory: robust mechanisms for rational secret sharing and multiparty computation. In: PODC 2006: Proceedings of the 25th annual ACM symposium on Principles of distributed computing, pp. 53–62. ACM, New York, USA (2006)
5. Lysyanskaya, A., Triandopoulos, N.: Rationality and adversarial behaviour in multi-party computation (extended abstract). In: Dwork, C. (ed.) CRYPTO 2006. LNCS, vol. 4117, pp. 180–197. Springer, Heidelberg (2006)
6. Maleka, S., Amjed, S., Pandu Rangan, C.: The deterministic protocol for rational secret sharing. In: SSN 2008: The 4th International Workshop on Security in Systems and Networks (to be published, 2008)
7. Dodis, Y., Halevi, S., Rabin, T.: A cryptographic solution to a game theoretic problem. In: Bellare, M. (ed.) CRYPTO 2000. LNCS, vol. 1880, pp. 112–130. Springer, Heidelberg (2000)
8. Franklin, M., Yung, M.: Communication complexity of secure computation. In: 24th ACM Symposium on Theory of Computing (STOC), pp. 699–710 (1992)
9. Osborne, M.: An Introduction to Game Theory. Oxford University Press, Oxford (2004)
10. Friedman, J.W.: A non-cooperative equilibrium for supergames. Review of Economic Studies 38(113), 1–12 (1971)

Distributed Private Matching and Set Operations

Qingsong Ye[1], Huaxiong Wang[1,2], and Josef Pieprzyk[1]

[1] Centre for Advanced Computing, Algorithms and Cryptography
Department of Computing, Macquarie University, NSW 2109, Australia
{qingsong,hwang,josef}@ics.mq.edu.au
[2] Division of Mathematical Sciences, Nanyang Technological University, Singapore

Abstract. Motivated by the need of private set operations in a distributed environment, we extend the two-party private matching problem proposed by Freedman, Nissim and Pinkas (FNP) at Eurocrypt'04 to the distributed setting. By using a secret sharing scheme, we provide a distributed solution of the FNP private matching called the *distributed private matching*. In our distributed private matching scheme, we use a polynomial to represent one party's dataset as in FNP and then distribute the polynomial to multiple servers. We extend our solution to the distributed set intersection and the cardinality of the intersection, and further we show how to apply the distributed private matching in order to compute distributed subset relation. Our work extends the primitives of private matching and set intersection by Freedman et al. Our distributed construction might be of great value when the dataset is outsourced and its privacy is the main concern. In such cases, our distributed solutions keep the utility of those set operations while the dataset privacy is not compromised. Comparing with previous works, we achieve a more efficient solution in terms of computation. All protocols constructed in this paper are provably secure against a semi-honest adversary under the Decisional Diffie-Hellman assumption.

Keywords: private matching, private set operation, homomorphic encryption.

1 Introduction

Freedman, Nissim and Pinkas [1] gave a protocol for private matching, a specialized version of oblivious polynomial evaluation [2], using a public-key homomorphic cryptosystem. We will call it the FNP protocol. This protocol enables one party, Alice, with a dataset A to interact with another party, Bob, for testing if Bob's input b matches any element in the Alice's dataset in an "oblivious" way. At the end of the protocol, Bob learns nothing about Alice's dataset, while Alice only learns whether $b \in A$ or not, and does not gain any additional information about b.

To run the above protocol in parallel with a set of elements $\{b_1, \ldots, b_n\}$ owned by Bob, the FNP protocol offers an efficient tool to solve the private set intersection problem. The private computation of the two datasets intersection is a useful primitive for various applications. For example, Alice may be a fruit-farm supplying fresh fruits to a collection of supermarkets in a town; while another local dairy-farm, Bob, supplies dairy products to another collection of supermarkets in the same town. For their mutual interests, Alice and Bob may agree to cooperate in order to deliver both fruits and dairy products to their shared supermarkets by a single truck. To obtain the list of their shared customers, they would like to perform a private set intersection operation on their databases without compromising their customers' privacy.

This private set intersection can be computed by using the FNP protocol directly. However, such an approach could be problematic if Bob outsources his database to a database service provider. In this case, Bob could risk his database privacy if he assumes that all database administrators act "professionally" and do not leak any information related to his database. To protect his database privacy, he could encrypt all the data stored in the provider's server with his public-key. In general, however, querying on such encrypted database could be extremely expensive; and in some cases this may not even be possible without letting a third party know the private key.

Motivated by the database outsourcing trend and the security and privacy concerns, this work extends the two-party private matching FNP protocol to the distributed setting. In such a setting, we distribute Bob's dataset, represented by a polynomial, to several servers using a (t, w)-Shamir secret sharing scheme. This way, any $t - 1$ or less servers cannot discover Bob's original dataset. Alice has to contact t servers to test if her input matches any element in Bob's dataset without revealing her input to him. In addition, she is going to obtain no additional information about Bob's dataset.

We further apply the distributed private matching scheme to private set operations. In the distributed setting, Alice, who owns a dataset, wishes to perform a set operation for both her and Bob's datasets. To do so, Alice runs the distributed private matching protocol in parallel for each element of her dataset. We consider the set intersection, the cardinality of set intersection and the subset relation problems in this paper. The security of our constructions is ensured as long as the underlying homomorphic cryptosystem is semantically secure.

1.1 Private Matching and Set Intersection Protocols in FNP

Polynomial Representation of Datasets and Private Matching. We briefly review the FNP protocol. Let $(\mathcal{K}, \mathcal{E}, \mathcal{D})$ be a semantically-secure public-key cryptosystem with additive homomorphic properties, such as Paillier's [3]. Recall that, given $\mathcal{E}_{pk}(a)$, $\mathcal{E}_{pk}(b)$ and a constant c, one can compute $\mathcal{E}_{pk}(a+b) = \mathcal{E}_{pk}(a) \odot \mathcal{E}_{pk}(b)$ and $\mathcal{E}_{pk}(a \cdot c) = \mathcal{E}_{pk}(a)^c$.

There are two parties in the protocol, namely, Alice and Bob. Bob owns a value b, while Alice possesses a dataset $A = \{a_1, \ldots, a_m\}$ and wants to test if $b \in A$ or not. Alice does not want to reveal A to Bob, and Bob is unwilling to disclose b to Alice.

The protocol runs as follows. Alice first presents her dataset A in the form of a polynomial $\mathcal{P}(y) = \prod_{a_i \in A} (y - a_i) = \sum_{i=0}^{m} \alpha_i y^i$ where $\alpha_m = 1$. Let (pk, sk) be Alice's public and private keys, respectively, applied in the homomorphic cryptosystem.

Alice encrypts her polynomial $\mathcal{P}$ with her public-key pk. Note that the encrypted polynomial $\mathcal{E}_{pk}(\mathcal{P})$ contains the encryptions of the coefficients α_i except α_m. Next she sends $\mathcal{E}_{pk}(\mathcal{P})$ to Bob. Because of the homomorphic properties, Bob can evaluate the polynomial at his input b as:

$$\mathcal{E}_{pk}(\mathcal{P}(b)) = \mathcal{E}_{pk}(\alpha_0) \odot \mathcal{E}_{pk}(\alpha_1)^b \odot \mathcal{E}_{pk}(\alpha_2)^{b^2} \odot \ldots \odot \mathcal{E}_{pk}(\alpha_{m-1})^{b^{m-1}} \odot \mathcal{E}_{pk}(1)^{b^m},$$

and sends $\mathcal{E}_{pk}(\gamma \mathcal{P}(b) + b)$ to Alice where γ is a random non-zero value. Note that $b \in A$ if and only if $\mathcal{P}(b) = 0$. When Alice receives the cryptogram, she decrypts it and checks if the decrypted message belongs to the set A; otherwise it is a random value.

Private Computation of Set Intersection. Suppose Alice and Bob, each has a private dataset of values denoted by $A = \{a_1, \ldots, a_m\}$ and $B = \{b_1, \ldots, b_n\}$ respectively, where the set cardinalities m and n are publicly known. Alice wishes to learn the intersection of two sets $A \cap B$. To compute the set intersection, we simply run the above private matching protocol m times in parallel for each of $b_j \in B$. In the end, Alice decrypts all the cryptograms and checks if each one is in A, and then establishes $A \cap B$.

We can also slightly modify the original FNP protocol to give a solution for evaluating the cardinality of the set intersection. That is, Bob sends $\mathcal{E}_{pk}(\gamma \mathcal{P}(b_j) + 0)$ to Alice for $j \in \{1, \ldots, n\}$, then Alice counts the number of ciphertexts received that decrypt to 0.

1.2 Overview of Our Construction on Distributed Private Matching and Set Operations

We consider distributed private matching and set operations. As in the basic FNP protocol, there are two parties, Alice and Bob. Bob has a dataset $B = \{b_1, \ldots, b_n\}$, represented by a polynomial $\mathcal{P}(y) = \prod_{b_j \in B}(y - b_j) = \sum_{i=0}^{n} v_i y^i$ with $v_n = 1$, while Alice possesses a value a, and wants to test if $a \in B$, i.e. to check whether $\mathcal{P}(a) = 0$. In our setting, a variant ElGamal encryption is used and the message space is over $\mathbb{Z}_q$. The details is given in Section 2.1.

In our distributed construction, Bob defines a bivariate polynomial $\mathcal{F}(x, y)$ to mask $\mathcal{P}(y)$, such that $\mathcal{F}(0, y) = \mathcal{P}(y)$. Using a (t, w)-Shamir secret sharing scheme, Bob then computes w shares of the function $\mathcal{F}$, denoted by $\mathcal{F}(1, y), \ldots, \mathcal{F}(w, y)$, and distributes $\mathcal{F}(\ell, y)$ (a set of shared coefficients) to the server S_ℓ.

To privately test if $a \in B$, Alice sends the encrypted a with her public key to t or more servers. Denote $\langle g \rangle$, the subgroup of $\mathbb{Z}_p^*$ generated by g and $f \in \langle g \rangle$. Each contacted server uses the homomorphic properties of the cryptosystem to obliviously compute $f^{\gamma \mathcal{F}(\ell, a)}$ in the encrypted form, and sends encrypted $f^{\gamma \mathcal{F}(\ell, a)}$ to Alice where γ is a random non-zero value chosen by Bob and known by all servers. When Alice decrypts received cryptograms, she uses Lagrange interpolation to compute $f^{\gamma \mathcal{F}(0, a)}$, and concludes $a \in B$ if and only if $f^{\gamma \mathcal{F}(0, a)} = 1$.

In a similar manner, the FNP two-party set intersection protocol can be extended to the distributed setting. Let Alice, who owns a dataset $A = \{a_1, \ldots, a_m\}$, runs the above distributed private matching protocol m times in parallel for each element in A against the Bob dataset B. Alice concludes that $a_i \in B$ if and only if $f^{\gamma \mathcal{F}(0, a_i)} = 1$ for $i \in \{1, \ldots, m\}$. At the end of the protocol, Alice is able to compute $A \cap B$.

We further extend our distributed set intersection solution to the cardinality of set intersection problem. Let Bob send his private permutation function π to all servers along with the shares of his polynomial $\mathcal{F}$ to evaluate the size of the intersection, rather than the intersection itself. Comparing with the intersection protocol, the only difference is that all contacted servers permute their computed cryptograms before sending them back to Alice. Alice is still able to find if any $f^{\gamma \mathcal{F}(0, a_{\pi(i)})} = 1$, but cannot identify the original index in the set A related to $\pi(i)$. Consequently, she could only discover the information of $|A \cap B|$.

In our distributed scheme, we are also able to test if $A \subseteq B$. The idea is that if $\sum_{i=1}^{m} \mathcal{F}(0, a_i) = 0$, then $A \subseteq B$. Indeed, note that

$$\sum_{i=1}^{m} \mathcal{F}(0, a_i) = \sum_{i=1}^{m} \sum_{j=1}^{t} c_j \mathcal{F}(\ell_j, a_i) = \sum_{j=1}^{t} \left(c_j \sum_{i=1}^{m} \mathcal{F}(\ell_j, a_i) \right), \quad (1)$$

where c_j's are Lagrange interpolation coefficients. So each contacted server S_{ℓ_j} only needs to return one encrypted value $\sum_{i=1}^{m} \mathcal{F}_{\ell_j}(a_i)$ to Alice. Then, Alice evaluates (1) to test if $A \subseteq B$ or not.

All protocols proposed in this paper require a single round. The communication and computation complexities of our distributed private matching scheme are $O(tm)$. It is about t times of the FNP protocol. For our distributed set intersection, the cardinality of the intersection and subset relation protocols, the communication and computation complexities are $O(tmn)$. All the protocols are secure against a semi-honest (also called honest but curious) adversary. The homomorphic encryption is based on the ElGamal scheme [4], which is semantically secure if the Decisional Diffie-Hellman (DDH) assumption holds [5].

1.3 Related Work

The problem of secure computation of the subset relation of two private datasets is another variant of the private set intersection problem where the intersection is one party's whole dataset. This can be computed by extending the FNP protocol. The applications of the subset relation was discussed in [6, 7]. Private disjointness tests of two datasets are considered in [8, 9]. The solutions still rely on oblivious polynomial evaluation techniques, but with somewhat different security requirements. Only one party can learn whether two datasets are disjoint or not and with no other information revealed. Protocols for private equality tests are a special case of the private disjointness tests, where each party has a single element in the database. These protocols were considered in [10, 2, 11].

Kissner and Song [12] present FNP-inspired schemes for various private set operation problems. In particular, they address set intersection, set union, threshold cardinality of the set intersection, and multiplicity test. They also suggest a multiparty model with the computation on a multiset. Sang et al. [13] use threshold homomorphic cryptosystem technique to further improve the communication and computation complexity on the set intersection protocol compared to Kissner and Song. Using the same technique, they provide a novel solution for private set matching problem in the multiparty model.

Recently, Ye, Wang and Tartary (YWT) propose a similar distributed scheme to compute private set intersection in [14]. YWT also uses secret sharing scheme and homomorphic encryption scheme. However, our approach is different from theirs and is more efficient. Our polynomial formulation is based on the representation of dataset as the roots of the polynomial (we follow the idea of the FNP protocol), while Ye et. al. present dataset as the coefficients of a polynomial. Accordingly, our computation relies on the oblivious polynomial evaluation in a distributed fashion. The private computation of the YWT protocol is based on private equality testing [10] in a distributed setting. The YWT protocol requires that one party checks each element of his/her dataset against all elements in another distributed dataset to see if there are matches between two datasets. It turns out that the computational complexity of our protocol is only one third of the YWT protocol. In addition, we also consider the distributed subset relation problem in this paper, while the paper by Ye et. al. only deals with distributed set intersection and the cardinality of set intersection problems.

Organization. The paper is organized as follows. In Section 2, we introduce the homomorphic encryption scheme, the model of the distributed setting, and our adversary model. In Section 3, we present a protocol for the distributed private matching and discuss its security. We extend our distributed private matching construction to distributed solutions for the set intersection, the cardinality of set intersection and the subset relation problems in Section 4. In that section, we also analyze the efficiency of our protocols and compare our solutions to other related schemes. Finally, we give concluding remarks and discuss possible future work in Section 5.

2 Preliminaries

2.1 Additively Homomorphic Encryption

Let $\mathcal{E}_{pk}(\cdot)$ denote an additively homomorphic encryption function with a public key pk. The cryptosystem supports the following operations, which can be performed without knowing the private key.

- Given $\mathcal{E}_{pk}(a)$ and $\mathcal{E}_{pk}(b)$, we can efficiently compute $\mathcal{E}_{pk}(a+b) = \mathcal{E}_{pk}(a) \odot \mathcal{E}_{pk}(b)$.
- Given a constant c and $\mathcal{E}_{pk}(a)$, we can efficiently compute $\mathcal{E}_{pk}(ca) = \mathcal{E}_{pk}(a)^c$.

In our schemes, the computations are carried out in $\mathbb{Z}_p$ where p is prime, and the message space is $\mathbb{Z}_q$, where $q = (p-1)/2$ is also a prime number. We note that all of our constructions can be based on the standard variant of ElGamal encryption. This variant has been employed recently for constructing protocols for privacy-preserving set operations (see, for example [8, 15, 11]). Let the triple $(\mathcal{K}, \mathcal{E}, \mathcal{D})$ be the variant of ElGamal where

- $\mathcal{K}$ is the key-generation algorithm. Given a security parameter $l = \lceil \log_2 p \rceil$, $K(1^l)$ generates the tuple (pk, sk), where the public-key $pk := \langle p, g, h, f \rangle$ and the corresponding secret-key $sk := \log_g h$ are such that g is an element of order q in $\mathbb{Z}_p^*$ and $h, f \in \langle g \rangle$;
- $\mathcal{E}$ is the encryption algorithm. Given the public-key pk and a plaintext $m \in \mathbb{Z}_q$, one encrypts as $\mathcal{E}_{pk}(m) = (g^r, h^r f^m)$, where $r \xleftarrow{R} \mathbb{Z}_q \setminus \{0\}$;
- $\mathcal{D}$ is the decryption algorithm. Given the secret-key denoted sk and a ciphertext (G, H) the decryption algorithm returns $G^{-sk}H \mod p$. Notice that this will only return f^m rather than m, however this suffices for our setting. In our protocols, we are only interested in testing whether $m = 0$, which is equivalent to testing if $G^{-sk}H \equiv 1 \mod p$.

Let $\mathcal{E}_{pk}(a) = (g^r, h^r f^a)$ and $\mathcal{E}_{pk}(b) = (g^{r'}, h^{r'} f^b)$. It is easy to see that $\mathcal{E}_{pk}(a) \odot \mathcal{E}_{pk}(b) = (g^{(r+r')}, h^{(r+r')} f^{(a+b)}) = \mathcal{E}_{pk}(a+b)$ and $\mathcal{E}_{pk}(a)^c = (g^{cr}, h^{cr} f^{ca}) = \mathcal{E}_{pk}(ca)$ for a given constant c.

2.2 Dataset Distribution

This section defines a polynomial representation of a Bob dataset and shows how a (t, w)-Shamir secret sharing is going to be used in our distributed protocols. The similar distributed construction can be also found in [16, 14].

Suppose that Bob holds a dataset $B = \{b_1, b_2, \ldots, b_n\}$, where $b_i \in \mathbb{Z}_q$. Let

$$\mathcal{P}(y) = (y - b_1)(y - b_2) \ldots (y - b_n) \equiv \sum_{i=0}^{n} v_i y^i \mod q,$$

where $v_n = 1$. Bob constructs a random masking bivariate polynomial in the following form:

$$\mathcal{Q}(x, y) = \sum_{j=1}^{t-1} \sum_{i=0}^{n} \alpha_{j,i} x^j y^i \quad \text{where } \alpha_{j,i} \xleftarrow{R} \mathbb{Z}_q.$$

He forms the bivariate polynomial $\mathcal{F}(x, y) = \mathcal{P}(y) + \mathcal{Q}(x, y)$. Note that we have $\mathcal{F}(0, y) = \mathcal{P}(y)$. For $1 \leq \ell \leq w$, Bob computes and sends $\mathcal{F}_\ell(y)$ to server S_ℓ as

$$\mathcal{F}_\ell(y) = \mathcal{F}(\ell, y) = \mathcal{P}(y) + \mathcal{Q}(\ell, y)$$
$$\equiv \sum_{i=0}^{n} (v_i + \vartheta_{i,\ell}) y^i \mod q, \text{ where } \vartheta_{i,\ell} = \sum_{j=1}^{t-1} \alpha_{j,i} \ell^j.$$

Let $\beta_{i,\ell} = v_i + \vartheta_{i,\ell}$, the server S_ℓ receives a shared-polynomial $\mathcal{F}_\ell(y)$ defined by the coefficients $\{\beta_{0,\ell}, \ldots, \beta_{n,\ell}\}$. By the Lagrange interpolation formula, we know that any coalition of t or more servers can reconstruct the original polynomial $\mathcal{P}$.

For the simplicity, we omit modulus p in the rest of the presentation, if no confusion occurs.

2.3 Security Model

We consider the semi-honest adversary (also called honest-but-curious) model. In this model, all involved parties honestly follow all prescribed steps of the protocol, but may try to learn extra information from the messages received during the protocol execution.

In our protocols, we assume that Alice does not interact with Bob directly. Instead Alice contacts a threshold of servers to perform private set operations. We assume also that no server colludes with Alice to cheat and only Alice learns the output of any operation. More precisely, the following conditions should hold.

Correctness. If Alice and the contacted servers faithfully follow the steps of the protocol, the protocol works and Alice learns the correct result of the operation specified in the protocol.

Alice's security. Given that each server gets no output from the protocol, Alice's privacy requires simply that any server cannot distinguish the client's inputs from random values.

Bob's security. Provided that no server colludes with Alice, the protocol ensures that Alice does not get any extra information other than the output of the operation. In addition, any t-1 or less servers should not able to find out any information about Bob's dataset.

3 Distributed Private Matching

Suppose that Alice has an input a and Bob owns a dataset B. The construction of the polynomial $\mathcal{F}$ from the dataset B, the initial shares construction and distribution are given in Section 2.2. In addition, Bob broadcasts $\gamma \xleftarrow{R} \mathbb{Z}_q \setminus \{0\}$ to the w servers. The purpose of γ is to prevent Alice learning extra information about $\mathcal{F}$ if $a \notin B$ by randomizing the result of $\mathcal{F}(0, a)$. Each server S_ℓ knows γ and a shared-polynomial $\mathcal{F}_\ell$ with the coefficients $\{\beta_{0,\ell}, \ldots, \beta_{n,\ell}\}$ for $1 \leq \ell \leq w$. Assume that $n = |B|$ is public.

We define the distributed private matching problem as follows. Alice contacts the threshold of t or more servers to test if $a \in B$. She must not gain any other information about the dataset B. The contacted servers do not learn any information about a.

The protocol is illustrated in Fig. 1. Note that the elements of the dataset B are represented as roots of a polynomial $\mathcal{P}$ and $\mathcal{F}(0, y) = \mathcal{P}(y)$ in our setting. The element $a \in B$ if and only if $\mathcal{P}(a) = 0$ (or equivalently $f^{\gamma \mathcal{F}(0,a)} = 1$).

Theorem 1. *The distributed private matching scheme described in Fig. 1 is correct and semantically secure against a semi-honest adversary if the Decisional Diffie-Hellman assumption holds.*

The proof of Theorem 1 is given in Appendix A.

Setup: Alice generates a key pair $(pk, sk) \leftarrow \mathcal{K}(1^l)$, $r_\tau \xleftarrow{R} \mathbb{Z}_q \setminus \{0\}$ for $\tau \in \{1, \ldots, n\}$. Bob constructs a polynomial $\mathcal{F}$ for the dataset B, computes the shares of the polynomial $\mathcal{F}$ and distributes the shares to w servers as in Section 2.2.

1. Alice broadcasts $\{\mathcal{E}_{pk}(a), \mathcal{E}_{pk}(a^2), \ldots, \mathcal{E}_{pk}(a^n)\}$ along with her public key pk to t servers $S_{\ell_1}, \ldots, S_{\ell_t}$.
2. For $j = 1, \ldots, t$, each contacted server S_{ℓ_j} computes

$$\mathcal{E}_{pk}(\mathcal{F}_{\ell_j}(a)) = \mathcal{E}_{pk}(1)^{\beta_{0,\ell_j}} \odot \mathcal{E}_{pk}(a)^{\beta_{1,\ell_j}} \odot \ldots \odot \mathcal{E}_{pk}(a^n)^{\beta_{n,\ell_j}}$$

and sends $\mathcal{E}_{pk}(\gamma \mathcal{F}_{\ell_j}(a))$ back to Alice.

3. Alice
   (a) computes $d_j \leftarrow \mathcal{D}_{sk}(\mathcal{E}_{pk}(\gamma \mathcal{F}_{\ell_j}(a)))$ for $j \in \{1, \ldots, t\}$,
   (b) computes $f^{\gamma \mathcal{F}(0,a)} \leftarrow \prod_{j=1}^{t} (d_j)^{c_j}$, where c_j's are Lagrange interpolation coefficients,
   (c) concludes $a \in B$ if $f^{\gamma \mathcal{F}(0,a)} = 1$.

Fig. 1. Distributed private matching protocol

4 Applications of Distributed Private Matching on Private Set Operations

Applying the distributed private matching protocol described in Section 3, we give solutions for private set operation problems in a distributed setting. That is the private set intersection, its cardinality and the subset relation.

Let the Alice dataset be $A = \{a_1, \ldots, a_m\}$. The random value γ, the Bob dataset B, its polynomial representation $\mathcal{F}$ and the distribution of $\mathcal{F}$ are the same as in Section 3. Suppose also that there exists a public pseudo-random number generator G_γ, using γ as a seed so that the outputs of G_γ are uniformly distributed in $\mathbb{Z}_q \setminus \{0\}$. Assume that the size of both datasets, $|A|$ and $|B|$, are public. Each server S_ℓ has the value γ and the shares of the polynomial $\mathcal{F}$, $\{\beta_{0,\ell}, \ldots, \beta_{n,\ell}\}$ for $1 \leq \ell \leq w$.

4.1 Distributed Set Intersection

The distributed set intersection problem is defined as follows. Alice contacts the threshold of t or more servers to compute the intersection of A and B. She must not gain any additional information about the set B. The contacted servers do not learn any information about A. The protocol, given in Fig. 2, is simply a m-fold application of our distributed private matching protocol. The properties of this protocol are stated in Theorem 2.

Theorem 2. *If Alice and the contacted servers follow the protocol faithfully, the distributed set intersection protocol is correct; and the privacy of Alice's dataset A is assured assuming the underlying homomorphic cryptosystem is semantically secure, while the privacy of Bob's dataset B is unconditionally secure.*

Setup: Alice generates a key pair $(pk, sk) \leftarrow \mathcal{K}(1^l)$, $r_\tau \xleftarrow{R} \mathbb{Z}_q \setminus \{0\}$ for $\tau \in \{1, \ldots, n\}$. Bob constructs a polynomial $\mathcal{F}$ for the dataset B, computes the shares of the polynomial $\mathcal{F}$ and distributes the shares to w servers as in Section 2.2.

1. Alice broadcasts $\{\{\mathcal{E}_{pk}(a_1), \ldots, \mathcal{E}_{pk}(a_1^n)\}, \ldots, \{\mathcal{E}_{pk}(a_m), \ldots, \mathcal{E}_{pk}(a_m^n)\}\}$ along with her public key pk to t servers $S_{\ell_1}, \ldots, S_{\ell_t}$.
2. For $j = 1, \ldots, t$, each contacted server S_{ℓ_j}
   (a) computes $\mathcal{E}_{pk}(\mathcal{F}_{\ell_j}(a_i)) = \mathcal{E}_{pk}(1)^{\beta_{0,\ell_j}} \odot \mathcal{E}_{pk}(a_i)^{\beta_{1,\ell_j}} \odot \ldots \odot \mathcal{E}_{pk}(a_i^n)^{\beta_{n,\ell_j}}$ for $i \in \{1, \ldots, m\}$,
   (b) generates γ_i for $1 \leq i \leq m$ from G_γ,
   (c) sends $\{\mathcal{E}_{pk}(\gamma_1 \mathcal{F}_{\ell_j}(a_1)), \ldots, \mathcal{E}_{pk}(\gamma_m \mathcal{F}_{\ell_j}(a_m))\}$ to Alice.
3. For $i = 1, \ldots, m$, Alice
   (a) computes $d_{i,j} \leftarrow \mathcal{D}_{sk}(\mathcal{E}_{pk}(\gamma_i \mathcal{F}_{\ell_j}(a_i)))$ for $j \in \{1, \ldots, t\}$,
   (b) computes $f^{\gamma_i \mathcal{F}(0, a_i)} \leftarrow \prod_{j=1}^{t}(d_{i,j})^{c_j}$, where c_j's are Lagrange interpolation coefficients,
   (c) concludes $a_i \in B$, if $f^{\gamma_i \mathcal{F}(0, a_i)} = 1$.
4. When this process concludes, Alice learns $A \cap B$.

Fig. 2. Private distributed set intersection protocol

Its proof is same as the one in Theorem 1 except the Bob's security. Since the information of $A \cap B$ is known to Alice, she can correct guess the Bob's polynomial $\mathcal{F}(0, y)$ from the result $\gamma \mathcal{F}(0, a)$ with the probability $\frac{1}{(q-|A \cap B|)^{|B|-|A \cap B|}}$.

4.2 Cardinality of Distributed Set-Intersection

As in [14], we can compute the cardinality of a set intersection by adding a permutation in our distributed set intersection protocol. In this protocol, Alice learns $|A \cap B|$, but does not know the actual contents of the set intersection.

Assume that Bob randomly chooses a private permutation π over $\{1, \ldots, m\}$, and sends it to w servers along with the shares of the polynomial $\mathcal{F}$. The protocol shown in Fig 2 needs to be upgraded by adding the following extra step just before the step 2.(c). We call it step 2.(c_0). Note that all servers permute m cryptograms according to the same permutation π.

---

2. (c_0) runs $\pi(\mathcal{E}_{pk}(\gamma_1 \mathcal{F}_{\ell_j}(a_1)), \ldots, \mathcal{E}_{pk}(\gamma_m \mathcal{F}_{\ell_j}(a_m)))$ and gets $(\mathcal{E}_{pk}(\gamma_{\pi(1)} \mathcal{F}_{\ell_j}(a_{\pi(1)})), \ldots, \mathcal{E}_{pk}(\gamma_{\pi(m)} \mathcal{F}_{\ell_j}(a_{\pi(m)})))$.

Clearly, the steps 3 and 4 in Fig. 2 ought to be replaced by the steps $3'$ and $4'$ as follows:

$3'$. For $\pi(i) = 1, \ldots, m$, Alice
  (a) computes $d_{\pi(i),j} \leftarrow \mathcal{D}_{sk}(\mathcal{E}_{pk}(\gamma_{\pi(i)} \mathcal{F}_{\ell_j}(a_{\pi(i)})))$ for $j \in \{1, \ldots, t\}$,
  (b) computes $f^{\gamma_{\pi(i)} \mathcal{F}(0, a_{\pi(i)})} \leftarrow \prod_{j=1}^{t} (d_{\pi(i),j})^{c_j}$, where c_j's are Lagrange interpolation coefficients,
  (c) checks if $f^{\gamma_{\pi(i)} \mathcal{F}(0, a_{\pi(i)})} = 1$.
$4'$. When this process concludes, Alice learns $|A \cap B|$.

Note that, this protocol works in the same way as the distributed set intersection protocol except the additional step $2(c_0)$. The permutations performed by t servers prevent Alice from learning $A \cap B$. However, the property of our distributed private matching scheme still allow Alice to determine $|A \cap B|$. That is $\gamma_{\pi(i)} \mathcal{F}(0, a_{\pi(i)}) = 0$ if and only if $a_{\pi(i)} \in B$ with unknown index $\pi(i)$.

The security proof for this protocol trivially follows from the distributed set intersection protocol.

4.3 Distributed Subset Relation

Based on our distributed set intersection protocol, we design a distributed subset relation, which enables Alice to decide whether or not her dataset A is a subset of B by contacting any t out of w servers. The idea follows from the fact that $A \subseteq B$ if and only if $A \cap B = A$ or in other words $\sum_{a_i \in A} \mathcal{F}(0, a_i) = 0$ from the construction of our private matching.

The protocol, given in Fig. 3, is the same as our distributed set intersection protocol for Step 1. In the second step, the servers $S_{\ell_j} (1 \leq j \leq t)$ first compute $\mathcal{E}_{pk}(\mathcal{F}_{\ell_j}(a_i))$ for $i \in \{1, \ldots, m\}$ as in the distributed set intersection protocol, and then compute $\mathcal{E}_{pk} \left(\sum_{i=1}^{m} \mathcal{F}_{\ell_j}(a_i) \right)$ by multiplying computed m cryptograms together. When Alice receives all $\mathcal{E}_{pk} \left(\sum_{i=1}^{m} \mathcal{F}_{\ell_j}(a_i) \right)$'s from t servers, she decrypts them and uses Lagrange interpolation to compute

$$\prod_{j=1}^{t} \left(f^{\sum_{i=1}^{m} \mathcal{F}_{\ell_j}(a_i)} \right)^{c_j} = f^{\sum_{i=1}^{m} \sum_{j=1}^{t} (c_j \mathcal{F}_{\ell_j}(a_i))} = f^{\sum_{i=1}^{m} \mathcal{F}(0,a_i)}.$$

The conclusion is obvious: if $f^{\sum_{i=1}^{m} \mathcal{F}(0,a_i)} = 1$, then $A \subseteq B$.

The security and its proof for this protocol is similar to the one in the distributed private matching protocol.

Setup: Alice generates a key pair $(pk, sk) \leftarrow \mathcal{K}(1^l), r_\tau \xleftarrow{R} \mathbb{Z}_q \setminus \{0\}$ for $\tau \in \{1, \ldots, n\}$. Bob constructs a polynomial $\mathcal{F}$ for the dataset B, computes the shares of the polynomial $\mathcal{F}$ and distributes the shares to w servers as in Section 2.2.

1. Alice broadcasts $\{\{\mathcal{E}_{pk}(a_1), \ldots, \mathcal{E}_{pk}(a_1^n)\}, \ldots, \{\mathcal{E}_{pk}(a_m), \ldots, \mathcal{E}_{pk}(a_m^n)\}\}$ along with her public-key pk to t servers $S_{\ell_1}, \ldots, S_{\ell_t}$.
2. For $j = 1, \ldots, t$, each contacted server S_{ℓ_j},
   (a) computes $\mathcal{E}_{pk}(\mathcal{F}_{\ell_j}(a_i)) = \mathcal{E}_{pk}(1)^{\beta_{0,\ell_j}} \odot \mathcal{E}_{pk}(a_i)^{\beta_{1,\ell_j}} \odot \ldots \odot \mathcal{E}_{pk}(a_i^n)^{\beta_{n,\ell_j}}$ for $i \in \{1, \ldots, m\}$,
   (b) caculates
   $$\mathcal{E}_{pk} \left(\sum_{i=1}^{m} \mathcal{F}_{\ell_j}(a_i) \right) = \mathcal{E}_{pk}(\mathcal{F}_{\ell_j}(a_1)) \odot \mathcal{E}_{pk}(\mathcal{F}_{\ell_j}(a_2)) \odot \ldots \odot \mathcal{E}_{pk}(\mathcal{F}_{\ell_j}(a_m))$$
   (c) sends $\mathcal{E}_{pk} \left(\sum_{i=1}^{m} \mathcal{F}_{\ell_j}(a_i) \right)$ to Alice.
3. Alice
   (a) computes $d_j \leftarrow \mathcal{D}_{sk} \left(\mathcal{E}_{pk} \left(\sum_{i=1}^{m} \mathcal{F}_{\ell_j}(a_i) \right) \right)$ for $j \in \{1, \ldots, t\}$,
   (b) finds $f^{\sum_{i=1}^{m} \mathcal{F}(0,a_i)} \leftarrow \prod_{j=1}^{t} (d_j)^{c_j}$, where c_j's are Lagrange interpolation coefficients and,
   (c) concludes $A \subseteq B$ if $f^{\sum_{i=1}^{m} \mathcal{F}(0,a_i)} = 1$.

Fig. 3. Privacy-preserving distributed subset relation protocol

4.4 Efficiency Analysis

All protocols in this paper require only a single round communication. The overall communication cost is measured in terms of number of elements that need to be transmitted during the protocol. Note that each of them can be represented over $\lceil \log_2 p \rceil$ bits. The computation cost is expressed by the number of multiplications, where one exponentiation takes at most $\lfloor \log_2(p-1) \rfloor$ multiplications using the Fast Exponentiation Algorithm from [17].

Distributed Private Matching Protocol. During a single round communication, Alice broadcasts her input as a set of encrypted n messages to t servers. Each contacted server responds with a single message. So the communication complexity of this protocol is $O(tn)$.

Our computations are done in the field $\mathbb{Z}_p$ and Alice needs $n+2$ modular exponentiations and n multiplications for encrypting her input; t exponentiations and multiplications, respectively for decryptions; t modular exponentiations and $t-1$ multiplications for the Lagrange interpolation. Each contacted server needs $2(n+1)$ exponentiations and $n+1$ multiplications for inputing its shares of the coefficients. So, the computation complexity of this protocol is $O(tn)$ multiplications.

For a fair comparison with a two-party case without distribution such as the one in [1], we assume that the variant of ElGamal is used to conduct the polynomial evaluation. Such an evaluation requires $O(n)$ multiplications and $O(n)$ communication. This shows that our protocol is just t times more expensive than the two-party case without distribution.

Distributed Set Intersection and the Cardinality of the Intersection Protocols. Our distributed set intersection protocol uses m parallel threads and each thread applies the underlying distributed private matching protocol. Therefore, the complexity of both communication and computation are $O(tmn)$. In the paper by Freedman et al., the two-party protocol requires $O(m+n)$ communication and $O(mn)$ multiplications. Note that our communication complexity is not $O(t(m+n))$. The reason is that in the FNP protocol, the Alice dataset is represented as a polynomial, while we represent the Bob dataset as a polynomial to suit our setting. As such, Alice has to send each of her encrypted element a_i as $\mathcal{E}_{pk}(a_i), \mathcal{E}_{pk}(a_i^2), \ldots, \mathcal{E}_{pk}(a_i^n)$ to t servers.

The protocol that enables two parties to compute the cardinality of distributed set intersection works in the same way as our protocol for distributed set intersection except the servers perform an additional permutation. Since the permutation cost is linear, it is negligible. As a result, the communication complexity is the same as the distributed set intersection protocol, and the computation cost is similar to that of the distributed set intersection.

Comparing our protocols to the ones developed by Ye et al. in [14], we can say that communication complexity of their protocols is similar to ours although the computation complexity is three times higher.

Distributed Subset Relation Protocol. Alice broadcasts her dataset as a set of encrypted mn messages to t servers. Each contacted server responds with only a single message. For computation cost, Alice needs mn modular exponentiations and the same number of multiplications for encrypting her input; t exponentiations and multiplications for decryption; t modular exponentiations and $t-1$ multiplications for the Lagrange interpolation. Each contacted server needs to perform $2m(n+1)$ exponentiations and $mn + m$ multiplications for inputing its shared-coefficients, then $2m$ multiplications for multiplying m cryptograms together. The overall cost for communication and computation are thus both $O(tmn)$.

5 Conclusion

In this paper, we proposed a protocol for the distributed private matching. We then applied this technique to solve several private distributed set operations: the set intersection, the cardinality of the set intersection and the subset relation. Our solutions rely on the polynomial representing of datasets, Shamir threshold secret sharing scheme and homomorphic encryption.

Our distributed protocols are useful in databases outsourcing while an individual server is not trusted by the data owner. All protocols constructed in this paper are provably secure against a semi-honest adversary if the Decisional Diffie-Hellman assumption holds.

As the future work, it would be interesting to extend the protocols in the semi-honest model to the case of active adversary, such as the cooperation of Alice and any server, malicious Alice, malicious servers or both.

Acknowledgment

The authors are grateful to the anonymous reviewers for their comments to improve the quality of this paper. This work was supported by the Australian Research Council under ARC Discovery Projects DP0558773, DP0665035 and DP0663452. Qingsong Ye's work was funded by an iMURS scholarship provided by Macquarie University. The research of Huaxiong Wang is partially supported by the Ministry of Education of Singapore under grant T206B2204.

References

[1] Freedman, M.J., Nissim, K., Pinkas, B.: Efficient private matching and set intersection. In: Cachin, C., Camenisch, J.L. (eds.) EUROCRYPT 2004. LNCS, vol. 3027, pp. 1–9. Springer, Heidelberg (2004)
[2] Naor, M., Pinkas, B.: Oblivious transfer and polynomial evaluation. In: 31st annual ACM Symposium on Theory of Computing (STOC 1999), Atlanta, Georgia, pp. 245–254 (May 1999)
[3] Paillier, P.: Public-key cryptosystems based on composite degree residuosity classes. In: Stern, J. (ed.) EUROCRYPT 1999. LNCS, vol. 1592, pp. 223–238. Springer, Heidelberg (1999)
[4] Gamal, T.E.: A public key cryptosystem and a signature scheme based on discrete logarithms. In: Blakely, G.R., Chaum, D. (eds.) CRYPTO 1984. LNCS, vol. 196, pp. 19–22. Springer, Heidelberg (1985)

[5] Tsiounis, Y., Yung, M.: On the security of elgamal based encryption. In: Imai, H., Zheng, Y. (eds.) PKC 1998. LNCS, vol. 1431, pp. 117–134. Springer, Heidelberg (1998)
[6] Laur, S., Lipmaa, H., Mielikainen, T.: Private itemset support counting. In: Qing, S., Mao, W., López, J., Wang, G. (eds.) ICICS 2005. LNCS, vol. 3783, pp. 97–111. Springer, Heidelberg (2005)
[7] Kiayias, A., Mitrofanova, A.: Syntax-driven private evaluation of quantified membership queries. In: Zhou, J., Yung, M., Bao, F. (eds.) ACNS 2006. LNCS, vol. 3989, pp. 470–485. Springer, Heidelberg (2006)
[8] Kiayias, A., Mitrofanova, A.: Testing disjointness and private datasets. In: S. Patrick, A., Yung, M. (eds.) FC 2005. LNCS, vol. 3570, pp. 109–124. Springer, Heidelberg (2005)
[9] Hohenberger, S., Weis, S.A.: Honest-verifier private disjointness testing without random oracles. In: Danezis, G., Golle, P. (eds.) PET 2006. LNCS, vol. 4258, pp. 277–294. Springer, Heidelberg (2006)
[10] Fagin, R., Naor, M., Winkler, P.: Comparing information without leaking it. Communications of the ACM 39(5), 77–85 (1996)
[11] Lipmaa, H.: Verifiable homomorphic oblivious transfer and private equality test. In: Laih, C.-S. (ed.) ASIACRYPT 2003. LNCS, vol. 2894, pp. 416–433. Springer, Heidelberg (2003)
[12] Kissner, L., Song, D.: Privacy-preserving set operaitons. In: Shoup, V. (ed.) CRYPTO 2005. LNCS, vol. 3621, pp. 241–257. Springer, Heidelberg (2005)
[13] Sang, Y., Shen, H., Tan, Y., Xiong, N.: Efficient protocols for privacy preserving matching against distributed datasets. In: Ning, P., Qing, S., Li, N. (eds.) ICICS 2006. LNCS, vol. 4307, pp. 210–227. Springer, Heidelberg (2006)
[14] Ye, Q., Wang, H., Tartary, C.: Privacy-preserving distributed set intersection. In: 2nd Workshop on Advances in Information Security (conjuncted with ARES 2008), Barcelona, Spain, IEEE Computer Society Press, Los Alamitos (2008)
[15] Aiello, B., Ishai, Y., Reingold, O.: Priced oblivious transfer: How to sell digital goods. In: Pfitzmann, B. (ed.) EUROCRYPT 2001. LNCS, vol. 2045, pp. 119–135. Springer, Heidelberg (2001)
[16] Naor, M., Pinkas, B.: Distributed oblivious transfer. In: Okamoto, T. (ed.) ASIACRYPT 2000. LNCS, vol. 1976, pp. 205–219. Springer, Heidelberg (2000)
[17] Pieprzyk, J., Hardjono, T., Seberry, J.: Fundamentals of Computer Security. Springer, Heidelberg (2003)

A Proof of Theorem 1

A.1 Proof of Correctness

For the correctness, we need to show that $a \in B$ if and only if $f^{\gamma \mathcal{F}(0,a)} = 1$ in our distributed private matching protocol.

Alice first encrypts her input a by using her public key as $\mathcal{E}_{pk}(a), \mathcal{E}_{pk}(a^2), \ldots, \mathcal{E}_{pk}(a^n)$ and broadcasts all encrypted elements to t servers. Then, each of the contacted servers S_{ℓ_j} $(1 \leq j \leq t)$ computes $\mathcal{E}_{pk}(\mathcal{F}_{\ell_j}(a))$ with the coefficients of the shared-polynomial $\mathcal{F}_{\ell_j}$ based on the homomorphic properties of the cryptosystem, and sends $\mathcal{E}_{pk}(\gamma \mathcal{F}_{\ell_j}(a))$ to Alice. Note that $\mathcal{F}_{\ell_j}(a) = \sum_{i=0}^{n} \beta_{i,\ell_j} a^i$. When Alice receives all cryptograms from the t servers, she decrypts them and uses the Lagrange interpolation coefficients c_j's to compute

$$\prod_{j=1}^{t} \left(f^{\gamma \mathcal{F}_{\ell_j}(a)}\right)^{c_j} = \prod_{j=1}^{t} f^{\gamma c_j \sum_{i=0}^{n} a^i \beta_{i,\ell_j}} = f^{\gamma \sum_{i=0}^{n} a^i (\sum_{j=1}^{t} c_j \beta_{i,\ell_j})} = f^{\gamma \mathcal{F}(0,a)}.$$

From Section 2.2, we know that $\mathcal{F}(0,y) = \mathcal{P}(y) = \prod_{b_i \in B}(y - b_i)$. So if $a \in B$, then we can get $f^{\gamma \mathcal{F}(0,a)} = 1$. On the other hand, if $f^{\gamma \mathcal{F}(0,a)} = 1$, then $\mathcal{P}(a) = 0$, that is, a is a root of $\mathcal{P}$. Due to the definition of $\mathcal{P}(y)$, we get $a \in B$.

A.2 Proof of Alice's Security

Given that each server has no output in the protocol, Alice's security requires that t servers cannot distinguish her input a, encrypted as $\mathcal{E}_{pk}(a), \ldots, \mathcal{E}_{pk}(a^n)$, from a random value if the DDH assumption holds.

To prove this, we will describe a simulator $\mathcal{S}$, who selects $s \xleftarrow{R} \mathbb{Z}_q \setminus \{0\}$ for $s \neq a$, executing this protocol. We will then demonstrate that Bob cannot infer the value s from $\{\mathcal{E}_{pk}(s), \mathcal{E}_{pk}(s^2), \ldots, \mathcal{E}_{pk}(s^n)\}$, or distinguish the value s from Alice's input a.

Let $\mathcal{S}$ generate a new key pair $(pk, sk) \leftarrow \mathcal{K}(1^l), r'_\tau \xleftarrow{R} \mathbb{Z}_q \setminus \{0\}$ for $\tau \in \{1, \ldots, n\}$. $\mathcal{S}$ broadcasts $\{\mathcal{E}_{pk}(s), \mathcal{E}_{pk}(s^2), \ldots, \mathcal{E}_{pk}(s^n)\}$ along with the public key pk to t servers $S_{\ell_1}, \ldots, S_{\ell_t}$.

From our cryptosystem discussed in Section 2.1, we know $\langle g \rangle$ is a subgroup of $\mathbb{Z}_p^*$ generated by g with an order q, and $h, f \in \langle g \rangle$. Note that the encryptions $\mathcal{E}_{pk}(a) = (g^{r_1}, h^{r_1} f^a)$ and $\mathcal{E}_{pk}(s) = (g^{r'_1}, h^{r'_1} f^s)$. Since r_1 and r'_1 are chosen uniformly at random over $\langle g \rangle$, the pairs (g^{r_1}, h^{r_1}) and $(g^{r'_1}, h^{r'_1})$ are uniformly distributed over $\langle g \rangle \times \langle g \rangle$.

As the discrete logarithm problem is assumed to be hard over $\mathbb{Z}_p$, any contacted server cannot compute r_1, r'_1 from $g^{r_1}, g^{r'_1}$ with non-negligible probability in polynomial time as a function of the bit size of p. Therefore, the pairs $(g^{r_1}, h^{r_1} f^a)$ and $(g^{r'_1}, h^{r'_1} f^s)$ are uniformly distributed over $\langle g \rangle$. Consequently, Bob cannot distinguish $\mathcal{E}_{pk}(a)$ and $\mathcal{E}_{pk}(s)$.

Using an identical argument, we can prove that the set of $\mathcal{E}_{pk}(s^i)$'s does not give any information about the value s. We choose $i' \in \{1, \ldots, n\}$, where $i' \neq i$. Let each contacted server know i' and i. As $r'_i, r'_{i'}$ are randomly picked over $\langle g \rangle$, the corresponding $(g^{r'_i}, h^{r'_i})$ and $(g^{r'_{i'}}, h^{r'_{i'}})$ are uniformly distributed over $\langle g \rangle \times \langle g \rangle$. Hence, t servers cannot deduce the value s from two uniformly distributed $\mathcal{E}_{pk}(s^{i'})$ and $\mathcal{E}_{pk}(s^i)$.

A.3 Proof of Bob's Security

The only message Alice receives from each contacted server is $f^{\gamma \mathcal{F}_{\ell_j}(a)}$ for $j \in \{1, \ldots, t\}$. Suppose that Alice knows the value $\gamma \mathcal{F}_{\ell_j}(a)$ from $f^{\gamma \mathcal{F}_{\ell_j}(a)}$. Since γ is uniformly distributed over $\mathbb{Z}_q \setminus \{0\}$, if $\gamma \mathcal{F}_{\ell_j}(a) \neq 0$, then there are $q^{n+1} - 1$ possible polynomials for each of $\mathcal{F}_{\ell_j}(y)$'s, where n is the degree of $\mathcal{F}_{\ell_j}(y)$. On the other hand, if $\gamma \mathcal{F}_{\ell_j}(a) = 0$, then there are still $q^n - 1$ possible polynomials for $\mathcal{F}_{\ell_j}(y)$. Therefore, the probability of Alice can correctly reconstruct $\mathcal{F}(0, y)$ from $\mathcal{F}_{\ell_j}(y)$'s is about $\frac{1}{q^{tn}}$.

Alice also knows $f^{\gamma \mathcal{F}(0,a)}$ after the interpolation. Assume also that Alice knows the value $\gamma \mathcal{F}(0, a)$ from $f^{\gamma \mathcal{F}(0,a)}$. The proof is the same as before. Since γ is uniformly distributed over $\mathbb{Z}_q \setminus \{0\}$, the probability that Alice correctly guesses $\mathcal{F}(0, y)$ from the value $\gamma \mathcal{F}(0, a)$ is about $\frac{1}{q^{n-1}}$.

In addition, the cooperation of less than t servers cannot compute Bob's polynomial $\mathcal{F}(0, y)$. This is guaranteed by the perfectness of Shamir secret sharing.

Computational Soundness of Non-Malleable Commitments

David Galindo[1,*], Flavio D. Garcia[2], and Peter van Rossum[2]

[1] Departament of Computer Science, University of Malaga, Spain
dgalindo@lcc.uma.es
[2] Institute for Computing and Information Sciences,
Radboud University Nijmegen, The Netherlands
{flaviog,petervr}@cs.ru.nl

Abstract. This paper aims to find a proper security notion for commitment schemes to give a sound computational interpretation of symbolic commitments. We introduce an indistinguishability based security definition of commitment schemes that is equivalent to non-malleability with respect to commitment. Then, we give a construction using tag-based encryption and one-time signatures that is provably secure assuming the existence of trapdoor permutations. Finally, we apply this new machinery to give a sound interpretation of symbolic commitments in the Dolev-Yao model while considering active adversaries.

1 Introduction

Over the last few decades, two main stream approaches have been developed for the analysis of security protocols. On the one hand, the cryptographic approach considers an arbitrary computationally-bound adversary that interacts with honest participants and tries to break a security goal. This model is satisfactory as it deals with every efficient attacker. On the other hand, the symbolic or Dolev-Yao approach idealizes the security properties of the cryptographic primitives, which are axiomatized in a logic. Moreover, the capabilities of the adversary are also specified by a set of inference rules. This approach is appealing because there are automated techniques for the verification of some security properties.

Abadi and Rogaway in [AR02] pioneered the idea of relating these two models and showed that, under appropriate assumptions on the underlying cryptographic primitives, a simple language of encrypted expressions is sound with respect to the computational model in the case of passive adversaries.

Such a relation maps symbolic messages m to distributions over bitstrings $[\![m]\!]$. This map then should relate messages that are observationally equivalent in the symbolic world to indistinguishable distributions over bitstrings. Such a map allows one to use formal methods, possibly even automated, to reason about security properties of protocols and have those reasonings be valid also in the standard computational model.

---
* Partially funded by the Spanish Ministry of Science and Education through the projects ARES (CSD2007-00004) and CRISIS (TIN2006-09242).

Several extensions to the original Abadi-Rogaway logic [AR02] have been proposed in the literature. These extensions deal with public key encryption [MW04, Her05], key cycles [ABHS05], partial information leakage [ABS05], active instead of passive adversaries [MW04, JLM05], and more realistic security notions [AW05]. Other extensions add new primitives to the logic such as bilinear pairings [Maz07], modular exponentiation [BLMW07] and hash functions [CKKW06, GvR06]. There are also frameworks dealing with generic equational theories [BCK05, ABW06, KM07]. So far there is no work in the literature, that we are aware of, that relates these two approaches for commitment schemes.

Commitment schemes are fundamental cryptographic primitives and are used in protocols like zero-knowledge proofs [GMW91], contract signing [EGL85], and can be used for bidding protocols. A commitment consists of two phases: the commitment phase where the principals commit to a message without revealing any information; and the opening phase where the principals reveal the message and it is possible to verify that this message corresponds to the value committed to during the commitment phase. After the commitment phase it should be infeasible to open the commitment to a different value than the one committed. This property is called binding. In the context of bidding protocols, non-malleability is also a desirable property. This means that an adversary cannot modify an intercepted commitment, say into a commitment to a slightly higher bid.

Our contribution. The first objective of this paper is to find sufficient security assumptions to give a sound computational interpretation of commitments schemes in the Dolev-Yao model, under active adversaries. Pursuing that objective we propose a new indistinguishability-based security definition for commitment schemes in the presence of adaptive adversaries. Then we give a novel generic construction for a non-malleable commitment scheme based on one-way trapdoor permutations. This construction is secure with respect to our new definition and has some additional properties such as being non-interactive, perfectly binding and reusable, which makes it of independent interest. This new definition allows us to prove soundness of the Dolev-Yao model extended with commitments, following the directions of Micciancio and Warinschi [MW04].

Overview. Section 3 introduces basic notation and definitions from the literature. Section 4 elaborates on different definitions of non-malleability for commitment schemes and discusses the relations among them. In Section 5 we propose a new commitment scheme and we give a security proof. Section 2 describes symbolic protocol executions, its computational counterparts and the map between them and also states the soundness result. Finally in Section 7 there are some concluding remarks.

2 Symbolic Protocols

We are going to apply this theory to give sound computational interpretation to symbolic commitments. Recall from the introduction that the symbolic approach to protocol verification deals with symbolic or algebraic messages and idealized cryptographic primitives. In this setting the adversary is unbounded in running time and has full control over the communication media but is completely incapable of breaking the underlying cryptographic primitives.

We now describe the message space and the closure operator. These messages are used to formally describe cryptographic protocols. The closure represents the knowledge that can be extracted from a message, and it is used to define what valid algebraic protocol runs are. Intuitively a protocol run is valid if every message sent by a principal can be deduced from its knowledge except maybe for some fresh randomness. Much of this is standard (see, e.g., [AR02, MW04, MP05, GvR06]), except that we model commitments and decommitments as well as encryption.

Definition 2.1. Let **Nonce** be an infinite set of *nonce symbols*, **Const** a finite set of *constant symbols*, **Key** an infinite set of *key symbols*, and **Random** an infinite set of *randomness labels*. Nonces are denoted by $n, n', \ldots$, constants by $c, c', \ldots$, keys by $k, k', \ldots$, and randomness labels by $r, r', \ldots$. Using these building blocks, *messages* are constructed using symbolic encryption, commitments, decommitments, and pairing operations:

$$\mathbf{Msg} \ni m := c \mid n \mid \{\!|m|\!\}_k^r \mid \mathrm{com}^r(m) \mid \mathrm{dec}^r(m) \mid \langle m, m \rangle.$$

A message of the form $\{\!|m|\!\}_k^r$ is called an *encryption* and the set of all such messages is denoted by **Enc**. Similarly, messages of the form $\mathrm{com}^r(m)$ are called *commitments* and the set of all these messages is denoted by **Com**. The messages of the form $\mathrm{dec}^r(m)$ are called *decommitments* and the set of all these messages is denoted by **Dec**. In a protocol run $\mathrm{dec}^r(m)$ is a valid decommitment of $\mathrm{com}^{r'}(m')$ only if $m = m'$ and $r = r'$. We say that elements in **Const** ∪ **Nonce** ∪ **Key** are primitive and we denote this set by **Prim**. For a public key k we denote its associated private key as k^{-1}.

The *closure* of a set U of messages is the set of all messages that can be constructed from U using tupling, detupling, commitment, decommitment, and encryption and decryption. It represents the information an adversary could deduce knowing U. Note that, due to secrecy of the commitment scheme, knowing $\mathrm{com}^r(m)$ does not provide an adversary with any information about m.

Definition 2.2 (Closure). Let U be a set of messages. The *closure* of U, denoted by $\overline{U}$, is the smallest set of messages satisfying: 1. **Const** $\subseteq \overline{U}$; 2. $U \subseteq \overline{U}$; 3. $m, m' \in \overline{U} \implies \langle m, m' \rangle \in \overline{U}$; 4. $m \in \overline{U} \land k \in \overline{U} \implies \{\!|m|\!\}_k^r \in \overline{U}$; 5. $\{\!|m|\!\}_k^r \in \overline{U} \land k^{-1} \in \overline{U} \implies m \in \overline{U}$; 6. $m \in \overline{U} \implies \mathrm{com}^r(m), \mathrm{dec}^r(m) \in \overline{U}$; 7. $\mathrm{dec}^r(m) \in \overline{U} \implies m \in \overline{U}$; 8. $\langle m, m' \rangle \in \overline{U} \implies m, m' \in \overline{U}$.

Next we need to find the right security notions to give sound computational interpretation to symbolic encryption and commitments.

3 Computational Setup

This section introduces syntaxis and security definitions for different cryptographic primitives. Much of this is standard, we refer the reader to [GM84, RS92] and [NY90] for a thorough explanation. Some of this primitives will be used to interpret algebraic operations and some of them are used as building blocks for our construction of Section 5.

3.1 Commitment Schemes

Definition 3.1. A *commitment scheme* is a triple $\Omega = (\text{TTP}, \text{Snd}, \text{Rcv})$ of probabilistic polynomial-time algorithms. TTP, the *trusted third party*, takes as input the security parameter 1^η and produces a common reference string σ. We require that $|\sigma| \geq p(\eta)$ for some non-constant polynomial p. Snd, the *sender*, takes as input σ and a message m and produces a commitment *com* to this message and a corresponding decommitment *dec*. Rcv, the *receiver*, takes as input σ, *com*, and *dec* and produces a message or $\bot$.

Meaningfulness$_\Omega(A)$:	**Secrecy**$_{\text{TTP},\text{Snd}}(A_1, A_2)$:	**Binding**$_{\text{TTP},\text{Rcv}}(A)$:
$\sigma \leftarrow \text{TTP}(1^\eta)$	$\sigma \leftarrow \text{TTP}(1^\eta)$	$\sigma \leftarrow \text{TTP}(1^\eta)$
$m \leftarrow A(\sigma)$	$m_0, m_1, s \leftarrow A_1(\sigma)$	$(com, dec_1, dec_2) \leftarrow A(\sigma)$
$(com, dec) \leftarrow \text{Snd}(\sigma, m)$	$b \leftarrow \{0, 1\}$	$m_1 \leftarrow \text{Rcv}(\sigma, com, dec_1)$
$m_1 \leftarrow \text{Rcv}(\sigma, com, dec)$	$(com, dec) \leftarrow \text{Snd}(\sigma, m_b)$	$m_2 \leftarrow \text{Rcv}(\sigma, com, dec_2)$
return $m \neq m_1$	$b' \leftarrow A_2(s, com)$	**return** $m_1 \neq \bot \neq m_2$
	return $b = b'$	$\land\ m_1 \neq m_2$

The following three conditions must hold.

1. For all probabilistic polynomial-time algorithms A, the probability $\mathbb{P}[\textbf{Meaningfullness}_\Omega(A)]$ is a negligible function of η.
2. For all probabilistic polynomial-time algorithms (A_1, A_2), the advantage $|\mathbb{P}[\textbf{Secrecy}_{\text{TTP},\text{Snd}}(A_1, A_2)] - 1/2|$ is a negligible function of η.
3. For all probabilistic polynomial-time algorithms A, the probability $\mathbb{P}[\textbf{Binding}_{\text{TTP},\text{Rcv}}(A)]$ is a negligible function of η.

Definition 3.2. A commitment scheme is said to be *perfectly binding* if for all unbounded algorithms A, the probability $\mathbb{P}[\textbf{Binding}_{\text{TTP},\text{Rcv}}(A)]$ is zero.

Definition 3.3. A commitment scheme is said to be *perfectly hiding* if for all unbounded algorithms (A_0, A_1), $|\mathbb{P}[\textbf{Secrecy}_{\text{TTP},\text{Snd}}(A_1, A_2)] - 1/2|$ is zero.

3.2 Encryption Schemes

Definition 3.4. An *encryption scheme* is a triple $\Pi = (\mathcal{K}, \mathcal{E}, \mathcal{D})$ of probabilistic polynomial-time algorithms. $\mathcal{K}$ takes as input the security parameter 1^η and produces a key pair (pk, sk) where pk is the public encryption key and sk is the private decryption key. $\mathcal{E}$ takes as input a public key pk and a plaintext m and outputs a ciphertext. $\mathcal{D}$ takes as input a private key sk and a ciphertext and outputs a plaintext or $\bot$. It is required that $\mathbb{P}[(\text{pk}, \text{sk}) \leftarrow \mathcal{K}(1^\eta); c \leftarrow \mathcal{E}(\text{pk}, m); m' \leftarrow \mathcal{D}(\text{sk}, c) : m = m'] = 1$.

```
IND-CCA$_\Pi(A_0, A_1)$:
(pk, sk) ← $\mathcal{K}(1^\eta)$
$m_0, m_1, s \leftarrow A_0^{\mathcal{D}}(\text{pk})$
$b \leftarrow \{0, 1\}$
$c \leftarrow \mathcal{E}(\text{pk}, m_b)$
$b' \leftarrow A_1^{\mathcal{D}}(s, c)$
return $b = b'$
```

Definition 3.5. An encryption scheme $\Pi = (\mathcal{K}, \mathcal{E}, \mathcal{D})$ is said to be *IND-CCA secure* if for all probabilistic polynomial-time adversaries $A = (A_0, A_1)$ the advantage of A, defined as $|\mathbb{P}[\textbf{IND-CCA}_\Pi(A_0, A_1)] - 1/2|$, is a negligible function of η. This adversary has access to a decryption oracle $\mathcal{D}$ that on input c' outputs $\mathcal{D}(\text{sk}, c')$ with the only restriction that $c \neq c'$.

3.3 One-Time Signatures

Definition 3.6. A *signature scheme* is a triple (Gen, Sign, Vrfy) of probabilistic polynomial-time algorithms. Gen takes as input the security parameter 1^η and produces a key pair (vk, sk) where vk is the signature verification key and sk is the secret signing key. Sign takes as input sk and a message m and produces a signature s of m. Vrfy takes as input vk, a message m and a signature s and outputs whether or not s is a valid signature of m.

```
OTS$_\Sigma(A_0, A_1)$:
(vk, sk) ← Gen($1^\eta$)
$m, s \leftarrow A_0(\text{vk}, 1^\eta)$
$\sigma \leftarrow \text{Sign}(\text{sk}, m)$
$m', \sigma' \leftarrow A_1(s, \sigma)$
return $\sigma \neq \sigma' \wedge \text{Vrfy}(\text{vk}, (m', \sigma'))$
```

Definition 3.7. A signature scheme $\Sigma =$ (Gen, Sign, Vrfy) is a *strong, one-time signature scheme* if the success probability of any probabilistic polynomial-time adversary (A_0, A_1) in the game **OTS**$_\Sigma(A_0, A_1)$ is negligible in the security parameter η.

3.4 Tag-Based Encryption

Definition 3.8. A *tag-based encryption scheme (TBE)* handling tags of length ℓ (where ℓ is a polynomially-bounded function) is a triple of probabilistic polynomial-time algorithms (KeyGen, Enc, Dec). KeyGen takes a security parameter 1^η and returns a public key pk and secret key sk. The public key pk includes the security parameter 1^η and $\ell(\eta)$; as well as the description of sets $\mathcal{M}, \mathcal{R}, \mathcal{C}$, which denote the set of messages, randomness and ciphertexts respectively. These descriptions might depend on the public key pk. Enc takes as inputs pk, a tag $t \in \{0,1\}^\ell$ and $m \in \mathcal{M}$. It returns a ciphertext $c \in \mathcal{C}$. Dec takes as inputs the secret key sk, a tag t and $c \in \mathcal{C}$, and returns $m \in \mathcal{M}$ or $\bot$ when c is not a legitimate ciphertext. For the sake of consistency, these algorithms must satisfy $\text{Dec}(\text{sk}, t, c) = m$ for all $t \in \{0,1\}^\ell$, $m \in \mathcal{M}$, where $c = \text{Enc}(\text{pk}, t, m)$.

Definition 3.9. Let $\mathcal{E} = (\text{KeyGen}, \text{Enc}, \text{Dec})$ be a TBE scheme. We say $\mathcal{E}$ is *IND-TBE-CCA secure* if for any 3-tuple of PPT oracle algorithms (A_0, A_1, A_2) and any polynomially-bounded function ℓ the advantage in the following game is negligible in the security parameter 1^η:

$A_0(1^\eta, \ell(\eta))$ outputs a target tag t. $\text{KeyGen}(1^\eta)$ outputs (pk, sk) and the adversary is given pk. Then the adversary A_1 may ask polynomially-many queries to a decryption oracle $\mathcal{D}(t', c') = \text{Dec}(\text{sk}, t', c')$ for pairs tag-ciphertext (t', c') of its choice, with the restriction $t \neq t'$. At some point, A_1 outputs two equal length messages m_0, m_1. A bit $b \leftarrow \{0, 1\}$ is chosen at random and the adversary is given a challenge ciphertext $c \leftarrow \text{Enc}(\text{pk}, t, m_b)$. A_2 may continue asking the decryption oracle for pairs tag-ciphertext (t', c') of its choice, with the restriction $t \neq t'$. Finally, A_2 outputs a guess b'.

$$\boxed{\begin{array}{l}\textbf{IND-TBE-CCA}_\mathcal{E}(A_0, A_1, A_2): \\ t, s_1 \leftarrow A_0(1^\eta, \ell(\eta)) \\ (\text{pk}, \text{sk}) \leftarrow \text{KeyGen}(1^\eta) \\ m_0, m_1, s_2 \leftarrow A_1^\mathcal{D}(s_1, \text{pk}) \\ b \leftarrow \{0, 1\} \\ c \leftarrow \text{Enc}(\text{pk}, t, m_b) \\ b' \leftarrow A_2^\mathcal{D}(s_2, c) \\ \textbf{return}\ \ b = b'\end{array}}$$

We define the advantage of A as $|\mathbb{P}[\textbf{IND-TBE-CCA}(A)] - 1/2|$.

3.5 Interpretation

Suppose we have an encryption scheme Π, a commitment scheme Ω and a function that maps symbolic constants to constant bitstrings. Then we can define a mapping $[\![\cdot]\!]$ from algebraic messages $m \in \textbf{Msg}$ to distributions over bitstrings $[\![m]\!] \in \textbf{Str}$. This interpretation maps nonces to random bitstrings of length η; encryptions are interpreted by running the encryption algorithm $\mathcal{E}$ and for interpreting commitments and decommitments we use the commit algorithm Snd.

In order to achieve sound interpretation we will explore the security requirements on these cryptographic primitives. For the case of encryption it is satisfactory to use any IND-CCA encryption scheme as shown in [MW04]. For the case of commitments, using standard security definitions is not straightforward as they are not strong enough nor indistinguishability based. To achieve sound interpretation of the idealized Dolev-Yao model, throughout the next section we elaborate on a convenient security definition for commitment schemes.

4 Definitions of Non-Malleability

As noticed by Fischlin and Fischlin [FF00], there are two different versions of non-malleability for commitment schemes, namely: NM with respect to opening (NMO) and NM with respect to commitment (NMC). NMC was the version originally proposed by Dolev, Dwork and Naor in [DDN91]. It means that given a commitment to a message m, the adversary is unable to build a different commitment to m', with m related to m'. This version of non-malleability is appropriate while considering perfectly binding commitments and only makes sense for schemes that are not perfectly hiding.

The other version NMO, seemingly weaker, means that an adversary that is first given a commitment to m and on a second stage its decommitment, is unable to find a different commitment-decommitment pair that decommits to a message m' related to m. This notion was studied by Di Crescenzo, Ishai and Ostrovsky [CIO98] and later by Di Crescenzo, Katz, Ostrovsky and Smith [CKOS01]. Intuitively a commitment scheme is non-malleable if the adversary can do no better than a simulator which has no information at all about the message that was committed to. Next we recall their definition.

NMO $_\Omega(A_1, A_2, D, R)$:
$\sigma \leftarrow \text{TTP}(1^\eta)$
$m_1 \leftarrow D$
$com_1, dec_1 \leftarrow \text{Snd}(\sigma, m_1)$
$com_2 \leftarrow A_1(\sigma, com_1)$
$dec_2 \leftarrow A_2(\sigma, com_1, com_2, dec_1)$
$m_2 \leftarrow \text{Rcv}(\sigma, com_2, dec_2)$
return $com_1 \neq com_2 \wedge R(m_1, m_2)$

SIM(S, D, R):
$m_1 \leftarrow D$
$m_2 \leftarrow S(1^\eta, D)$
return $R(m_1, m_2)$

Definition 4.1 (Non-malleability [CIO98, CKOS01]). Let $\Omega = (\text{TTP}, \text{Snd}, \text{Rcv})$ be a commitment scheme. Ω is called *non-malleable* if for all PPT adversaries (A_1, A_2) there is a PPT simulator S such that for all distributions D and all relations R,

$$\mathbb{P}[\mathbf{NMO}_\Omega(A_1, A_2, D, R)] - \mathbb{P}[\mathbf{SIM}(S, D, R)]$$

is a negligible function of η.

Remark 4.2. To prevent that the adversary trivially wins, by refusing to decommit, the following restriction over the relation R is imposed: for all messages m, we have $R(m, \bot) = 0$.

4.1 NMC-CCA: Non-Malleability against Chosen Commitment Attacks

The previous definition deals with non-malleability with respect to opening. For the relation between symbolic and computational cryptography we need the stronger notion of non-malleability with respect to commitment. Intuitively, this is because in the algebraic setting $\text{com}^r(m')$ cannot be deduced from $\text{com}^r(m)$, with m' somehow related to m. Therefore we adapt the NMO definition to non-malleability with respect to commitment and we strengthen it by incorporating active adaptive security, allowing the adversary to mount *chosen commitment attacks* (CCA in short). Specifically, we empower the adversary with access to a decommitment oracle $\mathcal{D}$. To do so, from now on, we restrict our attention to non-interactive, perfectly binding trapdoor commitment schemes. The oracle $\mathcal{D}$ has access to the trapdoor information. It takes as argument a commitment c with the restriction that c is not equal to the challenge commitment com_1. Then if the commitment c has been correctly generated, the oracle returns a decommitment d which opens c, and otherwise it outputs $\bot$.

NMC-CCA$_\Omega(A_0, A_1, R)$:	**SIM-CCA**$_{\text{TTP}}(S_0, S_1, R)$:
$\sigma \leftarrow \text{TTP}(1^\eta)$	$\sigma \leftarrow \text{TTP}(1^\eta)$
$D, s_1 \leftarrow A_0^{\mathcal{D}}(\sigma)$	$D, s_1 \leftarrow S_0(\sigma)$
$m_1 \leftarrow D(\sigma)$	$m_1 \leftarrow D(\sigma)$
$com_1, dec_1 \leftarrow \text{Snd}(\sigma, m_1)$	
$com_2, s_r \leftarrow A_1^{\mathcal{D}}(s_1, com_1)$	$com_2, s_r \leftarrow S_1(s_1)$
$dec_2 \leftarrow \mathcal{D}(com_2)$	$dec_2 \leftarrow \mathcal{D}(com_2)$
$m_2 \leftarrow \text{Rcv}(\sigma, com_2, dec_2)$	$m_2 \leftarrow \text{Rcv}(\sigma, com_2, dec_2)$
return $com_1 \neq com_2 \wedge R(s_r, m_1, m_2)$	**return** $R(s_r, m_1, m_2)$

Definition 4.3 (NMC-CCA). Let $\Omega = (\text{TTP}, \text{Snd}, \text{Rcv})$ be a commitment scheme. Ω is called *NMC-CCA secure* if for all PPT adversaries (A_0, A_1) there is a PPT simulator (S_0, S_1) such that for all relations R (with the same restriction as in 4.2),

$$\mathbb{P}[\textbf{NMC-CCA}_\Omega(A_0, A_1, R)] - \mathbb{P}[\textbf{SIM-CCA}_{\text{TTP}}(S_0, S_1, R)]$$

is a negligible function of η.

4.2 An Indistinguishability Based Definition

Next we introduce an equivalent formulation of NMC-CCA that is more convenient to prove soundness of the Dolev-Yao model with respect to commitment schemes.

IND-COM-CCA$_b(A_0, A_1)$:
$\sigma \leftarrow \text{TTP}(1^\eta)$
$m_0, m_1, s_1 \leftarrow A_0^{\mathcal{D}}(\sigma)$
$com_1, dec_1 \leftarrow \text{Snd}(\sigma, m_b)$
$b' \leftarrow A_1^{\mathcal{D}}(s_1, com_1)$
return b'

Definition 4.4 (IND-COM-CCA). Let $\Omega = (\text{TTP}, \text{Snd}, \text{Rcv})$ be a commitment scheme. Ω is said to be *IND-COM-CCA secure* if for all PPT adversaries (A_0, A_1)

$$\mathbb{P}[\textbf{IND-COM-CCA}_1(A_0^{\mathcal{D}}, A_1^{\mathcal{D}}) = 1] - \mathbb{P}[\textbf{IND-COM-CCA}_0(A_0^{\mathcal{D}}, A_1^{\mathcal{D}}) = 1]$$

is a negligible function of η.

Next we show that NMC-CCA and IND-COM-CCA are equivalent. We discuss it briefly as it is basically the proof that NM-CCA and IND-CCA are equivalent, adapted to commitment schemes.

Theorem 4.5. *Let $\Omega = (\text{TTP}, \text{Snd}, \text{Rcv})$ be a commitment scheme. Then Ω is IND-COM-CCA secure if and only if Ω is NMC-CCA secure.*

Proof. (IND-COM-CCA $\Leftarrow$ NMC-CCA) Let (B_0, B_1) be an adversary for IND-COM-CCA. Then we build the following adversary (A_0, A_1) against NMC-CCA.

Algorithm $A_0^{\mathcal{D}}(\sigma)$:	**Algorithm** $A_1^{\mathcal{D}}((\sigma, m_0, m_1, s_1), c_1)$:
$m_0, m_1, s_1 \leftarrow B_0^{\mathcal{D}}(\sigma)$	$b \leftarrow B_1^{\mathcal{D}}(s_1, c_1)$
$D \leftarrow U(\{m_0, m_1\})$	$c_2 \leftarrow \text{Snd}(\sigma, m_b)$
return $D, (\sigma, m_0, m_1, s_1)$	**return** c_2, ϵ

where U is the uniform distribution. Now take the relation $R(s_r, m_1, m_2)$ as m_1 equal to m_2. It should be clear, after unfolding (A_0, A_1) in the **NMC-CCA** game, that this adversary has the same advantage that (B_0, B_1) has against IND-COM-CCA.

(IND-COM-CCA $\Rightarrow$ NMC-CCA) Let (A_0, A_1) be an adversary for NMC-CCA. Then we build the following adversary (B_0, B_1) against IND-COM-CCA.

Algorithm $B_0^{\mathcal{D}}(\sigma)$:	**Algorithm** $B_1^{\mathcal{D}}((\sigma, m_0, m_1, s_1), c_1)$:
$D, s_1 \leftarrow A_0^{\mathcal{D}}(\sigma)$	$c_2 \leftarrow A_1^{\mathcal{D}}(s_1, c_1)$
$m_0, m_1 \leftarrow D$	$m \leftarrow \mathcal{D}(c_2)$
return $m_0, m_1, (\sigma, m_0, m_1, s_1)$	**if** $m = m_1$ **then return** 1
	else return 0

Again, just by unfolding these adversaries in the IND-COM-CCA game, it is easy to verify that they have the same advantage that (A_0, A_1) has against NMC-CCA. □

It remains to show that such a security notion for a commitment scheme is achievable. In the next section we give a practical construction that achieves IND-COM-CCA security.

5   The Construction

We now propose a new construction for IND-COM-CCA that is computationally hiding, perfectly binding, reusable, non-interactive, non-malleable under adaptive adversaries, and provably secure under the assumption that trapdoor permutations exist.

Next we outline the idea of our construction. As pointed out by Di Crescenzo, Katz, Ostrovsky and Smith [CKOS01], an IND-CCA secure public key encryption scheme can be converted into a perfectly binding non-malleable commitment scheme. Let $\Pi = (\text{KeyGen}, \text{Enc}, \text{Dec})$ be an indistinguishable against adaptive chosen-ciphertext attacks secure public key encryption scheme. The idea is to commit to a message m by encrypting it using random coins r; commitment is set to be the ciphertext $c = \text{Enc}(pk, m; r)$; de-commitment is set to be the pair (m, r); finally the opening algorithm takes (c, m, r) and checks whether $c = \text{Enc}(pk, m; r)$. When trying to directly use this construction to instantiate an IND-COM-CCA commitment scheme one might not be able to simulate the de-commitment oracle. The reason is that given a ciphertext/commitment c, one recovers the purported embedded message m by using the decryption algorithm, but not necessarily the randomness r. One way to break through this situation is to include in the commitment a second ciphertext $c' = \text{Enc}(\text{pk}', r; r')$ encrypting the randomness r used in the first ciphertext $c = \text{Enc}(\text{pk}, m; r)$. This is the key idea of our construction. We additionally use one-time signatures and this together with tag-based encryption schemes ensure the de-commitment oracle does not leak vital information.

Let $\Pi = (\text{KeyGen}, \text{Enc}, \text{Dec})$ be a tag based encryption scheme and let $\Sigma = (\text{Gen}, \text{Sign}, \text{Vrfy})$ be a signature scheme. Define (TTP, Snd, Rcv) as follows:

- TTP runs $\text{KeyGen}(1^\eta)$ twice to obtain $(\text{pk}_1, \text{sk}_1)$ and $(\text{pk}_2, \text{sk}_2)$. The common reference string includes pk_1, pk_2.
- To commit to a message m, the sender Snd computes and outputs the commitment $C = (\text{vk}, c_1, c_2, s)$ where $c_1 = \text{Enc}(\text{pk}_1, \text{vk}, m; r_1)$, $c_2 = \text{Enc}(\text{pk}_2, \text{vk}, r_1; r_2)$, with $r_1, r_2 \leftarrow \mathcal{R}$, $(\text{vk}, \text{sk}) \leftarrow \text{Gen}(1^\eta)$ and $s \leftarrow \text{Sign}(\text{sk}, (c_1, c_2))$. The decommitment is set to be (m, r_1).
- To de-commit ciphertext $C = (\text{vk}, c_1, c_2, s)$ using (m, r_1), the receiver Rcv first checks if the signature on (c_1, c_2) is correct, and afterwards whether or not $c_1 = \text{Enc}(\text{pk}_1, \text{vk}, m; r_1)$.

We assume $\mathcal{R} = \mathcal{M}$.

Theorem 5.1. *Assume that* $(\text{KeyGen}, \text{Enc}, \text{Dec})$ *is an IND-TBE-CCA secure tag based encryption scheme and that* $(\text{Gen}, \text{Sign}, \text{Vrfy})$ *is a one-time strongly unforgeable signature scheme. Then* (TTP, Snd, Rcv) *is an IND-COM-CCA secure commitment scheme.*

Proof. We transform an adversary A against the IND-COM-CCA security of the commitment scheme into adversaries against the TBE and the OTS. Next we will describe a sequence of games following the methodology advocated in [Sho04, BR06]. Let X_i be the event that A learns the challenge bit b in the i-th game.

Game 0. This is the unmodified IND-COM-CCA game. Trivially, $|\mathbb{P}[X_0] - 1/2|$ equals the advantage of A against IND-COM-CCA.

Game 1. In this game we disallow decryption queries $C = (\text{vk}, c_1, c_2, s)$ s.t. $\text{vk} = \text{vk}^\star$ where $(\text{vk}^\star, c_1^\star, c_2^\star, s^\star)$ is the challenge commitment. Then, we get that $|\mathbb{P}[X_1] - \mathbb{P}[X_0]|$ is less or equal than the advantage any PPT algorithm has in breaking the one-time strong unforgeability security of the OTS.

Game 2. Still decryption queries with $\text{vk} = \text{vk}^\star$ are forbidden. In this game we use the IND-CCA security of the second instance of the TBE scheme. The components $c_1^\star$ and $c_2^\star$ of the challenge ciphertext are changed to $c_1^\star = \text{Enc}(\text{pk}_1^\star, \text{vk}^\star, m_b^\star; r_1)$, and $c_2^\star = \text{Enc}(\text{pk}_2^\star, \text{vk}^\star, r')$ where $r', r_1 \leftarrow \mathcal{R}$. Now, we have $|\mathbb{P}[X_2] - \mathbb{P}[X_1]|$ is less or equal than the advantage any PPT algorithm has in breaking the selective IND-CCA security of the TBE.

Finally it is shown that $|\mathbb{P}[X_2] - 1/2|$ is bounded by the advantage any PPT algorithm has in breaking the selective IND-CCA security of the first instance of the TBE.

Putting everything together, we get that $|\mathbb{P}[X_0] - 1/2|$ is bounded by the advantages in breaking the OTS scheme plus twice the advantage in breaking the selective IND-CCA of the TBE scheme. Next we describe the concrete adversaries,

Game 0 $\approx$ Game 1. Assume that there is an adversary (A_0, A_1) that is able to distinguish the environments of Game 0 and 1. Then we build an adversary (B_0, B_1) against the one-time strong unforgeability of the signature scheme.

Algorithm $B_0(1^\eta, \text{vk})$:
$\text{pk}_1, \text{sk}_1 \leftarrow \text{KeyGen}(1^\eta)$
$\text{pk}_2, \text{sk}_2 \leftarrow \text{KeyGen}(1^\eta)$
$m_0, m_1, s_1 \leftarrow A_0^\mathcal{D}(\text{pk}_1, \text{pk}_2)$
$b \leftarrow \{0, 1\}$
$r_1 \leftarrow \mathcal{R}$
$c_1 \leftarrow \text{Enc}(\text{pk}_1, \text{vk}, m_b; r_1)$
$c_2 \leftarrow \text{Enc}(\text{pk}_2, \text{vk}, r_1)$
return $(c_1, c_2), (s_1 ||\text{vk}||c_1||c_2||\text{sk}_1||\text{sk}_2)$

---

and $B_1((s_1||\text{vk}||c_1||c_2||\text{sk}_1||\text{sk}_2), s) = [b' \leftarrow A_1^\mathcal{D}(s_1, (\text{vk}, c_1, c_2, s))]$. Calls to the decommitment oracle $\mathcal{D}(\text{vk}', c_1', c_2', s')$ are simulated by firstly verifying the signature $\text{Vrfy}(\text{vk}', (c_1', c_2'), s')$. If the verification succeeds then the oracle returns the pair $(\text{Dec}(\text{sk}_1, \text{vk}', c_1'), \text{Dec}(\text{sk}_2, \text{vk}', c_2'))$ and otherwise it outputs $\bot$. If the adversary eventually performs a query $\mathcal{D}(\text{vk}', c_1', c_2', s')$ with $\text{vk}' = \text{vk}$ then the execution of the adversary is aborted and B outputs $((c_1', c_2'), s')$, thus breaking the one-time strong unforgeability of the signature scheme.

Game 1 $\approx$ Game 2. Assume that there is an adversary (A_0, A_1) that is able to distinguish the environments of Game 1 and 2. Then we build an adversary (B_0, B_1, B_2) against the IND-CCA security of the second TBE. Take $B_0(1^\eta, \ell(\eta)) = [(\text{vk}, \text{sk}) \leftarrow \text{Gen}(1^\eta); \textbf{return } \text{vk}, (\text{vk}||\text{sk})]$ and $B_1(s_1, \text{pk}_2) = [r', r_1 \leftarrow \mathcal{R}; \textbf{return } r', r_1, (s_1||r'||r_1||\text{pk}_2)]$ and

---
Algorithm $B_2^{\mathcal{O}_{\text{sk}_2}}((\text{vk}||\text{sk}||r'||r_1||\text{pk}_2), c_2)$:
$\text{pk}_1, \text{sk}_1 \leftarrow \text{KeyGen}(1^\eta)$
$m_0, m_1, s_1 \leftarrow A_0^\mathcal{D}(\text{pk}_1, \text{pk}_2)$
$b \leftarrow \{0, 1\}$
$c_1 \leftarrow \text{Enc}(\text{pk}_1, \text{vk}, m_b; r_1)$
$s \leftarrow \text{Sign}(\text{sk}, (c_1, c_2))$
$b' \leftarrow A_1^\mathcal{D}(s_1, (\text{vk}, c_1, c_2, s))$
if $b = b'$ **then return** 1
else return 0

Calls to the decommitment oracle $\mathcal{D}(\text{vk}, c_1, c_2, s)$ are simulated by firstly verifying the signature $\text{Vrfy}(\text{vk}, (c_1, c_2), s)$. If the verification succeeds then the oracle returns $(\text{Dec}(\text{sk}_1, \text{vk}, c_1), \mathcal{O}_{\text{sk}_2}(c_2))$ and otherwise it outputs $\bot$.

Finally we show that $|\mathbb{P}[X_2] - 1/2|$ is bounded by the advantage any PPT algorithm has in breaking the selective IND-CCA security of the first instance of the TBE. Assume that there is an adversary (A_0, A_1) for Game 2. Then we build an adversary (B_0, B_1, B_2) against the IND-CCA security of the first TBE. Take $B_0(1^\eta, \ell(\eta)) = [(\text{vk}, \text{sk}) \leftarrow \text{Gen}(1^\eta); \textbf{return } \text{vk}, (\text{vk}\|\text{sk})]$ and

> **Algorithm** $B_1^{\mathcal{O}_{\text{sk}_1}}((\text{vk}\|\text{sk}), \text{pk}_1)$:
> $\text{pk}_2, \text{sk}_2 \leftarrow \text{KeyGen}(1^\eta)$
> $m_0, m_1, s_1 \leftarrow A_0^{\mathcal{D}}(\text{pk}_1, \text{pk}_2)$
> **return** $(m_0, m_1), (\text{vk}\|\text{sk}\|\text{pk}_1\|s_1\|\text{pk}_2\|\text{sk}_2)$

> **Algorithm** $B_2^{\mathcal{O}_{\text{sk}_1}}((\text{vk}\|\text{sk}\|\text{pk}_1\|s_1\|\text{pk}_2\|\text{sk}_2), c_1)$:
> $r' \leftarrow \mathcal{R}$
> $c_2 \leftarrow \text{Enc}(\text{pk}_2, \text{vk}, r')$
> $s \leftarrow \text{Sign}(\text{sk}, (c_1, c_2))$
> $b' \leftarrow A_1^{\mathcal{D}}(s_1, (\text{vk}, c_1, c_2, s))$
> **return** b'

Calls to the decommitment oracle $\mathcal{D}(\text{vk}, c_1, c_2, s)$ are simulated by firstly verifying the signature $\text{Vrfy}(\text{vk}, (c_1, c_2), s)$. If the verification succeeds then the oracle returns $(\mathcal{O}_{\text{sk}_1}(c_1), \text{Dec}(\text{sk}_2, \text{vk}, c_2))$ and otherwise it outputs $\bot$. □

6 Protocol Execution and State Traces

We now prove that it is possible to port proofs in the symbolic framework to the computational one. First, for the sake of self-containment we describe the adversarial model and the execution environment following the directions of Micciancio and Warinschi [MW04]. We refer the reader to this paper for a thorough explanation.

The message space and the closure operator were defined in Section 2. Messages are used to formally describe cryptographic protocols. The closure represents the knowledge that can be extracted from a message, and is used to define what valid algebraic protocol runs are. Intuitively a protocol run is valid if every message sent by a principal can be deduced from its knowledge except maybe for some fresh randomness. In this setting an adversary is in control of the communication media and is able to interact with honest participants. Consider then an adversary that has access to an oracle that will play the role of the honest participants. This adversary can start new sessions of the protocol and send messages to a principal of a given session and get the respective answer back. Formally, the adversary A can perform one of the following queries to the execution oracle $\mathcal{O}$.

1. $\text{newsession}([I_1 \ldots I_n])$ that takes a list of user identities I_i and returns a new session identifier s.
2. $\text{send}(s, I, m)$ that delivers the message m to the principal I of session s. Then $\mathcal{O}$ updates I's state and returns the answer to the adversary.

In case that the adversary performs a query that is not according to the protocol, for the specific state of the receiver, the oracle aborts the execution of this session.

In a formal protocol, the messages exchanged are algebraic expressions from the message algebra. A formal adversary A^f will interact with the formal oracle $\mathcal{O}^f$ in a symbolic protocol run.

On the other hand, a computational adversary A^c is a probabilistic polynomial-time Turing machine that operates on bitstrings. For a fixed value of the security parameter there is a set of primitive bitstrings for constants and nonces denoted by $\mathbf{Prim}_\eta$. The set of bitstrings $\mathbf{Msg}_\eta$ is build from $\mathbf{Prim}_\eta$ by tupling, encryptions, commitments and decommitments. There is a set $\mathbf{Sid}$ of *session identifiers*; a set $\mathbf{Uid}$ of *user identities* and a set $\mathbf{Vars}$ of *variables* in the abstract protocol description.

Let $F: \mathbf{Sid} \times \mathbf{Uid} \to (\mathbf{Vars} \to \mathbf{Msg}, \mathbb{N})$ be the state maintained by the formal oracle $\mathcal{O}^f$. On input (s, I) it returns the state of principal I in session s together with his *instruction pointer*. The instruction pointer indicates on which step of the abstract protocol this principal is. Similarly, $C: \mathbf{Sid} \times \mathbf{Uid} \to (\mathbf{Vars} \to \mathbf{Msg}_\eta, \mathbb{N})$ is the state maintained by the computational oracle $\mathcal{O}^c$. Assume without loss of generality that all the sessions are created at the beginning. Then, a formal adversary A_f is just a sequence of send(s, I, m) queries. We say that a formal adversary A_f is a valid Dolev-Yao adversary ($A_f \in \mathbf{DY}$) if each message he sends to the oracle is in the closure of his initial knowledge plus the answers he gets from the oracle $\mathcal{O}^f$. A protocol execution, thus, is the sequence of states $F_0, F_1, \ldots$ of the formal oracle O^f and is denoted by trace$(A_f, \mathcal{O}^f)$. After fixing the randomness of the adversary and that of the oracle environment to τ_A and $\tau_\mathcal{O}$, we can similarly define a computational execution trace trace$(A_c(\tau_A), \mathcal{O}^c(\tau_\mathcal{O}))$ as the sequence of states $C_0, C_1, \ldots$ of the computational oracle $\mathcal{O}^c$.

Definition 6.1. We say that $[\![\cdot]\!]: \mathbf{Prim} \to \mathbf{Prim}_\eta$ is an *interpretation function* if it is injective and structure preserving (i.e., maps formal nonces to nonce bitstrings, formal commitments to commitments and so on).

Definition 6.2. Let $F = F_0, F_1, \ldots$ be a formal execution trace and let $C = C_0, C_1, \ldots$ be a concrete execution trace. We say that $F \preceq C$ if there exists an interpretation function $[\![\cdot]\!]$ such that $[\![F_0]\!] = C_0, [\![F_1]\!] = C_1, \ldots$.

The following theorem shows that a computational adversary has no more power than an algebraic adversary.

Theorem 6.3. *Let* $(\mathrm{TTP}, \mathrm{Snd}, \mathrm{Rcv})$ *be an IND-COM-CCA secure commitment scheme and let* $(\mathcal{K}, \mathcal{E}, \mathcal{D})$ *be an IND-CCA secure encryption scheme. For any computational adversary* A_c, *the probability*

$$\mathbb{P}[\exists A_f \in \mathbf{DY}: \mathrm{trace}(A_f, \mathcal{O}^f) \preceq \mathrm{trace}(A_c(\tau_A), \mathcal{O}^c(\tau_\mathcal{O}))]$$

is overwhelming. Here the probability is taken over the random choices τ_A of the adversary and $\tau_\mathcal{O}$ of the oracle.

Proof. First fix the randomness τ_A and $\tau_\mathcal{O}$. Running the computational adversary A_c, it produces a sequence of queries/answers to/from the computational oracle. Because we know all the trapdoor information that the oracle generates and because the adversary has to send properly typed messages, we can de-construct any message sent into primitive terms. Choosing new algebraic terms for each distinct primitive bitstring encountered we build a sequence of algebraic queries which constitutes an algebraic adversary A_f. Note that for different random choices of τ_A and $\tau_\mathcal{O}$ we get the same A_f (up to renaming) with overwhelming probability.

It remains to show that the adversary we just built is Dolev-Yao. Suppose that it is not. Then A_f must, at some point, send a query that contains a non-adversarial nonce $n^\star$ that is not in the closure of the messages he received before. If this nonce occurs inside an encryption (with an unknown key) then one can build an adversary breaking the IND-CCA security of the encryption scheme [MW04]. Assume then that it occurs inside a commitment. We now build an adversary that breaks the IND-COM-CCA security of the commitment scheme.

This adversary simulates the environment to A_c using the de-commit oracle when necessary except for the query that contains $n^\star$. There it generates two interpretations (n_0, n_1) for $n^\star$ and gives them as challenge plaintext for the IND-COM-CCA game. The challenger gives back a commitment to n_b where b is the challenge bit. This commitment to n_b is used to answer the oracle queries. At the moment A_C outputs the interpretation of $n^\star$ we can check whether it is n_0 or n_1. □

A formal security notion is a predicate $\mathsf{P_f}$ on formal traces. A protocol $\Pi \models_f \mathsf{P_f}$ if for all adversaries $A_f \in \mathbf{DY}$ holds that $\mathrm{trace}(A_f, \mathcal{O}^f) \in \mathsf{P_f}$. Similarly, a computational security notion is a predicate $\mathsf{P_c}$ on computational traces. A protocol $\Pi \models_c \mathsf{P_c}$ if for all probabilistic polynomial-time adversaries A_c holds that $\mathrm{trace}(A_f, \mathcal{O}^f) \in \mathsf{P_c}$ with overwhelming probability (taken over the random choices of the adversary and the ones of the oracle environment). The proof of the following theorem follows as in [MW04].

Theorem 6.4. *Let* (TTP, Snd, Rcv) *be a IND-COM-CCA secure commitment scheme and let* $(\mathcal{K}, \mathcal{E}, \mathcal{D})$ *be an IND-CCA secure encryption scheme. Let* $\mathsf{P_f}$ *and* $\mathsf{P_c}$ *be respectively formal and computational security notions such that for all formal traces ft and all computational traces ct it holds that* $(ft \in \mathsf{P_f} \wedge ft \preceq ct) \Longrightarrow ct \in \mathsf{P_c}$. *Then*

$$\Pi \models_f \mathsf{P_f} \Longrightarrow \Pi \models_c \mathsf{P_c} \, .$$
□

7 Conclusions

We presented two equivalent security notions for commitment schemes: a simulation based definition and a indistinguishability based one. We then gave a concrete scheme satisfying this security notion. This construction is of interest on itself as it is generic and has some interesting features like being reusable, perfectly binding and secure against adaptive chosen-commitment attacks. We then applied this new machinery to give sound interpretation of symbolic commitments while considering active adversaries.

References

[ABHS05] Adão, P., Bana, G., Herzog, J., Scedrov, A.: Soundness of formal encryption in the presence of key-cycles. In: de Capitani di Vimercati, S., Syverson, P.F., Gollmann, D. (eds.) ESORICS 2005. LNCS, vol. 3679, pp. 374–396. Springer, Heidelberg (2005)

[ABS05] Adão, P., Bana, G., Scedrov, A.: Computational and information-theoretic soundness and completeness of formal encryption. In: CSFW 2005, pp. 170–184. IEEE Computer Society Press, Los Alamitos (2005)

[ABW06] Abadi, M., Baudet, M., Warinschi, B.: Guessing attacks and the computational soundness of static equivalence. In: Aceto, L., Ingólfsdóttir, A. (eds.) FOSSACS 2006 and ETAPS 2006. LNCS, vol. 3921, pp. 398–412. Springer, Heidelberg (2006)

[AR02] Abadi, M., Rogaway, P.: Reconciling two views of cryptography (the computational soundness of formal encryption). J. Cryptology 15(2), 103–127 (2002)

[AW05] Abadi, M., Warinschi, B.: Security analysis of cryptographically controlled access to XML documents. In: Proceedings of the 24th ACM Symposium on Principles of Database Systems, pp. 108–117. ACM Press, New York (2005)

[BCK05] Baudet, M., Cortier, V., Kremer, S.: Computationally sound implementations of equational theories against passive adversaries. In: Caires, L., Italiano, G.F., Monteiro, L., Palamidessi, C., Yung, M. (eds.) ICALP 2005. LNCS, vol. 3580, pp. 652–663. Springer, Heidelberg (2005)

[BLMW07] Bresson, E., Lakhnech, Y., Mazaré, L., Warinschi, B.: A generalization of DDH with applications to protocol analysis and computational soundness. In: Menezes, A. (ed.) CRYPTO 2007. LNCS, vol. 4622, Springer, Heidelberg (2007)

[BR06] Bellare, M., Rogaway, P.: The security of triple encryption and a framework for code-based game-playing proofs. In: Vaudenay, S. (ed.) EUROCRYPT 2006. LNCS, vol. 4004, pp. 409–426. Springer, Heidelberg (2006)

[CIO98] Di Crescenzo, G., Ishai, Y., Ostrovsky, R.: Non-interactive and non-malleable commitment. In: STOC 1998, pp. 141–150. ACM Press, New York (1998)

[CKKW06] Cortier, V., Kremer, S., Küsters, R., Warinschi, B.: Computationally sound symbolic secrecy in the presence of hash functions. In: ArunKumar, S., Garg, N. (eds.) FSTTCS 2006. LNCS, vol. 4337, pp. 176–187. Springer, Heidelberg (2006)

[CKOS01] Di Crescenzo, G., Katz, J., Ostrovsky, R., Smith, A.: Efficient and non-interactive non-malleable commitment. In: Pfitzmann, B. (ed.) EUROCRYPT 2001. LNCS, vol. 2045, pp. 40–59. Springer, Heidelberg (2001)

[DDN91] Dolev, D., Dwork, C., Naor, M.: Non-malleable cryptography. In: STOC 1991, pp. 542–552. ACM Press, New York (1991)

[EGL85] Even, S., Goldreich, O., Lempel, A.: A randomizing protocol for signing contracts. Comm. ACM 28(6), 637–647 (1985)

[FF00] Fischlin, M., Fischlin, R.: Efficient non-malleable commitment schemes. In: Bellare, M. (ed.) CRYPTO 2000. LNCS, vol. 1880, pp. 413–431. Springer, Heidelberg (2000)

[GM84]   Goldwasser, S., Micali, S.: Probabilistic encryption. J. Computer and System Sciences 28(2), 270–299 (1984)

[GMW91]   Goldreich, O., Micali, S., Wigderson, A.: Proofs that yield nothing but their validity and a methodology of cryptographic protocol design. J. ACM 38(1), 691–729 (1991)

[GvR06]   Garcia, F.D., van Rossum, P.: Sound computational interpretation of symbolic hashes in the standard model. In: Yoshiura, H., Sakurai, K., Rannenberg, K., Murayama, Y., Kawamura, S.-i. (eds.) IWSEC 2006. LNCS, vol. 4266, pp. 33–47. Springer, Heidelberg (2006)

[Her05]   Herzog, J.: A computational interpretation of Dolev–Yao adversaries. Theoretical Computer Science 340(1), 57–81 (2005)

[JLM05]   Janvier, R., Lakhnech, Y., Mazar, L.: Completing the picture: Soundness of formal encryption in the presence of active adversaries. In: Sagiv, M. (ed.) ESOP 2005. LNCS, vol. 3444, pp. 172–185. Springer, Heidelberg (2005)

[KM07]   Kremer, S., Mazaré, L.: Adaptive soundness of static equivalence. In: Biskup, J., López, J. (eds.) ESORICS 2007. LNCS, vol. 4734, Springer, Heidelberg (2007)

[Maz07]   Mazaré, L.: Computationally sound analysis of protocols using bilinear pairings. In: WITS 2007, pp. 6–21 (2007)

[MP05]   Micciancio, D., Panjwani, S.: Adaptive security of symbolic encryption. In: Kilian, J. (ed.) TCC 2005. LNCS, vol. 3378, pp. 169–187. Springer, Heidelberg (2005)

[MW04]   Micciancio, D., Warinschi, B.: Soundness of formal encryption in the presence of active adversaries. In: Naor, M. (ed.) TCC 2004. LNCS, vol. 2951, pp. 133–151. Springer, Heidelberg (2004)

[NY90]   Naor, M., Yung, M.: Public-key cryptosystems provably secure against chosen ciphertext attack. In: STOC 1990, pp. 427–437. ACM Press, New York (1990)

[RS92]   Rackoff, C., Simon, D.R.: Non-interactive zero-knowledge proof of knowledge and chosen ciphertext attack. In: Feigenbaum, J. (ed.) CRYPTO 1991. LNCS, vol. 576, pp. 433–444. Springer, Heidelberg (1992)

[Sho04]   Shoup, V.: Sequences of games: a tool for taming complexity in security proofs. Cryptology ePrint Archive, Report 2004/332 (2004), http://eprint.iacr.org/

Square Attack on Reduced-Round Zodiac Cipher

Wen Ji and Lei Hu

State Key Laboratory of Information Security,
Graduate School of Chinese Academy of Sciences,
Beijing 100049, China

Abstract. Zodiac is a block cipher with 128-bit blocks and designed for the Korean firm SoftForum in 2000. This paper discusses the security of Zodiac against the Square attack. We first construct two 8-round distinguishers to build a basic Square attack against the reduced 9-round Zodiac with 128-bit keys, and then extend this attack to 12, 13, 14, and 15-round Zodiac, which finds their round keys with the complexities $2^{92.3}$, $2^{124.8}$, $2^{157.2}$, and $2^{189.5}$, respectively. Moreover, our attack can find the round keys of the full 16-round Zodiac with 256-bit keys with a complexity of $2^{221.7}$ which is better than the exhaustive search and in this attack we just need $2^{16.5}$ chosen plaintexts. This result shows that the Square attack is not only applicable to Square-like ciphers but also to ciphers with Feistel structure once more.

Keywords: block cipher, Zodiac, square attack.

1 Introduction

Zodiac [1] is a block cipher designed in 2000 by Chang-Hyi Lee for the Korean firm SoftForum and this algorithm was submitted to the ISO/IEC JTC1/SC27-Korea in September of the same year. This cipher has a 16-round Feistel structure with an initial and final key whitening, and in its design there are an initial permutation and a final permutation before the first round and after the last round, respectively. The round function of the Zodiac cipher includes a linear transformation layer which consists of just exclusive or operations and includes a nonlinear transformation layer, namely the S-box.

Up to now, the most efficient method analyzing Zodiac is the impossible differential cryptanalysis [2]. This attack uses two 14-round impossible characteristics to derive the 128-bit master key of the full 16-round Zodiac with the complexity of 2^{119} encryption times and in this attack $2^{103.6}$ chosen plaintext pairs are used.

Square attack [3] or integral attack is a chosen plaintext attack, which was originally designed as a dedicated attack against the Square cipher and is later applicable to similar block ciphers based on Substitution-Permutation networks such as Crypton [5] and AES [6]. This attack is also one of the most effective attack against AES. To apply Square attack on the Feistel structure, Lucks introduced the saturation attack in the FSE'01 conference [4], which is a variation of the Square attack, and in the same paper he used it to attack the Twofish cipher. Since then, his method has been applied to a number of other ciphers, including Skipjack [9], Fox [10], and Camellia [8, 11].

This paper proposes two 8-round distinguishers for Zodiac and uses them to construct a basic Square attack against the reduced 9-round Zodiac with 128-bit keys (denoted Zodiac-128). Further, we extend this attack to the reduced 12, 13, 14, and 15-round Zodiac-128 and find all round keys of each of such versions of Zodiac with complexities of $2^{92.3}$, $2^{124.8}$, $2^{157.2}$ and $2^{189.5}$ cipher executions, respectively and they correspondingly need $2^{15.1}$, $2^{15.6}$, 2^{16} and $2^{16.3}$ chosen plaintexts. This paper also shows that we can obtain all round keys of the full 16-round Zodiac-256 (Zodiac with 256-bit keys) with a complexity of $2^{221.7}$ encryption times which is faster than the exhaustive key search and in this case we just need $2^{16.5}$ chosen plaintexts. Therefore, 12, 13-round Zodiac-128, 14, 15-round Zodiac-192 and the full-round Zodiac-256 are not immune to the attack presented in this paper. The result shows again that the Square attack is not only effective for structure similar to Square-like ciphers but also for Feistel-type ciphers.

This paper is organized as follows. In section 2 we describe the Zodiac cipher briefly. Two 8-round distinguishers of Zodiac and the basic 9-round Square attack are discussed in section 3. Section 4 extends the basic 9-round attack to 12, 13, 14, 15, and the full 16 rounds, and the corresponding complexities are analyzed. The last section concludes the paper.

2 Description of the Zodiac Cipher

The design of Zodiac is based on a 16-round Feistel iterated structure. The block size of Zodiac is 128 bits and this cipher supports 128, 192, and 256-bit keys. Within its design, there are key whitening layers and an initial and a final permutations Π before the first round and after the last round, respectively. Since the initial and final permutations do not affect the properties of the input and the output values, we ignore these two transformations in the sequel discussion. In addition, the key whitening can be incorporated into the internal round keys, so we will also ignore this transformation.

For $0 \leq r \leq 15$, let $X_L^{(r)}$ and $X_R^{(r)}$ be the left and the right halves of the $(r+1)$-th round inputs, respectively, $K^{(r)}$ be the r-th round key. With these notations the Feistel structure of Zodiac can be written as

$$X_L^{(r+1)} = X_R^{(r)} \oplus F(X_L^{(r)} \oplus K^{(r+1)})$$
$$X_R^{(r+1)} = X_L^{(r)}, \text{ for } 0 \leq r \leq 15.$$

Figure 1 shows the overall structure of Zodiac [2].

The round function $F : \mathrm{GF}(2^8)^8 \to \mathrm{GF}(2^8)^8$ adopts the substitution and permutation structure, and is defined as the composition of permutations S and P:

$$X \to S(P(X)),$$

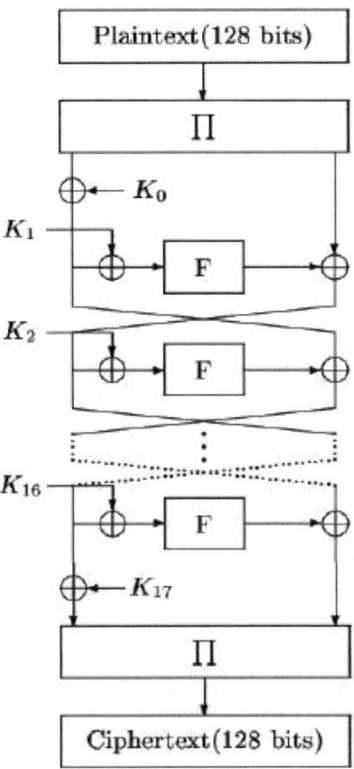

Fig. 1. The structure of Zodiac

where the substitution function $S : \mathrm{GF}(2^8)^8 \to \mathrm{GF}(2^8)^8$ is an one-to-one transformation defined by

$$(x_0, \cdots, x_7) \mapsto (S_1(x_0), S_2(x_1), S_1(x_2), S_2(x_3),\\ S_1(x_4), S_2(x_5), S_1(x_6), S_2(x_7)),$$

here $x_i \in \mathrm{GF}(2^8)$ and the two S-boxes S_1 and S_2 are generated by the following functions $h(x)$ and $g(x)$, respectively:

$$h(x) = h_0(h_0(x)), \text{ where } h_0(x) = (45^x \bmod 257) \bmod 256,$$
$$g(x) = (170 + x)^{-1} \text{ in } \mathrm{GF}(2^8), \text{with irreducible polynomial}$$
$$x^8 + x^4 + x^3 + x + 1.$$

The function $P : \mathrm{GF}(2^8)^8 \to \mathrm{GF}(2^8)^8$ is a linear permutation which maps $(y_0, y_1, y_2, y_3, y_4, y_5, y_6, y_7)$ to $(z_0, z_1, z_2, z_3, z_4, z_5, z_6, z_7)$, where

$$z_0 = y_2 \oplus y_3 \oplus y_4, \quad z_1 = y_0 \oplus y_1, \quad z_2 = y_1 \oplus y_2, \quad z_3 = y_2 \oplus y_3,$$
$$z_4 = y_6 \oplus y_7 \oplus y_0, \quad z_5 = y_4 \oplus y_5, \quad z_6 = y_5 \oplus y_6, \quad z_7 = y_6 \oplus y_7.$$

The key schedule algorithm of Zodiac is basically constructed from its round function. For the detail, see [1].

3 Basic Square Attack

The concept of Λ-set is the base of the Square attack. Let Λ be a collection of state vectors $X = (x_0, \cdots, x_{n-1})$ where $x_i \in \mathrm{GF}(2^8)$ is the i-th byte of X. If the i-th bytes of vectors in Λ are pairwisely distinct, then the i-th byte is called an "active" byte; and if the i-th byte of each vector in Λ correspondingly has a same value, then this byte is called a "passive" byte. The i-th byte in a collection Λ is balanced, if $\bigoplus_{X \in \Lambda} x_i = 0$. Below is a strict definition of Λ-set.

Definition 1. *Let Λ be a set of n-byte vectors and λ be the index set of the state bytes. If*

$$\forall x, y \in \Lambda \Rightarrow \begin{cases} x_i \neq y_i & for\ i \in \lambda \\ x_i = y_i & for\ i \notin \lambda \end{cases}$$

holds, then the collection Λ is said to be a Λ-set and λ is the index set of active bytes.

From the definition of Λ-set and the three basic functions in Zodiac, namely key exclusive or (XOR) transformation, nonlinear transformation S, and linear transformation P described in the previous section, it is easy to see that S and key XOR convert a Λ-set to a Λ-set with invariant index set λ, but P dose not necessarily transform a Λ-set into a Λ-set. Additionally, if the input of S-boxs S_i ($i = 1, 2$) is an active (passive) byte of a Λ-set, then the output of it is also active (passive). However, the output of S_i ($i = 1, 2$) may be not balanced when its input is balanced.

3.1 8-Round Distinguishers

In this paper we only consider Λ-sets in which only one byte is active, and then trace the evolution of this active byte through 8 rounds to construct two 8-round distinguishers for Zodiac cipher.

Let $X_L^{(r)}$, $X_R^{(r)} \in \mathrm{GF}(2^8)^8$ be the left and right inputs of the $(r+1)$-th round. Select two Λ-sets called Λ-set 1 and Λ-set 2 to be the input plaintexts.

The Λ-set 1 has the form:

$$X_L^{(0)} = (C, C, C, C, C, C, C, C),\ X_R^{(0)} = (C, A, C, C, C, C, C, C),$$

and the Λ-set 2 has the form:

$$X_L^{(0)} = (C, C, C, C, C, C, C, C),\ X_R^{(0)} = (C, C, C, C, C, A, C, C),$$

where each letter C denotes a constant byte (it is distinct at different positions); A is an active byte and ranges over all possible values in $\mathrm{GF}(2^8)$.

By the structure of the Zodiac cipher, we can find how the states of the vectors in these two Λ-sets evolute round-dependently. See Tables 1 and 2. Table 1 is for vectors of Λ-set 1 and Table 2 is for vectors of Λ-set 2. In these two tables, the notation "B" denotes a balanced byte, which means the XOR of all bytes of the Λ-set occur at this position is zero, and the symbol "?" stands that we do not know what characteristic the byte can possess. After an iteration of 8 round transformations, we will not know any characteristic of byte in every position, so we get two 8-round distinguishers for the cipher.

Table 1. Distinguisher 1

Round Num.	Left 64 bits	Right 64 bits
0	(C,C,C,C,C,C,C,C)	(C,A,C,C,C,C,C,C)
1	(C,A,C,C,C,C,C,C)	(C,C,C,C,C,C,C,C)
2	(C,A,A,C,C,C,C,C)	(C,A,C,C,C,C,C,C)
3	(A,B,?,A,C,C,C,C)	(C,A,A,C,C,C,C,C)
4	(?,?,?,?,A,C,C,C)	(A,B,?,A,C,C,C,C)
5	(?,?,?,?,?,A,C,C)	(?,?,?,?,A,C,C,C)
6	(?,?,?,?,?,?,A,C)	(?,?,?,?,?,A,C,C)
7	(?,?,?,?,?,?,?,A)	(?,?,?,?,?,?,A,C)
8	(?,?,?,?,?,?,?,?)	(?,?,?,?,?,?,?,A)
9	(?,?,?,?,?,?,?,?)	(?,?,?,?,?,?,?,?)

Table 2. Distinguisher 2

Round Num.	Left 64 bits	Right 64 bits
0	(C,C,C,C,C,C,C,C)	(C,C,C,C,C,A,C,C)
1	(C,C,C,C,C,A,C,C)	(C,C,C,C,C,C,C,C)
2	(C,C,C,C,C,A,A,C)	(C,C,C,C,C,A,C,C)
3	(C,C,C,C,A,B,?,A)	(C,C,C,C,C,A,A,C)
4	(A,C,C,C,?,?,?,?)	(C,C,C,C,A,B,?,A)
5	(?,A,C,C,?,?,?,?)	(A,C,C,C,?,?,?,?)
6	(?,?,A,C,?,?,?,?)	(?,A,C,C,?,?,?,?)
7	(?,?,?,A,?,?,?,?)	(?,?,A,C,?,?,?,?)
8	(?,?,?,?,?,?,?,?)	(?,?,?,A,?,?,?,?)
9	(?,?,?,?,?,?,?,?)	(?,?,?,?,?,?,?,?)

3.2 Basic 9-Round Square Attack

In this subsection we exploit the two 8-round distinguishers to derive a basic Square attack on the reduced 9-round Zodiac. Let $X_{L_i}^{(r)}, X_{R_i}^{(r)}$ be the i-th byte of $X_L^{(r)}$ and $X_R^{(r)}$, respectively. From distinguisher 1, the byte $X_{R_7}^{(8)}$ ranges over all possible values of $GF(2^8)$, so the XOR of these values is zero. For distinguisher 2, the byte $X_{R_3}^{(8)}$ has the same property.

According to the structure of the round function in Zodiac, we can get the following equation:

$$X_{R_7}^{(8)} = X_{L_7}^{(9)} \oplus S_2(X_{L_6}^{(8)} \oplus X_{L_7}^{(8)} \oplus K_6^{(9)} \oplus K_7^{(9)}), \qquad (1)$$

and
$$X_{R_3}^{(8)} = X_{L_3}^{(9)} \oplus S_2(X_{L_2}^{(8)} \oplus X_{L_3}^{(8)} \oplus K_2^{(9)} \oplus K_3^{(9)}). \tag{2}$$

Below we will only discuss the distinguisher 1, the distinguisher 2 can be considered in the same way from the equation (2).

Since $X_L^{(8)} = X_R^{(9)}$ and $(X_L^{(9)}, X_R^{(9)})$ is exactly the ciphertext, $X_{L_6}^{(8)}$ and $X_{L_7}^{(8)}$ can be obtained easily. By the equation (1), if we guess a value for $K_6^{(9)} \oplus K_7^{(9)}$, then for each element of Λ-set 1, the value in the position of $X_{R_7}^{(8)}$ can be calculated from this equation. If the XOR of these values is not zero, then the guessed byte is incorrect. In the worst case, we must check all 2^8 possible values of $K_6^{(9)} \oplus K_7^{(9)}$ to get the correct one. For each guessed value, the calculation of $X_{R_7}^{(8)}$ from equation (1) are not more complicated than the encryption, so the complexity is $2^8 \times 2^8 = 2^{16}$ cipher executions. Since the case of distinguisher 2 is similar to distinguisher 1, we can obtain the correct values of $K_6^{(9)} \oplus K_7^{(9)}$ and $K_2^{(9)} \oplus K_3^{(9)}$ after $2 \times 2^8 \times 2^8 = 2^{17}$ cipher executions with $2 \times 2^8 = 2^9$ chosen plaintexts.

4 Attacks on Reduced-Round Zodiac

In this section we extend the basic 9-round Square attack to 12, 13, 14, 15 and the full 16-round Zodiac.

As we know, if the round key of each round is obtained, then the cipher can be decrypted entirely. This means that we can attack the cipher successfully without the master key.

4.1 Extended Attack to the 12-Round Zodiac

In this subsection, we discuss the Square attack on the reduced 12-round Zodiac and obtain all round keys according to the testing bytes in the traces of the two distinguishers by 8-step operations.

Step 1: Similar to the 9-round case, we exploit the testing bytes in the 8th round of the two distinguishers. From the round transformation, to compute the values of $X_{R_7}^{(8)}$ on Λ-set 1, and $X_{R_3}^{(8)}$ on Λ-set 2, we need to guess the bytes which are shown in Table 3. Then we check whether the XOR of these values in the position $X_{R_7}^{(8)}$ on Λ-set 1 (or $X_{R_3}^{(8)}$ on Λ-set 2) is zero or not.

From Table 3, to compute the values in the position $X_{R_7}^{(8)}$ or $X_{R_3}^{(8)}$, we need to guess 10 bytes shown in the 1st and 2nd column of Table 3, respectively. And to get the 12th-round round key, we need to consider the two distinguishers simultaneously. Obviously, the computation complexities of the two distinguishers are the same to each other. For distinguisher 1, we need to guess $2^{10 \times 8}$ bits, which is also the time of 12-round Zodiac encryption. By checking a single Λ-set of plaintexts leaves about $1/256$ incorrect values as possible candidates, so the whole process must be repeated for 10 different Λ-sets with the same structure, that is, we need $10 \times 2^8 \times 2 = 2^{12.3}$ chosen plaintexts. Thus we can get the round key for the 12th round with a complexity $10 \times 2^{10 \times 8} \times 2^8 \times 2 = 10 \times 2^{89} \approx 2^{92.3}$ encryptions.

Table 3. Values needed in Step 1

$X_{R_7}^{(8)}$	$X_{R_3}^{(8)}$
$K_6^{(9)} \oplus K_7^{(9)}$	$K_2^{(9)} \oplus K_3^{(9)}$
$K_5^{(10)} \oplus K_6^{(10)}$	$K_1^{(10)} \oplus K_2^{(10)}$
$K_6^{(10)} \oplus K_7^{(10)}$	$K_2^{(10)} \oplus K_3^{(10)}$
$K_4^{(11)} \oplus K_5^{(11)}$	$K_0^{(11)} \oplus K_1^{(11)}$
$K_5^{(11)} \oplus K_6^{(11)}$	$K_1^{(11)} \oplus K_2^{(11)}$
$K_6^{(11)} \oplus K_7^{(11)}$	$K_2^{(11)} \oplus K_3^{(11)}$
$K_4^{(12)} \oplus K_5^{(12)}$	$K_0^{(12)} \oplus K_1^{(12)}$
$K_5^{(12)} \oplus K_6^{(12)}$	$K_1^{(12)} \oplus K_2^{(12)}$
$K_6^{(12)} \oplus K_7^{(12)}$	$K_2^{(12)} \oplus K_3^{(12)}$
$K_0^{(12)} \oplus K_6^{(12)} \oplus K_7^{(12)}$	$K_2^{(12)} \oplus K_3^{(12)} \oplus K_4^{(12)}$

Step 2: Decrypting the 12th round with the round key obtained in Step 1, we get the output of the 11th round. In this case, we use the testing bytes $X_{R_6}^{(7)}$ in distinguisher 1 and $X_{R_2}^{(7)}$ in distinguisher 2, which are all active bytes. To compute $X_{R_2}^{(7)}$ and $X_{R_6}^{(7)}$, we need the bytes presented in Table 4. Since some of them has shown in Table 3, we only guess the bytes newly appeared in this table. By computation, we get the 10th and 11th-round round key with complexity of $6 \times 2^{6 \times 8} \times 2^8 \times 2 = 6 \times 2^{57} \approx 2^{59.6}$ encryptions, and the number of chosen plaintexts is $6 \times 2^8 \times 2 = 2^{11.6}$.

Table 4. Values needed in Step 2

$X_{R_6}^{(7)}$	$X_{R_2}^{(7)}$
$K_5^{(8)} \oplus K_6^{(8)}$	$K_1^{(8)} \oplus K_2^{(8)}$
$K_4^{(9)} \oplus K_5^{(9)}$	$K_0^{(9)} \oplus K_1^{(9)}$
$K_5^{(9)} \oplus K_6^{(9)}$	$K_1^{(9)} \oplus K_2^{(9)}$
$K_4^{(10)} \oplus K_5^{(10)}$	$K_0^{(10)} \oplus K_1^{(10)}$
$K_5^{(10)} \oplus K_6^{(10)}$	$K_1^{(10)} \oplus K_2^{(10)}$
$K_0^{(10)} \oplus K_6^{(10)} \oplus K_7^{(10)}$	$K_2^{(10)} \oplus K_3^{(10)} \oplus K_4^{(10)}$
$K_4^{(11)} \oplus K_5^{(11)}$	$K_0^{(11)} \oplus K_1^{(11)}$
$K_5^{(11)} \oplus K_6^{(11)}$	$K_1^{(11)} \oplus K_2^{(11)}$
$K_6^{(11)} \oplus K_7^{(11)}$	$K_2^{(11)} \oplus K_3^{(11)}$
$K_0^{(11)} \oplus K_6^{(11)} \oplus K_7^{(11)}$	$K_0^{(11)} \oplus K_6^{(11)} \oplus K_7^{(11)}$
$K_2^{(11)} \oplus K_3^{(11)} \oplus K_4^{(11)}$	$K_2^{(11)} \oplus K_3^{(11)} \oplus K_4^{(11)}$

Step 3: Decrypting the 10th and 11th round with their corresponding round keys obtained in Step 2, we get the output of the 9th round. Then we use the

testing bytes $X_{R_5}^{(6)}$ in distinguisher 1 and $X_{R_1}^{(6)}$ in distinguisher 2, and check whether the XOR of the values in these two positions, which are computed from their corresponding Λ-sets, are zero or not. To compute these values, we need the bytes shown in Table 5 and guess the bytes which do not appear in Tables 3 and 4. After computation we obtain the correct round key of the 9th round with the complexity of $4 \times 2^{4 \times 8} \times 2^8 \times 2 = 2^{43}$ encryptions, and the number of chosen plaintexts needed in this step is $4 \times 2^8 \times 2 = 2^{11}$.

Table 5. Values needed in Step 3

$X_{R_5}^{(6)}$	$X_{R_1}^{(6)}$
$K_4^{(7)} \oplus K_5^{(7)}$	$K_0^{(7)} \oplus K_1^{(7)}$
$K_4^{(8)} \oplus K_5^{(8)}$	$K_0^{(8)} \oplus K_1^{(8)}$
$K_0^{(8)} \oplus K_6^{(8)} \oplus K_7^{(8)}$	$K_2^{(8)} \oplus K_3^{(8)} \oplus K_4^{(8)}$
$K_4^{(9)} \oplus K_5^{(9)}$	$K_0^{(9)} \oplus K_1^{(9)}$
$K_5^{(9)} \oplus K_6^{(9)}$	$K_1^{(9)} \oplus K_2^{(9)}$
$K_6^{(9)} \oplus K_7^{(9)}$	$K_2^{(9)} \oplus K_3^{(9)}$
$K_0^{(9)} \oplus K_6^{(9)} \oplus K_7^{(9)}$	$K_0^{(9)} \oplus K_6^{(9)} \oplus K_7^{(9)}$
$K_2^{(9)} \oplus K_3^{(9)} \oplus K_4^{(9)}$	$K_2^{(9)} \oplus K_3^{(9)} \oplus K_4^{(9)}$

Step 4: Decrypting the 9th round with its round key obtained from Step 3, we get the output of the 8th round. In this step we use the testing byte $X_{R_4}^{(5)}$ in distinguisher 1 and $X_{R_0}^{(5)}$ in distinguisher 2, which are all active. Similarly to Step 3, for computing $X_{R_4}^{(5)}$ and $X_{R_0}^{(5)}$, we need the values shown in Table 6. Since some of these values were determined in previous steps, we only guess the remaining bytes. By computation, the 7th and 8th-round round keys can be

Table 6. Values needed in Step 4

$X_{R_4}^{(5)}$	$X_{R_0}^{(5)}$
$K_0^{(6)} \oplus K_6^{(6)} \oplus K_7^{(6)}$	$K_2^{(6)} \oplus K_3^{(6)} \oplus K_4^{(6)}$
$K_5^{(7)} \oplus K_6^{(7)}$	$K_1^{(7)} \oplus K_2^{(7)}$
$K_6^{(7)} \oplus K_7^{(7)}$	$K_2^{(7)} \oplus K_3^{(7)}$
$K_2^{(7)} \oplus K_3^{(7)} \oplus K_4^{(7)}$	$K_0^{(7)} \oplus K_6^{(7)} \oplus K_7^{(7)}$
$K_1^{(8)} \oplus K_2^{(8)}$	$K_0^{(8)} \oplus K_1^{(8)}$
$K_2^{(8)} \oplus K_3^{(8)}$	$K_1^{(8)} \oplus K_2^{(8)}$
$K_4^{(8)} \oplus K_5^{(8)}$	$K_2^{(8)} \oplus K_3^{(8)}$
$K_5^{(8)} \oplus K_6^{(8)}$	$K_5^{(8)} \oplus K_6^{(8)}$
$K_6^{(8)} \oplus K_7^{(8)}$	$K_6^{(8)} \oplus K_7^{(8)}$
$K_0^{(8)} \oplus K_6^{(8)} \oplus K_7^{(8)}$	$K_2^{(8)} \oplus K_3^{(8)} \oplus K_4^{(8)}$

obtained in this step with complexity of $5 \times 2^{5 \times 8} \times 2^8 \times 2 = 2^{51.3}$ encryptions and $5 \times 2^8 \times 2 = 2^{11.3}$ chosen plaintexts.

Step 5: Decrypting the 7th and 8th rounds with their round keys we get the output of the 6th round. In this step we exploit testing bytes $X_{R_0}^{(4)}$ and $X_{R_1}^{(4)}$ of distinguisher 1 and $X_{R_4}^{(4)}$ and $X_{R_5}^{(4)}$ of distinguisher 2. From Tables 1 and 2, we know that $X_{R_0}^{(4)}$ and $X_{R_4}^{(4)}$ are active and that $X_{R_1}^{(4)}$ and $X_{R_5}^{(4)}$ are balanced. In order to compute these four bytes from the values in their corresponding Λ-sets, we need the bytes shown in Tables 7 and 8, but we only guess some of them with prior knowledge of Table 6.

After computation we obtain the round key for the 6th round with a complexity of $3 \times 2^{3 \times 8} \times 2^8 \times 2 + 2 \times 2^{2 \times 8} \times 2^8 \times 2 \approx 2^{34.6} + 2^{26}$ cipher executions and $3 \times 2^8 \times 2 + 2 \times 2^8 \times 2 = 2^{10.6} + 2^{10}$ chosen plaintexts are needed in all.

Table 7. Values needed in Step 5 (A)

$X_{R_0}^{(4)}$	$X_{R_4}^{(4)}$
$K_2^{(5)} \oplus K_3^{(5)} \oplus K_4^{(5)}$	$K_0^{(5)} \oplus K_6^{(5)} \oplus K_7^{(5)}$
$K_1^{(6)} \oplus K_2^{(6)}$	$K_5^{(6)} \oplus K_6^{(6)}$
$K_2^{(6)} \oplus K_3^{(6)}$	$K_6^{(6)} \oplus K_7^{(6)}$
$K_0^{(6)} \oplus K_6^{(6)} \oplus K_7^{(6)}$	$K_2^{(6)} \oplus K_3^{(6)} \oplus K_4^{(6)}$

Table 8. Values needed in Step 5 (B)

$X_{R_1}^{(4)}$	$X_{R_5}^{(4)}$
$K_0^{(5)} \oplus K_1^{(5)}$	$K_4^{(5)} \oplus K_5^{(5)}$
$K_0^{(6)} \oplus K_1^{(6)}$	$K_4^{(6)} \oplus K_5^{(6)}$
$K_2^{(6)} \oplus K_3^{(6)} \oplus K_4^{(6)}$	$K_0^{(6)} \oplus K_6^{(6)} \oplus K_7^{(6)}$

Step 6: Decrypting the 6th and 7th round with their round keys, we get the output of the 5th round. From Tables 1 and 2, in this step we use the testing bytes: $X_{R_3}^{(4)}$, $X_{R_1}^{(3)}$, and $X_{R_2}^{(3)}$ in distinguisher 1, and $X_{R_7}^{(4)}$, $X_{R_5}^{(3)}$, and $X_{R_6}^{(3)}$ in distinguisher 2. They are all active. To get the round key of the 5th round, we

Table 9. Values needed in Step 6 (for distinguisher 1)

$X_{R_1}^{(3)}$	$X_{R_2}^{(3)}$	$X_{R_3}^{(4)}$
$K_0^{(4)} \oplus K_1^{(4)}$	$K_1^{(4)} \oplus K_2^{(4)}$	$K_2^{(5)} \oplus K_3^{(5)}$
$K_0^{(5)} \oplus K_1^{(5)}$	$K_0^{(5)} \oplus K_1^{(5)}$	
$K_2^{(5)} \oplus K_3^{(5)} \oplus K_4^{(5)}$	$K_1^{(5)} \oplus K_2^{(5)}$	

need to guess some of the values shown in Tables 9 and 10. The computation complexity is $2 \times 2^{2 \times 8} \times 2^8 \times 4 + 2^8 \times 2^8 \times 2 = 2^{27} + 2^{17}$ encryptions and the number of chosen plaintexts is $2 \times 2^8 \times 4 + 2 \times 2^8 = 2^{11} + 2^9$.

Table 10. Values needed in Step 6 (for distinguisher 2)

$X_{R_5}^{(3)}$	$X_{R_6}^{(3)}$	$X_{R_7}^{(4)}$
$K_4^{(4)} \oplus K_5^{(4)}$	$K_5^{(4)} \oplus K_6^{(4)}$	$K_6^{(5)} \oplus K_7^{(5)}$
$K_4^{(5)} \oplus K_5^{(5)}$	$K_4^{(5)} \oplus K_5^{(5)}$	
$K_0^{(5)} \oplus K_6^{(5)} \oplus K_7^{(5)}$	$K_5^{(5)} \oplus K_6^{(5)}$	

Step 7: Decrypting the 5th round, we get the output of the 4th round. In this step, we exploit the testing bytes $X_{R_1}^{(2)}$ and $X_{R_1}^{(0)}$ in distinguisher 1, $X_{R_5}^{(2)}$ and $X_{R_5}^{(0)}$ in distinguisher 2. From Tables 1 and 2, they are all active, and we need the values presented in Tables 11 and 12 to compute these testing bytes. Considering Tables 9 and 10 in mind, we only guess some of them. After computation, with complexity $2 \times 2^{2 \times 8} \times 2^8 \times 2 + 7 \times 2^{7 \times 8} \times 2^8 \times 2 = 2^{26} + 2^{67.8}$, the 4th-round round key can be obtained and $2 \times 2^8 \times 2 + 7 \times 2^8 \times 2 = 2^{10} + 2^{11.8}$ chosen plaintexts must be used in this step.

Table 11. Values needed in Step 7 (for distinguisher 1)

$X_{R_1}^{(2)}$	$X_{R_5}^{(2)}$
$K_0^{(3)} \oplus K_1^{(3)}$	$K_4^{(3)} \oplus K_5^{(3)}$
$K_0^{(4)} \oplus K_1^{(4)}$	$K_4^{(4)} \oplus K_5^{(4)}$
$K_2^{(4)} \oplus K_3^{(4)} \oplus K_4^{(4)}$	$K_0^{(4)} \oplus K_6^{(4)} \oplus K_7^{(4)}$

Step 8: As for the 1st, 2nd and 3rd-round round keys with the relation between them in Tables 11 and 12, we can get them by using key scheduling algorithm three times. According to [1], the main transformation of key schedule includes only two round transformations of the encryption algorithm, so, the complexity of computing the first three round keys can be ignored. Thus, with the results obtained from the previous steps, the complexity of getting a round key for each round of the reduced 12-round Zodiac cipher can be computed as follows:

$$2^{92.3} + 2^{59.6} + 2^{43} + 2^{51.3} + 2^{34.6} + 2^{26} + 2^{27} + 2^{17} + 2^{26} + 2^{67.8} \approx 2^{92.3}.$$

And the whole process needs

$$2^{12.3} + 2^{11.6} + 2^{11} + 2^{11.3} + 2^{10.6} + 2^{10} + 2^{11} + 2^9 + 2^{10} + 2^{11.8} \approx 2^{15.1}$$

chosen plaintexts.

Table 12. Values needed in Step 7 (for distinguisher 2)

$X_{R_1}^{(0)}$	$X_{R_5}^{(0)}$
$K_0^{(1)} \oplus K_1^{(1)}$	$K_4^{(1)} \oplus K_5^{(1)}$
$K_0^{(2)} \oplus K_1^{(2)}$	$K_4^{(2)} \oplus K_5^{(2)}$
$K_2^{(2)} \oplus K_3^{(2)} \oplus K_4^{(2)}$	$K_0^{(2)} \oplus K_6^{(2)} \oplus K_7^{(2)}$
$K_0^{(3)} \oplus K_1^{(3)}$	$K_4^{(3)} \oplus K_5^{(3)}$
$K_1^{(3)} \oplus K_2^{(3)}$	$K_5^{(3)} \oplus K_6^{(3)}$
$K_2^{(3)} \oplus K_3^{(3)}$	$K_6^{(3)} \oplus K_7^{(3)}$
$K_0^{(3)} \oplus K_6^{(3)} \oplus K_7^{(3)}$	$K_0^{(3)} \oplus K_6^{(3)} \oplus K_7^{(3)}$
$K_2^{(3)} \oplus K_3^{(3)} \oplus K_4^{(3)}$	$K_2^{(3)} \oplus K_3^{(3)} \oplus K_4^{(3)}$
$K_0^{(4)} \oplus K_1^{(4)}$	$K_1^{(4)} \oplus K_2^{(4)}$
$K_1^{(4)} \oplus K_2^{(4)}$	$K_2^{(4)} \oplus K_3^{(4)}$
$K_2^{(4)} \oplus K_3^{(4)}$	$K_4^{(4)} \oplus K_5^{(4)}$
$K_5^{(4)} \oplus K_6^{(4)}$	$K_5^{(4)} \oplus K_6^{(4)}$
$K_6^{(4)} \oplus K_7^{(4)}$	$K_6^{(4)} \oplus K_7^{(4)}$
$K_0^{(4)} \oplus K_6^{(4)} \oplus K_7^{(4)}$	$K_0^{(4)} \oplus K_6^{(4)} \oplus K_7^{(4)}$
$K_2^{(4)} \oplus K_3^{(4)} \oplus K_4^{(4)}$	$K_2^{(4)} \oplus K_3^{(4)} \oplus K_4^{(4)}$

4.2 Extended Attack to the 13 and More Round Zodiac

In this subsection the above attack for the 12-round Zodiac is extended to the 13-round Zodiac by adding an additional round at the end. To build the relationship between $(X_{R_7}^{(8)}, X_{R_3}^{(8)})$ and the ciphertext $(X_L^{(13)}, X_R^{(13)})$, we need to guess the bytes presented in the first and second columns of Table 13, respectively. Similarly to the case of the 12-round Zodiac, we need to check whether the XOR of 256 values of $X_{R_7}^{(8)}$ on Λ-set 1 and 256 values of $X_{R_3}^{(8)}$ on Λ-set 2 are zero or not. As Table 13 shown, both $K_0^{(13)} \oplus K_6^{(13)} \oplus K_7^{(13)}$ and $K_2^{(13)} \oplus K_3^{(13)} \oplus K_4^{(13)}$ occur in column 1 and column 2. In order to decrease the computational complexity, we just need to guess one of them in the first column and the other in the second column, that is, we may guess $K_0^{(13)} \oplus K_6^{(13)} \oplus K_7^{(13)}$ in distinguisher 1 and $K_2^{(13)} \oplus K_3^{(13)} \oplus K_4^{(13)}$ in distinguisher 2, respectively. By computation, we get the 13th round key with a complexity of $14 \times 2^{14 \times 8} \times 2^8 \times 2 = 2 \times 14 \times 2^{15 \times 8} \approx 2^{124.8}$ encryptions and using

$$14 \times 2^8 \times 2 + 2^{11.6} + 2^{11} + 2^{11.3} + 2^{10.6} + 2^{10} + 2^{11} + 2^9 + 2^{10} + 2^{11.8} \approx 2^{15.6}$$

chosen plaintexts we can obtain all round keys of the 13-round Zodiac.

Further, we extend this attack to the 14-round Zodiac and get the 14th-round round key by adding a further round at the end of the 13-round Zodiac. To complete the computation we need to guess more values shown in Table 14 besides those in Table 13. It is easy to find that there are repeated bytes in the two columns of Table 14. With the same consideration to Table 13, we only need

Table 13. Values guessed for the 13th round

$X_{R_7}^{(8)}$	$X_{R_3}^{(8)}$
$K_6^{(9)} \oplus K_7^{(9)}$	$K_2^{(9)} \oplus K_3^{(9)}$
$K_5^{(10)} \oplus K_6^{(10)}$	$K_1^{(10)} \oplus K_2^{(10)}$
$K_6^{(10)} \oplus K_7^{(10)}$	$K_2^{(10)} \oplus K_3^{(10)}$
$K_4^{(11)} \oplus K_5^{(11)}$	$K_0^{(11)} \oplus K_1^{(11)}$
$K_5^{(11)} \oplus K_6^{(11)}$	$K_1^{(11)} \oplus K_2^{(11)}$
$K_6^{(11)} \oplus K_7^{(11)}$	$K_2^{(11)} \oplus K_3^{(11)}$
$K_4^{(12)} \oplus K_5^{(12)}$	$K_0^{(12)} \oplus K_1^{(12)}$
$K_5^{(12)} \oplus K_6^{(12)}$	$K_1^{(12)} \oplus K_2^{(12)}$
$K_6^{(12)} \oplus K_7^{(12)}$	$K_2^{(12)} \oplus K_3^{(12)}$
$K_0^{(12)} \oplus K_6^{(12)} \oplus K_7^{(12)}$	$K_2^{(12)} \oplus K_3^{(12)} \oplus K_4^{(12)}$
$K_4^{(13)} \oplus K_5^{(13)}$	$K_0^{(13)} \oplus K_1^{(13)}$
$K_5^{(13)} \oplus K_6^{(13)}$	$K_1^{(13)} \oplus K_2^{(13)}$
$K_6^{(13)} \oplus K_7^{(13)}$	$K_2^{(13)} \oplus K_3^{(13)}$
$K_0^{(13)} \oplus K_6^{(13)} \oplus K_7^{(13)}$	$K_0^{(13)} \oplus K_6^{(13)} \oplus K_7^{(13)}$
$K_2^{(13)} \oplus K_3^{(13)} \oplus K_4^{(13)}$	$K_2^{(13)} \oplus K_3^{(13)} \oplus K_4^{(13)}$

Table 14. Values guessed for the 14th round

$X_{R_7}^{(8)}$	$X_{R_3}^{(8)}$
$K_1^{(14)} \oplus K_2^{(14)}$	$K_0^{(14)} \oplus K_1^{(14)}$
$K_2^{(14)} \oplus K_3^{(14)}$	$K_1^{(14)} \oplus K_2^{(14)}$
$K_4^{(14)} \oplus K_5^{(14)}$	$K_2^{(14)} \oplus K_3^{(14)}$
$K_5^{(14)} \oplus K_6^{(14)}$	$K_5^{(14)} \oplus K_6^{(14)}$
$K_6^{(14)} \oplus K_7^{(14)}$	$K_6^{(14)} \oplus K_7^{(14)}$
$K_0^{(14)} \oplus K_6^{(14)} \oplus K_7^{(14)}$	$K_0^{(14)} \oplus K_6^{(14)} \oplus K_7^{(14)}$
$K_2^{(14)} \oplus K_3^{(14)} \oplus K_4^{(14)}$	$K_2^{(14)} \oplus K_3^{(14)} \oplus K_4^{(14)}$

to guess half of these bytes in one column and the remains in the other column for decreasing the computational complexity.

The complexity of getting the 14th-round round key is

$$18 \times 2^{18 \times 8} \times 2^8 \times 2 = 2 \times 18 \times 2^{19 \times 8} \approx 2^{157.2}$$

encryptions and we can get all round keys of the reduced 14-round Zodiac with

$$18 \times 2^8 \times 2 + 2^{11.6} + 2^{11} + 2^{11.3} + 2^{10.6} + 2^{10} + 2^{11} + 2^9 + 2^{10} + 2^{11.8} \approx 2^{16}$$

chosen plaintexts.

For attacking on the 15-round Zodiac, we need to guess values in Table 15 and the values present in Tables 13 and 14. And for the repeated bytes we just guess half of them in the first column and another half in the second column in each table. Thus, the computation complexity is

$$22 \times 2^{22 \times 8} \times 2^8 \times 2 = 2 \times 22 \times 2^{23 \times 8} \approx 2^{189.5}$$

and

$$22 \times 2^8 \times 2 + 2^{11.6} + 2^{11} + 2^{11.3} + 2^{10.6} + 2^{10} + 2^{11} + 2^9 + 2^{10} + 2^{11.8} \approx 2^{16.3}$$

chosen plaintexts are used to obtain all the round keys of the 15-round Zodiac.

Table 15. Values guessed for the 15th round

$X^{(8)}_{R_7}$	$X^{(8)}_{R_3}$
$K_0^{(15)} \oplus K_1^{(15)}$	$K_0^{(15)} \oplus K_1^{(15)}$
$K_1^{(15)} \oplus K_2^{(15)}$	$K_1^{(15)} \oplus K_2^{(15)}$
$K_2^{(15)} \oplus K_3^{(15)}$	$K_2^{(15)} \oplus K_3^{(15)}$
$K_4^{(15)} \oplus K_5^{(15)}$	$K_4^{(15)} \oplus K_5^{(15)}$
$K_5^{(15)} \oplus K_6^{(15)}$	$K_5^{(15)} \oplus K_6^{(15)}$
$K_6^{(15)} \oplus K_7^{(15)}$	$K_6^{(15)} \oplus K_7^{(15)}$
$K_0^{(15)} \oplus K_6^{(15)} \oplus K_7^{(15)}$	$K_0^{(15)} \oplus K_6^{(15)} \oplus K_7^{(15)}$
$K_2^{(15)} \oplus K_3^{(15)} \oplus K_4^{(15)}$	$K_2^{(15)} \oplus K_3^{(15)} \oplus K_4^{(15)}$

Finally, we extend the attack to the full round Zodiac. In this case we need to guess the bytes shown in Tables 13–16. Also, the bytes in these tables are not guessed repeatedly. After computation, we can obtain the 16th-round round key with the complexity

Table 16. Values guessed for the full 16th round

$X^{(8)}_{R_7}$	$X^{(8)}_{R_3}$
$K_0^{(16)} \oplus K_1^{(16)}$	$K_0^{(16)} \oplus K_1^{(16)}$
$K_1^{(16)} \oplus K_2^{(16)}$	$K_1^{(16)} \oplus K_2^{(16)}$
$K_2^{(16)} \oplus K_3^{(16)}$	$K_2^{(16)} \oplus K_3^{(16)}$
$K_4^{(16)} \oplus K_5^{(16)}$	$K_4^{(16)} \oplus K_5^{(16)}$
$K_5^{(16)} \oplus K_6^{(16)}$	$K_5^{(16)} \oplus K_6^{(16)}$
$K_6^{(16)} \oplus K_7^{(16)}$	$K_6^{(16)} \oplus K_7^{(16)}$
$K_0^{(16)} \oplus K_6^{(16)} \oplus K_7^{(16)}$	$K_0^{(16)} \oplus K_6^{(16)} \oplus K_7^{(16)}$
$K_2^{(16)} \oplus K_3^{(16)} \oplus K_4^{(16)}$	$K_2^{(16)} \oplus K_3^{(16)} \oplus K_4^{(16)}$

$$26 \times 2^{26 \times 8} \times 2^8 \times 2 = 2 \times 26 \times 2^{27 \times 8} \approx 2^{221.7}$$

cipher executions. In this case we need

$$26 \times 2^8 \times 2 + 2^{11.6} + 2^{11} + 2^{11.3} + 2^{10.6} + 2^{10} + 2^{11} + 2^9 + 2^{10} + 2^{11.8} \approx 2^{16.5}$$

chosen plaintexts to obtain each round key of the full round Zodiac.

The computational complexity of the Square attack on different cases of reduced-round Zodiac ciphers is listed in Table 17.

Table 17. Complexity and the number of plaintexts

Round Num.	Plaintext	Complexity
12	$2^{15.1}$	$2^{92.3}$
13	$2^{15.6}$	$2^{124.8}$
14	2^{16}	$2^{157.2}$
15	$2^{16.3}$	$2^{189.5}$
16	$2^{16.5}$	$2^{221.7}$

5 Conclusion

The Square attack on the Zodiac cipher is discussed in this paper. We presented a basic 9-round attack and extended it detailedly to 12, 13, 14, 15 and the full round Zodiac. The corresponding complexities of attack on the 12 to 16-round Zodiac are $2^{92.3}$, $2^{124.8}$, $2^{157.2}$, $2^{189.5}$, and $2^{221.7}$ encryptions. And in order to obtain all the round keys of the full round Zodiac we just need $2^{16.5}$ chosen plaintexts, which is much smaller than the case $2^{103.6}$ of impossible differential cryptanalysis. The attacks presented in this paper show again that the Square attack works not only against block ciphers with similar structure as the Square cipher but also against the Feistel-like ciphers.

References

[1] Lee, C., Jun, K., Jung, M., Park, S., Kim, J.: Zodiac Version 1.0 (revised) Architecture and Specification, Standardization Workshop on Information Security Technology, Korean Contribution on MP18033, ISO/IEC JTC1/SC27 N2563, 2000 (2000), http://www.kisa.or.kr/seed/index.html
[2] Hong, D., Sung, J., Moriai, S., Lee, S., Lim, J.: Impossible Differential Cryptanalysis of Zodiac. In: Matsui, M. (ed.) FSE 2001. LNCS, vol. 2355, pp. 300–311. Springer, Heidelberg (2002)
[3] Daemen, J., Knudsen, L., Rijmen, V.: The Block Cipher Square. In: Biham, E. (ed.) FSE 1997. LNCS, vol. 1267, pp. 149–165. Springer, Heidelberg (1997)
[4] Lucks, S.: The Saturation Attack - a Bait for Twofish. In: Matsui, M. (ed.) FSE 2001. LNCS, vol. 2355, pp. 1–15. Springer, Heidelberg (2002)

[5] D'Halluin, C., Bijnens, G., Rijmen, V., Preneel, B.: Attack on Six Rounds of Crypton. In: Knudsen, L.R. (ed.) FSE 1999. LNCS, vol. 1636, pp. 46–59. Springer, Heidelberg (1999)
[6] Ferguson, N., Kelsey, J., Lucks, S., Schneier, B., Stay, M., Wagner, D., Whiting, D.: Improved Cryptanalysis of Rijndael. In: Schneier, B. (ed.) FSE 2000. LNCS, vol. 1978, pp. 213–230. Springer, Heidelberg (2001)
[7] Knudsen, L., Wagner, D.: Integral cryptanalysis. In: Daemen, J., Rijmen, V. (eds.) FSE 2002. LNCS, vol. 2365, pp. 112–127. Springer, Heidelberg (2002)
[8] Yeom, Y., Park, S., Kim, I.: On the Security of Camellia against the Square Attack. In: Daemen, J., Rijmen, V. (eds.) FSE 2002. LNCS, vol. 2365, pp. 89–99. Springer, Heidelberg (2002)
[9] Hwang, K., Lee, W., Lee, S., Lee, S., Lim, J.: Saturation Attacks on Reduced Round Skipjack. In: Daemen, J., Rijmen, V. (eds.) FSE 2002. LNCS, vol. 2365, pp. 100–111. Springer, Heidelberg (2002)
[10] Wu, W., Zhang, W., Feng, D.: Improved Integral Cryptanalysis of FOX Block Cipher. In: Won, D.H., Kim, S. (eds.) ICISC 2005. LNCS, vol. 3935, pp. 229–241. Springer, Heidelberg (2006)
[11] He, Y., Qing, S.: Square Attack on Reduced Camellia Cipher. In: Qing, S., Okamoto, T., Zhou, J. (eds.) ICICS 2001. LNCS, vol. 2229, pp. 238–245. Springer, Heidelberg (2001)

Analysis of Zipper as a Hash Function

Pin Lin[1,3], Wenling Wu[1], Chuankun Wu[1], and Tian Qiu[2,3]

[1] The State Key Laboratory of Information Security, Institute of Software,
Chinese Academy of Sciences
[2] National Key Laboratory of Integrated Information System Technology,
Institute of Software, Chinese Academy of Sciences
[3] Graduate School of Chinese Academy of Sciences

Abstract. At CRYPTO 2005, Coron etc. proposed several modified methods to make the usual hash functions based on MD method indifferentiable from random oracles. However, the compression functions used in Coron's schemes are supposed to be random oracles. This assumption is too strong. To achieve Coron's goal in the real world, Liskov proposed Zipper structure and implemented a new scheme indifferentiable from random oracle based on this structure. Unlike Coron's schemes, the indifferentiability of Liskov's scheme does not depend on strong compression functions and insecure compression functions can be used to implement Liskov's scheme. In this paper, we show that the security of Liskov's scheme is not ideal as a hash function. We also analyze those Zipper schemes whose compression functions are insecure PGV compression functions instead of Liskov's weak compression functions, and we find that some insecure PGV compression functions whose security is stronger than Liskov's weak compression function cannot be used to build indifferentiable and collision-resistant Zipper schemes.

Keywords: Zipper, Hash Function, Compression Function.

1 Introduction

A hash function is a mapping from an arbitrary-length input to a fixed-length output and it can be described as follows.

$$H : \{0,1\}^* \to \{0,1\}^n$$

Merkle-Damgård method (abbreviated to MD method) is an important method which is widely used to build hash functions [4,15]. Most hash functions used in practice are based on this method, such as MD4 [17], MD5 [18], SHA-0 [5], SHA-1 [6] etc. These hash functions are also called MD hash functions. MD method is also named iterated method and can be described as follows.

$$h_0 = IV$$
$$h_i = f(h_{i-1}, m_i), 1 \le i \le l$$
$$H(m) = h_l$$

where f and IV denote respectively a compression function and the fixed initial value of the hash function, $h_1, \cdots, h_l$ denote chain values, H denotes the hash function built on f, $m = m_1, \cdots, m_l$ denotes the input message which is padded with some padding rule and divided into l blocks. The most important padding rule is called MD-Strengthening rule which appends 1 to the message and then appends enough 0s to make the padded length a multiple of $|m_i|$ and finally stores the binary length of the original message into the last block i.e. m_l. Lai etc. pointed out that if the message processed by a hash function is not padded with MD-Strengthening rule, it is possible to construct an effective attack to find its collisions [12].

A secure(ideal) hash function must resist collision attack, pre-image attack and second pre-image attack. The three types of attacks can be described as the following [11].

Definition 1 (collision attack). *Given a hash function H and its initial value (IV) h_0, find m and m' where $m \neq m'$ such that $H(h_0, m) = H(h_0, m')$.*

Definition 2 (pre-image attack). *Given a hash function H and its initial value(IV) h_0 and a randomly selected value σ, find m such that $H(h_0, m) = \sigma$.*

Definition 3 (second pre-image attack). *Given a hash function H and its initial value(IV) h_0 and m, find $m' \neq m$ such that $H(h_0, m) = H(h_0, m')$.*

In the above, H denotes a hash function, m and m' denote different messages, h_0 denotes the initial value. Assuming the output length of a hash function is n bit, the complexity to find a collision and a (second)pre-image for a secure(ideal) hash function should be $O(2^{\frac{n}{2}})$ and $O(2^n)$ respectively. The secure hash function above is also called collision resistant and (second)pre-image resistant hash function. The three attacks above are also called generic attacks. Except the generic attacks mentioned above, there are some other attacks on hash functions.

Definition 4 (multicollision attack). *An r-way collision is an r-tuple messages: $m^1, m^2, \cdots, m^r$ such that $H(IV, m^1) = H(IV, m^2) = \cdots = H(IV, m^r)$, where H denotes a hash function and IV is the initial value of it.*

Here H denotes a hash function, IV denotes the initial value, $m^1, \cdots, m^r$ denote different messages. If a hash function behaves randomly, the complexity to find r-way collision for it should be $O(2^{\frac{n(r-1)}{r}})$ [19]. However, Joux has shown that the complexity to find 2^t-way collision for a usual MD hash function is only $O(t2^{\frac{n}{2}})$ [8]. Kelsey etc. made use of Joux's tricks to construct an effective second pre-image attack [10] and herding attack [9] for usual MD hash functions, both of them are based on multicollision attack. Therefore, if a hash function which could resist multicollision attack is used, Kelsey's attacks will fail. Lucks proposed a double-pipe hash function and a wide-pipe hash function to resist multicollision attack [14]. Lucks improved the complexity of finding a collision for a compression function from $O(2^{n/2})$ to $O(2^n)$ by extending the length of chain values from n bit to $2n$ bit. This trick makes the usual multicollision attack impossible.

Merkle and Damgård proved that if the compression function is collision resistant, the MD hash function built on it is also collision resistant. Therefore, a secure compression function is the most important component in a MD hash function. However, sometimes, a secure compression function is insufficient to ensure the security of a MD hash function. The **MAC** scheme described below is a widely known example.

$$\mathbf{MAC}(K, m) = H(IV, K\|m)$$

where m denotes the message, H denotes a MD hash function, K denotes the secret key and $\|$ denotes the concatenation of two binary strings. Obviously, secure hash functions cannot guarantee the security of this scheme. Assuming we have got $h = H(IV, K\|m)$, then we can forge the **MAC** of $m\|y$ by computing $H(h, y)$ without knowing the secret key. However, if the hash function is a random oracle, the forgery is computationally infeasible. Coron etc. modified the usual MD method and made hash functions based on the modified methods indifferentiable from random oracles. If a hash function is indifferentiable from random oracle, it can be used as a substitution of random oracle without decreasing the security level. The definition of indifferentiability is as blow.

Definition 5. *[3] A Turing machine C with oracle access to an ideal primitive G is said to be $(t_D, t_S, q, \varepsilon)$ indifferentiable from an ideal primitive F if there exists a simulator S, such that for any distinguisher D it holds that:*

$$|Pr[D^{C,G} = 1] - Pr[D^{F,S} = 1]| < \varepsilon$$

where an ideal primitive is a block-box whose internal details are unavailable such as a random oracle or a compression function. The simulator has oracle access to F and runs in time at most t_S. The distinguisher runs in time t_D and makes at most q queries. Similarly, C^G is said to be (computationally) indifferentiable from F if ε is a negligible function of the security parameter k (for polynomially bounded t_D and t_S).

Coron etc. proposed four modified methods coming from the original MD method. However, the compression functions used in Coron's schemes are supposed to be random oracles. This assumption is too strong. To achieve Coron's goal in the real world, Liskov proposed Zipper structure and implement a new scheme indifferentiable from random oracle based on this structure [13]. Unlike Coron's schemes, Zipper can be implemented with insecure compression functions instead of random oracles. In this paper, We firstly review Zipper structure and Liskov's scheme and then in section 2 we show that Liskov's scheme is not ideal as a hash function under pre-image attack and second pre-image attack. We also analyze those Zipper schemes which are implemented with insecure PGV compression functions instead of Liskov's weak compression functions, and we find that some insecure PGV compression functions whose security is stronger than Liskov's weak compression functions cannot be used to build indifferentiable and collision-resistant Zipper hash functions.

1.1 Description of Zipper Structure and Liskov's Zipper

Unlike the usual MD hash functions, Zipper structure iterates two weak compression functions and can be described as the following.

$$Mid = f_0(m_l, \cdots, f_0(m_3, f_0(m_2, f_0(m_1, IV))) \cdots)$$
$$Out = f_1(m_1, \cdots, f_1(m_{l-2}, f_1(m_{l-1}, f_1(m_l, Mid))) \cdots)$$

where f_0 and f_1 are two different compression functions. See figure 1 for a more clear description. In Liskov's scheme(Liskov's Zipper), f_0 and f_1 are two weak

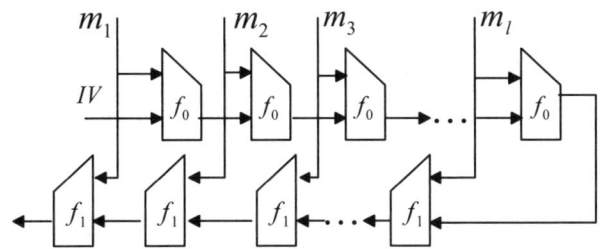

Fig. 1. Zipper structure description

compression functions. Likov showed that a weak compression function is a kind of compression function which has the following two oracles [13].

1. querying f^{-1} on input (x, z), the oracle f^{-1} returns a random value y such that $f(x,y) = z$.
2. querying f^* on input (y, z), the oracle f^* return a random value x such that $f(x,y) = z$.

In the above, f denotes a compression function, f^{-1} and f^* denote two oracles of f. Obviously, weak compression functions are susceptible to any generic attack. Weak compression functions cannot be used simply in MD method. It has been shown that Liskov's Zipper hash function which is based on weak compression functions is indifferentiable from random oracle. However, Liskov's Zipper is not sufficiently ideal as a hash function, and we give analysis in detail in the following sections.

2 Security Analysis of Liskov's Zipper as a Hash Function

As mentioned above, a secure hash function should be collision attack resistant, pre-image attack resistant and second pre-image attack resistant, and in some special circumstance, a hash function needs to be indifferentiable from random oracle or resist multicollision attack. It has been shown that Liskov's Zipper is indifferentiable from random oracle, which implies collision attack resistant. In the remaining part of this section, we analyze the security of Liskov's Zipper under pre-image attack, second pre-image attack and multicollision attack. We will show that the security of Liskov's Zipper under pre-image attack and second pre-image attack is not ideal and its security under multicollision attack is weaker than the usual MD hash functions.

2.1 Notation

We define a number of notions that are used in this section. $x \leftarrow y$ denotes assigning the value of y to x. $x \xleftarrow{\$} \{0,1\}^n$ denotes randomly selecting a value from $\{0,1\}^n$ and assigning it to x. f denotes a weak compression function and f^*, f^{-1} denote the random oracles mentioned above. $h_{out}, h_{i,j} (i=0,1; j=1,\cdots,l)$ and IV denote the chain values. n denotes the bit length of output and H_S denotes the set of chain values.

2.2 Security Bound of Liskov's Zipper under Pre-image Attack

Our pre-image attack on Zipper can be described as follows.

Step 1. $h_{out} \xleftarrow{\$} \{0,1\}^n$. The following steps below will find a pre-image for h_{out}

Step 2. $h_{1,1} \xleftarrow{\$} \{0,1\}^n$, query oracle f_1^* on $(h_{out}, h_{1,1})$ to get a message pair $(m_1, m_1^{'})$ such that

$$f_1(h_{1,1}, m_1) = f_1(h_{1,1}, m_1^{'}) = h_{out}$$

Then for each $i \in \{2, 3, \cdots, n/2-1\}$, $h_{1,i} \xleftarrow{\$} \{0,1\}^n$, query f_1^* on $(h_{1,i-1}, h_{1,i})$ to find a pair $(m_i, m_i^{'})$ such that

$$f_1(h_{1,i}, m_i) = f_1(h_{1,i}, m_i^{'}) = h_{1,i-1}$$

Step 3. Assuming that the message is padded by MD-Strengthening padding rules and the last block needs to store the length of the whole message, so the last message block $m_{n/2+1}$ remains intact. Then query f_1^{-1} oracle on $(h_{1,n/2-1}, m_{n/2+1})$ to get $h_{1,n/2}$ such that

$$f_1(h_{1,n/2}, m_{n/2+1}) = h_{1,n/2-1}$$

Query f_1^{-1} oracles $2^{n/2}$ times to get a set H_S which contains $2^{n/2}$ values for $h_{1,n/2}$.

Step 4. At last, the output value of the f_0 line should fall in the set H_S according to the figure of Zipper. Let C denote the event that the output value falls in H_S then $\mathbf{Pr}[C] = \frac{1}{2^{n/2}}$. After step 2, there are $2^{n/2}$ different messages for choice and make the probability $\mathbf{Pr}[C]$ innegligible.

In the attack above, the first step randomly selects a target value for which a pre-image will be found, the second step uses the f^* oracle to construct a collision at each step, the third step constructs a sufficiently large set of chain values for the next step and the fourth step finds a matching in the set. From the attack demonstrated above, the following theorem can be concluded.

Theorem 1. *The complexity of pre-image attack for Liskov's Zipper is* $n + (\frac{n}{2} + 1)2^{n/2}$.

Proof. In step 2, the number of queries on oracle on f_1^* is n. In step 3, the number of queries on oracle on f_1^* is $2^{n/2}$. In step 4, to find the matching in the set, all the $2^{n/2}$ messages may be processed and each of them has $n/2$ blocks. Thus the total number of queries on oracles will be $n + (\frac{n}{2} + 1)2^{n/2}$.

Figure 2 illustrates the above pre-image attack in a clear way.

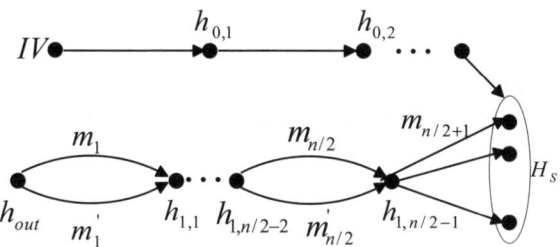

Fig. 2. pre-image attack and second pre-image attack on Liskov's Zipper

2.3 Security Bound of Liskov's Zipper under Second Pre-image Attack

Our second pre-image attack is similar to the above pre-image attack and can also be described in figure 2. The difference is only at the first step. Our second pre-image attack can be shown as follows.

Step 1. Randomly chose message M and then compute $h_{out} = Z(IV, M)$, where Z denotes a Liskov's Zipper hash function. The attack will find another message M' such that $Z(IV, M') = h_{out}$.

Step 2. $h_{1,1} \xleftarrow{\$} \{0,1\}^n$, query oracle f_1^* on $(h_{out}, h_{1,1})$ to get a message pair (m_1, m_1') such that

$$f_1(h_{1,1}, m_1) = f_1(h_{1,1}, m_1') = h_{out}$$

Then for each $i \in \{2, 3, \cdots, n/2-1\}$, $h_{1,i} \xleftarrow{\$} \{0,1\}^n$, query f_1^* on $(h_{1,i-1}, h_{1,i})$ to find a pair (m_i, m_i') such that

$$f_1(h_{1,i}, m_i) = f_1(h_{1,i}, m_i') = h_{1,i-1}$$

Step 3. Assuming that the message is padded by MD-Strengthening padding rules and the last block needs to store the length of the whole message, so the last message block $m_{n/2+1}$ remains intact. Then query f_1^{-1} oracle on $(h_{1,n/2-1}, m_{n/2+1})$ to get $h_{1,n/2}$ such that

$$f_1(h_{1,n/2}, m_{n/2+1}) = h_{1,n/2-1}$$

Query f_1^{-1} oracles $2^{n/2}$ times to get a set H_S which contains $2^{n/2}$ values for $h_{1,n/2}$.

Step 4. At last, the output value of the f_0 line should fall in the set H_S according to the figure of Zipper. Let C denote the event that the output value falls in H_S then $\mathbf{Pr}[C] = \frac{1}{2^{n/2}}$. After step 2, there are $2^{n/2}$ different messages for choice and make the probability $\mathbf{Pr}[C]$ innegligible. If it is done, a second pre-image is found.

In the first step, the target value for which a second pre-image will be found is selected, in the second step, f^* oracle is used to construct a collision at each step, in the third step a sufficiently large set of chain values is constructed for the next step and in the fourth step a matching in the set is found. It should be noted that the second pre-image found in the attack above does not need to be as long as the original message. Actually, the second pre-image attack and the pre-image attack in this paper is only related to the final output value. The following theorem gives the complexity of our second pre-image attack.

Theorem 2. *The complexity of second pre-image attack for Liskov's Zipper is* $n + (\frac{n}{2} + 1)2^{n/2}$.

Proof. the proof is the same as the one for theorem 1.

It should be noted that we used a padding rule in the two attacks above. However, in [13], no padding rules are recommended. Actually it does not affect the complexity of the two attacks whether a padding rule is used. We use the padding rule just because it is needed in practice.

2.4 Security of Liskov's Zipper under Multicollision Attack

The messages for Zipper can be regarded as $M = m\|p(m)$, where $p()$ is a permutation, and in Zipper, $p()$ reverses the order of original message blocks. Zipper can be regarded as nested two hash functions such that

$$Z(IV, m) = H_1(H_0(IV, m), p(m))$$

where H_0 denotes the hash function built on f_0, H_1 denotes the one built on f_1 and Z denotes a Zipper hash function. Hoch etc. proved that all schemes in concatenated or nested way cannot resist multicollision attack [7]. The hash functions discussed in [7] are usual MD hash functions whose compression functions are random oracles. However, the compression functions in Liskov's scheme are weak compression functions, so the multicollision attack on Liskov's scheme is much easier than on the scheme which combines two usual MD hash functions. In the following analysis, it is shown that the complexity to find 2^t collisions for H_0 is only $O(t)$ instead of $O(t2^{n/2})$ if weak compression functions are used. Our multicollision attack on Liskov's scheme can be shown as follows.

Step 1. $h_1 \xleftarrow{\$} \{0,1\}^n$, query oracle f_0^* on (IV, h_1) to get a message pair $(m_1, m_1^{'})$ such that
$$f_0(IV, m_1) = f_0(IV, m_1^{'}) = h_1.$$

Then for each $i \in \{2, 3, \cdots, l-1\}$, $h_i \xleftarrow{\$} \{0,1\}^n$, query f_0^* on (h_{i-1}, h_i) to find a pair (m_i, m_i') such that

$$f_0(h_{i-1}, m_i) = f_0(h_{i-1}, m_i') = h_i$$

After $l-1$ steps, there are 2^{l-1} messages whose outputs are h_l.

Step 2. For H_1, divide the $l-1$ message blocks except the last block into $\frac{2(l-1)}{n}$ groups each of which contains $\frac{n}{2}$ message blocks. According to the message blocks found at step 1, there are $2^{n/2}$ different messages in each group. Then a birthday attack can be implemented to find a collision for each group with a high probability. Assuming $\frac{2(l-1)}{n} = t$, then 2^t collisions for H_1 are found.

In the first step, 2^l collisions are found for H_0 and in the second step, those message blocks found in the first step are divided into t groups to find 2^t collisions for H_1. Figure 3 describes this attack in a more clear way.

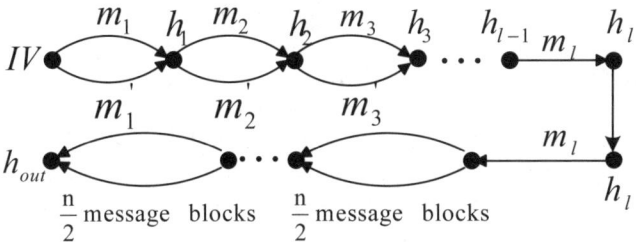

Fig. 3. multicollision attack on Liskov's Zipper

Theorem 3. *The complexity to find 2^t collisions for Liskov's Zipper is $O(t2^{n/2})$ if $\frac{2(l-1)}{n} = t$, where l is the amount of message blocks and n is the output length.*

Proof. The complexity to find multicollision in step 1 is $O(l)$ which is negligible. The complexity to find a collision for each group in step 2 is $O(2^{n/2})$ and there are t such groups. It can be concluded that The complexity to find 2^t collisions is $O(t2^{n/2})$.

The concatenation of any traditional MD hash function cannot resist multicollision attack [7]. Liskov's Zipper is weaker than the concatenation of two MD hash functions. Moreover the analysis of the second pre-image attack and the pre-image attack shows that Liskov's Zipper as a hash function is a weaker hash function than a MD hash function. However, Liskov's Zipper can be used when the message blocks are too few to implement our attacks. For example, Liskov's Zipper can be used to build an ideal compression function as follows:

$$f(h_{i-1}, m_i) = Z(IV, h_{i-1} \| m_i)$$

where h_{i-1} denotes the chain value, m_i denotes a message block and Z denotes a Liskov's Zipper hash function.

3 Implementation of Zipper Hash Function

Practicability is one of the most important aspects for a hash function. Without considering the strength of compression functions, Zipper can be implemented with all compression functions used in practice. It essentially requires two traditional compression functions, yet if the traditional compression functions are employed, Zipper hash function will be slower than a MD hash function. However, the compression function used in Zipper can be a weak one, therefore, if weak compression functions run faster than those stronger ones, the problem will be well solved. In this paper, we focus on 64 PGV schemes [16]. PGV schemes are compression functions based on block ciphers and firstly discussed by Preneel etc. who focus on attacks on those schemes instead of the formal proofs. They claimed that 12 of the 64 schemes are secure. Afterwards, Black etc. proved the security of all PGV schemes in the black-box model and find that 20 of the 64 schemes are collision resistant and the others are not [2]. The 20 collision-resistant schemes, however, need to schedule the keys for block ciphers at each step because the keys for each step should be different. It is widely accepted that scheduling keys at each step makes the hash functions base on block cipher slow. Among the remaining 44 insecure schemes, some do not need to schedule the keys at each step and they are faster than those stronger ones. We call these faster compression functions highly efficient compression functions. These schemes are listed in table 1. In table 1, E denotes a block cipher, i and j denote respectively the index in this paper and the corresponding index in Black's paper, Y and N denote whether the scheme can be used or cannot be used to implement Zipper. Obviously, there is only one key for these scheme, so key schedule is not necessary.

Liskov used weak compression functions to implement a Zipper hash function which is indifferentiable and collision resistant. In table 1, we find that the weaker ones such as the first 7 schemes whose security is weaker than Liskov's compression functions cannot be used to implemented Zipper and the stronger ones such as the 8-th scheme cannot either. Comparing the 8-th scheme with Liskov's weak compression function, it is obvious that the former is stronger. For example, for a weak compression function $f(x, y) = z$, querying oracle f^* on (y, z), the oracle randomly returns a value x' such that $f(x, y) = f(x', y) = z$. It is impossible to find two different x and x' such that $E_v(x) \oplus y = E_v(x') \oplus y$ if E is an ideal cipher.

For the 8-th scheme in table 1, its output is independent of the sequence of the message blocks. If a MD hash function H is built on this compression function, we have

$$H(IV, (m_1, m_2, \cdots, m_l)) = H(IV, (m_{i_1}, m_{i_2}, \cdots, m_{i_l}))$$
$$= E_v(m_1) \oplus E_v(m_2) \oplus \cdots \oplus E_v(m_l) \oplus IV$$

where $\{i_1, i_2, \cdots, i_l\}$ denotes a permutation on $\{1, 2, \cdots, l\}$. If it is used to implement Zipper, it is easy to find a collision. For example, $m = (m_1, m_2, \cdots, m_l)$ and $m' = (m_l, m_{l-1}, \cdots, m_1)$ are two collision messages. The 9-th scheme and the 10-th scheme are the same as the 8-th one.

highly efficient compression functions [1]. Actually it is impossible if the messages are processed only once by these highly efficient compression functions, but in Zipper, the messages are processed twice. Zipper partly and positively answers the question whether there are collision-resistant hash functions based on highly efficient compression functions although the scheme is not sufficiently efficient.

The speed comparison between the highly efficient compression functions and the secure compression functions when they are used in Zipper structure is shown in figure 4. We choose the 8-th scheme in the table as the highly efficient PGV function and choose $E_{m_i}(h_{i-1}) \oplus h_{i-1}$ as the secure PGV function. Figure 4 shows time cost of the two functions when the same message blocks are processed. It is obvious that the weaker one is more efficient.

4 Conclusion

In this paper, we analyzed the security of Liskov's Zipper as a hash function. It is shown that the complexity of second pre-image and pre-image attack on this scheme is $O(2^{n/2})$ instead of the ideal one $O(2^n)$. Actually, Liskov's scheme can be indifferentiable from random oracle and it could be used to build ideal compression functions when the input message blocks are too few to implement our attacks. The result in this paper does not contradict the properties of Liskov's Zipper, and shows that only indifferentiability is not sufficient to build a secure hash function. On the other hand, Zipper is a good method to build collision-resistant hash functions using weak compression functions. Since the compression functions are weak, it should be more careful to implement Zipper. In this paper, we find that some compression functions whose security is stronger than Liskov's weak compression function cannot be used to implement a Zipper hash function which is collision resistant and indifferentiable from random oracle. Another defect of Zipper is its low efficiency. Compared with the traditional MD method, Zipper has lower efficiency even employing highly efficient compression functions. As a future research point, we focus on improving the efficiency of Zipper. Another interesting future work is to find a weak compression function to build a secure Zipper hash function where 'secure' means collision attack resistant, second pre-image attack resistant and pre-image attack resistant.

Acknowledgement

We would like to sincerely thank Prof. X. Lai and those anonymous reviewers for their valuable comments. This work is supported by National Natural Science Foundation of China (Grant No. 90604036), Major State Basic Research Development Program of China (973 Program, Grant No: 2004CB318004) and National High-Tech Research and Development Program of China (863 Program, Grant No: 2007AA01Z470).

References

1. Black, J., Cochran, M., Shrimpton, T.: On the Impossibility of Highly-Efficient Blockcipher-Based Hash Functions. In: Cramer, R.J.F. (ed.) EUROCRYPT 2005. LNCS, vol. 3494, pp. 526–541. Springer, Heidelberg (2005)
2. Black, J., Rogaway, P., Shrimpton, T.: Black-box analysis of the block-cipher based hash function constructions from PGV. In: Yung, M. (ed.) CRYPTO 2002. LNCS, vol. 2442, pp. 320–335. Springer, Heidelberg (2002)
3. Coron, J., Dodis, Y., Malinaud, C., Puniya, P.: Merkle-Damgård revisited:How to Construct a Hash Function. In: Shoup, V. (ed.) CRYPTO 2005. LNCS, vol. 3621, pp. 55–70. Springer, Heidelberg (2005)
4. Damgård, I.B.: A Design Principle for Hash Functions. In: Brassard, G. (ed.) CRYPTO 1989. LNCS, vol. 435, pp. 416–427. Springer, Heidelberg (1990)
5. FIPS 180-1, Secure Hash Standard, Federal Information Processing Standard, Publication 180-1, NIST (1995)
6. FIPS 180-2, Secure Hash Standard, Federal Information Processing Standard, Publication 180-2, NIST (2003)
7. Hoch, J., Shamir, A.: Breaking the ICE-Finding Multicollisions in IteratedConcatenated and Expanded(ICE) Hash Functions. In: Robshaw, M.J.B. (ed.) FSE 2006. LNCS, vol. 4047, pp. 179–194. Springer, Heidelberg (2006)
8. Joux, A.: Multicollisions in Iterated Hash Functions: Application to Cascaded Constructions. In: Franklin, M. (ed.) CRYPTO 2004. LNCS, vol. 3152, pp. 306–316. Springer, Heidelberg (2004)
9. Kelsey, J., Kohno, T.: Herding Hash Functions and the Nostradamus Attack. In: Vaudenay, S. (ed.) EUROCRYPT 2006. LNCS, vol. 4004, pp. 183–200. Springer, Heidelberg (2006)
10. Kelsey, J., Schneier, B.: Second Preimages on n-Bit Hash Functions for Much Less than 2^n Work. In: Cramer, R.J.F. (ed.) EUROCRYPT 2005. LNCS, vol. 3494, pp. 474–490. Springer, Heidelberg (2005)
11. Knudsen, L., Lai, X., Preneel, B.: Attacks on Fast Double Block Length Hash Functions. J. Cryptology. 11, 59–72 (1998)
12. Lai, X., Massey, J.: Hash Functions Based on Blcok Ciphers. In: Rueppel, R.A. (ed.) EUROCRYPT 1992. LNCS, vol. 658, pp. 55–70. Springer, Heidelberg (1993)
13. Liskov, M.: Constructing an Ideal Hash Function from Weak Ideal Compression Functions. In: Biham, E., Youssef, A.M. (eds.) SAC 2006. LNCS, vol. 4356, pp. 331–349. Springer, Heidelberg (2007)
14. Lucks, S.: A Failure-Friendly Design Principle for Hash Functions. In: Roy, B. (ed.) ASIACRYPT 2005. LNCS, vol. 3788, pp. 474–494. Springer, Heidelberg (2005)
15. Merkle, R.: One Way Hash Functions and DES. In: Brassard, G. (ed.) CRYPTO 1989. LNCS, vol. 435, pp. 428–446. Springer, Heidelberg (1990)
16. Preneel, B., Govaerts, R., Vandewalle, J.: Hash Functions Based on Block Ciphers: a Synthetic Approach. In: Stinson, D.R. (ed.) CRYPTO 1993. LNCS, vol. 773, pp. 368–378. Springer, Heidelberg (1994)
17. Rivest, R.L.: the MD4 Message-Digest Algorithm. In: Menezes, A., Vanstone, S.A. (eds.) CRYPTO 1990. LNCS, vol. 537, pp. 303–311. Springer, Heidelberg (1991)
18. Rivest, R.L.: the MD5 Message-Digest Algorithm, RFC 1321, Internet Activity Board, Internet Privacy Task Force (1992)
19. Wagner, D.: A Generalized Birthday Problem. In: Yung, M. (ed.) CRYPTO 2002. LNCS, vol. 2442, pp. 288–304. Springer, Heidelberg (2002)

On the Importance of the Key Separation Principle for Different Modes of Operation

Danilo Gligoroski[1], Suzana Andova[2], and Svein Johan Knapskog[1]

[1] Centre for Quantifiable Quality of Service in Communication Systems, Norwegian University of Science and Technology, O.S. Bragstads plass 2E, N-7491 Trondheim, Norway
danilo.gligoroski@q2s.ntnu.no, Svein.J.Knapskog@Q2S.ntnu.no
[2] Department of Mathematics and Computer Science
Technische Universiteit Eindhoven
P.O. Box 513, NL-5600 MB Eindhoven, The Netherlands
s.andova@tue.nl

Abstract. The key separation principle for different modes of operation of the block ciphers is a cryptographic folklore wisdom that states: *One should always use distinct keys for distinct algorithms and distinct modes of operation*. If this principle is violated, then there are generic attacks that can recover the whole or a part of the encrypted messages. By the advent of software packages and libraries that offer some or all modes of operation of block ciphers, the violation of this principle is really possible in practice. We show that under the same key, OFB mode of operation is a special case of the CBC mode of operation, and that if CBC and CTR modes of operation are interchangeably used under the same secret key - then the security of the encryption process is seriously weakened. Moreover in the chosen plaintext attack scenario with interchanged use of CBC and OFB mode under the same key, we give a concrete list of openssl commands that can extract the complete plaintext without knowing the secret key.

Keywords: block ciphers, modes of operation, quasigroup string transformations.

1 Introduction

Block cipher modes of operation were introduced to allow block ciphers to provide data confidentiality and/or authentication. In 1980, NIST (at that time National Bureau of Standards) approved confidentiality modes of operations for the DES block cipher [11]. Later, with the advent of new block ciphers such as the AES, new modes needed to be developed and standardized. Several block cipher modes of operation for confidentiality and/or authentication have been proposed: Accumulated Block Chaining (ABC) by Knudsen [9], Rogaway's Parallelizable Authenticated Encryption (OCB) [16], Key Feedback Mode proposed by Håstad and Näslund [4], eXtended Ciphertext proposed by Gligor and Donescu, Block Chaining (XCBC) schemes [3] and a parallelizable encryption mode with message integrity by Jutla [8].

As a result of an extensive public discussion (including two public workshops) and vast number of suggestions and comments given by numerous cryptographers and practitioners in the field, in 2001 NIST compiled the Special Publication 800-38A (SP800-38A in short) "Recommendation for Block Cipher Modes of Operation" [13]. In this document NIST recommends and fully specifies five modes of operation: Electronic Codebook (ECB), Cipher Block Chaining (CBC), Cipher Feedback (CFB), Output Feedback (OFB), and Counter mode (CTR).

Wide international information security community, has also recognized the importance of precisely defined modes of operations for the block ciphers. Thus, in 1991 ISO/IEC adopted the first ISO/IEC 10116 standard [5] for modes of operations of n-bit block cipher, and have updated the standard in 1997 [6] and in 2006 [7]. The latest update from 2006 has the same five modes of operation that are defined in the NIST SP-800-38A.

Both international standards thoroughly discuss the particular use and the security concerns of all five modes. However, it is a very surprising fact that they do not mention the security flaws that may occur if different modes of operation are used interchangeably under the same encryption key, even though the so-called **Key Separation Principle** is well known in the cryptographic folklore. It states that *One should always use distinct keys for distinct algorithms and distinct modes of operation.*

This principle is mentioned in two other NIST documents: NIST Special Publication 800-21 2005, "Guideline for Implementing Cryptography In the Federal Government" and NIST Special Publication 800-57 2007, "Recommendation for Key Management Part 1: General (Revised)" [14,15]. In the first document on page 14 Sec. 3.3 the mentioning of this principle is like this: "Keys used for one purpose shall not be used for other purposes. (See SP 800-57)". In the second document this principle is mentioned on page 44 Sec. 5.2 with the following sentence: "In general, a single key should be used for only one purpose (e.g., encryption, authentication, key wrapping, random number generation, or digital signatures)". Further on in that section, it is stated that one of the reasons for applying the key separation principle is that "Some uses of keys interfere with each other", but the interference is explained only by interchangeable use of one key for key transport and digital signatures.

On the other hand in the ISO/IEC 10116 standard [7] there is just a brief mentioning that: "How keys and starting variables are managed and distributed is outside the scope of this International Standard". However, the examples that are given for the modes of operations in that standard are very misleading since they are actually breaking the key separation principle and all examples that explain different modes of operation use a same encryption key.

In the open literature there is no mentioning of possible interference between modes of operation of the block ciphers when the keys are the same. While it is a well known fact that keystream reuse within the same mode is insecure, (and the SP8000-38A elaborates on this matter several times where the recommendations of how to choose initial values for modes are given), it is perfectly possible and allowed by the NIST and ISO/IEC recommendations for two modes to use the same secret key. Then, the following situation may emerge: a keystream is produced for the first time in one of the modes of operation, and the same keystream is produced by the other mode in form of a ciphertext (under the same secret key). Thus, the request for not reusing a keystream within a particular mode is certainly obeyed, but yet the same keystream has been produced by another mode of operation. And this may cause complete or partial disclosure of the plaintext because the principle of key separation has been violated.

Therefore, the key separation principle is essential and it must be included in any forthcoming new updates of documents such as SP800-38A or ISO/IEC 10116. One possible short and elegant intervention in these documents would be to use the following phrase for every mode of operation: "The key should be secret and should be used exclusively for this mode of operation". Additionally, the examples in the ISO/IEC 10116 standard certainly should be changed to be in a compliance with the key separation principle. Moreover, findings and claims in this paper can be used as a technical support for addressing the key separation principle in more detail than it is done in the key management documents SP800-21, and SP800-57 [14,15] to avoid unnecessary risk of confidentiality violation.

It is natural to raise the question: "Is the interchanged use of several modes of operation under the same secret key possible in practice?" We think it is possible. One scenario is software packages or libraries offering a set of block ciphers, with the option to use the five standardized modes of operation (e.g. OpenSSL – http://www.openssl.org/ or Crypto++ – http://www.cryptopp.com/). Neglecting the problem may easily bring the users to the undesirable situation of performing insecure communication.

As a formal framework for our results in this paper we use the algebraic concept of quasigroup string transformations. We show that all the three modes of operation, CBC, OFB and CTR can be represented as quasigroup string transformations. Using these representations we observe that the OFB mode is a special case of the more general CBC mode. This implies that software packages that offer both CBC and OFB modes of operation, and yet fully comply with the NIST or ISO/IEC recommendations, are insecure as the interplay between the two modes opens up a scenario for a possible attack. We show that an attacker without knowing the secret key can successfully extract parts or the entire plaintext from the ciphertext. In addition, we describe a possible attack on the CTR mode when it is used together with the CBC mode if they both use the same secret key. We emphasize that the described scenario is allowed by the NIST or ISO/IEC recommendations, but as the key separation principle is not obeyed, the confidentiality property is broken without having any knowledge about the secret key.

The organization of the paper is the following: In section 2 we give a short introduction, some basic definitions and some properties of the quasigroup string transformations. We also shortly describe the three modes of operations used in the paper, CBC, OFB and CTR, and describe their representation as quasigroup string transformations. In section 3 we give several scenarios in which the attacker is able to extract the complete or partial plaintext without having any knowledge of the secret key. In addition, we list a concrete sequence of openssl commands that results in breaking the OFB mode when used interchangeably with CBC. Section 4 concludes the paper.

2 Basic Definitions

2.1 Quasigroup String Transformations

Here we give just a few definitions related to quasigroups and quasigroup string transformations. A more detailed explanation can be found in [1,2,10,17].

Definition 1. *A quasigroup $(Q, *)$ is a groupoid satisfying the law*

$$(\forall u, v \in Q)(\exists! \; x, y \in Q) \quad u * x = v \; \& \; y * u = v. \tag{1}$$

Thus, if $(Q, *)$ is a quasigroup, for each $a, b \in Q$ there is a unique $x \in Q$ such that $a * x = b$. $*$ induces an other binary operation on Q, called *left parastrophe*, defined as $x = a \setminus_* b$ iff $a * x = b$. It is obvious that $(Q, \setminus_*)$ is a quasigroup and that the algebra $(Q, *, \setminus_*)$ satisfies the identities

$$x \setminus_* (x * y) = y, \quad x * (x \setminus_* y) = y. \tag{2}$$

Definition 2. *Let $(Q, \cdot)$ and $(Q, *)$ be two quasigroups with the same carrier. Quasigroup $(Q, \cdot)$ is autotopic to quasigroup $(Q, *)$ iff there are bijections $\alpha, \beta, \gamma : Q \to Q$, such that $\gamma(x \cdot y) = \alpha(x) * \beta(y)$ for each $x, y \in Q$. Then the triple (α, β, γ) is called an autotopism from $(Q, \cdot)$ to $(Q, *)$.*

Note that if $(Q, \cdot)$ is autotopic to quasigroup $(Q, *)$ then the operation $\cdot$ is fully defined by $*$ and the corresponding bijections (α, β, γ). As a consequence, both quasigroups $(Q, \cdot)$ and $(Q, *)$ have the same algebraic properties. Sometimes bijections α and β are interpreted as rows and columns rearrangements of the multiplicative scheme of $(Q, *)$ and the bijection γ is interpreted as a renaming of elements of $(Q, *)$ (see [17] p. 5).

Consider an alphabet (i.e., a finite set) Q. By Q^+ we denote the set of all nonempty words (i.e., finite strings) formed by the elements of Q. In this paper, depending on the context, we use two notations for elements of Q^+: $a_1 a_2 \ldots a_n$ and $(a_1, a_2, \ldots, a_n)$, where $a_i \in Q$.

Definition 3. *Let $(Q, *)$ be a quasigroup and $M = a_1 a_2 \ldots a_n \in Q^+$ For each $l \in Q$ we define two functions $e_{l,*}, d_{l,*} : Q^+ \longrightarrow Q^+$ as follows:*

$$e_{l,*}(M) = b_1 b_2 \ldots b_n \iff b_1 = l * a_1, \; b_2 = b_1 * a_2, \ldots, \; b_n = b_{n-1} * a_n,$$

$$d_{l,*}(M) = c_1 c_2 \ldots c_n \iff c_1 = l * a_1, \; c_2 = a_1 * a_2, \ldots, \; c_n = a_{n-1} * a_n,$$

The functions $e_{l,*}$ and $d_{l,*}$ are called a quasigroup string e–transformation (or e–transformation for short) and a quasigroup string d–transformation (or d–transformation for short) of Q^+ based on the operation $*$ with leader l.

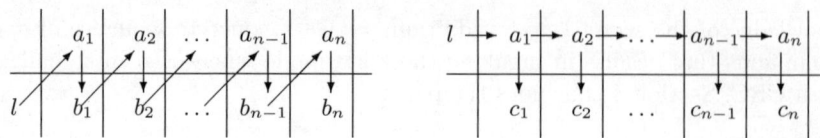

Fig. 1. Graphical representations of the $e_{l,*}$ and $d_{l,*}$ transformations

Graphical representations of e–transformation and d–transformation are shown in Fig. 1.

Using Definition 3 and the identities (2) it is easy to prove the following theorem.

Theorem 1. *If $(Q, *)$ is a finite quasigroup, then $e_{l,*}$ and $d_{l,\backslash_*}$ are mutually inverse permutations of Q^+, i.e.,*

$$d_{l,\backslash_*}(e_{l,*}(M)) = M = e_{l,*}(d_{l,\backslash_*}(M))$$

for each leader $l \in Q$ and for every string $M \in Q^+$. □

2.2 Representation of CBC, OFB and CTR Mode as Quasigroup String Transformations

We will use the same terminology and notation as is defined in SP800-38A [13].

– The forward cipher function of the block cipher algorithm under the key K applied to the data block X is denoted as $CIPH_K(X)$.
– The inverse cipher function of the block cipher algorithm under the key K applied to the data block X is denoted as $CIPH_K^{-1}(X)$.
– The bitwise exclusive-OR of two bit strings X and Y of the same length is denoted as $X \oplus Y$.
– The plaintext will be denoted as a sequence of n blocks $P = P_1, P_2, \ldots, P_{n-1}, P_n$ where every P_i has the length in bits that is characteristic for a particular block cipher.
– The ciphertext will be denoted as a sequence of n blocks $C = C_1, C_2, \ldots, C_{n-1}, C_n$ where every C_i has the length in bits that is also characteristic for a particular block cipher.
– The block size in bits is characteristic for each block cipher and will be denoted with b. (For AES $b = 128$.)
– The key size in bits will be denoted with k. (For AES $k = 128, 192, 256$.)
– The string consisting of all zero bits will be denoted as **0**.
– The set of all blocks of b bits will be denoted by $Q = \{0,1\}^b$.

Some modes of operation allow the last plaintext block P_n or the last ciphertext block C_n to be of a smaller length than the block size, and in the NIST publication they are denoted as P_n^* and C_n^*. However, without a loss of generality concerning the security issues, throughout this paper we will apply the ISO/IEC approach, namely we will assume that the last blocks of the plaintext and ciphertext have exactly the length of the block size.

Definition 4. Let $K \in \{0,1\}^k$. We define the following binary operation on $Q = \{0,1\}^b$, for every $A, B \in Q$

$$A *_K B \equiv CIPH_K(A \oplus B). \tag{3}$$

In the sequel, we will omit the subscript K in $*_K$ if it is clear from the context and any use of $*$ will refer to Definition 4 if not stated differently.

Theorem 2. $(Q, *)$ is a commutative quasigroup for any key K.

Proof. The commutativity of the operation $*$ follows immediately from the commutativity of the operation $\oplus$. Namely, for any chosen key K the following holds:

$$A * B = CIPH_K(A \oplus B) = CIPH_K(B \oplus A) = B * A.$$

Next, to prove that $(Q, *)$ is a quasigroup, it is sufficient to show that the equation $A * X = B$ (and similar for $X * A = B$) has a unique solution on X, for any $A, B \in \{0,1\}^b$. This follows directly from the fact that the block cipher function $CIPH_K(\cdot)$ is a bijection on $\{0,1\}^b$. Therefore, the equation $A * X = B$, which is equivalent to the equation $CIPH_K(A \oplus X) = B$, has $X = CIPH_K^{-1}(B) \oplus A$ as its unique solution. $\square$

Proposition 1. The operation $CIPH_K^{-1}(B) \oplus A$ is the left parastrophe operation that corresponds to the operation $*_K$, that is:

$$A \setminus_{*_K} B \equiv CIPH_K^{-1}(B) \oplus A.$$

Proof. Again, we omit the subscript K on $*$. We have to prove that identities (2) are satisfied. We have,

$$A \setminus_* (A * B) = CIPH_K^{-1}(A * B) \oplus A = CIPH_K^{-1}(CIPH_K(A \oplus B)) \oplus A = (A \oplus B) \oplus A = B,$$

and

$$A * (A \setminus_* B) = A * (CIPH_K^{-1}(B) \oplus A) = CIPH_K(A \oplus (CIPH_K^{-1}(B) \oplus A)) =$$

$$= CIPH_K(CIPH^{-1}(B)) = B. \square$$

Representation of the CBC mode. According to SP800-38A: "The Cipher Block Chaining (CBC) mode is a confidentiality mode whose encryption process features the combining (chaining) of the plaintext blocks with the previous ciphertext blocks. The CBC mode requires an initial vector IV to be combined with the first plaintext block. The IV need not be secret, but it must be unpredictable. Also, the integrity of the IV should be protected." The CBC mode encryption and decryption are defined in the following way:

CBC Encryption: $\quad C_j = CIPH_K(C_{j-1} \oplus P_j), \quad j = 1, \ldots, n$

CBC Decryption: $\quad P_j = CIPH_K^{-1}(C_j) \oplus C_{j-1}, \quad j = 1, \ldots, n$

where $C_0 = IV$ is the initial vector.

Theorem 3. *The encryption and decryption in the CBC mode of operation is a pair of e and d quasigroup string transformations on $Q = \{0,1\}^b$ defined as:*

CBC Encryption: $\quad C = e_{IV,*}(P_1, P_2, \ldots, P_n),$

CBC Decryption: $\quad P = d_{IV,\backslash_*}(C_1, C_2, \ldots, C_n),$

Proof. It follows directly from the definition of the e–transformation and d–transformation (Definition 3) by taking the initial vector IV as the leader in both transformations. □

Representation of the OFB mode. According to SP800-38A: "The Output Feedback (OFB) mode is a confidentiality mode that features the iteration of the forward cipher on an IV to generate a sequence of output blocks that are exclusive-ORed with the plaintext to produce the ciphertext, and vice versa. The OFB mode requires that the initial vector IV is a nonce, i.e., the IV must be unique for each execution of the mode under the given key." The OFB mode is defined as follows (supposing that the plaintext has length that is a multiple of the block size):

OFB Encryption: $\quad I_1 = IV;$
$\qquad I_j = O_{j-1}, \quad$ for $j = 2, \ldots, n;$
$\qquad O_j = CIPH_K(I_j), \quad$ for $j = 1, \ldots, n;$
$\qquad C_j = P_j \oplus O_j, \quad$ for $j = 1, \ldots, n;$

OFB Decryption: $\quad I_1 = IV;$
$\qquad I_j = O_{j-1}, \quad$ for $j = 2, \ldots, n;$
$\qquad O_j = CIPH_K(I_j), \quad$ for $j = 1, \ldots, n;$
$\qquad P_j = C_j \oplus O_j, \quad$ for $j = 1, \ldots, n;$

Note that in OFB mode the encryption of the plaintext is performed "stream cipher style" by XORing blocks of plaintext with blocks of keystream bits. In the sequel we will use the shorthand notation $C_{OFB} = OFB_{K,IV,encrypt}(P)$ for OFB encryption of plaintext P with key K and initial value IV.

Theorem 4. *The encryption and decryption of the OFB mode of operation is a pair of e and d quasigroup string transformations on $Q = \{0,1\}^b$ given as:*

OFB Encryption: $\quad C = e_{IV,*}(\mathbf{0}) \oplus P,$

OFB Decryption: $\quad P = e_{IV,*}(\mathbf{0}) \oplus C,$

Proof. From Definition 3, by performing an e–transformation with leader IV on the string $\mathbf{0}$ we will obtain the corresponding values of the ciphertext C and the plaintext P. □

From the last theorem it is clear that the OFB mode is a special case of the CBC mode. Namely, OFB encryption is indeed CBC encryption applied on the zero string $\mathbf{0}$. This situation opens up several possibilities to define attacks with chosen plaintext, that employ interchanged use of CBC and OFB modes of operation. Such attacks are described in the next section.

Representation of the CTR mode. According to SP800-38A: "The Counter (CTR) mode is a confidentiality mode that features the application of the forward cipher to a set of input blocks, called counters, to produce a sequence of output blocks that are exclusive-ORed with the plaintext to produce the ciphertext, and vice versa. The sequence of counters must have the property that each block in the sequence is different from every other block. This condition is not restricted to a single message: across all of the messages that are encrypted under the given key, all of the counters must be distinct." The counters for a given message will be denoted $T_1, T_2, \ldots, T_n$. Given a sequence of counters, $T_1, T_2, \ldots, T_n$, and supposing that the plaintext has length that is multiple of the block size, the CTR mode is defined as:

CTR Encryption: $\quad O_j = CIPH_K(T_j), \quad$ for $j = 1, \ldots, n$;
$\qquad\qquad\qquad\qquad C_j = P_j \oplus O_j, \quad$ for $j = 1, \ldots, n$;

CTR Decryption: $\quad O_j = CIPH_K(T_j), \quad$ for $j = 1, \ldots, n$;
$\qquad\qquad\qquad\qquad P_j = C_j \oplus O_j, \quad$ for $j = 1, \ldots, n$;

Since for every block of a plaintext a new counter is required, the plaintext may have the maximum length of 2^b blocks, so $n \leq 2^b$. In the remainder, we write $C_{CTR} = CTR_{K,T_1,encrypt}(P)$ as a shorthand notation for CTR encryption of plaintext P with key K and initial counter value T_1.

Note that in the CTR mode the plaintext is encrypted by XORing each plaintext block by the encryption of the counter that corresponds to the processed block of the plaintext. As a consequence, the CTR encryption of plaintext $P = P_1 P_2 \ldots P_n$ with counters $T_1, T_2, \ldots, T_n$ can be written as

$$CTR_{K,T_1,encrypt}(P) = (CTR_{K,T_j,encryp}(P_j))_{j=1,\ldots,n},$$

for $P_j, T_j \in \{0,1\}^b, j = 1, \ldots, n, n \leq 2^b$.

One of the essential observations used to reason about the CTR mode in terms of quasigroups is that the CTR encryption function produces exactly the encryption of the counter if the zero string with length b-bits, $\mathbf{0}$, is taken as the input plaintext.

Definition 5. *We define function $\gamma : Q \to Q$ as $\gamma(t) = CTR_{K,t,encrypt}(\mathbf{0})$ for every $t \in Q = \{0,1\}^b$.*

Lemma 1. *For every $t \in Q = \{0,1\}^b$, $\gamma(t) = CIPH_K(t)$.*

Proof. It follows directly from the definitions of γ, CTR encryption and $\oplus$ operation. $\square$

Recall that the set of all b-bit blocks $Q = \{0,1\}^b$ under the exclusive-OR operation forms a quasigroup, i.e. that $(Q, \oplus)$ is a quasigroup.

Theorem 5. *The quasigroup $(Q, \oplus)$ is autotopic with the quasigroup $(Q, *)$ where the operation $*$ is defined by equation (3). The autotopism is $(\mathbf{1}_Q, \mathbf{1}_Q, \gamma)$, where $\mathbf{1}_Q$ is the identity map on Q, and γ is defined by Definition 5.*

Proof. For any $x, y \in Q$ from Lemma 1 we obtain that:

$$\gamma(x \oplus y) = CIPH_K(x \oplus y) = x * y = \mathbf{1}_Q(x) * \mathbf{1}_Q(y).$$

□

We illustrate the previous theorem with the following example.

Example 1. For the example we fix $b = 4$. Thus, $Q = \{0, 1, \ldots, 15\}$ where the numbers $0, 1, \ldots, 15$ are represented as 4-bit nibbles. Let the encryption function be given by the bijection $CIPH_K : Q \to Q$:

$$CIPH_K = \begin{pmatrix} 0 & 1 & 2 & 3 & 4 & 5 & 6 & 7 & 8 & 9 & 10 & 11 & 12 & 13 & 14 & 15 \\ 12 & 2 & 13 & 6 & 7 & 10 & 5 & 14 & 3 & 9 & 11 & 1 & 15 & 8 & 0 & 4 \end{pmatrix}.$$

The quasigroups $(Q, \oplus)$ and $(Q, *)$ are given in Table 1.

Table 1. Two autotopic quasigroups $(Q, \oplus)$ and $(Q, *)$

$\oplus$	0	1	2	3	4	5	6	7	8	9	10	11	12	13	14	15
0	0	1	2	3	4	5	6	7	8	9	10	11	12	13	14	15
1	1	0	3	2	5	4	7	6	9	8	11	10	13	12	15	14
2	2	3	0	1	6	7	4	5	10	11	8	9	14	15	12	13
3	3	2	1	0	7	6	5	4	11	10	9	8	15	14	13	12
4	4	5	6	7	0	1	2	3	12	13	14	15	8	9	10	11
5	5	4	7	6	1	0	3	2	13	12	15	14	9	8	11	10
6	6	7	4	5	2	3	0	1	14	15	12	13	10	11	8	9
7	7	6	5	4	3	2	1	0	15	14	13	12	11	10	9	8
8	8	9	10	11	12	13	14	15	0	1	2	3	4	5	6	7
9	9	8	11	10	13	12	15	14	1	0	3	2	5	4	7	6
10	10	11	8	9	14	15	12	13	2	3	0	1	6	7	4	5
11	11	10	9	8	15	14	13	12	3	2	1	0	7	6	5	4
12	12	13	14	15	8	9	10	11	4	5	6	7	0	1	2	3
13	13	12	15	14	9	8	11	10	5	4	7	6	1	0	3	2
14	14	15	12	13	10	11	8	9	6	7	4	5	2	3	0	1
15	15	14	13	12	11	10	9	8	7	6	5	4	3	2	1	0

$*$	0	1	2	3	4	5	6	7	8	9	10	11	12	13	14	15
0	12	2	13	6	7	10	5	14	3	9	11	1	15	8	0	4
1	2	12	6	13	10	7	14	5	9	3	1	11	8	15	4	0
2	13	6	12	2	5	14	7	10	11	1	3	9	0	4	15	8
3	6	13	2	12	14	5	10	7	1	11	9	3	4	0	8	15
4	7	10	5	14	12	2	13	6	15	8	0	4	3	9	11	1
5	10	7	14	5	2	12	6	13	8	15	4	0	9	3	1	11
6	5	14	7	10	13	6	12	2	0	4	15	8	11	1	3	9
7	14	5	10	7	6	13	2	12	4	0	8	15	1	11	9	3
8	3	9	11	1	15	8	0	4	12	2	13	6	7	10	5	14
9	9	3	1	11	8	15	4	0	2	12	6	13	10	7	14	5
10	11	1	3	9	0	4	15	8	13	6	12	2	5	14	7	10
11	1	11	9	3	4	0	8	15	6	13	2	12	14	5	10	7
12	15	8	0	4	3	9	11	1	7	10	5	14	12	2	13	6
13	8	15	4	0	9	3	1	11	10	7	14	5	2	12	6	13
14	0	4	15	8	11	1	3	9	5	14	7	10	13	6	12	2
15	4	0	8	15	1	11	9	3	14	5	10	7	6	13	2	12

Note that the bijection $CIPH_K : Q \to Q$ appears as the first row of the quasigroup $(Q, *)$. Moreover, although the two quasigroups are different, since they are autotopic, they have the same structure. For example, the main diagonal in $(Q, \oplus)$ is filled with the element 0, while in the $(Q, *)$ that element is 12, which is encryption of 0. Actually, the autotopism is just element renaming, while the structure remain the same. This property, and the fact that the quasigroup $(Q, *)$ is defined only by its first row will be used in the next sections for mounting different attack scenarios when the same key is used interchangeably between CBC and CTR.

3 Scenarios of Attacks with Chosen Plaintext on the Interchanged Use of the CBC, OFB and CTR Modes of Operation

From the definitions, properties and theorems in the previous section it is clear that the following theorem holds.

Theorem 6. Let $K \in \{0,1\}^k$ be a secret key and let $IV \in \{0,1\}^b$ be an initial value. Let $C_{CBC} = e_{IV,*}(\mathbf{0})$ be a cipher text obtained by the encryption of the plaintext $P_{CBC} = \mathbf{0}$ in the CBC mode of encryption, with the secret key K and initial value IV. Then, any ciphertext C_{OFB} obtained by the OFB mode of operation with the same secret key K and the same initial value IV can be decrypted simply by the operation

$$P = C_{CBC} \oplus C_{OFB}.$$
□

Recall that, as long as it appears as a nonce, the use of one IV under OFB mode which has been used under CBC as well, complies with the NIST or ISO/IEC recommendations.

Fig. 2. Screen dumps for original, encrypted and extracted file

In the remainder of the section we will discuss four variants of a known plaintext attack, where interchanged use of the CBC, OFB or CTR modes of operation are performed, and where the requirements of the NIST or ISO/IEC recommendations are adhered to.

Attack 1 is just a step-wise application of Theorem 6.

Attack 1

Step 1. The attacker Eve knows[1] the encryption of the string **0**, i.e. she knows $C_{CBC} = e_{IV_{CBC},*}(\mathbf{0})$. She also knows the initial value IV_{CBC} of the encryption, but does not know the secret key K.

Step 2. Alice and Bob possess the secret key K, and decide to perform a secure communication using the OFB mode.

Step 3. Alice and Bob decide to use IV_{CBC} as an initial value for the OFB mode. According to the NIST recommendations, the use of IV_{CBC} is allowed since it has never been used in OFB mode before.

Step 4. Alice encrypts the plaintext P performing $C_{OFB} = OFB_{K,IV_{CBC},encrypt}(P)$.

Step 5. Eve extracts the plaintext without the knowledge of the secret key K simply applying $P = C_{CBC} \oplus C_{OFB}$.

Example 2. With this example we demonstrate possibility of the Attack 1. to occur in practice. We give a concrete set of openssl commands and the corresponding screen dumps showing the effects of those commands.

We will use the `aes-128-cbc` and `aes-128-ofb` options of the "`enc`" command in the openssl. For the purpose of this example we have prepared a short plaintext file containing the song of Dire Straits, "Once Upon A Time In The West" from the album "Communiqué" from 1979.

- The command "`vi OnceUponATimeInTheWest.txt`" displays the content of the file and the screen dump of that operation is shown in Figure 2a.
- The command "`dd if=/dev/zero of=zero.txt bs=4096 count=1024`" creates a file of length 4 MBytes all with zeroes.
- The command "`openssl enc -aes-128-cbc -in zero.txt -out zero.bin -K 01234567890123456789012345678901 -iv 0123456789abcdef0123456789abcdef -nopad`" encrypts the file zero.txt in CBC mode using key K and initial vector IV. This is the part of the known plaintext attack done by Eve.
- The command "`openssl enc -aes-128-ofb -in OnceUponATimeInTheWest.txt - out EncryptedDoc.bin -K 01234567890123456789012345678901 -iv 0123456789abcdef0123456789abcdef -nopad`" encrypts the file OnceUponATimeInTheWest.txt in OFB mode with the same key and IV used in the CBC encryption. The resulting ciphertext file is named EncryptedDoc.bin.
- By applying the command "`vi EncryptedDoc.bin`" the content of the encrypted file is displayed and the screen dump of that operation is shown in Figure 2b.

---

[1] There are a number of ways that a cryptanalyst can get knowledge about the encrypted version of a specifically formatted plaintext, e.g. by participating in cryptanalytic challenge.

- The command "./XORFiles zero.bin EncryptedDoc.bin Extracted.txt" invokes a program that XORs two files and produces the third file. The length of the produced file is same as the length of the smaller file. Note that the command ./XORFiles is not a part of any operating system and it should be specially prepared (programmed).
- By applying the command "vi Extracted.txt" we can see the content of the file and see the extracted plaintext. The screen dump of that operation is shown in Figure 2c. As expected, the file contains the original text from OnceUponATimeInTheWest.txt file.

A variant of the Attack 1 can be launched even if the IV_{CBC} is not used in the OFB mode.

Attack 2

Step 1. The attacker Eve knows the encryption of the string **0**, i.e. she knows $C_{CBC} = e_{IV_{CBC},*}(\mathbf{0})$. She does not know the secret key K.

Step 2. Alice and Bob possess the secret key K, and decide to perform a secure communication using the OFB mode.

Step 3. They choose to use an IV that has never been used in any OFB session before, but it happens that this IV is identical to a block of the ciphertext C_{CBC} that Eve possess. According to the NIST recommendations, the use of such an IV is allowed since it has never been used in OFB mode.

Step 4. Alice encrypts the plaintext P performing $C_{OFB} = OFB_{K,IV,encrypt}(P)$.

Step 5. Represented as concatenation of blocks, the ciphertext that Eve possess looks like: $C_{CBC} = C_1, \ldots, C_{j-1}, IV, C_{j+1}, \ldots, C_N$. She checks and finds out that the used IV is a block of her ciphertext, thus she cuts the first part of the ciphertext C_{CBC} (the first part including IV) obtaining the string $C'_{CBC} = C_{j+1}, \ldots, C_N$. She extracts the plaintext (all or parts of it) without having any knowledge of the secret key K simply applying $P = C'_{CBC} \oplus C_{OFB}$. If the lengths of C'_{CBC} and C_{OFB} are different, then by convention, the output of $\oplus$ operation will have a length that is equal to the smaller length of the two input strings C'_{CBC} and C_{OFB}.

The third attack does not even require that the known plaintext have to consist of all zeroes. Actually it is sufficient that the plaintext has many zero-blocks i.e. is of the form: $P = P_1, \ldots, P_{i_1-1}, \mathbf{0}_{i_1}, \ldots, \mathbf{0}_{i_2}, P_{i_2+1}, \ldots P_{i_3-1}, \mathbf{0}_{i_3}, \ldots, \mathbf{0}_{i_4}, P_{i_4+1}, \ldots$.

Attack 3

Step 1. The attacker Eve knows the encryption of the string P, i.e. she knows $C_{CBC} = e_{IV_{CBC},*}(P) = C_1, \ldots C_{i_1-1}, \mathbf{C}_{i_1}, \ldots, \mathbf{C}_{i_2}, C_{i_2+1}, \ldots C_{i_3-1}, \mathbf{C}_{i_3}, \ldots, \mathbf{C}_{i_4}, P_{i_4+1}, \ldots$. The parts of the ciphertext that are the result of the CBC encryption of the zero-block parts are denoted in bold. Eve does not know the secret key K.

Step 2. Alice and Bob possess the secret key K, and decide to perform a secure communication using the OFB mode.

Step 3. They chose to use an IV that has never been used in previous OFB sessions, but it happens that this IV is a part of the ciphertext blocks $\mathbf{C}_j$ that Eve possesses. According to the NIST recommendations, the use of such an IV is allowed since it has never been used in OFB mode.

Step 4. Alice encrypts the plaintext M performing $C_{OFB} = OFB_{K,IV,encrypt}(M)$.

Step 5. Similarly, as in the Attack 2, Eve extracts the part of the ciphertext C_{CBC}, $\mathbf{C}_j$, that is identical to the used IV, and obtain the string C'_{CBC}. She extracts the plaintext (all or parts of it) without the knowledge of the secret key K simply by applying $M = C'_{CBC} \oplus C_{OFB}$.

In the fourth attack there is no need for the known plaintext to have any particular structure, i.e., it is just of the form: $P = P_1, \ldots, P_N$.

Attack 4

Step 1. The attacker Eve knows the encryption of the string P, i.e. she knows $C_{CBC} = e_{IV_{CBC},*}(P) = C_1, \ldots C_N$. Eve does not know the secret key K.

Step 2. Alice and Bob possess the secret key K, and decide to perform a secure communication using the CTR mode. They chose to use a sequence of counters $T_1, T_2, \ldots, T_n$ following the NIST recommendations.

Step 3. Eve also knows the values of the counters. She checks whether there are values C_{i-1} and P_i such that $C_{i-1} \oplus P_i = T_j$, for some $i \in \{1, \ldots, N\}$ and for some $j \in \{1, \ldots, n\}$.

Step 4. Alice encrypts the plaintext $M = M_1 M_2 \ldots M_n$ performing $C_{CTR} = CTR_{K,T_1,encrypt}(M)$.

Step 5. Eve extracts the part M_j of the plaintext that corresponds to the counter T_j. As she has C_{i-1} and P_i such that $C_{i-1} \oplus P_i = T_j$, she can simply obtain the value of M_j as
$M_j = CTR_{K,T_j,encrypt}(M_j) \oplus C_i = CTR_{K,T_j,encrypt}(M_j) \oplus (C_{i-1} * P_i)$
$= CTR_{K,T_j,encrypt}(M_j) \oplus CIPH_K(C_{i-1} \oplus P_i),$
where the last equation holds due to Theorem 5.

4 Conclusions

In this paper we have represented two popular modes of operation of block ciphers (CBC and OFB) as quasigroup string transformations, and also established the relations between quasigroups and the CTR mode of operation. We have shown that the OFB mode is a special case of the CBC mode of operation where the encryption of a string of all zeroes is performed. We have also shown that the quasigroup obtained by the CBC mode of operation is autotope with the linear quasigroup of bitwise XOR-ing of b-bit words. From this, under the assumption that the principle of key separation was not properly applied, we have constructed several successful attacks.

The attacks in question are not probabilistic, and does not go against the cipher algorithms or their modes of operation as such. The underlying problem is that the operating procedures do not properly address the key separation principle in either of the two dominating standards referenced in this paper. In fact, both standards have presented suggestions or examples that are suited to mislead a prospective user/implementer of different modes of operation, even to a degree where complete extraction of the plaintext without any knowledge of the secret key can be made, and the implementation may still not be in violation with either standard. From the formal point of view, in those attacks, the NIST or ISO/IEC recommendations for the nature of IVs and counters were followed, but still by employing these attacks we were able to reconstruct the plaintext without having any knowledge of the secret key.

This highlights the necessity to urgently adopt and publish a new and more detailed key separation principle both in the ISO/IEC 10116 standard and in the NIST recommendations SP800-38A, SP800-21 and SP800-57.

References

1. Belousov, V.D.: Osnovi teorii kvazigrup i lup, "Nauka", Moskva (1967)
2. Dénes, J., Keedwell, A.D.: Latin Squares. In: New Developments in the Theory and Applications, North-Holland Publishing Co, Amsterdam (1991)
3. Gligor, V.D., Donescu, P.: Fast Encryption and Authentication: XCBC Encryption and XECB Authentication Modes. In: Matsui, M. (ed.) FSE 2001. LNCS, vol. 2355, pp. 1–20. Springer, Heidelberg (2002)
4. Håstad, J., Näslund, M.: Key Feedback Mode: A Keystream Generator with Provable Security, http://csrc.nist.gov/CryptoToolkit/modes/workshop1/papers/hastad-Naslund-kfb.pdf
5. ISO/IEC 10116:1991, Fisrt Edition 1991, Information technology - Security techniques - Modes of operation of n-bit block cipher (1991)
6. ISO/IEC 10116:1997, Second Edition 1997. Information technology - Security techniques - Modes of operation of n-bit block cipher (1997)
7. ISO/IEC 10116:2006, Third Edition 2006, Information technology - Security techniques - Modes of operation of n-bit block cipher (2006)
8. Jutla, C.S.: Encryption Modes with Almost Free Message Integrity. Cryptology ePrint Archive: Report 2000/039 (2000)
9. Knudsen, L.R.: Block chaining modes of operation. Technical Report, Department of Informatics, University of Bergen, Norway (2000)
10. Markovski, S., Gligoroski, D., Bakeva, V.: Quasigroup String Processing: Part 1. Maced. Acad. of Sci. and Arts, Sc. Math. Tech. Scien. XX 1-2, 13–28 (1999)
11. National Bureau of Standards, DES modes of operation, Federal Information Processing Standard (FIPS), Publication 81, National Bureau of Standards, U.S. Department of Commerce, Washington D.C. (December 1980)
12. National Institute of Standards and Technology, Modes of Operation Home page, http://csrc.nist.gov/CryptoToolkit/modes/
13. National Institute of Standards and Technology, Special Publication 800-38A 2001, Recommendation for Block Cipher Modes of Operation Methods and Techniques, 66 pages (December 2001)

14. National Institute of Standards and Technology, Special Publication 800-21 2005, Guideline for Implementing Cryptograph. In: The Federal Government. 89 pages (December 2005)
15. National Institute of Standards and Technology, Special Publication 800-57 2007, Recommendation for Key Management - Part 1: General (Revised), 142 pages (March 2007)
16. Rogaway, P.: OCB Mode: Parallelizable Authenticated Encryption. Comments to NIST concerning AES Modes of Operation, Draft (October 6, 2000), http://csrc.nist.gov/CryptoToolkit/modes/workshop1/papers/rogaway-ocb1.pdf
17. Smith, J.D.H.: An introduction to quasigroups and their representations. Chapman and Hall, Boca Raton (2007)

Author Index

Anckaert, Bertrand 86
Andova, Suzana 404
Armknecht, Frederik 29
Asokan, N. 161

Bao, Feng 71
Bellot, Patrick 218
Bringer, Julien 56
Brown, Andrew 233

Cappaert, Jan 86
Chabanne, Hervé 56

De Bosschere, Koen 86
Demaille, Akim 218
Deng, Robert H. 71
Ding, Xuhua 71

Escalante B., Alberto N. 29

Feng, Dengguo 248

Galindo, David 361
Garcia, Flavio D. 361
Gligoroski, Danilo 404

Hakuta, Keisuke 304
Hong, Jin 131
Hu, Honggang 248
Hu, Lei 377

Jeong, Kyoochang 203
Jeong, Kyung Chul 131
Ji, Wen 377
Joye, Marc 116

Kim, Hyogon 176
Kim, Sangjin 278
Knapskog, Svein Johan 404
Kwon, Eun Young 131
Kwon, Minjin 203

Le, Quoc-Cuong 218
Lee, Dong Hoon 101
Lee, Heejo 176, 203

Lee, In-Sok 131
Lim, Jihwan 278
Lin, Pin 392
Löhr, Hans 29

Ma, Daegun 131
Madou, Matias 86
Maleka, Shaik 334
Manulis, Mark 29

Oh, Heekuck 278
Okamoto, Eiji 45, 290
Okamoto, Takeshi 45
Osterhues, André 161
Ouafi, Khaled 263

Pandu Rangan, C. 334
Park, Jong Hwan 101
Park, Keun 176
Pasupathinathan, Vijayakrishnan 14
Phan, Raphael C.-W. 263
Pieprzyk, Josef 14, 319, 347
Pointcheval, David 56
Preneel, Bart 86

Qiu, Tian 392

Ryan, M.D. 1, 233

Sadeghi, Ahmad-Reza 29, 161
Salaiwarakul, A. 1
Sato, Hisayoshi 304
Seo, Dongwon 176
Shareef, Amjed 334
Shirase, Masaaki 290
Smith, Sean W. 146, 188
Stüble, Christian 161

Takagi, Tsuyoshi 290, 304
Tang, Qiang 56
Tsang, Patrick P. 146, 188
Tso, Raylin 45

van Rossum, Peter 361

Wang, Huaxiong 14, 319, 347
Wang, Xingang 248
Wolf, Marko 161
Wu, Chuankun 392
Wu, Wenling 392

Xu, Zhen 248

Yang, Yanjiang 71
Ye, Qingsong 319, 347
Yoo, Jaewon 176
Yuan, Jin 319

Lecture Notes in Computer Science

Sublibrary 4: Security and Cryptology

For information about Vols. 1– 3856
please contact your bookseller or Springer

Vol. 4991: L. Chen, Y. Mu, W. Susilo (Eds.), Information Security Practice and Experience. XIII, 420 pages. 2008.

Vol. 4965: N. Smart (Ed.), Advances in Cryptology – EUROCRYPT 2008. XIII, 564 pages. 2008.

Vol. 4948: R. Canetti (Ed.), Theory of Cryptography. XII, 645 pages. 2008.

Vol. 4939: R. Cramer (Ed.), Public Key Cryptography – PKC 2008. XIII, 397 pages. 2008.

Vol. 4896: A. Alkassar, M. Volkamer (Eds.), E-Voting and Identity. XII, 189 pages. 2007.

Vol. 4893: S.W. Golomb, G. Gong, T. Helleseth, H.-Y. Song (Eds.), Sequences, Subsequences, and Consequences. X, 219 pages. 2007.

Vol. 4890: F. Bonchi, E. Ferrari, B. Malin, Y. Saygin (Eds.), Privacy, Security, and Trust in KDD. IX, 173 pages. 2008.

Vol. 4887: S.D. Galbraith (Ed.), Cryptography and Coding. XI, 423 pages. 2007.

Vol. 4886: S. Dietrich, R. Dhamija (Eds.), Financial Cryptography and Data Security. XII, 390 pages. 2007.

Vol. 4876: C. Adams, A. Miri, M. Wiener (Eds.), Selected Areas in Cryptography. X, 409 pages. 2007.

Vol. 4867: S. Kim, M. Yung, H.-W. Lee (Eds.), Information Security Applications. XIII, 388 pages. 2008.

Vol. 4861: S. Qing, H. Imai, G. Wang (Eds.), Information and Communications Security. XIV, 508 pages. 2007.

Vol. 4859: K. Srinathan, C.P. Rangan, M. Yung (Eds.), Progress in Cryptology – INDOCRYPT 2007. XI, 426 pages. 2007.

Vol. 4856: F. Bao, S. Ling, T. Okamoto, H. Wang, C. Xing (Eds.), Cryptology and Network Security. XII, 283 pages. 2007.

Vol. 4833: K. Kurosawa (Ed.), Advances in Cryptology – ASIACRYPT 2007. XIV, 583 pages. 2007.

Vol. 4817: K.-H. Nam, G. Rhee (Eds.), Information Security and Cryptology - ICISC 2007. XIII, 367 pages. 2007.

Vol. 4812: P. McDaniel, S.K. Gupta (Eds.), Information Systems Security. XIII, 322 pages. 2007.

Vol. 4784: W. Susilo, J.K. Liu, Y. Mu (Eds.), Provable Security. X, 237 pages. 2007.

Vol. 4779: J.A. Garay, A.K. Lenstra, M. Mambo, R. Peralta (Eds.), Information Security. XIII, 437 pages. 2007.

Vol. 4776: N. Borisov, P. Golle (Eds.), Privacy Enhancing Technologies. X, 273 pages. 2007.

Vol. 4752: A. Miyaji, H. Kikuchi, K. Rannenberg (Eds.), Advances in Information and Computer Security. XIII, 460 pages. 2007.

Vol. 4734: J. Biskup, J. López (Eds.), Computer Security – ESORICS 2007. XIV, 628 pages. 2007.

Vol. 4727: P. Paillier, I. Verbauwhede (Eds.), Cryptographic Hardware and Embedded Systems - CHES 2007. XIV, 468 pages. 2007.

Vol. 4691: T. Dimitrakos, F. Martinelli, P.Y.A. Ryan, S. Schneider (Eds.), Formal Aspects in Security and Trust. VIII, 285 pages. 2007.

Vol. 4677: A. Aldini, R. Gorrieri (Eds.), Foundations of Security Analysis and Design IV. VII, 325 pages. 2007.

Vol. 4657: C. Lambrinoudakis, G. Pernul, A.M. Tjoa (Eds.), Trust, Privacy and Security in Digital Business. XIII, 291 pages. 2007.

Vol. 4637: C. Kruegel, R. Lippmann, A. Clark (Eds.), Recent Advances in Intrusion Detection. XII, 337 pages. 2007.

Vol. 4631: B. Christianson, B. Crispo, J.A. Malcolm, M. Roe (Eds.), Security Protocols. IX, 347 pages. 2007.

Vol. 4622: A. Menezes (Ed.), Advances in Cryptology - CRYPTO 2007. XIV, 631 pages. 2007.

Vol. 4593: A. Biryukov (Ed.), Fast Software Encryption. XI, 467 pages. 2007.

Vol. 4586: J. Pieprzyk, H. Ghodosi, E. Dawson (Eds.), Information Security and Privacy. XIV, 476 pages. 2007.

Vol. 4582: J. López, P. Samarati, J.L. Ferrer (Eds.), Public Key Infrastructure. XI, 375 pages. 2007.

Vol. 4579: B.M. Hämmerli, R. Sommer (Eds.), Detection of Intrusions and Malware, and Vulnerability Assessment. X, 251 pages. 2007.

Vol. 4575: T. Takagi, T. Okamoto, E. Okamoto, T. Okamoto (Eds.), Pairing-Based Cryptography – Pairing 2007. XI, 408 pages. 2007.

Vol. 4567: T. Furon, F. Cayre, G. Doërr, P. Bas (Eds.), Information Hiding. XI, 393 pages. 2008.

Vol. 4521: J. Katz, M. Yung (Eds.), Applied Cryptography and Network Security. XIII, 498 pages. 2007.

Vol. 4515: M. Naor (Ed.), Advances in Cryptology - EUROCRYPT 2007. XIII, 591 pages. 2007.

Vol. 4499: Y.Q. Shi (Ed.), Transactions on Data Hiding and Multimedia Security II. IX, 117 pages. 2007.

Vol. 4464: E. Dawson, D.S. Wong (Eds.), Information Security Practice and Experience. XIII, 361 pages. 2007.

Vol. 4462: D. Sauveron, K. Markantonakis, A. Bilas, J.-J. Quisquater (Eds.), Information Security Theory and Practices. XII, 255 pages. 2007.

Vol. 4450: T. Okamoto, X. Wang (Eds.), Public Key Cryptography – PKC 2007. XIII, 491 pages. 2007.

Vol. 4437: J.L. Camenisch, C.S. Collberg, N.F. Johnson, P. Sallee (Eds.), Information Hiding. VIII, 389 pages. 2007.

Vol. 4392: S.P. Vadhan (Ed.), Theory of Cryptography. XI, 595 pages. 2007.

Vol. 4377: M. Abe (Ed.), Topics in Cryptology – CT-RSA 2007. XI, 403 pages. 2006.

Vol. 4356: E. Biham, A.M. Youssef (Eds.), Selected Areas in Cryptography. XI, 395 pages. 2007.

Vol. 4341: P.Q. Nguyên (Ed.), Progress in Cryptology - VIETCRYPT 2006. XI, 385 pages. 2006.

Vol. 4332: A. Bagchi, V. Atluri (Eds.), Information Systems Security. XV, 382 pages. 2006.

Vol. 4329: R. Barua, T. Lange (Eds.), Progress in Cryptology - INDOCRYPT 2006. X, 454 pages. 2006.

Vol. 4318: H. Lipmaa, M. Yung, D. Lin (Eds.), Information Security and Cryptology. XI, 305 pages. 2006.

Vol. 4307: P. Ning, S. Qing, N. Li (Eds.), Information and Communications Security. XIV, 558 pages. 2006.

Vol. 4301: D. Pointcheval, Y. Mu, K. Chen (Eds.), Cryptology and Network Security. XIII, 381 pages. 2006.

Vol. 4300: Y.Q. Shi (Ed.), Transactions on Data Hiding and Multimedia Security I. IX, 139 pages. 2006.

Vol. 4298: J.K. Lee, O. Yi, M. Yung (Eds.), Information Security Applications. XIV, 406 pages. 2007.

Vol. 4296: M.S. Rhee, B. Lee (Eds.), Information Security and Cryptology – ICISC 2006. XIII, 358 pages. 2006.

Vol. 4284: X. Lai, K. Chen (Eds.), Advances in Cryptology – ASIACRYPT 2006. XIV, 468 pages. 2006.

Vol. 4283: Y.Q. Shi, B. Jeon (Eds.), Digital Watermarking. XII, 474 pages. 2006.

Vol. 4266: H. Yoshiura, K. Sakurai, K. Rannenberg, Y. Murayama, S.-i. Kawamura (Eds.), Advances in Information and Computer Security. XIII, 438 pages. 2006.

Vol. 4258: G. Danezis, P. Golle (Eds.), Privacy Enhancing Technologies. VIII, 431 pages. 2006.

Vol. 4249: L. Goubin, M. Matsui (Eds.), Cryptographic Hardware and Embedded Systems - CHES 2006. XII, 462 pages. 2006.

Vol. 4237: H. Leitold, E.P. Markatos (Eds.), Communications and Multimedia Security. XII, 253 pages. 2006.

Vol. 4236: L. Breveglieri, I. Koren, D. Naccache, J.-P. Seifert (Eds.), Fault Diagnosis and Tolerance in Cryptography. XIII, 253 pages. 2006.

Vol. 4219: D. Zamboni, C. Krügel (Eds.), Recent Advances in Intrusion Detection. XII, 331 pages. 2006.

Vol. 4189: D. Gollmann, J. Meier, A. Sabelfeld (Eds.), Computer Security – ESORICS 2006. XI, 548 pages. 2006.

Vol. 4176: S.K. Katsikas, J. López, M. Backes, S. Gritzalis, B. Preneel (Eds.), Information Security. XIV, 548 pages. 2006.

Vol. 4117: C. Dwork (Ed.), Advances in Cryptology - CRYPTO 2006. XIII, 621 pages. 2006.

Vol. 4116: R. De Prisco, M. Yung (Eds.), Security and Cryptography for Networks. XI, 366 pages. 2006.

Vol. 4107: G. Di Crescenzo, A. Rubin (Eds.), Financial Cryptography and Data Security. XI, 327 pages. 2006.

Vol. 4083: S. Fischer-Hübner, S. Furnell, C. Lambrinoudakis (Eds.), Trust and Privacy in Digital Business. XIII, 243 pages. 2006.

Vol. 4064: R. Büschkes, P. Laskov (Eds.), Detection of Intrusions and Malware & Vulnerability Assessment. X, 195 pages. 2006.

Vol. 4058: L.M. Batten, R. Safavi-Naini (Eds.), Information Security and Privacy. XII, 446 pages. 2006.

Vol. 4047: M.J.B. Robshaw (Ed.), Fast Software Encryption. XI, 434 pages. 2006.

Vol. 4043: A.S. Atzeni, A. Lioy (Eds.), Public Key Infrastructure. XI, 261 pages. 2006.

Vol. 4004: S. Vaudenay (Ed.), Advances in Cryptology - EUROCRYPT 2006. XIV, 613 pages. 2006.

Vol. 3995: G. Müller (Ed.), Emerging Trends in Information and Communication Security. XX, 524 pages. 2006.

Vol. 3989: J. Zhou, M. Yung, F. Bao (Eds.), Applied Cryptography and Network Security. XIV, 488 pages. 2006.

Vol. 3969: Ø. Ytrehus (Ed.), Coding and Cryptography. XI, 443 pages. 2006.

Vol. 3958: M. Yung, Y. Dodis, A. Kiayias, T.G. Malkin (Eds.), Public Key Cryptography - PKC 2006. XIV, 543 pages. 2006.

Vol. 3957: B. Christianson, B. Crispo, J.A. Malcolm, M. Roe (Eds.), Security Protocols. IX, 325 pages. 2006.

Vol. 3956: G. Barthe, B. Grégoire, M. Huisman, J.-L. Lanet (Eds.), Construction and Analysis of Safe, Secure, and Interoperable Smart Devices. IX, 175 pages. 2006.

Vol. 3935: D.H. Won, S. Kim (Eds.), Information Security and Cryptology - ICISC 2005. XIV, 458 pages. 2006.

Vol. 3934: J.A. Clark, R.F. Paige, F.A.C. Polack, P.J. Brooke (Eds.), Security in Pervasive Computing. X, 243 pages. 2006.

Vol. 3928: J. Domingo-Ferrer, J. Posegga, D. Schreckling (Eds.), Smart Card Research and Advanced Applications. XI, 359 pages. 2006.

Vol. 3919: R. Safavi-Naini, M. Yung (Eds.), Digital Rights Management. XI, 357 pages. 2006.

Vol. 3903: K. Chen, R. Deng, X. Lai, J. Zhou (Eds.), Information Security Practice and Experience. XIV, 392 pages. 2006.

Vol. 3897: B. Preneel, S. Tavares (Eds.), Selected Areas in Cryptography. XI, 371 pages. 2006.

Vol. 3876: S. Halevi, T. Rabin (Eds.), Theory of Cryptography. XI, 617 pages. 2006.

Vol. 3866: T. Dimitrakos, F. Martinelli, P.Y.A. Ryan, S. Schneider (Eds.), Formal Aspects in Security and Trust. X, 259 pages. 2006.

Vol. 3860: D. Pointcheval (Ed.), Topics in Cryptology – CT-RSA 2006. XI, 365 pages. 2006.

Vol. 3858: A. Valdes, D. Zamboni (Eds.), Recent Advances in Intrusion Detection. X, 351 pages. 2006.